JUSTICE, LAW, AND VIOLENCE

JUSTICE, LAW, AND VIOLENCE

Edited by James B. Brady and

Newton Garver

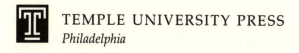 TEMPLE UNIVERSITY PRESS
Philadelphia

Temple University Press, Philadelphia 19122
Copyright © 1991 by Temple University. All rights reserved
Published 1991
Printed in the United States of America

The paper used in this publication meets the minimum
requirements of American National Standard for Information
Sciences—Permanence of Paper for Printed Library
Materials, ANSI z39.48-1984 ⊚

Library of Congress Cataloging-in-Publication Data
Justice, law, and violence / edited by James B. Brady and
   Newton Garver.
      p. cm.
   Includes bibliographical references and index.
   ISBN 0-87722-843-4
     1. Violence—Philosophy—Congresses.   2. Violence—
Moral and ethical aspects—Congresses.   I. Brady, James B.,
1939– .
II. Garver, Newton, 1928– .
HM281.J87 1991
303.6—DC20   91-10277

Chapter 7, "Limits of Legitimation and the Question of
Violence," by Bernhard Waldenfels, was first published in the
German language in Der Stachel des Fremden, by Bernhard
Waldenfels (Frankfurt am Main: Suhrkamp Verlag, 1990).
Reprinted with the permission of Suhrkamp Verlag.

Chapter 15, "Terrorism, Rights, and Political Goals," by
Virginia Held, was first published in Violence, Terrorism, and
Justice, edited by R. G. Frey and Christopher Morris (New
York: Cambridge University Press, 1991). © 1991 Cambridge
University Press. Reprinted with the permission of
Cambridge University Press.

For Diane and Anneliese

CONTENTS

PREFACE

The focus of this book is on questions about the legitimation or justification of violence. To address such questions we have brought together writers from a wide variety of backgrounds and philosophical viewpoints. Both Anglo-American and Continental philosophy are represented by authors from several nations: Canada, Finland, Germany, and Italy, as well as the United States. The main thrust of the inquiry is conceptual or philosophical, but inquiry into the problems concerning the relations among violence, law, and justice can never remain confined within any single discipline. We present these somewhat specialized studies to all who share an interest in the health and welfare of our social order.

Events such as the various explosions in the Middle East and the unrest in Eastern Europe and the Soviet Union all give a sense of urgency to the question of the justifiability of violence. We have, however, avoided direct focused discussion of these current problems, fearing that the discussion might become politicized and partisan. We do believe that participants in such discussions could profit from the understanding of the underlying concepts and perennial issues considered here.

These essays were presented and discussed at a conference entitled "Law and the Legitimation of Violence," held at State University of New York at Buffalo in March 1989. We would like to thank those at SUNY who provided the funds that made the conference possible: the Marvin Farber Memorial Fund, the Baldy Center for Law and Social Policy, Conversations in the Disciplines, Conferences in the Disciplines, the Deans of the Faculty of Law and Jurisprudence and the Faculty of Social Sciences, the Department of Philosophy, and the Graduate Group on Human Rights Law and Policy.

We also want to thank those participants in the conference who, in addition to the authors collected here, made valuable contributions to the discussion: Jacob Adler, John Arthur, Wray Bailey, Guyora Binder, Paul Brietzke, C. A. J. Coady, Margaret Coady, Victoria Cooley, Robert Dentan, Charles Ewing, Alan Freeman, Ray Frey, Gail Goodman, Michael Gorr, Anthony Graziano, Bart Gruzalski, Paul Guinn, Thomas Headrick, William Herbrechtsmeier, Richard Hull, Virginia Leary, Tibor Machan, Elizabeth Mensch, David Nyberg, Samuel Paley, Lansing Pollock, and Thomas Wartenberg.

We are indebted to Charlotte Hamilton, Assistant to the Chair, Department of Philosophy, for her work in organizing the conference and helping to prepare the essays, and to Marie Fleischauer and Judy Wagner for their secretarial assistance. A special word of thanks is due Peter Hare, Chair of the Department of Philosophy, who supported and encouraged us in this project from the very beginning. We are also grateful to Jane Cullen and anonymous readers at Temple University Press for useful suggestions about organizing and editing the material so that it would become more than simply the proceedings of a conference.

The essay by Virginia Held, "Terrorism, Rights, and Political Goals" (Chapter 15), was first published in R. G. Frey and Christopher Morris, eds., *Violence, Terrorism, and Justice* (New York: Cambridge University Press, 1991). We thank the editors and Cambridge University Press for permission to include the article here. All the other material, in its present form, appears here for the first time, although the essay by Bernhard Waldenfels (Chapter 7) has appeared in German translation in his *Der Stachel des Fremden* (Frankfurt am Main: Suhrkamp Verlag, 1990).

The contributors have been most gracious in agreeing to editorial changes that were sometimes severe, and for this we are grateful. Headings and subheadings have been introduced in many of the essays, and numerous footnotes have been replaced by brief parenthetical references for which full bibliographical details will be found in the Bibliography, except for the legal references in the contributions of Eike von Savigny (Chapter 3) and Lance Stell (Chapter 16), where the details are appended to the essays. Passages in square brackets are translations supplied by the editors.

JUSTICE, LAW, AND VIOLENCE

INTRODUCTION
TO THE ISSUES

AN OVERVIEW OF THE PROBLEM

Our aim in gathering these essays together has been to make a focused contribution to the discussion of the role of violence in modern society, and in particular its relation to justice. Like nearly everyone else, we deplore violence and wish to restrain it, we applaud justice and wish to promote it, and we are confused about the relation between what we deplore and what we applaud. On the one hand we are inclined to condemn the use of violence to promote justice, since justice promoted in this way is not only contaminated by its means but also becomes embattled and contested rather than integrative—attacked by those on the other side who are friends, relatives, and allies of the victims of the violence. In this all-too-human predicament, whose dynamic Bernhard Waldenfels and Elizabeth Wolgast elaborate in their contributions to this volume, we can see the truth of the remark of Camus (1946) that "victims and executioners are brothers in the same distress." On the other hand we are strongly drawn to approve, in the name of justice, the use of physical force (even lethal force) to restrain or dethrone criminals, bullies, tyrants, and other oppressors.

If there were a clear distinction between "force" and "violence," as Betz (1977) has suggested, we might say that injustice sanctions the use of force but not violence. "Force" and "violence" are not, however, objectively distinguishable in empirical terms; in many cases the destruction caused by police or armed forces far exceeds the measurable destruction or injustice that it was designed to correct, even in cases where the use of armed force succeeds as planned and intended. It makes sense to argue that the Civil War or the Second World War was justified, but it seems absurd to insist that the allegedly justified destruction was not real violence. So there is no easy way out of our dilemma about the role of violence in society.

We decided to sharpen our focus by concentrating on patterns of argumentation by which interested parties seek to *legitimate* (to use Max Weber's term), to *justify*, or (as Freud might say) to *rationalize* contested and contestable forms of action. The idea is this: If there are uncontested forms of justification or legitimation, they will point to the uses of violence that accord rather than conflict with the demands of justice. Our special focus has been to try to understand violence in relation to law, and hence (inevitably) in relation to justice and justifiability.

A further sharpening of our focus involves methodology. We do not mean to compete with the superb dramatic study of the rhetoric of legitimation that T. S. Eliot puts into the mouths of the four knights in *Murder in the Cathedral*. The contribution of these essays is conceptual and analytical. They are meant to throw light on the *concepts* of justice, of law, and of violence. The same public problems that motivate these essays might also be studied empirically or historically, and, indeed, they need to be. That the considerations brought to bear in this volume are conceptual or philosophical implies no disrespect for or disinterest in the substantial work sociologists and psychologists have done over the years to help define and direct attention toward these issues. The volume *Sanctions for Evil* (1972), edited by the sociologists Nevitt Sanford and Craig Comstock, was one of the previous works that stimulated this collection, even with its different aim and different motivation.

Nor do these essays include much moral condemnation of violence, such as one commonly hears from clerics and politicians. Indeed, the insistence that there can be no automatic condemnation of violence, or even of terrorism, is a recurring theme. This is partly because such condemnation often goes hand in hand with the authorization or approval of counterviolence, which seems to us to be part of the problem rather than part of the solution. And it is partly because in some senses and in some contexts, as becomes evident in very different ways in the essays of Waldenfels, Jan Narveson, and Hugo Bedau, violence seems inevitable: It seems, whether we like it or not, to constitute a component of social order in general and of punishment in particular. It is also partly because we are more perplexed than outraged by violence. This is not a value-free posture. On the contrary, we deeply deplore the excess of violence in human affairs—the way it tends, as Hobbes put it, to make life "nasty, brutish, and short"—and we have a commitment to its reduction, because of the burden it puts on humanity. But this attitude leads us, as it led Hobbes (1651), to inquiry rather than condemnation.

The question that prompted this collection is one about the sanctions or legitimations our society offers for the use of violence in the primary sense, that is, the sudden, destructive, potentially lethal use of physical force. That question, however, is much too broad. There are many dimensions to society and different sorts of sanctions in the different dimensions. Religions, for example, have frequently sanctioned violence—not just through crusades and Shiite assassinations but also in the recent and very interesting guise of liberation theology. The patterns of justificatory argument used in religion differ so radically from those in everyday affairs, medicine, or law, that they would certainly (as Réné Girard [1977] has demonstrated) deserve at least a volume on their own. It was apparent, therefore, that we needed to narrow the question.

We decided to focus on one facet of the relation of law and violence. There are two main facets of this relationship, and we chose the narrower one. The broad aspect of the relation of law and violence is that violence is stemmed by law. Especially in those systems characterized by just procedures and relatively easy access, legal remedies provide a nonviolent alternative to instrumental violence. That is arguably—although Waldenfels and perhaps Narveson would express reservations—law's most important social role: Hobbes certainly thought so. Our focus is on the other side of the relationship: the extent to and manner by which laws justify or legitimate violence. The clearest examples of such legitimation are the normal provisions in every national legal system for military defense and for criminal punishment, as well as for the exoneration of homicide in police work, military action, and self-defense. How is it that law at the same time provides among the most sophisticated alternatives to violence and among the most elaborate justifications for violence? This question, even for those contributors who insist on a wider perspective in order to throw light on it, remains the focus of the book.

Part One contains essays that discuss the nature of violence. As will quickly be seen, however, that brief characterization is both somewhat inaccurate and somewhat misleading. It is inaccurate because the contributors are quite unable to agree on any analysis or characterization that could be stipulated authoritatively at the outset, and no definition is deduced at the conclusion; on the contrary, it will be apparent that different contributors employ different conceptions of violence. It is misleading because all the chapters in this section also consider justifications and legitimations; the first topic is not discussed in isolation from the second.

Because we are not going to give a definition of violence, and believe that we cannot do so, we can shed light on the subject only by moving around it and illuminating it from different angles. Such a procedure has no obvious or necessary point of departure. There is no reason to believe that starting at the north will lead to clearer understanding than starting at the south, or that circling to the left will illuminate more than circling to the right. We choose to begin with essays having a narrow focus, leading up to the far more general philosophical considerations presented by Sergio Cotta and Kenneth Baynes. The first four essays are obviously and explicitly devoted to less than the whole problem. These well-focused discussions have, however, important general implications about how we should think about violence and about the use of the word 'violence'.

John Ladd focuses on collective violence, thus leaving aside private violence and largely ignoring the paradigm cases of rape, mugging, and murder. In the first part of the chapter he gives a splendid account of the confusions that arise from the common habit of thinking of collective violence on the model of private violence, a habit he labels "Platonic projection" because of the famous analogy between personal character and government in Plato's *Republic*. In the latter part of his essay he focuses on one aspect of collective violence, namely, its intractability. His careful analysis of five premises of the sort of ideological framework that sustains such intractability is, even though it touches only a narrow part of the whole problem, one of the highlights of the whole collection.

Eike von Savigny's essay is perhaps even more narrow; it is certainly more esoteric. He discusses the extension of the range of the concept of violence in West German judicial decisions, to the point where an admittedly nonviolent direct action now counts as "violence." The extension has occurred through a plausible but (he argues) fallacious process of judicial reasoning, which he likens to the Sorites fallacy, first identified by ancient Greek logicians.

The essays by Robert Holmes and Thomas Pogge comment on those of Ladd and Savigny. Holmes insists on the unavoidable ambiguity of the term 'violence', and on the importance of maintaining a moral perspective while discussing social and political questions about violence. Pogge's contribution is a fine illustration of the difficulty of establishing a firm conclusion even with respect to a narrow and clearly defined aspect of this general topic.

The essay by Cotta, which Kenneth Baynes helps to put into better focus, is an entirely different sort of contribution—general rather than specific, abstract rather than concrete, dense rather than clear, Continental rather than Anglo-American. Rich in the European tradition that stems from Heidegger, this essay addresses the broad problem of violence both in relation to the meaning of human life and more specifically in relation to patterns and practices of justification. We will say more about its theme and terminology in the introduction to Part One.

There is, in the ordinary sense, no conclusion of this first section. Readers will, we hope, draw some conclusions of their own. One possibility might be that the violence discussed here is a distinctly human phenomenon. It has little or nothing to do with volcanoes or earthquakes or "nature red in tooth and claw." It is, on the contrary, inseparable from language and the use of language. This is closely related to the point with which Waldenfels begins his contribution in Part Two, when he speaks of the "double violence" entailed by justifying the harm inflicted, that is, that the victim of violence is made to suffer social or psychological as well as physical harm by being told that the physical harm was "what you deserved" or "what you asked for." The classic case of such double violence is when a rape victim is found by judicial proceeding to have been responsible for the rape; Waldenfels generalizes this familiar pattern to human violence in general. Nowhere in nature, by contrast, are there to be found dichotomies such as that between violence and counterviolence, or between crime and punishment, in terms of which nearly all human violence is moralized.

This moralizing, this inseparability of human violence from language and patterns of discourse, means that a discussion of human violence is inevitably (although often implicitly and unknowingly) a discussion of the *concept* of violence. A philosophical discussion makes this hidden implicit dimension explicit. Consequently each of the essays proffers a definition or in some other way discusses and illuminates our concepts as well as the phenomena.

The role of definitional questions should not be misunderstood. The aim is not to pin down the idea of violence or legitimation or justice definitively, to cast it in bronze, so to speak, so that we will all finally be using the same definition. Quite the contrary. The aim is to get on with the discussion of a particular issue by making precise how the words are being used on a particular occasion. When the authors discussed each others' essays, therefore, it was natural (though not always easy!) for each of the discussants to use the definition of the essay under discussion rather than the definition in the discussant's own essay; to use, that is, the definition in terms of which a particular issue was defined rather than some absolutely superior one.

It will be apparent from these comments about definitions that there is diversity as well as unity in this volume. Our aim has been to include diverse perspectives on the single broad question we have described above. Part of the diversity comes from including relatively unpopular perspectives, such as the anarchism discussed by Bedau and Narveson. Another part of the diversity comes from including European perspectives. Cotta, for example, has a style and perspective entirely different from those of Carl Wellman, although both are among the foremost philosophers of law in their respective countries. We have also been pleased to discover instructive diversity not only between the Americans and Europeans, but also among the Europeans themselves.

In the essays of Cotta and Waldenfels, both of whom rank among Europe's foremost philosophers, the reader will find a confrontation of considerable philosophical depth and subtlety, one that throws the problem of the definition or conception of violence into sharp focus. As is the case with most antagonists, they have much in common. Both come to the question through a study of Nietzsche, Husserl, and Heidegger (a rather different route from that of the American contributors), both are phenomenologists whose style makes notable demands on the reader, and both agree that violence is a matter of degree. They would also agree in practice about most concrete situations. Where they differ, almost diametrically, is about what violence is, that is, about its definition. Waldenfels sees all sorts of order (*Ordnung*) as essentially violent (though not always in the same degree), and he joins Foucault in regarding the imposition of order as one of the significant forms of violence in contemporary society. Cotta, on the other hand (esp. Cotta, 1978), sees *disorder* (violation of *misura*) as the crucial element in all violence. *Misura* is the ordinary Italian word for "measure," although it has a somewhat broader use; the sense here is perhaps best captured when we speak in English of "a measured response." It is, of course, not exactly the same thing as *Ordnung;* and Cotta's fine distinction of three sorts of *misura* (internal, external, and purposive, depending on whether the source of the rule by which the action is judged comes from the action itself; from a natural, conventional, or civil law; or from the end or purpose the agent has in mind) introduces further important subtleties. With such reservations taken into account, it seems clear that both would agree that the justification or legitimation of such violent acts as beating, incarceration, and homicide, as is almost universally allowed in cases of parental and judicial punishment (also self-defense), superimposes *moral order* on the punitive violence itself. At this point they differ sharply. Cotta sees the imposition of moral order as a restoration of *misura* (i.e., purposive *misura*) and therefore a lowering of the level of violence. (Phenomenologically, this explains why many people do not consider just punishment to be an act of violence at all.) Waldenfels, on the other hand, sees it as a further violence, and he therefore speaks of a "double violence" in these cases. (One should not overlook the subtlety of Waldenfels's view: Although it implies that we should deplore the self-righteous justification of punishment as well as punitive violence itself, it does not imply that punishment is wrong or unjustified.) The opposed conceptions of violence therefore lead us to think of the familiar phenomenon of punishment in very different ways.

Although this confrontation shows our definitions and conceptions to be of vital importance, it does not mean that all our thinking need begin with and be based on definitions. On the contrary, the phenomena also need to be discussed in their own right. Before deciding between Cotta's idea of violence and that of Waldenfels, it would be wise to clarify ideas about the justification of punitive violence, as Bedau and André Maury attempt to do in their contributions to Part Three. The first half of Ladd's contribution also provides a fine example of how paying attention to the phenomena can check hasty but plausible definitions.

Part Two contains essays that discuss the way in which law and demands for justice provide legitimations of violence. The first essay addresses the issue in broad terms, hoping to throw light from a more distant vantage point. Waldenfels speaks generally about the nature of justifying or legitimating anything. Wojciech Chojna, to throw light on Waldenfels's essay, discusses the nonviolent alternatives developed in the recent Polish liberation movement. Newton Garver uses Isaiah Berlin's Agnelli Lecture as his starting point to analyze—disparagingly—one of the great legitimating ideas behind revolutionary violence, the notion of a perfectly just ideal society. Elizabeth Wolgast, with rich reference to the Greek tragedies, shows how insistence on "getting even" generates an endless cycle of violence, not because punishment or retribution fails to justly balance the offense, but because each punishment or retribution does harm to some third party, who then wishes to get even in turn.

Narveson makes a transition to more precisely defined issues having to do with law. While there is no doubt that law justifies the use of violence in defined conditions, its doing so is only the beginning, not the end, of Narveson's investigation. Legal justification of violence does not constitute moral justification. Quite the contrary. Narveson shows how it raises questions (here left unresolved) about the moral justification of law. Discussion of this closely defined set of problems found at the focal point of our concerns is continued by Wellman. Wellman's contribution, which closes Part Two, is one of the most systematic of the volume. It separates clearly four different questions implied in the general problem about law and the legitimation of violence and then addresses each of them in turn.

In Part Two the most general problem with respect to justice, law, and legitimacy is whether there are some sorts of order that require no justification, or that are beyond any serious dispute; or (this is perhaps a rewording of the same question) whether there are some sorts of disorder or disruption that are beyond justification. In language, for example, it would seem that order is often (not always, as racist epithets show) nonviolent and nonconstraining. There is an order, or a set of rules and regularities, that makes up Tamil. If I do not know that order, I may be inconvenienced but not violated by my ignorance. My ignorance is, in any case, not a rule or an order but the absence of rule and order—and certainly there is often violence in disorder. If I then learn Tamil and subject myself to its rules, it certainly seems that I am in no way harmed or damaged; on the contrary, I certainly seem to be strengthened rather than impaired by learning to subject myself to the rules of a language. Can there be a kind of order, with respect to behavior other than language, that is in this way empowering rather than constraining?

Two sorts of problems arise when we try to give to this question the simple affirmative answer that all our social commitments seem to require. One is a doubt whether even linguistic order is free of elements of violence. Waldenfels and Chojna argue that it is not. The other is whether problems of justice or of the enforcement of justice involve elements of violence or divergent perspectives that make the problems of justice and just social order different from the problems of linguistic order. Wolgast, Garver, and

Narveson all argue—each in a somewhat different way—that they do. We will come back to these questions in the introduction to Part Two.

None of the contributions in this volume discusses the negative version of the question, that is, whether there are some sorts of distress, disorder, or disruption that are beyond justification. A reader wishing to pursue this question further might turn to Stuart Hampshire's *Innocence and Experience* (1989). Hampshire would agree that no political order is or can be beyond dispute, but he proposes a nonrelativistic conception of basic justice, based on avoidance of human evils, evils that he convincingly presents as beyond justification in terms of any conception of the good.

The chapters in Part Three discuss more concrete instances of the general problem. The three areas to which these papers make contributions are among the acknowledged trouble spots of our contemporary society: punishment, terrorism, and self-defense. To some extent the lessons from these instances constitute applications of the general principles. To an equal extent, however, they stand on their own as cases to which the principles must conform; that is, they work from the bottom up. As in scientific thinking, there is a sense in which the general must defer to the concrete, just as our understanding the concrete must be in general terms. While different concrete problems might have been chosen, we do not believe that a volume on this topic could be complete or useful without some contributions of the sort we have collected in this part.

Consider what happens, for example, when we think about crime and punishment. The two sorts of acts cannot be distinguished by the harm or damage or injury done deliberately to another human being: punishment may be either more or less hurtful to the criminal than the underlying crime to the victim. Trying to achieve a balance is, as Wolgast shows in her essay, a pretty hopeless affair because of differing perspectives about what balances what. Worse still, as Maury shows, is uncertainty about whether the crime itself might be a punishment in a wider perspective (as Raskolnikov thought), or the punishment really a crime. Lance Stell's consideration of self-defense in the case of battered women makes the difficulty of any abstract definition of 'crime' even more anguishing. And yet, as becomes evident from Bedau's very careful discussion, we simply cannot get along in society without punishment. While acknowledging an element of violence in both, Bedau argues that we cannot have a society or social structure at all without distinguishing crime from punishment. And because these are ideas that are regularly put into practice, the distinction will have to be more than just abstract and verbal: It will also need to be anchored in concrete and uncontroversial instances.

Terrorism is an entirely different form of violence: Violence clothed as punishment is generally approved, whereas terrorism enters public discussion as intolerable. Here again, however, as Virginia Held's essay shows, a close look at the concrete phenomena helps to understand the interaction of violence with familiar patterns of justification. Held considers acts of violence, whether by terrorists or by governments, to be violations of human rights, and hence subject to being weighed in the scales of legitimacy and illegitimacy along with the other violations of human rights that contribute to the overall circumstances in which the acts of terrorism occur. Seen and judged in this perspective, terrorism can no longer automatically be condemned, because it may involve a decrease rather than an increase in violence or violation of rights. Judgments about terrorism, like those about punishment, therefore need to be anchored in concrete considerations rather than determined by the concept alone.

These conclusions from Part Three cannot override all the abstract considerations from Parts One and Two. There remains, for example, Waldenfels's insistence that any social order contains elements of violence. Cavell's remark (1979, 20) that our search for criteria is a search for community may be especially true, and especially poignant, with respect to the criteria and paradigms for the subcategories of violence and legitimation. However much we search for a universal, all-inclusive community, it may nevertheless turn out that we cannot form a community, a society, without excluding someone, that is, without violence. If so, the conclusion of Waldenfels, that our aim should be the reduction rather than the elimination of violence, is neither so despairing nor so unwelcome as it may at first appear. The concrete instances are essential for reaching such insights.

RESULTS AND CHALLENGES

There is no single lesson to be learned from this stimulating set of studies. There are, however, some results. Some of them are negative, or sound negative; but all are to be welcomed for their contribution to our understanding of problems of violence and of patterns of its legitimation.

One result is that there is no agreed definition of violence. This is not so discouraging as it might seem, because it is also apparent that the absence of an agreed general definition is no insuperable barrier to fruitful discussion. This is not to imply that the problems can or should be discussed naively, in blithe innocence of the tricky semantics involved. It does imply that sufficient precision can be attained for discussing particular problems, without inferring that precision from a general definition.

Part of the messy semantics of the concept of 'violence' has to do with problems of justification or legitimation. The semantics is messy partly because 'violence' is a quasi-moral concept: Violence is not wrong by definition; it is justifiable, but it always stands, as Hannah Arendt perceptively observed (1969, 51), in need of justification. The semantics is also messy partly because this need is so regularly met: Violence is instantly moralized or rationalized, so that, as Waldenfels puts it, the victim receives a double violence, first being harmed concretely and then stigmatized as deserving the harm received. A second result is thus that problems of violence cannot fruitfully be discussed in isolation from problems of justification.

A third result is that there is no general definition of 'legitimation' or 'justification', there is no single pattern into which justifications fall, and there is no criterion that infallibly distinguishes sound from fallacious justificatory claims. Justifications considered in the various essays are based on legal rights, on moral rights, on necessity, on goals or ideals, on ideology, and (in Bedau's comments on punitive violence) on considerations that do not fall easily into any of these categories. The fact that justificatory claims are always involved makes the problems of violence even more complex than they first appear, and the variety of patterns of justification increases the difficulties.

A fourth result is that violence seems an ineradicable feature of human life. None of the contributors envisages a society with no violence at all, and at least five of them (Bedau, Garver, Narveson, Wolgast, and Waldenfels) give reasons for thinking there never can be such a society.

Inevitability, however, does not entail justification, and the fifth result is that justifications normally given for acts of violence are highly suspect. Only Waldenfels and Chojna argue that violence is never justified, but all the contributors give reasons for thinking that many of the claims to justification are invalid, or arguably invalid. It is true that Stell argues for the validity of a relatively new pattern of justification, that both Bedau and Maury argue for the justifiability of punishment, that Held considers terrorism justifiable if state violence is, and that Wellman defends certain sorts of violence (or force) on the basis of moral or legal rights. In each of these cases, however, specific conditions must obtain if the claims of justification are to be sound, and such conditions obtain less frequently than might be thought. Overall the thrust of the papers is to sustain the *possibility* of justifying force and violence, but to question whether very much of the actual violence we see in the world is *really* justified. People frequently resort to the patterns of discourse of possible justifications on occasions when such patterns of discourse are inapplicable. In such cases the justificatory arguments are invalid.

That there is unsound reasoning in arguments that purport to justify violence may seem an instance of proving the obvious. It is, however, a result worth pondering, for it suggests serious intellectual work that still needs to be done. What needs to be done is to give serious consideration to those arguments. Some are unsound patterns of argument, some employ false or dubious general premises, and some make use of highly improbable particular premises: They are not all unsound in the same way. Nor is it likely that they are all *known* to be unsound by their proponents. There is both anger and anguish in the memorable words of Octave in Jean Renoir's film *Les regles du jeu*: "In this world there is one terrible thing, and that is that everyone has his reasons." We seem, at the time of action, perfectly justified in the pain we inflict. The anguish occurs only later, when we come to understand how thin and fragile our rationalization was. It is a nearly universal anguish. In *Little Gidding* T. S. Eliot counts such tardy realization as among the normal pains and hardships of old age, a time when "fools' approval stings, and honor stains." There must be many, politicians and others, who are no more perceptive than young Eliot. Refusal to take their misguided arguments seriously truncates dialogue, and truncated dialogue is itself a part of the problem. We rarely give to apparently despicable rationalizations the sort of detailed attention that Ladd gives to the ideology of collective violence. His essay is a model for the sort of work that needs to be done. As a measure of how great the task is we need only consider how incomplete his diagnosis is: Although he has clarified the structure of the arguments and identified hidden premises, he has not yet given questions about the warrant for the premises (their truth) the sort of careful scrutiny he has given to the overall argument.

Some of the work has been done by other books that have appeared since these essays were written. Two deserve special mention. The volume *Violence, Terrorism, and Justice* (1991), edited by Frey and Morris, makes a useful complement to this work. It contains contributions by Held and Narveson as well as a particularly fine essay by Annette Baier on expressive violence, the use of violence by a minority group to make themselves heard. Stuart Hampshire's *Innocence and Experience* (1989) is an elegant and carefully constructed essay with two main themes. The first is to insist on the reality of real evil, the denial of which is an objectionable form of innocence. The other is that evil can rarely if ever be dealt with by eliminating the evil persons, the case of Hitler being a misleading guide. Hampshire argues that there is, and can be, no overall conception of the good, one compatible with every ideal and every admirable aspiration. What we require to respond to evil is, therefore, not perfection but experience, guided by steadfast adherence to minimal procedural justice and to imaginative ways of looking at things.

The essays collected here are exploratory rather than definitive; they say neither the first nor the last word. The book simply scratches the surface of a significant social and intellectual problem. It does do that, and we are, frankly, enormously gratified that it does that much. We hope that Sanford and Comstock find it a useful continuation of the work they pulled together in *Sanctions for Evil* (1972). No accomplishments, however, can blot out the huge residual problems. Beyond their accomplishments the essays collected here point to a vast opportunity to address the problem of contemporary violence by challenging the currently received legitimations for violence.

PART ONE
Violence

It is perhaps to be expected that a word like 'violence' should lack a clear and agreed definition. That it does lack such a definition is one of the themes of the essays in Part One. Some of the contributors go so far as to suggest that violence is the sort of concept that never can be defined, and that its usefulness even depends in part on its not being pinned down by a definition. That situation is no doubt due in part to the moral or emotive dimension to the concept: Whatever deserves to be called "violence" stands in need of justification, and therefore everyone naturally endeavors, even by specious definitions, to avoid being seen as having done violence. There is no reason to suppose that we will not time and again see repetitions of the sort of remarks made twenty-five years ago by Malcolm X and Lyndon Johnson, who both denied any involvement with violence. Malcolm *did* believe in self-defense, by lethal force if necessary; but in an interview a few weeks before he was assassinated he explained that lethal force used as a response to violence initiated by others is not what he considers real violence. And Johnson energetically pursued the Vietnam War but did not consider "police action" to be violence. Certainly Gandhi and King had entirely different operating definitions of 'violence'!

These essays demonstrate, however, that the high contestability of definitions of violence is not an insuperable barrier to a better understanding of the concept. The key to understanding violence, as is shown over and over again in different ways, is understanding the ways in which violence is justified—or even, as Eike von Savigny shows, the ways in which uses of the word are justified.

Part One does not begin with an abstract discussion of the semantics of the word 'violence', even though semantics can never be left entirely aside. It does not begin, either, with a survey of the phenomena comprised under the heading *violence*. It begins with a much narrower perspective, namely John Ladd's discussion of collective violence. It may seem strange to leave aside the paradigm cases of mugging, murder, and rape in order to discuss a narrow, though admittedly widespread, sort of violence. The reason for beginning here is that certain features of violence become clearer. In particular, it is easier to see a pattern in the rationalizations for collective violence than in the justifications offered for rape, mugging, and murder.

15

For one thing, collective violence always has an explicit rationalization or moralization. The rationalization takes the form of an ideology, whose normal characteristics Ladd describes in convincing detail.

By seeing the premises that normally occur in the legitimation of collective violence, we begin to get a better perspective on the general phenomenon. That is because the phenomena of violence belong to the moral dimension of our lives rather than to the impersonal and amoral world of nature, which includes tornadoes and earthquakes. In the case of human violence, whether collective or private, the violent action is invariably accompanied by condemnations and justifications—which would make little sense in the case of the violence of nature, no matter how poignant its destruction. Ladd's essay provides a good introduction to this aspect of violence, which is then kept in focus throughout the book.

Robert Holmes (Chapter 2), emphasizing lines of thought expressed more fully in his recent book *On War and Morality* (1989), extends Ladd's insights and at the same time raises certain reservations. On the matter of definitions of violence he notes the ideological bias toward the establishment that occurs if one removes legitimate or necessary force or coercion from the range of what one considers violence; this seems to Holmes sufficient reason for avoiding such definitions. While this would certainly imply a criticism of the definition of 'violence' Carl Wellman gives in Part Two, it is in accord with some of the cautions Ladd makes about definitions of violence. With respect to the relations between individuals and collectivities there seems to be a more substantial difference between Holmes and Ladd. Ladd believes it essential for clear thought on the problem of collective violence not to reduce it to instances of individual violence: The victims are not attacked for what they have done as individuals, and the agents (e.g., soldiers) do not bear moral responsibility in the same way as they would for the same acts committed as private violence. Holmes, while agreeing that "Platonic projection" is a mistake, is no more willing to absolve the agents from moral responsibility than he is to absolve governments from responsibility for the "legitimate and necessary" force and coercion they employ. It is a subtle point, echoing one of philosophy's perennial problems. Fortunately it in no way impugns the diagnosis Ladd gives of the premises implicit in the ideological thinking that normally legitimates collective violence.

In Chapter 3 Savigny looks at the way the concept of violence has been applied in German High Court decisions, being extended in small steps from uncontroversial instances to peaceful sit-ins. Savigny shows the parallel of the legal reasoning to a familiar classical paradox, one in which the reasoning also proceeds in small increments. Some people might call it "proceeding down a slippery slope." If there is a fallacy in such reasoning, as there seems to be, it is difficult to diagnose. That such reasoning occurs with the concept of violence is, however, not surprising. Every concept that is contestable (in a sense derived from Gallie, 1956) is necessarily applied to new instances via reasoning by analogy from paradigms—and is therefore subject to just the sort of paradox Savigny demonstrates in these lines of court cases. Although his topic is narrow, his lesson is broad.

Thomas Pogge points out in Chapter 4 that a recognition of coercion as a form of violence, or certain other considerations, might rescue the jurists from the fallacy in reasoning that Savigny attributes to them. Coercion, however, is not always a sort of violence—the other necessary conditions can probably be specified only vaguely—and Pogge acknowledges that the sit-ins probably did not disrupt the normal and needful activities of the military enough to constitute violence. Pogge's comments, not only about the problematic relation of violence to coercion but also about "structural" violence, further illustrate how intrinsically contestable the concept of violence is.

Sergio Cotta's essay (Chapter 5) which extends the line of thought found in his remarkable book *Why Violence?* (1978), is among the more difficult in this volume, partly because of his sometimes technical terminology and partly because of the subtlety of his argument. He starts by noting that nonviolence is as natural as violence: Both occur in nature. That seems to leave us with a standoff, if we assume that what is natural is not altogether wrong. Using terminology derived from Heidegger, he characterizes these facts as "ontic" rather than "ontological"; that is, they pertain to factual or scientific findings rather than to what is "normal" or what belongs to the distinctive aims and achievements (the essence) of being human. Although Cotta's terminology is derived from Heidegger, readers familiar with the history of philosophy will find the approach similar to that of Aristotle. By pursuing the matter at a deeper ontological level, Cotta finds that acts of violence always negate a portion of the person who acts violently; that is, violence goes against what is distinctive and essential about being human. To act violently is, therefore, a partial denial of oneself. This self-negation, however natural it may be ontically (as reflected in common practices), is unnatural ontologically. This is so, if we have understood Cotta right, because a part of each person (conceived ontologically rather than ontically) is always involved with other persons with whom the person has dealings; so by brutalizing those others, however advantageous or necessary it may be superficially, one is brutalizing a deeper and more important aspect of oneself.

This conclusion requires a distinction, and Cotta says that violence is naturalistic (empirically familiar, or ontically real) but not really (ontologically) natural. It is easy to see that this conclusion continues and amplifies discussion of the moral dimension of violence, which was introduced in Ladd's essay.

Cotta frames his central idea metaphysically, as a return from an ontic to an ontological conception of human beings. Kenneth Baynes (Chapter 6) has great appreciation for this approach but shares some of the modern and postmodern apprehensions about metaphysics. One is whether this metaphysical perspective gives sufficient room to politics, economics, and other institutional realities; another is about the relative importance of will and dignity in Cotta's conception of a person; a third is whether the approach does not underestimate the validity of contemporary criticisms of metaphysics, as exemplified in this volume especially by Waldenfels. Pressing these questions, which are familiar enough to Cotta, helps to distinguish Cotta's thought from other familiar lines of Continental thought, and thereby to make its special character stand out.

The salient conclusion that emerges from these discussions of violence is that we can barely even identify the phenomena without making moral judgments. It emerges equally that this moral dimension, however inescapable, is not a serious barrier to careful analysis that contributes to greater intellectual understanding of the concepts and the phenomena involved.

1

THE IDEA OF COLLECTIVE VIOLENCE

John Ladd

John Ladd

COLLECTIVE AND PRIVATE VIOLENCE

The Problem of Collective Violence

This essay is about what I shall call "collective violence," that is, the kind of violence that is practiced by one group on another and that pertains to individuals, as agents or as victims, only by virtue of their (perceived) association with a particular group. Racism, when it reaches the stage of violent destruction it did with the Nazis, is an example of what I mean by 'collective violence'. To say that it is violence means that it involves the deliberate and excessive destruction of persons and of the things they value most highly. I hold excessive destructiveness to be of the essence of violence, although that is not all that needs to be said about it.

There is no question that our contemporary world is rampant with this kind of collective violence. We live in a turbulent world of terrorism, mass murders, massacres, pogroms, and genocide. These are typically connected in one way or another with deadly religious, ethnic, and racial conflicts, although they are not always of this kind. The list of places of collective violence is a long one: in India between Sikhs and Hindus or between Hindus and Moslems, in Sri Lanka between Sinhalese and Tamils, in Palestine between Israelis and Palestinians, in South Africa between blacks and Afrikaners, in Northern Ireland between Protestants and Catholics, in Iraq between Iraqis and Kurds—and we could (see Horowitz [1985] for details) extend the list indefinitely.

It should be observed that collective violence is often state run, that is, run by governments or at least espoused and supported by governments, often covertly. In such instances, it is collective violence because the government represents one group, the dominant group, meting out violence to another group, a minority. But whether it comes from a government or not, modern collective violence, unlike most private violence, is carried out by highly organized groups, whose operations are well financed and who are armed with technologically sophisticated instruments of destruction.

Collective violence is not a monopoly of underdeveloped societies or despotic governments; it is also practiced by respectable democratic nations such as our own, which has been called by Pierre van den Berghe and others (see Frederickson, 1987, 61) a *Herrenvolk* democracy. Witness our bombing in World War II of Hiroshima and Dresden,[1] our war in Vietnam, the bombing of Libya, not to mention the legally institutionalized collective violence (splendidly chronicled by Takaki, 1979) inflicted in the last century by whites on Indians and blacks in the form of genocide, expulsion, and slavery. Australia, another liberal democracy, has over the years through its various institutions, as Barta (1987) has shown, effectively committed genocide on the aborigines.

If there is any doubt about our national penchant for collective violence, along with other democratic nations, we need only remind ourselves that as a nation we are committed to the policy of total destruction in retaliation to a nuclear attack (MAD). Inasmuch as massive nuclear retaliation as a destructive act has no military purpose whatsoever, the acceptance of this ultimate solution as national policy simply amounts to an endorsement of collective violence as a political modality. Typically, however, in the American case, our national commitment to violence is conveniently and typically camouflaged by all sorts of denial, usually (see Bundy, 1988; Ladd, 1987) a plea of military or political necessity.

The pandemic of collective violence, that is, the excessive, destructive use of coercion, is an international problem; indeed, a global problem. Collective violence is, of course, not new to humanity, for both the Old Testament (the Book of Judges) and the *Iliad* exalt it; what is new is that the instruments of violence have become much more powerful and deadly and, at the same time, more readily available. Although in the past collective violence was generally local and contained, nowadays, as a result of advanced technology, every instance of collective violence becomes a globally significant event with widespread repercussions. In sum, collective violence is an urgent and pressing world problem not only because it is ubiquitous, but because it is more and more dangerous and threatening to human survival.

Collective violence also produces another kind of problem, a theoretical or philosophical problem, calling for conceptual analysis. There is a special and peculiar sort of absoluteness and intractability attached to collective violence that makes it difficult to subsume under more familiar categories of political philosophy and ethics. In this chapter I shall be particularly concerned with this problem, which might be called "the intractability problem." In considering the intractability problem, we need to ask such questions as, Why is collective violence intractable? In what ways is it so? What are the ethical, social, and political implications of the kind of intractability that characterizes collective violence?

These are difficult and puzzling questions. I do not pretend to have definitive answers to them. Much less do I plan to present a solution to the practical problem of collective violence, if indeed there is one. My principal objective is to call attention to some ways in which our understanding of collective violence might be developed.

Part of my argument is that the full significance of the intractability of collective violence is frequently unappreciated and underrated both by politicians and philosophers. This is because collective violence as a political and social phenomenon is commonly reduced to other categories, that is, to other more familiar uses of coercion, and assimilated to other political modalities that are more easily understood and that are, at least in theory, more tractable. Some of the issues I shall be concerned with will become clearer if I begin with a few preliminary remarks about some distinctive aspects of collective violence as contrasted, say, with private violence.

The Fallacy of Confusing Collective with Private Violence

There are many reasons why it is a mistake to try to understand collective violence by comparing it and assimilating it to private, individual violence, that is, violence between individuals. When violence takes place between groups it has a quite different form, meaning, and motivation from violence between individuals or small groups of individuals. One of the differences, for example, is that it tends to be heavily symbolic and ideological. This aspect of collective violence will be addressed in more detail later.

The difference between collective and private violence becomes clear if we compare how the victims of each are selected. Take racism as an example, in which collective violence is practiced by one racial group on another. Here the selection of victims is impersonal in the sense that the only pertinent reason for attacking or destroying particular individuals is that they belong to the targeted group, for example, they are members of a race or a sect. The individual victims may in fact possess all sorts of acceptable personal attributes; for example, they may be helpful, friendly, and peaceful, or they may even be children, women, or elderly persons. Such personal attributes make no difference as far as the point of the attack is concerned. Individual "guilt" or "innocence" is beside the point.

Thus, the Jews rounded up by the Gestapo became victims *only* because they were Jews—not because of anything that could be attributed to them as individuals. Where collective violence is concerned, "guilt" or "innocence" of the victim is immaterial, unless simply belonging to a group (e.g., being Jewish or black) makes one guilty. The same disregard of the personal attributes of individual victims is found in other instances of collective violence; the only "fault" of the victims in Hiroshima was that they lived in Hiroshima and were members of an enemy nation (the target). Collective violence is indiscriminate in that it fails to recognize the category of innocent victim, except in the sense that the victim may have been mistakenly chosen through some confusion about his or her group identity.

All this is quite unlike private violence, for example, domestic violence or street violence, in which the victims are selected by the attacker because of some relationship the attacker has to the victim or because of something about the victim that makes him or her a desirable target, such as having money or being a woman (rape). Except in unusual or bizarre cases, and making the usual necessary allowances for borderline cases, group membership (e.g., in a racial or religious group) is not the sole or the crucial factor, as it is with collective violence.

By the same token, the motivation for the two kinds of violence is different. Private violence is often undertaken for gain or, say, as an angry response to a particular situation, an injury or threat. Here the motives are personal just as the choice of victims is personal. In contrast, collective violence bypasses personal motivation: The motives for collective violence are nonpersonal and include such things as loyalty, faith, or allegiance to the group. If we listen to what people who are involved in collective violence say, they practice collective violence more often than not out of a "sense of duty" or "obedience to God," and other motives like that, ones that, as it were, transcend their individual interests and desires, hates, and fears.[2]

In the same vein, collective violence often requires self-sacrifice; private violence, except in strange cases, does not. That is why to victims and to third parties, collective violence is usually perceived as the work of fanatics, the obsessed, and the possessed; they find this self-sacrifice to strange gods unintelligible.

For these reasons, as well as others, our ways of understanding private violence and of responding to it, coping with it, and controlling it are inapplicable to collective violence. To compare a terrorist act to a private crime of rape or murder is dangerously to miss the point and foolhardily to lock oneself into a misdirected and inappropriate mode of response.

Throughout this essay I shall argue that the assimilation of collective violence to private violence is a fallacy that not only has absurd practical and political consequences, but that is also morally mischievous as well (to use Bentham's felicitous expression). I shall call it "the individualization fallacy."

Some of the mischievous consequences of the individualization fallacy may be mentioned right away. It was often thought that the violence slave owners practiced on their slaves was due to some especially sinister quality of the slave owner or to some especially delinquent behavior by the slave. The situation is individualized, that is, it is construed as a relationship between individuals. The individualization fallacy involved here leads to a denial of the reality, namely, that the treatment of the blacks was the systematic, institutionalized collective violence of one group, the whites, on another group, the blacks. There were, of course, nice whites and not-so-nice whites, but the "peculiar institution" had collective violence built into it. It was collective! Mutatis mutandis the same thing could be said of our treatment of the Indians. We practiced violence as a group against those groups, just as the Nazis' project to exterminate the Jews was a group project practiced on a group.

The failure to recognize collective violence for what it is blinds us to the realities and the objectives of the attacking group, which typically aims at the expulsion, extermination, or enslavement of the other group. Declarations of innocence on the part of individual victims—"We have done nothing wrong"—are simply beside the point. It is tragically easy for victims and third parties to miss the point because they have been misled by the individualization fallacy.

In this connection, it should be observed that one of the reasons the individualization fallacy is so seductive is that it provides a façade or cover-up for the reality of collective violence. By passing the blame along to individuals, it gives us a way to duck the difficult task of dealing with the collective violence of a group. Accordingly, we find racism attributed to a few individual racists and Middle Eastern terrorism attributed to Abu Nidal and Khadafy. As far as Americans are concerned, the massacre at My Lai (see French, 1972; Hersh, 1973) is a good illustration of this; it surely was a case of collective violence, but in order to save face for the army (and American society) it was turned into an assortment of private acts of violence of particular individuals.

Another mischievous consequence of the individualization fallacy is the attribution to groups of the kind of moral characteristics that are only appropriate for individuals. Groups are said to have the same sort of rights, responsibilities, obligations, virtues, and vices as individuals have. They are treated as big individuals. Private morality is "blown up" or "writ large" for groups. (This kind of interpretation might be called the "Platonic projection," a concept I discuss extensively in my essay "Corporate Mythology and Individual Responsibility" [1984].) The "writ large" line of reasoning leads to such absurd notions as "collective guilt" and "collective punishment," notions that we often find used to vindicate outrageous acts of collective violence performed under the rubric of retaliatory punishment.

An Illustration of the Fallacy: The Just War Theory

An excellent illustration of the mischievous way the individualization fallacy leads to handling groups as if they were individuals is provided by the classical just war theory. Since its early formulation by Augustine, the just war theory has assumed that there is an analogy between individual crimes and the crimes of states; and between the just response to individual crime, that is, retributive punishment, and the just response to the crimes of states (and nations), that is, the punishment of a just war. Thus, Aquinas, in his discussion of the just war, writes:

> Just as in punishment of criminals they (the rulers) rightly defend the state against all internal disturbances . . . so also they have the duty of defending the state, with the weapons of war, against external enemies. . . . Those wars are generally defined as just which avenge some wrong, when a nation or a state is to be punished for having failed to make amends for some wrong done, etc. (*Summa Theologica* IIaIIae qu 40, art 1)

The implicit ideology in the assimilation of collective violence to private violence (crime) and of retaliatory collective violence to punishment gives us a foretaste of the sorts of rationalization of collective violence that have now become common. "Our" violence is simply punishment in retaliation for "your" violence. (Later I shall call this kind of rationalization of violence a "vindication.")

The obvious objection to this extension of the concept of punishment to include punishing a group, a whole community or even an entire nation, as proposed in the just war theory, is that it is a conceptual and moral absurdity. Only individuals can be punished, and only those who have been found guilty in accordance with established judicial procedures ought to be punished; the punishment of "surrogates," who are innocent, violates all the ordinary moral notions of punishment. For these reasons, it makes no sense to apply the term 'punishment' to groups—especially to groups consisting of a huge diversity of different individuals, some of whom may have had nothing to do with the original evil that provides the ground for the punishment. To claim that the bombing of a village and the killing of women and children is punishment for terrorist acts makes nonsense out of the concept of punishment. You cannot punish an "evil empire"!

Again, attempts to rescue the just war notion of punishment by differentiating between combatants as the guilty, whom it is right to punish, and noncombatants, who ought not to suffer, does not make any sense in today's world. It is impossible to differentiate the innocent from the guilty, say, among the victims of a terrorist attack or, if you wish an example closer to home for Americans, among the victims of a bombing attack (e.g., on Hiroshima) or of a search-and-destroy mission (in Vietnam).[3] The just war model simply does not fit the realities of collective violence or modern war; built into the operations themselves is the virtual impossibility of discriminating between victims. The *just war theory is simply an excuse for collective violence.* The punitive rationale for collective violence will be discussed later.

Groups and Individuals: Targets and Victims

The issues just discussed bring out the more general question concerning groups and individuals, implied in notions like collective guilt and collective punishment as well as in collective violence; namely, what is a group and how is the relationship between the individuals belonging to a group and the group itself to be construed?[4] As far as the relationship is concerned it is sometimes said to be that of part to whole, an explanation that does not really explain anything. Again, the relationship is sometimes said to be that of membership or representation. What counts as membership or representation? These are thorny issues that are important for an understanding of collective violence. Different ideologies connected with collective violence have quite different answers to these questions. Obviously, how they are answered has consequences for who gets hurt when one group uses violence against another as well as for who is responsible for the violence.

At this point, it will be useful to draw a distinction between the *target* and the *victims* of an incident of violence. The target of a bombing attack on a village might be the terrorists hiding there, but the victims would be all those who are actually killed or injured, including nonterrorists. When Ronald Reagan ordered the attack on Libya the prime target was Khadafy, as the leader of the "guilty" nation, but others close to him, even physically, were probably also intended targets. It is hard to think that the women and children that were killed were other than victims.

To understand the rationale of an incident of violence it is necessary to identify the targets, not the victims. Sometimes the target is an organization and its leaders, while in other cases of collective violence the target is the whole group, which might be identified as including all the members of a race, an ethnic group, or sect. In racism, the target is usually the whole group, that is, all members of the race—men, women, and children. Often it is not clear what the target is, and the givers and receivers of violence have different ideas about that. On the other hand there are occasionally "misfires," that is, cases in which the violence ends up harming the wrong people, such as, for example, members of one's own group or of third parties. How the line is drawn here is crucial for an understanding of collective violence in particular cases.

This point about targets and victims shows the important role of the ideological framework in structuring any particular incident of collective violence because the determination of targets, for example, group members, representatives, or leaders, is part of the ideological setting for the collective violence exercised by one group on another. Later we will discuss the role of ideology in providing a rationale for collective violence.

What Is Violence?

Having briefly examined some of the specific points of difference between collective and private violence, I shall now turn to a consideration in more general terms of violence itself.

In asking what violence is, it might appear that we are asking for a definition. There are, however, obvious difficulties in trying to find a definition of 'violence', and philosophers are well aware of the traps of definitions of this kind. Some special difficulties in defining 'violence' might be mentioned here.

First, numerous senses of 'violence' are candidates for incorporation into a definition. A multiplicity of meanings and uses of 'violence' are listed in standard English dictionaries, but it is even more evident if we consider possible translations of the term in other languages. Thus, Zimmerman (1983, 436 n.7) lists the following as synonyms in Latin, German, French, and Italian: "*Gewalt, potestas, maiestas, Macht, Kraft, violentia, facultas, auctoritas, coercio, potentia, vis, vehementia, impetus, Stärke, Zwang, forza, vehemenza, potenza, commando, pouvoir, pouissance.*"

Lists like this of different senses of 'violence' make it clear there is no standard meaning of the word and that there will therefore be some arbitrariness in selecting which of the various possible senses of 'violence' will be the one to be defined.

The problem of definition is compounded, however, by the fact that 'violence', at least in the political context, is what W. B. Gallie (1956; 1964, chap. 8) calls an "essentially contested concept." Hence, to define it is to take a position on a controversial issue.

In this regard it is usually assumed that violence is something that, other things being equal, one ought to be against, should disapprove of and condemn. So let us grant, for the time being, that violence is "by definition" intrinsically undesirable or unacceptable. Assuming, then, that violence is by general consent a bad thing, then we should not be surprised to find politicians and writers defining 'violence' in such a way that it does not apply to them and to their conduct but only to their enemies and to those whose conduct they find objectionable. Thus, we find them making up their own definitions of 'violence' so as to capture "the high ground," so to speak, over violence. In this regard, 'violence' resembles 'terrorism', so that "one person's terrorist is another person's freedom fighter."

This consideration suggests that there is something relativistic about the notion of violence, and indeed we find that it is usually the victims and third parties who perceive a set of acts as violence while the protagonists themselves do not recognize it as such. The relativity, and bias, of the usage should put us on guard against self-interested and self-protective definitions of 'violence', of which there are many.

Along this line, we find at the very beginning of our discussion of violence a whole family of theories of violence that define 'violence' in such as way as to make violence an antiestablishment activity and something that respectable and civilized people do not participate in. These establishment-oriented definitions commonly refer to violence as coercion or destruction targeted at the establishment or at least disapproved of by it.

I shall argue that definitions of this type, which I shall call "conventional definitions," take private violence as their model and so miss the point of collective violence. In addition, of course, they tend to be question begging, ethnocentric, and hypocritical.

A second set of theories I will examine is associated with Marxism and adopts an "instrumentalist" view of violence. According to these theories, some violence is justified and some unjustified, even though violence in general is always illegitimate in the eyes of the establishment.

The instrumentalist view uses war as its model, a model that, as I shall argue, is unable to account for peculiar attributes of collective violence, namely, such things as its intractability. Again, like the conventionalist view, the instrumentalist view is question begging.

Having given a preview of the theories (or definitions) to be discussed, a few more remarks about violence in general and collective violence in particular are in order.

A Relatively Uncontroversial Aspect of Violence: Its Destructiveness

One aspect of violence that almost all writers agree on, even though they do not always realize what it implies by way of consequences, is that violence by its very nature involves extreme actions leading to excessive physical injury and destruction. The intended object (or side effect) of violence is destruction, and more particularly unlimited and irreversible destruction, such as killing, maiming, or destroying property and sacred objects. In other words, *destructiveness is the essence of violence*. It is its outcome—intended and actual.

It follows that when there is no actual destruction, there is no violence.

Unpleasant, undesirable, antisocial, and obnoxious behavior, as long as it does not involve destruction, is not violence. Someone has to be hurt in a rudimentary way for there to be violence. Thus, for example, although they may be illegal, protests including sit-ins are not violent, as long as no one is hurt.

Moreover, the destruction is not of unimportant and replaceable objects, but of something of supreme and irreplaceable value to the victim. In addition to taking away a person's life or limb, violence may destroy valuable things such as religious objects (e.g., a synagogue) or an individual's honor, self-respect, or identity as a person. The point may be put bluntly by saying that, in its typical sense, violence aims at the destruction of the whole person—life, values, and personhood.

In other words, the psychological side of violence is as important as the physical side. Thus, slavery is institutionalized violence, for it systematically deprives the slaves of all the perquisites of personhood. When American slaves were whipped, the aim was to harm them both physically and psychologically, to break them down. Accounts of the Nazi concentration camps bear witness to the same goal of destructiveness of personhood. The purpose of undertakings like these was to downgrade, to denigrate, or to cast out—"delegitimize"—the person or party that is the target of the violence and to demote the individuals concerned to nonpersonhood, to what Orlando Patterson (1982), in his discussion of slavery, calls a "social death."

I shall take these aspects of violence to be basic for the present inquiry and assume that any theory that does not provide for the absolute destructiveness of violence is not a satisfactory theory. As the discussion unfolds, I shall attempt to show why destructiveness in this absolute sense is an essential ingredient in collective violence.

SOME CURRENT DEFINITIONS AND THEORIES OF VIOLENCE

Force Versus Violence

Although violence is often identified with any use whatsoever of coercion that involves destruction, for example, deliberate killing and injury, for several reasons this kind of definition is much too general and is palpably unusable for most purposes that require finer discrimination.

To begin with, generally speaking, no viable political theory can seriously rule out the use of coercion and destruction under certain circumstances. For example, states sometimes have to use coercion to contain violence or to secure other worthy goals, such as the protection of life and liberty or obedience to the laws. Even war, one might argue, which is per se a use of coercion and destruction, need not and ought not to consist of violence. As in police action, it would seem that violence applies to the way and the purpose for which a war is fought, its excesses or its goals, rather than to the mere fact that it involves coercion and destruction.

Hence, we may grant that, unlike violence, some uses of coercion and destruction are acceptable, that is, reasonable, legitimate, legal, or moral—depending on the particular theory one espouses. That means that we need to look for a narrower definition of violence that will mark it off from generally acceptable uses of coercion. Following Cotta (and Dewey, as Betz [1977] shows), I shall use the term 'force' to distinguish acceptable uses of coercion and destruction from 'violence', which, by contrast, may be regarded as unacceptable.

Conventional Definitions of Violence: Force Versus Violence

The purpose of conventional definitions of 'violence' is to provide some way of distinguishing force from violence. They do this by reference to norms of one sort or another that are generally accepted in the society and that define those forms of coercion that are acceptable, that is, are to be considered force, and those that are not, that is, are to be considered violence.

There are several definitions of 'violence' that follow this general approach. The following are examples:

1. Definition in terms of law: *Violence is the illegal use of coercion.* Thus (Hook, quoted by Zimmerman [1983, 12]), violence is "roughly defined as the illegal employment of methods of physical coercion for personal or group ends"; or as "a considerable or destroying use of force against persons or things, *a use of force prohibited by law* and directed to a change in policies, personnel, or system of government, and hence to changes in society" (Honderich, 1976, 9, 98, my emphasis).

The legal definition of 'violence' immediately raises questions about what is covered by law. For example, do we mean by 'law' simply the positive law, such as legislative or judicial enactments, or norms embodied in the constitution? Some might restrict the legal definition of violence to laws in a democracy; others might try to link the law in question to the natural law in some version or other. But I shall leave these questions to one side. (Incidentally, the legal definition is one that Kant [1965b] would accept as long as the law in question is based on the natural law.)

The obvious difficulty with the legal definition is that in the usual sense of law (positive law) that links it with government, law often condones violence or sometimes even commands that violence be done. After all, slavery was legally enforced for a long time in American history, and this "peculiar institution" was regarded both as constitutional and as consistent with the natural law. Australian genocide of the aborigines was also legal, not to mention apartheid and other similar legally sanctioned institutions. If, on the other hand, we bend the notion of law to fit our own ethical conceptions of the difference between force and violence, then we have moved the discussion to another level and have abandoned the purely legal definition of violence.

2. Definition in terms of legitimacy: *Violence is the illegitimate use of coercion.* Thus, Wilkinson (1974, 23–4) defines violence as "the illegitimate use or threatened use of coercion resulting, or intended to result in, the death, injury, restraint or intimidation of persons or the destruction or seizure of property."

The term 'legitimacy' is a somewhat broader and less determinate concept than 'legality.' It may be defined by reference to norms that are generally accepted or approved in the society (or culture). (In this sense, it is perhaps the same as Austin's positive morality.) It is clear that acts may be disapproved by society even though they are not illegal and many illegal acts are not disapproved by society. In some jurisdictions, for example, rape by a husband is not illegal, but it might nevertheless be considered an illegitimate use of coercion, that is, violence. Furthermore, like law, social norms determining legitimacy often condone or even mandate some forms of immoral and violent conduct; for example, whipping (e.g., of children, wives, or slaves) was and still is approved by society in some places and thus must be considered legitimate.

There are obvious difficulties with the concept of legitimacy as used here. It is a hard notion to pin down in any satisfactory way. It is also relativistic and invites ethnocentric interpretations. Indeed, both the legal and the legitimacy approaches foster a cynical attitude toward conceptions of violence in general because they appear to countenance many arbitrary social prejudices embedded in our social institutions, for example, racism and sexism.

3. Definition in terms of rights: *Violence is the use of coercion that violates rights* or some other moral principle such as the principle of justice. "Violence is physical force applied for committing injustice," writes Bhagwat Charan (1987).

The difficulty with "ethical" definitions of violence is that their validity and usefulness depend on the prior acceptance of a particular moral theory or of a set of enshrined moral concepts. Hence, they are not likely to be accepted by someone who questions or rejects the theory or the concepts in question. Ethical definitions of this kind beg all the pressing and controversial questions about violence. In view of such considerations, the utility of ethical definitions for a general analysis of violence is severely limited.

4. Cultural definitions: *Violence is the violation of cultural (or civilized) norms.* Such definitions are based on certain postulated cultural values of

"civilized" society, such as moderation and civility ("civilized society" = Western society?). I take it that something like this is what Cotta has in mind when he introduces the notion of 'measure' as a key term in his analysis.[5] Thus he writes: "Violence is 'contra-action' [coercion, destruction?] that is disorderly, unruly, involving incomplete presence of measure, etc."

The advantage of definitions like these is that, as in Cotta's analysis, they focus on the characteristic extremism, excess, and disproportionality generally associated with violence. They make use of general cultural or philosophical categories that help to capture what I shall later refer to as the "intractability" of violence.

The disadvantage of this approach for our purposes is that it tends to be individualistic and psychological rather than social and political. Furthermore, Cotta's approach in particular rests on a controversial philosophical position that rejects philosophical views of what might be called "romantic individualism," that is, views such as those of Nietzsche and Sartre that advocate a revolt against conventional cultural standards (Cotta calls them "subjectivism" and "nihilism"). Using their rather idiosyncratic language, writers like Nietzsche and Sartre find something self-fulfilling in the kind of "violence" that is suppressed by our Western culture. Be that as it may and apart from the intrinsic importance of the general philosophical issues involved in debates like these, it is difficult to see how they are relevant to the broader problem of pandemic violence that is the concern of this essay.

General Comments on Conventional Definitions

All these definitions assume that the legal or constitutional, political, social, cultural, or ethical status quo, some body or other of accepted norms, provides the touchstone for differentiating between the acceptable use of coercion (force) and the unacceptable use of coercion (violence). As far as those who practice collective violence are concerned, when it is defined in these ways, the resulting views and evaluation of violence must be simply irrelevant and beside the point.

Accordingly, their usefulness as general definitions is limited, because they are question begging and depend on Western categories that lack credibility in the rest of the world, where collective violence is endemic. Like some definitions of 'terrorism', these conceptions of violence construe it to be by definition incompatible with the norms of the liberal democratic state. A critic might add that they can be and often are used by the status quo to cover up our own culturally condoned forms of violence.

Furthermore, these definitions are primarily negative definitions, because they focus on what makes violence distinguishable from force, that is, why it is *not* force. In other words, these approaches concentrate on the unacceptability of violence, as it is perceived by the antiviolence framers of the definitions, rather than on what violence is, as it might be conceived by those who use it. For a number of reasons that have already been mentioned, these conventional definitions do not advance our understanding of collective violence.

In addition, it should be observed that the conventional approaches to violence tend to identify violence with private violence, the violence of a common criminal or deviant whose use of coercion is inconsistent with public safety, the public or social order, the standards of propriety, or the values of civilization. The commitment to the private, individualistic model of violence has certain consequences that are worth pointing out.

First, violence is taken to be something abnormal, aberrant, or even pathological. Like criminal behavior, it exhibits what Durkheim (1953) calls "anomie." It is measured against the normal social order and found to be wanting. Being simply a departure from the norm, violence is just an anomaly or a form of deviance—something to be avoided, to be prevented, or to be treated as well as lamented, deplored, and condemned. It is easy therefore for us to compare protagonists of what *we* call "violence" to savages, animals, or crazies.

The implications of the private violence model of collective violence for such things as the Nazi concentration camps, the American treatment of the Indians, or terrorism are simply zero or, perhaps more accurately, dangerously deceptive. For this model deludes us about the realities (and threats) of collective violence and leads us to think that the right way to respond to collective violence is to treat it like the private violence model of criminal behavior. Accordingly, the ideal way to handle terrorism, for example, is to lock up the terrorists like common criminals, or the way to handle Nazism is to hang the Nazi war criminals.

Second, another consequence of conventional definitions of violence like these is that they make the notion of state violence, that is, the violent destruction of individuals or groups in pursuance of the ends of the state or of society, that is, the political regime, logically incoherent. Because violence is defined intrasystematically, that is, by reference to a system of values represented by the state or accepted by the society (i.e., its institutions), state-imposed violence or society-approved violence (e.g., apartheid) is ruled out by definition. Violence does not apply to Negro slavery, because it was accepted by the society, it was legal and legitimate. It is a mistake to tie collective violence too tightly conceptually to the political order or the state.[6]

Third and finally, these definitions are unable to account for interstate violence: What happens when one state (society, group) inflicts violence on another? Is it not violence? Even if we admit that war is not per se to be equated with violence, nevertheless in war, violence against the enemy, such as mass killings and massacres, is not uncommon.[7]

Again, it is unclear how these definitions help us understand intrastate violence, such as that described by Horowitz (1985) and Takaki (1979), when parties (e.g., religious or ethnic groups) within a state inflict violence on each other: Hindus versus Sikhs, Tamils versus Sinhalese, or in our past, whites versus blacks and whites versus American Indians.

In sum, these definitions are not helpful in furthering an understanding of collective violence in a deeper way as a distinctive political phenomenon.

Instrumental Conceptions of Violence

Another set of theories about violence, while explicitly or implicitly accepting some conventional or other definition of violence, such as one of those just discussed, focuses on the purposes for which violence can, might, and should be used. That is, these theories assign an instrumental function to it that "justifies" its use. This is basically the Marxist–Leninist position. Thus, Hannah Arendt writes, "Violence can be justifiable, but it will never be legitimate. . . . Legitimacy, when challenged, bases itself on appeal to the past, while justification relates to an end that lies in the future" (1969, 52).[8] She adds: "Violence always needs justification" (77). By this she means that some sort of ideological justification of violence is required, although it might not be an acceptable justification. She uses racism as an example of a justifying ideology.

Instead of using the private violence model, these theories use a war model to explain and justify violence. Thus, Sorel explicitly compares the general strike to war. He writes: "The analogy which exists between strikes accompanied by violence and war is prolific of consequences." He argues that the war analogy "excludes all abominations which dishonored the middle-class revolution of the eighteenth century." (1961, 274)

In other words, according to Sorel, when violence is conceived of as war fought by armies, then evil feelings (e.g., of creative hatred) must be eliminated because they are dishonorable and diversionary. The emphasis must be on the end to be achieved and not on degrading sentiments. In that sense, the approach to violence has to be objective, that is, dispassionate and rational.

Here the Clausewitzian dictum about war could be applied to violence, namely, that, like war, it is "an act of policy . . . a continuation of policy by other means" (1984, 87). But following Clausewitz (1984, 81), we need to add that "the political object determines both the military objective to be reached and the effort it requires." In other words (see Ladd, 1987), we are dealing with a strict means–end relationship here.

When applied to ends and means, rationality requires that the means be adapted to the end and be designed to achieve the end at minimum cost. The instrumentalist view of violence, then, prescribes strict attention to the effectiveness of the means (violence) in achieving one's political ends. Cost-effectiveness is critical. It follows (Ladd, 1987) that any purported means that is in fact counterproductive or even of no avail must immediately be abandoned.

The Clausewitzian war model of what he calls war "in practice" is easily applied to the instrumental view of violence, which, like war in practice, must always be limited; it is constrained by the ends, the means, the costs, the resources, the probabilities, the alternatives, and so on. In this sense, it is always conditional.

Collective violence, such as genocide and terrorism, does not fit this model, for by its nature it is unconditional, unconstrained, and unlimited. A simple examination of the cases of collective violence that have been mentioned earlier in this paper will show that, in contrast to the Clausewitzian model of war, they are counterproductive, disproportionate, and excessive.

For example, the Final Solution, the Nazi mass extermination of the Jews, did not serve any political or military purpose for Germany during the Second World War; indeed, it has often been pointed out that it contradicted political and military objectives. By the same token, massacres and mass murders, such as My Lai, could not be considered the kind of violence that the instrumental model is designed to account for. In this connection, Walliman and Dobkowski write of genocide (1987, 15) that where it is associated with a belief, a theory, or an ideology, "it seems clear that genocide was carried on in spite of tremendous costs to the perpetrators, costs that can be measured in economic, political, and developmental terms."

A survey of notorious cases shows that in general most, if not all, collective violence is not directed at a political objective at all, much less at an economic objective; for if it were, more effective and less costly means would be chosen. Furthermore, as political strategists from Machiavelli down through Clausewitz have emphasized, it is imprudent and inexpedient for political leaders to undertake military measures that destroy the object for which they are fighting, for example, a city like Beirut or a polity like South Africa. Terrorism is, in this sense, counterproductive—as are the other cases of collective violence.

For all these reasons, then, we must conclude that the instrumental model does not apply to the kind of collective violence that concerns us here, because collective violence is simply not undertaken as a means to a political end. *It is not instrumental at all!*

Summary

Both the conventional and the instrumental approaches to violence assume, either consciously or unconsciously, that to understand and deal with violence as a social or political phenomenon, it is necessary to assimilate it to other more familiar, intelligible, and tractable categories, such as deviant criminal behavior or war.

These reductions (or models), however, miss the key point of violence, especially collective violence, namely, its vehemence, its extremism, its disproportionality, and its excess, not to mention its passion and its "irrationality" (in the conventional sense).[9]

I shall now turn to a consideration of these attributes of violence, which apply especially to collective violence.

THE IDEOLOGICAL BASIS OF COLLECTIVE VIOLENCE

Two Special Attributes of Violence: Vehemency and Intransigency

There are several meanings of 'violence' found in dictionaries like the *Oxford English Dictionary* that are not covered in the analyses examined earlier. They provide us with clues for a richer analysis. Among these are notions like "passion," "anger," "brutality," "cruelty," "bestiality," "extremeness," and "excess." They may be collected together under the term 'vehemency'.

As I shall try to show, vehemency in these various senses is connected in an important way with the two other characteristics of violence that we have already noted, namely, intransigency and intractability. Careful attention to this family of notions will add another dimension to our understanding of collective violence.

The Anger Model

Let us begin by exploring the affinities between anger, that is, angry outbursts and attacks, and violence, especially in relation to vehemency and intransigence.

The first observation is that angry actions, like violent actions, are usually excessive; they are not "measured" in Cotta's sense. Nor are they instrumental in the usual sense; instead, they tend to be disproportionate in that they generally go far beyond what would be required to remedy a situation, and frequently they are actually counterproductive. In fact, angry actions are often as injurious and costly for the angry person himself as they are for the object of his anger, often more so.

For these reasons, acting from anger is considered per se not "rational" or sometimes even "irrational." Thus, we generally assume that a person who is angry, as long as he is angry, cannot be "reasoned with" by the person who is the object of this venom or by third parties. To use Cotta's words (1978, 60), anger, like violence, is "non-dialogical." Much the same can be said of notions related to anger, such as revenge, resentment, vengeance, and vindictiveness.

Group anger or collective violence is like individual anger or private violence in these regards. For example, an angry, destructive attack by one group on another, a case of collective violence, as in an incident of communal conflict in India, would be vehement and intransigent. It would be irrational in the sense that it is not instrumentally motivated and not limited by considerations of cost or likelihood of success. Instead, the objective of that kind of angry attack of collective violence appears simply to be the destruction of the target, that is, something to be done, as it were, for its own sake and not for its consequences. One is inclined to say that the action is valued for the harm it brings to the other party (target or victim) rather than for the benefit it brings to the attacker.

On the other hand, angry and violent attacks like those we are considering, whether by individuals or groups, are not adequately explained through psychological models like stimulus–response, operant conditioning, or frustration–aggression, which, incidentally, are also applicable to animals. Rather, as typically human actions, angry acts and violence have a *rationale*. As I have already indicated, however, their rationale is different from other common sorts of rationale that are thought to make actions "rational" in the sense mentioned above, that is, as involving considerations of ends and means or as relating the actions to (culturally) accepted norms, considerations that are ordinarily used to *justify* actions.

The special type of nonjustifying rationale that is offered in defense, say, of an angry action, will be called a "vindication." A vindication is a noninstrumental reason for what would otherwise be considered an irrational mode of conduct, for example, an angry, destructive attack on another person. In contrast to most justifications, vindications are usually backward looking rather than forward looking, except in the extended sense that they might involve reference to a transcendent or apocalyptic final end, such as the coming of the Messiah or the extermination of the forces of evil.

The typical form that vindications take is illustrated by the following examples. An angry person might try to defend, explain, or vindicate her angry attack on another by saying: "That guy started it," "He deserved it," "He is the guilty one," "I was acting in self-defense," "He insulted me,"

"He violated my rights," "This will teach him a lesson," "This is sending him a message," "I need to uphold my honor," "He is just an animal," "He is a brute, stupid and irrational," "You can't talk to him," and so on.

Defenses like these are not only likely to be backward looking, but they also include derogatory personal remarks blaming the victim himself. All this is no accident, for the language of vindications has much in common with the language of punishment, retribution, retaliation, and vengeance. They are all typically framed in the terminology of blame.

For the angry actors and their associates, vindications give meaning, structure, value, and validity to their aggressive, destructive actions, their violence. It should be noted at once that vindications are characteristically unilateral; they are neither intended to convince nor do they usually succeed in convincing third parties or the victims of the attack that their actions are right.[10] Vindications of angry acts are in a special and peculiar way actor-centered. In technical, philosophical jargon, they are perhaps not "universalizable."

There are obvious parallels between the kind of vindication individuals use to explain or defend their angry attacks on other individuals and the vindications offered by groups for their destructive attacks on groups, that is, for their collective violence. Again, the punishment language is common in both.

We must be careful, however, not to press the analogy between the individual anger and collective violence too far. Collective violence, even if it is taken as the "angry" behavior of a group, is different in important respects from anger between individuals. To reduce one to the other is to commit the individualization fallacy. A group is not an individual and so cannot be angry in the same sense that an individual is angry. Therefore, although the behavioral component might be comparable (for example, they both involve killing and destruction), a psychological analysis appropriate for individuals is inappropriate for groups. In collective violence, for example, subjective anger may be entirely absent, and the actions are unlikely to be spontaneous. Rather, as the studies by Arendt (1963) and by Walliman and Dobkowski (1987) make clear, collective violence is planned and organized; it is often carried out by bureaucrats who approach their grisly task in a "professional" or "businesslike" manner, regarding it as a job to be done quite dispassionately and unemotionally.

The main purpose of introducing the anger model at this juncture is to call attention to a special kind of rationale used both for anger and for extreme and excessive violence, a rationale that I have called a "vindication." If we accept my thesis that a vindication is a distinctive kind of rationale that is separate and distinct from the ordinary kind of rationale used to justify actions, then to claim that violence is irrational on the grounds that it is excessive, disproportionate, and noninstrumental is simply a *non sequitur*.

It ignores the concept of vindication. The rest of this essay will be devoted to the clarification of this concept.

The Violence of Groups

When we move from individuals to groups we enter a new domain, that of symbolism and ideology. Consider as an example the invasion by the Indian army of the Golden Temple in the Punjab on June 4, 1984, and its aftermath: At least one thousand people were killed by the army and this was followed by retaliatory death and destruction wrought by the Sikhs, including the assassination of Indira Gandhi. The collective violence of this sequence of events is replete with symbolism, beginning with what the Golden Temple means to the Sikhs and why it was chosen as a target by Gandhi.[11] The collective violence on both sides cannot be understood without reference to the symbolism. More generally, it should be evident on reflection that collective violence, whenever it occurs, is composed in large part of a concatenation of symbolic acts and relationships set in the conceptual frame of an ideology.

The term 'ideology' is used here to stand for a body of general beliefs and values that are shared by members of a particular group and that are used by them as a basis for social norms, institutions, and policies and through them as a ground for actions and projects.[12] An ideology as intended here approximates what Durkheim (1953) calls the "collective mind."[13] Ideologies in this sense tend to define groups, and groups tend to be defined by their ideology. In Parsons's words (1951, 349), "To constitute an ideology there must exist the additional feature that there is some level of evaluative commitment to the belief as an aspect of membership in the collectivity."

As I have argued throughout this chapter, the group side is an essential element in collective violence; that is, it is violence practiced by, for, and on behalf of a group and its values. What this means in specific cases and how it is articulated and carried out is a function of the symbolism in the group's ideology. Because collective violence is group-oriented and a group enterprise, it is perceived by the individual actor as transpersonal or superpersonal rather than as subjective and personal. This is why, as I pointed out at the beginning, the aims of collective violence and the motives for it are in important ways distinguishable and separable from the aims and motives of private individuals, which may be personal and not shared by others. The differences between the two emerge clearly if we contrast the collective violence of a group of terrorists planting a bomb with the private violence of an individual in a robbery.

An Ideological Framework for the Vindication of Collective Violence

We turn now to a brief examination of a typical framework of arguments that are used to vindicate collective violence. I call it a "framework" to emphasize that it is simply a schema or formal structure to be fleshed out by particular ideologies. It is therefore designed to provide a general structure rather than a specific account, and the examples are simply intended as illustrations of the main points. (I make no claim to historical accuracy in referring to them.)

Before proceeding further, two notes of caution are in order. First, my proposed analysis aims at comprehensiveness and eschews what I conceive to be parochialism. I believe that a parochial approach to the "rationality" of violence is bound to lead to a dangerous misunderstanding and misperception of the issues. Therefore, what follows may appear alien to "civilized" Westerners unaccustomed to thinking in different categories, categories that are accepted by many people in other societies but that they themselves find unacceptable. Furthermore, if we are forthright and candid about it, we need to acknowledge that our own ethical, political, and social values, that is, those of a liberal democratic society, are also part of an ideology. As I have argued earlier, conventional and instrumental views of violence have an ideological bias that is narrower and more ethnocentric than we care to admit.[14]

Second, the analysis presented here is intended only as an illustration of a particular kind of framework. It obviously does not fit, without modification and qualification, all the various kinds of collective violence that have been mentioned earlier or that ought to be included in a comprehensive discussion. In particular, it needs to be expanded and revamped to cover American domestic ideologies, especially as they relate to politico-military ventures and racism.[15] For it is characteristic of nations that consider themselves "civilized" to deny that they are using violence while at the same time imputing violence to their enemies. For example, Afrikaners charge the blacks with being violent, as the Israelis charge the Palestinians. A method needs to be developed to deal with denial and self-deception, even cover-ups, by one or other of the parties. This application of the theory will have to wait until my next essay! In the meantime, the analysis here may serve as a sort of mirror to make us more aware of our own ideological commitment to violence.

Five Parts; or, "Premises" of the Ideological Framework

The ideological framework of concepts used to vindicate collective violence may be divided into five parts, which will loosely be called "premises." The first is the Doctrine of Bifurcation. This is the assumption that the two opposing groups, one of which uses violence against the other, are irretrievably separated and divided—"Never the twain shall meet." They are perceived as having incomparable "natures" and belonging to different categories morally speaking. Racial categories used by racists are an example. For purposes of discussion, the groups will be referred to respectively as the "Chosen Group" and the "Other Group." More often than not, those who claim to be the Chosen Group are also the politically dominant group, the majority, the group in power, or the state, for example, whites versus blacks and Indians, Nazis and Jews, Afrikaners and blacks. There are, of course, other social and political bifurcations that pit two groups against each other, with each regarding itself as the Chosen Group and the other as the Other Group.[16]

The second premise is the Doctrine of Moral Disqualification. The bifurcation principle is based on the Chosen Group's perception of the Other Group as outside the pale, as moral outcasts. The bifurcation is typically grounded in the Chosen Group's conviction that members of the Other Group are morally incompetent and so lack the minimum attributes necessary for being members of the moral community, or even for being human.

Thus, they (the Others) may be considered by the Chosen to be innately deficient in such morally necessary attributes as intelligence, education, moral character, temperament, religious faith, or divine election. They are then, as Takaki (1979) and Frederickson (1987) show in detail, relegated to the status of animals, beasts, savages, barbarians, infidels, servants of Satan, vermin (the Jews in Hitler's view), or, as with the blacks under slavery, child–savages, Sambos, subhumans.

Here it is pertinent to observe that the Chosen Group, the group practicing violence on another group, itself lays down its own specifications of who, for its purposes, is to count as a member of the Other Group, the target group, and who is not. For example, the Chosen Group often unilaterally prescribes that children of mixed parenthood shall belong to the Other Group. Against this, however, it is common to find that the Others, the victims, identify themselves quite differently from the way they are identified by the Chosen Group. This unilaterality of group definition by the Chosen Group is illustrated by the Nazis' definition of who is a Jew and the definition of who is a Negro that was imposed by the whites in America.[17]

The third premise, which is a corollary of the preceding, is the Doctrine of the Double Standard. Having identified the Others as moral incompetents, the Chosen place them, like animals, outside the community of moral beings. Therefore, the Chosen need to adopt a double standard; one for their relationships to those like themselves, who are within the moral community, and another standard for relationships to those outside the community, who are not deemed human. Accordingly, the Chosen have a separate set of moral norms for dealing with Others whom they conceive as nonhuman creatures with no human rights and no claim to equality, liberty, justice, or responsibility. This third standard permits acts like killing, maiming, taking away liberty, exporting, and exterminating Others, acts that would be immoral if they were performed on ordinary human beings who are members of the moral community and of the Chosen Group.[18]

A further consequence of the Others' alleged incapacity to accept and understand morality or to act in accordance with its precepts is that it is taken to be impossible for the Chosen ever to enter into a "dialogue" or "to reason" with them as human beings concerning moral matters involving their differences and the relations between them. In that regard, they are like animals.

In sum, a theological, metaphysical, epistemological, biological, psychological, political, or economic doctrine, highly mythological in content, is introduced to justify the adoption of a permissive double standard by the Chosen in their relations to the Other. This might be called the negative side of the ideological framework.

The fourth premise, the positive side, is the Doctrine of Group Mission, which assigns a plenary mission, often divinely commanded, to the members of the Chosen Group to protect the Chosen Group and its values from perceived threats to it by the Other Group. This mission confers a sacred duty on individuals in the Chosen Group to be "warriors of God," "defenders of liberty," or "avengers," and to carry out any and every possible kind of violence against the Other, including expelling or destroying the Other Group as a whole—as a "final solution."[19] Individuals who sacrifice their lives in doing this duty are honored in the community as heroes and will be rewarded, for example, in the next life with eternal bliss.

Finally, there is a fifth premise that joins the issue: It is that the Chosen Group and the Other Group are positioned against each other in a zero-sum struggle; that is, they are locked in a conflict for which compromise or reconciliation are absolutely inconceivable—"No coexistence is possible." Often the focus of the conflict is a piece of land, as is the case, for example, in the struggle between the Israelis and the Palestinians or between the whites and the Indians in America in the last century. Sometimes it is religious objects (including hallowed land or rituals) that are at issue. Of course, there can be irresoluble conflicts over political or economic power, social or cultural prestige, and so on.

Whatever kind of thing is the source of conflict, the contention is perceived by the Chosen Group as a deadly threat couched in absolutist terms. It is an either/or; it's either us or them! In Al Fatah's words: "One of the two has to be liquidated."[20]

Because third parties generally do not interpret the issues in such absolutist and zero-sum terms and do not agree with the extreme claims of either side, they often find themselves unsympathetic to both of them. In this regard, it is worth noting that outsiders commonly fail to grasp and understand the fundamental issues, which depend on perceptions and ideology to which they are not privy. As a result, they tend to underrate the intensity and passion (vehemence) that characterizes the attitudes of the opposing parties toward each other and the pertinacity and consistency of their faith in their respective ideologies.

The failure to pay sufficient attention to the ideological background of the conflicts that give rise to violence explains the vogue of reductionist explanations of the violence, such as those that interpret it in terms of conflicts of economic interests or other nonideological sources of conflict that are the substance of social science studies of conflict.[21]

Intractability

If we examine the premises of the ideological framework just portrayed, it is obvious that, from a purely logical point of view, an impasse is inevitable. The ideology of a Chosen Group is so laid out that no meeting of minds with the Other Group is logically permitted. The line between the groups is drawn sharply and absolutely—at least by the Chosen Group; or, if the Other Group also regards itself as a Chosen Group, by both groups. As a consequence, the differences between the two groups and the violence between them are, at least at the ideological level, intractable.

In the final analysis, the intractability comes from the fact that Chosen Groups choose as their point of departure a hermetically sealed value system that automatically and for logical reasons excludes members of the Other Group from consideration as equal human beings. Along with the other premises, the logic of the argument makes the Others the natural and rightful targets of collective violence. Given the premises, the conclusion follows with ineluctable necessity.

The basic issue here is a methodological one and one that is worth discussing for the light it throws on the logical side of the vindication of collective violence. In considering the ideological framework from the methodological point of view, we must return to the Doctrine of Moral Disqualification. This doctrine, which has important ethical, political, and social consequences, postulates a sharp division between those who are ethically competent and those who are not. This postulated division, in turn, follows from a narrowly and exclusively defined set of criteria for having ethical "knowledge."[22] Because it is ordinarily and probably correctly assumed that a person's capacity for moral conduct, responsibility, and virtue is contingent on his or her "intellectual" capacity for moral "knowledge," the way that capacity is established and validated becomes a critical issue from the point of view of ethics.

What is important here is that the answer to the question of how competence and incompetence are identified depends on one's view of the nature and source of ethical "knowledge." If, for example, this knowledge is thought to come from God, then competence depends on religious qualifications such as divine election, faith, authority, or membership in a religious group. If, on the other hand, the knowledge is thought to depend on the intuitions of self-evident truths, which are in fact accessible only to educated middle-class white males, like the Founding Fathers, then those who do not have these intuitions or who do not have the social qualifications, such as blacks and Indians, are presumed ethically incompetent. There are numerous other possible illustrations (see Ladd, 1982), but these examples should suffice to make the point clear.

Philosophically, the underlying methodological category implied in the competent/incompetent distinction may be called "absolutism." Generally speaking, methodological absolutism in its numerous forms is based on the assumption that, for logical reasons, ethics must by its very nature be a hermetically sealed system (known as the "autonomy of ethics") and that therefore its first principles are not open to dispute or challenge from the outside, that is, by incompetents, ignoramuses, and people from other traditions. An absolutist system of ethics, especially religious ethics (see Ladd, 1988), is irrefragable.

What I would like to suggest here is that some form or other of methodological absolutism, *irrefragability,* is an essential component in the ideological framework of collective violence, because the ideology's first principles as well as its "facts," its interpretations, and its myths, cannot be disputed, controverted, or gainsaid. This characteristic of methodological irrefragability explains why collective violence is intractable and why the groups involved in it are intransigent.

In sum, I have tried to show that there is a certain basic logical structure in the thinking that lies behind collective violence, a structure that makes the claims of protagonists and their followers impregnable or, more specifically, makes them irrefragable to counterarguments, to appeals to reasonableness, to self-interest, to threats, or to other sorts of "realistic considerations." It should be evident by now that the other theories of violence that I examined previously fail to make room for this aspect of collective violence and so misconstrue the basic issues and underestimate the problematic character of collective violence.

Lessons

Before concluding this chapter, I should like to add some remarks about the significance of the kind of analysis presented here.

The basic assumption of this essay is that ideas are important, not only our own ideas, which we fondly believe to be reasonable and true, but also the ideas of others, ideas that we are prone to dismiss as plainly silly, absurd, superstitious, or dangerous. The value systems comprising ideas, true and false, that drive people to help or harm others are an important area of investigation, not only for practical, political, and social reasons, but also for philosophical and ethical reasons.

It has been said that the big mistake that we in the Western democracies made about Hitler was not to take seriously what he said in *Mein Kampf* and in his public utterances about his ideology and his program. Instead, we took what he said to be the empty rhetoric of a raving madman, an uneducated housepainter. We discovered only too late that the premises of his ideology pointed consistently, logically, and inexorably to the Final Solution, the extermination of the Jews. What happened is that we dismissed the Nazis' ideas as inconsequential because they did not fit in with our own ideas of what is reasonable. We could not believe that a "civilized people" like the Germans would resort to collective violence, genocide, and so we did not believe that what Hitler prophesied would actually be carried out. Our naiveté was our undoing.

By now we should recognize that we ignore other people's ideas at our peril, and that means not only ignoring what they say but also ignoring the inherent consistency of their thinking, its logical framework. A cavalier attitude toward other people's ideas, as we are now finding, is not only unrealistic and dangerous but, I am prepared to argue, is also immoral.

The exact methodology to be followed in investigations of this type is a complicated matter, for on the one hand we do not want to deny that people often do not do what they say they ought to do; there is a kind of slippage as well as hypocrisy that needs to be taken into account. Behavior does not always match theory. In general, the extent to which the analysis presented here is or is not reflected in political and social behavior must be left up to those better equipped to deal with empirical realities.

On the other hand there are questions involving distinctions of one sort or another between people's conscious and explicitly recognized ideas and those implicit in their ways of thinking, their customs, and their institutions. Some sort of reconstruction of underlying but unstated beliefs, and of the logical connections between them, is required. Elsewhere (Ladd, 1957) I have suggested a methodology that might be used here.

A few final words about the more strictly ethical pertinence of this kind of study will round out the picture. The position adopted here might be regarded by some as relativistic. If it is, it is not relativistic in a vicious sense; rather, it is critical and reflective. It would be better (see Ladd, 1982) to call it nonabsolutistic or, better still, antiabsolutistic.

An important consideration about the methodology of ethics is germane to this question. In ethical argumentation, which I take to be an essential component of the ethical life, there are two methods of arguing against erroneous or evil ideas, such as the idea that collective violence is right and a duty. That is, there are two kinds of ethical counterarguments, which are discussed at greater length in my essay "Philosophy and the Moral Professions" (1985, 16–18).

First, there is the kind of counterargument that argues that an ethical idea is false (unacceptable, mistaken, erroneous) on the grounds that it contradicts an ethical idea that is taken to be true. For example, the argument might be that violence is not right but wrong because it violates human rights. I call this kind of counterargument a "confutation."

In contrast to confutations, there is another kind of counterargument which I call a "refutation." It argues that the ethical idea under attack is false (unacceptable, mistaken, erroneous) on the grounds that the premises, the beliefs, and the lines of reasoning on which it rests are themselves false, groundless, or unproven.

Confutation argues that such (evil) ideas are wrong because ours are right. Refutation argues that they are wrong because their conclusions do not stand up: Their grounding is fallacious and false. Confutation is dogmatic, because it presupposes that we have the right ethics. Refutation, on the other hand, is skeptical, because its purpose is to undermine the credibility of a false position.

The premises used to vindicate collective violence are generally, perhaps invariably, flawed. This provides a basis for a refutation. We do not need to make use of premises drawn from our own ethics or value system to disprove an ethics of collective violence. Nevertheless, to disprove and refute a particular ethics of collective violence, we do need to know, to understand, and to analyze in detail the ideological position that provides its underpinning. Hence, a successful refutation of an ethics of collective violence requires a lot of hard work!

NOTES

1. See Bundy (1988, 64ff.) on the bombing of cities. A thoroughgoing critique of the American addiction to the use of air power is to be found in Sherry (1987).

2. For quotations by Jewish writers who say genocide is commanded in the Torah, see Harkabi (1988, 142ff.).

3. See Walzer (1977) and the critique by Bundy (1988, 94–96).

4. See May (1987) for an interestingly full discussion of subjects like this.

5. Cotta (1978, 81). I have found this book to be extremely helpful in working through the ideas in this essay.

6. For a critique of the legal definition of violence, see a criticism of Gurr reported in Zimmerman (1983, 62) that "he has taken over the point of view of the authorities."

7. Incendiary bombings of cities by the United States during World War II provide an example, albeit a controversial one. For a discussion, see Bundy (1988, 53–97).

8. Note that the last two sentences in the quotation are reversed in order from the original text.

9. These are some of the distinctive attributes of violence that are captured in Cotta's analysis (1978) when he characterizes violence as "passional" (63), "unruly" (64), "depersonalizing" (64), "non-dialogical and non-coexistential" (66).

10. Except, of course, when the victim is overcome with guilt!

11. For a summary of these events, see Murray J. Leaf, "The Punjab Crisis," in Laqueur and Alexander (1987), 318–26. In his analysis, Leaf downplays the ideological side of the conflict—mistakenly, in my opinion.

12. For a somewhat similar definition, see Parsons (1951, 348–51). For a general account of theories of ideology, see McLellan (1986).

13. Durkheim defines 'conscience collective' as "the set of beliefs and sentiments common to the average members of a single society (which) forms a determinate system that has its own life." Quoted in Lukes (1985, 4).

14. On ideologies, see McLellan (1986). Takaki (1979) shows in detail how American democratic ideologies, which he calls "iron cages," serve as a propadeutic for racism, slavery, and genocide.

15. See Sherry (1987) and Ladd (1987) on military ideologies. For a discussion of racism, see Ringer (1983) and Takaki (1979).

16. Horowitz (1985) classifies them as unranked groups. Obvious examples are Jews and Arabs, Hindus and Moslems.

17. See Walliman and Dobkowski (1987, 14–15) on selecting victims for genocide. Horowitz (1985, 46–48) has an interesting empirical account of how individuals are identified as members of a group.

18. Incidentally, double moral standards are not restricted to this context. Readers of the essay "On Liberty" should recall that Mill himself, the "apostle of liberalism," writes that his doctrine of liberty does not hold "for backward states of society in which the race itself may be considered in its nonage." Similarly, Frederickson (1987, 323) writes that the proslavery writers in the South maintained that "blacks were actually submen suited only for slavery, to whom the Declaration of Independence obviously did not apply."

19. To get the flavor, one only needs to read *Mein Kampf*, or Harkabi's account of the fundamentalist Jewish writers who advocate genocide because it is commanded in the Torah (1988, 149): "God declares a holy jihad." "The day will yet come when we will all be called to fulfill the divinely ordained war to destroy Amalek." They identify the Arabs with the biblical Amalek (Deut. 25:17–19.)

20. Quoted in Laqueur and Alexander (1987, 149). See also pp. 315–18.

21. Horowitz (1985, 131) concludes after a thorough investigation of ethnic conflicts that "it remains difficult to tie significant aspects of ethnic violence to economic interests. On the contrary, what emerges quite clearly is the willingness of ethnic groups to sacrifice economic interest for the sake of other kinds

of gain." Horowitz's thesis is that ethnic conflicts are basically struggles for relative group worth based on comparisons of self-worth between groups.

22. As a philosopher I am well aware of the pitfalls of using the expression "ethical knowledge." I do not intend to beg any metaethical questions here. My only purpose in using the term in this context is to convey the strong sense of conviction and of certainty that characterizes a person's ethical commitments in contrast to, say, that person's beliefs, opinions, and thoughts. As I use the term here, it is relativistic in the sense that individuals' and groups' "knowledge" may contradict one another.

2

EMOTIVENESS AND ELUSIVENESS IN DEFINITIONS OF VIOLENCE

Robert Holmes

SOME CONSTRAINTS ON DEFINITIONS OF 'VIOLENCE'

Definitions of 'violence' tend to be relatively unhelpful. They present an array of conflicting analyses that often introduce more confusion than clarity into the substantive issues of most concern in connection with violence. Still, there are some important observations that can be made about the meaning of the concept.

On the one hand the term 'violence' has a strong evaluative force to it. Even a casual survey of the ways in which it is used reveals that considerable stake is placed on being able to attach it to actions or policies of which one disapproves and to withhold it from those of which one approves. It has, if you like, a pronounced emotive meaning (a convenient label I shall use without implying the rest of the emotivist analysis of language from which it derives). Just as there may be uses of the term in which emotive meaning figures prominently, so there may be analyses (or definitions) of the concept in which the emotive meaning predominates. The term is then, let us say, persuasively defined (again borrowing a convenient term from the emotivist vocabulary without implying all the particulars of its use there). In other words, it reflects certain *evaluations:* the judgments in which it occurs are not neutral.

On the other hand the notion of violence also has descriptive (or conceptual or cognitive) meaning, whether that be a single meaning, and whether it be clear or confused. And just as there may be uses in which this aspect of its meaning predominates, so there may be definitions or analyses that emphasize this aspect of its meaning. Matters are complicated further by the fact that, if one stresses the conceptual meaning, one can do so either by trying to explicate it in morally neutral terms (say by reference to notions like force and destruction) or in morally (or at least normatively) laden terms like 'legitimacy' or 'violation'.

Different accounts of violence, from Newton Garver's pioneering essay in 1968 through Sergio Cotta's (1978) book-length study stress various aspects of its meaning and do so in different ways. But the term 'violence' is sufficiently vague and ambiguous, I suggest, as to make it difficult to say with confidence that either of these approaches is the only defensible one; or that any one of the various avenues open within either approach is the only correct one.

It is one of the merits of John Ladd's account in Chapter 1 that it sensitizes us to ways in which certain definitions may conceal ideological biases. What he calls conventional accounts, for example, "define 'violence' in such a way as to make violence an antiestablishment activity and something that respectable and civilized people do not participate in." He seems to want to explicate violence in a way that neutralizes the advantage defenders of the status quo often seek for themselves by defining it (explicitly or implicitly) in a way that enables them to characterize opposition to them as violent and to refrain from so characterizing their own resistance to this opposition. At the same time, Ladd includes a definite evaluative element in his own account.

> Generally speaking, no viable political theory can seriously rule out the use of coercion and destruction under certain circumstances. For example, states sometimes have to use coercion to contain violence or to secure other worthy goals, such as the protection of life and liberty or obedience to the laws. Even war, one might argue, which is per se a use of coercion and destruction, need not and ought not to consist of violence. . . .
>
> Hence, we may grant that, unlike violence, some uses of coercion and destruction are acceptable, that is, reasonable, legitimate, legal, or moral—depending on the particular theory one espouses. That means that we need to look for a narrower definition of violence that will mark it off from generally acceptable uses of coercion.

As I understand this, it is saying that, indeed, the term 'violence' does have a strong evaluative meaning, tied to the notion of legitimacy; and that the account of the descriptive meaning must be tailored to accord with this.

At this point I would diverge from Ladd (as well as, I might add, from Cotta, with whom Ladd here expresses agreement). For while one must recognize, and cannot by any plausible analysis remove, what I have called the emotive meaning of the term 'violence', one *can* assign the term a descriptive or conceptual meaning that is largely neutral from a moral standpoint. At the least, one can give it a descriptive meaning that is neutral with regard to the more controversial issues over which questions of the justifiability of the use of violence might be raised. For if the conventional definitions are biased in the ways Ladd indicates, I suggest that the constraint proposed in the passages just quoted is biased against the anarchist and the pacifist as well. It would require conceding the legitimacy of the use by governments of the kind of force that in the hands of others would usually be labeled violence; and it would commit us (so Ladd says one might argue, though he does not so argue himself) to saying that war itself need not involve the use of violence. Not only, then, is the negative emotive meaning of the term withheld from governmental force, destruction, and killing (at least when they are considered legitimate), but the very definition of anarchism as "the theory that all forms of government rest on violence, and are therefore wrong and harmful" by someone like Emma Goldman, becomes incoherent, as do definitions of war (like Clausewitz's) explicitly by reference to violence.

I would prefer to leave all the substantive moral questions about the justifiability of the use of violence open. This would mean that the legitimacy of government violence cannot be ruled out by definition simply because government has a monopoly on the major instruments of violence. It would also mean that warfare cannot be shown to be wrong simply because it represents a large-scale use of organized violence. But it would also mean that those who defend the state, or who defend war, cannot ease the burden of justifying the killing and destruction war and the state entail by denying that it constitutes violence. They cannot quietly substitute less emotively charged words like 'force' and 'coercion' for the term 'violence'. Let us, I say, recognize that the use of violence is generally accepted; that modern nation–states probably cannot exist without using it (or at least without being willing and prepared to use it) and that warfare cannot exist without it. Let those who oppose the institutions of government and warfare not be able to dismiss them simply on the grounds that they entail violence; and let those who wish to defend those institutions not be allowed to do so without confronting the fact that they have committed themselves to the use of violence.

These observations are not so much a criticism of Ladd's account of violence as suggestions regarding how to cut through some of the unnecessary complications that attend the attempts to define it. In fact, I am not sure that the account Ladd offers really conforms to the above constraint anyway; it may be that he ends up more nearly emphasizing the noncognitive than the cognitive or descriptive aspects of violence. If so, these observations may be regarded as an invitation to him to clarify some of these points.

THE MORAL ASSESSMENT OF COLLECTIVITIES

The other aspect of Ladd's discussion I wish to comment on is what he considers a "mischievous consequence" of the individualization fallacy (that of assimilating collective violence to private violence). This is "the attribution to groups of the kind of moral characteristics that are only appropriate for individuals." He says in this connection: "Groups are said to have the same sort of rights, responsibilities, obligations, virtues, and vices as individuals have. They are treated as big individuals. Private morality is 'blown up' or 'writ large' for groups." It is hard to know which comes first here, whether this "Platonic projection," as he calls it, of moral attributes onto groups is a result of the individualization fallacy, or whether the assimilation of collective to private violence is a result of the Platonic projection. I suspect it works the second way, and that what leads people to view collective violence in the same terms as private violence is the fact that they have antecedently begun to think of collectivities as though they were superpersons. In any event, there are further complications in this process of Platonic projection that need to be noted.

We commonly speak of the conduct of groups or collectivities in the same way we do of that of individuals. This way of speaking is so deeply embedded in our language that we can hardly avoid it. For this reason it is important to ask whether it is intelligible to try to assess the conduct of collectivities in moral terms. A common criticism of the conduct of nations has been that it falls short of the standards of the conduct of individuals. This tacitly recognizes that there are two "moralities," if you like, an individual morality governing the conduct of individuals, and a collective morality governing that of groups. It is just that the standards of the one (or, perhaps the degree of compliance with the one) fall short of the other.

One might, however, acknowledge a distinction between individual and collective morality but contend that the collective morality is the higher of the two. One might say that it overrides individual morality when and if the two conflict (as they may, for example, when individual rights are weighed against the imperatives of state power). This was the view of Heinrich von Treitschke in the nineteenth century, and it found its way into the fascist philosophy of *Mein Kampf*.

There is a third possibility here, however. Rather than giving priority to either individual or collective morality, one might agree with Ladd that it is a mistake to attribute moral notions to the behavior of groups. But then one might contend that what follows from this is that we simply cannot intelligibly judge the conduct, say, of nations, from a moral standpoint; and hence that the large-scale organized violence of warfare cannot be subjected to moral assessment. The just war theory, which Ladd recognizes as simply providing an excuse for collective violence, would on this view be wrongheaded in a very fundamental way. It would consist of trying to assess the conduct of nations in waging war by categories and concepts that are simply inapplicable to such conduct. This is an extreme version of so-called political realism.

I find all three of these alternatives unsatisfactory. I agree with Ladd that the Platonic projection is a mistake. Collectivities simply are not persons. To ascribe conduct to them in a literal sense is misconceived. Accordingly, both the view that would assign priority to individual over collective morality and the view that would assign priority to collective over individual morality I believe to be mistaken. But I find even more disturbing the position of those political realists (it does not include them all) who would try to exempt the conduct of collectivities from moral assessment and who find the introduction of moral categories into discussions of international affairs naive. For just as it is important to avoid the unnecessary hypostatization of collectivities, it is important to insist on the relevance of morality to the so-called conduct of nation–states and other collectivities. Both these concerns can be met by analyzing the behavior of collectivities ultimately in terms of the conduct of individuals, because the conduct of individuals is always susceptible to moral assessment. And if the conduct of groups inevitably consists ultimately of actions by individuals, then that conduct is susceptible to moral assessment as well.

This is a kind of reductionism, to be sure, but of a limited and I believe, benign sort. It does suggest, however, that *in some sense* the collective violence of groups must be understood ultimately in terms of the violence of individuals, which on the face of it is at odds with Ladd's account. I say "on the face of it," because I believe one can defend this kind of reductionism without falling into the various confusions he cautions against. We need not take the models of private violence, as he calls it, to be the appropriate ones for understanding collective violence. We need only recognize that individuals play different roles, and that in some of these roles (as, say, government or corporate leaders), they have obligations and responsibilities that differ from those they have when playing other roles in interpersonal relations.

This does not require that we recognize a public and a private morality (at least, not unless we mean nothing more by this than what I have just stated). It requires only that we understand collective violence as consisting ultimately of the actions of individuals in the performance of certain roles of power and authority. This suffices to avoid the conceptual and metaphysical problems of the Platonic projection. But at the same time it enables us to judge violence fully, whether of collectivities or of individuals. The very nature of morality demands that we do no less.

3

PASSIVE DISOBEDIENCE AS VIOLENCE: Reflections on German High Court Decisions

Eike von Savigny

PEACEFUL SIT-INS AS VIOLENCE

Passive disobedience first became a widespread phenomenon in West Germany when in the early eighties the peace movement (*Friedensbewegung*) began systematic sit-ins in driveways of U.S. military installations lodging Pershing or cruise missiles. This was part of a consistent strategy of demonstrations, lasting for several years and practiced all over the Federal Republic, against the NATO decision to station high-accuracy, middle-range missiles in Western Europe in order to force the Warsaw Pact to mutual disarmament with respect to these weapons. The sit-ins were planned and performed in ways that highlighted them as particularly peaceful enterprises: Some people sat down in the driveway, having announced the hour and place to the police as well as to the commanding U.S. officer some days in advance (so that other driveways could be used); they made room for ambulances, though not for any other military vehicles; if the police carried them away, they did not in any way resist; they had even received special training in not being provoked and in avoiding any movement of self-defense even if the police behaved rudely.

In due course, many of these people had to appear in court, charged for what in the German criminal code is called '*Nötigung*', a word I shall translate as "constraint." Although the translation may be fair enough, what matters is the legal description of the crime, whose essential features, as given in Article 240, are: By *Gewalt* (originally meaning "violence"; see the discussion by Waldenfels in Chapter 7), or by a severe threat, one person brings it about that another person does or omits something against his or her own will. (There is an additional culpability proviso that will concern us later.) The term '*Gewalt*' occurs in other articles, too, usually where violent ways of committing a crime are distinguished (for the purpose of more severe punishment) from nonviolent forms of what is substantially the same crime, as robbery in contrast to theft, rape in contrast to sexual abuse, or fierce resistance to policemen in contrast to mere disobedience.

Historically (see Jakobs [1986] for more details), the prohibition of violence in Article 240 originated from the need to suppress the tendency, widespread among powerful families even down to the time of the Enlightenment, to obtain satisfaction or justice or whatever they believed they had a claim to, by self-help rather than by appeal to the authorities. This behavior, known as *crimen vis* in Roman law, constituted a constant threat to public peace, and it was originally to secure public peace that violence was prohibited. Later on, the purpose shifted, as Jakobs makes clear, and Article 240, as one of the laws protecting personal freedom, is now intended to protect the individual person's free choice against specific illicit kinds of constraint.

All the same, the very term '*Gewalt*' signals which specific kinds of behavior free choice is to be protected against. There are plenty of cases in which people are forced by others to do this or that, cases that are socially absolutely normal; just consider being forced to overbid in an auction if you want to get the painting, or doing what your boss orders you unless you want to be fired, or stopping your car if the car ahead stops for completely mysterious reasons. Other cases are socially unacceptable, and out of these socially unacceptable cases, Article 240, by referring to violence as a means, selects the most severe ones for criminal punishment.

Now whereas the text of the criminal code is rather stable, opinions as to what counts as socially acceptable change more quickly; and the more types of behavior that come to be regarded as unacceptable, the stronger the pressure on the courts to enlarge that subsection of socially unacceptable cases of constraint against which people are to be protected by criminal law, rather than being left with the cumbersome and risky procedure of suing the offenders for damages.

I shall now give a sample of some decision sequences, stretching over a period of about one hundred years, in which the courts had to decide whether or not violence was involved.[1] This list is representative of how they reacted to the pressure just noted; in fact they gave in, and the only way open to them was to enlarge the scope of what they counted as violence, with the result that '*Gewalt*' comes less and less to mean something like "violence." The decisions in my sample are not all concerned with Article 240, but this does not matter. Although it is sometimes claimed that one and the same word may mean different things in different articles, it is a general rule that considerations about what it means in one article are relevant to what it means in a different one; and in the interpretation of one article there is regular cross-reference to other ones. Within the sequences (which are more or less in chronological order), the weakening of the concept of violence is pursued in different directions, corresponding to different similarity bridges. As a starting point, there were three clear-cut cases of violent behavior:

- The victim was knocked down, his fist was pulled out of his pocket and was unclenched to get at the money (*RG* 2:184 [1880]).[2]
- The victim was seized by his chest, his hat was struck from his head, a box was pulled out of his hands (*RG* 4:124 [1881]).
- The victim's hands were held on to, in order to take something out of his pocket (*RG* 4:429 [1881]).

1. Our first sequence widens the scope of violence in the direction of pressure:

- Setting the dog on a night watchman to prevent the latter from stopping the defendant's noisy singing in the night counted as violence (*RG* in *GA* 37:158 [1889]).
- In wintertime, the defendants had removed windows and doors from a flat to force the tenants to move out (*RG* 7:269 [1882]; *RG* 9:58 [1883]).
- The defendant had fired a loaded gun in the air (*RG* 60:157 [1926]).
- The defendant had fired a blank pistol in the air (*RG* 66:353 [1932]).
- The defendant had fired a tear-gas pistol when his victim was out of its range (*BGH* in *GA* [1962], 145).

2. Our second sequence has to do with threatening as well as with robbing someone of his or her composure:

- The defendant had driven a motor car toward the victim in such a way that the latter had to leap aside (*BGH* in *NJW* [1953], 672; *BGH* in *MDR* [1955], 145).
- In the passing lane of an Autobahn, for several kilometers, the defendant had followed the car ahead at a distance of two meters and at a speed of 105 km/h, constantly blowing the horn and flashing the headlights, although the car ahead was the last in a line of cars that, all at the same speed, were overtaking some slow trucks. The driver ahead became extremely nervous and finally took shelter in the right lane (*BGH* 19:263 [1964]).
- Students had shouted and otherwise made a din in a university lecture until the professor's nerves could not take it any longer and he gave up and broke off the lecture (*BGH* in *NJW* [1982], 189).

3. Violence is also affirmed in cases where freedom of choice is affected:

- The defendant had caused the victim erroneously to believe that the victim was locked up (*RG* 13:49 [1885]). Here one might speak of a shift from violence to wiliness.
- A policeman had been locked up (*RG* 27:405 [1895]).

- The defendant had applied an inhaled narcotic to the sleeping victim (*BGH* 1:145 [1951]). With this decision, the Federal High Court explicitly dissented from a much older decision by the former German Supreme Court, thus signaling the meaning change that had taken place in between.

4. Depriving someone of freedom of choice may indeed be achieved by bodily resistance; here begins our last sequence, which eventually leads up to violence in the form of peaceful sit-ins:

- In a Catholic churchyard, the defendants (they were a big group) had crowded together in such a way that a suicide's funeral procession simply could not pass through to reach the grave that had been dug in consecrated soil (*RG* 45:153 [1911]).
- The defendant had blocked the path of a cart by advancing toward it in the middle of the road (*RG* in *DJZ* [1923], 372).
- High school and university students had organized a demonstration against an increase in the streetcar fare in Cologne, the demonstration involving sit-ins on the streetcar rails, with active resistance to being removed by the police (*BGH* 23:46 [1969]). The streetcar driver could have passed through, but only at the cost of committing manslaughter.
- Finally, the sit-ins of the peace movement described in the beginning were subsumed under '*Gewalt*' (*OLG* Stuttgart in *NJW* [1984], 1909; *BGH* in *NJW* [1986], 1883).

THE SORITES FALLACY

These series of decisions transfer the concepts of violence and force, via similarities between neighboring cases, from uproar and wild fighting to completely passive behavior of people who had even been given special training in suppressing the natural urge for self-defense. They immediately call to mind the classical Sorites fallacy, by which you can prove both that one grain of wheat constitutes a heap of wheat and that a collection of 10,000 grains of wheat is not a heap of wheat after all. As reported by Diogenes Laertius (1972, 7:82), you prove that one is many, rather than proving that one grain makes a heap; but although the former is a manifest contradiction, the result will be seen to be no less disastrous in the latter case. The result is that you can no longer use the word 'heap' in communication: It loses its role in distinguishing one thing from another, thus becoming devoid of descriptive meaning. This is precisely what German courts have done to the words 'violence' and 'force'; the terms have lost their descriptive meanings. Now a legislating body must be in a position to rely on descriptive meaning if it is to enact norms and thereby regularize behavior via the respect for these norms in society. The effect of depriving a word of its descriptive meaning, if that word occurs in a law, thus amounts to depriving the legislating body of its constitutional role.

In order to show that the Sorites fallacy suspicion is warranted in our case, let me outline the fallacy. There are different reconstructions of it; I shall rely on the one by Jonathan Barnes (1982, esp. 27–32). By describing its tradition since antiquity, he was able to show that his discussion concerned the real classical fallacy; and he reduced it to the use of minimal premises, which leaves us with few options if we want to avoid the disastrous conclusion.

I shall stick to the heap example. Let us choose a finite number of grains, large enough for everyone to agree that this number of grains, if collected on the smallest possible area, makes up a heap of grains. (The condition that the grains cover the smallest possible area is necessary because otherwise they might be spread all over the ground rather than forming a heap. How large the area has to be depends on the angle the heap will form.) I have never counted grains in a heap and have, therefore, no idea how large the number ought to be; let us assume, therefore, that 10,000 grains will do. Thus we have premise (1):

> (1) *A collection of 10,000 grains that covers the smallest possible area is a heap.*

Now a difference between 10,000 grains and 9,999 grains does not make a difference in "heapness"; this evident premise is stated as an if-then sentence, our premise (2):

> (2) *If a collection of 10,000 grains that covers the smallest possible area is a heap, then a collection of 9,999 grains that covers the smallest possible area is a heap, too.*

From these two premises, by *modus ponens* we can infer an intermediary theorem:

> *A collection of 9,999 grains that covers the smallest possible area is a heap.*

Keep in mind that this is not an additional premise; it is a theorem derived from the first two premises by the most indispensable of inference rules. With this theorem in mind, we go on to the next step, that a difference of one grain will not change a 9,999-grain heap into a 9,998-grain non-heap. We state this as our premise (3):

> (3) *If a collection of 9,999 grains that covers the smallest possible area is a heap, then a collection of 9,998 grains that covers the smallest possible area is a heap, too.*

We can see now how this is going to continue. In a long, cumbersome process, we successively derive for collections of grains, each one grain less than its predecessor, the theorem that they are heaps. For each single inference, we need a new premise that states that if the collection proved to be a heap in the latest step is a heap, then the collection containing one grain less is a heap, too. So the end of the process looks like this. We will have just proved as a theorem:

A collection of two grains that covers the smallest possible area is a heap.

Then we need our last premise (10,000):

(10,000) If a collection of two grains that covers the smallest possible area is a heap, then one grain is a heap, too.

From this we derive our disastrous conclusion:

One grain is a heap.   Q.E.D.

Now this is false; one grain does not make up a heap. The conclusion has been derived from:

- our first premise, stating that 10,000 grains make a heap;
- 9,999 'if-then' premises; and
- 9,999 applications of one and the same rule of inference, modus ponens.

Thus either our first premise is false, or at least one of the 9,999 if-then premises is false, or modus ponens is an invalid form of inference, or it is not to be applied 9,999 times in succession. There is no easy way out; it is extremely hard to see how the starting premise could fail to be correct, or why any one of the transition premises should be false, or how one could doubt the validity of modus ponens or impose restrictions on the number of its successive applications.

Should there be any doubt that 10,000 grains make a heap of wheat, we can choose any greater number, say 100,000; the only difference will be that the derivation will take considerably longer.

Nor can there be any doubt that our transition premises are as obvious as one might wish. It is true that, if we compare the first with the last, the self-evidence seems to be of a different kind. In (2), 'if-then' has the force of 'since' or 'because': 9,999 grains make up a heap since 10,000 do. On the other hand although we may agree that 1 grain will certainly constitute a heap if 2 grains do so, the force of 'if-then' is quite different in this sentence. The difference can be brought to light by switching to the subjunctive, which is much more appropriate here: if 2 grains made up a heap, 1 grain would do so, too. This is self-evident, for sure, though not in the sense of licensing the proof that 1 grain is a heap, but rather in the sense of inviting the conclusion that since 1 grain does not make up a heap, neither will 2. This switch in our transition premises, from a tendency toward what might be called forward reasoning to a contrary tendency toward backward reasoning, ought to alert us to the possibility that there is something odd about our use of if-then sentences as transition premises. But what?

The fallacy has nothing to do with numbers. It can be duplicated with any quality, provided this quality admits of differences such that, if two items differ by the smallest difference which is just noticeable, either both items have the quality or both lack it. Another example, also noted by Barnes (1982, 35), is colors. By the Sorites fallacy, you can prove that everything red is blue by either moving slowly through adjacent shades of purple, lilac, and violet, or with a little more patience, through orange, yellow, and green. The number of transition premises will depend on the capacity of your victim for discriminating between different shades of colors; and your success will depend on your victim's agreeing, in each step, to the purely logical reasoning: "These two cards differ in color, but they could not differ less; therefore, if the first is red, then the second is red, too"—which is true, even if both cards are green.

A further important point (which it took me great pains to be convinced of) is that the fallacy does not in the least depend on any general if-then premise, say of the kind: "If a collection of n grains that covers the smallest possible area is a heap, then a collection of $n-1$ grains that covers the smallest possible area is a heap, too." From this single general premise, there would of course follow all the particular if-then premises we have been using. However, the general premise also entails the following general consequence: "If a collection of n grains that covers the smallest possible area is a heap, then any smaller collection of grains that covers the smallest possible area is a heap, too." Since this consequence immediately alerts one to the disastrous conclusion that one grain is a heap, the general premise from which it follows fails to be self-evident (at least on reflection). Rejecting it and thereby rejecting the general premise from n to $n-1$ grains looks like the most natural way out. It will not work, however, because the apparent truth of the particular if-then sentences actually used in our derivation would remain intact, and we would not have gotten rid of the fallacy.

Nor will it work to look for a solution by falsifying one or several of the particular if-then premises. One has the feeling that somewhere, say between 40 and 15 grains, the quality of heapness should fade away. The idea is that the pernicious chain ought to have a weak link where it can be broken. But the sad fact is that you will neither find a definite number, say 29, nor will you be able to state lower and upper limits, say 15 and 40, such that above 40 the premises are manifestly true, manifestly false below 15, and dubious in between. The feeling arises from the observation that 'heap' seems to denote a concept with blurred edges, such that it might be the case that less than 15 grains do not make up a heap, that more than 40 do, and that in between one cannot say anything for certain. Even if true, this would not help us at all, because we did not use as premises any statements to the effect that this or that collection of grains is a heap—except for our starting premise, where the heap can be as large as we please. What counts is *not* that 29 grains make up a heap; what counts is, rather, that they do *if* 30 do.

A SOLUTION THROUGH CONTEXT-RELATIVITY

For our problem, what counts is the self-evidence of the smallest steps; for it is just their self-evidence that the courts appealed to. Whatever convincing force the courts' arguments have—if one abstracts from the fact that a decision may be well founded by virtue of independent evaluative reasons, or reasons related to crime prevention—derives from pronouncements like the following: "If behavior in that case was the exercise of violence, then so is the behavior presently under consideration." (I shall give references below.) The arguments never rely on a dubious general premise like, "If any two kinds of behavior are at most minimally distinct with respect to either constituting or not constituting exercise of force or violence, then if one of them constitutes exercise of force or violence, so does the other." We do indeed face the problem of accepting the self-evidence of the smallest steps and of avoiding the disastrous conclusion all the same.

The solution I suggest consists in denying the applicability of *modus ponens* to our singular if-then premises. I shall argue that, in the examples suitable for Sorites, the facts that are usually expressed by if-then sentences are relational facts in terms of predicate logic, atomic facts in terms of the propositional calculus, rather than being conditionals. The facts to be expressed are of the kind that relative to a heap of 10,000 grains, a collection of 9,999 grains is a heap; that relative to a heap of 29 grains, a collection of 28 grains is a heap; and that relative to a heap of 2 grains, 1 grain makes up a heap, too. One may even assume quite generally that relative to a heap of n grains, a collection of $n - 1$ grains makes up a heap. No harm will result because from the facts that A is a heap, and that B is a heap relative to the heap A, all you can derive is that B is a heap relative to the heap A; what you cannot derive is that B is a heap. Therefore, even if it is true that C is a heap relative to the heap B, and that B is a heap relative to the heap A, and that A is a heap, it does not follow that C is a heap (or that C is a heap relative to the heap A).

To show that no such entailment holds, let us consider a politician, B, and two of his political friends, A and C, who are both conservatives. Now compared with his political friend A, B is liberal; compared with his political friend C, B is reactionary. If from the fact that compared to conservative A, B is liberal, we might infer that B is liberal, and if from the fact that compared to conservative C, B is reactionary, we might infer that B is reactionary, we might infer that he is both liberal and reactionary, which is impossible or senseless. (We do indeed say such things as: "Mrs.

Thatcher is both liberal and reactionary." But then what we understand is, of course, that in a sense she is liberal, and in a sense she is reactionary.) We can do the same faulty derivation with numbers: Relative to 9, 7 is small; relative to 5, 7 is large. Because we must not derive that 7 is both small and large, we must avoid either derivation. Now as regards 'small' and 'large', it has been known since antiquity that these words denote context-relative concepts—a tall girl may be a small basketball player. The same holds for many other words, like 'old' and 'young', 'useful' and 'useless', 'conservative' and 'revolutionary'; their use is known to presuppose tacitly supplied frames of reference, or contexts. A pupil who is called old is so called relative to the average age in his form; a tool that is called useful is so called relative to the task it is used for; a politician is called conservative relative to the spectrum of political opinions in the political theater he or she is engaged in.

The same holds for heaps and colors. A collection of 4 grains may be a heap on a game board with collections of 4, 5, and 6 grains on some of its squares, single grains on some of the other squares, paths connecting the squares, and an instruction to the players to reach as many and as large heaps as possible but to avoid squares with single grains. And a collection of 10,000 grains may fail to be a heap in a rural freight station where there are several collections of 10,000 grains and several ones of 100,000, and where in the course of loading the foreman tells one of the workers to start with the heaps. As to colors, it is well known that background plays an enormous role, background being just a special case of neighborhood and context. A piece of paper that is green if attached to a blue background may be blue if attached to a green one; when we say that it is "really" turquoise, what we mean is that it is turquoise if attached to a white background. Psychologists sometimes count such phenomena as optical illusions; this is as good metaphysics as it would be to say that 7 is "really" middle-sized and that it is a numerical illusion to think it small if compared to 9 and large if compared to 5.

It is quite normal linguistic usage to express relational facts by if-then sentences. If my mother is old, then surely my grandmother is—for my grandmother is old relative to her daughter. However, if my grandfather is surprisingly young, surely my grandmother is, for she is young if compared to her husband. If President Bush is a right-wing politician, then Vice President Quayle is—this means nothing but that Quayle is as far to the right as the President is.

ATTRIBUTIONS OF VIOLENCE AS CONTEXT-RELATIVE

Let us not multiply examples beyond necessity. What I need for establishing my diagnosis of the German High Courts' handling of violence as an instance of the Sorites fallacy is evidence for the assumption that this and related concepts are context-relative. The assumption can be established by describing behavior and contexts such that, independent of any moral evaluations, the behavior clearly constitutes exercise of violence or of force, or constraint, in one context while failing to constitute such in a different context. I shall rely on the heuristic principle that behavior that is normal in its context fails to constitute violence, whereas it can tend to do so in contexts where it is statistically rare; however, this heuristic guide is not a theory of contexts because I do not have any such theory.

First, violent behavior: A boxer who in a standard fight deals his partner heavy blows and finally knocks him out is not behaving violently. If we say that he is behaving violently, what we mean is that boxers behave violently as compared to, say, wrestlers, or to people who have an average disagreement with one another. That is, we locate boxing in a wider context, not in the context of a standard boxing match. Let us now have this professional fighter copy his behavior exactly in knocking out a burglar who was trying to rob his apartment—his identical behavior is now in fact violent, although possibly morally approvable (as the case may be). My tentative suggestion for explaining the difference is that most boxers, in fights, behave in that way and are expected to so behave, whereas most people in the face of burglars do not so behave and are expected not to do so. Violence, then, would involve descriptive abnormality with respect to what is to be expected in the relevant context.

Second, exercise of force (when exercise of force involves forcing—I am not, of course, referring to a physicalistic description of surmounting mechanical resistance). Here, heavy athletics (like wrestling) provides instances; one does not need the typical example, namely, policemen who, because of the state's monopoly on force, provide the most frequent cases of normal exercise of physical strength where one would not speak of the exercise of force, for example, where a crowd is pushed back for purposes that are either approvable (like making room for the firemen) or disapprovable (like protecting an execution according to the laws of a dictatorship). It is easy to change the context in such a way that the policemen are off-duty and are simply trying to make room for their morally approvable, though unadvertised, charity soccer game against the firemen in an overcrowded public park; this is, in fact, exercise of force.

Third, constraint: The owner of a snack bar in some corner of a large automobile exhibition hall sells his hamburgers for three dollars each; this is about the same price as in the other snack bars in the hall. A customer shows up and tells our snack bar owner that he is really very, very hungry, but that he has only three dollars left and needs one for riding home in the subway: "Let me have one for two bucks, man!" The owner refuses: "Take it or leave it." The customer, hungry enough, takes it and walks home. This is not an instance of constraint, I suggest. Now let us change the context. The snack bar is somewhere in the street, the normal price of a hamburger is one-and-a-half dollars, but the owner, at midnight, requests three dollars of this particular customer because he correctly calculates that the other is so hungry that he cannot help but take it. This, I submit, is in fact an instance of constraint, even if the customer is known to be a millionaire short of cash, and even if the snack bar owner needs every penny for paying the doctor who is to cure his baby (so that his behavior may well be morally approvable). Again, a change of context has effected a change in the nature of the behavior as being or not being a case of constraint. Thus I take it that these concepts are context-relative.

As a final piece of evidence for my diagnosis I sketch a sample of arguments taken from the decisions referred to in the first section of this chapter (or from parallel decisions). These arguments are only parts of the reasons given in each case—just those, regardless of whether or not the case had to be decided in a certain way for independent reasons, that were intended to establish that the decision was still in keeping with the real meaning of '*Gewalt*':

- If the defendant, without himself behaving violently, can exercise violence by using a dog in order to intimidate a night watchman, as was decided in an earlier case, then he can exercise violence by using only a little of his own physical strength in locking up a policeman (*RG* 27:405; *RG* 69:327).
- If blocking the path of a cart by advancing toward it in the middle of the road is exercise of violence, as was decided in an earlier case, then all the more so is firing in the air with a loaded gun (*RG* 60:157).
- If firing in the air with a loaded gun is exercise of violence, as was decided in an earlier case, then so is firing in the air with a blank gun (*RG* 66:353).
- If exercise of violence is constituted by behavior involving natural muscular force, as was decided in an earlier case, then so it is by behavior involving other natural forces, like the chemical force of a narcotic (*BGH* 1:145) or the kinetic energy of a motor car (*BGH* in *NJW* [1953], 672).
- If it is sufficient for the exercise of violence that a force has effects on the victim, as was decided in earlier cases, then violence can be exercised by the effect of psychological forces (*BGH* 19:263).

I think the parallel to Sorites reasoning is obvious. Each single decision argues for the claim that the present case, as compared to a case decided earlier, is not significantly different, and from this reasoning incorrectly concludes, first, that it is a case of violence, too; and, second, that there is now a new precedent for the courts to appeal to in the same fallacious way next time.

A final remark. At the beginning I referred to a culpability proviso that, from cases of violence, selects, as cases of culpable constraint, a smaller subclass. The operative condition is that "the exercise of violence . . . is repugnant, given its purpose." I have chosen the word 'repugnant' because I assume that it is not a legal term of British or American English; for neither is its German equivalent, *'verwerflich'*, which means much the same as the colloquial 'mean'. The clause has been added fairly recently (1953, when it was substituted for a Nazi clause from 1943), and was intended by the legislators as a brake to restrict the courts' unrestrained interpretation of 'violence'. The effect has been nil, for one cannot substitute purely evaluative words as a remedy for a descriptive meaning that has been lost. The result has been that the courts can now punish any kind of constraint, under the label of violence, provided they do not like it.

NOTES

1. For finding the decisions, I relied on Ihl (1988). In addition, I thank Professor U. Neumann, Saarbrücken, for helpful information. In German jurisprudence, the development is usually construed as a unilinear sequence of four or five stages, each stage stressing different features of *Gewalt*. For the diagnosis to be given below, unilinearity does not matter; a similarity net will do just as well, as long as any one similar case still precedes the one to be decided.

2. The following abbreviations have been used in citations given parenthetically in the text for this chapter and omitted from the Bibliography:

RG: *Entscheidungen des Reichsgerichts in Strafsachen*
GA: *Goltdammers Archiv für die gesamte Strafrechtswissenschaft*
BGH: *Entscheidungen des Bundesgerichtshofes in Strafsachen*
NJW: *Neue Juristische Wochenschrift*
MDR: *Monatsschrift für deutsches Recht*
DJZ: *Deutsche Juristenzeitung*
OLG: *Oberlandesgericht*

4

COERCION AND VIOLENCE

Thomas Pogge

Wer einen anderen rechtswidrig mit Gewalt oder durch Drohung mit einem empfindlichen Übel zu einer Handlung, Duldung oder Unterlassung nötigt, wird mit Freiheitsstrafe bis zu drei Jahren oder mit Geldstrafe, in besonders schweren Fällen mit Freiheitsstrafe von sechs Monaten bis zu fünf Jahren bestraft.

Rechtswidrig ist die Tat, wenn die Anwendung der Gewalt oder die Androhung des Übels zu dem angestrebten Zweck als verwerflich anzusehen ist.

Der Versuch ist strafbar.

Let me begin with an English translation of the German statute.

Whoever illegally coerces another person—either through violence or through threat of a significant *Übel* [evil, harm, damage, cost]—shall be fined, or punished with imprisonment of up to three years and in severe cases between six months and five years.

The action is illegal if the use of violence or the threat of *Übel* for purposes of attaining the intended end is rightly seen as repugnant.

The attempt is punishable.

The German *Gewalt*, here translated as "violence," also covers aspects of 'force' (e.g., in military contexts). However, the word is generally used in interpersonal contexts and not, for example, when force is discussed in physics (though one may speak of the *Gewalt* of an explosion).

Identifying coercion as a form of conduct, the statute defines it through three necessary and jointly sufficient conditions:

1. Coercion seeks to induce another person to *do, tolerate,* or *abstain from* something. This condition concerns the *end* of the conduct to be proscribed. It is formulated in very broad terms. In particular, the statute considers it irrelevant what the cost of compliance is to the other person. I may be coercing you into doing, tolerating, or abstaining from something even though you are not even inconve-

nienced by compliance. In fact, what I coerce you to do may have been your first choice all along.

2. Coercion works either through violence or through the threat of a significant *Übel*. This condition concerns the *means* of the conduct to be proscribed and is disjunctive. Neither violence nor the threat of a significant *Übel* is necessary; one of the two suffices.

3. The conduct as a whole—considering both means and end—must be repugnant. Here the term 'repugnant' has consistently been interpreted in objective rather than subjective terms. The state of mind of the purported coercer is not at issue; except, of course, insofar as is necessary for determining the situation-specific end and means of his conduct. Thus the court has deemed it irrelevant, for example, *for what further purpose* those participating in the sit-in were seeking their immediate end (to block traffic).

In opposition to recent West German High Court decisions, Savigny has claimed that it is implausible under the quoted statute to regard a sit-in as an instance of coercion, or, at any rate, that it is implausible to regard it as an instance of violence (as the court had done in order to find that coercion had taken place). Objecting to both these claims, I will try to show that some sit-ins can plausibly be regarded (1) as coercive, and even (2) as instances of violence.

CULPABLE COERCION WITHOUT VIOLENCE

Savigny tends to overstate the extent to which the statute relies on violence. The sit-in cases he is primarily concerned with can more convincingly be defended as cases of coercion as defined if they are viewed as involving the threat of a significant *Übel*. This brings out an interesting type of coercion, one that is overlooked, for example, in Nozick's (1972) seminal essay on this subject. A would-be coercer need not rely on her own capacity to use violence, but may instead draw on the latent violence embedded in existing practices, centrally including legal rules and their enforcement. Thus, instead of parking a large truck in front of your driveway to prevent your leaving with your car, I might also peaceably sit there, daring you (expressly or implicitly) to run me over, while we both know that your maiming me in the process would expose you to a very significant *Übel* in the form of legal prosecution. It would seem that the latter course of conduct is no less coercive than the former; and that the law, which is bound to prohibit and punish such exploitations of itself, can plausibly do so under the rubric of coercion.

Let me add here that Nozick (1972, 108) does recognize the case in which "someone sets things up so that damage is automatically inflicted if Q does A." But the case I have described is different. Our hypothetical sitter is not setting up anything. He merely exploits the fact that things are *already* so set up that damage will automatically be inflicted. He manipulates his victim into a situation such that her doing A will automatically trigger legal punishment, and thereby coerces her not to do A.

The conclusion of my first objection is that the German High Court has no need to refer to violence at all. It can reach the controversial decisions by finding that the sit-in demonstrators, by blocking an access road to a military facility, had implicitly threatened others with a significant *Übel* (criminal prosecution), thereby coercing them to abstain, however briefly, from using the relevant entrance.

Would this defense expose German jurisprudence to other sorts of attack? I can see two potential objections to the German practice. First, one might argue that condition (1) of the previously mentioned statute, the condition concerning the end, is too broad. We should not regard the threat of a significant *Übel* as coercive when the cost of compliance is trivial or nonexistent. I would, however, deem the statute defensible on this point. Second, one might argue that condition (3), the repugnancy clause, should be interpreted so that the court must take into account the remoter purposes of the alleged coercer. This issue is well known from discussions of civil disobedience, such as Dworkin's (1978) essay in *Taking Rights Seriously*. German jurisprudence, like that in most other countries, takes the standard position that statutes should be formulated without reference to such motives and that those who practice civil disobedience should be willing to pay the price for their transgressions. Since Savigny does not raise these two objections, I will not pursue them further.

PSYCHOLOGICAL AND STRUCTURAL VIOLENCE

Unfortunately, the reasoning offered by the German High Court in the cases at issue does not square with the rationale I have suggested. The court—although it plausibly could have found that the defendants had used a threat of a significant *Übel*—did in fact find that they had used violence. Is Savigny right to reject this finding as implausible?

Allow me once again to play devil's advocate by proposing a definition of violence that is *moralized* (in terms of our earlier discussions). Let me propose to say that a person uses physical violence if he deliberately acts in a way that blocks another's exercise of her legitimate claim-rights by physical means, or at least makes such exercise very costly or very difficult. Correspondingly, a person uses psychological violence if he deliberately acts in a way that makes it psychologically impossible or very costly or difficult for another to exercise her legitimate claim-rights. For the sake of brevity, I am skipping consideration of liberty rights (in the sense of

Hohfeld, [1919, 35–64]). Their exclusion from the definition is, I think, plausible, at least for the most part: You are not using violence if, for hours on end, you occupy the best spot from which to view the *Mona Lisa*, even if your doing so deprives me of the best view of her.

The proposed rough definition of violence makes this concept parasitic on the given legal, or on the proper moral, distribution of claim-rights. If the military, qua property owner, has a valid *legal* claim-right to use the entrance to some base, then blocking such use constitutes, legally speaking, violence. If South African blacks have a *moral* claim-right to freedom of movement within South Africa, then blocking their exit from their "homeland" constitutes, morally speaking, violence—even if their exit is blocked not by tanks but by a white crowd peaceably occupying some vital bridge. Whether this blockade constitutes *physical* violence is a further question, which I will not try to decide here. It certainly constitutes psychological violence on my definition, since it would be psychologically impossible or very costly to force one's way through the white crowd (e.g., by means of a truck).

Let me confess that my proposal has a consequence that may strike Savigny as being the very bottom of the slippery slope: You can commit physical violence by merely constructing a wall as an equivalent means of keeping the blacks inside their "homeland." Those who build such a wall, and those who preserve it in existence later, are inflicting continuous violence on blacks (provided, again, that these blacks have a moral claim-right to leave). In this way my definition enables an account of what has often been called *structural* or (Garver, 1968) *institutional* violence. A claim of structural violence would amount to this: Some poor citizens (of Honduras, for example) have less access to the resources of their country than they have a moral claim-right to have. This reduced access is not *accepted* by them (on the basis of some religion or ideology, say), but is *imposed* on them by physical means (including walls and fences, as well as armed personnel). The violence, though physical, is also structural, because it is organized through social institutions (that of property, especially). In such cases the violence inflicted on the poor may have many contributors *none* of whose conduct would constitute violence if he were the only one acting as he does. So reconstructed, I find the concept of structural violence plausible and am willing to defend it.

A last point. My definition clearly will not do as it stands. It would entail, for example, that you are using physical violence against me if you place a rock on my meadow. By placing the rock you are physically blocking my exercise of a claim-right of mine, namely, of my right to walk over the spot on which you placed the rock. If we want to use the term 'violence' in the way I have suggested, then we must take account of the cost the actor is imposing on her victim. I can *easily* and (almost) *costlessly* avoid the space occupied by the rock, and so your placing it, and your leaving it there, do not constitute violence. Similarly, I am not using violence if I stand in your driveway so that you can walk or drive around me, or if I lock one of your exit doors while leaving the other open. Blocking the exercise of a claim-right can count as violence only if this exercise is truly needed or highly valued. This leads me to embrace something like Savigny's conclusion, but on somewhat different grounds. My conclusion has the form of a dilemma. There *is* a plausible "moralized" definition of violence on which an access-blocking sit-in may constitute violence. But on this definition, the cost imposed by the agent or agents must be taken into account. With other entrances to the base remaining open, and with demonstrators quickly and predictably carried off by police, this cost was clearly too small to qualify the blockade as violence. The other horn of the dilemma was developed by Savigny: There may be plausible definitions of violence that do not take into account the cost the relevant actor imposes, but on such, typically "nonmoralized" definitions, a peaceful sit-in would not qualify as constituting violence.

5

THE NIHILISTIC SIGNIFICANCE OF VIOLENCE

Sergio Cotta

In my earlier book (Cotta, 1978) I note the historical ebb and flow of violence, remarking that our present century is distinguished from its predecessor by a singular dominance of violence over nonviolence. The main theme of that book is to ask the reason for this surge of violence; hence the title *Why Violence?* After characterizing the phenomenology of violence as a defiance of different sorts of measure (*misura*) and hence a counter-action or "action against" some norm, even when it is an implementation of some other norm, I argue that the predominance of violent solutions to human problems can be attributed in large part to two widespread philosophical ideas, antilegalism and the doctrine of the absolute subject.

I am gratified that a book expounding such a range of unpopular views has been as well received as it has. The causal scheme implied is so radically unlike Humean causation that it must be anathema to contemporary sociologists. The reservations about absolute subjectivity must offend not only Nietzsche's or Sartre's followers but also those who hold a Hobbesian doctrine of political sovereignty. The other point puts me at odds with that growing band of philosophers and postmodernists who see legalism rather than antilegalism as a form of violence. Despite the controversial nature of these arguments and conclusions, however, I wish here to stand by them and stand on them rather than to rehearse them or defend them.

In this essay I shall examine the *significance* of violence. My argument will be that violence in human affairs, although it occurs all too often in the natural world, is in an important ontological sense not a natural form of behavior. That is, of course, an uphill argument and cannot be neatly summarized. The leading idea similar to that of someone (e.g., Goethe) who might say that although deformed oak trees occur in nature, the deformity is nonetheless not the oak's natural shape.

The theme of violence—or more precisely, of violent human action, since I do not deal at all with violence in nature—is dealt with here from a philosophical rather than a sociological or historical point of view. I have therefore excluded from my investigation any research on the empirical and social causes that can provoke its insurgence. I propose instead to ascertain its *existential* dimension and thereby the theoretical and ethical problems it raises.

I would like to suggest a sufficiently broad preliminary definition of violence to cover its general manifestations in human affairs. I define it as "voluntary *acting-against* the will of another subject for the agent's own end." The scope of this definition excludes an involuntary action, however much it may be against the will of another, from the domain of violence. It also raises the question of whether it is correct to qualify as violence an act that the agent commits either (1) against him- or herself, as in the case of suicide; or (2) with the consent or on the request of the subject, as in the case of euthanasia. In neither case is there the requisite conflict of wills or divergence of ends. These, however, are exceptional cases, which I will not examine here in order to concentrate on the general phenomenon of violence, which is primarily interpersonal. Although the very mention of violence usually provokes an emotional reaction of repudiation and condemnation, concrete questions about it are not nearly so simple, especially with the widespread approval of it we find today, which I will discuss later on.

THE NATURALNESS OF VIOLENCE

Based on empirical observation, violence appears as such an obvious, widespread, and persistent phenomenon that it could be considered natural. It is ever-present throughout the course of human history, in the form of both individual and collective violence. Therefore, all cultures have made it an object of knowledge and evaluation. Psychoanalysis confirms its naturalness, tracing it back to the natural aggressive impulse that Freud associated with death (*thanatos*). From this perspective it appears prima facie a *necessary* behavior, and it appears born of natural necessity, not only because it is found universally among humans but also because it occurs in some animal species.

But another empirical and very similar observation shows, with equal evidence, the constant, ubiquitous presence throughout history of a phenomenon that is the opposite of violence, however we name it. In negative and generic terms it is nonviolence; in positive and more specific ones it is respect, harmony, or love. This other phenomenon is also an object of knowledge and appraisal for all cultures, to no lesser degree than the former. Psychoanalysis in its turn refers it to the aggregative impulse (*eros*), this also being present in animal species.

The two opposing modes of behavior, violent and nonviolent, are therefore both natural, in the sense that both originate in the empirical nature of living beings. Thus, nature does not deterministically compel such beings to either violence or nonviolence. Therefore, these two ways of behavior are, at the level of empirical analysis, natural *possibilities* alternatively practicable according to needs and circumstances. Violence, then, is not an *exclusive* natural necessity, but a possible and not unnatural behavior.

Acknowledging the possibility of violence as well as of its opposite requires a shift of attention from facts to acts, that is, to the agents who opt between the opposing possibilities. Acting within this wider range of possibility involves a sort of choice that appears to be an important quality in humans but not in animals. It is true that animals too have some possibility of choice: The carnivore can (has the possibility to) choose the easier or the more delectable prey, just as the bee can choose the more appetizing flower. But this choice is contained within narrow and impassable limits: The carnivore cannot cease to eat meat nor the bee suck nectar if they are to survive. Humans, on the other hand, can not only choose their food (they can be carnivorous or vegetarian) but can even produce artificial nourishments.

Furthermore, we humans have at our disposal a variety of possibilities that are not only larger in scope but of a different and higher quality: We have the capability to devise projects (realized and realizable) that surpass the usual natural conditions of life, with regard to both our habitat and our performances. Thanks to this extended power to invent the artificial, we can live above the ground or under water; we can increase our capacity for mental operations by means of the so-called artificial intelligence of electronic computers. No animal has similar capacities.

Finally, human potentiality reaches its highest level, a level unobtainable by any other living being, in *symbolic operations*. The two manifestations that in my opinion are the most significant are the tomb and the temple, which clearly do not depend on the progress of knowledge, as they have been coeval with humans since the most remote antiquity; tombs in fact date back to prehistory. The tomb, in its very material form, symbolically expresses our sense of immortality; otherwise there would be no reason to enclose and preserve in it that which is known to become bones and dust. The purpose of preserving the corpse from the avidity of animals is not a sufficient explanation. The tomb symbolically reveals our awareness that it is our sense of immortality that marks our essential difference from every other earthly being. With the temple—whose exterior and interior structure (not every building is a temple!) is already a symbol of untouchable sacredness—we humans push our own symbolic capacity into the sphere of the impossible: We want to hold the infinite transcendence of the divinity within the enclosed space of the temple.

The outline sketched here, of the degrees of extension and of the qualitative levels of our human possibilities, shows the radical difference between *our* nature and that of all other living beings. All these levels and degrees—above all the last and highest, that of symbolic operation— bring out clearly the structure of the human ego. It is a dual structure, an ontological duality that I have discussed in detail elsewhere (Cotta, 1985, chap. 3), of limitation and transcendence of limitation, or of finitude and infinity, to use a formula more suggestive if less precise. In one sense the ego is finite, destined to death and subject to the decay of the body; in another it is capable of transcending the *material* conditions of dwelling, producing, living, feeling, and thinking. In short, the ego lives its own finite and empirical reality under a continual strain to transcend it. From a metaphysical perspective, this duality constitutes the ontological basis of human possibility and characterizes it as our specific human nature, that is, as something *natural* for human beings.

As far as action is concerned, the possibilities stretch between two extreme poles: one of inflicting (or self-inflicting) death and one of operating for (giving or promoting) life. Both, in spite of their opposition, draw their origin from the dual structure of the ego and its nature. Within this general framework lies violence, which is oriented toward the pole of death and culminates in it, that is, in the possibility opposed to that of life, which the ego has at its disposal because of its ontological duality. Violence, then, seems natural not only on the empirical level, but on the ontological level as well. Is the problem of violence then resolved, in the sense that a nonviolent person would be only half human, that is, that the refusal of violence would bring about the loss of one natural possibility, thus diminishing human potentiality?

The problem has to be deepened, since the reasoning developed so far gives rise, as a logical consequence, to another question. If it is true that there are two possibilities of natural (ontological) origin, and not just one, it follows that neither can be seen as deterministically necessitated behavior. Therefore, because violence is not the *only* possibility, it is subject to judgment directing the choice for or against it. This judgment (about whether and under what conditions violence may be justified) is expressed and argued in all cultures.

In this regard it is useful, in my opinion, to draw a clear distinction, within the scope of Western thought and probably also of common feeling, between *classical* and *contemporary* judgments about violence. I will examine them now in broad outline to point out their differences with regard both to their philosophical foundation and to their evaluative conclusions.

THE CLASSICAL ASSESSMENT OF VIOLENCE

In the steadiest line of classical thought, which continues up to our day, violence is assigned to the domain of evil, of transgression, even when it is considered natural. If at times it is not condemned, absolution is generally limited by very precise terms and to specific cases: Violence is justified only when it is an *indispensable means* of defending a right or a value. The chief value that justifies violent means is, in classical thought, justice, understood as harmony—thought of in both cosmic and human terms by the Greeks and in more strictly human terms by Christianity. It must be emphasized that justice is considered a more radical (more basic) value than liberty: Violence is justifiable in the name of liberty only because it is *unjust* to deprive a people, a class, or individuals of their liberty. Violated justice, that is, justice to which violence has been done, authorizes and legitimizes (i.e., categorizes as conforming to the "law" of justice) such violence as is indispensable for restoring itself.

In such a case, however, violence undergoes a clear overturning of sense so that one can discern within the uniform factual materiality of violence a specific form of it open to a different evaluation. From violence it is turned into *counterviolence*, from acting-against into *counter-acting*, a reaction to evil, to the transgression that has upset the harmonious order of justice, and is therefore a legitimate defense, whether it is personal or collective. Counterviolence thus acquires legitimacy that primal violence can never attain. It is not accidental that on every violent act (belligerent, revolutionary, repressive, or personal) that results in oppression or domination there weighs a negative sentence without appeal—that of being an act-against that subverts the just order of coexistence. Such violence, devoid of justice, is thus reduced to an existing-for-itself of the violent agent, be the agent an individual person, a class, or a corporate body. Counterviolence may be the only way to restore the broken harmony.

Despite its meaning and legitimation as an *indispensable* means, counterviolence, or the violence of reaction, continues to be considered a sort of evil, even if only a *minor* one. Counterviolence for personal defense is in fact exposed to the risk of exceeding legitimate defense. Collective counterviolence incurs the same risk, that its violent reaction will reach the innocent as well as the guilty, harming or killing the innocent and often unjustly accusing them of sharing "collective guilt" for an evil for which they are not responsible. The classical justification of violence is therefore limited by two conditions: first, that it is a counter-action done genuinely for the sake of justice; second, that its application does not exceed the limits of equity. Juridical thought concerning war has defined both the *jus ad bellum*, determining who has the right, and under what conditions, to resort to war; and the *jus in bello*, establishing legal rules to be respected even during war. In terms of law, war is legitimate and justified only when it is a controlled counterviolence proportioned to the initial violent action. The same applies in the case of private self-defense. Consequently, in classical thought the justification of possible (natural) violence is subject to very strict limits imposed by the value of justice.

The discussion, however, does not end here; in fact it opens up into further questions about the consistency of the means with the end. If the condition for the justification of the means is the end, then one cannot justify the indiscriminate use of any means, but only of those homogeneous with the end by complying with it and conforming to its value. Otherwise the means not only produce negative collateral effects (which might well appear negligible compared to the preeminent value of the end), but also deprive the value itself of its inner sense, since they demonstrate its inability to regulate the action. Our values are a leading and regulatory axiological principle of action; it would therefore be contradictory if they authorized or flatly required means that do not conform to them. It is, in fact, obviously contradictory to want to restore justice and law by means of injustice and illegality: The means discredit the end. Similar reasoning also works in the case of technical operations: If the means are not adequate to the end, they are inefficient or wrong and not to be used. So if counterviolence is a means to achieve justice, it cannot be described as fully justified if it involves (as often happens) some degree of injustice. We arrive then, in large part because of this threat of contradiction, at the question of whether recourse to counterviolence is truly indispensable.

Highlighting the ontological duality, and the double alternative it gives rise to within the sphere of action, allows us to resolve the question. Although justice condemns the injustice of violence, it does not, however, make counterviolence *obligatory*, limiting itself to making it *permissible*. This leaves open the other possible choice, that of nonobedience, of passive nonviolent resistance, or even of a fully aware, noble acceptance of death. It is a choice that has always been present in human consciousness and is illuminated by illustrious and well-known examples. Counterviolence, then, is neither a deterministic necessity following initial violence nor an indispensable means of justice. Indeed, the presence of possible nonviolent alternatives excludes its falling within the sphere of strict duty. Counterviolence is, in my opinion, a *duty* only in the case of defense, not of oneself, but of someone else (if innocent). Gandhi himself did not hesitate to uphold this opinion.

THE PRESENT-DAY ASSESSMENT OF VIOLENCE

Although the classical judgment discussed above evidently continues to be accepted (in full or in part) in our time, it is no longer the only or even the dominant one. An opposing opinion has developed into a cultural tradition that neither maintains the limited and limiting classical justification of counterviolence nor takes the option of nonviolence into consideration. This trend reaches its most distinct and radical formulation in the judgment—made by certain Marxist, existentialist, and pragmatist philosophers who are also social activists—that not only accepts violence but exalts it as the propellant of human history or as the essential characteristic of a creative–destructive nature. In addition to this drastic and rigorously consistent position, other philosophies, while sharing its premise, that is, the preeminence of Becoming and Acting over Being, are nevertheless more cautious or timid, and certainly less consistent. They do not appreciate all the consequences of this premise; they therefore broaden beyond measure the motives that can justify violence, to the point of rendering them uncertain or completely inconsistent.

It is not my intention to draw here a precise and detailed picture of these positions. I am interested instead in highlighting the chain of theoretical principles that—quite apart from the difference between coherent and prudent philosophies—make it impossible rigorously to condemn violence and so to confute its supporters, and that therefore render acceptable its approval and even its exaltation.

To better understand such an extraordinary reversal of classical judgment, it is opportune to underline the latter's pivotal points. I have said that the classical judgment was based on the value of justice. In truth, the term 'value' is unknown to the classical world in its exclusively ethical meaning, which is altogether modern, in fact, very recent. Therefore, 'value' renders badly, or even misrepresents, the meaning the term 'justice' had for classical cultures, which is made up of two elements consistent with each other. On a theoretical level, justice is the explanatory principle of the world order based on Being (*Sein*) and not just on an empirical–factual 'being' (*Dasein*). On a practical level it designates a virtue, actually the *highest virtue*, that guides man toward respecting the order of Being. Seen in this way, values (to keep using the modern term) have, in classical culture, an objective and universal character, because of their theoretical and practical connection to Being. They always have an ontological foundation and character.

The new assessment of violence comes to maturity within a cultural orientation about which I will limit myself here to indicating the two theoretical principles that are, in my opinion, most relevant to the question I am dealing with. These principles deeply alter the classical conception of the human world and therefore allow an understanding of the altered assessment of violence.

The Ontic Foundation of Values

With the progressive (although not total) neglect of ontological enquiry in modern thought, the foundation of values is sought on the ontic or empirical–phenomenal level of human experience. Beyond this level, that is, if it is not interpreted exclusively in its naturalistic–physical determination, Being is declared an unrecognizable or senseless "metaphysical" expression. We then face the fact, however, that an acceptable notion of value cannot be inferred from this purely naturalistic reality. The only reality that can without question be reached in the world of human experience, interpreted in an exclusively ontic way, is the (feeling, thinking, active) *subject;* indeed the plurality of subjects gathered together in the formal category of *subjectivity.* This latter consequently constitutes the only possible field for a foundation (or origin) of values.

Subjectivity, however, expresses itself in two forms: individual and collective. Philosophies limiting their research to the ontic level generally distinguish themselves on the basis of this duality, thus affirming a foundation (or characterization) of values that is either individualistic or collectivistic, but always subjective. Such subjectively founded value is considered as expressing the subject's need for self-realization, either individual or collective. Presented in this way, however, it is not understandable why the subject should have this need, since an ontological analysis, transcending empirical facts, would be necessary for such understanding.

If values and self-realization are based on an ontic subject (in its dual aspect), their *objectivity* is lost in the case of individual values and is greatly reduced in the case of collective values. In both cases, on the contrary, they reveal themselves as particular and relative in their determination as well as in their capacity of orienting and directing action, therefore losing their *universality.* Ethics is fragmented not only in terms of fact but also in terms of principle. In my opinion (see Cotta, 1978, chap. 6) the modern doctrine of the "absolute subject" is at the root of the subjectivization of values, and hence of the fragmentation of ethics. It is true that Kant endeavored to maintain the universality of values (and therefore the unity of ethics), but in quite *formal* terms and limited to the one value (or better, "dignity": *Würde* and not *Wert*) of a rational moral law and a rational subject able to understand and follow it. But deprived of an ontological foundation, this purely formal universality and rationality (strictly limited to the moral *law* and its pure criterion of universalization) could not raise a resistance strong enough to stem the spreading of the potentialities inherent in the ontic subjectivism of values. The *form* says nothing about the *content* of values; therefore, the subject is always able to claim the concreteness of his own particular and relative values against this form and its universality.

Hegel was certainly not the last to hold this thesis. So the fragmentation of ethics remains unaltered and quite legitimized; it does not authorize a reunifying dialogue but opens instead the way to conflict.

This situation could still be *made* acceptable by resorting to tolerance. Tolerance is a pragmatic attitude, certainly useful and commendable in many circumstances, but it equalizes all subjective values into a sort of nebulous morality. It is thereby capable of hiding or (more dubiously) of minimizing their contradictory nature but not of resolving the conflict that arises when the values emerge in a decisive affirmation. The only possible solution then becomes violence, which is also an expression of subjectivity, because it severs the dialogical and coexistential relation among people and establishes the domination of one subject over the others. Like subjective values, violence too is enclosed within the framework of particularity relativity; it is homogeneous with them in expressing the pure limitation of human beings, denying their capacity to transcend it.

The Absolute Value of the "New"

The neglect of ontological enquiry, and the consequent exclusion of an ontological foundation of values, find their apex in theoretical and practical historicism, where thinking and existing have an exclusively historical character, that is, particular, relative, and contingent. To be sure, the earliest historicism, born at the beginning of the nineteenth century, does not consider this character—which would reduce history, and with it truth and values, to a contradictory chaos—to be absolute, but rather intends to highlight historical and evolutionary continuity. The earliest historicism could be called, therefore, *retrospective*, because it tries to *recover* the connection (and often the value as well) of the past to the present. Moreover, it holds that it is possible to understand the truth of an action only when it has reached its termination, its "sunset." This conception of historicism finds its highest expression, as is well known, in the works of Hegel, from the *Phenomenology of Spirit* to the *Lessons* (on the philosophy of religion, the history of philosophy, and the philosophy of history) of his Berlin period.

But with the transition from Hegel to Marx, and in a peculiar way to Nietzsche (to cite the most influential thinkers), historicism loses its retrospective character. Philosophy does not rise any more at "sunset" but at "dawn," and it understands history as the producer of the *new*. History is of value if, and only if, it generates the new: That which lasts throughout time is a sign of motionlessness, a dead weight, something that has been, which allows only repetition and not the dynamic power of innovation. History is (and its value lies in) innovating thought and action. Within the framework of this historicism the particularity and relativity of subjective values fully reveal their intrinsic contingency. The presence and content of values (individual and collective) depend completely on the innovative dynamism of history. They appear, disappear, and change depending on the variation of vital historical experience (the *Lebenswelt*) of either the individual or the society.

The innovative dynamism of history finds its acme, according to the most consistent historicism, in the radical form of revolution. In this form neither the past nor the present transmit any permanent truth. On the contrary, if the new is a (fuller) truth, it will be all the more "true" as it differs more from what has been before. In this sense the truest "new," so to speak, is exactly that produced by revolution, that is, the action that overturns the present order (conveyed by the past) in anticipation of a "new order," of which the revolution is the beginning. Revolution is thus the beginning of a new history, as much for the individual who acts egocentrically (thus beginning a "new life") as for the collective subject that carries out (or undergoes) the revolution. And the "new history" will be all the more rich with change as the revolution is more *permanent* and its "new order" therefore more temporary. This means, as I have argued more fully in Cotta (1986), that the new order will generate its own disorder and thus its self-negation. Permanent revolution implies permanent violence.

The neglect or condemnation of the temporal dimension of *duration*, already implied in the more moderate idea of evolution, thus reaches its apex as values are attributed exclusively to the "new," which is continually renewed. I have previously maintained (Cotta, 1978, chap. 5) that this neglect of the temporal dimension of duration is the principal source of the antilegalism so widespread at present. Here we see that the purely formal *infinity* (*endlessness*) of innovative motion, far from hiding the temporal finiteness of concrete novelties, fully reveals it. Just as in the case of the subjectivity of values, the finite dimension of man is emphasized once more, thus opening the way to conflict.

VIOLENCE AS A SCISSION-NEGATION OF THE EGO

The analysis carried out so far has sought to highlight, in the field of contemporary thought, the linking of two principles (the ontic foundation of values and the absolute value of the "new") and their common roots within the finite dimension of man, of which both are consistent expressions. This allows us to understand why, within the sphere of thought characterized by the above-mentioned principles, it is impossible to condemn violence except either occasionally, when it endangers our own interests and judgments, or inconsistently, because it is absurd to deny its novelty, even if brutal, in relation to the existing order. If the conflict of subjective values is taken seriously in its implications, it appears as the principal condition, the very humus, of the rise and spread of violence. In its turn the attribution of an absolute value to the "new"—above all when it gives rise to the radical and continuous revolutionary innovation—involves the acceptance of violence. It even involves an approval of it, which extends to its glorification as a cathartic purification–liberation from the burden of what has already been done, of that which has fallen into the dead immobility of the past, and of a purely repetitive present.

But no catharsis is conclusive for finite man; otherwise it would indicate his entrance into the kingdom of the infinite, of the absolute. Therefore catharsis continually renews itself, and with it violence, which consequently reproduces and justifies itself in an endless cycle, or as Nietzsche said, "an eternal [destructive–creative] return of the same."

I have now reached the crucial question. In my opinion, if an analytic look shows us the undeniably ontological *duality* of the ego, synthetic thought reveals to us in an equally undeniable way a deeper ontological truth. The ego *is* ontologically, and *lives* existentially, only in the synthetic unity of the two dimensions I have already pointed to, finitude and infinity (infinity meaning transcendence of finiteness). The scission between these two dimensions and the consequent considering of now one and now the other dimension as absolute (theoretically or practically) involve the exclusion of the subject from the human ontological order, the end of the synthetic ego, that is, the end of personhood. When infiniteness is considered as absolute we have a flight from reality into a phantasmic dream: It is the false infiniteness of a false consciousness, which is contradicted by the actual active and temporal finiteness of the mortal ego. When on the other hand finiteness is considered as absolute, the ego is reified and reduced from being a subject into being an object.

This reduction is produced by violence, openly on those who suffer it, but, in a more primary though less evident way, also on those who carry it out. The latter, in so acting, turn themselves—whatever may be their motives, impulsive–passionate or cathartic—into a sort of destructive vitalistic organism, whether individual or collective. They become, in other words, a "force of nature," precisely as Nietzsche thought. But at this moment the distinctively human, the ego-subject, is suppressed. On the other hand the continuous "return" of violence is eternal only in a formal sense, and therefore the expression of a false infiniteness, because violence always remains finite in its concrete realization.

In his paper on violence presented to the Twelfth International Wittgenstein Symposium, Newton Garver (1988) has rightly suggested that violence occurs when there is infringement of a human being's "status as person." I interpret this status as that of the "synthetic ego." It is an ontological status, pertaining to every person because of a *specific* nature beyond any empirical difference of sex, race, social condition, nationality. Therefore its infringement may be qualified as *basic* violence, that is, the violence annihilating every possibility of human coexistence, and consequently of any right social order.

In short, confronted with this basic status, the choice of violence is the choice of death, not only of some persons but of humanity itself. And so the very possibility of violence, which is rooted in human existence, ends by being annihilated. In fact a person is and exists only as the synthetic unity of the ego. Human capacity for thought and action springs forth from this unity, within which it finds its insuperable limit, beyond which it would be annihilated. It follows that the ontological and existential truth of the ego qualifies violence as an event that is *naturalistic*, and destined therefore to end in death and nothingness, but not humanly *natural*, that is, corresponding to human openness to life. On this ontological–existential foundation, disclosing the nihilistic significance of violence, the ethical condemnation of violence can be firmly based, beyond every utilitarian or emotive evaluation, which is always swinging ambiguously from approval to condemnation.

6

VIOLENCE AND COMMUNICATION: The Limits of Philosophical Explanations of Violence

Kenneth Baynes

It is difficult to say anything substantive or illuminating about violence in general. Initially, at least, there seems to be little reason to think that a terrorist attack on a passenger airline, a state's refusal to grant political asylum to refugees from "friendly" authoritarian regimes, and teenage suicide should share anything in common. Thus at the end of his extensive and detailed survey of theories of civil violence, Rule (1988, 264) concludes, "The search for *general theories* of civil violence . . . may simply be the wrong search." Yet, if ordinary linguistic usage is to serve as a guide, these various acts may all be regarded as acts of violence. And, if ordinary usage can be still further trusted, such acts are not inevitable but (to a greater or lesser extent) stem from individual or collective choices. Thus, acknowledging both reasonable reservations about relying too heavily on ordinary usage (see Teichman, 1989) and the heavy burden of proof on those who choose violence, we may nevertheless conclude that (at least in some cases) the decision to act violently is open to justification. Beyond this, however, what people commonly say does not seem to be a reliable guide for an analysis of violence in general. We too often break apart into lamentations about inexplicable personal tragedy or senseless acts of terror, are silenced by the official management of the news, or yield the floor to the specialized discourses of the social sciences. If philosophy is to contribute a clarification of violence, it will have to do so either by staking out a terrain of its own or by mediating between the specialized discourses of the social sciences and the unilluminating popular discourse on violence (e.g., that of the mass media).

In Chapter 5 and more fully in *Why Violence?* (1978) Sergio Cotta, who is inclined toward the first of these philosophical approaches, examines the nature, causes, and significance of the increasing recourse to violence and its more positive assessment in the contemporary world. His analysis is stimulating and provocative. On the one hand it challenges recent philosophical reflection, which tends to view violence primarily as a means for the realization of various social and political ends. On the other hand it endeavors to return to a more classical conception of violence, which generally viewed with greater caution the use of violence. At the same time, however, Cotta's discussion reflects what seems to be an inherent weakness in the attempt to provide a philosophical explanation of violence in isolation from a general conceptual framework based on empirical claims derived from social and political theory.

His discussion can be summarized in three steps: First, he presents a phenomenological analysis in which violence is defined as the "absence of measure." He then describes some manifestations of the contemporary assessment of violence and offers an account of its philosophical or cultural roots. Finally, in moving from phenomenology to ontology, he assesses its philosophical significance and suggests steps that must be taken to curb the pervasiveness of violence and its positive assessment.

COMMUNICATION AND RECIPROCITY AS COMMON "MEASURES"

The most intriguing aspect of Cotta's work is his analysis of violence as an "absence of measure" (1978, 64). This analysis is part of a tradition of thought that construes violence as "an offense against a norm," to which Honderich (1980) and Stanage (1975a) belong and on which Ladd comments in Chapter 1. What is unique here is that violent action is not simply an offense against a norm or standard external to the action, but exhibits a lack of measure along several axes. In particular, Cotta identifies three "modes of measure" in connection with which a violent act should be assessed. There is an internal measure (in the sense that one acts with measure); an external measure (in the sense that one acts in accordance with a social, moral, or legal norm); and a purposive measure (the plan or goal for which one acts).

Violent action is then shown to consist not in the absence of all measure, but in the absence of measure with respect to various combinations of its modalities. In fact, the presence of measure in any one or two modes may even result in a more dangerous or brutal form of violence. Thus, the violence of an action that lacks purposive measure may be heightened by the presence of internal and external measure (the orderly conduct of bureaucratic or public officials in carrying out the extermination of a people). Similarly, the presence of internal and purposive measure without external measure (the self-disciplining of a revolutionary cadre) will not ensure a less violent action. Finally, even if it is only internal measure that is lacking there is no guarantee that violence will be diminished: Acts of self-defense in which both external and purposive measure are present are not any less violent for that reason alone, as Judith Thomson (1986, 33–48) makes clear with her extreme hypothetical examples. Thus, one must speak of violence with reference to an absence of measure along a variety of axes or a different combination of "modes of measure." Only if measure is present in each mode can one speak of a complete exclusion of violence.

An analysis of violence along these lines has certain advantages. On the one hand it provides a way of distinguishing between force and violence. For while a coercive act is always an act against an individual will (such as a coercive juridical act), it is not necessarily lacking in measure and thus may not be violent (Cotta, 1978, 83). It also presents an alternative to the view (elaborately detailed by Foucault [1975; 1980] and further articulated by Waldenfels in Chapter 7) that discovers an element of violence at the root of all forms of social interaction and within all the interstices of social life. Most important, however, it offers a means for assessing violence in other than merely instrumental terms, that is, in terms of whether or not the ends it pursues are just.[1]

To speak of violence as an absence of measure, however, is so far to offer a purely formal characterization. If the definition is to be useful for identifying specific acts of violence, the relevant modes of measure will have to be given more content. Cotta pursues this in two related, but distinct, ways. On the one hand he emphasizes the dialogical nature of human existence and "the measure" of communication itself. Communication presupposes a norm of reciprocal recognition and a willingness to listen to the voice of the Other.

> Dialogue, the complete and authentic form of communication (not verbal alone but practical and behavioral as well), necessarily requires a common measure. And it is this very measure that is lost in violence, which, being unruliness, denies at the root the dialogical nature of existence, and so constitutes the most explicit and radical breakdown in communication. (1978, 65–66)

Violence, on this view, would be the flagrant transgression of a fundamental norm of reciprocity inherent in the structure of communication. It may either take the form of a forceful interruption of ordinary processes of communication (perhaps itself symbolic, as in some acts of political terrorism) or itself appear as the effect of such disturbances. Thus Schmid and de Graaf (1982, 108): "Terrorism . . . is best understood as a form of communication. It can be explained in terms of a felt lack of access to communication by ordinary means." Wellmer (1984) makes a similar claim in describing terrorism as a social pathology to be understood *both* as a "structural violence" maintained by the social system *and* as a deliberate isolation of terrorist groups from "the needs, experiences, and learning processes of their social surroundings." Cotta (1978, 67) sums up as follows: "We are therefore totally in the domain of Weilian *pesanteur:* mutual incomprehension, refusal to concern oneself with the Other, arbitrary and absolute imposition."

At the same time, Cotta attempts to deepen the notion of a common measure through an unusual blend of substantive natural law and Heideggerian metaphysics. In contrast to modern natural-right theory and its individualism, Cotta calls for an ontological reinterpretation of the ego as "I-with-the-Other" and a renewal of the objective values of justice and law based on the order of Being. On this view there exists an independent natural law that can be discovered by reason or intuition: "Justice is the explanatory principle of the world order based on Being (*Sein*) and not just on an empirical–factual 'being' (*Dasein*)" (Chapter 5). This law is in turn to serve as a guide or standard for human law, rather than itself being subordinated to the political realm as positive law (1978, 106). Violence, on this interpretation, is understood as a transgression of "the harmonious order of justice" and as a "scission-negation" of the ontological status of the ego as both finite and transcendent (Chapter 5); that is, as under the law but capable of knowing the law, thus raising itself above bare material existence.

Although it may be that these two attempts to provide the notion of a common measure with content need not be opposed—Cotta indeed speaks of "the authentic sense of law as an interpersonal mode of living the *Mitsein*" (1978, 103)—the return to substantive natural law raises certain well-known epistemological problems. In particular, it apparently rejects the distinction between fact and value and becomes embroiled in conflicting interpretations about the natural end (*telos*) of human being. To the extent that these natural laws are not self-evident to all, it also conflicts, at least potentially, with the principle of a democratic justification of norms, which I have discussed in more detail elsewhere (Baynes, 1988).

However, it is also possible to emphasize the dialogical nature of human existence and a norm of reciprocity without advocating a return to classical natural law and metaphysics, as has been done by Habermas (1984–87; 1990). The idea would be to analyze the norms of communication more directly in connection with the various (often counterfactual) suppositions of validity that speakers make in their interaction with one another. To be sure, not every violation or infraction of a norm of communication constitutes an act of violence; it would at least be necessary to speak of a continuum of greater and lesser transgressions of such norms. Not every transgression of a rule of conversational implicature, for example, would constitute an act of violence, but the systematic silencing of or refusal to listen to the voice of another would. The crucial point is that violence should not be restricted to physical assault on a person, but also viewed in terms of disturbances to the processes of communication responsible for the formation of rational (i.e., discursive) individual and collective identities. In contrast to Cotta's return to a blend of classical natural law and metaphysics, however, it is also important that the identification of possible transgressions and the question of their justifiability be self-reflexively linked to formally and informally institutionalized processes of communication and democratic will formation.

Of course, much more needs to be said about the different types of individual and collective identity formation and the various levels of interaction between them. Recent attempts to rethink the relation between the state and civil society in connection with autonomous civil associations that limit or check collective identities managed "from above" by a centralized state or mass-party political system would be relevant in this context, as would other attempts to reconceptualize the complex interplay and balancing of law, politics, and morality in the formation of social and cultural identities (see Baynes, 1989; Arato and Cohen, 1991). There is, however, no guarantee that in a pluralist and decentralized democracy based on a principle of reciprocity or mutual recognition conflicts will not erupt within the context of multiple and diverse identities. The most that may be hoped for is that mechanisms for communication and conflict resolution that individuals regard as fair are institutionalized at various levels and thus that the frequency of recourse to individual and collective violence can thereby be diminished.

EMPIRICAL AND INTELLECTUAL ASPECTS OF VIOLENCE

In *Why Violence?* Cotta (1978) also inquires into the causes of the perceived increase in violence and its more favorable assessment. He considers these to be primarily philosophical or cultural—the "metaphysics of subjectivity" and the relativization of values. By the former he means an absolutization of the self in which the existence of objective standards of truth and moral evaluation is denied and the subject is held to be the sole author and judge of what has value. The fragmentation and conflict of values that characterize the modern world are thus construed as fundamentally irresolvable except through an act of violence, or the subjugation of others (and nature) to the instrumental calculation of individual self-interest. According to Cotta (1978, chap. 5) this is especially reflected in the "antilegalism" of this century, in which the notion of law as *ratio* has been displaced by the notion of law as the expression of an arbitrary private will (*voluntas*).[2] But it is also evident in contemporary challenges to the classical notion of the *res publica*, in which the public sphere is distinct from the private sphere and each operates according to an internal logic of its own: "The private no longer wants to be protected in its privacy from the intrusion of the public; it wants, instead, to impose publicly on everyone the absolute arbitrariness of its own will, to receive public recognition . . . of the sovereignty of its own doing" (1978, 118).

Comparable attempts to interpret the modern world through a critique of the metaphysics of subjectivity have been made in several different keys, ranging from Heidegger and the early critical theory of Adorno and Horkheimer, to Leo Strauss and Hannah Arendt, to French deconstruction and Jürgen Habermas. Each of these analyses identifies the metaphysics of subjectivity or instrumental reason as a contributing factor to the contemporary malaise, but they disagree on the diagnosis of its effects and prognosis for its reform. They also disagree among themselves about whether the metaphysics of subjectivity has its beginnings with the origins of Western (Platonic) thought, with the "new sciences" in the sixteenth century, or with the spread of capitalism in the seventeenth and eighteenth centuries. It is thus necessary to be more precise than Cotta is in the identification of the intellectual causes and not to insist too quickly on direct causal links between (fairly esoteric) intellectual ideas and specific manifestations of violence. Cotta (1978, 118) is apparently confident, for example, about interpreting the demand for abortion rights as an expression of the metaphysics of subjectivity rather than (as in MacKinnon, 1987) as a possible (legal) means for combating a predominantly patriarchal metaphysics of subjectivity.

In particular what is noticeably absent from Cotta's analysis is any treatment of the social and political institutions that might mediate between the metaphysics of subjectivity (or instrumental reason) and various manifestations of violence. There is also no discussion of how transformations within these institutions have shaped public and private life. I have in mind studies such as Arendt's *The Origins of Totalitarianism* (1951), which sees the loss of a public space for thinking and acting as a precondition for the rise of totalitarian regimes, or Habermas's *The Structural Transformation of the Public Sphere* (1989), which traces the "depoliticization" and "reprivatization" of the bourgeois public sphere during the nineteenth century. The idea would then be to interpret the recourse to violence in the twentieth century against the background of this earlier erosion of time-honored cultural and religious traditions, yet simultaneous failure in the development of literary, civic, and political institutions of a modern public sphere that could help mediate the new forms of social conflict and contention and thus enable the formation of new (modern) social solidarities. Such an analysis would continue to employ a model of violence as the flagrant transgression of the norms of communication responsible for the formation of individual and collective identities. But it would also be able to proceed more empirically and fallibly in formulating hypotheses about changes in forms of publicity and privacy and their connection to civil violence. It may thus be that the recourse to violence in this century has more to do with the restriction of forums for public deliberation about social ends and a "colonization" of cultural life by the market and bureaucratic state than with the "absolutization of the subject" and relativization of values per se, a line of thought that Wellmer (1984) makes use of in his interesting analysis of West German terrorism.

VIOLENCE AS TRANSGRESSION OF HUMAN COMMUNICATIVE STRUCTURES

Instead of pursuing a critique of the metaphysics of subjectivity in connection with the decline of public life or a theory of communicative action along these lines, Cotta advocates a return to a "metaphysics of being" as a way of confronting the contemporary recourse to violence and its nihilistic significance. But, as in the case of the return to substantive natural law, it is difficult to see how such a metaphysics can be reconciled with a principle of democratic justification or with the various institutional differentiations (between science and morality, on the one hand, and morality, politics and law, on the other) that have come to characterize modern societies. For these reasons a philosophical and social-theoretic approach that analyzes violence in connection with disturbances to the general structures of communication responsible for the formation of individual and collective identities seems more promising. This is not to deny that socialization as a process of "normalization" is frequently accompanied by violence (as thinkers such as Foucault have emphasized). Nor is it to envision a concrete utopia in which all social interactions are fully "communicative" and from which all violence has been excluded. It is to claim that processes of cultural reproduction, socialization, and identity formation need not be conceived as inherently violent, but (to varying degrees) that they institutionalize norms of communication and reciprocity that can themselves be used in identifying instances of violence; this is a line of thought that Minow (1987) uses in her interesting critique of Cover (1986). At the same time, however, the task of defining the "measure" that violence offends would not be assigned to a renewed metaphysics of being, but would be linked to normative social criticism and, in the last analysis, the reflexive process of democratic will formation itself.

Finally, an approach informed by social and political theory in this way would also leave the question of the justification of violence more open than in Cotta's analysis. Arendt (1969, 52) may be right that violence can never be legitimate, but its justification has a great deal to do with the legitimacy of the specific collective identities toward which it is directed, and the legitimacy of the individual and collective identities on whose behalf it is perpetrated, as has been argued by Walzer (1970) and Held (1984b). In general, the more societies have institutionalized processes of communication and created "public spaces" in Arendt's sense, the less likely it is that violence would be justifiable or, for that matter, necessary. On the other hand, to the extent that collective identities are sustained through systematic distortions to communication, it is more likely that individual and collective violence will ensue—and perhaps also with greater justification.

These remarks are admittedly quite programmatic. I began, after all, with the caution that it was difficult to say anything substantive or illuminating about violence in general. Nevertheless, if progress is to be made toward understanding the nature and significance of violence in our time, it is necessary to proceed with a broad conceptual framework so that the brute reality can be comprehended in the variety of its manifestations. It is important above all that the definition of violence not be restricted to isolated acts of terror or physical assault upon individuals, but be understood more generally as a flagrant transgression of the dialogical or communicative structure of human existence. We are indebted to Cotta's analysis for deepening this insight.

NOTES

1. Even Hannah Arendt subscribes to this assessment of violence: "Violence is by nature instrumental; like all means, it always stands in need of guidance and justification through the end it pursues" (1969, 51). For an original critique of instrumental assessments of violence, see Benjamin (1979).

2. For a different analysis of the way in which law is both *ratio* and *voluntas*, and of the reprivatization of law beginning at the turn of the century, see Neumann (1957, 22–68).

PART TWO
Law and Legitimation

One of the "language-games" that is universal in human society is that of justifying action, or of showing that what is offensive or disagreeable is nonetheless legitimate. As we have already said, the problem of violence in human affairs is sharply different from any problem about violence in nature just because of this common fact. While there is, no doubt, value in discussing violence abstractly and attempting partial definitions, the role of violence in human affairs cannot be understood without explicit consideration of our procedures for allowing what we know to be harmful and destructive.

The common presupposition of any sort of justification is some sort of social order or practice, a set of rules and procedures implemented on a regular basis. The chapters by Bernhard Waldenfels and Wojciech Chojna argue that this very general presupposition entails that violence is inevitable in human affairs, even from the strictest theoretical point of view. This conclusion may at first appear cynical or shocking, but we need to look as carefully at this assessment as at the structure of Waldenfels's argument.

Waldenfels's conclusion in Chapter 7 is in fact part of a concrete hope for humanity. True, it rules out any possibility of a truly nonviolent society, as do Elizabeth Wolgast and Newton Garver in rather different terms, and thus it rejects any generalization to the whole of society of the philosophy of nonviolence of Gandhi and King. But the argument is that this was never really possible in the first place. Because it was never possible in the first place, advocacy of a nonviolent society is nothing but a debilitating distraction, an illusory ideal. Insisting on complete nonviolence neglects the indisputable fact that 'violence' is a quantitative concept, that it admits, as Aristotle puts it in the *Categories*, of a more and a less. Given this indisputable fact, it is more reasonable to focus on the reduction than the elimination of violence. The illusory ideal of complete nonviolence often blinds us to elements of violence that are in subtle ways crippling other people. The hopeful side of the conclusion Waldenfels reaches is that, by paying attention to its quantitative nature and its subtle dimensions, we will be better able to achieve a genuine reduction in levels of human violence.

The argument, which hangs together with a point of view elaborated more fully and eloquently in *Ordnung im Zwielicht* (1987), depends on presuppositions about the concepts of 'violence' and 'order'. The conception of violence is broad, agreeing with that of Cotta (1978) and Garver (1968) in seeing its essence more in violation of persons than in sheer force, and therefore concurring with Thomas Pogge (Chapter 4) that structural or institutional violence is an important part of the general phenomenon. So violence is part, at least sometimes, of the normal everyday way of doing things. The conception of order is highly pragmatic: Rules and possibilities can never be determined abstractly or conceptually, but only in concrete social or historical situations. This conception allows no reality to Tamil considered as a system of semantic and syntactic rules; as a language it has reality in concrete situations in which actual behavior depends on knowing and practicing those rules. In such a situation the ordinary linguistic practice does violence to those who are inept in Tamil: It shackles them, and may even exclude them from a wide range of normal activities. The practice thus violates these other persons; that is, it violates their basic human rights. There can therefore be *no* social order that does not involve elements of violence: Violence is always and necessarily part of the normal everyday way of doing things. In some ways this critique of "order" is more radical than the anarchist perspective discussed by Jan Narveson and Hugo Bedau.

It should be apparent that however difficult this argument may be, and whether or not it is ultimately sound, its basis lies not in any cynicism, but rather in a profound respect for the dignity of individual human beings, as well as in a sense of repugnance at putting rules above compassion. Chojna (Chapter 8) shows how phenomenological redescription of "justified" violence can facilitate such compassion—although it would seem equally able to facilitate punitive harshness.

A key point in the argument, which we can here only indicate and not properly discuss, is the insistence that there are gaps in any actual justification. In actual practice after-the-fact justifications *do* come to an end. Otherwise, as Wittgenstein has pointed out, they would not be capable of justifying. So the question arises how there can nonetheless be real gaps; how it can be, as Chojna puts it, that "any order . . . itself stands in need of justification." Such a gap seems abstract rather than concrete; or, in the terms Garver (Chapter 10) borrows from Kant, seems to involve constitutive use of regulative ideas. But such a problem is too complex to be resolved here and should not distract from serious consideration of the profound perspective of Waldenfels and Chojna. The insistence that "nonviolent reason" is a contradiction in terms, and that an absolutely nonviolent social order is an illusory ideal, remains sobering.

The point made by Waldenfels and Chojna may be salutary as well as sobering. The editors confess, however, that they remain unconvinced.

One problem is that the phenomena considered by Waldenfels extend far beyond the phenomena considered by John Ladd or by Bedau; we are not sure whether what can be said with confidence about one narrow range or the other applies with equal confidence to the two narrow ranges combined, let alone to the broader range considered by Waldenfels. It is surely not the case that the justifications one might give for the institution of punishment, for example, those one finds in Bedau's paper, fall into the same patterns as the deplorable ideological thinking Ladd describes. Another, and perhaps more critical, problem is our lingering uncertainty about whether common practices always need justification. We cannot see that we need ever offer any justification for being able to speak the languages we are able to speak; nor that anyone need ever offer any justification for the existence of such languages. (Having to apologize for *not* being able to speak a certain language, for not having mastered its rules, is an entirely different matter.) It is hard to see, concretely, that any demands are satisfied by the existence of such languages, nor that there are other demands violated or frustrated by them. Although these considerations leave us unconvinced, the stimulation of Waldenfels's paper is unforgettable, and we doubt that we could offer an altogether satisfactory rebuttal. The viewpoint is one that emphatically needs to be included in any discussion of the legitimation of violence.

Let us mention in passing that the essay by Waldenfels not only offers a challenging and substantially divergent perspective but also is especially helpful in integrating the volume. On the one hand he makes half a dozen references to other contributors and therefore enables readers to pursue the details of the divergences themselves. On the other hand he provides an analytic perspective on the concept of violence, partly by distinguishing it from related concepts and partly by noticing how different are the Latin roots of the English word 'violence' (from *violare*) and the German word *Gewalt* (from *valere*).

The essays by Wolgast (Chapter 9) and Garver (Chapter 10) discuss specific forms of justification. Wolgast discusses "getting even" in terms of ways in which we generally defend rights of self-defense and our intuitive insistence that punishment and counterviolence are qualitatively different from crime and original violence. Garver discusses the character of ideals that are invoked as ends in means–ends arguments in which violence serves as the instrumental means. The essays are parallel in that both disparage the arguments they consider. They also agree in doubting whether there is or ever can be any coherent concept of a perfectly just society.

Wolgast, as is usual in her work, eschews technicalities in her contribution. She argues in terms of the familiar everyday idea of getting even. This idea implies some objective or interpersonal conception of balance, and the crux of her argument is that no such conception is available. The main reason that no such conception is available is that balance is always in part a matter of perspective, and perspective always varies because of divergent points of view and interests. So what is balance (justice) to one party will be provocation (violence) to another. One can easily see in this argument, although it is conducted in entirely different terms, a convergence with the conclusion of Waldenfels and Chojna that imposing a certain order of discourse always involves an element of violence. The inevitability of such divergences, given that we do have different perspectives, leads Wolgast, naturally enough, to the conclusion that perfect justice is an illusory and incoherent ideal.

Garver's paper, although original in its details, is an elaboration of a main thesis of Isaiah Berlin. Berlin, in his Agnelli Lecture, notes that no plan for a utopia has ever worked out in practice and argues that this failure rate is due to the very idea of social ideals. Reasonable persons will, therefore, aim in practice at compromises rather than utopian ideals. Garver notes the Kantian character of this argument, then applies it to the ideal of a just society. He argues that every such ideal is incoherent. A main consideration is that justice is a regulative ideal and that the concept of a just society seems legitimate only by illicitly making constitutive use of it. His conclusion is that the term 'justice' always refers in part to a process rather than an outcome, and that the ideal of a just society can therefore not be used to justify violence as an instrumental means.

These two essays, because they are both powerful and provocative, need to be considered with caution, as R. G. Frey and John Arthur have done in unpublished discussions of them. Frey suggested that "getting even" sounds to a utilitarian more like vengeance or retribution than like justice, that justice can operate without an arithmetic of exact balances, and that Wolgast's heavy stress on perspectives brings her closer than she cares to admit to the sort of relativism she disavows. Arthur, speaking from a deep respect for traditional philosophy of law, pointed out ways in which justice does serve as an ideal for the judicial process; and he raised a question (which Garver avoids in his paper) about what changes, if any, these provocative considerations imply for jurisprudence and judicial practice. These are useful matters to bear in mind while reading these two essays.

Jan Narveson (Chapter 11) and Carl Wellman (Chapter 12) address fundamental questions concerning the relations between law, violence, and rights. One is whether rights legitimate violence. That is, does the violation of a right, or the protection of a right, justify acts of violence? The other main question is whether law, which is often seen as the main defender of the citizen against acts of violence, is itself implicated in violence; and if so, whether this connection between law and violence is a necessary one.

Narveson displays a deep skepticism about the legitimation of state violence. He believes, with Robert Holmes and Wellman, that normative questions must not be precluded by a definitional move. But "force," "coercion," and "violence" are very often deplorable, and Narveson sees a common thread in objections against their use. What is wrong about all of these is that, in Narveson's terms, the victim's "menu of alternatives" is unilaterally revised in such a way that the victim's rights are violated. This raises the fundamental question, of course, of just what rights a person has, and Narveson offers a libertarian account of those rights in the second section of his essay.

In these first sections of his essay, therefore, Narveson provides his answer to the first question posed above, about to what extent the protection of rights justifies acts of violence.

His response to the second question, about whether law is necessarily coercive, elaborates a theme of his recent book, *The Libertarian Idea* (1989): While law is not necessarily illegitimate, it almost always is. A combination of empirical and theoretical considerations leads him to conclude that laws themselves, together with actual practice in the administration of the law, will almost certainly violate rights that people have—that the law itself is in practice a sort of violence.

In these matters Narveson largely agrees with the contention of Waldenfels that some degree of violence is implicated in any and every legal order. At the same time Narveson wishes to reduce the level of violence in human lives and believes the law, ideally, is similarly committed. This uneasy balance is something we must learn to live with: The law, which in principle deserves our respect and support, must in its day-to-day operations always be viewed with suspicion. While several of the essays in this collection view the use of violence by the state as suspect, Narveson's develops the most thoroughgoing skepticism about the legitimacy of the state's use of force and violence.

Wellman offers a detailed analysis of the relation of violence to both legal and moral rights. One criterion of a good definition of violence is that it not prejudice moral issues; but unlike Holmes and Garver, Wellman believes this criterion requires avoiding any emotive or evaluative terms in explaining what violence is. He defines violence in a primary sense as action "characterized by the exertion of great physical force." It should be noted, as the other contributors agreed, that this definition provides Wellman with a clear question to consider; and that others can easily join him in the consideration of this issue, even though they define 'violence' differently in their own work.

Does violence in this sense necessarily violate basic legal or moral rights? Wellman's answer to this question might be thought of as an application of J. L. Austin's dictum that moral philosophy has much to learn from the law. Like Austin's work, his essay makes it clear that there is no simple answer to this apparently simple question. Violent acts do often violate rights; but not always *because* of their violence, and not to the same degree in the case of legal rights as in the case of moral rights. On the other hand they sometimes do not. A high point of Wellman's essay is the way he distinguishes various ways in which a violent action may fail to be a violation of a legal or moral right.

Wellman also considers whether rights legitimate or justify violence. Again, the analysis distinguishes legal and moral rights. Basic legal rights that legitimate violence include war powers, police powers, self-defense, and defense of others. There are four basic moral rights, analogous to these legal rights, that provide a moral legitimation of violence. Of particular interest in this section is his discussion of the moral right of an individual to use violence in defense of others as analogous to the state's right to police society.

Wellman's essay gives the most thorough account to date of the general problem of the relation of rights to the legitimation of force and coercion. Other essays in this book that also focus on rights in a more limited way are those of André Maury, Virginia Held, Lance Stell, and Narveson. Other contributors use other basic normative concepts as their touchstone, including some (such as Waldenfels and Chojna) whose normative touchstone is violence itself. The essays in Part Two thus illustrate the variety of starting points one may choose when considering whether or not violence can be justified.

7

LIMITS OF LEGITIMATION AND THE QUESTION OF VIOLENCE

Bernhard Waldenfels

One may destroy a man who makes war upon him or has discovered an enmity to his being, for the same reason that he may kill a wolf or a lion; because such men are not under the ties of the common law of reason, have no other rule but that of force and violence, and so may be treated as beasts of prey, those dangerous and noxious creatures, that will be sure to destroy him whenever he falls into their power.
—John Locke, *Second Treatise of Government*, 3:16

Generally human violence is opposed to reason. It seems to lack legitimation except in cases of counterviolence, when someone is forced to defend reason against its enemies. This is accurate enough for one form of violence, that which occurs within an existing order. But there is another form that opposes one order to another. In the latter case the legitimation may refer to a true and total order, to a just and fundamental order, or simply to a factual order. But because every order is selective and exclusive, each contains some element of violence and none can be legitimated in a complete way. If one nevertheless tries to rationalize such violence, there will arise a new specific form of violence used in the name of reason and resulting from a kind of overlegitimation. Against all forms of such pseudosolutions we would be better off treating violence as an open question. If violence consists in disregarding the otherness of the Other, we need a speech that renounces the first word as well as the last word.

It is beyond question that even today human beings not only resort to violence but also try to legitimate it; if not completely, then at least partially. We could speak of a "double violence," as we speak of a double truth. Take, for example, just war, revolutionary violence, the monopoly of legitimate coercion attributed to the state, or the private use of violence in cases of self-defense or emergency aid: In all these cases violence is *not simply* violence. But it remains violence even if the victims of violence are resurrected by monuments. The old saying *"Inter arma silent musae"* should not suggest that the Muses start singing afterward as if nothing had happened. The attempt to legitimate violence worries us because elements come together that at first glance do not fit together and whose combination remains in a certain sense unthinkable. Trying to "think the unthinkable," as Hannah Arendt (1969, 6) put it,[1] strains the limits of reason, and we are not sure whether—as Kant (1968b, 229) claims—the *"Grenzgott"* of morality really resists the *"Grenzgott"* of violence. Throughout the following reflections, the question of violence will be explicitly treated in connection with the question of its legitimation. By doing so we try to avoid the danger of imputing to violence a nature, an end, or an origin of its own that it, per se, does not really have.

Human violence cannot be reduced to natural violence, which is beyond every kind of justification. It refers to violent, or perhaps nonviolent, forms of speaking and acting that take place within certain orders. In other words, human violence always arises in the framework of specific discourses, whose orders change in correspondence to the challenges to which they respond. In this sense our interrogation of violence will be guided by the idea of a possible or impossible legitimation of violence. But in the background there is a further question referring to violence as such. We have to ask ourselves if we may really presume a discourse about violence that is not in itself affected by some elements of violence. I shall argue that there is no such pure form of discourse because of the unavoidable limits of legitimation.

REASON AND VIOLENCE

The Great Divorce Between Reason and Violence

The pure claim to legitimate violence starts from a great divorce. Since the time of the ancient Greeks, on the one side of the borderline we find agencies of order such as Reason (*Nous*), Law (*Nomos*), or Right (*Dikè*) confronted with chaotic, blind, and brute forces of pure Violence (*Bia*) on the other side. Some examples may be sufficient to illustrate this. In his tragedy *Prometheus Bound* Aeschylus introduces the figures of *Kratos* and *Bia*. They get the first word, but the last word is given to Prometheus's *Technè*, by means of which the fetters get untied. In the *Laws* (645a) Plato praises argumentation as a kind of drawing that is "beautiful and gentle, and not violent [*biaiou*]." Later, in *On Duties* (I, 11, 34), Cicero distinguishes between two ways of overcoming conflicts, namely, *disceptatio*, a human way of arguing and negotiating, and *vis*, a bestial or brutish way of dispute. Behind such distinctions there is a certain trend aiming at an "unviolent reason," which subdues and transforms "unreasonable violence." If reason in the end keeps some element of violence it does so only in the form of a *bia en tō logō* (Aristotle, *Met.* IV, 6, 1011 a 15), that is, in the form of a cogency of arguments. For reasonable beings this cogency ceases to be coercive because once we have become reasonable, there is no longer any reason to resist.

The Clash of Reason and Violence

The great divorce between reason and violence suffers from the fact that reason and violence do not live in different worlds. The claims of right and reason and the effects of violence clash *within this one world*. If reason wants not only to be valid but to survive and to realize itself, it cannot, as matters stand, restrict itself to the soft forces of its own. It resorts perforce to violence that is not just in itself but has to be justified. Furthermore, this conflict not only separates one's own world from the world of others; it passes through *somebody's own existence*. Being *simul justus et peccator* or "citizen of two worlds" (both saint and sinner), the human being is exposed to allurements and assaults of violence coming from the inside. Plato and Freud have sufficiently shown that the conflict enters the human soul, able to increase to the point of a civil war within one's own soul. Consequently, reason, which by itself rebuts violence, reaches for violence when threatened. Being unable to justify violence as violence for its own sake, it is compelled to justify it in reference to violence that is already given. When violence is justified, it becomes qualified as 'counterviolence', a concept prominent in the 1960s but already found in Kant (1968b, 156), albeit with negative connotations. There is no doubt that counterviolence has a different status than violence in courts of popular and even rational judgment; but what shall we do when counterviolence stands against counterviolence, as it does in the ideologically charged struggles, whose dynamic is discussed in the papers of Ladd and Wolgast, and which are so typical of our century?

Violence Within an Order and Violence Between Orders

First we have to distinguish between two different kinds of violence, one that grows out of the *grounds of an existing order* and another that is used *in favor of* or *against growing orders*. In the first case we have to do with offenses and crimes that violate laws, but without contesting them. These forms of violence can be duly treated within the framework of an existing order. The representatives of order who react to violence by means of a legitimate or legal counterviolence claim to defend order against *disorder*. The criminal is finally expected to accept the consequences of punishment and to make good for what has been done. Following Hegel (1821, sec. 100), the demand that the criminal accept punishment as well deserved, and thus interiorize it in terms of self-punishment, constitutes the "honor" of the criminal. The so-called fraternal wars that aim at conquest or retaliation without undermining the other's form of life also apply here. Consequently, Plato makes the distinction between discord (*stasis*), in which Greeks confront Greeks who are "friends by nature," and war (*polemos*), in which Greeks confront barbarians who are "enemies by nature" (*Rep.* V, 470b–c). In a similar way Cicero (1969, I, 12, 38) distinguishes between two types of warfare; in the first case the existence of one or the other state is at stake (*uter esset*), in the other case domination is at stake (*uter imperaret*). In the second case, which transgresses the limits of a given order and which is well known from the different friend–enemy images, one order opposes other orders. This opposition arises when one's own form of life has to be defended against an alien one, or when a new form of life is exchanged for an old one.

The conceptual distinction between "intraordinal" and "interordinal" conflict does not exclude the fact that the alien or new order is often already rumbling within the familiar and well-established order. We have to reckon with what Max Weber (1976, 15) called "fluent transitions," a lot of examples of which are to be found in the *The Real Life of Alejandro Mayta* (1986), the story narrated by Mario Vargas Llosa about a Peruvian revolutionary. The "same" action, for example, a bank robbery, may be taken as crime or as revolutionary act; or the "same" collective events, such as the Budapest events in 1956, may be classified as 'counterrevolution' or reinterpreted as 'revolt of the people'. Such reinterpretations are well known as having far-reaching consequences, political as well as juridical ones. They show that neither intra- nor interordinal conflict ever pits *pure* reason against *pure* violence. Pure violence would mean a form of violence detached from any *logos*, from any order of speaking and acting; it would be, following honorable men like Cicero or liberal men like Locke, no longer human but bestial or brutish. But stigmatizing human beings as beasts is, apart from the crude misunderstanding of animal life, in itself an act of social violence that cuts the other short. Thus there is no chance for reason to whitewash itself.

Every action, even war, is symbolic, as Merleau-Ponty (1955, 293–94) puts it. As in Lima's museum of the inquisition, which Vargas Llosa minutely describes in *The Real Life of Alejandro Mayta*, so also in history "higher" and "lower" forms of violence dwell side by side. But violence may also appear in the harmless-looking garment of governmental administration based on economic mechanisms. So in New York's Indian Museum we meet with a Minnesota General Order of 1863 which offers, in administration's finest letters, one hundred dollars of head money to be paid for each killed Indian, "independent of age and sex." This way of killing is certainly not "antilegal." Even the killing machines of Hitler's camps took care that everything got its ideological pretexts and its bureaucratic correctness, up to the scrupulously arranged button collections, gathered from the clothes of the gassed, which are exhibited in Auschwitz. The more the "technology of subtle, efficient and economical forms of violence" increases, the more we keep distance from the purely bestial.[2]

JUSTIFICATION

Varieties of Justification

The distinction between violence within an order and violence between different orders helps us to sharpen the problem. As long as we remain on the ground of an existing order, we may, in case of conflict, refer to a mediating and legitimating instance. As soon as the common ground cracks under the assault of alien or new orders, the legitimation instance itself becomes questionable. This is the situation from which Hobbes's thinking and that of his followers starts. In this case violence can only be justified by a legitimation of second degree, mediating between conflicting orders.

This second-degree legitimation proceeds in different ways. It may take the form of "totalization," which refers to a true and total order. Violence appears as *part or phase of a highest good* justified in and by itself, for example, as cosmic order, as plan of salvation, as reign of freedom, as classless society, or simply as creative and destructive forces of life. Violence turns into a *felix culpa* on the background of a religious or secularized economy. Furthermore, legitimation may take the form of universalization referring to a just and fundamental order. In this context violence becomes an unavoidable evil that has to be put up with in realizing a right order. Thus in Kant's *Anthropologie* (1968a, 686) the republican constitution is characterized as "violence combined with freedom and law"; violence must be added to "guarantee success" of the two other principles. Finally, one may defend the positivity of an order by referring to a factual order that is handed down by tradition, introduced by pure decision or functioning in a pragmatic way. It could be argued that without some order whatsoever humankind could not survive and prosper. Thus, violence is accepted as an unavoidable fact.

Justification After the Fact

Before asking in which way the legitimation of violence is limited, we should consider how legitimation functions.[3] Who legitimates or justifies what vis-à-vis whom if a discourse about violence takes place? Legitimation includes different items, none of which seems to be dispensable: An *advocate* justifies an *agent* (who may also be the advocate) *for some action* or deed done to *another*, and he does so *in the presence of a third party* by giving *reasons* for what he has done. The question to what extent the role takers are individualized or conversely become anonymous may be put aside here, because it involves special problems, for example, the problem Ladd (Chapter 1) addresses of how to distinguish between individual and collective violence.[4] Moreover, it does not matter whether the different roles are taken by different persons or by one and the same person. If I justify myself vis-à-vis myself, I carry on an internal discourse in such a way that the difference of roles is retained.

First, it should be mentioned that justification in its explicit form comes after the fact (*après coup*).[5] The speech of justification belongs to the genre of forensic speech that—as Aristotle puts it in his *Rhetoric*—is connected with the dimension of past. In this way the act of violence becomes a topic that we dispute, putting violence on the one side and arguments on the other. In this process law (justification) seems to go its way, free from violence. Those who have done violence and those who have suffered from it need not even take part personally in the process of legitimation. Defense attorney, prosecutor, and judge can settle the case among themselves, and this necessarily occurs when a historical event has to be judged. But such a transformation of violence into a subsequent topic cannot deceive us about the difference between violence about which we dispute from the perspective of a mediating *third* party, and violence we do *to the other*. Therefore Kant makes a strict distinction between moral action and historical event. A legitimation of violence that goes to the roots of things would have to include the perspectives of agent and victim. That means there must be an open possibility for the agent of violence to justify herself not only face to face with a third party but also face to face with her victim, even if de facto it may be too late: One cannot justify oneself vis-à-vis a corpse.

But this is not all. The possibility just mentioned presupposes that the act of violence is performed between speaker/agent and addressee, and is *done to* somebody. This implies a minimal form of allocution. If what has been done would totally fuse with whom it has been done to, there would be nothing left to be justified because nobody would be left whose demands could be violated. The act of violence would degrade to a mere act of damage or destruction of things.[6] But if on the contrary the act of violence refers to an addressee—if, that is, even offense or the pure labeling of persons includes an element of intercourse or even bodily harm or murder includes an element of interaction—then violence and speech meet on one and the same level and intertwine. The great divorce underlying the justification of violence as something purely nonviolent or purely verbal vanishes at this point. The verbal or nonverbal act of violence lacks the distance capable of making justification possible. By the way, the same has to be said of the verbal or nonverbal act of love, although in the latter case we do not look so much for justification. Taking up a distinction made by Emmanuel Levinas (1974, 58ff., and chap. 5), we could claim that not only does saying exceed what is said, but also doing exceeds what is done. A process of justification that clings to what is said and what is done cedes the words to the third party, taking it right out of the other's mouth. Every speech that transforms violence into a pure topic we speak about becomes ventriloquial, as if the discourse about violence were dubbed; or again as if it were a voice-over, like a tape we erase. The playing down of violence begins by justifying it.

The Unavoidable Gaps of Justification

Certainly, one should concede that, to a certain extent, treating violence takes place on the level of pros and cons, looking for reasons that may support what is said and done even if what is said and what is done do not catch up with the very process of saying and acting. But even here legitimation shows its own limits, which I have described in more extensive reflections in *Ordnung im Zwielicht* (1987, especially chap. C). The presupposition of this can only be referred to, not fully explained in this context. Every order, I would argue, from the order of feeling, perceiving, and moving, through the order of speaking and acting, to the encompassing orders of life, society, and world, is *selective and exclusive,* realizing certain possibilities and simultaneously excluding others. Every sort of rationality points, as Merleau-Ponty made clear (1945, preface), to the basic fact that "there is rationality"; and every sort of ordering, as Foucault (1966, preface) has shown us, goes back to the basic event that "there is order." This "there is" (*es gibt; il y a*) allows for reasons but not for a sufficient reason. This means that the second-degree legitimation charged with settling the case between conflicting orders will never come to an end. The shifting event and fact of order, mixing rationality and contingency, can not be integrated in a comprehensive order, regulated by an absolutely fundamental order, or reduced to an empirical fact. To this extent *no order* can be legitimated in a complete way.

These gaps of justification, incapable of being filled up, create a problem of power that cannot be resolved by mere power of reason. One order is established instead of others, without being backed by sufficient reasons. Because no order is capable of complete legitimation, each of them contains some element of violence (*etwas Gewaltsames*); that is, every order violates certain demands (*Ansprüche*) just by satisfying others, and this preference cannot be oriented on an optimum, for example, the best of all worlds. As Merleau-Ponty (1955, 75; trans. 1973, 53) states in his analysis of Western Marxism, "Violence is necessary only because there is no final truth in the contemplated world; violence cannot therefore pride itself on having an absolute truth."[7] This problem, to be found in Hobbes or Nietzsche as well as in Max Weber, Walter Benjamin, Raymond Aron, Merleau-Ponty, Levinas and Foucault, has nothing to do with an irrational, anarchic, existential, or subjectivistic hostility against law and order, nor with an obsession with freedom. On the contrary, it has to do with problems of order and reason itself first arising in the beginning of modern time and displaying their consequences today under the rather helpless catchword of postmodernity. As Musil (1952, 19) remarks in his half-ironical way, we become more and more aware that even God speaks in form of a *conjunctivus potentialis*. What some call "existential antilegalism" is nothing more than a short-winded reaction against a long-lasting transformation of rationality.[8]

COMING TO TERMS WITH VIOLENCE

Violence and Its Conceptual Surroundings

A short categorical interplay may be useful to clarify the matter and terminology at hand.

1. Following the example of Max Weber, Heidegger, and Merleau-Ponty, we prefer the adjective "violent" (*gewaltsam*) to the substantive "violence" (*Gewalt*).[9] Thus we try to avoid the misinterpretation that violence (or power) might be some mythical or quasi-mythical entity, able to replace sense, truth, reason, or law. Indeed, that which is violent in our sense is speaking and acting itself, and this not only by offending order but also by fulfilling and changing it. In this careful way we may distinguish between elements of *actual violence*, which appear within a certain order; elements of *structural violence*, which are attached to the structures of a certain order; and finally elements of *transcendental violence*, which concern order as such.[10] As to the last form of violence, we reaffirm that violence, lurking in the interstices between different orders, refers to the possibility of sense and not only to an empirical garbage of non-sense.

2. In general, violence is understood as a kind of violation as suggested by the Latin word *violentia*. More precisely we think of a "violation" of demands that are to be responded to. Injustice in the sense of violation of juridical or quasi-juridical claims that are to be fulfilled already constitutes a more specific form of violation.[11] Violence as violation of demands presupposes a certain form of circumscribed integrity, otherwise we would speak of mere damage. Insofar as the victim of violence realizes his integ-

rity by embodiment, and insofar as the body is enlarged through a proper world of things, we have to assume that by violence against the body and by violence against things the person himself is more or less affected. Instead of contrasting physical and psychical violence or violence against things and against persons, we would do better to distinguish between peripheral and central, direct and indirect forms of violence. The point of attack changes from one case to the other, but the use of violence is not divided into different domains. As each child knows, even by doing nothing other than remaining silent, a wall of violence may be set up.

3. The concept of violence proposed in (2) makes sense only if located in an interregnum of dialogue where we speak to someone and do something to someone. I am not convinced that this sphere of demands must be restricted to human beings, but I put aside all questions concerning our relation to nature and the possibility of a new kind of eco-ethic. In any case, the process of order, combining selection and exclusion, would degenerate into a mere game if the demands of others were left out. In contrast to Lyotard (1983), we should not speak of violence or even of injustice when the only thing at stake is the exclusion of possibilities by the realization of anything whatsoever. From a simple modal ontology we find no answer to the question why, in the case of difference (*différend*), one possibility *ought* to be realized instead of the other.[12]

4. Finally there are complications of the immediate linguistic context that are responsible for many misunderstandings. Whereas the English term 'violence' is etymologically related to *violentia*, which clearly derives from *violare*, the corresponding German term *Gewalt* is related to *valere* and originally means something like the "having disposal of something" (*Verfügungsfähigkeit*) in a nonlegal sense. Only later the sense of '*Gewalt*' is split into two senses, one corresponding to *potestas* and the other to *violentia*, which creates a highly seductive ambiguity.[13] The central term 'violence' is surrounded by neighboring words such as 'conflict', which means the clash between interests or efforts; 'force' (*Kraft*), which means, among other things, a certain *élan* attributed to things as well as to ideas; 'coercion' or 'constraint' (*Zwang*), which means that the free space of action is restricted; 'obstacle' (*Hindernis*), which points to the occlusion of an initiative; and so on. Finally, 'violence' comes close to the term 'power' (*Macht*), which has to do with the ability and productivity of acting and which socially, following Max Weber's famous definition (1976, 28), means the "chance to carry through (*durchzusetzen*) one's own will within a social relation, even against resistance (*Widerstreben*)." What in our context is discussed in terms of violence has obviously much to do with problems that authors like Arendt (1969) and Foucault (1982) discuss as the social form of power or *pouvoir*. So much for eluding some of the most strik-

ing misunderstandings. To be sure, more subtle distinctions of concepts and further translations between concepts are required, but in the present context what has been done should be sufficient.

Rationalization of Violence

Provided it is true that every legitimation of violence comes after the fact and reduces the saying and doing to what has been said and done, and further provided it is true that the legitimation of what has been said and done offers not more than *insufficient* reasons, we will run into an empty space incapable of being filled by any kind of legitimation. If, nevertheless, one tries to fill the empty space by excluding all aspects of violence and by introducing some kind of all-encompassing "super-discourse," specific forms of violence will arise resulting from the very attempt of *overlegitimation*. We find many examples in the Western attempts of rationalization that tend toward a totalization and universalization. One invokes a *prima ratio* sanctifying or justifying all means, or at least and more modestly one refers to an *ultima ratio* whenever the good weather ceases, a social tempest arises, and soft means begin to fail. The distinction between right and wrong, progressive and regressive, life-increasing and life-lessening violence clears up the frontiers by invoking the great divorce of which we spoke in the beginning. Conflicts between one order and the other are played up as part of the struggle between order and disorder. By stigmatizing the criminal as pure malfeasant, the political rebel as pure criminal, the enemy as "underman" or underdog, a good conscience is preserved in a society that *nolens volens* does violence to others. The representatives of society defend themselves, refusing even answers to their enemies. The law creates "outlaws" without questioning what kind of "out" this is. The justification of violence is compensated for by self-righteousness of reason, which cedes to its own violence the more this process is disguised by rationalization. In this point a thinker like Foucault seems to be right.

Violence as an Open Question

We find a first way out of the dead-ends such pseudosolutions offer if we try to leave the presumed super-discourse behind, turning to the intertwining and interfering of *specific discourses* whose limits coincide with the limits of legitimation. Thinking the unthinkable requires questioning origins, motives, and conditions of violence, and showing what it—right or wrong—does in the world. The question of legitimacy or illegitimacy comes only later. By postponing the question in cases of emergency, not so much would be lost. It is a common dilemma that those who ought to listen to arguments do it the least. Listening to the voice of reason presupposes a capability and readiness that cannot be grafted by arguments. In the long run, an "indirect treatment" of violence, including liberating laughter, may have better effects than a direct form of combat and condemnation pursuing the phantom of a final solution, an *Endlösung*.

If the heart of the violence consists in disregarding the otherness of the Other and in cutting the Other short, we need a speech that renounces the first word as well as the last word. We need a kind of *Sagen/dire* ready for a perpetual *Entsagen/dédire*, as Levinas (1974, 195ff) indicates when he speaks of an incessant process of *dire* and *dédire*. In this context excuses, pardon, and reconciliation find their private and public, their ordinary and extraordinary place, as Garver (1988, 222) has suggested. Such symbolic gestures do not intend to justify what has been said and done, nor to restore an order in the view of a third party; they rather try to renew the dialogue with the other and to continue speaking and acting in spite of all that has been said and done. Even such a kind of speaking and acting would not be totally free from "elements of violence," from *Gewaltsamkeiten*, but these would not so quickly congeal to an irrevocable "institution of violence," of *Gewalt*.[14] This does not mean that the thinking of the unthinkable finds a solution, but at least it does find a support.

NOTES

1. Arendt's attempt to think about power and violence has been very attractive for my own reflections, though I do not follow her in many points, for example, in her orientation on the classical conception of reason.

2. See Foucault (1975, 105). To these subtle, efficient, and economical forms of violence correspond similar forms of verbal violence. Take as example this document from the Gestapo prison in Lublin: "Lublin 19. Juli 1944. Aufstellung der Häftlinge, die hier wegen kommunistischer Betätigung einsitzen und bei Räumung des Gefangenenhauses Lublin der Sonderbehandlung zugeführt werden können." (Lublin July 19, 1944. Exhibition of prisoners residing here because of Communist activity and presented at a special offering through cleaning out the Lublin prison.)

3. Because I generally focus on *quaestiones iuris,* especially on the sufficient or unsufficient character of de jure questions, I do not clearly distinguish between 'legitimation', which points to the reasoning of public institutions and procedures, and 'justification' (*Rechtfertigung*), which points to personal forms of rendering account and of finding out what is right. On the whole the term 'legitimation' seems to me more appropriate to keep the debate open. By its Weberian connotations it points to the institutional framework without which no action, not even the so-called moral action, may be possible.

4. Concerning this distinction, which Ladd ably defends, I should plead for a certain continuity rather than a dichotomy, because every interindividual behavior takes place within a social field, being never *completely* individual.

5. Should we presuppose implicit forms of justification that function *simultaneously*? Here we could think of a kind of acting accompanied by a consciousness of the law that affords reasons whenever wanted; Schütz's 'stock of knowledge' would be complemented by a 'stock of reasons'. But I would speak of justification only in cases where the legitimacy of an action, performed really or by imagination, is contested and defended against this contestation. The 'afterwards' has especially to do with what above I call "legitimation of second degree," that is, with cases in which a granted stock of reasons is just lacking.

Another problem, raised by Savigny (Chapter 3), consists in the fact that every kind of justification implies a skill, more or less available for the person just concerned. Otherwise the sophisticated teacher and writer of speeches would not have had such a big clientele, and otherwise many attorneys would be breadless. So the skill of *giving* reasons cannot be simply identified with *having* good reasons.

6. The question whether something like that exists or, on the contrary, whether all damage to things is more than *pure* damage to things, may remain open in the context of our present discussion.

7. We may add that neither can violence pride itself on having an absolutely "true coexistence," as Merleau-Ponty had been inclined to presume in *Humanisme et terreur* (1947). The necessity of violence cited has to be taken in its literal sense as the inevitability of a problem, not as the expression of an essence or a fact, even a simple fact of life that we just have to accept.

8. On this point I disagree with Cotta. I can accept neither the way he answers the question, What is violence? nor the way he resolves the problem of violence, namely, by turning away from the modern "metaphysics of subjectivity" and coming back to a postmodern "metaphysics of being" (see the epilogue of *Why Violence?* [1978]). As many others before him Cotta leaves behind the problem about the "great divorce" I have mentioned. The alternative is restricted to the opposition of right measure and excessiveness, of sufficient reason and arbitrariness; in Cotta's work, consequently, we find good *force* and bad *violence* confronting each other like regularity and unruliness (see 64). He presents an order without shadow and twilight, to which I oppose a much more restricted form of order. This does not prevent us from learning from Cotta's sophisticated phenomenology of violence, which has many fruitful aspects.

9. See, for example, Weber (1976, 29): "Für politische Verbände ist selbstverständlich die *Gewaltsamkeit* weder das einzige noch auch das normale Verwaltungsmittel. . . . Aber ihre Androhung und, eventuell, Anwendung ist allerdings ihr *spezifisches* Mittel und überall die ultima ratio, wenn andre Mittel versagen." [For political units the *element of violence* is, of course, neither the only nor the normal means of administration. . . . But its threat and possible use is certainly the means *specific* to it and is everywhere the ultimate resource when other means fail.] Or see Heidegger ([1926] 1953, 311–12): "Die existenziale Analyse hat für die Ansprüche bzw. die Genügsamkeit und beruhigte Selbstverständlichkeit der alltäglichen Auslegung ständig den

Charakter einer *Gewaltsamkeit* [Existential analysis regularly has, for the demands or satisfaction and easy self-evidence of everyday exegesis, an *element of violence*]," because every understanding, sustained by a certain interpretation, has the "Struktur des Entwerfens [structure of a design]." Merleau-Ponty (1945, 415, 438; 1969, 195, 197–98) calls perception, human existence, and/or human speech an "acte, passage, ou movement violent." And finally Foucault (1971, 55): "Il faut concevoir le discours comme une *violence* que nous faisons aux choses, en tout cas comme une practique que nous leurs imposons." [One must think of discourse as a *violence* that we impose on things; in any case as a practice that we impose on them] (my emphasis). These passages call for interpretation and not for hasty repudiation.

    10. See Derrida's article on Levinas, "Violence et métaphysique," in *L'écriture et la différence* (1967), esp. 173ff.

    11. On this point my reflections join those of Garver (1988) and Cotta (1985; 1986), who define violence as the violation of persons and as the violation of measure.

    12. Compare Lyotard's (1983) definition of the différend, shifting from a modal–logic model (difference between realized and not realized phrases) to a legal–moral model (difference between two parties or between complaint and victim).

    13. See the article "Gewalt" by Röttgers (1974).

    14. See Levinas (1974, 223): "Le vrai problème pour nous autres occidentaux, ne consiste plus tant à récuser la violence qu'à nous interroger sur une lutte contre la violence qui—sans s'étioler dans la non-résistance au Mal—puisse éviter l'institution de la violence à partir de cette lutte même." [The real problem for us Westerners consists less in condemning violence than in doing research on a struggle against violence that—without wilting down to nonresistance against evil—may avoid the institutionalization of violence as a result of that struggle itself.]

8

THE PHENOMENOLOGICAL REDESCRIPTION OF VIOLENCE

Wojciech Chojna

The thesis I shall defend in this essay is that violence can never be legitimized—neither in theory nor in practice—and that the only sound approach to it is one aimed at its elimination, or at least its drastic reduction. This, I want to argue, can be achieved by redescription. I will examine Waldenfels's proposal to redescribe violence in a phenomenological way and then comment on the alternative form of practical redescription exemplified by the happenings of the "Orange Alternative" movement.

LEGITIMATION AS PHENOMENOLOGICAL DESCRIPTION

Waldenfels's essay (Chapter 7) is concerned with the form of legitimation of a violent action within an "after-the-fact" (*après coup*) structure. Being after the fact means that *One* justifies one's violence done to an *Other* in the presence of a *Third* by means of *reasons*, and that the whole procedure takes place *after* the violent action has been performed.[1] "In this way," says Waldenfels, "the act of violence becomes a *topic* that we dispute, putting violence on the one side and arguments on the other." Such a justification would succeed—violence could be legitimated—if the separation between violence and reason, seen by the ancients (Aeschylus, Plato, Cicero, and Aristotle), were real. In actuality, it is not. Violence and reason always go together. To ensure its success, a violent action has to be guided by reason. To ensure its dominance, reason has to resort to violence. Pure violence and pure reason are unintelligible. Thus, there is no distance between violence and *logos*, and, since the *après coup* structure of justification requires such a distance, there is no hope for its success.

Furthermore, by justifying violence *après coup*, we not only soften its moral impact but play it down as well. After all, we can only look at its effects and not live through the process, which always carries more meanings than those contained in the outcome.

A more important point is that it belongs to the essence of "legitimation" to be carried out within a given order, or in reference to some higher order ("second-degree legitimation"). The problem with any order is that it itself stands in need of justification; or to put it more bluntly, that indeed, as Waldenfels credits Merleau-Ponty and Foucault with having shown, "*no order* can be legitimated in a complete way." If so, then every order contains some element of violence, for it has to violate *some* demands by justifying *some others*, and there is no highest order to justify this choice. This element of violence in a *not fully legitimated* order is carried over to the act of justification itself.

Thus the conclusion of Waldenfels's essay is not only that violence can never be justified, but also that every act of justification necessarily creates more violence. What is the solution? Let me quote: "Thinking the unthinkable requires questioning origins, motives, and conditions of violence, and showing what it—right or wrong—does in the world. The question of legitimacy or illegitimacy comes only later." In my opinion, Waldenfels points here in the direction of Husserl's famed phenomenological description. If we substitute 'description' for 'justification', nothing is lost but a lot is gained. Following Husserl and Merleau-Ponty, we might say that if there is a good reason for an act of violence, it has to be constituted in noncontradictory perceptions of shifting perspectives. If these perceptions blend, or as Husserl says, "coincide," then a common meaning emerges: The reason that does not contradict itself. There is no way, however, as Merleau-Ponty (1945, preface) shows, that we could separate the reason from these perspectives and set it up in an independent realm, ideal or mundane. Any appeal to an order by which *après coup* justification proceeds does exactly this, theoretically ending in infinite regress and practically multiplying violence.

Phenomenological description, instead of explaining away, describes violence in the process of its happening, not only from the perspectives of the actors and victims but also from the perspectives of various historical orders at the intersection of which the violence took place. This seems to mean that we have to abandon the hope of ever legitimating our actions, because descriptions, if sound, are free from evaluative presuppositions. In other words, if phenomenological description is the only possible (and nonviolent) solution, then Waldenfels's hope that "the question of legitimacy or illegitimacy comes only later" is bound to be frustrated.

Phenomenological description, however, separates itself from value only in the sense that no value, of one order or another, is presupposed. Instead, value is constituted at the end as the positive or negative result of the description itself. If what has been described exhibits some *reason*, in the sense of Husserl's and Merleau-Ponty's noncontradictory blend of perceptions, then we have understood the nature of the described event (violence, in this case), and the need for its occurrence.

Anticipating a possible objection, I will add that no phenomenological description can ever be completed; so its final value correlate, the legitimacy or illegitimacy of the violent action, will never be established once and for all. What we have instead is an unending quest for truth. Unlike an *après coup* justification—for which there is an *Endlösung* (final solution) that, like a court verdict, is rarely reversed—a phenomenological description can always be adjusted; it carries the possibility of redescription in itself, as does every normal perception.

There is, however, one more important gain from the phenomenological description. After all, the reason we are interested here in the possibility of justification of violence is to reveal the nature of the violent act itself and not the nature of its justification. In case our suspicion is correct, that is, in case no violence can be justified in any possible way, we should focus on the more important task of eliminating violence itself from the domain of human actions. And, because it is true, as Waldenfels says, that "those who ought to listen to arguments do it the least," we have to proceed in such a way that the violence would be explicitly *shown*, and *seen*, as defeating its own purpose.

Phenomenological description, which by its very nature does not have argumentative structure, is best suited for the purpose. It provides us with the undeniable, because self-evident, data that no argument can offer. And like all the data, it carries the evidence of the Now, without the false pretense to necessity that every argument has. Besides, description focuses on the process itself and not only on the outcome, and it does so from the perspective of a third party, who sits above and is able to see the whole battlefield without taking part in the battle, and without taking sides with the actors. In a similar vein Arendt (1969; 1970) shows how great acts of violence in history, for example revolutions, although aiming at the betterment of human fate, have always resulted in greater unhappiness and more violence.

PRACTICAL REDESCRIPTION
AS AN ALTERNATIVE TO VIOLENCE

Had Lenin understood correctly the meaning of Marx's famous Eleventh Thesis, he would not have taken it as an imperative, but rather as a prediction that (like all inductive reasoning) entails no necessity. A lot of violence, mundane and discursive, could have been avoided. Marx's familiar thesis, "Philosophers have only interpreted the world in different ways; the point is to change it," is the shortest commentary on the end of Hegel's *Phenomenology of Mind*. If Hegel reached Absolute Knowledge, then the only thing left to be done was to actualize it. Reason—or in Marx's prediction the emancipation of humanity—will be brought about by the proletariat, not quite conscious of its role. Lenin took Marx's prediction for the call for direct revolutionary action, regardless of the fact that the conditions for such action, as delineated in Marx's theory, were not present. The result is that at the end of the twentieth century, after seventy years of violence, Russia is in no less miserable condition than at the beginning.

Similarly, had Christianity understood correctly Christ's famous Sermon on the Mount, as for example Joseph Brodsky (1986) understands it in "A Commencement Address," much aggression could have been halted before it even got started, by revealing its absurdity. It did not happen, for "turning the other cheek" in an act of passive resistance is in itself a violent action, which cuts the other short, saying: "Look, this is only the body that you are hitting, you cannot reach my soul." No wonder then, that the aggressor accepted the challenge! Besides, we have to remember what Auden (1979) taught us in "September 1, 1939": "Those to whom evil is done/Do evil in return."

What one can do instead is to take the adversary by the hand and show him the absurdity of his own actions—not by a convincing argument, but by the careful description of how this very act of violence looks from different perspectives, so that the adversary might realize that he is in fact one of the victims of his own, or another's, narrow-minded interpretation of history, and thus might realize the absurdity of his actions and perhaps abandon them altogether.

It is not difficult for the state to outlaw its political enemy on the basis of an evidence, real or prepared. It is even easier for officers of the state to fulfill orders diligently when the enemy and the evidence are part of the description of the orders. But when you realize, all of a sudden, that the enemy you are interrogating is not only willing to answer all your questions but to supply additional "incriminating" information as well, and then, after the interrogation, they thank you for the nice evening and offer you flowers, you begin to reflect on what has happened—the sense of absurdity has crept in, and both the evidence and the enemy have to be redescribed.

The Orange Alternative happenings, to which I am referring here, had the power of showing the absurdity of violent actions through dwarfing the "crime" and exaggerating the punishment.[2] People were arrested in this happening for wearing red, or for carrying portraits of Communist officials. In another one they were taken to prison for making toasts with red strawberry juice. The organizers of these happenings had obviously read Christ's Sermon carefully, not stopping at the famous line about turning the other cheek but continuing (Matt. 5:40–41):

> And if any man will sue thee at the law, and take away thy coat, let him take thy cloke also. And whosoever shall compel thee to go a mile, go with him twain.

Brodsky is right when he says (1986, 389) that the meaning of the above lines is "anything but passive, for it suggests that evil can be made absurd by excess." That is certainly what the Orange Alternative managed to achieve. After one of the happenings the participants, having formed their own police troops, helped the riot police arrest their fellow demonstrators and then jumped into the police cars themselves. How are such people to be treated—especially if, in addition to all this, they thanked their oppressors for a very nice evening, expressed the hope of seeing them again, and promised to celebrate joyfully the "Day of the Policeman"?

What is thematized here is the *way* the state always wanted its people to behave: to take the violence that is done to them with gratitude, that is, as a sign of care. But when the violence is shown as violence, and gratitude as gratitude, the absurdity creeps in again. After all, *they* cannot *really* be grateful for what we *do* to them. This, all of a sudden, becomes obvious, even to the dullest enemy—who, in effect, might begin to perceive himself, by analogy, not as a saviour but as an actor in an absurd play, and might be tempted to leave the stage before the next act. The hope is, of course, that nobody likes his actions to be absurd.

NOTES

1. 'After' does not necessarily refer here to the real time the events take place. One justifies a violent action within the structures that are already present, and one can do it before the action actually takes place. Nevertheless, whether an action has been performed, or is to be performed, the structure, as the *possibility* for justification, remains the same.

2. The Orange Alternative movement was originated in Wroclaw by Waldemar "Mayor" Frydrych after the Polish government crushed the real independent and nonviolent mass revolution aimed at the democratization of economic and political forces in Poland in 1981. The organizers hoped that by involving a great number of people in the mock celebrations of the official state holidays, like the anniversary of the Bolshevik Revolution, or the "Day of the Policeman," a twofold gain could be achieved: First, the state would realize the absurdity of actions with which nobody really identifies; and second, the citizens would realize that only active engagement, which is neither violent nor passive, is able to get them out of the spell of hopelessness that the all-powerful state has cast. As the recent events in Poland and all over Eastern Europe have now shown, these two objectives have been fully realized.

9

GETTING EVEN

Elizabeth Wolgast

We can learn something about justice by observing its place in many long-term, ongoing conflicts. There it shows properties, dynamic properties, that are not otherwise visible. I focus here on one recurring feature of protracted conflicts, namely, that both sides act in protest against injustice.

THE DIALECTICS OF JUSTICE

Justice as Getting Even

The origins of long-term conflicts are often ambiguous or disputed. But once they begin the following pattern frequently develops:[1] One side, feeling offended and wronged, acts in the name of justice in order to set the balance straight, which is to say avenge the offense. But that provokes the other side, which now feels unjustly used, and this sets a process going in which each party acts in turn to remedy injustice, with counter-action leading to counter counter-action, and so on without termination. All in the name of justice.

One *should act* against injustice if possible. That is required by an understanding of what injustice is, for unconcern and passivity suggest acquiescence or an infirm moral sense; protesting against a wrong, the power of whose appeal I discuss in detail in chapters 6 and 7 of *The Grammar of Justice* (1987), goes hand in hand with action to redress it. What kind of action? Injustice seems to require payment proportional to the offense: It requires getting even. These two propositions sometimes seem to be tautologies. That is partly due to the analogy between injustice and debt and, in turn, the role of arithmetic in debt. If A does something hurtful in x degree to B, then B should do something hurtful in x degree to A to put the equation back into balance. Thus, getting even presupposes an arithmetic of justice; it is, as Bradley (1927) makes clear in the essay "The Vulgar Notion of Responsibility," the arithmetic commonly invoked by retributivists on punishment. Using that arithmetic, when a proportional reaction is effected, the score will be settled. The parties will be back to even, to zero, which is the point of stability and peace.

In real life, however, the attempt to get even often works in the opposite direction, against stability and settlement and toward further conflict. This happens whenever the getting even of one side is interpreted as a fresh wrong by the other, and thus provokes a new effort to get even. In such cases it appears that the two sides are computing differently, by different arithmetics, and thus that the very idea of a just settlement is crucially ambiguous. This characteristic of disputes needs to be accounted for in a theory of justice.

How can we account for such differences? They first suggest some lack of understanding about the nature of the wrongs, as if each side already had a theory. And then the problem would be too many theories rather than the lack of one. It is a curious issue and not easily answered by the observation that all such things are relative, that different cultures take different views of morality: The same kind of problem develops within a culture with a single idea of morality, with the Hatfields and the McCoys for instance.

I believe we can account for this instability in disputes by seeing that demands for justice in this kind of situation may work dialectically, calling on different frameworks rather than a common one. Thus, in an ongoing conflict every action may have ambiguous significance. I will argue that once a conflict between parties having different frameworks begins, it is unclear how any theoretical resolution will help. In that case reliance on an arithmetic of justice is unhelpful and misleading; and the phrase "getting even" is a misdescription of the process set in motion by actions prompted by appeals for justice. My ambition here is to understand how this happens and to find a more illuminating way to describe the process.

We also need to determine whether the instability of such conflicts is a necessary feature of the grammar of justice or an accidental feature of people's conflicts.

The Dialectics of Justice in the Oresteia

The dialectical working of justice can be seen most clearly in events that are both distant in time and that have tenuous claim to historical truth, as in the epic stories of ancient Greece. These events have the advantages of historical distance and scope, but they have the hazard of substituting fiction for fact, of using the playwright's own ethical point as if it represented a "neutral" historical account. I will consider this point later. For the moment, however, I will present the stories to show how the nexus of demands for justice propels the action on both sides into unresolved and morally ambiguous conflict.

First look at the story of Agamemnon, king of Achaea and leader of the Achaean forces in the war against Troy. The story begins with his reckless boast of superiority to Artemis, the goddess of wild things. Artemis waits for the moment to punish him, to get even, and that moment comes when his ships and company of Achaean warriors are assembled at Aulis ready to sail to Troy. There, thanks to the goddess, unruly winds prevent them from sailing, and they must dig into provisions meant for their journey and siege, waiting for better winds and the chance to sail. The frustration of the others rises; Agamemnon's leadership and the expedition itself are in jeopardy. At this point Agamemnon must choose between sacrificing his youngest, dearest daughter or giving up an expedition that was a matter of personal, communal, and kingly honor.[2]

Facing this dilemma, Agamemnon reluctantly chooses to pay Artemis's price; when he does, the winds become firm and the mission to Troy proceeds to a victorious climax. Could one, at the point of Agamemnon's sacrifice, say that now Artemis's injury has been compensated, the debt canceled, the score back to zero? She extracted her revenge, and with his debt paid, Agamemnon went on to accomplish his mission. What is the matter with that?

But we are not finished with justice. For in sacrificing his daughter Iphigenia, Agamemnon profoundly wounded and offended his wife, Clytemnestra. Unconcerned with the incident in Artemis's grove, she attempted to dissuade him from sacrificing Iphigenia; and failing, remained bitter and unforgiving. She sees things neither from Agamemnon's perspective nor from Artemis's, but from a third. Thus, when she takes a lover while Agamemnon is off fighting and plots with him to assassinate the king, the development is understandable as an indirect consequence of Agamemnon's offense against Iphigenia and herself.

With Clytemnestra we encounter a new perspective on, and context for, Agamemnon's action. Artemis's view focused on her pride and honor as a goddess; while Agamemnon's involved only *his* fate, his dilemma, his leadership, and his reluctant repayment for a moral travesty. Now Clytemnestra introduces the framework of a mother less concerned with national honor than with her youngest child, and unforgiving of the slaughter of that child. She joins with her lover to kill the king.[3]

One might think that now, with Agamemnon's murder, the story has finally come to an end. As he offended and was punished by Artemis, now he is punished for offending his wife through paying Artemis's price. It is ironic but now it is finished. Justice was in the wings throughout, since Agamemnon's dilemmas and his fate are all indirectly determined by what he has done. The scales are in balance.

But we are not finished. Just as Clytemnestra does not see the murder of Iphigenia from the view of either Artemis or Agamemnon, so her children see the assassination of their father in a still different view, that of his children and the only ones left to avenge him.[4] So Orestes and Electra set out to avenge his murder, just as Clytemnestra avenged the death of Iphigenia, and just as Artemis avenged Agamemnon's offense.

At the end of each phase of the story, where one might have thought that the design was closed and finished, a new phase opens up and needs to be finished in turn. And finishing that leads to another, with each new cycle of demanding justice and satisfaction evolving from the one prior and creating another to follow. Appeals to justice are embedded in a changing process with ever new coordinates, a process without a logical end.

But when all the action of the *Oresteia* is done, when all the circles are closed, *then* perhaps we have the sense that the computations balance out, neat as an equation. Then perhaps nothing is left dangling, and the scores are all settled.

Not so. For at the end of the *Oresteia* we have two young adults who managed to avenge their father's death but must now live with the guilt of matricide. It is an uneasy end, its peace the peace of exhaustion, and it leaves us tormented still by questions of justice and its passions. With this we feel a general sadness for the inability of humans to find their way out of a self-generating process of destruction.

Take another aspect of the long story of the Trojan war, that sequence beginning when Paris referees the rivalry of the goddesses and culminating in the defeat of Troy. In exchange for judging that Aphrodite was fairest (and perhaps she was), Paris rightly and justly received his promised reward, the most beautiful of mortal women. In this turn of the wheel, justice is done when he takes Helen, wife of Menelaus the royal Achaean and returns to Troy.

But Paris' perspective is not the only one. The Achaeans see the abduction of Helen as a flagrant insult to their city, and they demand repayment. Justice requires that they attack Troy, punish the Trojans, and bring Helen home. But as they advance on Troy a third perspective emerges. Not having been party to Paris' adventures, the Trojans view themselves as accidental victims of attack by the ferocious, war-disposed Achaeans. In the course of fighting, both sides offend justice repeatedly, notably the Achaeans in their deceitful use of the wooden horse, and Patroclus's slaughter and mutilation by Trojans.

Considering the major line of action we ask, Where is justice really, where can we locate it? But we are baffled how to reply. It is no answer that the whole chain should never have gotten started, although that is no doubt true. The answer must lie in some single framework or perspective. Yet what we have is three, each in its way plausible, each suited to one part of the sequence and justified within it.

The war eventually comes to an end and the Achaeans are avenged:

Troy is devastated. Does that mean that now there is a just resolution of the original offense? Not at all. On the contrary, the excitement of battle over, peace shows the misery of the conflict bare and repugnant, and in the end much of our sympathy lies with Hector's wife and son and with other Trojans who must suffer incidentally. The war itself seems the greatest injustice, and in *The Trojan Women* Euripides spells out his condemnation of war: It fails to be justified or make moral sense for either side, he seems to say. Its nature is to corrupt, destroy, wound, betray. If what ought to emerge at the end of the story is justice, then the saga fails utterly.

Look at one more example. In *Antigone* Polynices suffers injustice at the hands of his brother Eteocles, who refuses to give Polynices his turn on the throne as agreed. So Polynices brings friends from Corinth to help him seize the throne by force. He means to restore justice and the order of royal rule to which both once agreed; justice here means his possession of what is rightfully his. From this limited framework one might say that, had Polynices dethroned his brother and taken power, justice would have been done. But in the view of Theban citizens, his bringing a band of Corinthians to invade their city was a betrayal, an act of treason. It was to be censured.

The siege of Thebes results in the death of both brothers, at which point leadership of the city goes to their uncle Creon. Creon is a man driven by fear for Thebes' stability. He must be strong, he reasons, even inflexible if necessary, to maintain order and peace. In his judgment the treasonous invasion by Polynices should be denounced as an example to others. Thus, by his decree the body of Polynices is denied a burial and left to be picked at by birds and wild dogs. Antigone, Polynices' sister, has a different view, however, one stemming from the religious requirements that the living owe the dead and that the family in particular owe them. In that view the exigencies of politics fail to compare with requirements of divine law. She must try as she can to bury her brother.

Antigone defies Creon's decree and performs burial rites over her brother, at which Creon displays intense concern with security and his own authority, not to mention his manly vanity. From his point of view, stability and Thebes' need for a strong leader are the overriding issues. Thus his stance, like Antigone's, involves a moral concern. Still another perspective is provided by the chorus, which counsels compromise and denounces acts of pride and anger as conducive to violence, to tragedy.

At the end of the play Antigone, sentenced by Creon to death, is dead by her own hand; Creon's son dies with her; the queen soon after. What is left is an abject Creon and a chorus who mourn that things worked as they did. Where is justice? It has been lost in the tragedy.

I have used these three complex chains of events to show the locked interrelations of differing views or frameworks. Avenging wrong might bring a resolution to the initial wrong *if* the choice of framework could be restricted, or if both—or all—sides subscribed to a single one. But it cannot be restricted: The poets are clear about that. Moreover to restrict it would mean taking sides from the outset and thus ignoring other perspectives, reasonable perspectives that call on justice from other angles and do so with some plausibility. One thing Homer and the dramatic poets show us is that any ultimate judgment about right and wrong, justice and injustice, is infernally difficult.

DIVERGENT PERSPECTIVES

Moral Perspectives

A note is needed about the term 'perspective', which ordinarily means the visual aspect of something from a certain place. A natural extension of the term would mean a personal point of view, a view from one's own *interested* place, a self-oriented viewpoint.[5] But that meaning does not capture all my examples, not those in which self and moral commitment become meshed as they do in Antigone's view of her obligations.

By 'perspective' I mean the understanding one has of a given situation and particularly of its moral implications. The facts included as relevant in two conflicting perspectives need not be the same: Creon's view does not include Antigone's family obligation; hers does not include the political stability of Thebes; and Polynices', focused as it is on the injustice done him, does not recognize the treasonous aspect of enlisting Corinthian help.

Thus, a perspective is a morally colored understanding of a situation, in which some things may be left out as irrelevant, while others are focused on and given emphasis. That emphasis is indeed part of the view, it is part of showing facts in a certain relationship. The ambiguity of perspectives on a given situation is analogous to our perception of an ambiguous visual figure. It is like the duck-rabbit used by Wittgenstein to illustrate how we can see a thing or concept in different aspects, how we can describe it differently and draw different conclusions about it depending on which aspect captures us. We cannot see the duck-rabbit *both* as duck and rabbit, but only as now one and now the other. When our vision moves from one aspect to the other and we see a whole new interpretation, then Wittgenstein says an aspect "dawns" on us. We suddenly see things differently.

Homer, Aeschylus, and Sophocles show us events from different perspectives, different *moral* perspectives, of a human situation. Take Oedipus's changed view of himself when he learns who his parents were and that he has slain his father and married his mother. Once the epitome of a proud hero–king, he no longer sees himself this way, although some

Thebans and the audience may want to. That view is gone for him; his actions are the same, but their significance is transformed. His perspective undergoes a sudden and utter shift: He now appears to himself as the most loathsome of mortals. We might say that new aspect has dawned and replaced the other entirely.

A plurality of moral perspectives need not signify different codes of morality. What we are concerned with is not the difference of cultural values. In the codes of both the Achaeans and the Trojans, for example, some forms of behavior in war were considered dishonorable, as was the treatment of Hector's body. Instead, the differences connect with moral convictions and the emphasis put on some features of the situation along with neglect of others.[6] It is easy to see why the perspective that will dominate a situation, looked at in a given moment, is not easily predictable.

Given different perspectives of a situation, what is getting even in one may be a provocation and an injustice in another. It is the differences in perspective of the two sides that lead them to calculate about justice differently. So the problem here is not moral relativism, but rather the fact that there is no single and definitive framework for measuring wrong or determining its corrective. The same facts may be fitted into different pictures.

"Getting Even" as a Further Provocation

The above examples of multiple perspectives are artistic products bent and shaped into lessons by the poet–moralists.[7] Yet a glance at major recent conflicts reveals similar patterns, the dynamic working of justice thanks to different perspectives on the same events. For example, the origins of World War II lay in the "just" resolution fashioned by the victors at the end of World War I. It was a resolution that, while it satisfied the victors' sense of justice, ignored the losers' humiliation with the penalties of defeat. Thus the latter righteously demanded respect through counter-action; and the peace laid the ground for new cries of injustice and a return to conflict.

Another example. Past injustices, a history of Jewish repression and persecution, are cited by Israel to justify its claim to a secure homeland and control of whatever territory this requires. At the same time, Palestinians see injustice in the confiscation of their land and in their precarious existence as noncitizens. Lacking a political voice, they protest through violence. In turn, Israelis respond with increasing repression and justifications of self-defense.[8]

In such cases each side calls for justice; but through its actions each provokes moral outcries against itself. As long as every action is illuminated differently by different perspectives, the machine—a machine driven by justice—has infinite endurance.

What can we infer from this pattern? One thing is this: Acting in the name of justice may be a morally ambiguous and chancy business, not sure to be understood or judged in the aspect under which actions are done. No wonder Hamlet felt such heavy uneasiness, uncertainty, and inertia about avenging his father's death. For despite one's righteous anger at wrong, there is danger that attempting to reestablish justice may open the door to further righteous protest.

The Contingency of Divergent Views

Is this general pattern part of the grammar of justice, an inevitable feature of actions taken to correct injustice? Not if that means that the two sides cannot have the same perspective and speak from the same moral stage. For surely they may. The differences of perspective are not grounded in a necessary difference between individual viewpoints; both parties may see an action of one of them as wrong. That would mean that one party accepts responsibility and condemns itself for its misdeeds. But in that circumstance the concern for justice is a concern about reparation, compensation, repentance, and perhaps forgiveness. At this point the opposing invocations of justice are gone; the moral focus has changed, and getting even is no longer the issue.

However, when conflicting parties have different perspectives, the demand for justice may generate new wrongs—or what are perceived as wrongs—in the course of redressing old ones. The common phrase "teach them a lesson" suggests that what is wanted is to get the others to see things as those who feel wronged do. But often the attempt is futile because the original difference of perspective further infects the understanding of whatever is done to correct it. Those differences keep the machine in motion, just as counterbalances sustain the movement of a wheel. And the question of whether justice and demands for it will always work dialectically has the answer: Although in practice it often will, that is not necessary and not a universal feature of conflicts.

INSTABILITY AND AMBIGUITY

Passion for Justice Promotes Instability

Let us look closer at the workings of this machine.

Indignation at wrongdoing is part of respect for justice: The abhorrence we feel at injustices is the other side of the same coin. Moreover, in the face of a wrong one ought to do something if possible; sitting idly signifies cowardice, indifference, or capitulation. But what does justice demand that we *do* in the face of an injustice, and how does it show us how to calculate a result that is just?

Wrongs can be avenged in exaggerated terms, overdone as when the wronged Medea murders Jason's betrothed and her own children. Or they can be addressed with gestures too small to give moral satisfaction, mere tokens. Therefore, it seems as if some action or actions must be appropriate, right, and just. One wants to insist that there must be such a response or range, for otherwise acting justly seems a vacuous idea. It is an axiom of the rubric of justice that there is some tit for tat, and for that an arithmetic of justice is needed. There must be a meaning to getting even although there may not be any practical path to it.

My argument suggests that, however compelling, this idea does not jibe with the way justice works in human history and the way we see it work before us. For assume that there is one correct perspective of justice in a given case. Then since the Achaeans and Trojans see things differently, neither can be presumed to be a good judge of what is right. Perhaps what is needed is a neutral outsider to look at both sides objectively and see where justice lies. From such a neutral position that person can do the arithmetic that neither side is able to do. Is that so?

Watching the Greek plays we resemble a judge in a courtroom: cool and observant from a distance; concerned with justice; experienced, thoughtful, compassionate. Then perhaps *we* can make the right computation and see what should have been done to even things up. But what do *we* say at the end of the *Iliad*? We say that demands for justice brought about tragedy in different forms, and many stupid and cruel actions, but it brought little in the way of heroism or admirable deeds. It yielded no finally just solution, no cause for either celebration or moral condemnation. At the end we look back with awe that such a long and bloody history should have transpired, but even we cannot define a path through the moral jungle, one that would have restored justice and evened things up. Throughout the process justice was never in sight.

The really neutral judge sees that there are several perspectives, irreconcilable aspects under which events are seen; that is part of his or her fair and detached view. But in that case how shall the judge cast judgment? One can describe the two perspectives neutrally, but any *moral* judgment will *involve* and employ some perspective: It will show some actions as morally objectionable, others not, through a view of their relations. Thus a judge's perspective will not be "neutral" if that means not morally charged. And this reintroduces the old questions about different perspectives.

Nonetheless a judge might be neutral in the sense of standing outside the action, of standing back and apart. Unlike the parties in conflict, a judge, not being compelled to act, can attain Butler's "cool hour" for the sake of evaluation. Judicial judgment will be that of a passive observer, and this can be useful. For if one can find a framework that can be respected by both sides, then one's role is important indeed. One will see at once the different perspectives, and the individuals who were guided by them, and where possibly they may come together and understand each other. This does not mean that the final and just calculation is now complete. It means that reconciliation may be sought in a framework of compassion for both sides and a sense of human frailties. Thus, a judge may need to find language that leaves these calculations behind. Such objectivity, if that is what we should call it, goes beyond getting even. But all this depends on not engaging the judge to decide the moral issue as it is presented.

When Oedipus discovers he has committed two cardinal offenses—parricide and incest—both he and the citizens of Thebes are shocked and dazed, for these offenses make him a moral pariah. But in the light of his fleeing from those very offenses, he is also a figure of desperate though impetuous virtue. Helpless, perhaps, but in that respect still virtuous and hardly culpable. We see both sides, both perspectives, much as in a modernist painting we might see all sides of a three-dimensional object. Like Picasso with his portraits, Sophocles triumphs in having kept both moral perspectives in sharp focus, thus presenting us with the dilemma facing the Thebans in its most intense form. They must face the truth that their adored and heroic leader is unwittingly but irredeemably corrupt, and by his own admission a burden to them. Oedipus's own perspective shows him that he cannot be himself without reconciliation with his moral code: He blinds himself. Yet the two aspects of his actions continue to hover, both with compelling claims to validity.

The Uncertainty of Moral Sanction

We are not yet finished with the self-propelling character of such conflicts. We still must explore the connection between the necessity to act and the multiplicity of frameworks that makes action ambiguous.

The language of justice, originating in protests against injustice, is intrinsically passionate and one-sided.[9] Such protests cannot be made with measured rational calculation and carry their full moral force. But this means that neither side can give full recognition to the other side's viewpoint. The language of justice is a language of righteous indignation, of wrath, and of absolute objection to injustice and wrong.

When anger is expressed, its expression is typically vehement, even hurtful and destructive. Raising one's voice in imprecations and insults, plunging impetuously into action, hitting, breaking things, are some of its natural expressions. One does not express anger by sitting down for a long friendly talk; that would belie one's indignation and wholehearted opposition to wrong. This is clear when opponents feel that speaking together is a betrayal of their righteous position, for communication suggests willingness to compromise, and compromise suggests lack of conviction. The rhetoric of justice thus quickly undermines negotiations and supports inarticulate action and violence.

As expressions of anger are normally absolute and vehement, anger at injustice is characteristically expressed in insult or harm to the wrong-doer. These carry the message that injustice is seriously protested, and the wrongdoer is morally condemned. It is easy to see how serious and intense expressions of righteous indignation are naturally violent.

Yet the term 'naturally' here raises a flag of suspicion. Is the natural-ness of violence supposed to justify it morally? No. But there is a sense in which violence is justified by what provokes it. Some powerful hurt or striking insult can make us understand and sympathize with a violent re-action, this happens with Billy Budd in Melville's story of that name. Billy, a mild and quiet young sailor, is so angered by the charges of the master-at-arms Claggart that in a moment of supreme frustration he strikes him; it is what a reader thinks anyone might do. The blow kills Claggart, and an inquiry determines that Billy must pay for it with his life. The reader here, as the reader of Oedipus, is of two minds: Billy's was a spontaneous and natural response to intolerable provocations.[10] The provocations com-pletely explain Billy's action and, as with Oedipus's slaying his father, we cannot condemn him for it. But this is not the same as saying that what Billy did was morally justified.

Violence and anger have a deep affinity, a grammatical affinity. It is the affinity of a very basic human feeling to its untrained and characteristic expressions. Just as weeping is a natural expression of sorrow, or laughter of amusement, or wincing of pain, so anger has its expression in gestures of violence. The connection between such primitive expressions and the emotion they express is, as Wittgenstein argues, grammatical or concep-tual. It is also grounded in the kind of beings we are. Thus, one who is very amused has an irrepressible inclination to laugh or smile or giggle. And someone who suffers a wrong feels anger and tends to show its char-acteristic expressions, inchoate and primitive expressions among which are gestures and actions of violence. Of course this does not mean that anger cannot be shown in nonviolent and nondestructive ways or that reason has no power to restrain. One *may* feel profound sorrow without tears, or be amused while keeping a straight face. Similarly, the natural expressions of anger can be restrained and other expressions substituted. Indeed, history shows the efforts of whole movements to protest injus-tice while practicing restraint. But the primitive and natural connection is still there.

The relation between injustice, anger, and violence appears then to be this. There is a grammatical connection between the perception of injus-tice and anger; you cannot understand and react morally to wrong without some indignation. There is also an affinity between anger and action, between indignation in the face of wrong and acting against the perpetrator. Thus, violent action, which is one primitive and unlearned expression of anger, is connected with righteous protest. Violent protests against injustice should not surprise us. They have a conceptual justification in the grammar of injustice. That is different, however, from moral sanction.

The Elusiveness of "Just Peace"

The impossibility of defining "getting even" in many conflicts implies that in a conflict where more than one perspective is at work, there may not be any path to a just peace. The expression 'just peace' will itself be as ambiguous and sensitive to multiple perspectives as the provocations were in the first place. Moreover, the appeal to justice may frustrate attempts at peace because what is just is not subject to negotiation, while negotiation is precisely what peace often requires. Thus, demands for justice on the one hand and peace on the other will often pull in different directions. Peace may need to be dissociated from the absolutes of justice as perceived by either side, which is to say, dissociated from justice simply, and to bring focus on assuaging wounds of pride and honor and arranging a cessation of conflict. This would mean putting aside the indignation and the moral ambiguities of getting even, relinquishing the search for justice through direct action, and forgetting about the scales being balanced. What then would be central is the state of peace for its own sake. When the focus is on justice, peace of an attainable kind may not be either possible or morally satisfying.

The concept 'just peace' thus has no unequivocal form. To both sides in a conflict, peace without justice means bowing to the original wrongs; while just peace means settling the matter righteously. But if the meaning of 'just peace' is itself disputed, then invoking it as a standard is unhelpful.

This conclusion is philosophically frustrating. But if demands for justice drive a machine—a machine grammatically grounded—by which people are treated brutally, demeaned, killed, and their moral sensibilities desecrated, then a demand for justice is not doing much good.

The Ineluctable Ambiguity of Moral Action

Among the implications of the foregoing discussion is this. There is very powerful reason for saying that an unjust condition demands correction, an efficient and effective correction. The demand to do *something* seems tied to injustice and to one's being a person of integrity and courage. Thus, when we are faced with injustice, our natural way of thinking is consequentialist. It concerns how to get from the one repugnant situation to a superior, more just and humane one, with the least ill effects in the process.

In making physical changes in the world, much can be said for direct action: Destroy or disassemble the old and replace it with the new. If a building is unsafe or deteriorating, we take it down and build a better, safer one. That is often the quickest and most effective thing we can do, for any other course wastes time and incurs problems in the meantime. The analogue in the social world to making such a radical and efficient change often (though by no means always) is to use violence. The French Revolution is one example; the American Civil War is another. These were violent transitions aimed at correcting unjust situations, and the means used were those of courageous, righteously indignant protestors. I do not question that in both cases the perceptions of what was wrong and what would be better were correct. Morally committed people could see the end they wanted to work toward and could see its moral superiority to the prevailing situation. Moreover I do not question the means–end reasoning per se; we *can* often envisage a clear path toward a specific goal.

The problem is this. In the course of getting from an unjust state to a future, more just one, there will be a change in the features relevant to a moral judgment. Especially when the change involves violence, a new perspective will reflect the character of that violent means. Thus, the perspective that shows this new situation in advance, and shows the means for getting there, cannot also show how it will appear morally after the fact. The idea that in the social world we can tear down the old house and build a new one, like turning a page, leaving the old one invisible, is fundamentally wrong.[11] For in the process of tearing down and rebuilding we bring new facts into being and new predicates. From the end perspective the goal will be seen not only in contrast to the original one but as reflecting the means used, as well as other unforeseen factors. In this way, a new regime brought about by revolution is a *revolutionary* regime; it has that origin and that stamp. Whatever its principles, its roots are fixed in violence, which now belongs to its perception, its image. The final judgment on such a transition is not controllable in advance.

If this is so then it shows why moral calculations about means and end, cost and benefit, are inherently chancy. The problem is not only uncertainty about the details and how the means will work to produce the end—the familiar calculations of benefit versus cost. What is problematic is the way the means affect the coordinates of one's future perspective— ours and others—how unpredictable these future coordinates are until we regard them in retrospect. Agamemnon's sacrifice of his daughter was not in retrospect only the means of making amends to Artemis, and so getting his troops launched. It is preeminently (we say with hindsight) the slaughter of a child dependent on Agamemnon's fatherly protection. Thus, I am not arguing that ends–means reasoning errs from lack of information to gauge the present situation against the future one. I argue rather that the process by which such a calculator figures to get from the unjust state to the more just one is impossible to ascertain. The means he uses will affect unpredictably the moral coloring and description of the result and thus the result itself.

The different lights that illuminate events from one time to another point to a curious disjunction of moral judgments and the actions based on them. We may rightly judge a situation unjust and morally in need of correction. And we may clearly see a condition that would be morally better. Also, we may see a way to reach that state by means that are, all things presently considered and calculable, acceptable. Nonetheless, when the actions are done and the transition process is over, what we often find is not the attainment of that goal simpliciter, but a state in a new perspective, one that looks quite different from what we aimed at and one that has been colored by the change itself.

Two factors are at work here. One has to do with time: We see things only in the perspective of the present, and that applies both to present injustice and to the future, better condition. What we cannot see is how our perspective and perspectives of others will change during the transition from the present to the future, how the means will help shape such new perspectives. In fact, the one thing we can say is that the new state will probably look quite different *when it exists* than it appears now.

The second factor is the tendency we have to detach means and end, to look at means as a coinage that can be used to purchase an effect. "Is it worth this price?" we ask. And if the answer is yes, then the only question is whether we are ready to pay it. All we want is the thing purchased; the medium of exchange is morally neutral and in this sense antiseptic. But the means we take to a goal are not like money with an independent existence and a morally neutral status, with no internal relation to what is purchased. Thus, we cannot make the means a separate matter capable of being balanced off against the end. Instead, what we do by way of getting to a desirable goal may affect the description of the final state. For example, one describes the Civil War as a war to end slavery: That was its point. But it was also a war of domination by one part of a nation over another that wanted to go its own way, a war in which brothers killed brothers, in which property was confiscated and a way of life was destroyed. And it was won by the strongest, economically most-powerful faction, leaving a heritage of resentment for many generations. At its conclusion, slavery was ended; but the state at the war's close cannot be described so simply as this.

One implication of this discussion of the various ways justice is perceived is to warn about our reasoning when we act to correct injustice. It is a warning about the security of reasoning in a straightforward, consequentialist way, even when all rational calculation shows a clear balance in favor of an end to which the means appear to be available. For means and end are not detachable in the way such reasoning requires, and their interconnection will influence the state attained and its appearance in a new perspective. We cannot feel confident, even when faced with clear and apparently correctable wrongs, that what we will be doing in correcting them will be seen under that description of our vision.

After his awful discovery, we still call up Oedipus's early view, his consultation with the oracle, his flight from parricide. Then, trudging the road from Delphi to Thebes, he encounters his arrogant royal father with an armed guard and is ordered to step aside. What was he to do? Back down? No: He was proud, able, and courageous, and indignant at being humiliated and overwhelmed. It is all understandable; but looking back one wishes Oedipus had hesitated over possibilities outside his immediate field of vision.

We want to deal rationally with injustice, and that seems to mean reacting proportionately. Yet reason, with its emphasis on calculations and objective comparisons, is more difficult to apply in moral matters than it appears. For we must deal with dual uncertainties, the uncertain exigencies of chance, and uncertainty about the moral perspective to emerge when the actions are done. When acting in the name of justice, a future change in view is only obscurely imaginable, and unpredictable. We are at the mercy of our own subsequent, retrospective, cool hour, an hour that may reveal things utterly different than they now appear with all their elements in very different relationships. In this respect we are all, like Oedipus, blind to the future.

In a realm where the language is one of absolutes, where action is the mark of commitment, and where anger is the appropriate spur to righteous action, these uncertainties give us powerful reason for caution. It is the heart of morality that we should act against injustice. Yet the danger is continual that such action may foster a new moral problem.

NOTES

Acknowledgments: I am indebted to members of the SUNY Buffalo symposium "Law and the Legitimation of Violence," especially Virginia Held and Anthony Coady, and most of all Carl Wellman, whose perspective on things always enriches mine.

1. One feature of just war theory is the moral culpability of whoever starts a conflict: See Walzer (1977, esp. chap. 4). But the beginning, and the question of what is the beginning, are often disputed. Thus, pinning responsibility on the original offender may be as morally ambiguous as other incidents

of conflict. The differences of perspective in my account explain why this happens. Such is the usual upshot of making neat Procrustean beds for unwieldy realities.

2. Since the abducted Helen was Agamemnon's sister-in-law, the issue is personal. Moreover a king such as Agamemnon was responsible for protecting the honor of his community as well as its security. Aristotle describes this kind of rule in *Politics* 1285b. Also see Bonner and Smith (1968), 1: 1–5.

3. I simplify here, since Clytemnestra's liaison with Aegisthus is a crucial element in the story, which also makes Clytemnestra's motivation ambiguous; for with the king dead, he and Clytemnestra assume the throne. Was it love of Aegisthus or of Iphigenia that moved her?

4. The need for avenging to be done by the family of the one wronged is characteristic of justice at this time and echoed in Antigone's reasonings with Ismene about the burial of Polynices. Also see Bonner and Smith (1968), 1: 17–18.

5. Winch (1972) uses the term 'perspective' in discussing the relation of a person to his or her action. Of his meaning he writes, "If I had to say shortly how I take the agent in [this] . . . situation to be related to [his] . . . perspective I should say . . . that the agent *is* this perspective" (178). That is a somewhat different idea. My use also differs from Nagel's (1986). Nagel argues that a perspective may be personal; there is also an objective view, a view from nowhere. Apart from sticking closer to the visual model, his use of 'perspective' also differs fundamentally from mine in that my perspectives are morally colored. I do not use the term 'aspect', because that suggests a property of what is seen, as if some human situations *had* particular characteristic aspects; I want to emphasize that the moral coloring of the perspective relates to the perceiver's angle of vision.

6. Such differences may coincide with differences in religion, as in the contemporary conflict between the Shiite and Sunni Moslems, whose mutual charges of past religious wrongdoing lay the grounds for repeated acts of violence. This is not moral pluralism, since it is not the moral values that distinguish the perspectives so much as the descriptions and omissions of historical events. The conflict in Northern Ireland is another such case of a pluralism of religious perspectives in a context where the principal moral values are shared.

7. It is widely acknowledged by scholars that the playwrights of Athens often used dramatic stories to make moral and political points. For an interesting argument about Sophocles' use of Oedipus see Knox (1957; 1964).

8. I refer the reader to Carlin Romano's article on this subject in the *Village Voice Literary Supplement*, June 1988, as well as Grossman's *The Yellow Wind* (1987).

9. The primacy of the concept of injustice over that of justice is argued in chapter 6 of my *Grammar of Justice* (1987). David Hume also argued that morality is grounded in passions, not reason, for the latter has no power to move us to act (1751, sec. 1).

10. Arendt (1969, 64) claims Billy is justified. She calls this "the classical

example" of "acting without argument or speech and without counting the consequences . . . to set the scales right again."

11. There is a strong tendency to compare the social and the physical realms; to compare social and medical experiments to physical ones, for example. Jonas (in Beauchamp and Walters [1982]) has some perceptive observations on this.

10

THE PURSUIT OF IDEALS

Newton Garver

THE VIOLENCE OF UTOPIAN POLITICS

The Problem of Idealistic Violence

East and west, north and south, violence and oppression are often matters of policy, sometimes to support the status quo and sometimes to overturn it. A vast proportion of the pain and injury and premature death inflicted on human beings is inflicted knowingly, with all due deliberation, for the purpose of achieving some end or goal. The concepts and arguments at work in these deliberations provide a special field for philosophical analysis. Sometimes the rationale for violence can be deflected by showing that the goal is unworthy, the means inadequate, or the side effects subversive of the goal. Thus, a defender of the Old South might argue that the force used to suppress the Freedom Marchers had the side effect of making martyrs and media heroes out of the marchers, thereby more than canceling its intended justificatory effect. Or a critic might argue that the Old South was not worthy of being defended, spiking the guns of the same means–end argument in another way. While both of these counterarguments have merit, we must bear in mind that they would not convince everyone, that they were not so convincing at the time as they are today, and that there are very many cases of putatively justified violence in which the goal does seem worthy and the means plausible. I therefore propose to examine the very idea of supposing noble goals to justify the employment of necessary but disreputable means.

I wish to review Isaiah Berlin's contributions to the consideration of the issues and to draw the discussion out a bit further. I shall do so by considering the pursuit of a just society, a noble ideal often cited as justifying various political and military measures. My aim will be to show the incoherence of the idea of a just or perfect society; that is, to discredit the "noble ideals" that motivate so much violence, without impugning the idea of justice itself.

Berlin's Kantian Argument Against Utopian Politics

There is a richness in the texture of Sir Isaiah's writing that is bound to be lost in summary. Part of this richness in his Agnelli Lecture (1988) comes from the course he traces of his own intellectual development, through Machiavelli, Vico, Collingwood, and others, and part comes from his acquaintance with an extraordinarily wide range of history and culture. For all the richness and subtlety, the essential message is clear and simple, namely, that the very idea of a just society or a perfect state is incoherent and full of danger:

> Utopias have their value, but as guides to conduct can prove literally fatal. Heraclitus was right, things cannot stand still.
> So I conclude that the very notion of a final solution is not only impracticable, but, if I am right, and some values cannot but clash, incoherent also. The possibility of a final solution—even if we forget the terrible sense which those words acquired in Hitler's day—turns out to be an illusion; and a very dangerous one. For, if one really believes that such a solution is possible, then surely no cost would be too high to obtain it: to make mankind just and happy and creative and harmonious forever—what could be too high a price to pay for that? (12–13)

It is worth paying attention to the argument behind this conclusion. Berlin cites Machiavelli, Vico, Herder, and Herzen in support of his position, but the form of his argument is strikingly Kantian. That is, it is Kantian in the sense of Kant's first critique, the *Kritik der reinen Vernunft* (1787), not in the sense of conforming to the ideas of Kant's moral philosophy. The illusions to which Berlin refers are analogous to the dialectical illusions of speculative metaphysicians. Berlin first notes, as did Kant, that the grand speculative schemes have never succeeded in practice, although they have been formulated by the brightest and most imaginative of philosophers. The cosmological ideas of Leibniz and Newton are devoid of the definitive impact of their mathematical and scientific ideas. "Liberty, Equality, Fraternity" proved to be the path to the imperial reign of Napoleon; the vaunted principle that "all men are created equal" was reduced to two thirds for slaves; the promise of Zion is cluttered with militarism, debt, and oppression; and so on. In these domains, failure is without exception our experience as human beings.

It is a stark experience. Once one is aware of it, one faces a very considerable challenge to avoid the twin perils of illusion and cynicism. Some moralists would insist—still under illusion—that we must get up and try, try again. Others, with an exaggerated skepticism bewitched by Nietzsche, argue that the collapse of ideals means the collapse of all moral values. But Kant argues, as does Berlin, that the trouble lies neither in imperfect effort nor in totally worthless ideas, but rather in attempting the impossible, that is to say, in attempting to use sound ideas in ways for which they are not suited. The ideals of reason, Kant argues (1787, B536–43), are illusions when they are taken as constituting a reality or possible reality, and the source of dialectical illusion is just such a constitutive use of regulative ideas.

This distinction between constitutive and regulative uses of ideas was a brilliant innovation on Kant's part and is of continuing importance. A constitutive idea is one that directly determines some reality, in that what it refers to or presupposes would not be the referent of any idea if it were not for the constitutive idea itself and the rules comprising it; whereas a regulative idea is one that presupposes the reality to which it applies. For example, the words 'today' and 'yesterday' express constitutive ideas, as does 'the day before yesterday'. Each of these ideas signifies, at any given time the words are used, a particular day that has reality within our experience. The idea of 'preceding days' is only a regulative idea: It indicates how we are to proceed in our thinking, using today (or some other day) as a base, allowing us by successive applications to signify any definite reality or possible past reality that could lie within experience.

Proper use of a regulative idea not only begins with a point in possible experience but also ends in such a point. That is, the operation implied by the idea of 'preceding days' leads to a day that, like any other ordinary day, also has a predecessor. If we use the idea to extrapolate to 'the first day of time' or 'the totality of time up to today', we illegitimately attempt to escape these empirical constraints by making constitutive use of this regulative idea. The reason this is fallacious is that the ideas of pure reason, being regulative, make sense only given certain conditions. Illusion arises when a metaphysician abstracts from those empirical conditions and proposes *unconditioned* (constitutive) use of an idea. In our example, the illusion consists both in using 'preceding days' in such a way that is no longer possible to get from our present experience to the signified days in any series of manageable steps, and also in the end product of the idea of a day without any predecessor.

Although Berlin does not refer to Kant, his criticism of the pursuit of the ideal makes use of this sort of Kantian critique. The noble ideals of political and social thought do not refer to definite constitutions or states of society. They are not constitutive ideas at all; they are, rather, regulative ideas. Their function is to criticize existing states of society, not to constitute or lay the blueprint for any new state of society. Their proper use thus presupposes historical conditions, and their employment to sketch a social ideal in abstraction from historical conditions results in illusion. Like the dialectical illusions of dogmatic metaphysicians, the utopian illusions of political thought are *unconditioned* ideals—that is, they illegitimately attempt to escape from the conditions that make such thought possible at all. The illusion consists partly in supposing that one must create or constitute a just society, or at least know how to create one, in order to respond to injustices; and partly in the very idea of a state or society that could not be further improved.

Both Kant and Berlin begin with recognition of the fact that a certain sort of thinking has not worked and then seek to explain the failure as the result of an understandable sort of illusion. So Berlin's thinking is essentially Kantian here.

CONFLICTING CONCEPTIONS OF JUSTICE

A Just and Harmonious Society as a Noble Goal

The problem at hand is one that was raised eloquently by Plato in the *Laws*:

> Life abounds in good things, but most of those good things are infested by polluting and defiling parasites. Justice, for example, is undeniably a boon to mankind; it has humanized the whole of life. And if justice is such a blessing, how can advocacy [the legal profession] be other than a blessing too? Well, both blessings are brought into ill repute by a vice which cloaks itself under the specious name of an art. (*Laws* xi.937d–e)

Plato, especially when the context is taken into account, seems to have in mind the sort of abuse that occurs when statutes and legal principles are used to subvert, thwart, or overturn the substance of justice—as when an attorney successfully pleads "statute of limitations" or "illegal search and seizure" to technically exculpate a known criminal; or conversely when a prosecutor uses an obscure regulation or an arbitrary definition to subject an upright citizen to criminal penalties or (as in the Soviet gulag) to psychiatric confinement.

Sometimes cases of abuse are easily discernible, but in general the situation is more complex than Plato envisaged. In addition to (1) cases in which the truth is discerned and acknowledged, and (2) cases in which the truth is discerned and hidden or denied, which are the two sorts of cases Plato seems to envision, there are also (3) societies in which there is an adversarial system of justice, and (4) endeavors to remake society, as Plato himself proposed, so as to eliminate injustice and disharmony. (1) and (2) are not problematic, except in practice; but (3) and (4) raise problems not foreseen by Plato and deserving of separate discussion. (3) raises deep and disturbing questions about the American legal system, of which Plato would probably be highly critical. Plato himself engaged in (4), of which Popper (1945) and now Berlin have been highly critical. In what follows I will leave (3) aside and will discuss (4) by considering the concept of justice and the ideal of a just society that that concept may seem to entail.

Drawing Up Plans for a Just Society

No one wishes to live in an unjust society, and a lively sense of the deeply entrenched imperfections in our own society encourages us to envision one that is perfectly just. Justice is a universally acknowledged value, not the special aim of a narrow sect. One need not be embarrassed or isolated in struggling for justice. Because in a just society there would be no racism, no sexism, no brutality, no vast differences of poverty and wealth, no slavery or apartheid, or any of the other forms of injustice, many of the barriers to loving fellowship would be removed. Living in such a just society, we are tempted to think, would be living in a "new society" or the "peaceable kingdom." Can the dream become a blueprint? Can we envisage a just society, with all its special form and content, and the obstacles we must overcome in order to sketch and implement it?

To these hopeful and aspiring questions a negative conclusion is implicit in the works of Cahn (1949; 1966) and is explicit in Wolgast (1987, esp. chap. 6), in Lucas (1980, esp. 16–19), and most recently and eloquently in Hampshire (1989). I have learned much from these works, as will be evident in what follows; but I shall not try to restate their arguments. In the following sections I will delineate three reasons why it is not possible to draw up a blueprint for a just society. All three of these reasons derive from the nature of the concept of justice. The first arises from its being derivative and privative, the second from its containing incompatible component criteria, and the third from its being essentially contestable. When these characteristics have been identified, it will be apparent that any program to create a perfectly just society must be based on a misunderstanding of the concept of justice.

Justice Is a Privative Rather Than an Empirical Concept

The first thing to notice is how very different our task is from that of describing a bird, a house, or a lake snuggled up against a mountain, that is, something seen, something with fairly definite features. I do not mean that it is easy to describe such concrete things, for all description is difficult. But in the case of a just society we have to start with things not there rather than with what is there. What are lacking, and what must be sketched and defined first, are injustices; for we understand justice derivatively, through the all-too-familiar injustices it deprives us of:

For what gives justice its special savor of nobility? Only the divine wrath that arises in us, that girds us to action whenever an instance of injustice affronts our sight. (Cahn, 1966, ix)

Justice is not . . . something with a given form, but is a creature of our effort, imagination, and demand. We craft responses to wrong, our purpose being not to satisfy some preconceived picture of justice but to address the snares of injustice. (Wolgast, 1987, 145)

Injustices come in various concrete forms that we encounter all the time and that we can describe on the basis of all-too-frequent experience. Justice is defined by contrast to this empirical experience. The way Cahn puts it (1949, 14–15) is that justice can be defined as "the *active process* of remedying or preventing what would arouse the sense of injustice." Even if we are not sure about justice being a process (though we will later find that there is no good alternative category) or have reservations about the subjectivity implied by the stress on the "sense" of injustice, the opposition of justice to injustice is surely right. We can then say, following Cahn, that justice is that which corrects or prevents injustices.

In this respect the concepts of justice and injustice are just the reverse of the words 'justice' and 'injustice': The word 'justice' is positive and the word 'injustice' is its negation; but the concept of injustice is the one with which we have direct experience and the idea of justice is derived from the negation or privation of that experience. As Lucas puts it:

It is only when somebody's rights and interests are in jeopardy that the unity and coherence of society is under strain, and it is only then that the issues of justice arise. That is to say, it is when *in*justice is in danger of being done that we become agitated. Injustice wears the trousers. And we should therefore follow the example of Aristotle, and adopt a negative approach, discovering what justice is by considering on what occasions we protest at injustice or unfairness. (1980, 4)

Because our understanding of justice is through conceiving the absence (or privation) of what we are familiar with, justice is what the logicians call a privative concept.

That the idea of justice is based on privation of injustices is not an insuperable obstacle to knowledge and sound judgment. The idea of health is similarly privative. A healthy person is one free from any disease or impairment. We have learned a great deal about what it means to be healthy. For the most part we have learned what we know by paying attention to unhealthy persons rather than by analyzing healthy ones. A doctor generally finds it much easier to give a precise description of a disease than a precise description of health. Knowledge of health is through theories and hypotheses rather than by direct experience; in terms of our experience, it is derivative and privative, but it is nonetheless knowledge. Doctors often certify that a person is in good health, and we know a good deal about what it means to be healthy. And similarly, as Wolgast points out (1987, 133), we know a good deal about justice.

Admitting all this does not dispose of the issue. The issue is not whether we know enough to correct deviations (cure patients), but whether we know enough to provide a *complete* and detailed description, such as we would need to build a genuinely ideal society, one with no latent injustices lurking unseen. Can we describe a healthy person in detail, specifying in positive terms just what the person's height, weight, blood chemistry, metabolism, and so forth would be, without mentioning diseases or impairments? No, we certainly cannot. Healthy people come in all sorts of sizes, shapes, blood types, metabolic rates, and so on. All that we know of health and disease is woefully inadequate to determine an ideal from among all these variations.

The lack of a specifically defined ideal is no problem at all for medicine, because human beings come already constructed. The medical problem is just to prevent and cure disease and disability among these already constructed beings. But such a complete and detailed description is exactly the sort of thing we would need if we are to build a just society: We have to say in detail what the structure of the society would be and how its institutions would function, and we have to say this in positive terms, without relying on the *absence* of police brutality; the *absence* of corrupt judges; the *absence* of prejudice, which excludes some people from a fair hearing; and the *absence* of other forms of injustice. We must proceed in this way because if the whole definition were negative, just in terms of privations, what we describe would not even be a society; it would be nothing at all. At this point the problem looms very large, and may be insuperable. But it is a problem that cannot be avoided, because unless we get down to the specifics of just how we imagine our "just society" to be organized and operated, the notion of a just society remains hopelessly vague.

Justice Contains Incompatible Component Criteria

The second problem arises when we come to work out the details of a just society: The concept of justice has incompatible components, as has been pointed out by Cahn (1949, 14–22), Lucas (1980, 14–19), and Wolgast (1987, chap. 6). Four such components that come to mind are principles for distributing the burdens and benefits of society.

One is that benefits and burdens should be distributed equally among members of the society, as in the case of universal suffrage, according to which each adult person is entitled to cast one and only one vote. This is also the principle that governs the kingdom of heaven, according to the parable of the workers in the vineyards, who were all paid the same amount whether they worked for one hour or twelve (Matt. 20:1–16). But if this principle were used to determine the wages in either the lettuce fields of California or the production lines of General Motors, the result would *clearly* be unjust.

Second, in the case of wages the principle for just compensation is "equal pay for equal work." In that case, of course, payments and penalties will not be equally distributed unless everyone does the same amount of work. But even if we could arrange it so that everyone did the same amount of work, equal compensation would still not be just in all cases, because of accomplishment and crimes.

To take account of accomplishments and failures, as well as of crimes and good behavior, we employ the third principle, that payments and penalties should be proportional not to effort but to achievement, or more precisely to achievements and contributions on the one hand and to crimes and damages on the other. Royalties for books and inventions are distributed according to this principle; it is absurd to suppose that an author should be compensated equally for a good book and a bad book just because she spent an equal amount of effort in writing both. It is also by virtue of this principle that the punishment is supposed to fit the crime: No one, I suppose, believes it would be just if all violators were punished equally, whether guilty of overtime parking or of murder. This principle also applies in schools and universities, where just grades are not distributed equally to all students, nor according to the amount of time spent studying, but according to achievement.

The fourth principle applies more easily to society as a whole than to individual activities. It is expressed in Marx's formula for a communist society, "From each according to his ability, to each according to his need." According to this principle, burdens and benefits will not be distributed equally because abilities and needs are unequal; and because need is not generally directly proportionate to either effort or merit, the results of this principle will differ from those of the second and third principles as well. The argument that certain aspects of welfare and Social Security are a matter of simple justice is based on this fourth principle.

According to which of these principles are we going to arrange our just society? The society we live in is a congeries of different activities and programs, and we use each of the principles for some of them. But we cannot ever use any two of the principles at the same time, with respect to the same activity or the same distribution problem. In order to envision a just society, we must define justice in terms explicit enough so that we can draw a blueprint from the definition. For these purposes the four incompatible principles present a very considerable obstacle.

We might meet the challenge by cataloguing all the activities possible in our new society and then specifying which of the four principles of justice applies to each. I am skeptical of this approach, both because of the inherent difficulty in giving a complete catalogue of anything and also because the procedure would seem to insure a static society devoid of innovation. But let us suppose that the task can be accomplished, and we succeed in envisioning a just society in all its complex detail. We encounter then the third problem, that of applying the blueprint to reality.

The Essential Contestability of Justice

In the case of architectural blueprints there are few problems about applying the blueprint to the real world, because there are few disputes about what counts as an inch, what counts as a foot, what is wood, what is aluminum, what is steel, what is a nail, what is a bolt, and so on. In the case of our blueprint for a just society, however, the analogous agreements are more problematic. Our vision will have to be sketched in abstract terms— we have no others—and its application will therefore depend on paradigms and criteria for equality, for effort, for merit, and for need. But such paradigms and criteria are either lacking or are incomplete or not authoritative. Does equal effort include travel time to and from the place of work, or not? How many hours of penal servitude (or judicially assigned community service) is equal to one month of imprisonment? or a $10,000 fine? Do persons include women and children, or only men? At what age, or at what stage of fetal development, does a human being begin to count as a person with respect to having some interest and representation in politics and other activities? Does a case of embezzlement merit an equal penalty to a case of rape? Is sophisticated medical care, or a university education, a genuine human need?

The propositions specifying these criteria and paradigms figure in moral argument as what Donagan (1977) usefully characterizes as "specificatory premises." These premises introduce great tension and flexibility into the system of absolute moral principles Donagan presents, or indeed in any set of principles; but he misleadingly suggests that they may all be scientific, rather overlooking their essential contestability. The character of such statements of paradigms and criteria is rather more like that that Cavell identifies (1979, 20), in a remark that has deeper Kantian roots than his readers generally acknowledge, when he says that our search for criteria (which we must have in common, and which must serve our common interests) is both a wish and search for *reason* and also a wish and search for *community*. It is because paradigms define community that they are bound to be contestable.

How will our vision of a just society cope with these niggling questions? I can see only two paths. One is to make the definition of a just society more and more precise, so that the answer to each of these questions is contained in our vision itself. But that would result in a tyranny of abstract concepts, in which there would be nothing left for us humans to do other than to submit to the concepts or to protest against justice itself. The other path would be to leave the questions open (as Waldenfels suggests at the end of his essay), trusting social processes to work out the necessary accommodations. But in that case we will not have given a vision of a just society, because in practice a dispute may turn out either way, or remain in a state of uneasy indeterminacy.

We often get along in our present imperfect society because we are more concerned with injustices we immediately recognize than with an explicit definition of justice. In such cases we use the concept of justice pragmatically, as a regulative rather than a constitutive ideal, to guide our discourse with one another toward an accommodation that corrects currently perceived injustices. As Lucas says (1980, 16): "The arguments of justice are essentially dialectical." In that respect the concept of justice is what Gallie (1956) has called an "essentially contestable concept." That is, it is a concept we deliberately leave without an explicit definition, so that we can argue problematic cases by analogy with paradigms. We have "contests" with one another, so to speak, about whether the contested concept shall apply to this case or that one. In the case of Social Security, for example, there are disputes about whether for some really needy persons to receive more than a thousand times their contributions to the system is just (fourth principle) or unjust (second or third principle), and about whether it is just (second and third principle) or unjust (fourth principle) for very wealthy persons to draw old-age benefits. Even if the paradigms are recognized all around the table, their respective analogies to present circumstances remain subject to dispute.

Our disputes among these various principles and criteria, or about their applicability, are moderated to a considerable extent by a fifth principle of justice, sometimes referred to augustly as the principle that *pacta sunt servanda* and more commonly familiar in the adage that it is not fair to change the rules in the middle of the game. Roger Scruton reminded me that this needs to be included in any balanced account of conflicting principles of justice; Lucas (1980, chap. 12) has a useful and balanced discussion of the principle and its limits.

This principle is, of course, not on a par with the previous four principles, because one could not begin to use it to describe or construct the basic structure of a society. In the terms of a distinction prominent in Hampshire (1989), it is a negative virtue, whereas the others are positive; that is, its merit lies not in what it achieves but in what it prevents. Each of the other four principles depends on, and might be justified in terms of, a conception of the human good. This principle is indifferent with respect to conceptions of the human good. It depends on, and might be justified in terms of, the conviction that abrupt change is injurious to plans and projects of every sort.

To some extent, this fifth principle *conflicts* with each of the other four principles, just because it prescribes holding with the *present* rules and procedures, whatever they are, rather than attempting to make them more just. For that reason alone, this principle is no more fit than any of the others to be absolute; it can serve to condemn abrupt change but not to rule out every change. Hence, one manifestation of this principle is the "due process" clause of the U.S. Constitution, which prevents abrupt or arbitrary changes of the rules of public life—after the dice have been thrown and the bets placed, so to speak—without insulating privileged groups against all change whatever. It can also serve, when the dispute between renovation and tradition depends on a subtle balancing of interests, to put justice on the side of tradition rather than change.

If such a conclusion sounds objectionably conservative and subservient to the status quo, one should bear in mind that we really do find it wholly unfair to change the rules smack in the middle of a game just because someone or other dislikes the outcome, whereas it is not unfair to insist afterward on not playing *that* game anymore.

Thus *pacta sunt servanda* muddies the waters even more. That is, it makes it all the more apparent that justice is a contestable concept rather than one with a clear definition and settled criteria of application.

Other essentially contestable concepts are the concepts of a champion, of a democracy, of a crime, of violence, of freedom, of discipline. It might be argued, for example, that an athlete is no "real champion" because of unusual tactics used in winning his bouts; or that Bobby Fisher is still the real chess champion of the world because no one has beaten him or could beat him. In each of these cases we agree both about whether the concept connotes something desirable or undesirable and also about certain paradigm cases. This complex agreement is the basis for our talking to one another, and for our "contests." Within this framework we then disagree about just where the concept rightly applies, that is, to just which cases and to just whose interests. For such purposes it is not necessary, nor even desirable, to have a clear explicit definition of the concept, because what the concept does is provide the framework for a discussion whose outcome is not determined by the concept but worked out by the participants.

Justice is a contestable and dialogical concept, and so to have a good grasp of the concept one must be willing to listen to other claims and to contest them in established forums, rather than to define the outcomes in advance. For that reason justice consists in, or resides primarily in, a process rather than outcome. As Lucas puts it:

> Instead of seeing justice as a simple static assignment of benefits, responsibilities and burdens, we should see it as a dynamic equilibrium under tension, wanting to treat the individual as tenderly as possible, yet being prepared, for sufficient reasons, to take a tough line. . . . Our rules of natural justice . . . are "process values" showing our great concern for the individual and that he should not be needlessly done down.[1] (1980, 18)

Insisting that justice is a process rather than a state is in keeping with a basic commitment to the moral sense of all persons, and to social relations determined by the common moral sense of all people rather than by rules and concepts.[2] Viewed in this manner justice defines the shape of dialogue but not of action, it poses questions rather than answers, it moves toward accommodations rather than predetermined goals.[3] In particular, justice cannot be used to justify the sort of brutality that has been done in the name of "justice" over the years. For though the force of arms may be used to enforce conclusions, it is powerless to bring about dialogue. It is precisely its insistence on dialogue and accommodation that differentiates this sort of commitment to justice from that of the Old Testament militancy and of modern political rhetoric, which John Ladd discusses so ably in Chapter 1.

Viewing justice as a process is also incompatible with envisioning a "just society" as a social condition or state toward which we might strive. A process cannot be a state, anymore than a pain can be a material object. They are two completely different kinds of things, and to treat a process as if it could be a state (to make constitutive use of a regulative concept, as Kant put it) is a recipe for futility and frustration.

BASIC JUSTICE AS PROCEDURAL

So three problems stand in the way of the description of a just society: that justice is a derivative and privative concept, that the idea of a just society contains incompatible criteria that rule out any practical blueprint, and that justice is a contestable rather than a descriptive concept. These are sufficient to make the project of defining and achieving a just society a dubious enterprise at best, and more probably a seductive and debilitating illusion.

This line of thought should give no special comfort to the growing chorus of libertarian and communitarian critics of Rawls's *Theory of Justice* (1971). Quite the contrary. Although my arguments have been formulated without reference to Rawls, and largely without his theory in mind, they are entirely compatible with his insistence on distinguishing a theory of justice from a theory of morality and with his aim at formulating a practical *political* conception of justice. Political conceptions naturally aim at accommodations rather than at ideal or final solutions. Here is how Rawls, in words that are readily compatible with what I have argued, states what he sees as the social outcome and practical objective of his theory of justice:

> The search for reasonable grounds for reaching agreement rooted in our conception of ourselves and in our relation to society replaces the search for moral truth interpreted as fixed by a prior and independent order of objects and relations, whether natural or divine, an order apart and distinct from how we conceive of ourselves. The task is to articulate a public conception of justice that all can live with who regard their person and their relation to society in a certain way. And though doing this may involve settling theoretical difficulties, the practical task is primary. (1980, 519)

Pogge (1989) has recently made a useful contribution toward "realizing" Rawls's theory (in both senses, appreciating and implementing). He remarks (5) that, from this practical perspective, one would not wish to grapple with abstract problems and concepts, such as those out of which utopian ideals are constructed, until one has "first grasped the political content of Rawls's criterion of justice, how it is to govern social institutions and guide their assessment and reform. Other matters are important only insofar as they affect the interpretation of this criterion or its justifications against competing criteria that are actually put forward in good faith." He also points out (9) that the main abstraction in Rawls's program is his abstracting questions about justice from the domain of theoretical ethics, where most philosophers have traditionally thought them to belong—an "abstraction" that moves toward rather than away from practical political questions.

Pogge's reading of Rawls is bound to be controversial, and I do not wish to foreclose debate with these few words. Nor can I now compare what I have argued with points made by Rawls. What is clear, however, is that there is no good reason to regard the line of thought developed here as removed from, indifferent to, or incompatible with the landmark work of Rawls.

The conclusion from the incoherence of the idea of a "just society" is not that we should tolerate injustice, nor that we should drop the word 'justice' from our vocabulary. On the contrary. The concept of justice has great importance in political and social controversies, but it needs to discard its sword and content itself with structuring an essentially nonviolent process of moving those controversies toward mutually agreeable accommodation of strange and puzzling aims and interests. The process eschews outward force and allows each party to appeal to the other's sense of right and wrong; it both demands and encourages a sensitivity to conscience and to persons. To serve in this manner, the concept of justice must remain open and contestable, and we are therefore *in principle* unable to define in sufficient concrete detail the character of a society toward which we might strive.

These remarks may engender an air of paradox. Perhaps the air can be cleared somewhat by Hampshire's *Innocence and Experience* (1989). Hampshire conceives of justice as an important and coherent concept but insists that it is a *negative* rather than a *positive* virtue. "There is a sense in which justice, both procedural and substantial, can be called a negative virtue, whether it is applied to individuals or to institutions or to policies: it is negative, in comparison with love and friendship, or courage, or intelligence. One has to ask, in a Hobbesian spirit, what it prevents rather than what it engenders" (68). The one cannot be reduced to the other, because there is agreement about human evils but not about human goods:

> Humanity is united in the recognition of the great evils which render life scarcely bearable, and which undermine any specific way of life and any specific conception of the good and of the essential virtues. The glory of humanity is in the diversity and originality of its positive aspirations and different ways of life, and the only universal and positive moral requirement is the application of procedural justice and fairness to the handling of conflicts between them. . . . It is neither possible nor desirable that the mutually hostile conceptions of the human good should be melted down to form a single and agreed conception of the human good. (107–9)

We should become more sensitive to the constructive dialogical role the concept of justice can play in our own imperfect society. In particular we must avoid embracing those claims of "justice" that are likely to be enforced with arms. Justice, as a basic procedural notion, invites the articulation of partisan claims—that is part of its role as a dialogical principle. But justice itself—the principle that gives structure to *this* kind of dialogue—is universal rather than partisan, and it demands primary commitment to dialogue rather than to parties. Hampshire's book is a wonderful articulation of these points, and of the philosophical reasons for them. In a world impatient for quick results, the process of accommodating conflicting interests needs all the valiant defenders it can get. We should be willing to discard the vision of a "just society" in order to join in that task.

Ideas certainly do have a social reality. They impinge on our lives as much and as often as ballots and bullets or as privilege and prejudice. But different ideas have different prospects of realization. In the case of noble ideals, means and ends are tragically mismatched in the way they are translated into social reality. Sir Isaiah is right that noble ideals are never realized, and never can be. This ought not to be a disheartening conclusion. A perfectly just society, with all our ideals realized, would be bound to be static, since there could be no reasonable justification for changing it. Constant change is one of the conditions of life; realistic ideals will not seek to abolish that condition but to guide us as we steer through the turbulence change entails. The point is that no change ever will be, or can be, the final one that perfects the conditions of human existence. That is why enthusiastic pursuit of the "ideal society" is more likely to impoverish our lives than to ennoble them.

NOTES

Acknowledgments: An earlier version of this essay was prepared for and presented at the international conference "Idea and Reality" held in Budapest on August 10–13, 1988, and is published in the proceedings (Nyíri and Mezei, 1990). I am indebted to Professor J. C. Nyíri not only for the invitation to present the paper but also for considerable encouragement generally over the past decade. I have made some changes in text in the light of comments made at both conferences, particularly those of John Arthur, Roger Scruton, and William McBride.

1. See also Cahn's (1949) definition, cited above. But Wolgast disagrees, refusing to identify justice with any substantive (1987, 128ff.) and responding to Cahn that "the demand for justice is not a demand for anything specific, not even for a process" (p. 138).

2. This is a characteristically Jeffersonian outlook. See Garver (1983a). See also Wills (1978). Here is an example of how Jefferson formulates this idea: "Man was destined for society. His morality, therefore, was to be formed to this object. He was endowed with a sense of right and wrong, merely relative to this. This sense is as much a part of his nature as the sense of hearing, seeing, feeling; it is the true foundation of morality. . . . The moral sense, or conscience, is as much a part of a man as his arm or leg. . . . It may be strengthened by exercise, as may any particular limb of the body. . . . State a moral case to a ploughman and a professor. The former will decide it as well and often better than the latter because he has not been led astray by artificial rules" (*Papers*, ed. Julian Boyd [Princeton 1955], 12:15).

3. Cf. Wolgast (1987, 135n:) "A. I. Melden seems to me right in saying that just policies are often compromises. . . . It *is* important to respect various concerns and not to insist on absolute standards: this argument concurs with my own. If justice were an ideal, it would not be subject to compromise." The reference is to Melden (1977, 111–13).

11

FORCE, VIOLENCE, AND LAW

Jan Narveson

LAW AND THE PROHIBITION OF VIOLENCE

Definitions

What is the relation of law to force and violence? There are two aspects of this matter to distinguish, both of which I shall address. One is violence on the part of private citizens; the other is violence on the part of the law itself, that is, of its agents. We may call the former "citizen violence," the latter "state violence." Regarding the former, we want to know what role law can and should play in relation to it; regarding the latter, whether there is a special problem due to the fact that agents of the law are or seem to be specifically authorized to engage in violence. The question of who, or what, guards the Guardians arises and, once raised, is not easy to answer.

Violence is an all-too-familiar phenomenon on the contemporary scene. It seems obvious that it can occur in the absence of functioning legal systems, but also that it can and does occur when such systems are functioning quite well. Many also suppose that legal systems, of approximately the kinds we are all familiar with, are actually necessary for the prevention, or at least minimization, of violence. It is an important question whether that is true, and what sort of necessity we would be invoking. But there is another important question (addressed also by Waldenfels in Chapter 7)—whether we can have law without violence. Can any actual system of law in human society abstain from violence? Or is violence, in some measure, an inherent and inescapable feature of human-made law? And if so, might the cure be worse than the disease?

Much clarification is needed regarding what we are to understand by the term 'violence', especially in relation to such terms as 'force' and 'coercion'. The very name has a negative ring to it; yet it is of little help to define 'violence' as, say, "wrongful use of force." For we then still need to know when the use of force is wrongful, and we will not have an answer if we say, "when it is violence." The proposition that violence is wrong should have some useful meaning; it should not be mere pleonasm. Trying to pin down just what we object to about violence—why we should think it wrong when it is wrong—is, in fact, a major and very difficult undertaking.

Then there is the question of what we are to understand by 'law'. This is a particularly difficult matter as it bears on our present concerns, for three reasons. First, there are many and very different legal systems. How would we know that all of them must involve the use of force? Second, there are also many kinds of law within any given legal system. Perhaps some of those kinds, at least, do not involve using force, in which case there would seem to be the possibility that a legal system might not need to use it. And third, there has long been the interesting idea that there might be, apart from any particular human institution of law, a "natural law" bearing on our subject. In at least some versions of this idea, invoking natural law would in effect short-circuit the need for law to be imposed or enforced; in which case, evidently, the answer to our question would obviously be in the affirmative: Law could exist without anything resembling violence. However, the intriguing but obscure idea of natural law also raises the question of whether anything that is in any clear sense "natural" can, in any reasonably clear and recognizable sense, be "law" at all; if not, then our easy affirmative answer becomes irrelevant.

I will begin, then, with the clarificatory questions posed and then proceed to the argument for the claim that law is inextricably wedded to the use of violence, or something similarly objectionable. We start with 'violence', 'force', and 'coercion'.

Following various authors, and my own previous (1986, 126) analysis, I am inclined to define 'violence' as "the intentional inflicting of damage, pain, injury, or death, contrary to the consent of the persons on whom it is inflicted," a definition not far from common usage, except that the latter additionally carries with it a suggestion that these damages were inflicted in a sudden and forcible way. On the definition given, killing someone with a slow-acting poison is an act of violence, though this is not the first word that comes to mind in ordinary usage.

What about 'force'? In its most general sense, this term signifies the utilization of energy, but that is much too broad for our purposes. Let us instead speak only of the interpersonal use of force. In this sense, an individual, A, "forces" another individual, B, to do something if A, by the utilization of appreciable amounts of energy, renders it impossible for B to do anything else, for example, by pushing B downstairs. There is another sense of the verb 'force' in which it is a synonym for 'coerce', which is discussed below.

Note that it is frequently possible to use force on persons or property without actual damage, pain, injury, or death. 'Force' is in this sense a more neutral term. Violence, for most of us, at least raises a moral question; force may not. Someone driving a stake into the ground with a sledgehammer uses force, but there may be nothing morally objectionable going on. Using force on persons is more likely to be objectionable, but it is still not necessarily so and often not even on the face of it so. Whenever we give someone a ride in our cars, we use force on someone: The person's whole body is, after all, carried irresistably off. However, when discussing morally interesting issues, the presumption is that the force is being used on someone contrary to that person's will, and many of us would indeed regard that as prima facie objectionable. Force exerted by one human on another is sometimes coercive and is sometimes intended to inflict damage of various kinds; but it need not be either.

Finally, we have 'coercion'. This is rather a vexed subject in the literature, but I think there is general agreement on some points. In particular, you coerce someone when you "make" her do what she did not want to do. But there are many ways of doing this, some violent and some not, some involving force and some not—and some morally objectionable and some not. The general idea is that you coerce someone by revising, without the coercee's consent, her set of available alternatives in such a way that all the others are worse, from the coercee's point of view, than the one you want to induce her to do; she otherwise would have had some clearly preferable ones, but given this new menu of options, she does what you want her to.

Attempted coercion is inherently resistible, in the sense that the victim always has a choice—it is not like being pushed downstairs—but the choice-situation forced on her by the coercer is worse than the status quo ante would have been. What the victim has no choice about in coercion, then, is the menu of alternatives: She has been deprived, without consent and without present power of revision, of the alternatives she otherwise would have had, some of which she definitely prefers to any of those now open to her.

What Is Wrong About Violence?

This is a normative inquiry into the law—we are not simply asking what the law actually says and does but what it ought to say and do. Thus we must go into the question of what the fundamental rights and wrongs are regarding the use of force, violence, and coercion—obviously a major project; but equally obviously one we cannot avoid. That could be a fairly long story, but I hope to make the story of medium length, if not short.

The short of it is that we cannot say that any of the three—coercion, force, or even violence itself—is necessarily and always morally prohibited. In sports and on various other occasions people agree to engage in actions some of which are certainly forcible, coercive in certain ways, and even sometimes violent. The boxer in the ring may well intend to inflict damage on his opponent, and the opponent is willing that he attempt to do so. Whenever there is an act of force, violence, or coercion, moral objection to it depends crucially on its not being agreed to by uncoerced, rationally acting individuals. If our public concern with these things exceeds that restriction, we run the danger of paternalism and deprivation of liberties that reasonable people would want.

Let us focus on coercion in particular. I have suggested that coercion is essentially a matter of fiddling with the menus of alternatives open to the victim in ways contrary to the latter's will. What is wrong with coercion, when it is wrong, has to be that the coercer had no right to limit the menu in the particular way that he does. Yet sometimes he will have this right. If A has for some time been extending a benefit to B, to which B has no prior claim, then A may be in a position to coerce B into doing x by threatening to withdraw this benefit if B does not comply. It is, I dare say, a familiar device among married couples and assorted friends: "If you don't do x, I won't love you any more!" will be a potent threat in some cases, although the threatener can rarely be said to have a moral obligation to love the threatened person. Coercion is wrong, however, when those aspects of the victim's menu that we subject to unilateral revision are protected by independently established rights.

A similar problem infects a general proscription of either force or violence. The wrongness of violence against someone's property presupposes that she has rights to that property, which therefore cannot be established simply by appeal to a general right against violence. How, then, are we to establish anything like a fundamental right against violence to the person?

Rather than become intimidated by such questions, we should stick with the view that what makes all these things wrong is what makes coercion wrong when it is. That, I suggest, is that the coercer has no business unilaterally revising the agenda for the worse, when the entries on A's menu of available options are generated by the otherwise legitimate activities of parties other than the coercer, including the victim herself.

Prima facie, on the other hand, unilaterally altering it for the better is not obviously a problem from the point of view of the affected individual. Choosing between existing options and new ones that might be better can, of course, be a nuisance; but when this is a legitimate complaint, it would have to be because the effect of the possibly well-intended addition to the menu is really to alter his situation for the worse on the whole. He may have preferred simply to continue sitting under the banyan tree watching the clouds drift by, instead of worrying his head about a set of new opportunities of whose properties he is uncertain. (Recent writers, such as Zimmerman (1983), have also worried about "coercive offers" in a different way; we will not be able to go into that matter here.)

Note that the interventions condemned on this proposal will be wrong-ful whether or not they are done for purposes of coercion in particular, that is, for the purpose of getting the victim to act differently than he otherwise would. Pure malicious violence, for example, alters the victim's situation for the worse with no intent to influence specific future behavior, except in the residual sense of making many future activities impossible and most of them painful or less efficient. (I speak here of his "situation" rather than his "options" for that very reason. Inflicting physical damage or pain will, however, influence the character of one's options, especially if we define options in terms of the use of existing facilities in roughly their current condition. If I can still play tennis, but with a very sore jaw or an intense headache, my options are affected relative to what they would have been had I been able to choose to play with no new aches and pains.)

I should like now to attempt a formulation of the fundamental right of security of the person. Following Locke (1937), Nozick (1974), and the recent work of David Gauthier (1986), my suggestion is that we can get a suitable recursive characterization of what is protected by the fundamen-tal rights of any given person, as follows. I will propose a version of J. S. Mill's Liberty Principle ([1859] 1968, 73): that A's liberty of action is not to be unilaterally restricted by others as long as A does not by those actions violate anyone else's similar rights. Putting it that way brings up the need for an effective and noncircular characterization of what those "similar rights" are. To see how this works, let us first note that the general liberty right is equivalent to a right over one's person, specifically, that A's body as a whole may not be impinged on contrary to A's preferences regarding it. Why so? Because, I submit, a property right is a right to a set of actions, just like any other liberty right—indeed, as I ultimately think, just like any other genuine right. What you can do by virtue of owning x is, in brief, anything you can do with x, as long as what you do does not in turn violate others' rights. (Or you may have a restricted right of this type, in which case various particular things it is possible to do with x are forbidden. We will not concern ourselves with such matters here.)

The right to one's own body, indeed one's own person, is the subject's right to do whatever he or she wishes with that entity, within the limits imposed by others' rights. Note that 'one's own body' does not here mean 'the body that you have a right to,' but rather, 'the body that is part of you' (or, on some views, all of you). The relation is that of inclusion, not ownership. The bodies of slaves did not (legally) belong to the slaves, in social systems where slavery existed; the sense in which a certain body was the body of a certain slave is that the body in question was included in the whole person who was that slave. The right to one's own person is, then, really equivalent to a general right of personal liberty.

Now let me extend the treatment to one's property. What we propose here is that A is prima facie at liberty to operate on the external environment in whatever way A sees fit, and so is everyone else. These operations relate A to particular bits of the world, such that A is understood to be "using" those bits and not others. Suppose that those bits were not previously enmeshed in the activities of any previous persons; then further persons who encounter A will be doing violence to A if they utilize those bits in ways inconsistent with A's utilizations, without A's consent. We suggest this as an interpretation of the elegantly formulated principle that Gauthier (1986, 206) calls the "Lockean Proviso," which holds that "no one is free to better his own situation through interaction worsening the situation of another." The question is, what is to count as a relevant sort of worsening. My partial answer is that A worsens the situation of B when A brings it about that the programs of action B is engaged in—B's "projects," to use Bernard Williams's apt term—are in some way made less feasible from B's point of view; B prefers the contemplated programs as they were in the status quo to what they will be given A's actions. A good example would be environmental deterioration in a respect pertinent to the success of B's various projects. If A's actions involve worsening B's situation as so characterized, then they violate the proviso in question.

Property rights as so conceived are easy enough to define in the uninteresting cases, as when A and B are on separate islands or universes or whatever—mainly because in those cases there is no problem whose solution depends on the definitions in question. But suppose A's and B's activities come into conflict: A's doing x, part of A's intended program of activity, is impossible if B does y, which is part of B's intended program. In such cases, the rule of "first come first serve" is of the essence. My restriction on doing things with a set of molecules that happen to occupy portions of your body is due solely to the happenstance fact that you "got there" first: Those same molecules could have been in my body instead, or in nobody's body, in either case making my employment of them unproblematic. But alas, they are not, having instead by chance taken up residence in your body; and my requirement to respect your rights obliges me to refrain from employing them without your agreement.

In many cases, we can readily imagine, it will not be clear who got there first; and in many more it will not be clear just which regions of the external world do figure in your pattern of activity. These will require negotiation, and the negotiation will in the main be along the lines of either clarifying the structures of activity that led to the problem, or of arriving at a fair allocation of resources to which both parties had a reasonable claim.

One important set of problems has to do with unintended adverse effects of one person's activities on those of others. Here the rule proposed has it that you are entitled to the resources involved in your program of activities in the condition they are in upon acquisition. Others are forbidden to make your situation worse (in *your* view of what is worse) than it would have been had they desisted. This too will lead to many difficulties and, indeed, quarrels. But it will also, as I have explained elsewhere (1989, esp. chaps. 6–8), resolve many difficulties and quarrels and also give some sense of direction for resolution of the quarrels that remain.

To sum up this part of my program, we can say that force, violence, or coercion is wrong whenever the act in question worsens the situation of the victim, V, in respects over which V had rightful authority as generated by an initial right to personal liberty plus whatever further accretions to V's legitimate agenda arose in the course of V's career, provided those accretions did not in turn violate the similarly defined rights of others.

For convenience, I will henceforth speak only of 'violence', understanding it to include more than just sudden and substantial alterations of someone's situation for the worse, but what is common to force and coercion as well, insofar as there is this sort of prima facie moral case against them.

Law

Let us turn, then, to the specific question before us: What has human law to do with violence? This, as noted, requires us to say at least something about what human law is. Again, this could certainly be a complex and lengthy inquiry on its own, on some understandings of what is involved. I hope, however, that much of that complexity can be sidetracked here— but not all can, to be sure. The point of definitions is communicational efficiency, which is not the same as philosophical insight, though hopefully it will pave the way to it. So the "definitions" I hope to come up with are literally intended to be that, and not disguised theories in the guise of definitions.

I have used the term 'human law' here to indicate that we envisage at least on the surface of things a distinction between it and what some would term 'moral law'. The latter is, indeed, a bit of a misnomer: Moral "laws" are not the laws of anybody—there is no "lawgiver" in their case; but that laws properly so called are the sort of things that are "given" or "laid down" by someone partly defines what we are talking about here.

Here we may accept the suggestion of Aquinas (quoted from Arthur and Shaw, 1984, 4) that law "is nothing else than an ordinance of reason for the common good, promulgated by him who has the care of the community." Aquinas's characterization is easy to misunderstand, evidently, for it appears that some people do not agree with it. Perhaps we can clear up the main sources of misunderstanding by bracketing off what the definition does not say from what it does say—granting that Aquinas himself could well be among those who were misled! I suggest the following (whether as interpretations or as revisions does not matter for present purposes).

First, I take it that the reference to an "ordinance of reason" can look a lot as though these "caretakers" were the very living embodiment of Reason; but that need not be claimed at all. What is claimed, rather, is that what purports to be a law must be issued under the aegis of a claim that there is good reason, for example, some sort of need, for the ordinance in question. Not just any old well-formulated imperative will do for a law, no matter how awesomely bewigged the promulgator may be.

Second, the suggestion that the ordinance in question is to be "for the common good" must, again, be understood as meaning only that the people who proclaim it do so under the aegis of some conception of community good, however ill-formulated or badly thought out. If the dictator orders, "Off with his head!" for what the dictator himself agrees is no reason at all, and more specifically no reason pertaining to some conception of community good, then his order, while it may be duly carried out by the dupes or minions to whom he shouts it, simply has to be understood to be, Aquinas claims, as some sort of perversion or marginal case—and on the far side of the margin, at that. An order that does not even purport to be justified in terms of the community interest rather than the simple interest, or even whim, of those in power just will not do as an instance of law. Were all "laws" like that, then we would indeed be unable to distinguish law from gang rule, and legal philosophy should simply close its doors. (One of the major problems of legal positivism is its need to avoid being stuck with the implication that the whims of dictators really are, somehow, all right.)

What does have to be said is (1) that the idea of the common good, while not a completely blank check, is nevertheless one that needs filling out by a good theory of that elusive object, and (2) that particular governments rarely have any such thing explicitly in hand. But they do have the need for one: A government unable or unwilling to at least try to tell us what good a given law aims to promote and why that should be thought to be a good is open to embarrassment. The smell of illegitimacy hangs over the governmental enterprise when it has no answers to those questions. In sum: If L is claimed to be a law, then L must be issued under the claim that there is a reason for issuing L, and that this reason concerns the common good of those governed.

Third, how a particular set of people come to have "the care of a community," indeed, what it is for them to have it, is a nice question. Again, though, we should distinguish the origins of the group in question, which can vary all over the map, from its perceived status, which can be generally explicated as involving, in Austin's dictum, something in the nature of a "habit of obedience" on the part of the people, this habit being not simply the tendency to just go ahead and do anything anybody tells them, but rather an ascription of putative authority to the persons in question to promulgate the ordinances in question. For the purported lawgiver to be the lawgiver is for it to be generally recognized as having authority to do so. (This, of course, raises the question of what we do when some members of the community do not cede such a group the authority in question. I do not pretend to answer it here.)

Fourth and finally, Aquinas leaves barely implicit in this formulation what later is made explicit, and what most directly brings us to our present subject, namely that an essential part of the package in some group's being (or being regarded as) a government is its having the general power to enforce the ordinances in question. We may take this to be implicit in the notion of an 'ordinance', just as we may also take to be implicit both in that term and in the previous reference to 'Reason' that the orders issued by this group have some sort of generality and order to them. Laws are rulings, and intended to rule, which means to *overrule* those who might wish to do something other than what the law directs them to do. They are not just pieces of advice.

Such, then, is law: A set of coercively enforceable directives (reasonably clear, general, and suitably published) from someone (the government) recognized as having the authority to do so, to a particular community, as pertaining to and promoting that community's common good, under some to-be-discussed conception of that common good.

Law's Office of Prohibiting Violence

We expect the laws, at a minimum, to prohibit assorted acts of violence. Why is this? Because, roughly, the idea of a truly common "good" that is at all recognizable as a good goes straight down the drain if the members of the community whose common good is in question are simply in open season to those who would wreak violence on them.

However, we can be more precise than this. Aquinas did not spell out the notion of common good very much, and in any case infused it with irrelevant theological notions. But if we are to identify a truly common good for a diverse community, then the paramount need is for a totally secular notion of that good, a notion that, among other things, will enable both the denizens of assorted and conflicting religions and the nonreligious to carry on with their lives on a basis of mutual respect, despite basic differences in belief. The essential secularity of the notion is due to both these sources, both the divergence among religions and the absence of religion among many. All these people are members of society, all must be accommodated there, and so the principles by which they can live together cannot depend on anything peculiar to any one set of beliefs. The "common good" must be genuinely common, that is, shared by all.

We have talked as though the common good were just out there, awaiting explication. It is not that way, of course. The common good that can animate the laws is, instead, a construction. All moral problems are your and my and every other particular person's problems. We each make our way through life in a social sea of others who differ more or less, but very often, more rather than less. A proper notion of common good must reach to you, to me, and to all the other uncommon people in that vast group— ultimately to all people everywhere—whose impingement on each other is the source of the problems (and solutions) of moral, political, and legal philosophy. The law occupies a major niche in the construction issuing from our concern with these problems.

Well, what "problems"? Those implied above: The problems that result when our paths cross, to the detriment of one or more parties. Now, our paths cross with lots of people, and given the phenomena and paraphernalia of contemporary life, they cross with increasing numbers in an increasing variety of ways. The need for "order" in all this is not due to an aesthetic taste for tidiness. Rather, the need, for each one of us, is literally to make our valued ways of living possible at all.

Clearly, the first requirement of pursuing a way of life is having a life in which to pursue it. This elementary requirement has the special feature of being invariant: To pursue a life, one must live, and this is true even of lives aimed at a certain kind of death. So important is this requirement that it becomes overwhelmingly plausible to argue as does Thomas Hobbes ([1651] 1968): The interest in one's continued living outweighs any advantage one might derive from being free to take the lives of others as one pleases. Yet everyone can do that—the weakest, as Hobbes observes, have strength enough to kill the strongest (chap. 13). It is thus a rationally good deal for anyone to make with everyone that they refrain from availing themselves of the other's life, just because to do so fits in better with the pursuit of their own. This becomes the most fundamental, rudimentary form of social cooperation: the practice, namely, of respecting the lives of sundry others, whatever beliefs, race, tastes, or any other variable property they exemplify. It is a form of cooperation, in my view; that is, we refrain from violence on condition that others do so as well, and we do so because we are all better off as a result of this mutual forbearance.

The importance of Hobbes's axiom for present purposes is underscored by the ongoing character of our vulnerability to the potentially lethal actions of others. Not only may we be destroyed at any time by anyone, as far as physical capability is concerned, but also we have gotten as far as we have in life because so many have refrained from exercising that capability in the past. The individual who makes free to kill others in adulthood has taken advantage of the forbearance of his fellows; he has come this far only because they have refrained from anticipating his bad example. He is, in truth, a "free rider."

Our story gets complicated when we extend it to miscellaneous depredations. I conjecture that the best arrangement anyone can make with all others is to respect Gauthier's Proviso: that we agree to refrain from pursuing our own way by worsening the lot of those we interact with. The path of wisdom is to cooperate in these vital respects, which means to be committed to settling disputes by negotiation rather than violent conflict. That is the only way that can be mutually agreed on as a communal rule of life by thoughtful persons of otherwise diverse proclivities. And it is, I believe, the fundamental basis of law. What this agreement does is to establish as the community baseline the good of peace. Departures from the status quo—that is, from the array of interactions we shall have when everyone respects everyone else's Lockean rights—must be justified by supplying reasons to suppose that the effects will be in everyone's ultimate interest, notably by observing what I call the moralized rule of Pareto: namely, to allow any changes that benefit some but harm none.

The problem is with imposed changes, those that benefit some at the expense of others. These in general are not allowed by the Lockean restriction. So if a change that appears to violate it is proposed, arrangements must be made to compensate, to their satisfaction, those who have borne the cost without adequate benefit this time around. They must in turn be the beneficiaries in future, in such a way that the costs borne by others in that new round are sufficiently compensated by the benefits they got back in Round One. In this way, we may continue to adhere to the genuinely common good. And we have a place for notions of equity, the reasonably equal sharing of any burdens that are necessary to the common good insofar as it is really common. The main such burden is, however, the commitment to nonviolence itself; and its main benefit is the very possibility of pursuing one's chosen life.

All this is the moral background to the law. My claim is not that law is unintelligible without precisely this account of its moral background but only that law is unintelligible without some such account. In respect of the genesis of moral proscriptions against violence and of the community concern with it, however, I believe it to be in essentials right.

JUSTIFICATIONS AND THEIR LIMITS

"Natural Law"

Here, in speaking of "the law," we have meant human, legislated law, not "natural law," if such a thing makes any sense. Does it?

What makes sense here, I think, is not some kind of ghostly Institution or Code existing in Plato's heaven, as we say, but instead a set of reasonable principles. In the absence of such a Realm of Essence, where could such things be said to "exist"? The answer, I think, is just where Aquinas claims they do, namely, in the souls of individual people—they are "written in the hearts of man," as he puts it. We may table the question whether a divine creator wrote it there (with a direction for a likely negative answer). In a way, it does not much matter how it got there. What matters is whether what is so "written" can serve as a basis for human institutions; and some things suggest that it can, though others admittedly suggest the opposite. One major factor in support is the "common law," evolving over centuries without specific legislation by governments. But more fundamental, I think, would be the ready availability of a good argument, showing that certain principles are in some sense obvious to all and thus available for appeal when differences need to be settled.

Here are three ways this might be thought to work: (1) Perhaps everyone simply does, on the surface, actually cite these principles in everyday contexts; or (2) one could follow up a kind of secular analogue of Aquinas's theological idea, by proposing that these principles are simply wired into our genetic makeup (thus "written in our hearts"); or (3) one could argue that these principles are what are called for by the great variety of purposes humans actually do pursue, as essential means to their efficient pursuit.

I take (1) to be empirically problematic. Both common sense and anthropological evidence suggest that at this surface level there is a good deal of variability. In the case of a deviant, what would there be to say? That "it is so 'written on your heart' only you cannot read"? Option (2) seems to me to face a serious problem of empirical meaningfulness. If a certain principle is wired into the frame of individual A, then what on earth is A doing ignoring or denying that principle in practice? What does it mean for us to be programmed to do x if we nevertheless often, in just the cases where x is called for, do y instead?

My preferred option, then, is (3). It has the great advantage of neither denying evident empirical facts nor of relying on exotic biological theory. If it can be shown that certain principles are the ones that people need to have, given their other pursuits, then the situation is in part as Aquinas says, namely, that the "natural law" is literally rational, implied by the common reason of all people. So if we do not find the principles already written on our hearts at the moment, we may instead find good reason, from our own point of view, why we should perhaps get our pencils out and write them there ourselves.

My theoretical surmise for the present enterprise is that the principles we will arrive at in this way will tell us to refrain from the use of force in pursuing our ends, except as necessary—assuming it ever is—to defend our pursuit against those who will not recognize such a right. And the reason we will arrive at those principles will be that we do better that way, given the nature of the creatures we interact with, namely, our fellow persons.

This brings us to our central concern, the normative status of violence vis-à-vis the law. The account given concerns the principles that underlie the law. Law always needs to be justified, though it sometimes, hopefully, is so. And here I again follow Aquinas, who proposed that human law, when properly carried through, is a kind of deduction or application of natural law, which we will refer to simply as "the moral background," or in short, "morality."

So how do they differ? Or, I should say, what is the status of law when it does its proper job?

Enforcement and the Rightful Use of Force

Law differs from morals in two ways: first, in being set forth in black and white, as it were. A suitably authoritative body sets down the content of law for all to know and be guided by. The idea, moreover, is that when the authoritative body does it, it is done, and not before: We now have a law where we did not before—an idea that hardly makes any sense in the case of morality. Second, the law is enforced by a definite, "official" set of agents whose official duty it is to do so.

In the absence of enforcement, would law be law? Let us note the further parallel. Is morality enforced? Certainly it is, but not essentially by the police. A given community's understanding of morality is enforced by that community in the sense that it is reinforced by all and sundry, in their day-to-day interactions. The "enforcement" of morality is via grass-roots initiative and is, of course, more or less haphazard and unreliable. The enforcement of law, by contrast, is (intended to be) organized, definite, precise—in principle. In particular, it is the citizen's understanding of law that it will be enforced and that enforcement is available, is in the offing, and will occur with a considerable degree of reliability. Enforcement is coercive. The law enforcers attempt to bring it about that nonconformity is not a viable option. Citizens "must" conform—or else. This brings us to the question of just what the "or else" can properly consist of. In particular it brings us to the question of whether law can be nonviolent, and if not, what that proves.

To get us into this issue, we must first raise the question of why enforcement of the law should be thought necessary. There are two reasons for at least some doubt on the matter. One is the pacifist appeal to the Inner Light: Can we not always settle differences by reason rather than by resorting to force? Why, in other words, do reasonable interpersonal rules require any enforcement at all? The second lies in a quite different direction: Why should law need official enforcement? Why not leave it to the citizen to do on his or her own, by arrangement with such as may go along? We shall take them in order.

Pacifism

There is a familiar, clichéd answer to the first question: "Differences often just will not be settled by reason. There are violent people in the world, no amount of reasoning will actually touch them, and thus we have no option but to deal with them at their own level. The pacifist idea is hopelessly impractical." It is an answer with some truth in it, but as it stands it is question begging and may seem arbitrary. I think this is because the real point of it has been misunderstood. The cliché implies that we have only two options: Use violence ourselves or allow violence to be done to some innocent while we attempt to trot out our appeals to sweet reason. But this is not quite it. For indeed, we do not know for certain that reason will not work. The pacifist is surely right about that. How could we possibly *know* that there are no nonviolent options, in the case of any given miscreant, that would induce him to desist?

True. But fortunately irrelevant. What we will often know well enough, in particular cases, is that we are not going to stop this miscreant in the near future with appeals of the type in question. We cannot know whether there is some gifted individual in the whole wide world who might have been able to bring it off. Nor do we know that we ourselves might not have succeeded, eventually, in talking him out of it. We do not know this, but the legitimacy in principle of our choosing the more violent route does not rest on our knowing it. It rests on something different: to wit, that our right to defend ourselves is not contingent on the attacker's coming out as nearly unscathed as possible. If I, the victim, can spare the attacker some damage by investing considerable resources of time and effort in acquiring the spiritual technology necessary for persuading him to desist by peaceful means, then it does not follow that I have a duty to make that effort. To whom, after all, would I owe it? Not, surely, to my attacker? Quite the contrary. After all, he has already violated my right to go about my own business; his claim to the protection he gets from our forbearance is invalidated by his use of violence. The most we can say for the rights of attackers is (1) that in cases where it is pretty clear that less violent methods would be effective, then we ought to take those; (2) that our initial response to threatened violence should have a reasonable upper bound, roughly, somewhere around the level of just enough to contain the threat; and (3) that it might be really nice if we generally took the less violent of two methods of securing our rights, but we do not have a duty to be really nice, and especially not to wrongdoers.

A further word about (2): If we really have the right, all things taken into account, to do x, what we may do is, I once argued and still think, whatever it takes to secure that right (Narveson, 1965). The upper limit mentioned in (2) is a limit to what we may do by way of an initial response.

I would argue that we could sometimes reasonably exceed this limit. But meanwhile, how do we establish this reasonable upper limit?

What suggests itself here is something analogous to the *lex talionis*. When someone threatens us with violence to level m, then the reasonable rule is that we may not respond above level m, pending a need for escalation as shown by the attacker's response. Obviously some of the securities that are prima facie due every person are no longer due an attacker, because what he does adversely affects portions of our lives that we have the right to pursue in the ways we are pursuing them. The point of rights is security; when someone threatens us, then the point of our extending security to that individual is defeated. So when someone proposes to use unlimited violence, by making clear threats of death, then all bets are off—we are in the Hobbesian state, and in principle there is nothing we may not do to him. What we do to him may or may not be motivated by retaliation. The point here is only that he has no complaint even if that is our motive and even if we consider retaliation prima facie disreputable, as indeed we should. For how would he get to complain about that?

Suppose the miscreant still persists. Since we then have a more serious threat to our security, we are entitled to a further response, an escalation, because that is evidently required by his persistence. For example, we can increase the penalty for a second offense; and against one who will persist no matter what we do, an extreme penalty would seem to be in order—possibly death, for example.

What Does and What Does Not Justify Force?

All this has been on behalf of the right of self-defense. But it would seem to apply equally, in principle, to the defense of others—friends, clients, or indeed anyone who needs and is willing to accept help in this respect. The qualification 'is willing to accept' is plainly essential though. A's defense of B is designed to prevent what B sees to be a harm; but B is the judge of that. If B does not want A's help, the indicated conclusion is that B judges the proposed "help" to be worse than the disease it is designed to cure.

Does anything else justify forcibly coercive response? This is a question I have tried to answer in "Terrorism and Morality" (1991); here, in somewhat different words, is what seems to me a plausible ordering of types of cases, from most to least plausible, that have been put forth in the way of justifying violence.

1. Immediate prevention of injury to self—out-and-out self-defense
2. Immediate prevention of injury to others—out-and-out other-defense
3. Longer-range or indirect defense of self or others

4. Securing of necessary conditions of a minimally acceptable life when no other means is possible
5. Promoting a better life for oneself, some favored group, or human-kind at large, over and beyond what is called for by (1) through (4)—for example, "promoting the general welfare," or bringing the group in question up to some sort of "equality," in welfare or some other measure of well-being, with some other group or groups.

Cases (1) and (2) we have already discussed. They provide the clearest cases, the paradigms, of justified use of violence, as an immediate offshoot of the most fundamental plank of the moral platform about violence: Those against whom violence is used in cases of type (1) or (2) are persons who are acting in violation of its basic provisions. The degree of violence they justify, I have proposed, is, simply, the minimum amount necessary to do the job.

But what about cases of type (3)? Suppose we claim to be protecting someone from a threat that is not immediate: How much may we do? May we engage in preventive warfare, "getting" them before they "get" us? Not, at least, unless the evidence is extremely strong that they do intend us harm in a way that poses a real, though temporally distant, threat, and there is no nonviolent way of effectively allaying this threat. If A intentionally puts B into a condition that will kill B in several years, does A presently deserve the penalties appropriate to murder? Is an AIDS carrier who knows himself to be such and has relations with someone he does not know to be one, without warning her, guilty of attempted murder or something like it? Clearly the victim has a case for compensation, at least, and that compensation may be exacted by force. But how much? Whatever we say here, our response can hardly be the same as for fatal shootings, stabbings, and other more ordinary methods of doing violence. We cannot pursue the awesome complexities of these cases, which are rightly among the main fare of the legal profession.

But the cases that concern us most here are (4) and (5). May we resort to force against B in order to get B to save C from starving to death? And if so, how much force? The trouble with thinking that it is very much is simple enough: If I threaten B with death to do this, then I am putting B in the same situation C is already in—an imminent threat of death—in order to get C out of it. And this though B had (in the case we are considering) nothing to do with getting her into it. How could that be justified, supposing that B legitimately came by the resources that would enable him to save C? Would rational persons give up that much liberty in order to secure even the minimal necessities of life for others? It seems to me not. Those others have no claim on B's resources; B was in no way resposible (we are assuming) for C's plight. To force B to help out seems to me a clear injustice. To do so in order to enable D to go from near-poverty to near-affluence is an even clearer one.

The assumption that B was "in no way responsible for" C's plight is essential, of course, for if he were, then A is in the position of defending C against what amounts to a form of violence by B, and this we agree to justify use or threat of force if necessary. Otherwise, though, for A to use force against B is for A to engage in unjustified violence: It is to disregard B's freedom to live the sort of life B chooses to live. What especially will not do here is to assimilate B's previous nonassistance to C as itself a form of "harm." Plainly if we take that line, then freedom has been denied from the start. My freedom to live as I please, whatever may be your situation, as long as I do not violate your similar freedom, is identical to my being your devoted slave if we insist that I do "violate your similar freedom" whenever I fail to do what your devoted slave would do if you had one!

State and Enforcement

This brings us back to the case of law, with the relevant questions much narrowed down. Is law necessarily coercive? My arguments above, I believe, imply that it is necessarily capable of being coercive—necessarily such as to justify coercion on some occasions. If it is the office of the law to protect us from violence, then in those cases where only the threat of violence will allay the attack, the law must be able to avail itself of it, just as may any private citizen in those circumstances. But then, this latter clause brings up the question of whether it is necessary for there to be officers of the law to do this, persons with distinctive authority to do it, and to deny others the power to do it themselves, even though those others do not want it done by these people and are ready and willing to make alternative arrangements for their security.

Here we must consider the arguments of the anarchist, who holds that we need no centrally coercive agency of the law to provide protection for us. On the contrary, says the anarchist, just as it is wrong for A to use force against B in order to prevent C from starving to death, so it is wrong for A to use it against B in order to prevent C from using force against D. In the absence of any special arrangement, B has no duty to assist D in this respect, even though that respect is the defense of D's clear rights. Now, the state undertakes not only to defend everybody, but also to require everybody to assist in this endeavor, at least by paying taxes to support it. The anarchist challenge is that this activity does not look morally satisfactory. For here A (the government) is holding a gun to the head of B (the taxpayer) in order to prevent C (the criminal) from violating the rights of D (the victim).

The direct connection between rights and defenses is this: If someone,

A, has a right to do something, then there is a range of defensive activities to which A, or any others willing to assist and whom A is willing to have assist, may rightfully resort. A's right entails duties on the part of certain others (those against whom A has the right), but it does not entail, just like that, a right to the defensive assistance of others in order to reinforce those duties. That is a separate item, calling for separate arrangements. Those whose assistance is unwanted are prima facie violating the rights of those whom they misguidedly endeavour to assist.

It is a familiar claim about the state that, whatever else it does, it has the general function and duty of enforcing the rights of its citizens, of protecting them and their property from the violent or forcible incursions of others. But this very function, reasonably regarded as the most basic of all legitimate public functions—if there are any at all—is called into question by the challenge we have just noted. If the inevitable effect of government enforcement of rights is to coerce some into assisting others to repel the wrongful exertions of still others, then it seems that government at its very core is engaged in wrongful activities. The guardians are predators themselves, violating some of the very rights they are supposed to be protecting.

If this is a challenge to be taken seriously—as it seems to me it is—then where do we go from here?

One response might be to deny that taxation really does involve coercion of the kind that violates rights. For example, some say that what is ours is not really our pretax income but our aftertax income, so that public agencies are not taking our money but rather simply administering the utilization for public purposes of what is already theirs. Render unto Caesar what is Caesar's—and if there's any left, you can do as you like with it! This view, I believe, makes a mockery of the whole idea of taxation. How would the government claim to be the legitimate owner of the resources it gets from taxation? Can government in any sense claim to have created the wealth in question? Even in the case of a government employee, the answer is clearly in the negative. Government gets its money, ultimately, either (1) by taking it from someone who did create the wealth it represents, or (2) by forcibly preventing others from taking advantage of opportunities that would otherwise be available to citizens, as when it operates some service as a monopoly. But this way of muscling out the competition is violence, rightly not permitted to private citizens.

To provide relevant contrast, let us consider how it could be different. For example, there can be "voluntary taxes," contributions determined on the basis of an allocational formula that the contributor approves of, by people she trusts, which she is not forced to pay, but which she does pay anyway because she approves of it and shares its purposes. Some deductions from my bank account are like that. I approved them, and they disappear automatically without my having to readdress myself to the issue every month. But I retain the right to withdraw my approval. This certainly contrasts with taxes, as I have argued (1989, 235–41, 248–49) in defending this idea against an interesting argument of Nagel's. With taxes, your personal approval of the formula or of anything else in the procedure is irrelevant. Only if your disapproval happens to be matched by enough other voters to get the set of laws that lead to the taxes revoked can you escape them. And while the right to a morsel of power, a tiny probability of getting your preferred policies realized, is no doubt better than no power at all, it is hardly what could reasonably be referred to as a right simpliciter with respect to the policy in question.

Another line people might take is that taxation does not really require violence. I have heard people seriously maintain this. The agents of the law, a conferee at a recent conference pointed out, need use no force against you. You can stand quietly by unmolested as they cart off your property in part payment of taxes owed. If you resist, of course, that is another matter: They will then have to use force, and possibly even threaten or employ violence. But then—so goes the argument—that is a matter of "self-defense" by the authorities owing to your rash act of resistance.

But if it is conceded that the property or the income in question is yours, then you certainly have no duty to stand quietly by and let people haul it away for their purposes. To have a right of any sort is for it to be the case that defense of that to which you have a right is prima facie legitimate. And so the items on your agenda that the police would be foreclosing are ones that are legitimately on your antecedent agenda; threatening to use force if necessary to foreclose those options is thus illegitimate, and so the defense of taxation along this line also falls.

The account here, it will be noted, flatly denies the independent authority of the state, which is to say, of laws made by some people to control, involuntarily, the actions of others. The laws of the state stand in contrast to the fundamental justificatory laws that we are agreeing to have the sort of function that Aquinas's natural laws have: to wit, laws based on what is genuinely common to all and have the rational agreement of all. Many thinkers (almost all, I surmise) would apparently argue that we must include in our idea of the common good a common power (or governing body) to ensure at least minimally acceptable behavior on the part of others, a power deriving its authority from the rational assent of all. But the argument that there is such assent in turn depends on a thesis that such authorized enforcing bodies are literally necessary for the common good. And the trouble is not only that this has not been shown and that attempts to show it have a way of being flatly question begging; but worse, it looks as though something like the opposite is more nearly the truth.

The anarchist's challenge is that the common good is incompatible with the alleged "authority" in question.

There is another matter contributing in no small way to our problem: the likelihood of error in the laws and their administration. This has two aspects. First, in particular where laws emerge from what passes for the "democratic process," there is the very real possibility that the wrong things will be made illegal. For example, if it is wrong for me to force you to assist someone else in warding off wrongful attack, it is still more obviously wrong for me to force you to refrain from inhaling a substance that would likely be bad for you in the longer run, unless you are my child. Aquinas speaks of him who "has the care of" the community and could take seriously the metaphor that the state has a parental relation to its citizens. But, obviously, the state is not and cannot be a parent; it can only be just some more of us, no better than we (and no worse, except that the agents of the state are armed; so we have to reckon with the tendency for power to corrupt). As mature men and women who may make, or ruin, our own lives, none of us has the right to force others to walk the right line in life, although we certainly have the right to see to it that those who choose ruin confine it to themselves, rather than inflicting their unhappy fates on the rest of us. When we consider the busybody tendencies in human nature, the high likelihood of misusing power when one has it, and the effects of "democracy"—which is taken to make the majority something like an absolute monarch—then the likelihood that the laws of any given state will be considerably, and probably overwhelmingly, in violation of the schedule of rights insisted on above is tantamount to certainty.

The second nearly inevitable feature of any system of administering the law is that those who carry it out down at the consumer end will respond not to what is right but to what their superiors tell them to do. Most laws, probably all laws, are necessarily rough—'stupid' is perhaps the more accurate term. The officer will be told to arrest anyone who is doing x, the law having been passed on the assumption that x is "harmful," even though at the time and in the circumstances x is quite unlikely to harm anyone in any way. As far as the officers are concerned, x is prohibited, and so their job is to prohibit x, however indirect, imperfect, or even plainly lacking may be its connection with the sort of harm properly to be prevented. And frankly, because it is far easier to prohibit x than to actually head off danger and prevent harm, the Officers' Union will naturally rally around the idea that the real object of law is Obedience to Law and Authority.

These two problems are so likely in any real system of law that we may as well rate them inherent and inevitable features of it. And they again amount to a general problem concerning any legal system: Any such system, in brief, is inevitably coercive in ways that are not fundamentally legitimate. Thus, if the laws made by the state are wrongly coercive, and if the machinery for enforcing those laws is wrongly coercive, then it would appear to follow that the law is inevitably coercive.

The impositions of authoritative persons with their inevitable coercions might be justified if indeed there is no other effective way to ward off assorted threats to our rights. This is a familiar line of argument, which conceivably might work. That seems to me much more doubtful than is commonly thought, especially when one looks at the normally question-begging structure of the arguments put forward on behalf of that claim. But at the very least, it seems that the institutions of the law operate under a pall of probable illegitimacy.

It is an occupational hazard of those involved in it to suppose that their exercises of force are just obviously legitimate, even necessarily so; for which purpose they construct such atrocious ideologies as those analyzed by Ladd (Chapter 1). It seems to me the part of wisdom to appreciate that just the opposite is much more nearly the truth; though what the appropriate remedy is, or if indeed there is any, is not easy to say, and certainly will not be gone into here!

In his fascinating book *Facing Social Revolution* (1987), Powelson argues that the problems of the poor in this world are largely due to the imposition of violence or what amounts to it: specifically, the sort of violence wielded by governments, be they of the "right" or the "left." "History—ancient, medieval, and what is going on right now—tells us that coercive governments always oppress, no matter what they say in advance and no matter how they behave when they first take power." (Powelson, 1987, 120). Perhaps we can add, on reflection, that this is no surprise.

12

VIOLENCE, LAW, AND BASIC RIGHTS

Carl Wellman

VIOLENCE AS THE VIOLATION OF RIGHTS

Our subject, "Law and the Legitimation of Violence," is a large and convoluted one. Only collectively can we hope to illuminate it to any significant degree. A single contributor, like myself, would do best to confine himself to some small portion of the philosophical issues involved. Because the only thing I know very much about is the theory of rights, I shall explore the relations between violence and basic rights.

The *Oxford English Dictionary* (OED) reminds us that the original, and for some time the only, meaning of the verb 'to legitimate' was "to render (a bastard) legitimate." This suggests that, strictly speaking, legitimation is possible only when it is necessary, only when without legitimation something would remain illegitimate. Why, then, might it be thought that violence needs legitimation? It is often alleged that violence violates basic rights. Is this true?

Does Violence Violate Basic Legal Rights?

One's answer depends on precisely what one means by 'violence'. Since this word is both vague and ambiguous in ordinary language and there is no established philosophical usage, I shall propose my own stipulative definition. Although this will require me to do some gentle violence to standard English and to reject the definitions of my philosophical colleagues, I shall endeavor to remain within the range of established meanings and to select those that do not prejudice important philosophical issues.

Let us begin by observing that for our purposes the word has an excessively broad denotation. The *Oxford English Dictionary* defines violence as "force or strength of physical action or natural agents; forcible, powerful, or violent action or motion (in early use frequently connoting destructive force or capacity)" (OED, sense 3). Hurricanes, tornadoes, forest fires, and earthquakes are familiar instances of violence. Although often destructive and sometimes catastrophic, none of these can significantly be said to be illegitimate; nor is there any conceivable way in which the law might legitimate such purely natural violence. Hence, I shall limit my discussion to human acts and shall define 'violence' in its primary sense as "violent human action." What renders an action violent, strictly speaking, is that it is "characterized by the exertion of great physical force or strength; done or performed with intense or unusual force, and with some degree of rapidity; not gentle or moderate" (OED, sense 4b).

Is violence necessarily destructive? On this score ordinary language vacillates. The *Oxford English Dictionary* includes this characteristic in some of its definitions and omits it from others. I will abide by the parenthetical remark quoted above: "in early use frequently connoting destructive force or capacity." Violent actions have the capacity to injure persons or damage property simply because of their violence. Thus, they tend to be destructive but are not inevitably so.

It is not accidental that violence encompasses emotion as well as action, for violent action typically springs from violent motivation. This association becomes entrenched in our language when the word 'violence' is used to mean "vehemence of personal feeling or action; great, excessive, or extreme ardor or fervor; also violent or passionate conduct or language; passion, fury" (OED, sense 5). Although this conjunction between violent feeling and violent action is frequent and of great practical importance, it is a matter of fact and not true by definition. The professional hit man may calmly and with all too little feeling blow out the brains of his victim. Hence, I shall add no reference to motivation in my definition of violence.

But is the cool, controlled action of the hit man really violent? If I were sent by the mob, I would probably pull the trigger with so much force that I would jerk the gun and miss my target. The professional gently squeezes the trigger and blows away his victim. Again, it may require a delicate touch to plant a powerful bomb and, when one's enemy gets into the car, no great physical force to press the button that detonates the high explosives by remote control. One can understand why some philosophers have denied that such actions constitute instances of violence, but let us draw an essential distinction here. The acts of squeezing a trigger, planting a bomb, or pressing a button are not violent; the actions of shooting a person or blowing up a car with driver are paradigms of violence. They clearly fall under my definition of violence as violent action, action characterized by the exertion of great physical force, force in these instances supplied by the instruments used by the human agents.

Before we move on to more substantive issues, let us pause to take note of a potentially misleading ambiguity in the word 'violence'. Although it is most often used in its primary sense of violent action, it has quite a different meaning in the idiom "to do violence to" someone or something. In this context, it means "to outrage or violate" (OED, sense 1b). It is natural, although perhaps not safe, to assume that to violate a person is to violate one or more of her rights and that to violate an object is to violate some property right of its owner. But *if* this is true, it is true by definition and a mere tautology. It simply would not follow that violence in the primary sense I have defined violates anyone's rights at all.

Do violent actions, then, violate basic legal rights? The short answer is that some do and that others do not. Our friend the hit man does violate his victim's constitutional right to life; the public executioner who kills a duly convicted criminal sentenced to die by the electric chair does not violate his victim's legal right to life. (What one should say about the victim's moral right to life may be, of course, another story.) When an enraged husband batters his wife, he presumably violates her basic common-law right to personal security; but when one prizefighter batters another in the boxing ring, he does not violate the legal right to personal security of the opponent, who freely consented to engage in a manly sport. If a burglar breaks down the door of my house with felonious intent, she violates my constitutional and common-law right to property; if I break into my own house, after inadvertently locking myself out, I violate no one's property rights. Clearly, violence may, but need not, violate one or more legal rights.

Confining our attention to basic rights, either constitutional rights or the most fundamental common-law rights, what legal rights might violence violate? The right to life springs first to mind. Although the act of murder need not be violent, it often is. The acts of shooting someone with a high-caliber rifle or handgun, blowing someone up with a car bomb, bludgeoning a woman to death, or lynching a suspected rapist all violate the legal right to life of their respective victims. Lesser crimes such as manslaughter or negligent homicide may be committed in violent ways and also violate the right to life.

Another basic right commonly threatened by violence is the common-law right to personal security. The policeman who tries to beat a confession out of a suspect violates this right as much as the robber who beats up a woman in order to take away her purse. Forcible rape violates this right also. Let us not dwell exclusively on such sordid examples. A surgeon may violate this right if she operates on a patient without his permission. So do I if I set a row of beer cans on my garden fence and engage in target practice so as to endanger the life or limb of my neighbor. Driving recklessly at high speeds is an all-too-common sort of violent action that violates the right to personal security when done in traffic or where pedestrians are present.

Kidnappers who seize their victim and hold her for ransom, a mob that captures a suspect and carries him away to their lynching spot, and an overzealous citizen who commits a false arrest by brute force all engage in violent actions that violate the basic legal right to liberty. So does the kind but misguided neighbor who, without legal authority, subdues an emotionally disturbed but not dangerous person and forces him, struggling all the time, to go to a mental hospital.

Other violent actions, or even the same ones, frequently violate the constitutional and common-law right to property. A successful, so to speak, car bombing may violate the property right of the owner of the destroyed vehicle at the same time it violates the right to life of the driver killed. Robbery by force violates both the victim's property right and her right to personal security. A rioter who throws a Molotov cocktail into a home and a looter who smashes the window of a shop both violate property rights by their violent actions. Although the demolition crew may not violate any property right of my neighbor, who has hired them to knock down his condemned apartment building with their powerful wrecking ball, they do violate my right to property if they thereby damage my home with flying debris or scatter bricks all over my yard. On a much smaller scale, if a vagrant breaks down my back door, while I am on vacation, in order to have a place to sleep, he also violates my legal right to property.

These are violent actions that do violate rights. What of those that do not? Indeed, how can it be that many acts of violence infringe no legal right at all? Rights by their very nature presuppose two parties, the possessor of the right and some second party against whom the right holds. Thus, the creditor's right to repayment is inconceivable without some debtor who is thereby obligated to repay the amount owed. But some violent actions affect no second party and, therefore, bear on no conceivable right. If Robinson Crusoe violently shatters a boulder while clearing ground that belongs to no one, his act could not violate anyone's right. When one person fires a rifle out to sea so that the bullet falls harmlessly into the ocean, no right is relevant simply because no second party is affected in any way. And if after an especially poor game John McEnroe violently smashes his tennis racquet, there is no second party whose right might be violated.

There are also violent actions that do have victims but that violate no right because those second parties are not right holders. Hunters annually kill or maim many deer or bears, but because wild animals have no legal rights, no legal rights to life or bodily integrity are thereby violated. And because wild animals have no owners, no property right is violated either. Whether or not trees should have standing, they have no legal rights under United States law. Hence, a property owner who dynamites a huge California redwood or a giant sequoia in order to improve her view violates no legal right. Even the citizen who violently kills someone who has been declared an outlaw violates no legal right because his victim has been placed outside the protection of the law and thereby deprived of his status as a legal right-holder.

A third reason why violent action may not violate any legal right is that the second party may have forfeited the relevant right. The use of violence, even to the point of deadly force, to stop a fleeing felon violates no right because the felon, unlike someone wanted for a misdemeanor, has forfeited his or her rights to life and personal security under the common law (Perkins, 1969, 981). Presumably the woman who violently beats off a rapist also violates no right because by his wrongful attack her assailant has forfeited his legal right not to be battered.

On other occasions a violent act may violate no legal right because the right-holder has waived his or her relevant right. Thus, one boxer who batters another does not violate his opponent's right to personal security, for the latter has waived this right by consenting to participate in a manly sport. For the same reason, a wrestler who pins her opponent to the mat by brute force does not violate the legal right to liberty of the second party, whose movements are thus constrained. In a related situation, the team trainer or physician who violently jerks the dislocated arm of a football player back into place violates no right to bodily security as long as the player has consented to this medical treatment. And if after the game the football player violently shoves an oblivious child out of the way of an approaching vehicle, thereby saving her life, her presumed consent is recognized by the law as waiving her basic common-law right to personal security, a right that would otherwise have been violated.

A fifth, and probably the most common, reason why violent action may not violate any legal right is that it is not of a *kind* that violates any right-based duty. The action of one person violates a legal right of some second party only when it violates a legal duty imposed by that right. For example, an act of murder violates the victim's right to life simply because it is a violation of the legal duty not to kill imposed on others by that basic right. Notice, however, that violence does not enter into either the definition of the right to life or the duty not to kill. The premeditated killing of another human being is murder whether committed violently or by the gentlest unsuspected poisoning. Negligent homicide is equally a crime, and equally a violation of the right to life, whether or not it is perpetrated violently. When violence does enter into the definition of a crime or tort, it typically does so as an aggravating circumstance. Thus, theft by violence is robbery, not mere larceny, and assault with a deadly weapon becomes aggravated assault. None of the basic legal rights threatened by violence is defined in terms of violence, and there is no basic right under United States law not to be treated violently. When violence does violate some basic legal right, as it often does, it is because the violent action is also of another kind, such as an act of battering or killing, that does fall within the definition of some right-based legal duty. Human actions, judged simply by their violence, fall outside the kinds of acts rendered illegal by our basic rights.

Finally, a violent action may not violate a legal right because the action falls within some exception to the duty imposed by that right. A person's legal right to life imposes a duty on others not to kill one, and a person's common-law right to personal security grounds a duty of others not to batter one. An exception, however, is the legal privilege to use force, even deadly force, to prevent the commission or consummation of a serious crime (Perkins, 1969, 990). Thus, violent actions reasonably intended to prevent crime may not violate the right to life or personal security because they are legally recognized exceptions to the duties imposed by these basic legal rights. Again, the owner's right to property grounds a legal duty of others not to damage or destroy one's property. But if a fire department dynamites a house to stop the spread of a conflagration that threatens to engulf an entire city block, their act is exempted from this duty because they can plead the privilege of necessity (Prosser, 1971, 125). Accordingly, the longer answer to the question, Does violence violate basic legal rights? is that violent actions often violate the rights to life, personal security, liberty, or property, among others, but that there are at least six reasons why other violent actions may not violate these or other rights.

Does Violence Violate Basic Moral Rights?

In *A Theory of Rights* (1985) I have tried to show that moral rights are analogous to legal rights. If this is so, and some will disagree, our answer to this question should parallel our answer to the corresponding question about legal rights. More specifically, violence often does violate the basic moral rights to life, personal security, liberty, or property. Violent actions violate no moral right, however, when they affect no second party, or their victim is not a moral right-holder, or their victim has forfeited or waived the relevant right, or the violent action is not of a kind that violates any right-based duty, or it is an exception to such a duty.

I could drop the subject here, for any story I could tell about moral rights will be reminiscent of the story I have already told about legal rights. But analogous rights are not identical rights, and it will repay us to examine briefly some of the differences between the realms of law and morals. Many basic legal rights recognize and protect even more fundamental moral rights. The definition of the legal right may not, however, precisely coincide with the definition of the corresponding human right or civic right it partially and imperfectly secures. Thus, the violent lynching of a suspected murderer does not violate the victim's constitutional right to due process because this right holds only against the federal and state governments and imposes no duty of procedural justice on private individuals. But lynching presumably does violate the victim's human right to "a fair and public hearing by an independent and impartial tribunal, in the determination . . . of any criminal charge against him" (Universal Declaration, art. 10). Similarly, private acts of violence that prevent citizens from publicly expressing their political convictions do not violate their constitutional right to free speech that holds only against federal or state action. Such violence would, however, violate their basic human right to free speech, for this imposes duties on private individuals as well as on states. Again, the Supreme Court has decided that electrocution need not violate the victim's constitutional right against "cruel and unusual punishments." But it could be argued that it violates the broader human right not to be subjected to "cruel, inhuman or degrading treatment or punishment" (Universal Declaration, art. 5). Accordingly, violence that does not violate some basic legal right may violate a similar, but not identical, moral right.

Conversely, it may be that some acts of violence that do violate a legal right may not violate the comparable moral right. Consider the husband who shot his incurably ill and grievously suffering wife at her repeated and urgent request. Because consent is not a legally recognized defense against an indictment for murder, he violated her legal right to life. But perhaps that pitiable woman did waive her human right to life; at least it seems inhumane to deny this. If so, an act of violence that violated her legal right to life did not violate her moral right to life.

Some basic moral rights have no close analogues in many legal systems. These, too, might be violated by legally permissible violence. Article 21 of the Universal Declaration of Human Rights proclaims that "everyone has the right to take part in the government of his country." In countries where there is no basic right to vote, state violence to prevent the introduction of democracy presumably violates this basic moral right. The first article of the International Covenant on Civil and Political Rights reads in part, "All peoples have the right of self-determination. By virtue of that right they freely determine their political status and freely pursue their economic, social and cultural development." Even though it may be true that no legal rights of the Palestinians are violated by the violent attempts of the Israelis to prevent them from creating an independent state in the West Bank, such violence may well violate this fundamental human right. Similarly, the efforts of a colonial power to maintain its domination over another people by brute force may constitute violence that violates that people's basic moral right to self-determination. I hesitate to issue any definite pronouncements on such actions, for the nature and definition of our human and civic rights remain obscure and controversial. What is clear is that violence may violate a basic moral right even when there is no comparable legal right to be threatened by it. For this reason, if for no other, it is probably true that violence violates basic moral rights even more often than it violates basic legal rights. Nevertheless, many violent actions violate neither legal nor moral rights.

RIGHTS TO USE VIOLENCE

Now let us turn to a very different relation between violence and basic rights, the way or ways in which rights might legitimate violence. We have already observed that in its original sense the verb 'to legitimate' meant "to render (a bastard) legitimate" (OED, sense 1). In a later and broader sense applicable to human actions, it meant simply "to render lawful or legal" (OED, sense 2). Still later it came to mean "to serve as justification for" (OED, sense 3). Because not every lawful action is morally justified, we now confront a problem of interpretation. Does the concept of legitimation belong to law or morals? My reading of the illustrative quotations cited in the *Oxford English Dictionary* suggests that the verb 'to legitimate' began as a purely legal term with no moral implications whatsoever but is now used in both legal and moral discourse. This ambiguity is confirmed by the definition of the cognate adjective 'legitimate' as meaning "conformable to law or rule; sanctioned or authorized by law or right; lawful; proper" (OED, sense 2). Being conformable to law, sanctioned or authorized by law, and lawful are explicitly legal matters. But rules, right, and properness are not exclusively legal; in the last analysis, they are determined by morals rather than legislation. Therefore, I propose to distinguish between legal and moral legitimation and to discuss each in turn.

Do Basic Rights Legally Legitimate Violence?

Clearly some basic legal rights render some violent actions lawful or legal. The most obvious example is military violence. Typical acts of war are killing enemy soldiers or even civilians; wounding or injuring persons by gunfire, bombing, or other violent means; and the destruction of property. Such violent actions are lawful as long as they are within the rules of war because they fall within the privilege of public authority (Perkins, 1969, 977). Thus, many violent actions of military personnel are legally legitimated by public authority. Public authority is not itself, however, a basic right; it is an authority conferred on the members of the armed forces by Congress, when it declared war, and the president, when he or his subordinates inducted them and ordered them to fight in the service of their country. These actions were in turn authorized by the war power of the federal government under Article I, Section 8 and Article II, Section 1, of the United States Constitution. The war power is a basic right, one of the fundamental rights of every sovereign state, and it is this right that in the end legally legitimates military violence.

Another species of violence that is similarly legitimated by public authority is police violence. The police are legally authorized to use force, when necessary and to a reasonable degree, to arrest a suspect or convicted person (Perkins, 1969, 977) and to prevent the commission or consummation of a crime (Perkins, 1969, 990). In the case of serious crimes, this public authority legitimates even violent police actions. This sort of authority is conferred on the police by their state governments in virtue of the police power "reserved to the States respectively" by the Tenth Amendment. The police power is another basic constitutional right that legally legitimates violent actions.

It does not, however, legitimate any and every act of police violence. "Police power is the exercise of the sovereign right of a government to promote order, safety, health, morals, and general welfare within constitutional limits and is an essential attribute of government" (*Marshall* v. *Kansas City*, Mo., 1962). Hence, violent actions to promote ends other than order, safety, health, morals, or the general welfare, or that violate constitutional limits, are illegitimate even when performed by the police in the performance of their duties. Sociological studies show that the police often treat suspects or even potential troublemakers violently to instill respect for the police (Westley, 1970, 151). Because this is not one of the ends to be promoted by the police power, this sort of violence is not and cannot be legitimated by it. Again, punishments that are so violent as to be cruel and unusual are not legitimated by the public authority derived from the police power because they violate the Eighth Amendment.

A third basic right that legally legitimates violence is the right to self-defense. Each individual has a legal right to use all necessary and reasonable force to defend him- or herself from an unlawful act of another that threatens personal harm (Perkins, 1969, 995). Deadly force may be reasonable when it is necessary to defend one's very life, but only nonlethal force may, as a rule, be used to defend one's limbs or bodily integrity. Still, this basic legal right often legitimates violent actions, for these are often reasonable acts to defend oneself from violent attacks that threaten one with grievous bodily harm or even death.

A similar legal privilege is the defense of others (Perkins, 1969, 1019). This would render lawful any violent actions intended to defend another from harm provided that that person is the innocent victim of an unlawful attack and the violence is reasonable in light of the seriousness of the threat. There is probably not, however, any basic legal right to defend others. This legal privilege has developed gradually in the common law from more fundamental sources so that today its grounds are somewhat uncertain. Because the defense of others tends to prevent the consummation of a crime, it may be derived from the police power of the state. Alternatively, it may rest on the right to personal security of the other person whom one is defending. Either way, a basic legal right—the state's police power or the individual's right to personal security—legally legitimates reasonable violence in the defense of others. It can hardly be doubted that some basic legal rights—at least the war power, the police power, the right to self-defense, and the right to personal security—legally legitimate some sorts of violent actions.

What can be doubted is whether any *moral* rights can *legally* legitimate violence. The existence of unjust laws, even grossly unjust legal systems, reminds us that positive law does not necessarily reflect and may violate fundamental human and civic rights. Hence, the mere existence of a moral right, no matter how basic, implies nothing whatsoever about what the law of this, or any other, nation actually is. If, however, a legal system were to recognize moral rights as authoritative sources of law, then it might be possible for a basic moral right to legitimate violence, not just morally, but legally also.

On one interpretation, the Ninth Amendment does incorporate fundamental moral rights into our constitutional law. It reads: "The enumeration in the Constitution, of certain rights, shall not be construed to deny or disparage others retained by the people." What are those other rights, the unenumerated rights retained by the people? Very probably they are, or at least include, the Lockean natural rights affirmed in the Declaration of Independence. Especially relevant to our subject is the following passage:

> But when a long train of abuses and usurpations, pursuing invariably the same Object, evinces a design to reduce them under absolute Despotism, it is their right, it is their duty, to throw off such Government, and to provide new Guards for their future security.

It is not impossible that the basic moral right to revolution would, via the Ninth Amendment, legally legitimate violent actions intended to overthrow a federal or state government that had become despotic.

Of course, it is hard to imagine our Supreme Court, especially given the recent Reagan and Bush appointments, explicitly affirming any constitutional right to revolution. The only major legacy of the Ninth Amendment to our constitutional law has been the right to privacy, about as nonviolent a right as one can imagine. Historically, our courts have preferred not to invoke the Ninth Amendment because of the unbounded judicial discretion it threatens to bring with it. Developments in other legal systems, however, suggest that our judges may have been too timid.

Appeals to natural justice, including natural rights, are not uncommon in the courts of France and the Federal Republic of Germany. A much closer analogue of our Ninth Amendment, however, is found in Article 40.3 of the Constitution of the Republic of Ireland. It reads in part: "The State guarantees in its laws to respect, and, as far as practicable, by its laws to defend and vindicate the personal rights of the citizen." In the landmark decision of *Ryan* v. *Attorney General*, a decision subsequently reaffirmed by the Irish Supreme Court, Justice Kenny wrote:

> I think that the personal rights which may be invoked to invalidate legislation are not confined to those specified in Article 40 but include all those rights which result from the Christian and democratic nature of the State.

In that case, the unspecified rights to marry, to travel within the state, and to bodily integrity were given legal recognition. In a series of later cases at least seven additional moral rights have been accepted as legally relevant by the Irish courts (Heuston, 1976, 220–21).

Although I make no predictions on this score, it would be a natural development for the Irish courts at some future date to decide that at least some of the violent actions of the IRA are lawful because they are protected by the basic moral right to resist oppression, in this case the British oppression of Roman Catholics in Northern Ireland. To be sure, in *The State (Ryan)* v. *Lennon*, Justice Fitzgibbon announced:

> "The Declaration of the Rights of Man and of Citizens" by the National Assembly of France on October 5th, 1789, that "liberty, property, security, and resistance to oppression are the natural and imprescriptible rights of man," cannot be invoked to overrule the provisions of a statute enacted in accordance with the provisions of a written Constitution.

But that was in 1922, long before the 1963 decision in *Ryan* v. *Attorney General*. By 1974, in *McGee* v. *Attorney General*, Justice Walsh could confidently affirm "They [Articles 41, 42, and 43] indicate that justice is placed above the law and acknowledge that natural rights, or human rights, are not created by law but that the Constitution confirms their existence and gives them protection." Accordingly, it is now in principle possible in Ireland, and perhaps under our own Ninth Amendment, for some basic moral right to *legally* legitimate some violent actions. Now let us proceed from the familiar domain of the law to the relatively uncharted territory of morals.

Do Basic Rights Morally Legitimate Violence?

I believe, although a pacifist would not, that the state has a moral right to wage war. To be sure, this right is not unlimited, nor do its boundaries precisely coincide with those of the corresponding legal right, for example, the war power as defined in the United States Constitution. Presumably, the moral right to wage war is the right to wage a just war only. Fortunately, we can set aside for the moment the task of defining a just war. What is relevant to our present purposes is the observation that the moral right to wage a just war would morally legitimate violent military actions in a manner analogous to the way in which the constitutional war power legally legitimates military violence authorized by it. One surmises, however, that the moral right to wage war legitimates a somewhat narrower range of violent actions because of the moral limits imposed by the rules of just warfare.

There are theoretical considerations to confirm my hypothesis that morally legitimate military violence is more restricted than violence legally legitimated by the war power. The legal limits to legitimate military violence are set by municipal law, especially constitutional law, and international law. Now, the United States Constitution can and does define a federal war power broader than any plausible just war doctrine. But no such unilateral provision of positive law can redefine or broaden in any way the moral right to wage war. The international law of war consists primarily of treaties, such as the Geneva Convention of 1906 and the Hague Convention of 1907 (Akehurst, 1977, 250). Because these are contractual agreements entered into by sovereign states, they have the legal effect of waiving certain portions of the war powers of these states. And because there is a moral obligation to abide by one's agreements, they can in principle waive some portion of the moral right to wage war of any state that consents to them. Thus, the law can reduce, but cannot extend, the state's basic moral right to wage war.

Another basic right that can morally legitimate violence is the state's right to police its society. The police power reserved to the several states under the Tenth Amendment is a rights package that includes at least the power-right to make laws for its citizens by legislation and adjudication, and the liberty-right to enforce these laws by its police force with the assistance of its citizens. Let us use the verb 'to police' as shorthand for "to exercise the rights in the police power or in any analogous rights package." It seems to me, and to most moral philosophers, that any sovereign state has a basic moral right to police itself, at least if its sovereignty is morally legitimate. This moral right to police a politically organized society is the right to enact and enforce legislation provided the laws aim at some morally permissible end and are not unjust in content and are enforced by morally permissible means only. One morally legitimate purpose of legislation, among others, is to protect the basic moral rights of the citizens, and one moral limit on legislation and enforcement is that the basic moral rights of those subject to the law not be violated. Now the state can act only through its agents, including police officers authorized to enforce its laws. Thus, violent actions of the police may be morally legitimated by the state's basic moral right to police its society provided those actions are necessary to carry out the task of enforcing just laws.

What is the ground of the state's moral right to police itself? One traditional justification for this right is that the police power is essential to the sovereignty of any possible state. But because the moral legitimacy of political sovereignty could be called into question, this seems little more than a circular argument. Both the Declaration of Independence and the Declaration of the Rights of Man and of the Citizen affirm that the justifying purpose of government is the protection of the natural rights of the individual citizens. Although I doubt that this is either the only or the ultimate ground of the basic moral rights of the state, I do believe that it is at least one ground of the moral right of the state to police itself. If so, this helps to define the content of this right. If the right to police is grounded on the rights of the citizens, it can morally legitimate police violence that protects these rights but not violence that invades them.

The American and French Declarations both presuppose a social contract theory of political sovereignty. Should we accept this theoretical framework and ground the basic rights of the state on a contract with or among its citizens? I think not. The difficulties inherent in every attempt to establish the existence of any actual social contract are notorious and, to my mind, insurmountable. Although hypothetical contract theories evade this problem, they must confront the equally difficult challenges of specifying in some nonprejudicial way the original position and demonstrating in some convincing manner precisely what the terms of the hypothetical contract would be under the ideal, that is, imaginary, conditions of the original position. Worse yet, I fail to see how this is the appropriate sort of argument to establish the grounds of moral rights. It seems much more at home when applied to the principles of just social institutions than when used to ground noninstitutional moral rights. Finally, this appeal to a social contract seems unnecessary. Why not ground the basic moral rights of the state directly on the even more fundamental moral rights of the individuals protected by state action?

The very nature of moral rights suggests this more direct justification for the state's moral right to police its society. The concept of a right defines three distinct roles (Wellman, 1985, 96–102). There is the role of the possessor of the right, the party on whom the right, if respected, confers some specific domain of dominion. There is the role of the second party against whom the right holds, the party on whom it imposes duties, liabilities, and disabilities. And there is the role of third parties in a position to intervene in any confrontation between the right holder and some second party threatening to violate her right. The state is such a third party and as such has a right to act to protect the fundamental moral rights of the individuals within its sphere of influence. Because one of the main ways in which a state can and should secure the human and civic rights of its citizens is by enacting and enforcing just laws, it has a basic moral right to police its society in this manner.

Individual citizens are as often in a position to play the third-party role implicit in basic moral rights as is the state. Hence, by an argument analogous to the one I have just given to ground the state's moral right to police its society, one can ground the basic moral right of the citizen to intervene to prevent the violation of the moral rights of other citizens. Here we find united, and on the more fundamental moral level, the two lines of reasoning we noticed earlier in the common law concerning the defense of others. Some courts have interpreted the defense of others to be an extension of the police power of the state to the citizen acting as a posse; others have reasoned directly from the right of personal security of the other person being defended to the liberty of the citizen to act to protect that right. The truth seems to be that the right of the individual citizen to intervene to prevent the violation of a basic moral right is grounded on the third-party role implicit in that right in the same way that the state's right to police is grounded on that role.

The most difficult, even awkward, problem confronting any moral philosopher like myself who asserts a moral right of the citizen to act to protect the moral rights of other citizens is to define the precise limits of this right. The right I have in mind is much more limited and oriented toward different practices than the similar right Locke ascribes to individuals in a state of nature.

> And that all men may be restrained from invading others' rights, and from doing hurt to one another, and the law of nature be observed, which willeth the peace and preservation of all mankind, the execution of the law of nature is in that state put into every man's hand, whereby every one has a right to punish the transgressors of that law to such a degree as may hinder its violation. (Locke, 1937, 7)

There are, however, serious disadvantages to conceding to private individuals any very broad liberty to enforce the moral law, especially by the use of violent force. Any such attempt is apt to be biased by the perspective of the individual and is likely to call forth an equally violent response. Accordingly, I would limit the moral right of the individual to intervene to prevent the violation of any moral right of another to situations in which there is a clear and present danger of violation of an important moral right and to actions that are a reasonable means of directly preventing the threatened violation and that use only that degree of force necessary to this end. This would exclude any attempt of individual citizens to punish past violations in order indirectly to protect rights by deterring similar violations in the future. Unfortunately, I am unable at this time to give a more precise definition of this right. Presumably it is broad enough to legitimate morally some violent actions of the citizen when defending a basic moral right against a severe threat; surely it will not legitimate any and every act of violence intended to protect a moral right.

What is the relation between the state's right to police its society and the citizen's right to protect the rights of other citizens? The state's right does not replace or extinguish the right of the individual as Locke believed.

> But because no political society can be or subsist without having in itself the power to preserve the property, and, in order there-unto, punish the offenses of all those of that society, there, and there only, is political society, where every one of the members has quitted this natural power (to preserve his rights and judge and punish offenders), resigned it up into the hands of the community in all cases that exclude him not from appealing for protection to the law established by it. (Locke, 1937, 56)

I do not believe that the state's right to police is conferred on society by any act whereby the citizens transfer their individual rights to the sovereign to act as their political agent. There is no historical evidence to suggest that any such actual social contract has been entered into by the citizens in our or almost any other society. Nor should one postulate any such hypothetical contract, for it would be irrational for all individuals to agree to it. It is not necessary for the individual citizens to give up their moral right to protect the basic moral rights of others, at least when defined as narrowly as I have defined it, in order to leave room for the state's moral right to police its society. And because no state can guarantee the complete security of individual rights, any society in which the citizens contracted to give up their individual right to intervene to protect moral rights would leave many individuals on many occasions with no one to defend their basic moral rights.

At the same time, the state's right to police, if effectively exercised, does reduce the number of occasions on which the individual's right to prevent the violation of the rights of others can morally legitimate violent actions. This is because it is a right to use only necessary force, and violence is less often necessary to protect moral rights when law and order prevail in a society.

The state's moral right to police also reduces by morally legitimate state regulation the extent of the citizen's moral right to intervene to prevent the violation of the moral rights of others. Laws will prohibit many sorts of intervention by private individuals, and if these are just laws, there is a moral duty of the citizen not to disobey them. Because a moral liberty consists in the absence of any contrary moral duty, this duty to obey just laws of one's society will limit the citizen's liberty-right to use force, including violent force, to protect the moral rights of others.

A fourth basic right capable of morally legitimating violent actions is the individual's moral right to self-defense. This fundamental human right is analogous to, although it need not coincide with, the citizen's legal right to self-defense. Hence, it can morally legitimate violent actions of the individual to defend her life or limb in a manner analogous to that in which the corresponding constitutional and common-law right legally legitimates some sorts of violence.

Can the law restrict or reduce the capacity of the moral right of self-defense to legitimate violence as in something like the way it can narrow the range of violent actions legitimated by the moral right to intervene to prevent the violation of the rights of others? I am inclined to think not, at least as far as defense of life goes, although I am not confident that I can explain why this should be so. Perhaps the reason is that to impose a moral duty on any individual to refrain from defending his or her very life would be to demand a morally excessive sacrifice. In any event, even Hobbes denied that his absolute sovereign has any power to extinguish or limit the individual's natural right to preserve his or her life from an immediate threat. It is probably true, however, that the law can narrow the moral right to self-defense in other respects, for example by laws prohibiting the use of violence to defend oneself from lesser threats to bodily injury.

Could the law extend the moral right to self-defense? The state of Oklahoma has recently expanded its legal right to self-defense by enacting its controversial "Make My Day" law to permit its citizens to use deadly force to protect their homes from intruders.

> Under existing statutory and case law, deadly force may be used only when necessary to prevent a felony or when serious bodily injury or death is threatened. The new law provides that deadly force may be used against an intruder who has unlawfully entered the dwelling as long as the "occupant has a reasonable belief that such other person might use any physical force, no matter how slight, against any occupant of the dwelling." (Smith, 1988, 542–43)

Since Oklahoma treats its defense of dwelling law as an aspect of its law of self-defense, this new legislation expands the legal right to self-defense of the citizens of that state. It does not thereby extend the individual's moral right to self-defense, however, because it ignores the moral requirement of proportionality, the requirement that the degree of force employed in self-defense be reasonable in the light of the severity of the threatened harm to oneself. Accordingly, the law is only a secondary factor in determining when or how the individual's basic moral right of self-defense can morally legitimate violence.

It appears, then, that there are at least four basic rights that can morally legitimate violence. These are the state's moral right to wage war, the state's moral right to police its society, the moral right of the citizen to intervene to prevent the violation of the moral rights of other citizens, and the human right to self-defense. Exactly what sorts of violent actions these basic rights morally legitimate depends primarily on their precise definitions, but to a lesser degree this may be modified by the content of just law as well as the effectiveness of its enforcement in the society.

We have been exploring the relations between violence and basic rights. I have argued that violence needs legitimation because it often, although not always, violates basic rights, either legal or moral rights. I have also explained how basic rights can legitimate some sorts of violent actions.

What is the role of law in legitimating violence? It is the law and the law alone that legally legitimates violent actions in any society. Thus, it is typically basic legal rights that legitimate violence legally. But some basic moral rights might, if and only if they are legally recognized, contribute to the legal legitimation of violence.

The moral legitimation of violence is another, although parallel, story. It is primarily basic moral rights that can morally legitimate violence. However, positive law can modify this capacity in several ways. When the law effectively protects basic moral rights, it is less often necessary to resort to violence to exercise or to protect those rights. When the law justly prohibits certain sorts of violent actions, basic moral rights may no longer morally legitimate these sorts of violence. What the law cannot do, however, is expand the range of violent actions morally legitimated by basic rights. For this we may be grateful, at least if our legislators and judges are conscientious persons.

PART THREE

Controversial Instances of Allegedly Legitimate Violence

The essays in this section continue the discussion of the justification of violence. The virtue of the discussion here is that the consideration of this question is not in the abstract terms of some of the earlier papers, for example those of Bernhard Waldenfels and Carl Wellman, but in relation to specific instances in which some practice or institution that involves violence is at stake. Hugo Bedau and André Maury question the justification of violence in the institution of punishment. Bedau's conclusion is that punishment, involving an essential element of violence, is justified because no alternative that protects the rights of the innocent is feasible. Maury's conclusion is that while punishment can be justified on a theory that treats rights as conventional or conditional, a true natural-rights theory cannot ever justify the punitive violence done to the offender. Virginia Held, using as her method a comparison of the severity of rights violations, argues that even terrorist forms of violence can be justified, if state violence to preserve the status quo can be, in order to achieve a more just society. Lance Stell argues that killing even a sleeping man may be justified as self-defense by a woman "suffering" from "battered-woman syndrome." Because these chapters deal with specific examples of justification, they are bound to be controversial as well as enlightening.

The issues involved here provide the opportunity to make explicit a distinction between justification and excuse. Both a justification and an excuse provide the accused person with a defense, in law as well as morality; but they do so in different ways and for different reasons. Quite briefly, to claim a justification is to claim that, under the circumstances, no wrong has been done. In contrast, when one advances an excuse, the claim is not that the conduct was right or permissible or warranted, but that the agent should not be held accountable, or not fully accountable, for the harm. Actions are justified; agents are excused. There is a good deal of contemporary interest in the justification/excuse distinction (see for example Fletcher, 1978; Robinson, 1984), inspired initially, perhaps, by Austin's (1961) discussion of these different defenses in "A Plea for Excuses." It is important to see that these defenses are distinct and that there are different implications for the "legitimation" of violence depending on which track, justification or excuse, one follows.

Justifications are in their very nature controversial. One is claiming, under a justification, that no wrong is done. It follows that any force opposed to justifiable force is illegitimate. If, for example, one is exercising lethal force in justifiable self-defense, any force that might be used to oppose that force is illegitimate. Parties to a dispute, therefore, are likely to disagree about whose force is justifiable and whose force is illegitimate. Justifications seem to admit no middle ground. So it is easy to see how the different perspectives on justifications may quickly lead to the endless cycle of violence and counterviolence described by Wolgast.

An attractive proposal is to argue that those who do violence should confess the inadequacy of their action and beg to be excused, rather than to claim justification. A more radical proposal that might be considered is to abandon the quest for justifications altogether and to argue that only excuses can be used as a defense to the charge of having used violence. These proposals have several advantages. Violence would always be categorized as wrong. Those engaged in violence might be excused, that is, the person might receive the benefit of exoneration, but the legitimacy of violence itself would never be asserted. Self-righteousness would thereby be limited, because an excuse is always based on the admission of some defect, such as ignorance or inability. Excuses also more readily admit of repentance, forgiveness, and reconciliation than do justifications. A justification is the claim that what was done was warranted. While the necessity of engaging in violence, under a justification, may be regretted, it is difficult to see how repentance would be in order. And reconciliation may be quite difficult if one still maintains that what one did was not wrong. All these considerations ought to lead, whenever possible, to offering excuses rather than justifications, and they lead philosophically to the question of whether we might do away with justifications for violence altogether.

Would it be possible, then, to abolish justifications and rely only on excuses? Maury argues in Chapter 14 that the institution of punishment may be justified only on theories that hold rights to be conventional or conditional, and he distinguishes between "conventional-" and "natural-rights" theories. One distinction is that the existence of conventional rights depends on a condition of others recognizing them. Another distinction is that, for Maury, natural rights are "unconditional" in another sense: They are inalienable. He discusses, for example, Locke's theory of natural rights to show that on Locke's theory, rights are "conditional" in the second sense and so not as "natural" as often supposed. On Maury's interpretation of a natural-rights theory no justification is possible. One cannot say that the criminal has by the crime forfeited or lost natural rights. Because natural rights are part of the definition of what it is to be a person, any punitive violence that overrides those rights treats the criminal as less than human. He does suggest, however, that while punishment can never be justified on a natural-rights theory, it may be excused.

Let us consider the position of the natural-rights theorist as described by Maury, who can only excuse but never justify the violence inherent in punishment. There may, of course, be past cases of punishment that, one might excuse; for example, one might argue that the execution of witches in the Middle Ages was due to excusable ignorance. It is difficult to see how the present, continuing system of punishment, which involves the intentional infliction of harm on the offender, could only be excused. One would have to view a system of punishment from some distance to be able to say that it should be excused. From a contemporary viewpoint, it would seem that the institution of punishment is to be either condemned or justified.

Bedau's essay (Chapter 13) is a powerful argument for the claim that punitive violence is indeed justified. Bedau is interested in the violence conceptually implied by punishment. The very concept of punishment implies the intentional infliction of harm on offenders. He considers several possible alternatives to punishment: substituting a system of rewards for not violating the law for the present system of sanctions for violations; forgiving offenders rather than punishing them; substituting a system of treatment, such as Lady Wootton has proposed, for a punitive system; "symbolic" punishment or denunciation.

His conclusion, based on certain empirical assumptions, is that the institution of punishment neither can nor should be eliminated and that the element of violence implicit in it is inevitable and justified. The key argument here is that punishment is more efficacious than any alternative in reducing the level of violations of the moral rights of the innocent. This is not an excuse for the violence in punishment, but a justification.

Held's essay (Chapter 15) is also concerned with justifications rather than excuses. Can a violation of the rights of some to secure the rights of others ever be justified? She envisages an example in which this might be the case. Consider two situations of a society. In a set of circumstances that could emerge from a typical political confrontation, which she labels "situation S_1," the human rights of members of one group, A, to x are effectively respected, but the human rights of members of another group, B, are not. In an alternative set of circumstances, S_2, the human rights to x are respected for members of both groups. If violations of rights of members of group A are necessary to transform society from S_1 to S_2, would this be justified? Her argument, subject to empirical findings, is that terrorism to bring about a more just society is justified on a principle of a comparison of rights violations. That is, if it is necessary to violate the rights of some by terrorism in order to bring about a more just society for all, it is more justifiable to violate the rights of those who have not been the subject of past rights violations. The victims of the oppressive system have suffered and continue to suffer rights violations. It is only fair, if necessary to bring about a more just society for all, to violate the rights of members of a group who have not suffered rights violations than to maintain the status quo and continue the rights violations of the oppressed. Held's argument is controversial because it is an argument about justification. Terrorist violence is not merely excused, but justified.

Stell in Chapter 16 considers the justification/excuse distinction in relation to a very specific situation involving individuals and not institutions. Should battered-woman syndrome be treated only as an excuse or should it be a justificatory defense? Courts have admitted expert testimony on battered-woman syndrome in support of a plea of insanity. This would be to treat the condition as relevant to an excuse; the woman suffering from such a syndrome is not to be held responsible, or fully responsible, for her actions because of a defect in the agent. She is not justified in the killing. Even in the circumstances, the killing is still wrong. Stell's argument is that a woman "suffering" from such a syndrome may have a "reasonable belief" that she is in "imminent danger" just because she is in constant danger, so that she may be *justified* in killing her abuser even while he is asleep. His essay does raise the controversial question of whether in these cases there should be an acquittal on self-defense grounds and not only an acquittal, or conviction of a lesser offense, on an excusing defense such as mental impairment. If these cases do fit into the traditional self-defense category, as Stell attempts to show, then it does seem prejudicial to exclude them from the category of justification.

A common thread in the essays by Bedau, Held, and Stell is the argument that justification is appropriate in some cases of violence. These essays are thus controversial because, as we noted earlier, the claim that one has a justification for violence is challenging in a way that a plea of excuse is not. All these essays may inspire further consideration of justificatory defenses in general. The essays do seem to show that we cannot eliminate all justifications in favor of excuses.

The essays by Held and Bedau are important in another respect. Too often discussions about the justifiability of violence take place with little consideration of the empirical findings necessary to support normative conclusions (see Brady, 1983). Both Held and Bedau identify the empirical findings necessary to support their conclusions and acknowledge that their positions are subject to change should the empirical assumptions turn out to be false. More needs to be done on empirical investigations, but that, perhaps, as Held suggested during the discussion of these essays, is the subject of another project.

13

PUNITIVE VIOLENCE AND ITS ALTERNATIVES

Hugo Adam Bedau

PUNISHMENT, VIOLENCE, AND COERCION

Violence as Essential to Punishment

Punitive violence comes in three major forms. One is the notorious abuses to which offenders are subjected while they are in the hands of the criminal justice system but that are not part of the punishment to which they were sentenced. These abuses, not authorized by law, are sometimes so extreme that judges have refused to sentence youthful offenders to prison lest they be victimized by hardened convicts. Other abuses have led other judges to condemn whole prison systems as "cruel and unusual punishment," in violation of the Constitution. I shall have no more to say about abuses of this sort. A second kind of punitive violence is the cruel and harsh modes of punishment authorized by statute and familiar from the history of punitive institutions: maiming, branding, flogging, forced labor, solitary confinement, and, of course, the death penalty in all its various forms. Violence of these sorts and their replacement by less brutal methods are also not my concern in these remarks.

Instead, I am preoccupied solely with the violence that seems to be essential to punishment itself. Our traditional conception of punishment is one in which harm to the convicted offender—whether that harm is described as "evil" (as by Hobbes, [1651] 1968, 353) or as "deprivation of rights" (as by Rawls, 1955, 10)—is essential to anything that can properly be called a punishment. Utilitarians and retributivists, who disagree about so much concerning punishment, agree on this: Punishments are like crimes in intentionally causing harm to the offender. This must be so for the utilitarian, because otherwise no punishment could accomplish either its incapacitative or deterrent effects, on which the utilitarian relies. And it must be so for the retributivist, because otherwise no punishment could pay back to the offender what the offender deserves for victimizing the innocent.

Since it is the harm or violence essential to punishment that I want to discuss, and not the harm or violence incidental to its infliction—the kind of harm that counts as an abuse or violation of the convicted offender's own rights—my focus is on two main questions. First, is it possible to get rid of punishment entirely, thereby eliminating the violence essential to this practice? (Cf. Bianchi and van Swaaningen, 1986; Ross, 1975, 67–100.) Second, is it really true that harm, deprivation, and violence are essential to whatever counts as punishment—or is punitive nonviolence no oxymoron but only a sadly and badly neglected option?

The Immorality of Coercion

I want to begin my approach to the first question by considering the kind of argument that a pacifist anarchist would direct against the very idea of punishment for crimes. The anarchist challenges us to justify in general the authority of some over others, and in particular of the state and its government over its citizens, because of the way those in authority use force, threats, and coercion to secure compliance. The target of the anarchist's concern of interest to us is the enactment and enforcement of laws that impose a liability to punishment when the laws are inexcusably or unjustifiably violated (Ritter, 1980, 72–76). What the anarchist must do is convince us that, on moral grounds, no one ever has or can acquire authority over another to *prohibit* conduct, however harmful, unfair, or ruinous to others it may be, and—even if this were false—that whatever authority some have over others, it never entitles them to *enforce* such prohibitions, should they be violated, with punitive methods. These two propositions raise several familiar questions, among them these three: Is using force against other persons always wrong? Or is it always wrong at least when it violates the person's autonomy? Are there no norms of sufficient importance that enforcing them to secure (not perfect but a reasonable level of) compliance is worth the costs necessary to do so?

It is difficult to see on what grounds a person should object to the use of force by one person against another when both parties have knowingly and voluntarily consented to it. If we believed otherwise, then we would have to regard such games as football, wrestling, or boxing as immoral. Even some requested medical treatments would have to be condemned. The usual grounds for objection to coercion are that the coerced person has not consented (e.g., is in a coma), or that the harm done would be so extreme that it cannot be rationally permitted (e.g., gladiatorial contests). But when these standard nullifying conditions are absent, there is little or no basis for interfering with the use of coercion or force by one person against another. Interpersonal violence gets the deservedly bad name that it has because its use is not always or even typically confined to cases of adequately informed mutual consent. As such, however, interpersonal violence is as morally indeterminate as interpersonal touching or interpersonal talking. Either of these, too, taken to extreme lengths (sexual harassment, defamation) can become morally objectionable; but they need not be.

The violence and liability thereto that the practice of punishment involves is suspect, I believe, because it seems so obviously to violate the autonomy of the person being punished. Rare is the offender who knowingly and freely consents to (much less seeks) punishment, who believes (as Socrates taught) that he or she will be better off by undergoing the pains of deserved punishment than by avoiding them. No wonder Kant, who taught us to value personal autonomy, went out of his way to try to show how the criminal not merely deserves punishment but in fact "wills" it, thereby relieving society of the charge that punishment violates the autonomy of the punished criminal.

But this heroic line of argument will not work. It is impossible to establish that the punishments imposed on those judged guilty of crimes are yet freely and knowingly willed—sought and chosen—by offenders, except in those rare cases (as in a Dostoevskian novel) where the offender manages to convince us that, indeed, they are. Instead, we have to argue that despite appearances to the contrary, punishing the offender either does not violate the offender's autonomy; or that, although it does, this does not suffice to make punishment in principle a wrongful use of coercion (even if excessive or cruel punishment of course would be). I believe the latter alternative is true, because it relies on the proposition that it is unfair to refuse to punish offenders.

It seems grossly unfair that some members of society should have to endure victimization—the violation of their rights at the hands of others—when the latter are free from any liability to punishment for having committed these violations. Yet this is precisely the license that this version of the anarchist argument would extend. The contemplation of such impunity is especially aggravating when there is reason to believe that some of these violations might have been prevented by nothing more than the liability to punishment plus moderately effective law enforcement. The anarchist, through excessive respect for the autonomy of the offender, in effect asks the rest of society to tolerate the risk of victimization, quite forgetting that this victimization is itself a violation of autonomy. Surely, if anything destroys or threatens one's autonomy it is the event of becoming another's victim. Crime, in violating my rights, not only violates my liberty, privacy, security, or other rights, but my autonomy as well. How can the anarchist fail to see this? Perhaps through believing that *any* form of forceful prevention or response (or the threat thereof) by the state is morally more objectionable than the violence the offender inflicts. This is not a popular doctrine, and it is not hard to see why. Nor is it possible to see how it could be persuasively argued, except by a nihilistic appeal to the moral worthlessness of the laws for which liability to punishment is imposed (a point to which I return in the paragraphs below).

A more forthright argument would be that in the long run, a system of punishment causes more harm and suffering than it prevents—an argument available to the anarchist only if the anarchist is also something of a utilitarian. But is such an empirical claim true? Few think so. Even if it were true, it seems to be the wrong sort of argument. For it would treat as equal in value a given quantity of undeserved harm suffered by an innocent victim and a comparable quantity of deserved harm suffered by a guilty offender. This presumed equivalence offends our intuitions of fairness to the innocent. Our sensitivity to the pain and deprivation typical of punishments should not be at the cost of blindness or indifference to the undeserved and frequently graver pain and loss endured by the victims of crime in the first place.

So the most that can be conceded to the anarchist is that in many, perhaps the majority of cases, coercion and the threat thereof are not in fact needed to secure compliance with the law, thus obviating recourse to punishment in many cases. But this cautious generalization, even if conceded, would not go far enough to warrant the elimination of punishment.

THE UNAVOIDABILITY OF PUNISHMENT

The Invalidity of Legal Norms

A related line of attack is to argue that there are no laws, rules of conduct, or norms of sufficient validity and importance to warrant trying to secure compliance with them by a system of punishment. It is important to take this nihilistic claim seriously. Were we to deny or seriously doubt the rough justice of the criminal law and yet continue to punish its violators, punishment would have been turned into a weapon of immoral violence. Of course, only the extreme nihilist is likely to go so far as to deny that there are any laws worth trying to enforce. The rest of us hold the conventional view that laws against murder, assault, arson, and the like— roughly, "the minimum content of natural law," as H. L. A. Hart (1961, 189) has called it—are of sufficient importance to human interests that it is worth some sustained effort to secure general compliance with them, including the use of liability to punishment, the coercive force of threats, and the violence of punishment itself as disincentives to their violation. It remains true, of course, that we could eliminate punishment if we would eliminate crimes; when there are no crimes—no norms whose violations are deemed criminal—nothing can count as their violation. Crime and punishment, to this extent, take in each other's washing. But the decision to regard all acts currently deemed criminal as no longer worthy of that designation, and to do so on purportedly moral grounds, is absurd.

We must insist, nevertheless, that to the extent the laws we enforce are not themselves just, or not capable of fair enforcement, we place in jeopardy the moral authority to punish anyone for their violation. We can all think of cases where conduct regarding sexual, political, and religious practices, for example, has been required (or forbidden) by the criminal law but where there is no moral authority for doing so. Conversely, the failure to enact criminal laws prohibiting environmental pollution and the failure to enforce laws against corporate crime, for example, place in doubt the seriousness and fairness of society's concern to protect the innocent and defend the rights of all equally. Such convictions as these, however, hardly qualify as concessions to the anarchist or nihilist.

The Possibility of Eliminating Crime

Consideration of the nihilistic version of the anarchist's argument against punishment suggests another line of reasoning by which to undermine a necessary condition of punishment. Whereas the nihilist attacks the liability to punishment, one might instead attack the eligibility for punishment. Punishment could be eliminated if no one were eligible for punishment; and no one would be if no crimes were committed. Without criminal acts (or omissions), there is no occasion to impose on anyone the deprivations characteristic of punishment.

Valid though this reasoning is, its impact is canceled by each of two very different reasons. One is the empirical point that there is little likelihood this eventuality will ever come to pass. It is too obviously one of those kinds of arguments for eliminating punishment that depends on empirical contingencies that are utterly improbable. The Bible assures us that the poor we shall always have with us. The rest of human experience tells us the same sobering lesson regarding lawbreakers, criminals, and the vicious who prey on the innocent and vulnerable.

The other objection, a conceptual one, is more important, even if only slightly less obvious. Even if tomorrow we could be assured that there would be no more crimes, and thus no one to punish, this would not by itself be enough of a reason for eliminating the practice or institution of punishment. We need to know more about why crime has ceased. Is it because opportunity for crime—thanks to target hardening, and social defense in general—has diminshed to zero? Is it because criminogenic factors—unemployment, anomie, and so on—have been eliminated? Is it because inclination and motivation have shifted, so that crime no longer holds out the prospect of excitement and easy profit? Or is it because liability to punishment has at last succeeded in discouraging every prospective defender from acting on criminal desires? The essence of the practice of punishment is creating the liability to punishment in the first place, in preserving the capacity to carry out punishment on those who incur that liability, and in making this capacity credible. Many would argue that the best way to go about assuring ourselves that we never actually have to punish anyone is to create liability to punishment for everyone who violates the law, and then to use this liability as the basis for convincing threats.

We have here in capsule form the visionary dream of every advocate of the deterrent use of penalties, from Beccaria to former Attorney General Meese: Make the liability to punishment so general, the eligibility conditions for its infliction so minimal, the severity of the punishments so acute, and the threat of their infliction so prompt and certain, that no one of right mind (i.e., no one not insane or without some other valid excuse) will commit a crime. Thus, in the present context, the very condition necessary to guarantee that no one is ever punished turns out (or may well turn out to be) a consequence of vigorous law enforcement and the threat of swift and even savage punishments. Were we to eliminate punishment in the sense that no one is in fact eligible for it, that might well be because we had left intact the entire system of punitive liability, poised always on the brink of application should anyone be so foolish as to bring down its sanctions on his or her head.

The Necessity of Liability to Punishment

This line of reasoning brings us into direct encounter with the fundamental issue posed by the project before us. This is whether the liability to punishment (coupled, perhaps, with the experience of being punished, or seeing others punished) is a necessary condition of developing a sense of public justice, including respect for the law and for the rights of others that the law is designed to protect. We live as though we knew that conformity to the law can be secured only by general deterrence, the inculcation of obedience through a rational calculation, that is, the belief by prospective offenders that they would suffer more harm through the punishment they risk for their criminal conduct than through their frustration in not securing illicit gains by violating the law. Such an approach forever regards the law as essentially an alien presence, something the classic contractarian thinkers (Locke, Rousseau, Kant) denied. Yet others, such as Gibbs (1982), have argued that the very development of conscience itself, internalized self-constraints that yield unalienated conformity to law, depends on a background of adverse sanctions for noncompliance. Unless this latter view is wrong—and it is clearly a question of fact whether it is—liability to punishment and to that extent the practice of punishment is ineliminable from human experience. We must ask, therefore, what are the alternative forms of social control that dispense with coercion and thus with punishment, even in the background, and yet can be counted on to achieve socialization and the internalization of the norms required for a just society. Only if there are such alternatives is punishment eliminable. To persist in punishment despite the known availability of such alternatives would testify to a deep perversity in human nature. (Of course, if human nature is deeply perverse and punishment one of the forms this perversity takes, punishment would then have been proved to be ineliminable for this reason.)

We must start with the fact that there seems to be the universal belief that without sanctions for violations, society would be unable to secure conformity with its norms. At least since Durkheim, as Toby (1964) makes clear, sociologists and criminologists have taken this principle as virtually an axiom of their sciences. Thus, all current studies of the deterrent effect of penalties begin by tacitly assuming that there is such an effect, and, therefore, the only problem is to measure differential deterrence (e.g., of a given pair of alternative punishments with respect to a certain class of possible offenders over a given time and in a given place). It is, of course, impossible to infer from the failure of punishment to deter in a given case, or to provide a desired level of deterrence, that punishment has no deterrent effect whatever. But the central issue is not whether a system of criminal law controls mainly via general deterrence, or even whether it exerts enough control to warrant a defense of punitive measures mainly on such grounds. For we know that conformity to law can be explained by reference to any of several patterns of motivation distinguishable from general deterrence, of which three—enculturation, habit, and internalization of norms (see Gibbs, 1975, 57–93)—are especially important in this context. The central issue is whether these mechanisms (enculturation, etc.) would develop at all, or develop as effectively (as rapidly, widely, durably, etc.) as they do, without the liability to sanctions for violation of norms anywhere in the social background and experience of those whose moral development is in question. This is the absolutely vital issue for the general elimination of punishment.

There are, to be sure, studies of moral development (e.g., Howell and Willis, 1989) that purport to show that internalized self-restraints growing out of genuine respect and affection for others and resulting in conformity to the requirements of social life in no way depend on the availability, even in the background, of the liability to punishment for nonconformity. But there is no evidence that such effects can be achieved in existing modern, industrialized and postindustrialized societies on a scale necessary to socialize the entire population of a nation. Anomie, temptation, inequality, relative deprivation, opportunity for illicit gain, low risk of detection and conviction, all would contribute to the defeat of any large-scale experiment to test this hypothesis in our society. Perhaps as a matter of empirical fact, the practice of punishment is thus ineliminable from modern society, and the transformations necessary to permit its elimination would themselves so totally alter modern societies as to make them unrecognizable—or uninhabitable by us. These conjectures apart, one must conclude that at present there are no adequate answers to the empirical questions now before us. We simply do not know whether societies like ours could, if they seriously tried, secure compliance with a just system of laws by nothing more than nonpunitive methods of social control.

In order to shed further light on this complex problem, I propose in the remainder of this paper to examine several such alternatives to punishment. (Not all of them are reasonably described as "methods of social control," however.) Unfortunately, what we know about how each operates is acutely affected by the fact that punishment is always a background factor; we have little or no experience with these alternatives in a social environment where the practice of punishment is unknown, in disuse, or rare. It also emerges that part of the problem in answering the question of whether punishment can be eliminated in favor of these alternatives is a certain vagueness in the very idea of punishment itself, a vagueness that has been suppressed in this discussion until now. Obviously, we cannot eliminate punishment or provide alternatives to it without knowing (or deciding) what is to count as punishment, and why. It is time now to undertake this part of the task.

PROSPECTS FOR NONVIOLENT ALTERNATIVES

Replacing Punishments with Rewards

By far the most radical alternative to punishment is the one addressed to everyone before any become offenders. It is the idea of using rewards or other incentives for compliance to replace punishment for noncompliance. The idea is at least as old as Jeremy Bentham's now largely forgotten book *The Rationale of Reward* (1825). It was popularized in another form more recently by B. F. Skinner in his didactic utopian novel *Walden Two* (1948). Skinner's ideal society was the product of adult efforts at rearing the young by means of exhortations and example, patience and praise, encouragement and reward, but not punishment. "We don't punish," Skinner's spokesman, Frazier, proudly declared. "We never administer an unpleasantness in the hope of repressing or eliminating undesirable behavior" (p. 92). Skinner thus viewed punishment (see also Skinner, 1971, 66) much as Marx viewed the state after the demise of capitalism and the onset of communism: It could be counted on to wither away.

It is tempting to dwell on the attractive features of this alternative to punishment. But there are grave problems, and it suffices here to consider only two of them. First, on cost–benefit or utilitarian grounds, punishment may well get the nod over the alternative of reward. As Bentham pointed out nearly two centuries ago, the cost of an effective system of reward (used as an alternative to punishment) in conjunction with the complexities of its administration would be staggering. The basic idea of such a system is that the government would undertake to pay each person in some kind of coin—money, food stamps, retirement credits, praise, whatever—every time the person does not commit a crime. In this way the desirable prospects of reward would serve as a positive incentive to comply with the law, replacing the undesirable prospect of punishments that serve as disincentives (or "aversive reinforcers," in the jargon of operant conditioning) to the same end. So far so good. But practical and theoretical problems immediately arise. Because the opportunities for crime in a modern society are enormously varied and virtually infinite, the occasions on which most people act (or could act, or have a motive to act) in a manner *not* in violation of the criminal law are comparably infinite. How are we to allocate rewards, given the range and variety of criminal acts *not* performed for which some kind of reward would be the appropriate response? By contrast, it seems much simpler to confine our efforts (as we do under a punishment system) to apprehending those who intentionally violate the criminal law, at worst a relatively small percent of the population, and mete out to them (in Ignatieff's telling phrase) "a just measure of pain" (Ignatieff, 1978). Even if sin or crime is not its own punishment, it may be best to inculcate the idea that virtue, and nothing more, is its own reward.

The other objection worth considering directs our attention to the empirical support for a policy of reward. The chief evidence in favor of the superior efficacy of reward over punishment in shaping conduct comes from two sources. One is laboratory experiments involving animals, in which schedules of positive reinforcement supposedly yield behavioral results superior to those achieved by aversive conditioning. The other is experiments involving alcoholics, child molesters, and others who have been subjected to regimens of behavioral modification in which rewards have been used with greater effect than punishments. Unfortunately (see Axelrod and Apsche, 1983), these empirical results fall far short, in different ways, of what is needed to vindicate the idea that a system of reward could supplant a system of punishment.

First, the animal experimentation evidence does not warrant unqualified confidence in the invariable superiority of reward over punishment. Even if it did, it would verge on the worthless for our purposes. There is no reason to believe that animals understand the behavior of experimenters that they call "reward" and "punishment" as we understand the behavior so called, or even as little children do. In particular, animals cannot be expected (as we can, and as we teach children) to grasp the concept of a wrong or a crime, much less the idea of the rights of others. But for us, punishment is conceptually connected to the commission of a crime, or more generally, to breaking a rule or disobeying a command by an act that inflicts harm on another without adequate justification or excuse. Animals no doubt understand the idea of acting in a manner that is followed by gratification or by frustration of desire (or by some comparable state of consciousness, e.g., pleasure versus pain). But this falls short of understanding that one is acting in compliance with or contrary to the imperative wishes of someone in a position to benefit or hurt oneself.

It follows that the harm that befalls an animal when it acts contrary to a command (or when it runs down the "wrong" rather than the "right" branch in a maze) cannot be identified with the harm that befalls you or me when we break a rule with the result that someone else is harmed, which in turn provides the occasion for a third party (typically) to bring harm in the form of punishment on us. Only harms in this setting, understood in this way, typically qualify as punishments, under the conception of punishment relevant to that practice as it is institutionalized in human society. Consequently, there is little reason to regard the results of experiments on the effects of animal training and "behavior shaping" through gratifications in preference to frustrations as adequate empirical evidence for the superiority of reward over punishment of human beings in securing compliance to a roughly just system of law.

The problem with the results of behavioral modification with human subjects is quite different. Here, again, the record is mixed regarding the superior effect of rewards over punishments. Even if it were not, it seems utterly utopian to suppose that *all* human behavior that is criminal could be eliminated in advance by proffering rewards for compliance. Furthermore, it is difficult to believe that it is always more efficient to aim at securing compliance with law by means of the prospect of rewards than by arousing the fear of adverse consequences. Even if some behavior of addicts and convicts (the typical experimental subjects) can be brought into conformity with the law through reward-dominated procedures of behavioral modification, this does not suffice to show that all convicted offenders could have been similarly influenced by rewards. Even if it did, it would fall far short of providing convincing evidence that entire populations could have their behavior shaped into compliance with the criminal law without recourse to punitive threats, as long as adequate reinforcement schedules of reward are provided. Even if we could avoid the administrative problems that discouraged Bentham, we are hardly in a position today to sketch out the general features of such a reward-oriented practice for our society, much less able to translate such a sketch into strategies and tactics for daily behavior. Eliminating punishment in favor of reward by this route at best lies in the distant future.

The Alternative of Forgiveness

Let us, therefore, return our attention to offenders and consider three general strategies for dealing with them, each of which avoids recourse to punishment. One such strategy lies in the proposal that wrongdoers should not be punished, because there is a better idea—forgiving them. By forgiveness, I do not mean indifference by the victim to having been victimized; nor do I mean pardoning by the authorities; and I certainly do not mean deliberate permissiveness that would tolerate or condone crime. Each of these attitudes or practices deserves some attention in its own right, and one or another may well be the best thing to do under the circumstances in certain cases. But none is the same as forgiveness and should not be confused with it.

The idea that wrongdoers should not be punished but should be forgiven would probably strike the average person in our society as sheer lunacy. However appropriate it may be for God to forgive us our sins, were society to forgive us our crimes, most of us are sure that this would only bring down on our heads yet more victimization. We need not dwell on what politicians and editorial writers would say of the idea were anyone so naive as to broach it seriously. The scorn they would shower on it would be reinforced by recent findings by Axelrod (1984) in his research on "the prisoner's dilemma." If we can rely on this research, it appears that social cooperation itself cannot develop through a policy of victim forgiveness. Instead, it develops only through a retaliatory policy of striking back in measured blows, a so-called tit-for-tat strategy. It is, of course, possible that this research proves very little, because all of it was carried out among persons reared and encultured in society as presently structured (or, rather, by computers programmed by persons so socialized).

It is useful, therefore, to consider at least two other objections that raise doubts about the very idea of forgiveness as a general strategy with which to replace punishment. First, only the victim is in a position to forgive the person who has victimized her; it would make no sense for a third party to offer forgiveness to the offender. Yet for many of the worst crimes either the victim cannot forgive the offender (the victim is dead) or the victim will not, and unwilling forgiveness is not forgiveness at all. Second, for anyone to be forgiven without prior repentance seems odd, or even absurd. Such forgiveness would verge on sheer indifference to victimization by the victim. Even if that were not so, it would defeat the point of forgiveness, which is reconciliation of the offender and the victim. Reconciliation is impossible as long as the offender fails to acknowledge wrongdoing, refuses to repent, does not ask to be forgiven. As things stand in our world, only an uncertain fraction of offenders is likely to repent, and it is quite uncertain how many of these would be likely to repent were their liability to punishment eliminated. Quite apart from whatever effect on the crime rate such a policy might have, these two considerations effectively destroy all hope of replacing the practice of punishment with a policy of forgiveness.

Before abandoning this strategy, however, it may be worth pausing a moment to say a few words in favor of forgiveness. For parents in dealing with their children, for adults in a neighborhood dealing with the children of their fellow residents, and even in some cases of stranger-to-stranger criminal encounters, it may be possible for forgiveness to play a useful role. No doubt, in all such cases, the appropriateness and effectiveness of forgiveness depends in part on evidence of apology, contrition, regret, repentance, and similar attitudes and acts by the offender.

I stress a moderately expanded role for forgiveness because I take it to be true that our morality is not indifferent to forgiveness. It is not a moral virtue to be of an unforgiving nature, even if unforgivingness is not a vice or as grave a moral defect as many others. Also, given the relatively small amount of harm done in some offenses, the absence of fully malicious motivation in some offenders, the prospects of bringing about a reconciliation between the offender and the victim, and the hope of reducing future harmful violence, every society needs to give more thought to forgiveness than might seem to be true at first glance. Nevertheless, however desirable it is to extend forgiveness to the fullest extent, and without denying that such an extension would make a general improvement overall in our moral economy, it is not in fact feasible to consider supplanting the practice of punishment with a practice of forgiveness.

The Therapeutic Alternative

A second major alternative to punishment is subjecting convicted offenders to nonpunitive treatment, in particular some form of therapeutic intervention. During the 1940s and 1950s, psychiatrists such as Karl Menninger in this country and social reformers such as Lady Barbara Wootton in England popularized the elimination of punishment (as they saw it) in favor of compulsory treatment of those who have caused unlawful harm to others, or who might cause such harm. The treatments advocated ranged from hormonal injections, psychosurgery, and electroconvulsive shock therapy to tranquilizers, with genetic modification looming on the horizon. The advocates of these interventions viewed them on analogy with public health and coercive control measures such as compulsory public education, military conscription, quarantine, and internment of enemy aliens in time of war. For advocates of this outlook, the ordinary ideas of guilt, personal responsibility, and the like were to be set aside in favor of concepts of stricter liability regardless of individual intent, *mens rea*, and other "mental elements" of traditional criminal conduct. What mattered, on this view, is what the offender did, or might do; other considerations about the offender's motivation, intention, or autonomy as an individual person were to be ignored, outweighed, or repudiated. As a consequence, the practice of punishment was supposed to disappear not only or even mainly because of the harm it caused but because of its inappropriateness.

Persuasive arguments against this therapeutic view, on various grounds, have been widespread, and there is no need to add to them here. These objections have made clear several points of importance for the present argument. First, one cannot seriously propose to treat someone for something that is not diagnosable as a disease, illness, or sickness— and it is far from evident that crime is such a "disease." Second, one cannot seriously believe that imposing treatment on a person always does less violence to the person's autonomy than does punishment.

There is another line of criticism, however, that is relatively under-stressed. Even if the two objections above were in error, the treatment alternative if conceived as a strategy designed to eliminate punishment trembles on the edge of irrelevance. The problem is that insofar as you must rely on detention or other measures imposed on offenders in order to subject them to therapeutic interventions, you have not yet given up co-ercive control over convicted offenders. Nor have you abandoned creating liability to such control. Nor has eligibility for these controls been freed from connection to (actual or probable) conviction of criminal offenses. For these purposes the police and the courts are still needed. At best, there-fore, we must regard all these therapeutic alternatives as quasi-punitive regimens, because their professed aim to produce some change for the better in offenders and to do so without the usual punitive methods or intentions nevertheless relies on some of the characteristic features of a system of punishment.

What is at stake in the treatment or therapeutic alternative, then, is partly a conceptual struggle over whether it is the *intention* in the interven-tion that determines the true character of the intervention or whether it is the *impact* of the intervention that is decisive. (Tacit reliance on this contrast was crucial to the effect achieved by Anthony Burgess's novel *A Clockwork Orange* (1965), in which the impact of ostensibly therapeutic intentions casts grave doubt on the plausibility of taking those intentions seriously.) Theorists of the first sort argue that because the dominant intention of the postconviction practice has changed from one of paying back offenders in harsh coin to one of trying to enable them to start new lives, the lingering presence of coercive controls must not distract us from the sea-change that has transpired in their purpose. Theorists of the second sort reply that this alleged change in intention is superficial and can be seen to be so by the facts that coercion remains central and not incidental—the person being treated is not free to choose whether or not to submit; and the class of persons deemed suitable for "treatment" is defined by reference to who has caused—or is believed likely to cause—criminal harms, rather than by any strictly medical or nonforensic diagnosis.

I am inclined to judge this latter line of reasoning the more persuasive of the two. Yet I confess to being torn over the dispute, owing to two very different reasons. One is my unfamiliarity with actual regimens of the "treatment" in question. Perhaps if I were more familiar with what goes on in hospitals where offenders are treated, in contrast to prisons where they are confined, I would find impressive differences that elude me as things stand now. Perhaps I would then be less inclined to see conventional punishment and "treatment" of offenders as no more than two extreme points on the same continuum. But there is another aspect to the problem altogether, and it helps account for my being pulled in the opposite direction. Over the past three decades many have argued that even if punishment could be eliminated in favor of the alternative of treatment, nevertheless it should not be (Allen, 1959; Wasserstrom, 1964; Morris, 1968). They have raised moral grounds favoring punishment over treatment, grounds that are not easy to dismiss. But this dispute presupposes that punishment of offenders, in contrast to their "treatment," is not merely another point on the same continuum; the two must be altogether independent practices. I confess I do not quite see how to resolve this dispute, and so conclude, as above, that the "treatment" of offenders may be no more than a quasi-alternative to punishment after all.

Denunciation

Is there, then, any truly nonpunitive alternative that might be introduced instead of various alternative kinds of punishment? The only candidate known to me is denunciation, verbal castigation, what some have called "symbolic punishment." One version of this idea, called "emphatic condemnation," was sketched briefly a few years ago as follows: "Suppose a public registry of convictions were established, and with suitable publicity and solemnity entries were made of each crime and its perpetrator. . . . For many . . . persons, public humiliation and loss of reputation would result from their registration, and might even equal in condemnation what they would suffer by imprisonment" (Gross, 1979, 406).

To make the proposal more vivid, we might imagine several variations on the scheme, such as requiring the daily newspapers to print the names of all such offenders for several weeks, or requiring television spot announcements showing the pictures of offenders and a report of the crimes of which they had been convicted. We might imagine these malefactors undergoing denunciatory and admonitory speeches thundered at them in the courtroom from the judge's bench, with the duration and content of such speeches a function of the gravity of the crime of which the offender has been found guilty.

Leaving aside entirely whether such methods might be adequate to play a causal role in reforming the future conduct of those offenders subjected to them or in other ways reducing the incidence of crime, we need to decide whether emphatic denunciation qualifies as a true alternative to punishment. The argument that it does seems to rest entirely on the idea that denunciation does not produce, nor is it intended to produce, the characteristically disabling and deprivatory effects of punishments. If, as the typical retributivist and utilitarian agree, something counts as a punishment only if it causes "pain" or constitutes a manifest disability or deprivation, then it is doubtful whether emphatic denunciation is a punishment. Running in the other direction, however, is the argument that persons undergoing judicial denunciation are undergoing a practice coercively enforced. They are experiencing something to which they have been *sentenced* because of their wrongdoing. But is not whatever a person is judicially sentenced to experience a punishment, regardless of what we choose to call it and however tolerable it may be to experience?

It is not easy to resolve this dispute and tell with assurance which side of the argument has the better of it. We might say, and I propose to say, that in the practice of emphatic condemnation or denunciation, we have a true borderline case, something that comes as close as anything can to being a nonpunitive practice while still retaining many of the features of practices that are incontestably punitive.

If you are willing to grant this much, then you can go on to ask whether it is not only possible but also desirable to eliminate punishment in favor of this nonpunitive alternative. (Hyman Gross, from whom I borrowed the sketch quoted above, clearly thought it was not.) Probably most of those who contemplate this idea would be inclined to think not. Why, it would be asked, would it be rational to undertake to supplant punishment by emphatic denunciation in a society where most of the criminal laws are just and, hence, violations of these laws prima facie violate the moral rights of the innocent, and where coercive liability to punishment can significantly reduce the level of violations and do so better than a system of authoritative denunciation would? I do not see a way clear to defend the denunciatory alternative in the face of these beliefs.

While it is true that much can be said against the practice of punishment as a device of moral education, and for this reason we should enlarge the role of denunciation (in conjunction, no doubt, with suitable explanations and admonitions), denunciation by itself seems a singularly unconvincing strategy to use with some offenders, such as hardened recidivists of any sort, and adult offenders guilty of the worst crimes against the person. The rationale for abandoning more familiar and more effective methods of incapacitation and general deterrence in favor of the proposed alternative remains elusive.

REDUCTION OF PUNISHMENT IS REALISTIC, ITS ELIMINATION IS NOT

So far, we have explored a series of alternative grounds and schemes with the aim of establishing whether at least one of them, if taken in isolation, might possibly serve as a basis for eliminating punishment. The conclusions we have reached are not encouraging. Yet the opponents of punishment need not despair entirely. They can argue that even if no one of these considerations by itself suffices to eliminate punishment, it may well be that some combination of them all, suitably orchestrated, will do the trick. This is a plausible suggestion, and there is not space here to do it justice. I will content myself with observing how unlikely I find this possibility to be. While it may be true that the extent of punishment in our society, or in any society, can be *reduced* through enhancing and orchestrating several of the strategies outlined so far, the practice of punishment itself cannot be—and should not be—entirely *eliminated*. The same can be said, although this is not the place to argue the point, in regard to imprisonment: Its role can be reduced, but it cannot be eliminated—as long as it is the sole effective general method of incapacitation short of unacceptably barbaric practices from our past, such as maiming and death.

Eliminating punishment turns out to be a complex matter with any number of hidden considerations lurking within it. I have tried to bring out all the major issues involved, whether they are empirical, conceptual, or normative. The conclusion I reach is this: If by eliminating punishment we mean primarily not inflicting punishment on anyone for anything, then there is little likelihood of that coming to pass and equally little likelihood that it would be an improvement over current practice if it did. The same is true if we mean removing the very liability to punishment in the first place.

Yet, as I have also tried to show, even these conclusions rest in part on empirical questions as yet unanswered in several respects. To that extent, we do not know whether punishment can be eliminated, nor whether if it could it would be an improvement over even the best punishment system imaginable. Thus, if I am right, we do not know whether punishment can be eliminated—but at least we now know *why* we do not know.

NOTE

Acknowledgments: An earlier and more primitive version of this paper was published without the author's permission in Cleary (1985, 168–79). For valuable editorial contributions to the present draft I am grateful to Constance E. Putnam.

14

CRIME AND PUNISHMENT

André Maury

VIOLATION OF RIGHTS IN CRIMES AND PUNISHMENTS

Crime and punishment share an element of violence. I shall consider here the conditions under which the violence involved in punishment is acceptable.

Crime is a violation of persons; but so is punishment, and it is even meant to be such. One way of upholding the difference at this point between crime and punishment is to think that the violent act involved in a crime is a violation of *rights*, whereas a similar act involved in a punishment is not. The question is how violence against persons can be acceptable at all if they have human rights.

The obvious way out is to hold that the criminal does not have rights. Even if the criminal had rights, he does not have them after the crime. However, this loss of rights is impossible if human rights are unconditional or, as I shall say, natural.

There is a difference between *natural* and *conventional* properties. In considering whether violence against persons can be acceptable, it is crucial to determine whether the right to one's body or freedom is natural or conventional. If punishment is to make sense at all, the answer will be that rights have to be regarded as conventional. The philosophical task is to account for a practice so that it comes out consistent. Consistency demands that the law cannot take human rights as natural. If it did, it would come out inconsistent, since it endorses punishment. The law is set up, if it is any good, to protect human rights. However, if the law did not avail itself of punishment, it would be without force. So, if we are to have any consistent law, we have to give up the idea of human rights as natural.

Some human rights have been called "natural rights," above all the exclusive right to one's body (and all that goes with that). That right, when natural, excludes violence by others against that body. The view that human rights are natural seems to give them a foundation. A natural right is one you have simply by being a person. Your natural rights are thus, as I shall say, unconditional.

This means that rights are not given to you by some institution or practice, or formed during the course of your life. It may take some effort or time to realize that you have them, yet they are there awaiting to be discovered. Anyone who treats you as if you did not have these rights violates the natural order of things. The rights also stay with you; they cannot be taken away, though they can be disregarded. You cannot lose them either. Or if that is possible, it means that you become less of a person than you were before.

When rights are made part of the definition of being human, punishing a person without violating the person's rights is possible only if we, indeed, assume that the person is less than fully human. This assumption seems to be part of our ordinary practice. Amnesty International does not in general list cases of legal punishment as violations of human rights. However, the assumption is counterintuitive. The courts surely convict *persons—human* beings, not something less than that.

I shall discuss two theories of rights that permit the lifting of rights. The first is based on Hegel's theories; the second is Locke's. I shall also briefly discuss the consequences of accepting a theory that takes rights as inalienable and consider the "measure of punishment." I shall exemplify the whole discussion by considering some central questions in Dostoevsky's *Crime and Punishment* and some recent views of rights. I shall begin with some general remarks on our attitude toward violence.

Our Attitude Toward Violence

Our attitude toward violence is surprisingly permissive, considering that violence goes against human rights. Yet we are staunch supporters of human rights. How is this possible? The only explanation seems to be that acceptable violence is directed toward people who do not have rights (for some reason).

Anyone familiar with history knows that the most important historical events involve violence, or at least our history books are written in such a way. Accounts of the French Revolution are not in the first place meant to arouse protests on moral or human grounds against the breaches of the rights of the counterrevolutionary forces. Accounts of Finland's short winter war against the Soviet Union sometimes glorify it. The most glaring instances of simple murder are presented as cases to be adored as examples of might, power, and courage. No mention of human rights. Indeed, I learned in the army that the enemy does not consist of men but of "living force." In accounts of the Russian Revolution, a stress on the abuses of power by the early Communist regime would be regarded as very conservative indeed. It would perhaps be seen as a political act, one of taking sides.

An account of most historical events from the point of view that human rights are natural would make sorry reading. Stressing human rights in these instances is, it is sometimes argued, to miss something. It is to construe things in the wrong way. The violence involved is not an end but a means for an end that is good, maybe even something perfect or ideal, as Garver discusses in Chapter 10. The point is not to crush human rights (if the adversary has such) just for the sake of crushing human rights, though perhaps the adversary has no rights. The rationalization for violence is either that it is necessary or that the adversary has no rights, so no further excuse or justification is really needed.

Justifying political violence by invoking an end that demands acceptance is common. Nobody sheds tears for the human rights of the tyrant who is killed. The end justifies the means, obviously. It is also often maintained that the end involves less overall violence than the situation that would follow if nothing were done. So more good than bad comes out of the violent act.

Consistently taking the attitude of human rights seems often to rob us of the only means for change, and so also for changes for the better. Of course, there are innumerable examples of acceptable violence against persons. Punishment, when legal, is a case in point.

Losing Your Rights

Even if you are for human rights, you can say that violence is not a breach of human rights if the adversary has, somehow, forfeited them. Supporters of law (and consistency) have to think in this way. But then human rights cannot just be natural properties of persons. They have to be properties of some other kind, indeed, less part of being human than naturalists think. They must be such that it makes sense to say they are lost, or at least temporarily lost. The reason punishment does not go against human rights is that the criminal has by committing the crime lost certain rights, so it seems. What kind of properties, then, must human rights be in order that violating the rights of another means losing them yourself?

I shall discuss two theories of human rights that try to make sense of this quite astonishing effect of a criminal act. Even if the effect—the loss of rights—were written into the law, that would not in itself be a justification for it. The question still remains what kind of properties human rights are, in light of the fact that they can be lost.

How is it that we have rights at all?

TWO THEORIES OF HUMAN RIGHTS

Human Rights and Anerkennung

I shall present a theory of properties implicit in Hegel's theory of *Anerkennung*, as presented in his *Phenomenology of Spirit* (1977), but I shall start by considering some of the most interesting things Hegel has to say on crime and punishment in his *Philosophy of Right* (1976).

Hegel's Philosophy of Right.   What worries Hegel in punishment is not human rights but the fact that it involves violence. He does not accept the standard "justification" for violence in punishment, namely, that its end is good. The end is some social or psychological end that is seen as justifying the punishment, and Hegel does not think that such consider-ations amount to a justification. For him there must be some "internal" connection between crime and punishment; thus, the right not heeded in the crime is restored by the punishment (Hegel 1976). He maintains that the crime "*eo ipso* contains its negation in itself and this negation is mani-fested as punishment." Hegel stresses that if the "implicit interconnection of crime and its negation . . . is not apprehended, then it may become possible to see in a punishment proper only an 'arbitrary' connexion of an evil with an unlawful action."

Hegel does not think that the "inner identity" in crime and punishment consists of something like the "qualitative and quantitative characteristics of crime and its annulment" being the same. No "absolute determinacy" is possible in this sphere. I shall come back to this theme in considering the question of the proper "measure" of punishment.

Hegel also remarks that crime and punishment are not rightly seen if they are treated as if they were "unqualified" evils, because it is unreason-able to will an evil merely because "another evil is there already" (a quote from Klein, in Hegel's text). This is a good point. The connection between a crime and the punishment for *it* cannot just be that it is followed by another evil. Even if the consequences of the second evil are good, that does not make the connection sought for, if the evil involved in a punish-ment must be a "*second* evil." In Hegel the point of the punishment cannot be something in the future, but rather the somewhat abstract "annulment" of the crime. Is that possible?

Hegel, for one, thinks it is. Crime is the "infringement of right as right" so punishment is the "righting of a wrong." That both crime and pun-ishment involve evil acts is not really relevant. Indeed "crime is to be annulled, not because it is the production of an evil, but because it is an infringement of the right as right." As far as punishment is concerned, it seems that *anything* that restores the wronged right could serve.

The notion of restoring of right is, of course, a problematic notion, and doubly so. *Restoring* is difficult to analyze, and Hegel's concept of *right* is very abstract. His discussion, although imaginative, is unsatisfactory from our point of view because he does not really say why the second evil is not in its turn an infringement of right. This omission can in part be made good, however, by considering his early theory of *Anerkennung*, which tells us something about properties.

Conventional Properties. There are natural properties, but there are also *conditional* properties. You have a property conditionally if your having it depends on *other people*.[1] Being a father or a mother is a case in point. Being one or the other depends on there being someone else to whom the man or woman stands in a certain relation. Being envious or jealous is also a case in point. Natural properties are different, however. Bodily or mental properties are not conditional (in the intended sense). Being a pianist or a swimmer demands something outside yourself, but these properties do not depend on other people, so they will not be called conditional. Only those properties that depend on relations to other people will count.

There is a kind of conditional property that is of special interest to us, namely, conventional property. A *conventional* property is conditional, but in addition to that it depends on other people's explicitly *recognizing* that property. Hegel, in his *Phenomenology of Spirit* (1977; see also Taylor, 1975), calls this *Anerkennung*.

A conventional property exists only insofar as it *is* recognized. A good example is being a state. A country (or something else) may declare itself a state; but even if it has all a state must have, it will not be a state without recognition from other states. Having a particular border is also a case in point. Countries have natural properties, the landscape, the climate, the characteristics of the inhabitants, and so on, but having a particular border is *not* a natural property (not even in the case where the border is said to be a natural one, like a river). The property is *conventional*, because the border must be recognized as such by some other country, that is, by those people in that country who have a right to give the *Anerkennung*. Hegel stresses that the recognition must come from those who are qualified to give it. If the other country for some reason stops recognizing the border, problems will follow. Its staying as a border presupposes that it is *treated as such*.

Many properties are conventional. Being a teacher is one. Being a good teacher is also one. For Hegel being human is, surprisingly, a conventional property. That property is indeed the one with implicit reference to which he introduces the whole notion of *Anerkennung*. I say "implicitly" because he says that self-consciousness exists only when recognized. For Hegel self-consciousness defines being human, so that property also exists only when recognized. Being a good human being is certainly also a conventional property. Indeed, judgments on the right and the good certainly depend for their truth on *Anerkennung*.

Human rights can surely be seen as properties that demand recognition, in the following way. Humans are born with certain needs and appetites. Saying that these needs are *rights* is not a remark on something that the child is also born with. To speak of rights is to see a person in the context of others. The notion of the person having rights regulates, as it were, *our* actions—it should exclude our treating that person in certain ways. Our recognition of rights does indeed produce them. Treat her as not having them, and she will not have them. Having a right to the "preservation of one's body" (Hobbes, 1651), the most fundamental right, means that a person is *as a matter of fact* treated in a certain way.

When a person starts to be treated in a way not compatible with basic needs, the person does not have this fundamental human right (anymore). *Infringement of rights* is construed as *lack of* recognition of his needs in actual practice. So when people in South America or South Africa are treated in a way that their "rights" are infringed, these people do not (in an important sense) have human rights yet. Amnesty International's recognition of them (from London) does not reach that far; Amnesty is not the body whose recognition counts.

The central question here is whose *Anerkennung* counts. Regarding rights as conventional raises the problem of when the *Anerkennung* is fulfilled, when the *right* exists in fact. But perhaps that is not a question of fact in itself. Perhaps conventional properties are in their very nature shaky. Leaving aside certain difficult questions, the *Anerkennung* theory of rights is in essence the doctrine that rights are functions of certain ways of acting toward other people, that is, acting in accordance with their needs.

Seeing human rights as conventional makes punishment possible; that is, punishment comes out as consistent. (This is not yet to say that punishment is a good.)

How does a loss of rights come about on this theory? Doing bodily harm against a person means that you do not recognize the person's rights. (Recognizing those rights would have meant treating the person differently.) You hit the person, fatally, let us suppose. Then surely that person is in no position to recognize your rights. But even if the violent act does not result in death (whereby *Anerkennung* would become technically impossible), the violent act in itself has, according to Hegel, the following result: By not recognizing the other person's rights, you (the criminal) cannot take *that person* to be in a position to recognize your rights. A person who has *no* rights cannot recognize rights. Why is this so?

Recognition must be mutual, Hegel stresses. The point gets more edge if we think that the criminal act is directed not just toward one, but toward all—through the existence of a law. Of course the act affects one, but it can be seen as a threat toward all (except the criminal). Infringing the rights of one means infringing the rights of all. The violent act disqualifies all others as such ones who could recognize rights. So the criminal loses her own rights. The criminal act is, as it were, a move outside the game of rights. The criminal starts to play another game, one in which the concept of right does not exist. The original game (here Hegel differs sharply from Hobbes) is one in which the mutual recognition of rights is essential.

Hegel's doctrine is not pure fancy. Far from that. I find it difficult, however, to argue for it in a straightforward way. The doctrine can be made less ambititious by assuming that the loss of rights comes about by our simply *stopping* to treat the criminal in ways that could be called "recognizing rights." Hegel's point, however, is more ambitious. When we stop treating the criminal as one who has rights, she indeed loses them. But Hegel says (in our interpretation) not just that we stop treating the criminal in this way, but that we could not even try to do so. We are not in the right position anymore, because only those who are treated as having rights *can* treat others as having rights.

When understood in the way Hegel meant his doctrine of *Anerkennung*, what is in question is not *just* some "action theory" of rights, though that feature is the one that can be understood most easily, but also a theory of *whose* action counts. That is the difficult part.

Nevertheless, *one* existence condition for rights is action by others. As a criticism of rights as natural this one condition is quite effective. The criminal starts to play another game in which rights do not count. This is not to say that the criminal is not a person anymore. She is a person, although one without rights. Let us assume that being a person is a natural property (*pace* Hegel). Rights still are not natural. However, losing a conventional property in no way means that some natural property is lost thereby. Natural properties do not demand this sort of "game" for their existence, a game Gewirth (1978, chaps. 1–3) describes ably in somewhat different terms.

Natural Rights

Locke's theory of natural rights is familiar to most people, so I shall not dwell on it too long. My point is just that rights, as conceived of in the *Second Treatise of Government* (1976), are not *so* natural as is usually supposed.

In the first chapter Locke suggests that rights derive either from a law of nature or from a positive law. Political power, which is Locke's theme, is the right of making laws with penalties, as he says. *This* right does not easily fit into the given scheme about the two sources of right, but it certainly is there only as a result of an act of recognition (like rights involved in positive law in general).

In Chapter 2 Locke suggests that in a state of nature there is perfect freedom and perfect equality between men. (I follow his wording as far as possible, but I leave out capital letters in nouns even in direct quotations.) The state of nature has a law of nature that governs it. This law is reason, which teaches that "all being independent, no one ought to harm another in his life, health, liberty or possessions."

There is one exception, though. You may "impair the life, liberty, health, limb or goods" of a transgressor of that law of nature. So criminals may be punished; that is, one person may "lawfully do harm to another." The punisher comes by "a power over another." (Locke gives an interesting list of some more or less natural relations of such power: father to child, master to servant, husband to wife, lord to slave, captain to crew, ruler to subject, magistrate to subject.)

The *measure* of punishment is also part of the law of nature, Locke asserts. He adds, however, that it is "beside his purpose to go into particulars" at this point. The upshot is that if a person "invades another's rights," anyone has a right to punish the transgressor according to a given, though unspecified, measure.

Why, then, does not the law of nature, which grants human rights, apply to the criminal? Locke's answer is that an offender of the law "declares himself to live by another rule than that of reason." Through the violent act he "declares himself to quit the principles of human nature" and may be destroyed as a lion or tiger. Locke refers to Cain: "And *Cain* was so fully convinced, that every one had a right to destroy such a criminal, that after the murder of his brother he cries out, *Everyone that findeth me, shall slay me;* so plain was it writ in the Hearts of all Mankind."

But the question is, Why is it that an act is criminal in one case and lawful in another? The harm, the evil, the violence is in one case a transgression of the law, in the other case that very law prescribes it. In the first case the violent act goes against rights, but in the second it does not.

The answer given by Locke seems to be that the criminal is less than a person, or less than a full human being; therefore, the law of nature that applies to persons, and grants them rights, does not apply. The violent act involved in punishment is not a violation of rights anymore than the killing of a tiger is a violation of *its* rights. By serving the prescribed sentence a criminal (if still alive) regains the rights that were lost or suspended. The pariah becomes human, once more.

Can rights be called natural on this theory? I think not. At least they are not unconditionally natural, since they can be lost and regained through *action*.

Only in the sense that rights are part of the definition of being human in Locke's theory are they natural. When rights are lost, given this definition, the individual loses (part of) his or her humanity too. One curious consequence is that being human turns out to be conditional! Hegel also draws that conclusion, but I do not think the view is correct.

My having rights *continually* depends on my relation to other people. So rights on Locke's theory turn out to be conditional after all. You have them as long as you observe them in others.

They are not conventional, however, not in the final analysis, at least. Rights are not accorded through action, as in the theory of rights as conventional. The obvious difference is that for Locke a right exists as long as we do no evil, and this is rather a nonaction theory of rights than an action theory of rights.

On both theories a crime, a violation of the rights of another, leads to a loss of rights on the part of the criminal. So violent action against the criminal is not wrong and does not lead to an inconsistency in thinking and action. Both theories get the rights of the criminal out of the way.

Let us contrast these theories with a theory that takes rights as inalienable, that is as natural in the full sense, namely, as unconditional.

Inalienable Rights

Suppose rights are part of the very definition of being human and they cannot be removed. Let us assume that Locke is wrong in taking the criminal as less than a person. Now, punishment will be inconsistent, *if* crime is defined as a violation of rights. Then the difference between crime and punishment must be made out *without* reference to rights, which seems almost impossible. So we would have to live with an inconsistency. That is possible, I suppose. Perhaps there are some such theories of the practice of ordinary law, namely, that it involves an inconsistency in its very nature—one that cannot be removed by changing the law but that is there as long as we have law and the necessary means for its enforcement.

Indeed, it is not difficult at all to see rights as unremovable. Suppose rights are a function of human needs. The necessity of upholding life and freedom creates rights according to the formula that it would be misplaced to put obstacles in a project in which one is involved oneself. So if rights follow upon needs, there is no particular reason to suppose that a criminal through her violent act suddenly *needs less than before*.

INTENTIONS AND ARBITRARY CONVENTIONS

The Intention in Punishment

Next I wish to point out one difference between crime and punishment that exists even on the deontological level, that is, when we leave out all consideration of consequences.

The difference between crime and punishment is great in actual practice. From a purely deontological point of view, however, the difference is not that great. Yet there is a difference on that level, too. The acts involved in crime and punishment have sometimes the same result, that a person is killed, say. If the result were always the criterion of what act is in question, crime and punishment would often be indistinguishable—as they also are for Raskolnikov (to be discussed shortly). Often, however, the criterion is provided by the *intention* in the act or action. When a person is killed as the result of a criminal action, it is not as a rule the case that the criminal has an intention to commit a criminal act. His intention is to kill for some reason or other—the reason not being in general to be a criminal! In a punishment the result may be the same and there certainly is an intention to kill. There is also the intention that the act be a punishment.

The intention of punishing does not depend on the existence of a law, as all parents know. Nor, for that matter, does the existence of a crime: Feinberg (1984, introduction) mentions a classical list of "natural" crimes, such as murder, rape, theft, and arson. Punishing, however, is an intentional act, whereas there is no intentional act called "criming." There is indeed no verb 'to crime'.

An exception to this would be a person who wants to commit a crime, *no matter what crime,* in order to defy the law for some reason or other. But this is marginal. Crime typically lacks the kind of double intention typical of punishment.

In a punishment the result—that a human being is put away or put to death—is important, but not all-important. The intention with which the act is done is all-important, however. This is partly so because the actual form of punishment is *arbitrary.* In these respects crime is different. However, the violent act involved in punishment does not become less violent because it is "meant" in a certain way. Yet the intention seems to excuse it. In crime this is seldom so. What makes it a crime *is* the violence.

The Measure of Punishment

Let us next discuss the measure of punishment, and its forms. As we saw, Hegel stresses that if we leave out the aspect of "right," the connection between crime and its punishment becomes arbitrary. I think, however, that punishment in a certain respect is always arbitrary, even if we pay due attention to the aspect stressed by Hegel. Locke, as we noted, speaks of a given "measure of punishment." He is probably right in holding that reason tells us how severe the punishment for a given sort of crime should be. So the crime itself seems to provide the measure for that.

Obviously there is still a question of what particular form the punishment should take. However, justifying a particular form of punishment by reference to the crime is difficult. If I cut a person's hand, why should my hand rather than my foot, say, be cut? It has happened that people who write poetry get several years of labor camp for that. This surely shows that there is some arbitrariness between crime and punishment.

Nevertheless, the forms of punishment have a history. The history of punishment shows that "natural" punishments have been important. We call a punishment natural when it in part at least repeats the criminal act— cutting limbs, for instance; capital punishment is the obvious example today. Imprisonment is not a natural punishment for most crimes. One of the few crimes for which imprisonment would be natural is kidnapping.

Let us take some examples from a classical source, which Locke in fact relied heavily on. In Genesis some forms of punishment are laid down in a general fashion, but also in great detail: "Thou shalt give life for life, eye for an eye, tooth for tooth, hand for hand, foot for foot, burning for burning, wound for wound, stripe for stripe. And if a man smite the eye of his servant, or the eye of his maid, that it perish; he shall let him go free for his eye's sake." The same, by the way, also applies in the case of teeth. Consider also this: "If a man shall steal an ox or a sheep and kill it, or sell it; he shall restore five oxen for an ox, and four sheep for a sheep."

There is an interesting transition here from natural punishment to complete arbitrariness (in the number of oxen or sheep). We also learn that although the crime suggests the punishment, there is nothing in the crime that *demands* a particular form of punishment. It is especially difficult with the degree of severity. When it comes to that, Locke seems certainly right. I want to stress only that the crime in no way entails a particular form of punishment.

In ordinary imprisonment the arbitrariness of the form of punishment is clear. Loss of freedom is wholly unrelated to rape or writing poetry. True, when in prison the criminal has less chance of repeating his crime. But, then, killing him would be more of a guarantee.

My reason for saying all this, which is quite obvious in itself, is that punishment is sometimes perhaps thought to be more well founded. Ending up with a theory, say, that takes punishment as an arbitrary form of harm directed toward creatures without rights is not much of a foundation. The arbitrariness of the form of punishment also shows something about the place of morals in punishment, or rather the lack of morals. If the form is arbitrary, how could one form be more right than another?

The point that punishment, quite like crime, has something chaotic about it, is beautifully brought out by Dostoevsky in *Crime and Punishment*, which I will briefly consider.

Imaginary Rights

In Dostoevsky's book the former university student Raskolnikov kills the pawnbroker Aljona Ivanovna. He also kills her sister when she happens to become a witness to the murder. In the end Raskolnikov gives himself up, having confessed his crime to his beloved Sonya. The police do not suspect him because another man has already confessed to the killings.

Raskolnikov is a madman who tries to be rational. The novel is an account of the unexpected consequences on a psychological and social level of his crime. The crime becomes too much for him to bear, though he has in a way a rational explanation or excuse for his act, which he refuses to call a crime. He asserts that he had a right to kill the pawnbroker. The killing of the sister is seen by him as pure accident, and he does not give that killing any separate consideration.

Raskolnikov has written an article in his university days, according to which some extraordinary people have rights that ordinary people do not have. Perhaps he sees himself as extraordinary. Yet his violent act has no clear end (which would justify the violent means). He does not kill for money, though that motive is mentioned; in fact, he loses interest in the small amount of money he takes. He asserts that he had a right to kill, so the killing is not a crime. He also had a right to kill *this* woman, because she is no more than a "louse." So any rights on the part of the victim do not set up an obstacle for the killing.

Of course, having a right to kill is not in itself an explanation of why he did it, what moved him to action. Indeed the very act comes in a way as a surprise to himself. This is, I think, part of Dostoevsky's philosophy in the book. In fact the ways in which people act in the book are not "explained" very much. Most actions seem to grow out of chaos. Excepting his sister Dunya and his beloved Sonya, people in the book do not in general display any normal reactions. They come up with the most unexpected things. Dostoevsky stresses the feature of chaos by taking into the story all sorts of quite irrelevant events.

It turns out that Raskolnikov's excuses for his act in no way explain it. His excuses—he had a right to kill someone who is no more than a louse—do not justify his act either, because they are obviously wrong. He takes his punishment, which is not very severe, and he finds happiness with Sonya.

Now, from our point of view, his regarding his victim as inhuman is important. Raskolnikov is in a way sensitive to rights. In another respect he is not. He sees his right to kill as natural. However, that right can be natural at most in the case of punishment, if we follow Locke. If not natural, it must be conventional, that is recognized. Raskolnikov does not really come to think of this. He *seizes* the right, but this is not the way in which rights are set up. So his right to kill is purely imaginary. Imaginary rights do not have the reality of natural rights or conventional rights.

Raskolnikov does make use of the conventions. He sometimes sees his act as a punishment of his victim. This is possible.[2] Crime and punishment do share the element of violence. They are distinguished by convention, not by nature.

Some Recent Views About Rights

For me 'natural' in 'natural rights' is used properly only if it means unconditional or, what comes to the same, inalienable. However, many writers want to treat rights as natural *and* conditional, quite like Locke. As pointed

222 | CRIME AND PUNISHMENT

out by Richards (1968; see also Brown, 1955) it is to misinterpret the tradition to think that Locke did *not* take that view.

Frankena (1955) holds that rights are only prima facie, and there is a question whether an individual has a "right" to that prima facie right. To my mind this is making rights conventional, since the second "right" depends on recognition.

Feinberg (1980) refers to Thomson (1976), who relativizes rights to an immense number of conditions. I would regard most theories of "rights with limitations" as theories of rights as conventional. On the other hand, it seems to be generally agreed that 'natural' in 'natural rights' means the same as "part of the definition of being human." So when rights are lost (through a crime) it means, as pointed out, that the criminal has become less human. This consequence has not been given due consideration in the literature. One (unwanted) consequence of the doctrine is that the criminal, the *person* who committed the crime, is no longer there (in the full sense).

Admittedly, taking rights as conventional makes them look shaky and less important than one would expect. Yet the view in a simple way saves the consistency and "rationality" of the law. To me that seems important. It means that when the "rights" of a criminal are overruled, some more powerful principle (than rights) is at work. To my mind, that principle has not yet been made explicit in the literature.

The theory of rights as inalienable, however, also appeals to me. But then punishment cannot be morally justified. Of course there will still be *excuses* for punishment, as Newton Garver has pointed out to me, but excuses only exculpate; they do not remove the moral wrong of the action. The point is that taking punishment as morally wrong is a thesis that would suit only a Don Quixote! So for the time being I am forced to conclude that human rights are conventional.

NOTES

1. 'Conditional' can be defined in many ways. The definition given here is central to my argument.

2. It is Raskolnikov's perspective. See Wolgast's discussion in Chapter 9 of perspective as central to questions of legitimate violence.

15

TERRORISM, RIGHTS, AND POLITICAL GOALS

Virginia Held

USAGE AND DEFINITION

An examination of usage is particularly unhelpful in deciding what terrorism is and whether it can be justified. Usage characteristically applies the term to violent acts performed by those of whose positions and goals the speaker disapproves and fails to apply it to similar acts by those with whose positions and goals the speaker identifies. And usage much more frequently applies the term to those who threaten established conditions and governments than to those using similar kinds of violence to uphold them. There is a tendency to equate terrorism with the *illegal* use of violence, but of course the questions of who can decide what is illegal and on what grounds are often the questions at issue.

Careful analysis can help clarify the issues surrounding terrorism and provide a basis for recommended interpretations. We can recognize that drawing distinctions is difficult and yet agree with Jenny Teichman when she says that "seemingly ambiguous kinds of violence can . . . be distinguished from one another." She suggests that "*revolutions* can be differentiated into the peaceful and the violent. . . . *Civil protest*, similarly, can be either peaceful or violent. *Guerrilla war* is simply small war. Whether *riots* are crimes or acts of war depends on the intention and the degree of organization of the rioters" (1986, 89–90). Whether or not one shares her ways of drawing these distinctions, one can agree with her conclusion that such distinctions are possible, and important, to make. Terrorism also, she believes, can be defined, despite being, in her view, "the most ambiguous concept in the list" (90).

Much recent philosophical discussion of the term 'terrorism' provides sufficient clarification, and demands sufficient consistency, to make persuasive the view that terrorism is not committed only by those opposed to governments and their policies. 'Terrorism' must be understood in such a way that states and governments, even friendly or democratic ones, can be held to engage in acts of terrorism, along with those who challenge the authority of and disrupt the order of such states and governments. But an adequate definition has not yet emerged in the philosophical literature.

R. M. Hare in his article "On Terrorism" (1979) does not even attempt a definition. Carl Wellman offers a wide definition: Terrorism is, he suggests, "the use or attempted use of terror as a means of coercion" (1979, 250). But this definition is so wide that, as he admits, it includes nonviolent acts that almost no one else would count as terrorism. Wellman writes that "I often engage in nonviolent terrorism myself, for I often threaten to flunk any student who hands in his paper after the due date. Anyone who doubts that my acts are genuine instances of the coercive use of terror is invited to observe . . . the panic in my classroom when I issue my ultimatum" (252).

Although this particular ultimatum may well be an instance of the coercive use of terror, it does not, for most of us, constitute an instance of terrorism, and the very conclusion that on Wellman's definition it would have to is enough to suggest to most of us, I think, that his definition is unsatisfactory. Violence seems an inherent characteristic of terrorism, so that Wellman's "nonviolent terrorism" seems to be something else than terrorism.

Furthermore, not only does Wellman's definition allow too many acts to be implausibly counted as terroristic, it excludes others that should not be ruled out. For Wellman, "coercion, actual or attempted, is of the essence of terrorism" (252). He does not mean only that terrorism is itself coercive, as is violence, for instance, but that it is a means to further coercion, as when terrorism against airline passengers is used by a given group to coerce a government into releasing certain prisoners. It follows that nothing not intended to coerce can be terrorism.

To build the goal of coercion into the definition of terrorism seems mistaken. Among other difficulties, it excludes what can be considered acts of expressive violence, as some acts can best be described. Some terrorism seems to be an expression of frustration more than a means to anything else, or it can have a variety of goals. Terrorism can be intended as punishment, or to call attention to a problem even when no ability to coerce anyone further is expected. If we say that punishment is coercive, we can still recognize that although one may have to coerce people in order to punish them, the two are not identical. Sometimes wrongdoers accept punishment voluntarily, and coercion is often not punitive, so the two terms have different meanings. In the case of terrorism whose purpose is to call attention to a problem, we can again agree that the violence involved is itself coercive, but not that it is for the purpose of further coercion. (On the meaning of coercion, see Held [1972].) If an effort to coerce people to pay attention, to force them against their wills to heed the terrorists' message, is to count as an intention to coerce further, we would have to consider a wide range of free speech to be a means of coercion, as orators and demonstrators speak and gather in public places in ways that others cannot easily avoid hearing and seeing. If forcing one's message on persons would be considered a means of coercion, rather than merely itself coercive, then so much free speech (and especially so much advertising) would be a means of coercion that the meaning of this term would lose its reasonable limits. Of course, terrorism is not merely free expression; but what else it is, is not necessarily a means of further coercion. The violence it involves is coercive, but it can be for the purpose of gaining a hearing for a view rather than for the further purpose of, say, extracting a concession from opponents.

One of the most useful discussions is that of C. A. J. Coady (1985), though I shall disagree with his definition of terrorism. He defines the word as "the tactic or policy of engaging in terrorist acts," and a terrorist act as "a political act, ordinarily committed by an organized group, which involves the intentional killing or other severe harming of noncombatants or the threat of the same" (52). The crucial component of terrorism, in his view, is intentionally targeting noncombatants. He does not think the intent to spread fear should be part of the definition of terrorism. Among his reasons are that instead of spreading fear and demoralization, the terrorist act may give rise to defiance and a strengthening of resolve.

In response to this latter point, one can point out that although of course a terrorist act may fail to have the intended consequence of spreading fear, any act can fail to produce its intended effect. The issue is whether an intention to produce fear as well as damage should or should not be built into the definition of terrorism. Unless we do build it in, we may lack a suitable way to distinguish terrorism from other forms of violence. Coady says that if we refer in the definition to an intention to spread fear there will be problems in ascertaining what the intention behind the act was; I do not think such problems will be much more severe in the case of assessing the intention to promote fear than in the case of assessing the intention to harm noncombatants, and this latter intention Coady does build into his definition.

A difficulty with confining terrorism to those acts involving the intentional harming of noncombatants is that it will exclude actions that seem among leading candidates for inclusion, such as the blowing up of the Marine barracks in Lebanon in October 1983. In this attack, in which a truck with explosives was driven into a Marine compound and exploded, 241 persons, most of them American Marines, were killed.[1] The drivers of the truck were killed as well. The Marines were clearly the intended target. On Coady's definition, this act could not be an act of terrorism, and this seems arbitrary.

Additionally, on Coady's definition, intentional harming of noncombatants by a resistance group as in, say, a long-term campaign of refusing to perform services (for example, being hospital orderlies) for an oppressing group would count as terrorism, because it would intentionally harm noncombatants, and this seems implausible. Coady cites the work of the Brazilian revolutionary Carlos Marighella, whose *Handbook of Urban Guerrilla Warfare* (1971) has been influential in Latin America with revolutionary groups. Marighella confines his discussion of terrorism (89) to only two paragraphs; he means by it "the use of bomb attacks." While this is certainly insufficient as a definition, it contains a core that should not be dismissed, and that core does not seem consistent with a claim that an intention to harm noncombatants is a necessary component of terrorism.

Another difficulty here is the drawing of the distinction itself between combatant and noncombatant. Coady calls various claims that one cannot distinguish the two "absurd and obscene" (59), but he unfairly loads his own descriptions of the distinction. He is surely right that inconsistency often operates here: Those who deny that the distinction can be made among their enemies in wartime fail to accept a comparable argument made by revolutionaries about *their* enemies. Still, the distinction is considerably more difficult to make, on both sides, than Coady admits, for reasons that will be touched on later.

Another useful discussion is Teichman's, though again I shall reject the definition offered in it. Teichman concludes that terrorism is not a matter of scale but that it is a style or method of government or of warfare and that it can be carried out by states as well as groups. "Terrorism," she writes, partially agreeing with Coady, "essentially means any method of war which consists in intentionally attacking those who ought not to be attacked" (1986, 96). She shows why those who ought not to be attacked may not be equivalent to the category of noncombatant, or to the innocent, as usually understood. Those responsible for the start and the conduct, as well as the carrying out of violence are not the improper targets the definition rests on. The major difficulty with her definition, however, in addition to the excessive focus on some version of the combatant/noncombatant distinction, is that it builds a moral judgment into the definition, an approach that I and many others reject for reasons to be discussed later.

My own view of what terrorism is remains, then, close to what it was in 1984, in an article (Held, 1984b) in which I focused on violence, rather than on terrorism itself.[2] I there defended the view that violence is "action, usually sudden, predictably and coercively inflicting injury upon or damage harming a person" (606). And I saw terrorism as a form of violence to achieve political goals, with the creation of fear usually high among the intended effects. For reasons similar to those subsequently argued by others, I limited violence and terrorism to harm to persons rather than to property; sometimes, though not always, one harms persons by harming their property, but the intention to harm persons must be present.

Judith Lichtenberg (see *QQ*, 1987, 2) is quoted on how terrorism *does* induce fear: Violence targeted at ordinary people makes ordinary people everywhere feel uneasy. In the case of the attack on the Marine barracks in Lebanon, the target was not ordinary people or noncombatants, but the aim to induce fear can also be present in such cases. The aim can be to induce fear among military personnel: Young American soldiers anywhere, and especially in the Middle East, can realize that the most expensive and sophisticated weaponry cannot protect them against the kind of attack that killed so many of their fellows.

I now think that we should probably not construe either the intention to spread fear or the intention to kill noncombatants as necessary for an act of political violence to be an act of terrorism. It does seem that both are often present, but not always. And there do not seem to be good reasons to make the latter a part of the definition while dismissing the former. Furthermore, there can be other motives. As Grant Wardlaw notes in his perceptive book on terrorism, "whilst the primary effect is to create fear and alarm the objectives may be to gain concessions, obtain maximum publicity for a cause, provoke repression, break down social order, build morale in the movement or enforce obedience to it" (1982, 41–42; see also Al-Azmeh, 1988).

I will not venture to suggest exactly what one factor or what combination of factors may be necessary to turn political violence into terrorism, but perhaps when either the intention to spread fear or the intention to harm noncombatants is primary, this is sufficient.

THE JUSTIFIABILITY OF TERRORISM

Sound Definitions Leave the Question Open

A second way in which usage and much popular and some academic discussion have been unhelpful in illuminating the topic of terrorism is that they have frequently built a judgment of immorality or nonjustifiability into the definition of terrorism, making it impossible even to question whether given acts of terrorism might be justified. Thus, news reports frequently equate terrorism with evildoing. Politicians often use the term as an automatic term of abuse. The British author Paul Wilkinson, in a book on terrorism, characterizes terrorists as persons who "sacrifice *all* moral and humanitarian considerations for the sake of some political end."[3] Benjamin Netanyahu goes even further. He describes the terrorist as representing "a new breed of man which takes humanity back to prehistoric times, to the times when morality was not yet born. Divested of any moral principle, he has no moral sense, no moral controls, and is therefore capable of committing any crime, like a killing machine, without shame or remorse" (1986, 29–30). The philosopher Burton Leiser says that by definition, terrorists consider themselves above law and morality; he equates terrorism with piracy and considers it invariably criminal and immoral.[4] Finally, Michael Walzer begins a discussion of terrorism with the assumption that "every act of terrorism is a wrongful act" (1988, 238), a position effectively criticized by Robert Fullinwider (1988).

Arguments against building unjustifiability into the definition of terrorism can follow similar arguments against holding violence to be by definition morally wrong. Not only is violence often used in ways usually accepted, as in upholding law, but one can easily cite examples of violence used against governmental authority that make meaningful the question whether such uses of violence were morally wrong or not. The 1944 bomb plot against Hitler is one obvious candidate. Even if examples of possibly justifiable acts of terrorism, as distinct from other forms of violence, are for many persons harder to acknowledge, we should still be able to *consider* the justifiability of terrorist acts. We should be able to treat such questions as open, and this requires that we not imagine the issues to be answerable merely by appealing to a definition.

Many of those who use 'terrorist' as a term of denunciation apply it, as noted before, to their opponents and refuse to apply it to the acts of their own government, or of governments of which they approve, even when such governmental action is as clearly violent, intended to spread fear, or expectably productive of the killing of noncombatants. The collection of essays edited by Netanyahu (1986) provides many examples of this practice. But one cannot effectively criticize the terrorism of those Third World revolutionaries who consider various terrorist acts to be admirable (Dugard, 1976) unless one also criticizes the terrorist acts included in campaigns of counterterrorism carried out by one's own government and the governments of states one considers "friendly."[5] What to consider "original offense" and what "retaliation" is of course a matter of political judgment. Many of those engaged in acts considered terroristic by existing governments consider themselves to be retaliating against unjustified and violent acts by those governments themselves, as in "reprisal raids" that predictably kill civilians.

In a balanced discussion of forms of violence, the philosopher Robert Holmes (1987) concludes that terrorism per se is morally no worse than many conventionally accepted forms of violence. Ordinary warfare often uses terror as a tactic, and we should remember that the numbers of persons killed in the terror bombings of Dresden, Hiroshima, and Nagasaki undoubtedly killed far more people than have been killed by all the terrorists, as conventionally so labeled, throughout the world in all the years since.

One can further argue, as does Falk, that one cannot be sincerely or consistently opposed to terrorism unless one is also opposed to the "tactics of potential or actual warfare that rely on indiscriminate violence or that deliberately target civilians" (1988, 37). Since those who defend preparing for nuclear war are not willing to reject such tactics, their opposition to terrorism seems more propagandistic than honest. However, the mistake of selective application can be corrected, as we become accustomed to the term 'state terrorism' and then reduce the bias so far manifest in usage concerning its application.

Some of those who define terrorism in terms of the intentional harming of noncombatants conclude that because of this, either by definition or not, terrorism is always wrong. Jan Schreiber (1978), Leiser (1979), and Coady (1985) fall into this broad category. Because we can rule out as inadequate the view that terrorism is by definition wrong, let us consider only those cases in which the judgment is not one of definition but is instead independently arrived at. Is intentionally harming noncombatants always wrong then, and terrorism always wrong because it involves this?

Let us consider some objections to the position that it is never justifiable to harm noncombatants. First, let us take up the question of harming noncombatants in wartime and focus on a recent example. Reports (e.g., Butterfield, 1988) suggest that the Iran–Iraq War may have cost some 1 million dead, 1.7 million wounded, and more than 1.5 million refugees. It is also suggested (Trainor, 1988) that Iran's decision to accept United Nations Resolution 598 calling for an end of the fighting was partly the result of demoralization within Iran brought about by the Iraqi bombing of Iranian cities.

Certainly from a moral point of view the war ought not to have been fought, and other means to achieve this outcome should have been found. Iraq was at fault in starting the war and in violation of international law in its use of poison gas (Trainor, 1988). But once the war was under way, was violence used against noncombatants beyond the possibility of moral justification, if it did in fact hasten the cessation of violence? However blameworthy the Iraqi leader Saddam Hussein has been on many counts, it should be possible to evaluate specific actions.

An argument can be made that no absolute right of noncombatants to immunity from the violence suffered by combatants should be granted, especially when many of the combatants have been conscripted or misled into joining the armed forces. Recent reports indicate that many who serve in armies around the world are children. Iran's conscription age was lowered to thirteen; the Contra rebels in Nicaragua recruited boys as young as twelve; and these are not isolated examples. Some 200,000 members of the world's armies, according to a UN report, are youngsters. Sometimes they are forcibly rounded up, sometimes they are urged by parents "to enlist in armies to gain food, jobs or payments if the child dies in battle."[6] Such "combatants" hardly seem legitimate targets while the "civilians" who support the war in which they fight are exempt.

Now let us apply this objection to terrorism. Is violence that kills young persons whose economic circumstances made military service seem to be almost their only option very much more plausibly justifiable than violence attacking well-off shoppers in a mall, shoppers whose economic comfort is enjoyed at the expense of the young persons who risk their lives in order to eat and thereby defend the shoppers? It is hard to see here a deep moral distinction between combatant and noncombatant. If the combatant is a conscript, the distinction between combatant and "ordinary person" is often difficult to draw. And while one may certainly hold that any child is innocent, it is still not clear why the children of one group should be granted an absolute right of exemption from the risk of violence when no such right is granted to the children of an opposing group, *if* the violence is justified on other grounds. When the police use violence to apprehend a suspected criminal and an innocent child is killed in the cross-fire, this is normally interpreted as an unfortunate tragedy, not a clear violation of the rights of the child. *If* an act of "unofficial violence" is otherwise justified and an innocent child is killed, it might, perhaps, be no more clearly a violation of the rights of the child. So we cannot conclude, it seems, that terrorism is necessarily always wrong even if the intention to harm noncombatants would always be present.

This is not to suggest that we should simply abandon the distinction between combatant and noncombatant. It is certainly harder to justify harming noncombatants than it is to justify harming combatants, other things being equal, and we can try to combine this distinction with usefully drawn notions of "those responsible." But as Coady notes, "if a revolution is unjustified, then any killing done in its name is unjustified whether of combatants or noncombatants" (1985, 63). And the same can be said of any repression of opponents of a regime. It is often more important to keep this in mind and to apply the judgments it provides than to rely on a distinction between otherwise legitimate and illegitimate targets.

Many of those who most bitterly denounce terrorism, such as Leiser (1979, 395), are entirely willing to sacrifice the innocent lives of hostages to uphold the principle that one should never negotiate with hostage takers. They judge that in the long run fewer lives will be lost if one upholds this principle. But this risks harm to innocent hostages and may rest on justifications quite comparable to those of hostage takers, who are willing to risk harming innocent persons to bring about a political goal such that in the long run, fewer lives overall will be lost if the goal is achieved than if intolerable oppression continues.

Lichtenberg and the anonymous author of the report on terrorism in

QQ (1987) suggest that we should refuse, in retaliating against terrorism, to sink to the tactics of the terrorist by risking the lives of the innocent. But—though they do not draw this conclusion—such concern for the lives of the innocent might then indicate that we must be willing rather than unwilling to negotiate with terrorists. The argument is always that negotiating with terrorists now risks more loss of innocent life later, but, of course, the sincere defender of terrorism makes a parallel claim, that a risk to innocent life now will avoid the further loss of innocent life later that must be expected if a repressive regime continues its unjust and violent repression.

Consequences Do Not Provide a Decisive Criterion

Most recent philosophical discussion avoids the mistake of making terrorism wrong by definition. Hare, Wellman, Coady, Holmes, and others agree that, as with violence, we ought to be able to consider whether terrorism can ever be justified. The question should be open, not ruled out by definition. But then, can terrorism be justifiable?

Burleigh Wilkins (1987) argues that consequentialism provides weak defenses against terrorism. To a consequentialist, terrorism would have to be justifiable if, on balance, it brings about better consequences than its alternatives. And though such consequentialists as Hare and Kai Nielsen think that terrorism is hardly ever justified, their arguments depend on empirical estimates that terrorism almost always produces results that are worse on consequentialist grounds than their alternatives (Wilkins, 1987). Others find the empirical claims on which such judgments rest to be questionable.

Reading the historical record is notoriously difficult. Some think, with Walter Laqueur (1988), that terrorist violence has tended to produce "violent repression and a polarization which precluded political progress" rather than the changes sought by the terrorists. The German philosopher Albrecht Wellmer (1984), building on the critical theory of Habermas, finds of the terrorism of the Red Army Faction in Germany in the 1970s that although it "reflects and brings to a head the pathologies of the system against which it is directed" (300), its net effect has been reactionary: It has provided legitimation for political repression and a defamation of the entire left.

Others think, with Charles Tilly (1969) and Lewis Coser (1966), that violent protests have been an almost normal part of the Western political process, and that they have often contributed to progressive developments. Concerning effectiveness, Richard Falk (1988) points out that the bombing of the Marine barracks in Lebanon is considered by some to be one of the most successful uses of force "in the history of recent international relations, leading a very strong power to accede to the demands of a very weak opponent" (34–35). The Marines had been deployed in Lebanon as the major expression of an American intent to support the Gemayel government, and, as a result of the bombing, were removed from Lebanon by President Reagan.

It may be almost impossible to predict whether an act of terrorism will in fact have its intended effect of hastening some political goal sought by the terrorist, or whether it will in fact do the terrorists' cause more harm than good. But as Wilkins asks, "Is there something special about acts of violence which makes them different from other acts where judgments about their consequences are concerned? We frequently do many things where the outcome is uncertain." If existing conditions are terrible, "they might prompt a prospective terrorist to reason that *any* chance of altering these states of affairs is worth the risk of failure and the near certainty of harm to property or persons that violence involves" (1987, 150).

Furthermore, states use violence and the threat of violence to uphold their laws, and some use terrorism. Many theorists still define the state in terms of its monopoly on the use of violence considered legitimate.[7] But if violence can be condemned on consequentialist grounds it can be condemned in unjustified state behavior as well as in the behavior of a state's opponents. On the other hand if violence or terrorism on the part of the state *can* be justified, it may be as impossible to predict its success as to predict the success of the violence or terrorism of its opponents. When a legal system violates the human rights of those on whom it imposes its will, the violence or terrorism it uses to do so is surely no more justified than the violence or terrorism used against it, and quite possibly it is less so. When the security forces of an unjust regime kill or brutalize detainees to deter future opposition, or shoot at random into groups of demonstrators, they engage in acts of terrorism. Even relatively legitimate legal orders on occasion violate the human rights of some; the violence or terrorism they use to uphold their authority against those they thus mistreat is not more justified than the violence or terrorism of their opponents. In both cases, predictions of success may be impossible to make accurately, but in another sense may be impossible to escape making.

TERRORISM AND RIGHTS

In my view (see Held, 1984a) we cannot adequately evaluate social action in consequentialist terms alone. The framework of rights and obligations must also be applied, and in the case of terrorism it is certainly relevant to ask, Are rights being violated, and can this be justified?

Against Hare and others who evaluate terrorism by applying utilitarian calculations, Wellman usefully considers the place of rights in evaluating terrorism. Wellman says that "certain fundamental human rights, the rights to liberty, personal security, life, property, and respect, are typically violated by acts of terrorism" (1979, 258). This does not mean that terrorism can never be justified, but that an adequate moral appraisal will have to take violations of rights into account along with any calculation of benefits and harms produced.

Coady (1985) rightfully notes the prevalent inconsistency in many discussions of terrorism. The use of violence directed at noncombatants is judged justifiable on utilitarian grounds if carried out by one's own or a friendly state, as in many evaluations of the justifiability of bombing raids in wartime in which civilians can be expected to be killed. At the same time, when revolutionaries and rebels use violence that harms noncombatants, such acts are judged on nonutilitarian grounds to be unjustifiable violations of prohibitions on how political goals are to be pursued. As Coady observes, consistency can be achieved either by applying utilitarian evaluations to both sides, or by applying nonutilitarian evaluations to both sides. He favors the latter, and concludes that terrorism is "immoral wherever and whenever it is used or proposed" (58). My own suggestion is for a nonutilitarian comparison of rights violations. It could reach a different conclusion.

One of the most difficult problems for political philosophy is the problem of how to evaluate situations in which human rights are not being respected. What are persons justified in doing to bring about such respect, and how should these actions be judged? Should "bringing about increased respect for human rights" be evaluated in consequentialist terms? But then how should this consequence be weighed against any violations of rights necessitated by the action to achieve this consequence? If we say that no violations of rights are justified, even in this case, this can become a disguised recipe for maintaining the status quo. If we permit violations, we risk undermining the moral worth of the very rights for which we are striving to achieve respect.

My suggestion is that we not yield to a merely consequentialist evaluation, but that we strive for reasonable comparative judgments. In a well-developed scheme of assured rights, rights should not be traded off against one another, or judged in comparative terms. We do not usefully speak of more of a right to vote or less of a right to vote, but of a right to vote. And we do not usefully try to determine whether a right to vote is more or is less important than a right to nondiscrimination in employment. When rights conflict, we may order them in terms of priorities or stringency; this, however, is not a matter of maximizing, but of seeking consistency. Some rights may be deemed to have priority over others, or to be more basic than others, but our aim is not to engage in trade-offs. We seek, rather, to arrive at a consistent scheme in which all the rights of all persons can be respected and none need be violated.

In a defective society, on the other hand, where rights are not in fact being respected, we should be able to make comparative judgments about which and whose rights violations are least justifiable. Is it more important, for instance, for blacks in South Africa to gain assurance of rights to personal safety than it is for white South Africans to continue to enjoy their property rights undisturbed? While blacks are denied respect for their most basic rights, it seems worse to continue these violations than to permit some comparable violations of the rights of whites participating in this denial.

Such an evaluation is not a consequentialist calculation, but it does allow us to compare rights violations. It requires us not to ignore the violations involved in maintaining an existing system, because of course charges of rights violation should not be applied only to those seeking change, while those upholding an existing system are exempt.

I shall use the expression 'effective respect for rights' to mean that an existing legal system recognizes the rights in question and effectively upholds respect for them. Of course, this does not mean that violations never occur; no legal system can secure perfect compliance with its norms. It means that violations are on the whole prevented by adequate education, socialization, and police protection, and that those who commit such violations are apprehended and dealt with to a sufficiently high degree to make respect for the rights in question generally high. There is no escape from the fact that effective respect for rights is a matter of degree, but it is quite possible to make an accurate empirical judgment that it is absent when a legal system does not even recognize a right in question as a legal right. When using the expression 'effective respect for rights', the type of rights in question should be specified; this can be done.

Let us consider the case in which a certain type of right is recognized as a human right by the major international documents and bodies establishing international norms concerning rights.[8] And consider when such a right is not recognized as a legal right for a certain group of persons in a given legal system. Clearly then there will be no effective respect for those rights of those persons in that legal system. An example would be the right to nondiscrimination on grounds of race recognized as a right in Articles 2 and 7 of the Universal Declaration of Human Rights adopted by the General Assembly of the United Nations on December 10, 1948. Under the system of apartheid in South Africa, especially before the reforms initiated by the government of F. W. deKlerk, this right was not recognized for South Africa's black population. Hence, very clearly there was for blacks in South Africa no effective respect for this right.

Frequently, rights are recognized as legal rights in a given legal system, but respect for them is not effective because law enforcement agencies are corrupt or prejudiced, or the government is inefficient or unfair in its administration, and so forth. The empirical judgment that effective respect for rights is absent may in such cases be difficult to make, and the lack of effective respect for rights can be as serious as in those cases where the right is not even recognized in the legal system. However, an advantage for purposes of moral theory in choosing a case of the latter kind, in which a human right is being violated and is not even acknowledged to be a legal right, is that there can be so little dispute at the empirical level that effective respect for rights is absent.

So let us consider this kind of case, imagining two groups A and B, and supposing that the failure to recognize the human rights of the members of Group B as legal rights in legal system L is advantageous to the members of Group A, in this case, and disadvantageous to the members of Group B, in terms of any further benefits and burdens that accrue to them in exercising or in failing to have the rights in question. However, the evaluation of comparative justifiability of rights violations will not be made in terms of these further benefits or burdens.

Now let us ask whether it can be morally justifiable to violate some rights to achieve effective respect for other rights. First, an aside: If there are legal rights in conflict with human rights such that we can judge that these legal rights ought not to exist, then what appears to be a violation of them will probably not be morally unjustified. That kind of case will not present the moral difficulties I wish to consider.

The difficult case is when achieving effective respect for the fundamental human rights of the members of one group, rights that ought to be respected, requires the violation of the fundamental human rights of the members of another group, also rights that seemingly ought to be respected. If terrorism can ever be justified, it would seem to present this kind of problem. When there is a lack of effective respect for the fundamental human rights of the members of one group, and *if* there is a reasonable likelihood that limited terrorism will significantly contribute to bringing about such effective respect, and no other effective means are available, can it be justifiable to violate the fundamental human rights of those who will suffer from such terrorism? Any act of terrorism is likely to violate their rights to "life, liberty and security of person," as specified in Article 3 of the Universal Declaration. Can this possibly be justified?

Let us specify two situations. In the first, S_1, the members of Group A have a human right to x, and they enjoy effective respect for this right in a given legal system, while the members of Group B also have a human right to x, but suffer a lack of effective respect for this right. In Situation S_2, in contrast, both the members of A and the members of B have a human right to x, and they enjoy effective respect for that right. Obviously S_2 is a morally better situation than S_1. It is the process of getting from S_1 to S_2 that is in question.

We can, it seems to me, make a number of comparative judgments. First, nonviolent methods not involving violations of human rights would certainly be morally superior to violent methods, other things equal. Defenders of nonviolence argue, often convincingly, that nonviolent pressures are in fact more successful, and lead to the loss of fewer lives, in moving societies from situations such as S_1 to situations such as S_2. It seems obvious that nonviolence is morally superior, if it can succeed.

I consider myself an advocate of nonviolence, by which I mean that one should recognize strong prima facie principles against the use of violence and always place the burden of proof, in a justification, on the violent course of action if it is claimed that violence is needed to prevent or to correct serious wrongs or violations of rights. More important, one should continually champion what Ruddick calls "a sturdy suspicion of violence" (1989, 138). One should strive to invent and to promote nonviolent forms of action and should try one's best to bring it about that nonviolent approaches are successful. It is often to this aim that our best efforts can be directed: to create and to sustain institutions that permit, encourage, and, when appropriate, are responsive to nonviolent forms of control or protest, thus deflecting tendencies on any side of a conflict to resort to violence (Harris and King, 1989).

To advocate nonviolence is to argue that there are prima facie principles against the use of violence to uphold a legal order as well as to challenge it. It may well be justifiable to forcefully intervene to prevent, say, violent assault, but force is not the same as violence, and violence usually need not and should not be used. The state has *many* means besides violence to uphold its legitimate authority and to bring about the effective respect of rights, and such nonviolent means should be developed far more than they have been. Strong prima facie arguments against violence should also apply to groups seeking changes in political and legal arrangements. Nonviolence is not acquiescence; it can be a stubborn refusal to cooperate with injustice and a determination to resist oppression, but to do so nonviolently. Feminists have added greatly to the case for nonviolence. As the author of one collection of essays writes, "Put into the feminist perspective, nonviolence is the merging of our uncompromising rage at the patriarchy's brutal destructiveness with a refusal to adopt its ways" (McAllister, 1982, iii).

In important ways that are brought out by Robin Morgan (1989), the terrorist often shares the worst *macho* aspects of his targets, mirroring the fascination with violence and the eroticization of force characteristic of the culture he seeks to attack. However, after this has been said, comparative judgments are still needed. If a judgment is made that in certain circumstances violence to uphold law is justifiable, cannot a judgment as plausibly be made that in certain other circumstances, violence to bring about respect for rights can be justifiable? And if violence can be justifiable, can terrorism, on occasion, be also? State terrorism to destroy legitimate movements of liberation exists. Can terrorism as a considered method to overcome oppression with as little loss of life as possible be, in contrast, less unjustifiable?

Gandhi is reported to have said that "it is best of all to resist oppression by non-violent means," but also that "it is better to resist oppression by violent means than to submit" (quoted in McAllister [1982, vi]). In his book on Gandhi, William Borman asserts that Gandhi "repeatedly and explicitly makes statements preferring violence to cowardice" (1986, xiv). Gandhi wrote that "my non-violence does not admit of running away from danger and leaving dear ones unprotected. Between violence and cowardly flight, I can only prefer violence to cowardice" (quoted in Borman [1986, 252–53]). This leaves us with the task of making comparative judgments concerning the use of violence among all those unwilling or unable to adopt "the summit of bravery," nonviolence, and preferring, on the various sides of any given conflict, violence to flight. It is these comparative judgments with which I am concerned.

Let us return to the example of trying to move from S_1 to S_2. If a judgment is made, especially in special circumstances, that nonviolence cannot succeed, but that terrorism will be effective in moving a society from S_1 to S_2, can engaging in terrorism be better than refraining from it? Given that it will involve a violation of human rights, can it be better to violate rights through terrorism than to avoid this violation?

Let's outline the situations and the alternatives:

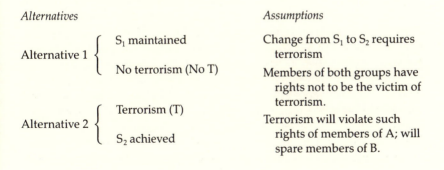

Alternatives		*Assumptions*
Alternative 1	S₁ maintained No terrorism (No T)	Change from S_1 to S_2 requires terrorism Members of both groups have rights not to be the victim of terrorism.
Alternative 2	Terrorism (T) S₂ achieved	Terrorism will violate such rights of members of A; will spare members of B.

Considerations	For Group A	For Group B
Alternative 1 $\left\{\begin{array}{l} S_1 \\[2ex] \text{No T} \end{array}\right.$	Human right to x Effective respect for this right No violations of rights vs. T	Human right to x No effective respect for this right Violations of rights to x
Alternative 2 $\left\{\begin{array}{l} \text{T} \\[2ex] S_2 \end{array}\right.$	Violations of rights vs. T Human right to x Effective respect for this right	No violations of rights vs. T Human right to x Effective respect for this right

S_1: Situation in which members of Group A have a human right to x and enjoy effective respect for this right in legal system, while members of Group B have a human right to x but no effective respect for this right and hence suffer violations of it.

S_2: Situation in which members of both groups have a human right to x and enjoy effective respect for that right.

Alternative 1 is to maintain S_1 and to refrain from terrorism; Alternative 2 is to employ terrorism and to achieve S_2. Both alternatives involve rights violations. The questions are: Can they be compared and can either be found to be less unjustifiable?

It has often been pointed out, in assessing terrorism, that we can almost never accurately predict that an outcome such as S_2 will be achieved as a result of the terrorism in question. But I am trying to deal with the moral issues *given* certain empirical claims. And *if* the empirical judgment is responsibly made that the transition is likely to achieve S_2, a situation that is clearly morally better than S_1, and that no other means can do so, can Alternative 2 be better than Alternative 1? Rights will be violated in either case. Are there any grounds on which the violations in Alternative 2 are morally less unjustifiable than the violations in Alternative 1?

It seems reasonable, I think, that on grounds of justice, it is better to equalize rights violations in a transition to bring an end to rights violations than it is to subject a given group that has already suffered extensive rights violations to continued such violations, if the degrees of severity of the two violations are similar. And this is the major argument of this essay: If we must have rights violations, a more equitable distribution of such violations is better than a less equitable distribution.

If the severity of the violations is very dissimilar, then we might judge that the more serious violations are to be avoided in favor of the less serious, regardless of who is suffering them, although this judgment could perhaps be overridden if, for instance, many different though less serious violations were suffered by the members of Group B, and this could outweigh a serious violation for the members of Group A. But generally, there would be a prima facie judgment against serious violations, such as of rights to life, to bring about respect for less serious rights, such as those to more equitable distributions of property above levels necessary for the satisfaction of basic needs.

The case on which I focus, however, involves serious violations among both groups. The human rights to personal safety of oppressed groups are, for instance, frequently violated. If a transition to a situation such as S_2 involves violations of the rights to personal safety of the oppressing group, why would this violation be less unjustifiable than the other? *Fairness would seem to recommend a sharing of the burden of rights violation*, even if no element of punishment were appealed to. If punishment is considered, it would seem more appropriate for those who had benefited from the rights violations of the members of a given group to suffer, in a transition, any necessary rights violations rather than to allow the further rights violations of those who had already been subjected to them. But punishment need not be a factor in our assessment. We can conclude that though nonviolence is always better than violence, other things being equal, one sort of terrorism—that carried out by the group that has reason to believe it can only thus successfully decrease the disregard of rights where such disregard is prevalent—is less morally unjustifiable than terrorism carried out by the group that maintains such disregard.

That justice itself often requires a concern for how rights violations are distributed seems clear. We can recognize that some distributions are unfair and seek to make them less so. Consider the following: The right to personal security, or freedom from unlawful attack, can be fully recognized as a right in a given legal community, and yet of course some assaults will occur. The community's way of trying to assure respect for such rights is likely to include the deployment of police forces. But if almost all the police forces are deployed in high-income white neighborhoods and almost none in low-income black neighborhoods, resulting in a risk of assault for inhabitants of the latter many times greater than the risk for inhabitants of the former, we can judge without great difficulty that the deployment is unfair. Or, if we take any given level of effort to protect persons from assault, and if cuts in protection are then necessary for budgetary reasons and the cuts are all made in areas already suffering the greatest threats of attack, again we can judge that such cuts are being made unfairly.

The basis for such judgments must be a principle of justice with respect to the distribution of rights violations, or of risks of such violations.[9]

This is the principle to which I am appealing in my argument concerning terrorism, and it seems clear that it is a relevant principle that we should not ignore.

What all this may show is that terrorism cannot necessarily be ruled out as unjustifiable on a rights-based analysis any more than it can on a consequentialist one. Depending on the severity and extent of the rights violations in an existing situation, a transition involving a sharing of rights violations, if this and only this can be expected to lead to a situation in which rights are more adequately respected, may well be less morally unjustifiable than continued acceptance of ongoing rights violations.

NOTES

Acknowledgments: I am grateful to the many persons who made helpful comments when this essay was presented at a philosophy department program at the Graduate School of the City University of New York; at a conference of the Greater Philadelphia Philosophy Consortium; at the conference "Violence, Terrorism and Justice" at Bowling Green State University, November 18–20, 1988; at the conference "Law and the Legitimation of Violence" at the State University of New York at Buffalo, March 16–18, 1989; and at presentations at Colgate University and at Hampshire College. I would especially like to thank Joseph Raz, Hans Oberdiek, Annette Baier, Jonathan Glover, Peter Simpson, C. A. J. Coady, Thomas Headrick, Bart Gruzalski, and Huntington Terrell.

1. See U.S. Department of State (1985). The State Department classified this attack as an act of terrorism.

2. For a useful discussion of the concept of violence, see Coady (1986).

3. Wilkinson (1974, 17), emphasis added. In a more recent book (1986) Wilkinson does not build moral judgment quite as directly into the definition. He defines political terrorism as "coercive intimidation. It is the systematic use of murder and destruction, and the threat of murder and destruction, in order to terrorize individuals, groups, communities or governments into conceding to the terrorists' political demands" (51). Then, on the basis of a useful though not unbiased survey of terrorist activity, he concludes that terrorism is "a moral crime, a crime against humanity" (66).

4. Leiser (1979, chap. 13). Leiser considers Palestinians to have provided the foremost examples of terrorist acts. Israeli "reprisals" and the children and noncombatants killed in them are not mentioned.

5. On this see especially Falk (1988).

6. *New York Times*, August 7, 1988, sec. A.

7. The classic statement is Max Weber's: "The state is considered the sole source of the 'right' to use violence. . . . The state is a relation of men dominating men, a relation supported by means of legitimate (i.e., considered to be legitimate) violence" (1958, 78).

8. See, for example, *Human Rights Documents* (1983), compiled by the U.S. Committee on Foreign Affairs. For discussion, see, for example, Nickel (1987).

9. This argument is in response to a comment by Rogers Albritton.

16

THE LEGITIMATION OF FEMALE VIOLENCE

Lance K. Stell

BIAS AND THE LAW OF SELF-DEFENSE

In 1978, Elizabeth Schneider and Susan Jordan outlined the legal problems a battered woman faces when she kills her batterer. These problems intensify should the battered woman prefer to plead justification rather than some form of excuse because, Schneider and Jordan claim, our traditional rules of self-defense are not gender-neutral. They are premised on male experiences with violence. Thus appearances of impartiality notwithstanding, the law of self-defense carries a sex-bias. They further claim that the recent trend for courts to listen to women's voices regarding violence has ironically reinforced sexist stereotypes.

Even the most cursory investigation of our legal history reveals significant asymmetries in the law's treatment of men and women when they use force. Traditionally, men enjoyed the protection of paramour statutes that permitted a husband to kill his wife's lover should he catch the adulterers *in flagrante delicto*.[1] Wives possessed no similar privilege. Both ancient Roman law and the English common law (see Oppenlander, 1981) have permitted husbands to use force to secure dominance over their wives. Prosecutors, judges, and juries have tended to treat a husband who kills his wife's lover more leniently than a woman who kills her rapist (Schneider and Jordan, 1978, 153). Legal authorization for husbands routinely to use force against their wives has gradually withered away; but women who use defensive force against their husbands still face certain distinctive problems should they attempt to argue that their use of force was legally privileged.

In a homicide trial where the defendant is a battered woman who pleads self-defense, the judge must make many decisions that may prejudice the outcome against her. For example, in the trial's discovery phase, the woman may indicate her desire to introduce expert testimony on battered-woman syndrome. The judge must decide whether to permit it, and may decide that such testimony, while relevant to an impaired mental-state defense, is irrelevant to an argument for justification. The reasoning might go like this. Testimony tending to show that the woman suffered from a "syndrome" could support a claim that her homicidal actions were motivated by a sincerely held but unreasonable belief. But such testimony could not conceivably establish that her motivating belief was reasonable. As a matter of law, anyone claiming a legal privilege to kill must produce evidence to show that the homicide was motivated by a reasonable belief in its necessity. So, as a matter of law, battered-woman syndrome testimony cannot be relevant.

For example, after extensive pretrial examination the trial court in *State* v. *Kelly* refused to permit expert testimony on battering in support of a self-defense plea. The trial court said it "would be appropriate to give testimony to a lay jury as to the consequences of the syndrome, but that's not the bottom line. The bottom line is, to put it vulgarly, so What? Because, under our law what would it go to? and that's what I want to ask you, What would that evidence go to? It does not go to self-defense."[2]

Plausible as this reasoning seems, it contains a questionable assumption, namely, that "syndromes" can distort powers of judgment (perhaps in excusable ways) but cannot enhance them. The definition of 'syndrome' does not imply this. To suffer from a syndrome is to display a grouping of symptoms typical of a physical or mental disease (see Gregory, 1987, 765). Although 'disease' connotes abnormality, or an overall subpar condition, that someone suffers from a syndrome does not preclude the possibility that one of its symptoms may be an acquired ability to apprehend a relevant reality more vividly and accurately than the average person. Such an eventuality may surprise us, but our prejudices should not blind us totally to the possibility.

Expert testimony on battered-woman syndrome seeks to explain how its victims can possess hypersensitivity to signals of grave danger and so apprehend danger more acutely than the average person. If a judge had a prejudice about women who kill their husbands (say, that women tend to respond to physical intimidation hysterically), this might tend to increase his or her skepticism about expert testimony about "syndromes." Prejudices need not show themselves in blatant ways. At their most subtle, they may simply increase our resistance to accepting what is novel but not unreasonable, or they may lend more credibility to a line of thought than it deserves, or they may seem to urge an interpretation of rules or principles that is not compelled logically.

Until quite recently, courts tended to exclude expert testimony on battered-woman syndrome in support of a self-defense plea. There are problems with such testimony, such as the tendency to convert criminal trials into a contest between the prosecution's experts and the defense's experts. There is also the more specific problem of having experts testify on "normative" questions; for we may think that a social scientist might give testimony tending to *explain* an action but also think that there is no such thing as expert testimony that could tend to *justify* it. Nonetheless it is now widely accepted that such testimony is relevant.[3]

In this essay, I consider seriously the possibility that sexist bias may exert an influence on judicial discretion, not in decisions about expert testimony, but in the decision whether to instruct the jury on self-defense. Occasions calling for the exercise of discretion provide a natural opportunity for a sexist bias to influence judgment. It is not my purpose to argue that such bias exists, although I think it does. Instead, I want to give justifying reasons for judges to give self-defense instructions when tradition would seem to be against it. An example of such instructions is the current practice in North Carolina, where a defendant is entitled to an instruction on perfect self-defense as justification for homicide in which, when viewed in the light most favorable to the defendant, there is evidence tending to show that at the time of the killing:

1. It appeared to defendant and she believed it to be necessary to kill the deceased in order to save herself from death or great bodily harm, and
2. Defendant's belief was reasonable in that the circumstances as they appeared to her at the time were sufficient to create such a belief in the mind of a person of ordinary firmness, and
3. Defendant was not the aggressor in bringing on the affray, she did not aggressively and willingly enter into the fight without legal excuse or provocation, and
4. Defendant did not use excessive force, that is, did not use more force than was necessary or reasonably appeared to her to be necessary under the circumstances to protect herself from death or great bodily harm.

(Note: I have taken the liberty of restating the rules in the feminine gender. Courts do not take this liberty. Does it make a difference?)

In the pretrial, discovery phase of the trial, a defendant under a homicide indictment may indicate that she plans to plead self-defense. The judge must decide to permit it or not on the basis of an assessment whether that defense is relevant and appropriate to the circumstances of the case. Even if the defendant secures the court's permission to pursue a strategy based on the theory of self-defense during the trial, the judge may refuse to instruct the jury on the law of self-defense when instructions on the law relevant to the case are given to the jury. This must happen if the judge finds that the defendant has failed in the end to provide any credible evidence that would tend to convince a reasonable person that the killing was legally privileged. On the other hand if the judge finds that there is some evidence (a very weak requirement) that might tend to convince a reasonable person that the killing was defensive within the legal meaning of the word, then the judge must either read to the jury the self-defense instructions prepared and submitted by the defense or substitute more appropriate instructions of his or her own.

My argument, in a nutshell is this: To enjoy a legal privilege to use deadly force requires that the would-be killer be motivated by a reasonable belief that the use of such force was necessary. Typically, the necessity requirement is interpreted as requiring of the defendant that her actions be motivated by the sincere, reasonably held belief that she was in "imminent danger" of death or great bodily harm when she killed. Taking inspiration from a recent court of appeals decision in North Carolina, I claim that years of victimization by a battering spouse may lead some women to believe reasonably that they are in "constant danger" of death or great bodily harm at his hands. If it is possible for her to believe this reasonably, then she believes that she may be killed or seriously harmed by him at any time. In some circumstances, to be in constant danger is also to be in "imminent danger." Whether the circumstances of a particular case exemplify this sort of congruence calls for a factual judgment, not a legal judgment. Factual questions are the province of the jury. Therefore, if a female defendant can produce some evidence to show that she was not unreasonable in thinking that she was in constant danger, the judge should instruct the jury on self-defense so it can decide whether the circumstances support as reasonable the defendant's belief that she was in imminent danger when she destroyed her batterer.

I shall not be arguing the radical idea that suffering from battered-woman syndrome confers on the victim of it a privilege to kill her batterer. Instead, I argue that living in constant danger of death or great bodily harm may lead a victim to the reasonable belief that destroying the threat to her life is necessary and that the facts of a particular case may support her acting on this belief even though the batterer is asleep when she kills him.

The Traditional Law of Self-Defense

The legal doctrine of self-defense stands as an important but carefully circumscribed exception to the prohibition against lethal self-help. Philosophers have asserted the privilege to kill in self-defense since antiquity. For example, Cicero asserted it (unsuccessfully) on behalf of a client as follows: "And indeed, gentlemen, there exists a law, not written down anywhere but inborn in our hearts; a law which comes to us not by training or custom or reading but by derivation and absorption and adoption from nature itself; a law which has come to us not from theory but from practice, not by instruction but by natural intuition. I refer to the law which lays it down that, if our lives are endangered by plots or violence or armed robbers or enemies, any and every method of protecting ourselves is morally right" (1969, 222). But contrary to many commentators, it seems not always to have enjoyed explicit legal recognition, at least not in England. Until 1532, all killings, of whatever sort, were legal wrongs against the king requiring the king's pardon (Hurnard, 1969, 298). Killers could argue that they killed for the sake of self-preservation and from necessity, but there was no right to acquittal even if their assertions were persuasive. Killers (even those who killed accidentally) needed the king's pardon, something the king had no duty to give. This exception apart, the doctrine answers to a near-universal sentiment that when an innocent defender, acting from a motive of self-protection, uses deadly force to preempt an aggressor's lethal threat, she does nothing the law should forbid. Both Hobbes and Locke seem to agree that the interest in self-preservation must be central to an account of what makes it rational and right for there to be a political order at all.

Controversy arises on several fronts. Even if we set aside Cicero's troublesome claims that the law of self-defense is "inborn in our hearts," and that when necessary we may do whatever it takes to neutralize deadly threats to ourselves, how can we justify a doctrine that permits intentional killing?[4] For present purposes, suppose that we can anchor a doctrine of self-defense to some fundamental, protectable interest. But even if this much be granted, many troublesome questions remain. We want to draw the rules conferring the privilege to use deadly force carefully. We must formulate rules to guide us in distinguishing permissible uses of defensive deadly force from impermissible uses of force even though they be defensively motivated. For example:

1. Must a defender's belief that the use of deadly force is necessary be true as well as reasonably arrived at and sincerely entertained? Or should we permit the defender some leeway for mistaken judgment in the light of what we know about deadly encounters (e.g., that often they do not lend themselves to sober, measured thought).

2. If the defender could have fled the trouble in complete safety but failed, has her defensive privilege disappeared? Or, should we hold, merely, that she not be unreasonable in failing to take a nonlethal option?

3. Must the defender refrain from using preemptive deadly force until the moment the aggressor's threat of death or great bodily injury is imminent? If so, when does that moment come? Does it come so late that, were the defender to delay any longer, the aggressor would succeed in killing or severely harming the defender? How strict do we want to be in requiring the defender to calculate this precisely?

There is nothing about the concept of self-defense that forces us to answer any of these questions one way rather than another. There are a range of more or less restrictive possible rules. In traversing the range we will pass a point where there will be no practical difference between restrictive permission to use defensive force and a prohibition of it. But I doubt we can say where that point is. Our concept of self-defense is fuzzy at the margins, so it will not give clear answers to questions about marginal cases.

When interests conflict, as they do in close encounters of the lethal kind, not only must the law decide which side to favor, it must decide how much to favor it. For example, suppose the law were to answer the first question negatively. Clearly, the defender would be better off than if it answered affirmatively. Why? The defender's burden of restraint would be lighter: The law's negative answer relieves the defender of the costs of (reasonable) mistake. Clearly, defenders would benefit if the law permitted the use of deadly force whenever they reasonably and honestly believed that it was necessary to forestall death or great bodily harm. Others would lose, however; for in some cases the law will permit defenders to kill innocent people (viz., when the defender's sincerely held, reasonable belief is false). Even a person who believed that the right to self-defense is conferred by natural law could not show that permission to kill innocent people is logically tied to the concept of self-defense.

Because no one can claim that the more permissive rule follows from the right to self-defense, it is tempting to suppose that if there is justification for answering the first question negatively, it must be a utilitarian justification. How might the reasoning go? Like this: Overall, society will be safer with the more permissive rule because rational aggressors will be less willing to initiate deadly assaults under the permissive rule. The rule is Pareto-efficient because those innocent people who will lose their lives to defenders exercising their deadly privilege under the permissive rule will have been (fully?) compensated *ex ante* by virtue of having lived in the safer society.

Notice that 'safer society' means "the society with fewer violent-encounter deaths for nonaggressors" and not "the society with fewer violent-encounter deaths overall." I also emphasize the argument's assumption that there is a causal connection between a society's rules about the use of force and a deterrent effect on the behavior of rational aggressors.

Imagine the following: Let R_1 be the comparatively permissive rule and R_2 be the comparatively restrictive rule. Suppose that with R_1, the number of violent-encounter deaths in society is 25,000, composed of 15,000 defenders and 10,000 aggressors. Suppose that with R_2, the number of violent-encounter deaths in society is 20,000, composed of 18,000 defenders and 2,000 aggressors. The safer society (for innocent defenders) is the one with R_1, even though total violent-encounter deaths are higher. (It might be thought that a utilitarian must be indifferent to who tends to die under R_1 and R_2, and restrict concern to minimizing aggregate violent-encounter deaths. But I fail to see why this should be so. It might be better for society overall if more aggressors are killed even if the rule's effect is to increase aggregate violent-encounter deaths somewhat.)

But utilitarian reasoning is not the only route to the more permissive rule. Suppose the law were to follow the more restrictive rule. Aggressors would be better off under it because law-abiding defenders would bear the extra burden that having sincerely held, reasonable, and true beliefs imposes. Since we know that aggressors generally enjoy an advantage in deadly encounters (for one thing, they tend to know their own malicious intentions before defenders can infer them), we can argue that it would be unfair to permit aggressors to gain even more from their law-abiding victims because of the law's burden that the victims take extra care in forming beliefs about their assailants. On such reasoning, we can argue that any reasonable person selecting rules for the society in which he or she would live would insist on the more permissive rule. This argument for the comparatively permissive rule fastens on its fairness and on the claim that it would be chosen by any reasonable person under circumstances that model a plausible conception of objectivity.

It is not my purpose to defend either of these putative justifications for the more permissive rule. A host of difficulties await whichever effort may seem more promising. My purpose has instead been to show that mere belief in the doctrine of self-defense is not sufficient to settle marginal perplexities with a legally useful statement of the doctrine. Possible rules can treat the interests at stake more or less fairly. They may also impose on some classes of defenders burdens that are greater than those imposed on others.

What I hope to show is that one cannot just rule out what I shall call "battered-woman defenses" (which are paradigmatically asserted when a battered woman kills her batterer when he sleeps) as incompatible with "our concept" of self-defense, that is, as ruled out as a matter of law on its plain meaning. I will suggest that in formulating and interpreting legal rules that enable us to work with the doctrine of self-defense, we should employ a theory that says what it means to secure equally the interests of men and women in not being victimized by violent assault. But I emphasize the point that we cannot settle the questions I have raised by attempting to reflect more deeply on our concept of self-defense.

Whither Bias?

The claim that the traditional law of self-defense is sex biased should not be confused with a claim that it "discriminates" in some constitutionally forbidden sense. The rules of self-defense do not categorize by sex nor do they stigmatize women. Certainly they do not do so explicitly. Because women are not precluded from claiming self-defense on account of sex, how could the law be sex biased?

Although the law does not preclude a woman's escaping criminal liability for homicide by asserting self-defense, carrying the burden of the defense is generally more difficult for women than it is for men. This is so because of stereotypes about women and violence, and also because of contingent facts about women.

Consider the latter first. Although the restraint the law imposes falls on all would-be defenders, it does not do so equally. It burdens smaller, weaker defenders more than larger, stronger ones. Because women tend to be smaller and weaker than men, they will, in general, be at a greater disadvantage than men because of the law's restraint requirements. Women tend to have their violent encounters with men, not with other women. (Of course male defenders tend to have *their* violent encounters with men, too.) If a violent encounter involves an escalating level of violence, the law forbids excessive force. Traditionally, judges have interpreted this idea under the notion of parity or proportionality of force. The law tends to withhold the right of deadly preemption until the *instant* it is reasonable to believe that the aggressor's use of deadly force is imminent. But if the defender is a law-abiding woman (i.e., a woman who refrains from using unlawful force), this interpretation would seem to offer her little chance of repelling her larger, more powerful aggressor's force, slap for slap, shove for shove, blow for blow. Her only hope of avoiding her own violent death may require that she preempt her assailant with a deadly weapon.

These conjectures seem confirmed by the facts. Jones (1980, 320–21) found that nine out of ten murdered women are murdered by men. Four out of five are murdered at home. Almost three out of four are murdered by husbands or lovers. The percentage of women killed by strangers is negligible. Because women tend to be weaker than the men who batter them, when they strike back they typically use a weapon as an equalizer. Browne (1987, 11) found that when men kill women, they tend to beat them to death.

It might be objected that there is nothing sexist in the law's restraint requirements. They fall on all smaller, weaker defenders, male or female. It is a price we must pay for taking a stand against the use of excessive force or precipitant use of deadly force. If a defender wants to enjoy the law's permission, she must not employ deadly force except as a last resort, when she is sure that it is absolutely necessary. That this handicaps a smaller, weaker defender more than a larger, stronger defender is unfortunate but not unfair.

What does this objection come to in practical terms? Do we want to require a woman to have good inductive, hence rational, grounds for deadly fear before permitting her to destroy her assailant if she can? Must she have survived a near-fatal beating at the hands of her spouse at least once before she has a right to early preemption next time round? But if she has already survived a brutal beating, does she not have good inductive grounds for supposing that she can survive the next one without resorting to deadly force? Must she have reason to suppose that the current attack threatens more harm than the one she previously survived before she may preempt? Does surviving a number of beatings gradually erode the basis for her claiming self-defense unless they were increasingly brutal? Does submitting to the brutality of her spouse make it unreasonable for her to decide to fight back now that there is evidence that he probably will not kill her?

REASONABLENESS AND THE BATTERED-WOMAN SYNDROME

Reasonableness

In appraising a woman's claim that she killed in self-defense, the law asks first whether she honestly believed the danger was grave and imminent and that nothing short of deadly force would eliminate it. Second, the law asks whether her belief was reasonable in light of all the circumstances. Not uncommonly, jurors apply the reasonableness test by imagining *themselves* in the defender's situation and then considering what *they* would have done. But so doing may distort the appraisal of a woman's defensive actions by failing to filter out common stereotypes about women who use force to defend themselves. Unless effective testimony challenging stereotypes about women and violence is presented at trial and properly treated by the judge, a jury might think that no innocent, reasonable woman would find it necessary to kill her spouse. Gender-based stereotypes might cause a jury to suspect that the defensive actions of a female killer must be faulty because she probably provoked the trouble (because she is whiny or a nagging bitch) or probably were unnecessary because even if he beat her as she claimed, a reasonable person could (and would) have left him, or the stereotype might lead a jury to agree unreflectively and unfairly with the prosecutor's argument that her acquiring a weapon was murderous, part of the preparation for a planned killing, because innocent women have nothing to do with the machines of violence. Our society stereotypes women as (naturally?) incompetent in handling the machines of violence. The first comprehensive, federally funded study of firearms and violence in American life (Newton and Zimring, 1969) dismissed women's defensive concerns in one sentence: "Women generally are less capable of self-defense [than men] and less knowledgeable about guns" (64).

Buttressing this stereotype, the media tend to react with amazement (and not uncommonly with an air of disapproval) to women who buy deadly weapons (especially handguns) and seek defensive proficiency in their use. As cast by the stereotype, women should be no better at managing the means of applying deadly force than it would have them be at handling mice or snakes or changing oil filters. We still live with a social perception that threatened women are hysterical and that armed threatened women are a danger to everyone except to their assailants.

A rash of violent assaults on women not uncommonly prompts chiefs of police and newspaper editorials to remind women of the repellent power of hat pins, house keys, fingernail files. They solemnly advise women to "buy a police whistle," to "tell him you have AIDS," or to "kick him where it hurts." What reasonable reassurance can a battered woman get from a defensive repertory like this, clutching her police whistle, limbering up her kicking motion, as she waits with her children in fear of the return of her drunken, brutal spouse? Can she think that authorities and opinion shapers have taken seriously her fears of victimization? Can we imagine the police chief giving similar advice to a male bank president friend who had received death threats? Or would he more likely offer to facilitate his friend's getting a "carry permit," offer to help him pick out a handgun, and urge him to take a course in safe gun handling and defensive gun use?

But with women and handguns it is different. A woman who asks about firearms for defense may hear someone say (usually a man, but not necessarily; many women buy the stereotype, too) that the gun she acquires for self-defense most likely will be used to kill or wound an acquaintance or family member. What irony! Anyone who has studied female victimization seriously (see Kates, 1979, 132; Jones, 1980, passim) would know that her spouse or other male acquaintances are the ones most likely to sexually assault her or try to kill her. Or she may hear that the gun she relies on for protection will be seized from her and used against her. Except in movies, this seems not to happen (Kates, 1979, 159). In fact, there are myriad instances in which women have used handguns to kill, wound, or frighten off their attackers. It is illuminating that police firearms instructors warn their students *never* to try to wrest a handgun from a person unless they have reason to believe that they will be shot anyway (in which case they have nothing to lose).

Overcoming these stereotypes presents challenges to courts, the media, and opinion shapers generally. Feminist lawyers and social scientists have done much to confront stereotypes about women and violence by successfully pressing courts to admit expert testimony on battered women. The media have produced dramatic presentations of women who kill the men who batter them. Social scientists have discovered that, contrary to the stereotype, females in increasing numbers are buying and learning to use firearms for defensive purposes, and because society cannot protect them, doing so may be the best alternative for some women.

Battered-Woman Syndrome

An old cliché says "Home is where the heart is." A newer cliché says "Home is where the hurt is." For many women, the newer cliché is too true to be good. Domestic violence haunts the lives of many women; the *State* vs. *Kelly* Amicus Briefs (251; see also Straus, Gelles, and Steinmetz, 1980) contend that wife battering occurs in approximately 1.8 million homes. The men in the lives of these women regularly beat and sexually assault them. Yet, a woman who uses deadly force against her batterer faces distinctive problems if she claims the killing was justified by her defensive privilege.

If she claims that her spouse brutalized her for years, the law will want to know why she had not defended herself on the first occasion or had not reported the assault to the police. A sordid story of continuous abuse invites the prosecutor to paint her use of deadly force as retaliatory, punitive, and premeditated rather than a reasonable response to fear of imminent peril. An untutored (even if sympathetic) jury may see a clear motive for revenge but fail to appreciate that the battered defendant could reasonably think of her life with her spouse as a reign of terror rather than as a series of isolated domestic spats.

It will be the prosecutor's duty to challenge the reasonableness of her belief that her use of deadly force was necessary on the ground that a reasonable person would have left such an unpleasant situation straightaway. Her own lawyer, anticipating this, may push her away from claiming that her use of force was reasonable in the circumstances and toward an argument that her use of force, while wrong, should be excused because she was temporarily insane, driven mad by the abuse she had learned to tolerate. This latter strategy, even if prudent (and ultimately successful) reinforces the stereotype that any woman who uses violence against her husband must be either murderous or off her rocker.

But are these suspicions not appropriate? Killers have an incentive to claim that they acted with justification. Not uncommonly, people have an extravagant view of what they may do in "self-defense." How is it sexist to suspect that a woman killer would respond to the same incentives as a man or suffer from the same illusions about her legal privilege? How can "expert testimony" serve any good purpose in dealing with these sensible suspicions?

Getting courts initially to admit expert testimony on what has become known as "battered-woman syndrome" faced certain obvious difficulties. First, courts had to satisfy themselves of the existence of expertise on the subject. And expertise requires that (1) the content of the testimony go "beyond the ken of the average layperson," (2) the state of knowledge be such as to reliably support a scientific opinion, (3) the individual in fact have valid claim to be an expert in the field (see *Dyas* v. *United States*, 1977).

Even when a court recognizes the existence of expert opinion on a subject, the judge must decide whether the testimony of the expert is relevant and material to the strategy of the defense. What legal benefit might an expert's testimony be to a battered woman?

An expert can speak generally about battering. According to Walker (1979), for example, there tends to be a cycle of violence in the battering of women: (1) a tension building stage; (2) an acute battering phase; and (3) a loving, contrite, reformist phase wherein the batterer begs forgiveness and promises "never again." The battering severely affects victims psychologically as well as physically and often involves psychological abuse and intimidation. An expert can also draw parallels between paradigm cases of battered women and the defendant, can render a professional opinion on whether the defendant suffers from the syndrome and in so doing explain actions by the defendant that otherwise might seem incredible to a jury. Specifically, the expert's testimony

1. may challenge successfully any disposition of the jury to suppose that a battered woman somehow deserves, enjoys, or provokes her beatings. (Even well-intentioned friends often counsel battered women to avoid saying or doing the things that trigger the beatings, encouraging the victim to suppose either that she causes her own trouble or that her friends think she does). The social tendency to find contributory fault in the victim of battering as well as the deterrent effect of spousal threats, when pointed out by the expert, may help the jury understand why victims tend to conceal the brutality. Not uncommonly, victims tend to label injuries requiring professional treatment as "accidents."
2. can offer an explanation why the woman failed to leave her spouse. Victims commonly lack income, and job skills, and have dependent children. Victims who flee their batterer often receive fiercer beatings and death threats.
3. can explain the woman's feelings of learned helplessness, her feeling that her batterer is omnipotent and that the society cooperates to keep her under his power. Ignorant but well-meaning friends may unwittingly contribute to perpetuating the brutality by revealing the whereabouts of the victim to a penitent-seeming batterer. Even

professionals may contribute to a woman's feelings of helplessness. Many social workers avoid placing blame on individuals. Instead of placing blame on wicked individual wrongdoers, they direct their attention to the dynamics of "problem relationships." This approach encourages the nonjudgmental idea that each side makes its own contribution to the trouble, when, in fact, in many instances it is the woman's sheer availability as much as anything that "provokes" the beatings she receives.

4. can explain the development of the woman's hyper-perceptivity to the "looks" and "sounds" presaging outbreaks of savage brutality.[5] Demeanor that might strike the average person as entirely innocent can be deadly warnings of imminent danger to a battered woman. Since a necessary condition for permitting "expert testimony" is that the matters in question fall outside the ken of the average layperson, there is an argument that a judge should not permit an expert on battered-woman's syndrome to testify about the hyper-perceptivity of battered women to the subtle signs of impending peril. It is "common sense" that a person's distinctive experience makes a difference in his or her ability to perceive and that intimates can detect in each other signs of amusement, annoyance, or anger that would be missed by outsiders. Thus, the argument: If such knowledge is common sense, then it is not outside the ken of the average layperson; if it is not outside the ken of the average layperson, then the judge should not permit an expert to testify about it; such knowledge is common sense, so judges should exclude it. The retort is that stereotypes concerning women and violence are likely to prevent jurors from employing their common sense on the matter in question and that permitting expert testimony can offset the effects of stereotypes to some degree.

Initially, courts were willing to admit expert testimony on battered-woman's syndrome in support of a plea of temporary insanity but not self-defense. It is not hard to see why. Expert testimony that the defendant suffered from a "syndrome" fits naturally with a diminished capacity, or a mental impairment defense. Yet certain characteristics of battered-woman syndrome, especially "learned helplessness," seem to support an argument that an act of destruction was necessary. If women suffering from the syndrome tend to feel that nothing short of a killing will release them from their torment, we can better understand the actions of a woman who has killed her batterer and perhaps think that she did not act unreasonably.

Expert testimony about the hyper-perceptivity of battered women toward apparently "innocent" events that in fact presage savage brutality is relevant to the traditional requirement that a righteous killer must honestly and reasonably believe that she faced imminent danger. This testimony helps a jury understand how a battered woman could perceive reality more acutely than the average person—something a jury might fail to ponder if left with nothing more than their common sense to guide them.

If the expert's testimony could only support the *honesty* of a battered woman's belief that her use of deadly force was necessary, then it would be useless to support a claim of reasonableness. But such testimony bids to reach much farther—right to the heart of the imminent danger requirement.

KINDS OF REAL DANGER

Danger and Preemption

Self-defense is not a legal version of "tit for tat." Successful self-defense involves preemption in the trivial sense that the defender must destroy the aggressor before what the aggressor threatens comes to pass. How early may the defender strike? Suppose the defender faces several aggressors at once, may the defender begin to use deadly force earlier than if there had been but one assailant? Presumably the defender should be able to use deadly force early enough to repel the (reasonably anticipated) attack of them all, otherwise the law would, in effect, condemn to death defenders facing several attackers. Repelling several may take more time than repelling one, so the onset of the defender's permissible use of deadly force should come earlier. Should the onset time be just a function of the number of attackers, or should we make allowance for facts about their armament, their reputation for brutality? Should smaller, weaker defenders enjoy earlier onset times than larger, stronger defenders?

Suppose a battered woman kills her batterer while he is asleep. But unlike Francine Hughes (made famous by Farah Fawcett in "The Burning Bed"), who (successfully) pleaded temporary insanity, she pleads self-defense instead. Apparently, juries have acquitted at least three times in such circumstances. With the batterer asleep, presumably there are no subtle signs that a hyper-perceptive women could reasonably judge to be symptoms of imminent danger (other than the possibly well-founded expectation that when he awakens he may beat her to death).[6]

A battered woman commonly perceives her batterer as comparatively invulnerable and thinks that resistance to his brutality is impossible while he is awake. Might she think reasonably that the only way to escape his brutality is to kill him while he sleeps? If the law refuses to privilege the killing of anyone not awake, then there is no way for a battered woman who thinks of her batterer as invulnerable while awake to also think of self-defense as a genuine option.

One alternative is to judge the battered woman's estimate of her husband's power as an honest but unreasonable belief. Her belief is clearly not on all fours with that of a person who honestly imagines that his daughter is possessed by demons and kills her in an exorcism. A battered woman is not imagining that her batterer counts as a genuine threat to her. Clearly he is. What is in question is the status of her belief that he is invulnerable when awake and the consequent belief that the only way of ending his reign of terror without increasing her peril requires that she strike while he sleeps. If she believes reasonably (even if falsely) that he is invulnerable, then the consequent belief is reasonable too. Should a judge instruct the jury on self-defense when a battered woman has killed her batterer while he slept?

Imminent Danger and Constant Danger: A Tale of Two Cases

Two battered-woman cases, one from North Carolina and the other from Kansas, that focus the question dramatically were decided in 1988. They are dramatic because they are in many respects mirror images of each other. Both involved battered women who, having endured years (in the former case twenty years and in the latter twelve years) of savagery of such magnitude as to strain the credulity of any decent person, killed their husbands while the husbands slept. Both pleaded self-defense.

In North Carolina, the trial court refused to instruct the jury on self-defense because as a matter of law no one can reasonably believe that a sleeping man presents an imminent danger. The woman was convicted of manslaughter but appealed, claiming that the trial court erred in refusing to instruct the jury on self-defense. The court of appeals agreed and remanded the case, holding that the facts presented at trial were such as to permit a reasonable person to find that the killing was legally privileged. The court of appeals swept aside the obstacle that had seemed insurmountable to the trial court, namely, the fact that the deceased was killed while he slept. It ruled unanimously that the deceased's being asleep was "but a momentary hiatus in a continuous reign of terror" (*State of North Carolina* v. *Judy Laws Norman*, 394).

In Kansas, the trial court, over the prosecution's objections, acceded to the defense's request that the jury receive a self-defense instruction. The jury acquitted. But the State appealed on the point of law asking whether the trial court erred in instructing the jury, because the deceased was asleep when he was killed. The Kansas Supreme Court agreed with the State, holding that "When a battered woman kills her sleeping spouse when she is in no imminent danger, the killing is not reasonably necessary and a self-defense instruction may not be given" (*State* v. *Stewart*). Because the North Carolina ruling had been cited by the defense as a reason for upholding the trial court, the Kansas Supreme Court responded as follows:

> There is no doubt that the North Carolina court determined that the sleeping husband was an evil man who deserved the justice he received from his battered wife. Here, similar comparable and compelling facts exist. But . . . to permit capital punishment to be imposed upon the subjective conclusion of the [abused] individual that prior acts and conduct of the deceased justified the killing would amount to a leap into the abyss of anarchy. Finally, our legislature has not provided for capital punishment for even the most heinous crimes. We must, therefore, hold that when a battered woman kills her sleeping spouse when there is no imminent danger, the killing is not reasonably necessary and a self-defense instruction may not be given. To hold otherwise in this case would in effect allow the execution of the abuser for past or future acts and conduct." (*State* v. *Stewart*)

It seems to me that the North Carolina Court of Appeals (although overturned) is right and Kansas Supreme Court wrong.[7] The years of savage beatings, death threats, and horrifying degradation established as fact in these cases meets the very weak requirement to produce some evidence tending to convince a reasonable person on the jury that the defendants may have believed reasonably that they could have been killed by their batterers at any time. If so, it was not unreasonable for these defendants to believe that deadly preemption was necessary when they in fact resorted to it.

This is not an argument for acquittal. It is an argument that evidence of constant danger should elicit a self-defense instruction from the judge. Then the jury must decide whether the facts together with the law of self-defense compel it to exonerate such desperate killers.

There is another argument. The North Carolina trial court held that it was unreasonable, as a matter of law, to consider a sleeping man an imminent danger. If we can give a paradigm case in which killing a sleeping man seems justified by our defensive privilege, then it will be a matter of factual judgment whether any other circumstance involving the killing of a sleeping man is sufficiently like the paradigm case so as to be similarly privileged. If so, it would be wrong to withhold jury instructions solely on the ground that it is unreasonable as a matter of law to believe that killing a sleeping man is necessary.

Can we produce such a paradigm case? Suppose a kidnapper tells his victim that he plans to beat her to death eventually and that gradually he will intensify the beatings until she comes to regard the prospect of death as a blessing. He takes her into her bedroom and administers the first beating. This is followed by a more brutal beating. And so on. He pauses to have a few beers, becomes sleepy, and dozes off. His victim dashes for the door. He awakens, intercepts her, and nearly beats her to death. He has a few more beers and dozes again. To escape the torment, she attempts suicide. He awakens to intercede, telling her that she will die when it pleases him and not otherwise. Again he dozes off. Finally, having concluded that she may be killed at any time and that escape and even suicide are futile, she eases a gun from his belt and shoots him as he sleeps.

It is *possible* that she could have slipped out the door and escaped instead of shooting him. It is *possible* that he was only bluffing when he said he was going to kill her. But can we claim, *on these facts,* that she recklessly, or negligently concluded that killing him was necessary? A negative answer is not logically compelled. But an affirmative answer would be sheerly unreasonable. To so answer would express an outrageous indifference to the legal benefit human predators would reap from such a restrictive interpretation of reasonableness. Such a restrictive interpretation would not differ effectively from a rejection of the doctrine of self-defense altogether.

CONCLUSION

I have accepted the claim that there is sex-bias in the way in which the traditional law of self-defense has been interpreted. However, I think there is hope for its elimination short of rewriting the law itself, although I am not completely confident that what I have urged amounts to an extension or a stretching of the law rather than a redefinition of it. My current view is that proper interpretation of the law we have will result in a greater willingness of judges to instruct juries on self-defense in battered-woman cases. This will be a step to more just treatment of women who kill the men who brutalize them. But it is a very small step. Social awareness of the routine battering of women remains low. More shelters for battered women would help. An increased willingness of police officers to arrest and incarcerate batterers would help, too.

But sexist stereotypes about women and violence will survive such palliatives. Most women (and many feminists, ironically) continue to believe that their physical safety should rest in the hands of men primarily and that it is unfeminine to take seriously the practical implications of assuming the responsibility for protecting themselves. Whatever other merits it may have, the "ethics of caring" so thoughtfully developed by some feminists does not address seriously the defensive needs of women, nor does it confront the fact that there can be no equality in a relationship in which one party depends for her physical safety on the other. Until women insist on providing for their own defense in the first instance, women's liberation will remain an unfulfilled dream.

Kates has described the situation aptly. "For men know that through-out all the prior ages of history the bottomline in male–female relations has always been woman's need for male protection. So they lived with a male protector and accepted his dictation of their role, either as a condition of receiving his protection, or because he would impose it upon them by physical force, or both" (1979). When women cease to vest responsibility for their physical safety in the hands of men, they will have taken another important step toward equality.

NOTES

Acknowledgments: In writing this paper, I received helpful comments from the following people: Carl Wellman, Al Mele, Don Kates, Dan Polsby, Elizabeth Wolgast, and Rosemarie Tong. For a variety of reasons, none of them agrees with me completely.

1. See the "Unwritten Law" as a Defense, ch. 303, secs. 2–4, 1963 N.M. Laws (repealed 1973).

2. Trial transcript at 2T 126; quoted in Schneider (1986, 208, n. 80). In this case the New Jersey Supreme Court ultimately vindicated the defense's contention that testimony on battering was necessary to offset common jury prejudices about women and battering.

3. See *Hawthorne* v. *State*, 408 So. 2d 801 (Fla. Dist. App.), rev. denied 415 So. 2d 1316 (Fla. 1982); *Com.* v. *Rose*, 725 S.W. 2d 588 (Ky. 1987); *State* v. *Anaya*, 438 A. 2d 892 (Me. 1981); *State* v. *Gallegos*, 104 N.M. 247, 791 P. 2d 1268 (N.M. App. 1986); *People* v. *Torres*, 128 Misc. 2d 129, 488 N.Y.S. 2d 358 (1985) and Annot., 18 A.L.R. 4th 1153. Of course, nothing follows from showing that courts now routinely permit expert testimony on battered-woman syndrome in support of defendants who plead self-defense. It may be a mistake. Ex-panding the use of expert testimony is problematic in itself. But in this case admitting it may help to offset social prejudices about women who have been battered.

4. The logically prior question is *whether* we can justify such a doctrine, but for present purposes I assume that it has an affirmative answer. For a provocative discussion, see Polsby (1986). But see also Stell (1986).

5. In *People* v. *Scott*, the victim tapped his wrist as he was talking on the telephone as a signal to his battered companion that she was to bring handcuffs to him, which he often used on her before beating her. She instead got a gun and shot him. She testified that she was afraid that the (anticipated? threat-ened?) beating might kill her. The trial court refused to instruct on self-defense because there was no evidence of imminent danger. The court of appeals held that the trial court erred in refusing to instruct on self-defense.

6. *People* v. *Diaz*, No. 2714 (Sup. Ct. Bronx Co., N.Y. 1983) and *People* v. *Melandovich* (Sup. Ct. Kings Co., N.Y. 1985). Cited in Blackman (1986, 235, n. 44). See also *State* v. *Stewart*.

7. On April 5, 1989, a divided North Carolina Supreme Court reversed

the appeals court. The appeals court order for a new trial for Judy Norman was overturned, and she began serving her sentence for manslaughter. On July 7, 1989, North Carolina Governor James Martin commuted her sentence. See *State of North Carolina* v. *Judy Laws Norman*, 89 N.C. App. 384, 366 S.E. 2d 586.

BIBLIOGRAPHY

Akehurst, Michael. 1977. *A Modern Introduction to International Law*. London: Allen and Unwin.

Al-Azmeh, Aziz. 1988. "The Middle East and Islam: A Ventriloqual Terrorism." In *Third World Affairs*, 23–34. New York: Third World Foundation.

Allen, Francis A. 1959. "Legal Values and the Rehabilitative Ideal." *Journal of Criminal Law, Criminology, and Police Science* 50:226–32.

Arato, Andrew, and Jean Cohen. 1991. *Civil Society and Social Theory*. Cambridge, Mass.: MIT Press.

Arendt, Hannah. 1951. *The Origins of Totalitarianism*. New York: Harcourt, Brace and World.

———. 1963. *Eichmann in Jerusalem*. New York: Viking Press.

———. 1969. *On Violence*. New York: Harcourt, Brace and World.

———. 1970. *On Revolution*. New York: Harcourt, Brace and World.

Arthur, John, and W. Shaw, eds. 1984. *Readings in the Philosophy of Law*. Englewood Cliffs, N.J.: Prentice-Hall.

Auden, W. H. *Selected Poems*. 1979. New York: Vintage Books.

Austin, J. L. 1961. *Philosophical Papers*. Edited by J. O. Urmson and G. J. Warnock. Oxford: Clarendon Press.

Axelrod, Robert. 1984. *The Evolution of Cooperation*. New York: Basic Books.

Axelrod, Saul, and Jack Apsche, eds. 1983. *The Effects of Punishment on Human Behavior*. New York: Academic Press.

Barnes, Jonathan. 1982. "Medicine, Experience, and Logic." In J. Barnes, J. Brunschwig, M. Burnyeat, and M. Schofeld, eds., *Science and Speculation*, 24–68. New York: Cambridge University Press.

Barta, Tony. 1987. "Relations of Genocide: Land and Lives in the Colonization of Australia." In Isidor Walliman and Michael N. Dobkowski, eds., *Genocide and the Modern Age: Etiology and Case Studies of Mass Death*. New York: Greenwood Press.

Baynes, Kenneth. 1988. "The Liberal/Communitarian Controversy and Communicative Ethics." *Philosophy and Social Criticism* 14:293–313.

———. 1989. "State and Civil Society in Hegel's *Philosophy of Right*." *Cardozo Law Review* 10:1415–26.

Beauchamp, Tom, and Leroy Walters, eds. 1982. *Issues in Bioethics*, second edition. Belmont, Calif.: Wadsworth.

Benjamin, Walter. 1979. "Critique of Violence." In Peter Demetz, ed., *Reflections*. New York: Harvest Books.

Bentham, Jeremy. 1825. *The Rationale of Reward*. London.

Berlin, Isaiah. 1988. *On the Pursuit of the Ideal*. The First Agnelli Lecture. Turin: Agnelli Foundation. Reprinted in *New York Review of Books*, March 17.

Betz, Joseph. 1977. "Violence: Garver's Definition and a Deweyan Correction." *Ethics* 87 (July): 339–51.

Bianchi, Hermann, and René von Swaaningen, eds. 1986. *Abolition: Toward a Non-Repressive Approach to Crime*. Amsterdam: Free University Press.

Blackman, J. 1986. "Potential Uses for Expert Testimony: Ideas Toward the Representation of Battered Women Who Kill." *Women's Rights Law Reporter* 9:227–57.

Bonner, Robert, and Gertrude Smith. 1968. *The Administration of Justice from Homer to Aristotle*. New York: Greenwood Press.

Borman, William. 1986. *Gandhi and Nonviolence*. Albany, N.Y.: State University of New York Press.

Bradley, F. H. 1927. *Ethical Studies*, second edition. Oxford: Clarendon Press.

Brady, James B. 1983. "The Justifiability of Hollow-Point Bullets." *Criminal Justice Ethics* 2 (Summer/Fall): 9–19.

Brodsky, Joseph. 1986. *Less Than One*. New York: Farrar, Straus and Giroux.

Brown, Stuart M., Jr. 1955. "Inalienable Rights." *Philosophical Review* 64 (April): 192–211.

Browne, Angela. 1987. *When Battered Women Kill*. New York: Free Press.

Bundy, McGeorge. 1988. *Danger and Survival: Choices About the Bomb in the First Fifty Years*. New York: Random House.

Burgess, Anthony. 1965. *A Clockwork Orange*. New York: Ballantine Books.

Butterfield, Fox. 1988. *New York Times*, July 25, sec. A.

Cahn, Edmund N. 1949. *The Sense of Injustice: An Anthropocentric View of Law*. New York: New York University Press.

———. 1966. *Confronting Injustice*. Boston: Little, Brown.

Camus, Albert. 1946. "Ni victime ni bourreau." *Combat*, November 19–30. Translated by Dwight Macdonald, under the title *Neither Victims Nor Executioners*. Chicago: World Without War Publications, 1972.

Cavell, Stanley. 1979. *The Claim of Reason*. New York/Oxford: Oxford University Press.

Charan, Bhagwat. 1987. "The Philosophy of the Bomb." In Walter Laqueur and Yonah Alexander, eds., *The Terrorism Reader*. New York: NAL Penguin.

Cicero. 1969. *Selected Political Speeches*. Translated by Michael Grant. Harmondsworth/Baltimore: Penguin Books.

Clausewitz, Karl von. 1984. *On War*. Edited and translated by Michael Howard and Peter Paret. Princeton, N.J.: Princeton University Press.

Cleary, R. E., ed. 1985. *The Role of Government in the United States: Theory and Practice*. Lanham, Md.: University Press of America.

Coady, C. A. J. 1985. "The Morality of Terrorism." *Philosophy* 60 (January): 47–69.

———. 1986. "The Idea of Violence." *Journal of Applied Philosophy* 3:3–19.

Coser, Lewis. 1966. "Some Social Functions of Violence." *Annals of the American Academy of Political and Social Science* 364 (March): 8–18.

Cotta, Sergio. 1978. *Perché la violenza? Una interpretazione filosofica*. Rome:

L'Aquila. Translated by Giovanni Gullace, under the title *Why Violence? A Philosophical Interpretation*. Gainesville, Fla.: University of Florida Press.

―――. 1985. *Il diritto nell'esistenza: Linee di ontofenomenologica giuridica*. Milan: Giuffré.

―――. 1986. "Innovation and the Public Good." In G. Feaver and F. Rosen, eds., *Lives, Liberties, and the Public Good*. London: Macmillan.

Cover, Robert. 1986. "Violence and the Word." *Yale Law Journal* 95: 1601–29.

Declaration of Independence. Reprinted in *Human Rights* (*see* Melden 1970). Also reprinted in *Inventing America: Jefferson's Declaration of Independence* (*see* Wills 1978).

Declaration of the Rights of Man and of the Citizen. Reprinted in *Human Rights* (*see* Melden 1970).

Derrida, Jacques. 1967. *L'écriture et la différence*. Paris: Seuil. Translated by Alan Bass, under the title *Writing and Difference*. Chicago: University of Chicago Press, 1978.

Diogenes Laertius. 1972. *Lives of Philosophers*. Cambridge, Mass.: Harvard University Press.

Donagan, Alan. 1977. *The Theory of Morality*. Chicago: University of Chicago Press.

Dreyfus, Hubert L., and P. Rabinow. 1982. *Michel Foucault: Beyond Structuralism and Hermeneutics*. Chicago: University of Chicago Press.

Dugard, John. 1976. "International Terrorism and the Just War." *Stanford Journal of International Studies* 12:21–37.

Durkheim, Emile. 1953. *Sociology and Philosophy*. Translated by D. F. Pocock. Glencoe, Ill.: Free Press.

Dworkin, Ronald. 1978. *Taking Rights Seriously*. Cambridge, Mass.: Harvard University Press.

Dyas v. United States. 1977. 376 A.2d 827 (D.C. 1977), *cert. denied*, 434 U.S. 973.

Falk, Richard. 1988. *Revolutionaries and Functionaries: The Dual Face of Terrorism*. New York: Dutton.

Feinberg, Joel. 1980. "Voluntary Euthanasia and the Inalienable Right to Life." In *Rights, Justice, and the Bounds of Liberty*. Princeton, N.J.: Princeton University Press.

―――. 1984. *Harm to Others*. New York: Oxford University Press.

Fletcher, George. 1978. *Rethinking Criminal Law*. Boston: Little, Brown.

Foucault, Michel. 1966. *Les mots et les choses: Une archéologie des sciences humaines*. Paris: Gallimard. Translated under the title *The Order of Things: An Archeology of the Human Sciences*. New York: Pantheon Books, 1970.

―――. 1971. *L'ordre du discours: Leçon inaugurale au Collège de France, prononcée le 2 décembre 1970*. Paris: Gallimard.

―――. 1975. *Surveiller et punir: Naissance de la prison*. Paris: Gallimard. Translated by Alan Sheridan, under the title *Discipline and Punish: The Birth of the Prison*. New York: Pantheon Books.

―――. 1980. "Two Lectures." In *Power/Knowledge* (*see* Gordon 1980).

―――. 1982. "The Subject and Power (Why study power? The question of the subject, How is power exercised?)." Afterword in *Michel Foucault: Beyond Structuralism and Hermeneutics* (*see* Dreyfus and Rabinow 1982).

Frankena, William. 1955. "Natural and Inalienable Rights." *Philosophical Review* 64 (April): 212–32.

Frederickson, George M. 1987. *The Black Image in the White Mind*. Middletown, Conn.: Wesleyan University Press.

French, Peter, ed. 1972. *Individual and Collective Responsibility*. Cambridge, Mass.: Schenckman.

Frey, R. G., and Christopher Morris, eds. 1991. *Violence, Terrorism, and Justice*. New York: Cambridge University Press.

Fromm, Erich. 1973. *The Anatomy of Human Destructiveness*. New York: Holt, Rinehart and Winston.

Fullinwider, Robert K. 1988. "Understanding Terrorism." In *Problems of International Justice: Philosophical Essays* (see Luper-Foy 1988).

Gallie, W. B. 1956. "Essentially Contested Concepts." *Proceedings of the Aristotelian Society* 56. Reprinted in *Philosophy and the Historical Understanding* (see Gallie 1964, 157–91).

———. 1964. *Philosophy and the Historical Understanding*. New York: Schocken Books.

Garver, Newton. 1968. "What Violence Is." *The Nation*, June 24.

———. 1983a. *Jesus, Jefferson, and the Task of Friends*. Wallingford, Pa.: Pendle Hill.

———. 1983b. "Towards a Just Society?" *Friends Journal*, February 3.

———. 1988. "Violence and Social Order." In Peter Koller and Ota Weinberger, eds., *Philosophy of Law, Politics, and Society*. Proceedings of the Twelfth International Wittgenstein Symposium. Vienna: Hölder-Pichler-Tempsky.

Gauthier, David. 1986. *Morals by Agreement*. Oxford: Clarendon Press.

Gewirth, Alan. 1978. *Reason and Morality*. Chicago: University of Chicago Press.

Gibbs, Jack P. 1975. *Crime, Punishment, and Deterrence*. New York: Elsevier.

———, ed. 1982. *Social Control: Views from the Social Sciences*. Beverly Hills: Sage Publications.

Girard, Réné. 1977. *Violence and the Sacred*. Translated by Patrick Gregory. Baltimore: Johns Hopkins University Press.

Gordon, Colin, ed. 1980. *Power/Knowledge*. New York: Pantheon.

Graham, Hugh Davis, and Ted Robert Gurr, eds. 1969. *Violence in America: Historical and Comparative Perspectives*. New York: Bantam Books.

Gregory, R. L., ed. 1987. *Oxford Companion to the Mind*. New York: Oxford University Press.

Gross, Hyman. 1979. *A Theory of Criminal Justice*. London/New York: Oxford University Press.

Grossman, David. 1987. *The Yellow Wind*. New York: Farrar, Straus and Giroux.

Habermas, Jürgen. 1984–87. *The Theory of Communicative Action*. Two volumes. Translated by Thomas McCarthy. Boston: Beacon Press.

———. 1987. *The Philosophical Discourse of Modernity*. Translated by Fred Lawrence. Cambridge, Mass.: MIT Press.

———. 1989. *The Structural Transformation of the Public Sphere: An Inquiry into a Category of Bourgeois Society*. Translated by Thomas Burger. Cambridge, Mass.: MIT Press.

———. 1990. *Moral Consciousness and Communicative Action*. Translated by Christian Lenhart and Shirley Weber Nicholsen. Cambridge, Mass.: MIT Press.

———, ed. 1984. *Observations on "The Spiritual Situation of the Age": Contemporary German Perspectives*. Translated by A. Buchwalter. Cambridge, Mass.: MIT Press.

Hampshire, Stuart. 1989. *Innocence and Experience*. Cambridge, Mass.: Harvard University Press.

Hare, Richard M. 1979. "On Terrorism." *Journal of Value Inquiry* 13:241–49.

Harkabi, Yehoshafat. 1988. *Israel's Fateful Hour*. New York: Harper and Row.

Harris, Adrienne, and Grestra King, eds. *Rocking the Ship of State*. Boulder, Colo.: Westview, 1989.

Hart, H. L. A. 1961. *The Concept of Law*. Oxford: Clarendon Press.

Hegel, George Friedrich Wilhelm. [1821] 1976. *Philosophy of Right*. Translated by T. M. Knox. London/New York: Oxford University Press.

———. 1977. *Phenomenology of Spirit*. Translated by A. V. Miller. London/New York: Oxford University Press.

Heidegger, Martin. [1926] 1953. *Sein und Zeit*. Tübingen: M. Niemeyer. Translated by John Macquarrie and Edward Robinson, under the title *Being and Time*. New York: Harper and Row, 1962.

Held, Virginia. 1972. "Coercion and Coercive Offers." In J. Roland Pennock and John W. Chapman, eds., *Coercion* (*Nomos* 14). New York: Aldine-Atherton.

———. 1984a. *Rights and Goods: Justifying Social Action*. New York: Free Press/Macmillan. Reprint. Chicago: University of Chicago Press, 1989.

———. 1984b. "Violence, Terrorism, and Moral Inquiry." *The Monist* 67, no. 4 (October): 605–26.

Hersh, Seymour M. 1973. *Cover-Up*. New York: Random House.

Heuston, R. F. V. 1976. "Personal Rights Under the Irish Constitution." *The Irish Jurist* 11:205–22.

Hobbes, Thomas. [1651] 1968. *Leviathan*. Reprint, edited by C. B. MacPherson. Baltimore: Penguin.

Hohfeld, W. N. 1919. *Fundamental Legal Conceptions as Applied in Judicial Reasoning, and Other Essays*. New Haven, Conn.: Yale University Press.

Holmes, Robert L. 1987. "Terrorism and Other Forms of Violence: A Moral Perspective." In Joseph C. Kunkel and Kenneth H. Klein, eds., *Issues in War and Peace: Philosophical Inquiries*. Wolfeboro, N.H.: Longwood Academic.

———. 1989. *On War and Morality*. Princeton, N.J.: Princeton University Press.

Honderich, Ted. 1976. *Political Violence*. Ithaca, N.Y.: Cornell University Press.

———. 1980. *Violence for Equality*. New York: Penguin.

Horowitz, Donald L. 1985. *Ethnic Groups in Conflict*. Berkeley, Calif.: University of California Press.

Howell, Signe, and Roy Willis, eds. 1989. *Societies at Peace: Anthropological Perspectives*. London: Routledge and Kegan Paul.

Hume, David. 1751. *Enquiry Concerning the Principles of Morals*. London.

Hurnard, Naomi. 1969. *The King's Pardon for Homicide Before 1307*. Oxford: Clarendon Press.

Ignatieff, Michael. 1978. *A Just Measure of Pain: The Penitentiary in the Industrial Revolution, 1750–1850*. London: Macmillan.

Ihl, W. 1988. *Nötigung, Gewalt, Sitzblockaden*. Saarbrücken: Institut für Rechts- und Sozialphilosophie.

International Covenant on Civil and Political Rights. 1983. *UN Treaty Series* 999:171.

Jakobs, G. 1986. "Nötigung durch Gewalt." In *Gedächtnisschrift für Hilde Kaufman*, 791–811. Berlin/New York: Walter de Gruyter.

Jones, Ann. 1980. *When Women Kill*. New York: Holt, Rinehart and Winston.

Kant, Immanuel. 1787. *Kritik der reinen Vernunft*. Second edition. Translated by N. Kemp Smith, under the title *Critique of Pure Reason*. New York: St. Martin's Press, 1965.

———. 1965. *Metaphysical Elements of Justice*. Translated by John Ladd. Indianapolis: Bobbs-Merrill.

———. 1968a. *Anthropologie in pragmatischer Hinsicht* [Anthropology from a pragmatic point of view]. In *Werkausgabe* 12 (*see* Kant 1968d).

———. 1968b. *Zum ewigen Frieden*. In *Werkausgabe* 11 (*see* Kant 1968d). Translated by H. B. Nisbet, under the title *Toward Perpetual Peace* (*see* Reiss 1970).

———. 1968c. *Über den Gemeinspruch*. . . . In *Werkausgabe* 11 (see Kant 1968d). Translated by H. B. Nisbet under the title *On the Old Saw: "That May Be Right in Theory, but It Won't Hold in Practice"* (*see* Reiss 1970).

———. *Werkausgabe*. 1968d. 12 volumes. Edited by Wilhelm Weischedel. Frankfurt am Main: Suhrkamp Verlag.

Kates, Don. 1979. *Restricting Handguns: The Liberals Speak Out*. Croton-on-Hudson, N.Y.: North River Press.

Knox, Bernard. 1957. *Oedipus at Thebes*. New Haven, Conn.: Yale University Press.

———. 1964. *The Heroic Temper: Studies in Sophoclean Tragedy*. Berkeley, Calif.: University of California Press.

Ladd, John. 1957. *Structure of a Moral Code*. Cambridge, Mass.: Harvard University Press.

———. 1982. "The Poverty of Absolutism." In Timothy Stroup, ed., *Edward Westermarck: Essays on His Life and Works*. (Philosophia Fennica 24). Helsinki: Societas Philosophica Fennica.

———. 1984. "Corporate Mythology and Individual Responsibility." *International Journal of Applied Philosophy* 2, no. 1 (Spring).

———. 1985. "Philosophy and the Moral Professions." In J. Swazey and S. Scher, eds., *Social Controls and the Medical Profession*. Boston: Oelgeschlager, Gunn and Hain.

———. 1987. "Computers and War: Philosophical Reflections on Ends and Means." In David Bellin and Gary Chapman, eds., *Computers in Battle: Will They Work?* New York: Harcourt Brace Jovanovich.

———. 1988. "Politics and Religion in America: The Enigma of Pluralism." In

J. Roland Pennock and John Chapman, eds., *Religion, Morality and the Law* (*Nomos* 30). New York: New York University Press.

Laqueur, Walter. 1988. *The Age of Terrorism*. Boston: Little, Brown.

Laqueur, Walter, and Yonah Alexander, eds. 1987. *The Terrorism Reader*. New York: NAL Penguin.

Leiser, Burton. 1979. *Liberty, Justice, and Morality*. New York: Macmillan.

Levinas, Emmanuel. 1974. *Autrement qu'être ou au-delà de l'essence*. The Hague: M. Nijhoff.

Locke, John. 1937. *Treatise of Civil Government and a Letter Concerning Toleration*. New York: Appleton-Century-Crofts.

———. 1976. *Two Treatises of Government*. Edited by Peter Laslett. New York/ Cambridge University Press.

Lucas, John R. 1980. *On Justice*. Oxford: Clarendon Press.

Lukes, Steven. 1985. *Emile Durkheim: His Life and Work*. Stanford, Calif.: University of California Press.

Luper-Foy, Steven, ed. 1988. *Problems of International Justice: Philosophical Essays*. Boulder, Colo.: Westview Press.

Lyotard, Jean François. 1983. *Le différend*. Paris: Minuit.

Marighella, Carlos. 1974. *Handbook of Urban Guerrilla Warfare*. Translated by John Butt and Rosemary Sheed. Harmondsworth: Penguin.

Marshall v. Kansas City, Mo. 1962. 355 S.W. 2nd 883.

May, Larry. *The Morality of Groups*. 1987. Notre Dame, Ind.: University of Notre Dame Press.

McAllister, Pam. 1982. "Introduction." In Pam McAllister, ed., *Reweaving the Web of Life: Feminism and Nonviolence*. Philadelphia: New Society Publishers.

McGee v. Attorney General. 1974. IR 284.

Mackinnon, Catharine A. 1987. *Feminism Unmodified*. Cambridge, Mass.: Harvard University Press.

McLellan, David. 1986. *Ideology*. Minneapolis, Minn.: University of Minnesota Press.

Melden, Abraham I., ed. 1970. *Human Rights*. Belmont, Calif.: Wadsworth.

———. 1977. *Rights and Persons*. Berkeley, Calif.: University of California Press.

Merleau-Ponty, Maurice. 1945. *Phénoménologie de la perception*. Paris: Gallimard. Translated by Colin Smith, under the title *Phenomenology of Perception*. London: Routledge and Kegan Paul, 1965.

———. 1947. *Humanisme et terreur: Essai sur le problème communiste*. Paris: Gallimard. Translated by John O'Neill, under the title *Humanism and Terror: An Essay on the Communist Problem*. Boston: Beacon Press, 1969.

———. 1955. *Les aventures de la dialectique*. Paris: Gallimard. Translated by Joseph Bien, under the title *Adventures of the Dialectic*. Evanston, Ill.: Northwestern University Press, 1973.

———. 1969. *La prose du monde*. Paris: Gallimard. Translated by John O'Neill, under the title *The Prose of the World*. Evanston, Ill.: Northwestern University Press, 1973.

Mill, John Stuart. [1859] 1968. *On Liberty*. Reprint. London: J. M. Dent/Everyman.

Minow, Martha. 1987. "Interpreting Rights: An Essay for Robert Cover." *Yale Law Journal* 96:1860–1915.

———. 1987. "The Supreme Court, 1986 Term—Foreword: Justice Endangered." *Harvard Law Review* 101:10–95.

Morgan, Robin. 1989. "The Demon Lover." *Ms* 17, no. 9 (March): 68–72.

Morris, Herbert. 1968. "Persons and Punishment." *The Monist* 52:475–501.

Musil, Robert. 1952. *Der Mann ohne Eigenschaften*. Hamburg: Rowohlt.

Nagel, Thomas. 1986. *The View from Nowhere*. New York: Oxford University Press.

Narveson, Jan. 1965. "Pacifism: A Philosophical Analysis." *Ethics* 75, no. 4 (July): 259–71.

———. 1986. "At Arms' Length." In Tom Regan, ed., *Matters of Life and Death*, second edition. New York: Random House.

———. 1989. *The Libertarian Idea*. Philadelphia: Temple University Press.

———. 1991. "Terrorism and Morality." In *Violence, Terrorism, and Justice (see* Frey and Morris 1991).

Netanyahu, Benjamin, ed. 1986. *Terrorism: How the West Can Win*. New York: Farrar, Straus and Giroux.

Neumann, Franz. 1957. "The Change in the Function of Law in Modern Society." In *The Democratic and the Authoritarian State*. Glencoe, Ill.: Free Press.

Newton, George, and Frank Zimring. 1969. *Firearms and Violence in American Life*. A staff report to the National Commission on the Causes and Prevention of Violence. Washington, D.C.: Government Printing Office.

Nickel, James W. 1987. *Making Sense of Human Rights*. Berkeley, Calif.: University of California Press.

Nozick, Robert. 1972. "Coercion." In Peter Laslett, W. G. Runciman, and Quentin Skinner, eds., *Philosophy, Politics, and Society*, fourth series, 101–33. Oxford/New York: Blackwell/Barnes and Noble.

Nyíri, J. C., and G. Mezei, eds. 1990. *Perspectives on Idea and Reality*. Budapest: A Filozófiai Figyelö kiskönyvtára.

Oppenlander, Nan. 1981. "The Evolution of Law and Wife Abuse." *Law and Policy Quarterly* 3:382–405.

Parsons, Talcott. 1951. *The Social System*. New York: Free Press.

Patterson, Orlando. 1982. *Slavery and Social Death: A Comparative Study*. Cambridge, Mass.: Harvard University Press.

People v. Scott. 1981. 97 Ill. App. 3d 899, 424 N.E.2d 70.

Perkins, Rollin M. 1969. *Criminal Law*. Mineola, N.Y.: The Foundation Press.

Plato. 1961. *Laws*. Translated by A. E. Taylor. In Edith Hamilton and Huntington Cairns, eds., *Plato: The Collected Dialogues*. Princeton, N.J.: Princeton University Press.

Pogge, Thomas W. 1989. *Realizing Rawls*. London/Ithaca, N.Y.: Cornell University Press.

Polsby, Daniel. 1986. "Reflections on Violence, Guns, and the Defensive Use of Lethal Force." *Law and Contemporary Problems* 49:89–111.

Popper, Karl R. 1945. *The Open Society and Its Enemies*. London: Routledge and Kegan Paul.

Powelson, Jack. 1987. *Facing Social Revolution*. Boulder, Colo.: Horizon Society Publications.

Prosser, William L. 1971. *Handbook of the Law of Torts*, fourth edition. Saint Paul, Minn.: West.

QQ. 1987. *Report from the Center for Philosophy and Public Policy* (University of Maryland) 7, no. 4 (Fall).

Rawls, John. 1955. "Two Concepts of Rules." *Philosophical Review* 64 (January): 3–32.

———. 1971. *A Theory of Justice*. Cambridge, Mass.: Harvard University Press.

———. 1980. "Kantian Constructivism in Moral Theory." *Journal of Philosophy* 77:515–72.

Reiss, Hans, ed. 1970. *Kant's Political Writings*. Translated by H. B. Nisbet. Cambridge: Cambridge University Press.

Richards, B. A. 1968. "Inalienable Rights: Recent Criticism and Old Doctrine." *Philosophy and Phenomenological Research* 29:391–404.

Ringer, Benjamin B. 1983. *We the People and Others*. New York: Tavistock.

Ritter, Alan. 1980. *Anarchism: A Theoretical Analysis*. New York: Cambridge University Press.

Robinson, Paul H. 1984. *Criminal Law Defenses*. Vols. 1 and 2. St. Paul, Minn.: West.

Ross, Alf. 1975. *On Guilt, Responsibility and Punishment*. Berkeley/Los Angeles: University of California Press.

Röttgers, K. 1974. "Gewalt." In *Historisches Wörterbuch der Philosophie* 3. Basel: Schwabe.

Ruddick, Sara. 1989. *Maternal Thinking: Toward a Politics of Peace*. Boston: Beacon Press.

Rule, James. 1988. *Theories of Civil Violence*. Berkeley, Calif.: University of California Press.

Ryan v. Attorney General. 1963. 1965 IR 294.

Sanford, Nevitt, Craig Comstock, and Associates, eds. 1972. *Sanctions for Evil: Sources of Social Destructiveness*. Boston: Beacon Press.

Schmid, Alex P., and Janny de Graaf. 1982. *Violence as Communication: Insurgent Terrorism and the Western News Media*. Beverly Hills: Sage.

Schneider, Elizabeth. 1986. "Describing and Changing: Women's Self-Defense Work and the Problem of Expert Testimony on Battering." *Women's Rights Law Reporter* 9:195.

Schneider, Elizabeth, and Susan Jordan. 1978. "Representation of Women Who Defend Themselves Against Physical or Sexual Assault." *Women's Rights Law Reporter* 4:149–63.

Schreiber, Jan. 1978. *The Ultimate Weapon: Terrorists and World Order*. New York: Morrow.

Shawcross, William. 1984. *The Quality of Mercy: Cambodia, Holocaust and Modern Conscience*. New York: Simon and Schuster.

Sherry, Michael S. 1987. *The Rise of American Air Power: The Creation of Armageddon*. New Haven, Conn.: Yale University Press.

Skinner, B. F. 1948. *Walden Two*. New York: Macmillan.

———. 1971. *Beyond Freedom and Dignity*. New York: Knopf.

Smith, Donna. 1988. "Oklahoma's 'Make My Day' Law." *Tulsa Law Journal* 23 (Spring): 533–45.

Sorel, Georges. 1961. *Reflections on Violence*. Translated by T. E. Hulme. New York: Collier.

Stanage, Sherman. 1975a. "Vilatives: Modes and Themes of Violence." In *Reason and Violence: Philosophical Investigations* (*see* Stanage 1975b).

——, ed. 1975b. *Reason and Violence: Philosophical Investigations*. Totowa, N.J.: Rowman and Littlefield.

State of North Carolina v. *Judy Laws Norman*. 1989. 89 N.C. App. 384.

State v. *Kelly*. 1984. 97 N.J. 178, 478 A.2d 364.

"*State* v. *Kelly* Amicus Briefs." *Women's Rights Law Reporter* 9: 251–57.

State (Ryan) v. *Lennon*. 1922. 1935 IR 170.

State v. *Stewart*. 1988. 243 Kan. 639, 763 P.2d 572.

Stell, Lance K. 1986. "Close Encounters of the Lethal Kind." *Law and Contemporary Problems* 49:113–24.

Straus, M., R. Gelles, and S. Steinmetz. 1980. *Behind Closed Doors*. New York: Doubleday.

Takaki, Ronald T. 1979. *Iron Cages: Race and Culture in Nineteenth Century America*. Seattle, Wash.: University of Washington Press.

Taylor, Charles. 1975. *Hegel*. New York: Cambridge University Press.

Teichman, Jenny. 1986. *Pacifism and the Just War: A Study in Applied Philosophy*. Oxford: Basil Blackwell.

——. 1989. "How to Define Terrorism." *Philosophy* 64:505–17.

Thomson, Judith Jarvis. 1976. "Self-Defense and Rights." The Lindley Lecture. Lawrence, Kans.: University of Kansas. Reprinted in *Rights, Restitution, and Risks*, 33–48 (*see* Thomson 1986).

——. 1986. *Rights, Restitution, and Risks*. Edited by William Parent. Cambridge, Mass./London: Harvard University Press.

Tilly, Charles. 1969. "Collective Violence in European Perspective." In *Violence in America: Historical and Comparative Perspectives* (*see* Graham and Gurr 1969).

Toby, Jackson. 1964. "Is Punishment Necessary?" *Journal of Criminal Law, Criminology, and Police Science* 55:332–37.

Trainor, Bernard. 1988. *New York Times*, July 19, sec. A.

U.S. Congress. House. Committee on Foreign Affairs. 1983. *Human Rights Documents*. H. 382–30. Washington, D.C.: Government Printing Office.

U.S. Department of State. 1985. *Patterns of Global Terrorism: 1984*. Washington, D.C.: Government Printing Office.

Universal Declaration of Human Rights. Reprinted in *Human Rights* (*see* Melden 1970).

Vargas Llosa, Mario. 1986. *The Real Life of Alejandro Mayta*. Translated by Alfred MacAdam. New York: Farrar, Straus and Giroux/Vintage Books.

Waldenfels, Bernhard. 1987. *Ordnung im Zwielicht*. Frankfurt am Main: Suhrkamp.

Walker, Leonore. 1979. *The Battered Woman Syndrome*. New York: Harper and Row.

Walliman, Isidor, and Michael N. Dobkowski, eds. 1987. *Genocide and the Modern Age: Etiology and Case Studies of Mass Death*. New York: Greenwood Press.

Walzer, Michael. 1970. *Obligations: Essays on Disobedience, War, and Citizenship.* Cambridge, Mass.: Harvard University Press.

——. 1977. *Just and Unjust Wars.* New York: Basic Books.

——. 1988. "Terrorism: A Critique of Excuses." In *Problems of International Justice: Philosophical Essays* (see Luper-Foy 1988).

Wardlaw, Grant. 1982. *Political Terrorism.* Cambridge: Cambridge University Press.

Wasserstrom, Richard A. 1964. "Why Punish the Guilty?" *Princeton University Magazine* 20:14–19.

Weber, Max. 1958. *Essays in Sociology.* Edited and translated by H. H. Gerth and C. Wright Mills. New York: Oxford University Press.

——. 1976. *Wirtschaft und Gesellschaft.* Tübingen: Mohr.

Wellman, Carl. 1979. "On Terrorism Itself." *Journal of Value Inquiry* 13, no. 4 (Winter): 250–58.

——. 1985. *A Theory of Rights.* Totowa, N.J.: Rowman and Allanheld.

Wellmer, Albrecht. 1984. "Terrorism and the Critique of Society." In *Observations on "The Spiritual Situation of the Age": Contemporary German Perspectives* (*see* Habermas, ed. 1984).

Wertham, Frederic. 1973. *A Sign for Cain: An Exploration of Human Violence.* New York: Paperback Library.

Westley, William A. 1970. *Violence and the Police.* Cambridge, Mass.: MIT Press.

Wilkins, Burleigh. 1987. "Terrorism and Consequentialism." *Journal of Value Inquiry* 21, no. 2: 141–51.

Wilkinson, Paul. 1974. *Political Terrorism.* London: Macmillan.

——. 1986. *Terrorism and the Liberal State.* Second edition. New York: New York University Press.

Wills, Gary. 1978. *Inventing America: Jefferson's Declaration of Independence.* New York: Doubleday.

Winch, Peter. 1972. *Ethics and Action.* London: Routledge and Kegan Paul.

Wolgast, Elizabeth H. 1987. *The Grammar of Justice.* Ithaca, N.Y.: Cornell University Press.

Wolin, Sheldon. 1988. "Collective Identity and Constitutional Power." In Gary Bryner and Dennis Thompson, eds., *The Constitution and the Regulation of Society*, 93–122. Provo, Utah: Brigham Young University Press.

Zimmerman, Ekkart. 1983. *Political Violence, Crises, and Revolutions: Theories and Research.* Boston: G. K. Hall.

ABOUT THE CONTRIBUTORS

KENNETH BAYNES is Assistant Professor of Philosophy at the State University of New York at Stony Brook and co-editor of the volume *After Philosophy: End of Transformation?* He is the author of an article in *The Monist* on Kant's theory of property rights and an article in *Philosophy and Social Criticism*.

HUGO ADAM BEDAU is Austin Fletcher Professor of Philosophy at Tufts University. He has published widely in social, political, and legal philosophy. His books include *The Courts, the Constitution, and Capital Punishment*; *The Death Penalty in America*; *Justice and Equality*; *Civil Disobedience*; and (co-author with Edwin Schur) *Victimless Crimes*. His latest book is *Death Is Different*.

JAMES B. BRADY is Associate Professor of Philosophy at State University of New York at Buffalo. His areas of interest include criminal law, ethics, and philosophy of law, particularly criminal culpability. His articles have appeared in numerous law and philosophy journals including *Analysis*, *Criminal Justice Ethics*, *Ethics*, *The Monist*, *Philosophy and Phenomenological Research*, and *Modern Law Review*.

WOJCIECH CHOJNA is Instructor in Philosophy at La Salle University. He was formerly Assistant Professor at the University of Maria Curie-Sklodowka (Poland). He is now completing a dissertation at Temple University on the problems of the identity and value of a cultural object.

SERGIO COTTA is Professor of Philosophy of Law and Director of the Institute for the Philosophy of Law at the University of Rome (Italy). A distinguished Italian jurist, he is the author of several books, including *Why Violence?* which was a major stimulus for this volume. His latest book is *Dalla guerra alla pace*.

NEWTON GARVER is Distinguished Service Professor of Philosophy and Co-director of Cooperation and Conflict Studies at State University of New York at Buffalo, where he has taught since 1961. His articles about Wittgenstein, Derrida, justice, violence, and other matters have appeared in *Mind*, *Ethics*, the *Humanist*, the *Journal of Philosophy*, *Philosophical Investigations*, *Philosophy and Phenomenological Research*, the *Encyclopedia of Philosophy*, and the *Encyclopedia of Ethics*. He is the co-editor, with Peter H. Hare, of *Naturalism and Rationality* and is completing a book on Wittgenstein.

VIRGINIA HELD is Professor of Philosophy at the City University of New York (Graduate School and Hunter College). She has been a visiting professor at UCLA, Hamilton, and Dartmouth and has also taught at Yale and Barnard. She is editor of *Property, Profits, and Economic Justice*. Her most recent book is *Rights and Goods: Justifying Social Action*, and she is currently working on a book on feminism.

ROBERT HOLMES is Professor of Philosophy at the University of Rochester. He has written on ethics, philosophy of war, and social and political philosophy. He is the co-author of *Philosophical Inquiry: An Introduction to Philosophy*. His latest book is *On War and Morality*.

JOHN LADD is Professor of Philosophy Emeritus at Brown University. He is a Kant scholar as well as a moral and social philosopher. His books include *The Structure of a Moral Code*, Kant's *Metaphysical Elements of Justice* (as editor and translator), *Ethical Relativism*, and *Ethical Issues Relating to Life and Death*.

ANDRÉ MAURY is Docent in Philosophy at the University of Helsinki (Finland). Author of monographs on Wittgenstein's *Tractatus* and *Philosophische Bemerkungen*, he has published and lectured widely on questions about political philosophy and personal identity that arise out of Hegel's work.

JAN NARVESON is Professor of Philosophy at the University of Waterloo (Canada). He is the author of numerous articles in philosophy, mainly on ethical theory. His books include *Morality and Utility* and *Moral Issues*. His latest book is *The Libertarian Idea*.

THOMAS POGGE, a native of Germany, received his undergraduate training at Hamburg and the M.A. and Ph.D. from Harvard. He is currently Associate Professor of Philosophy at Columbia University and author of the recent book *Realizing Rawls*.

EIKE VON SAVIGNY studied at Oxford as well as at Munich. He is Professor of Philosophy at Bielefeld (Germany) and has written extensively on ordinary language philosophy. The first volume of his commentary on Wittgenstein's *Philosophical Investigations* appeared in 1989, the second volume in 1990.

LANCE K. STELL is Professor and Chair of the Philosophy Department at Davidson College. Recently a fellow at the National Humanities Center, he has published in a variety of areas, including ethics, medical ethics, and legal philosophy.

BERNHARD WALDENFELS, the foremost German exponent of recent French philosophy, is Professor of Philosophy at Bochum (Germany) and has been a visiting professor in France, Japan, the Netherlands, and the United States. He is co-editor of the journal *Philosophische Rundschau* as well as co-editor of a series of scholarly books, *Übergänge*. The latest of his books are *Ordnung im Zwielicht* and *Der Stachel des Fremden*.

CARL WELLMAN is Hortense and Tobias Lewin Distinguished Professor in the Humanities at Washington University (St. Louis). He recently completed a five-year term as Chair of the American Philosophical Association's Committee on Philosophy of Law. He has published several books, including *The Language of Ethics* and *Welfare Rights*. His latest book is *A Theory of Rights*.

ELIZABETH WOLGAST is Professor of Philosophy at California State University at Hayward and was recently honored with a fellowship at the Rockefeller Center in Bellagio (Italy). Her wide-ranging writings include *Paradoxes of Knowledge*, *Equality and the Rights of Women*, *The Grammar of Justice*, and *The Artificial Person*.

INDEX OF NAMES

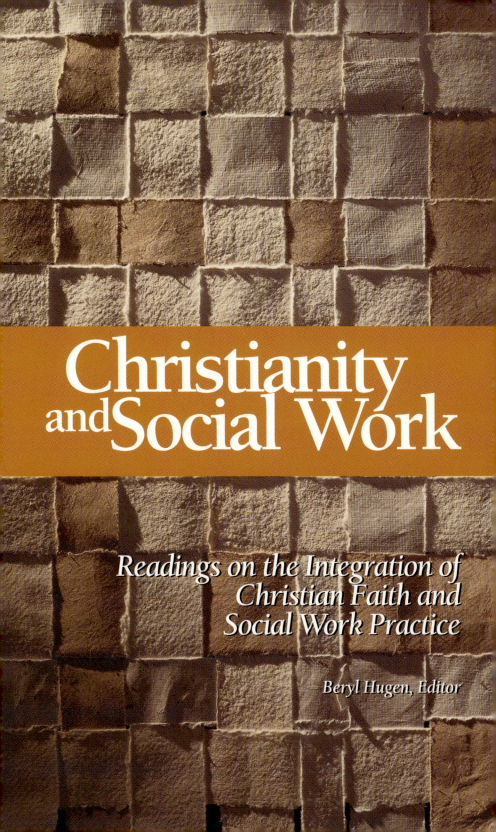

Christianity
and Social Work

Readings on the Integration of Christian Faith and Social Work Practice

Beryl Hugen, Editor

Christianity and
Social Work

Christianity and Social Work

Readings on the Integration of Christian Faith and Social Work Practice

Editor
Beryl Hugen

Copyright 1998
North American Association of Christians in Social Work
P.O. Box 121
Botsford, CT 06404-0121

ISBN 0-9623634-6-4

CONTENTS

Worldviews and Plumblines

Spiritual Aspects in the Helping Process

Humility and Competence

PREFACE

I have been teaching social work on the undergraduate level at Christian colleges for several years. While teaching social work, I have used what I felt were the best introductory texts on the market. However, these texts were produced for the secular market and have been at best neutral and at times antagonistic to Christian concerns. For the past few years I have felt a need for a text that would not only offer a Christian perspective on the social work profession as a whole, but also on specific topics within the profession. In discussions with some of my colleagues, I sensed that they saw a similar need.

After some research and discussion it seemed that the best approach was to produce a collection of articles dealing with a variety of topics and issues related to the practice of social work. To accomplish this I decided to recruit Christian social workers from a wide variety of colleges and universities who would address topics in which they were most competent.

The contributors, therefore, represent a variety of academic settings, along with a broad range of theological and social work perspectives. The common denominator for all of them is a commitment to social work as a profession and a commitment to integrating social work with their Christian faith. The contributors were not given a strict outline to follow, but rather were supplied with the basic purpose of the book and general stylistic guidelines. As editor, I have attempted to allow the authors' ideas to stand with as few editorial changes as possible.

This collection has been written so that it may either be used by itself in the classroom, supplemented by lecture material, or used as a supplement to standard texts. Perhaps its best usage is as a text where selected articles are addressed in differing courses throughout the curriculum of the social work program.

The reader may agree with some of the contributors and disagree with others. It is my hope that the reader, whether agreeing or disagreeing, will be stimulated to integrate his or her Christian worldview with the professional social work perspective on helping. I know all the contributors sincerely hope that the reader will catch a glimpse of the potential contributions that being a Christian in social work can make to the competent and wholistic practice of professional social work and, not incidentally, to the furtherance of the gospel of Jesus Christ and the growth of His Kingdom.

Acknowledgements

Special thanks are due the contributors. I have had the entirely enjoyable task of working with a group that without exception not only produced substantive manuscripts, but shared a clear commitment to the integration of Christian faith and social work practice.

I thank my colleagues at Calvin College for their editorial help and the support of the Calvin Faculty Research Fellowship Program. Special thanks go to Carla Goslinga at Dordt College and Maxine Comer at Calvin College for their secretarial assistance along with Bob Alderink from Publishing Services (Calvin College) for his work on the layout.

I also wish to acknowledge the influence of Alan Keith-Lucas on the initial thinking and development of this project. Both his life and writings continue to provide encouragement and motivation for many social workers in the continuing effort to integrate their Christian faith and social work practice.

CHAPTER 1

INTRODUCTION

Beryl Hugen

One of the developments in social work in the second half of the 20th century has been a marked decline in the recognition of the Christian religion in the teaching and practice of professional social work. The secularization of the social work profession, the notion of religion in both an ideological and institutional sense having little or no part in forming or informing the world of social work, has been very extensive. In fact, the profession has at times been outright hostile toward persons and institutions that profess a Christian orientation to practice. Even presently, when spirituality is being recognized by the profession as a legitimate area of inquiry, Christianity, as one spiritual voice, is recognized only hesitantly.

This is unfortunate for a number of reasons. First, social work once used the language of Christianity as a basis for its existence. Historically, such language was widely and eloquently used by both social work educators and practitioners. Second, spirituality, and to a large degree Christian spirituality, is very much part of our culture and continues to play a significant role in providing moral rationale and reasoning to our political, social, and charitable institutions. As a result, many individuals who seek to be social workers want to know what role Christian faith plays in a helping profession—specifically, the professional existence and activities of social work. The purpose of this book is to help respond to this question.

For many in the social work profession, this question of the relationship of Christian faith and social work is inconsequential, irrelevant, and for some, even an inappropriate topic for professional investigation. For others, it is simply outrageous. George Marsden recently published a book entitled, *The Outrageous Idea of Christian Scholarship*. Why is Christian scholarship an outrageous idea? Many academics (including social workers) regard Christian belief as an affront to reason. They argue that people may hold religious beliefs in the privacy of their own homes, but to propose that such antiquated notions should inform one's scholarship and practice is truly outrageous.

Ironically, throughout history and particularly in the history of charity, the opposite has been true. It would be hard for anyone to deny that the Christian church is one of the true originators of charity. Out of ancient Israel's concern for justice and mercy toward the sick, the poor, the orphaned, the widowed — from Micah and Hosea, Jeremiah and Isaiah — grew the compassion of Jesus and the devotion of Paul. The justice and love of God set forth and exemplified in the Judeo-Christian tradition has given drive and direction to much of western culture's charities. Historically the whole shape and operation of organized welfare is inexplicable apart from this religious conviction and commitment. Jewish, Catholic, and Protestant thought have all along continuously shaped the ideological basis of social work practice. One writer has suggested that these religious traditions, along with the secular philosophy of humanism, are the four foundational roots out of which has emerged the value base of the profession (Kohs, 1966). So it is today that many social workers find the assumptions, beliefs, and values of the Christian faith helpful in providing a frame of reference for understanding and responding to both individual and societal problems.

There are many social workers who are Christians who do not hold to the idea that there is such a thing as Christian social work—only Christians in social work (I am one of them). They do believe, however, that one's Christian perspective comes into play in social work practice when one is deciding *what* to do, *when* to do it, *how* to do it, and *why* one should do it. They clearly identify with those who seek to follow Christ in a servant role for the alleviation of pain and suffering and the establishment of justice and peace in the world. It is for this significant group of social workers (perhaps you are one of them), whose motivations to enter the profession and whose desire is to develop approaches to helping that reflect and are informed by their Christian faith, that this book is written.

The Changing Context for Practice

Social work as a profession has undergone a variety of changes in the twentieth century. Many of these reflect both significant material and technological changes in our society, along with a shift in our ideas about the relationship between people and their social environment, particularly government. The early twentieth century was fertile ground for the development and expansion of broad governmental responsibility for social welfare. The idea of the welfare state and of the centrality of government and public service seemed both inevitable and probably necessary.

But the latter part of the twentieth century has been much less hospitable to the concept of the welfare state. The country has lost the political enthusiasm and conviction that problems can be fixed through public processes and public action. Ideas of limited government, volunteerism, and privatization are now in vogue, and seem not to be some passing fancy.

Private, sectarian, and faith-based organizations are now being asked and expected to fill in the gaps left by this shrinking public response. Churches, sectarian agencies, and Christian voluntary organizations are being increasing called upon to participate more fully in providing community-based social welfare services. Social workers, therefore, who are able to understand and relate to both the professional(public) and faith-based communities are now in an important and advantageous position to contribute by developing policies and programs, and delivering services to help meet the social welfare needs in their communities. Several chapters of the book are focused on this changing environment of social work practice.

Worldviews and Plumblines

It is increasingly being recognized that social work, while its preoccupation in the last half century has been with "science" and with developing objective and empirically validated practice techniques, is also a normative discipline (Siporin, 1982, 1983). Normative means that social work also is concerned with how persons ought to behave "on principle," and that the goals of the profession are guided by particular values. A normative principle is an objective rule which when properly applied distinquishes between right and wrong. Such rules may be applied to the behavior of individuals, whether client or professional, or to social processes and their associated outcomes. So when the social work profession advocates for a redistribution of resources that are deemed valuable to society, a philosophical basis or normative principle for such a redistribution is needed. For example, to promote a national health plan because it is believed that adequate health care is a right, requires a standard or principle informing others as to what is the basis for such a right. So also human behavior, both individual and collective, is socially defined as good or bad, normal or deviant. Whether one chooses as a social worker to enforce these norms or advocate for their change, the essential "morality" of these norms or standards requires justification. Social work has always been guided by such normative principles, although they have rarely been clearly and completely explicated.

For the Christian, the standard or "plumbline" (Amos 7:8) used to make judgements has always been the principles set forth in the Bible. Hence it is important and necessary for Christian social workers to relate or test the values of the profession with the principles of a Christian worldview. To be explicit about such moral principles provides an opportunity to reconnect with the profession's religious bearings and roots. To do so may also help recover dimensions of social work teaching and practice that have been alienated from their theological roots. Articulating these Christian principles or "plumblines" — helping the reader develop a Christian worldview related to social work — is another one of the focuses of this book.

Spiritual Aspects in the Helping Process

Today there is also a small but growing movement within the social work profession that affirms that spirituality and religious beliefs are integral to the nature of the person and have a vital influence on human behavior. These spiritual and religious dimensions are being increasingly recognized as important features of social work practice, at all phases of the social work helping process and in all areas of practice. This perspective embraces a holistic conception of the person, with this view more recently being elaborated as the bio-psycho-social-spiritual perspective. This perspective reintroduces spiritual issues as a legitimate practice focus and provides for a more complete understanding of client strengths, weaknesses, and problems. As a result, there is now a need for the development of theoretical frameworks, including assessment tools, intervention models, and evaluation methods that flow from this perspective.

Social work research has also shown that although many social workers see religious and spiritual issues as important parameters in practice and important in their own lives as well as in the lives of their clients, many are hesitant to initiate discussion of spiritual issues with clients (Derezotes & Evans, 1995; Joseph, 1988). Much of this hesitation is due to the lack of knowledge and skill in this area. Greater sensitivity to the concerns of the religious client has also been shown to be related to the social worker's own spiritual awareness — the ability to integrate the personal, spiritual and religious self with the professional self. Again, there has been a reluctance to incorporate such knowledge into social work education, considering such discussions as an intrusion into a private sphere.

With this wider movement within the profession to embrace a bio-psycho-social-spiritual focus in practice and the promotion of a professional learning environment that is more supportive of personal religious and spiritual experiences, Christian social workers now have the opportunity to truly minister to the whole person. Several chapters in the book also address these spiritual aspects of the helping process.

Humility and Competence

These tasks — adapting to the changing landscape in social welfare, articulating the principles of a Christian worldview related to social work, and developing spiritual frameworks related to the differing aspects of the helping process and a professional use of self related to spirituality — also provide challenges. One is to apply a Christian message to the realities of the contemporary practice context, and not assume that a Christian understanding and response to social problems from an earlier time period is applicable for today. This also means that Christians in social work do not have all the answers. The Bible may provide principial guidance, but does not always provide clear and specific direction for the sometimes confusing moral and ethical situations social workers encounter in practice. As Christian social workers, we know that we live and practice in a broken world, and that our only real comfort is that we are not our own, but we belong, body and soul, in life and in death, to our faithful Savior Jesus Christ.

It is also easy to assert the evident Christian goodness of helping people. And it can be easier still to assume that a Christian perspective on the profession of social work furthers that good. But goodness of motivation may be and frequently is unrelated to outcome. There is always the possibility that our Christian perspectives are no more than self-serving rationales (promoting judgmentalism, discrimination and selective helping motiffs) rather than the product of a thoughtful analysis. This book, therefore, attempts to offer a Christian perspective for social work that is within the parameters of contemporary models of social work research and scholarship — clearly the social work profession can also inform the Christian community. The book's final chapter, written in a narrative form, illustrates these themes of humility and competence.

References

Derezotes, D.S. & Evans, K.E.(1995). Spirituality and religiousity in practice: In-depth interviews of social work practitioners. *Social Thought, 18*(1), 39-54.

Joseph, M.V.,(1988). Religion and social work practice. *Social Casework, 60*(7), 443-452.

Kohs, S.C. (1966). *The Roots of Social Work*. Association Press.

Siporin, M.(1982). Moral philosophy in social work today. *Social Service Review, 56*, 516-38.

Siporin, M. (1983). Morality and immorality in working with clients. *Social Thought, 15,*(3/4), 42-52.

CHAPTER 2

CHURCH SOCIAL WORK

Diana R. Garland

Early in my professional career, I went from being a clinical social worker in a small community mental health center to being a clinical social worker in a small church-related counseling center. I continued to work with clients seeking help with marital conflict, grief, troubled and troubling children, chemical addictions, depression, and an assortment of other life challenges. I did not see much difference in the clients and their problems which presented themselves to me in my new practice setting, nor, I must admit, even in the cozy, informal atmosphere of the centers.

The only difference I noticed was the source of referrals. In the community mental health center, clients came from inpatient psychiatric referrals and local physicians, or they came on the advice of friends and pastors. In the pastoral counseling center, pastors were far more often the referral sources. The work did not seem to change very much, however. In both settings, clients' problems and strengths were tangled together with the family and community in which they lived, and in the philosophical and spiritual frameworks through which they interpreted their world, themselves, and the meaning of life and suffering. Unfortunately, because I saw no difference in the contexts of my work, I missed opportunities for more effective work with my clients and in the churches and community that supported my work. I simply did in the church-related agency what I had done in the community mental health center.

Over time, however, I began to wonder if anything about my work *should* be different. How should I be defining my responsibilities as a social worker in a church-related setting? In both settings, I dealt with spiritual issues when they came up in relationship to the problems and struggles clients presented. Was it simply that spiritual concerns were more often a part of the focus in the church agency, because clients sought us out as a place where these concerns would be considered appropriate and important? Was it that the staff could initiate discussions of spiritual matters when we felt that spirituality was relevant to the client's presenting problem? Or should there be something different about the very nature and purpose of our work? Should I be defining my work in relationship with the congregations that sent us referrals, or should I let the referrals be the boundaries of my professional responsibility?

Those questions started my search for defining what church social work is and can be, whether it happens in a pastoral counseling agency, a congregation, or denominational headquarters. If I could go back to my practice in that pastoral counseling center now, I would define my role and responsibilities very differently, and I would do that defining in conversation with the churches that related to our agency. As you read this chapter, think about how you would define social work practice in such a setting.

****

More than any other helping profession, social work recognizes that the context for work has a dramatic impact on that work, both in positive and negative ways. The context can be both a barrier and a resource for change. When the context is ignored, barriers remain hidden and resources go unused. Even the value of social work to the host institution itself may be lost in the process.

Congregations can be a tremendous resource in working with social work clients. The congregation can be a community of support that can make all the difference to a family coping with stressful experiences such as chronic illness, for example. The congregation can provide (1) friendship, concern, and the mentoring of others who have been through such experiences, (2) respite care for the ill family member that supports the caregiver and spreads the burden of care to a wider group, (3) hot meals brought to the home and help with household chores, and (4) a framework for interpreting the meaning and significance of the stress the family is experiencing. The church social worker sensitive to these resources can nurture and strengthen them.

Congregations also provide access to social services for persons who would otherwise be difficult for social service agencies to reach. For example, families will involve themselves in educational programs such as parenting classes or marriage seminars offered by their church who might never seek out such a program offered by a community mental health agency.

At the same time, the church context for social work practice can also present significant barriers to practice and complicate a client's difficulties. For example, a family going through a divorce may sense gossip and even rejection instead of compassion and support by a congregation. A single adult may feel odd and out of place in a congregation which emphasizes the nuclear family as the ideal lifestyle ordained by God. A teenager struggling with questions of sexual orientation or a couple in the throes of family violence may consider the church—and a social worker related to the church—the last place where help can be found.

Certainly, the setting of church social work often dictates that the social worker will deal with spiritual and religious issues more often and in more depth than in other practice settings. But there is much more to it than that.

What Is Church Social Work?

Roselee is Director of Christian Social Ministries, a full time staff position at First Baptist Church. Her responsibilities include developing and administering a diversity of programs sponsored by this large congregation, including a counseling center staffed with full-time and part-time mental health professionals, an emergency assistance program, a therapeutic day care program for children who have emotional difficulties as a result of traumatic life experiences, a feeding program for homeless persons, a prison ministry, an after-school recreational program for community teenagers, and a myriad of support groups for persons experiencing a variety of life crises and challenges. Her work includes supervising the professional staff and providing consultation and support for a very large group of volunteers who work in these programs.

David is a social worker in a counseling center supported by the local denominational association of congregations. He provides individual and family counseling for members of the supporting congregations as well as for others in the community. He also leads marriage enrichment, parent education, and other educational programs for congregations too small to have staff able to provide this kind of leadership, and he is organizing a family resource center for the churches to use. It will have videotapes, books, and audiotapes on a variety of topics related to family life.

Martha directs a church-sponsored community center in an inner-city slum. The center offers recreational and after-school tutoring and child-care programs for community children and youths, job placement and training programs for older youths and adults, a resource center and micro-loan program for small business development by residents of the community, crisis counseling and emergency assistance, a variety of support groups, and a food co-op. Martha trains and supervises a whole army of volunteers from suburban churches who provide staff for the various programs.

Often, the Center is involved in organizing the community and its supporting congregations to advocate for the needs of children and their families living in poverty in the community.

Ricardo directs the Christian Social Ministries Department in the national headquarters of the denomination. He supervises the work of staff all over the United States. His board of directors determines which mission sites to found and support, including community centers in inner cities, rural areas, and with various ethnic minority groups. By writing articles in denominational magazines and the curricula of the denomination's educational programs, Ricardo helps churches of his denomination examine the social issues of the day and advocate for justice. He also is a frequent speaker at regional church conferences and meetings.

Church social work is social work which takes place under the auspices of a church organization, whether that organization is a congregation, denominational agency, or ecumenical or parachurch organization. To understand church social work, then, requires understanding the church.

The Church is a Human Organization

Churches are human organizations, sharing many of the characteristics of other human organizations. They have *structures* which divide responsibility and privilege between persons (clergy and lay persons, congregations and denominations, deacons and membership). They have *tasks* to be performed—worship, missions and ministry, care of the membership, outreach/evangelism, and administration of the church's physical and human resources. They have *processes, rules and norms* for performing these tasks; some of these are overt and formal, but many are also informal and unspoken. Finally, churches and church organizations have *bodies of beliefs codified in creeds and doctrines* which define their culture. These characteristics need to be understood in all their particularity in each setting for effective social work practice.

For example, as Martha works with the congregations which partner with her community center, she seeks involvement of the persons who provide leadership to their congregations and can move those congregations toward greater action. That means understanding how roles and power are defined and distributed in each congregation. In some churches, power rests with the pastor, but in others, power may be vested in a women's organization, or the board of deacons. As she works with these various leaders, she describes her work using the language of the church. For example, she describes the community center's work as missions and evangelism, a way that their members can grow and strengthen their faith by serving others.

Depending on the processes of each congregation, Martha may work informally with individual leaders over coffee or provide formal presentations of the work of the center at church committee meetings. She provides ongoing consultation with volunteers, helping them relate their volunteer work to their own faith journeys. As she talks with leaders and members of congregations, she is sensitive to and uses language which is congruent with their doctrine and their use of scripture.

The Church is the Body of Christ

Of course, the church is also something other than a human organization. It is also a creation of God, the Church to which all followers of Jesus Christ in the past, present, and future belong. This Church is the body of Christ, and its parts each have indispensable functions (Romans 12:3-8; 1 Corinthians 12). In another image, Christians together are members of the "household of God" who, with Christ as the cornerstone, serve as a holy temple, a dwelling place for God (Ephesians 2:19-22). The Church is in process of being and becoming this creation, this dwelling place for God. The tension between current reality and theological ideal motivates and guides the continuous modifications and development of church organizations—and thus the context for church social work practice.

Church Social Workers as Leaders of Christian Social Ministries

Church social workers often provide leadership in the social ministries of congregations and denominations. Social ministries are activities carried out by Christians (both professional church leaders and members of congregations) to help persons in need and to work for greater social justice in communities and the larger society. These ministries are considered central responsibilities of the church and of individual Christians, growing out of Jesus' teaching (1) that neighbors are to be loved as we love ourselves and that all persons are our neighbors, (2) that responding to the needs of persons is a way to respond faithfully to God's love, and (3) that God is less concerned with religious ritual than with social justice.

The Settings of Church Social Work

Church social workers practice in various settings. These include congregations and parishes, denominational organizations, ecumenical organizations, and parachurch organizations. Each of these have somewhat different characteristics that give definition to social work practice in that setting. *Congregations* are groups of persons who voluntarily band together for religious purposes, and who share an identity with one another. They often have a central meeting place and may be referred to as the group which meets in that place (First Baptist Church, The Church of the Redeemer) despite the frequent disclaimer that a church is not a building, it is the people. A *parish* is the geographic community served by the congregation. The term parish is often also used to refer to local governmental jurisdictions (like a "county"), reflecting a time when one church body was overwhelmingly the dominant religious institution and when geographic location and congregational membership were synonymous.

A *denomination* is an organization which governs many congregations who share certain beliefs and practices. Denominations vary dramatically in their government structures. In some denominations, congregations are subsystems of the larger denomination and are not seen as independent, autonomous entities apart from the denomination (e.g., Roman Catholic). In other denominations, congregations are independent entities which voluntarily participate in the denomination because the denomination can help them achieve goals which they could not on their own (e.g. Baptist). Because their participation is voluntary, congregations in these denominations can also choose to disaffiliate themselves if they become dissatisfied or alienated by the work or policies of the denomination. Through the denomination, congregations support mission ventures, social service and social action projects, educational institutions (universities and seminaries), publication houses, and financial and other support services for clergy and congregations.

Denominations are often organized into local, state, and national levels of government and service programs. Church social workers are employed by denominational agencies such as residential child care and treatment programs, shelters for homeless persons and families, pregnant teens, and abused family members; community-based family service agencies; housing, nutrition, and socialization programs for aging families; adoption and foster care programs; hospitals; refugee relief programs; and disaster and world hunger relief agencies. Social workers are also commissioned as missionaries with specific cultural groups in this country and in international contexts.

Ecumenical organizations are organizations of denominations, individual congregations, and even individual church members. The organizations attempt to transcend theological, ecclesiological, and historical differences between churches and denominations in order to work toward common purposes. For example, community ministry agencies are local community-based organizations of churches from various denominations who share the same community. The congregations cooperate with one another in the ecumenical community ministry in order to provide social services to their communities which few congregations could provide with only their own resources—child day care, adult day care, emergency assistance, feeding programs for senior adults or homeless persons, counseling services, etc. The National Council of Churches and the World Council of Churches represent the national and global levels of ecumenical organization. These organizations often strive to be inclusive of denominations and religious organizations with a broad spectrum of theological and political viewpoints, sometimes extending to non-Christian faith groups and organizations.

Finally, there are *parachurch organizations*. Parachurch organizations resemble ecumenical organizations in their inclusion of persons and congregations from differing denominations. However, parachurch organizations sometimes are limited to congregations and denominations that consider themselves more conservative theologically and politically than those who are comfortable participating in the diversity present in many ecumenical organizations. Parachurch organizations also are often special interest networks with a specific purpose rather than the comprehensive organizations which ecumenical organizations represent. Examples of parachurch organizations are World Vision, Bread for the World, Youth for Christ, Prison Fellowship, Focus on the Family, and the Christian Coalition.

It should be clear by now that *church social work* and *Christian social work* are not equivalent. The personal faith of the social worker does not define that worker's practice as church social work; church social work is defined by the context in which the social worker practices.

What Makes the Church a Distinctive Context for Social Work Practice?

Churches and their agencies are distinct from other practice settings in that they represent (1) a host, rather than primary, setting for social work; (2) a social community; (3) a source of programs and practices which often become, through a process of secularization, part of the dominant society; and (4) voices of advocacy for social justice. These

primary characteristics of the churches and their agencies, taken together, make it a context unlike any other for social work practice.

Churches and their agencies are *host settings* for social services.

Churches are not primarily social service agencies. Instead, they are
host settings, settings in which social work is a "guest," invited in for a
reason. Host settings are those which have purposes other than or beyond
the primary purposes of the social work profession, but these purposes
which can be enhanced by what social work can offer. For example, hospitals and schools are also "host settings" for social work. They are not primarily social service agencies, but their purposes—treating illness and educating students— are furthered by providing social services to their patients/
students. Hospitals use social workers to help plan for care after a patient
leaves the hospital, or to help families deal with the crises of difficult diagnoses and with making care plans. Schools use social workers to address
family and community factors that keep children from succeeding in school.

If social workers in a host setting forget that they are there to help
the organization achieve its goals, and instead try to transform the setting into a *primary* setting, one which is primarily committed to providing social services and advocating for social justice, the welcome of the
host setting may be withdrawn. Hospital social workers can address the
needs of patients and their families, and may even be able to advocate
for their needs with community structures and even the hospital itself.
But they probably cannot expect the hospital to support their spending
time working with street gangs in order to decrease the violence in the
community. Even though such work may be related to the health of
patients and their families, the hospital will probably see it as peripheral, not an activity to invest in if it means less energy is directed toward
the direct care needs of patients and their families.

Social ministry and social action are central to the mission of the
church. Church social workers must keep in mind, however, that social
ministry and social action are important for the church because they
point to the kingdom of God, because they are the fulfillment of Jesus'
teachings, and because engaging in them grows the faith of Christians.
Social service and social action are not ends in themselves; they must
always be securely anchored in and reflective of the church's mission.

Churches are *social communities*.

A *community* is the set of personal contacts through which persons
and families receive and give emotional and interpersonal support and

nurture, material aid and services, information, and make new social contacts. The people in a community know us. They are people we can borrow from or who will take care of a child in an emergency. They are the ones from whom we can obtain news and gossip so that we know the significant and not so significant information that gives shape to our lives. Community includes the physical environment that communicates a sense of belonging because it is familiar. The smells of the river or the factory or the pine trees down the street are much like the smell of Grandma's house, part of the canvas of daily experience so familiar that it is hardly noticed until we are in different surroundings and miss them. We sit in the same pew on Sunday and look at the same stained glass windows from the same angle, and can predict who else will sit where. We hardly think about or recognize community until it is changed, or we absent ourselves. Upon return from a long absence, the sights, smells and greetings from familiar people may flood us with emotion. All these point to the familiar niche that community is. It consists of people, organizations, and physical environment that keep us from depending solely on persons within our family to meet all our personal, social, physical, and spiritual needs, and who communicate, "this is your place; you belong here."

The African proverb "It takes a village to raise a child" became a political slogan pointing to the importance of community for children, but it does not quite go far enough. *All* persons, both children and adults, need community. Because children are so dependent on others for their survival, their vulnerability in the absence of community is more apparent. Adults, too, however, need to live in and experience community, although some seem to need community more than others. Even self-sufficient adults living alone seek the company of others, if only for recreation and social support. Even seemingly independent adults need community when they become ill, injured, or feel threatened.

In our world of automobiles and our society of expressways and work and school separated from home and neighborhood, community is frequently no longer defined geographically. In many ways, marking the path of a person's automobile over the course of a week—from work to home to school to recreation to church to extended family and so on—will map that person's community. To the extent that the congregation is a significant emotional and interpersonal node in that tracing, the church is community. It may be the only institution in which all members of a family or friendship group participate together. For many, it is a place where they regularly worship, study, eat, engage in recreation, conduct business, socialize with others, and care and are cared for (Garland, forthcoming).

Both in congregations and in church agencies, church social workers have the task of building and strengthening communities. The most effective outreach ministries of the church (i.e., "evangelism") are those which extend the hospitality and care of the church community to those who do not have such a community. For example, one downtown congregation in a metropolitan area has "adopted" a nearby middle school. They provide tutoring, mentoring, enrichment classes, and stock a reduced-cost store in which students can purchase needed items. In the process, the church members developed relationships with the school's students. A large church-related family service agency trains church volunteers as family mentors and then pairs them with families in crisis. In the Chicago area, church women take gift baskets of baby items and small gifts for new mothers to young single mothers in the hospital whom nurses identify as having few or no visitors. The basket includes coupons for two evenings of free in-home child care by the women of the church and monthly visits to bring toys on loan and to discuss child development. Some of the women have subsequently become friends with these young mothers and "grandmas" to their babies. A program developed by church social workers in Louisville, Kentucky pairs the families of mothers with AIDS with volunteers who will provide support and friendship. They work with the mother to make permanent plans for children in the event of her death. In short, these programs wrap the community around families and individuals both inside and outside the congregation.

The focus of the church social worker is not simply using the community of faith to meet the needs of social work clients, but through service and caregiving, to build and strengthen the community itself. Dieter Hessel concludes that "the primary role of professional church workers is to equip a faithful *community* to intervene compassionately in the social system and to enhance caring interpersonal relations in ways that are consistent with Christian maturity" (Hessel, 1982, p. 125).

Church social workers are often expected to be active members and leaders of the denominations and congregations they serve. In some settings, the social worker may be ordained or in other ways recognized by the church as a leader. Because communities encompass both formal and informal ties between people in a web of relationships, it is difficult to separate formal—professional—relationships from informal relationships. Professional relationships with clients sometimes originate in church activities such as church committees, groups, and church programs led by the social worker. Boundaries of client/professional relationships and between professional and private life therefore are much less well defined then in some other professional contexts. At times, they are virtually absent. Consequently, clients and church members have greater access to the social worker than in other social service settings. The social worker also has greater potential knowledge of clients' and members' social networks and other resources and barriers for intervention. Often, however, the social worker has to cope with personal or organizational confusion of roles and the results of being almost constantly, if informally, "on duty" (Ferguson, 1992; Wikler, 1986; Wikler, 1990; Wigginton, 1997).

Churches *spin off programs and services* to their societal context.

Sometimes churches start ministries which take on a life of their own, outgrowing the congregational setting where they began. For example, All Saints Church in Los Angeles began an AIDS ministry before any programs for AIDS patients and their families existed. Over time, they were able to obtain funding from government and private sources outside the congregation. Volunteers began working with the AIDS ministry from outside the congregation. The program grew and became incorporated separately, and then became independent of the church.

Ed Bacon, Rector of All Saints, has pointed out that when the church gives birth to a ministry, then successfully calls on society to support that ministry, and finally the ministry is secularized and integrated into society, then the church has facilitated social transformation (Bacon, 1996). Many of the child welfare agencies in this nation began through volunteer organizations of church women. Over time they hired professional staff and became increasingly independent of the birthing church (Garland, 1994).

One of the difficult tasks for church social workers is leading the church in deciding when to hold on to ministries and when to let go of them. The church social worker can help this become a decision-making process which is inclusive of both professionals and church members and leaders who have invested themselves in the ministry. The decision needs to be made with clarity about the mission of the church and its purposes in beginning the ministry, and how that mission and sense of purpose have evolved through service.

In many respects, the profession of social work is itself a "spin off" of the church. It was a social transformation begun in the church. Long before the social work profession's birth, the church concerned itself with human needs and served poor, oppressed, and marginalized persons. The direct forerunners of social work were the voluntary societies which church groups and individuals formed in the eighteenth and nineteenth centuries. These societies and agencies addressed the problems of hunger, slum life, unemployment, worker's rights, mental illness, prison reform, and the care of widows and orphans. Many early social workers were ministers and other church leaders. For example, in the early years of the 20th century, Jane Addams rejected a foreign missionary career to become a pioneer social worker in the settlement house movement in Chicago (Garland, 1995; Hinson, 1988). Social work has become increasingly secularized over the past century. The relationship between the church and the social work profession has sometimes been rocky. The church has moved from being the primary host setting for social work practice to being one of many places where social workers practice. Nevertheless, perhaps the church needs to celebrate the social transformation it created by giving birth to and nurturing the social work profession as it became a part of the mainstream of our society.

Churches are (or should be) advocates for the poor and oppressed and committed to social justice.

The church not only serves oppressed persons; it is sometimes their advocate. An advocate is one who pleads the case of another, who speaks out for those who have no voice. Advocates seek to bring about change in unjust social systems in addition to ministering to those who are harmed by the injustice.

For churches, advocacy most often grows out of ministry. For example, the Christian Service Program (CSP) in Canton, Illinois, assists seniors in completing their Medicare and health insurance forms, offers volunteer income tax assistance, and meets similar simple clerical needs. The program is staffed by volunteers. They deny any interest in engaging in "advocacy"; they just want to help senior adults in their community. Social justice is not their chosen priority. But when they learned that the county ambulance service in Canton was being curtailed, they led the charge for a new ambulance service to take its place. When they found some insurance companies were ignoring or hassling their clients, they pressured the companies to improve their care of senior citizens. And when they realized that one of the many forms for the Social Security Administration made no sense, they leaned on the agency until Social Security changed its form (Dudley, 1996).

At other times, churches have been advocates because it was their own people who were victimized by injustice. During the period of slavery and in the time of racist oppression which has followed, the Black Church not only gave birth to new social institutions such as schools, banks, insurance companies, and low income housing, but it also provided the arena for political activity to address the larger society's racism as well as the needs of the community. Black churches had a major role in establishing the black self-help tradition during a time when there were no public social welfare agencies and private philanthropy was reserved for other groups.

One of the most challenging tasks of church social workers is leading congregations and denominations from ministry into advocacy for social justice (Garland, 1994,1996). As Harvie Conn states:

> ...the task of the church, until that glorious day, is to be co-workers with God in the formation of the new creation. This is why the church is not content merely to change individuals: God is not so content. One day soon God will create a wholly new environment in which the righteousness of His people will shine.... We labor in the knowledge that God alone can build it. But, in Pannenberg's words, our "satisfaction is not in the perfection of that with which we begin but in the glory of that toward which we tend...." What will be the instrument of the church in effecting this change? Not simply charity but also justice. Charity is episodic, justice is ongoing. One brings consolation, the other correction. One aims at symptoms, the other at causes. The one changes individuals, the other societies (Conn, 1987, p. 147).

Jesus made the declaration of Jubilee central to his mission and identity. His salvation includes not only deliverance from sin and physical healing; it also involves a gift of economic and social well-being for the poor and downtrodden of the world (Campolo, 1990).

What Else do Church Social Workers Need to Know?

Churches, then, are (1) host settings for social services, (2) social communities, and (3) contributors to the justice and well-being of the world as they spin off services and programs into mainstream society and as they advocate for societal change. To work with congregations and other church practice settings, however, social workers need to know more than how to provide social services in a host setting, how to develop and nurture community, how to help churches determine their ongoing relationship with social services, and how to motivate and lead in advocacy for social justice. Churches are voluntary, mission-driven organizations with a unique culture. Each of these characteristics suggests knowledge and skills needed by the church social worker.

Churches are *voluntary organizations.*

Particularly in American society, church membership and participation is voluntary. If people do not like what is happening in one congregation, they simply move to another, or stop participating altogether. In some denominations, even congregational participation in the denomination is voluntary. If the congregation does not like what the denomination is doing, it may choose to withdraw and to affiliate with another denomination, to remain independent, or simply to withhold its financial support from the denomination. Dealing with conflict and maintaining interpersonal relationships therefore have much greater import in church social work than in other settings.

At the level closest to many church social workers, the work of many church social service and social action programs are carried out by church members—volunteers. Supervising and consulting with volunteers is dramatically different than supervising and consulting with employees. Volunteers have to continue to see the significance of what they do in order to be motivated; there is no paycheck at the end of the week which keeps them coming even when they are tired and discouraged. Just as challenging, volunteers are not hired, so they cannot be fired. Dealing with difficulties in the work of volunteers requires considerable skill and sensitivity.

Nurturing the relationship with congregations and their leaders is an ongoing, significant aspect of church social work. Speaking and writing are arenas of church social work that have much greater import than in other social work specializations. The most effective church social workers often preach or in other ways provide worship leadership to churches and church groups, provide stimulating educational presentations, and write about what they do and about the role of the church in social issues of the day. They write for church newsletters, Christian education curriculum, denominational magazines, and specialized publications.

Churches and their agencies are *mission-driven organizations*.

The church is a mission driven organization. That is, it is not motivated primarily by serving the needs around it but by the mission to which it feels called. The church is not ultimately responsible for effectively meeting all the needs of society. Instead, the church is responsible for being faithful to its mission, a mission of telling the story of its faith and serving as a living witness to the love of God as demonstrated in the life, death, and resurrection of Jesus Christ. Church social workers must first be clear about and then articulate the relationship between their work and this overarching mission of the church.

Too often, social workers approach the church from the perspective of *social work's* mission, which is addressing the needs of persons in their environment and advocating for social justice. When one begins with social work's mission, the church is seen as a resource to be mined in accomplishing the mission of social work. After all, the church has money, and volunteers, and some political clout. The volunteer service of church members is a tremendous resource to social services in our society; it has been estimated that churchgoers donate about 1.8 million hours of services in the United States annually (Filteau, 1993). It is not surprising, then, that social workers try to finesse the church's involvement and support of what they are doing. Sometimes this works, and both the social work professional and the church are enhanced, because their missions are congruent with one another.

On the other hand, sometimes social workers end up strip-mining the church, taking their resources of money for emergency assistance, or volunteers for their social service programs, with little thought for the impact on the church itself. The focus is on getting needed help in the social service program, rather than the reverse—helping the church achieve its mission. The money is spent, but the church may feel little connection with what happened to the money, and they become discouraged that their little bit makes so little difference in a sea of need. Volunteers find the work hard and do not connect that serving the needs of others is a fulfillment of Jesus' teaching, regardless of the response. The harassed social worker may have no time to work with the volunteers, to pray with them, to connect what they are doing with their spiritual lives. As a consequence, the church's resources are diminished rather than nurtured. As for the social worker, there may be a growing resentment over time as the church loses its interest in being involved and the resources dry up.

Church social work, therefore, must begin with the church's mission and how the mission of social work can be used in service of that mission. Working with volunteers must thus be bi-focal—both on the provision of needed services by the volunteer as well as on the nurture of faith and commitment in the volunteer (Garland, 1994).

Churches are *cultural groups*

It should be clear by now that churches are in many respects subcultures. They have their own language, nonverbal symbols, norms, and patterns of relationships. They have historical identities that shape their current understanding of themselves. These identities reflect not only an overarching denominational heritage but also the unique histories of a particular congregation. Like families, churches develop over time, going through organizational stages that partially shape their current life together (Moberg, 1984; Carroll, Dudley, & McKinney, 1986; Garland, 1994).

The church social worker operates within and uses the language and cultural patterns of the church community. The Bible, theology, and Christian values are keys to understanding and working effectively in this context. For example, the concepts of the "family of God" and Christian hospitality provide the ground for social action in behalf of homeless and isolated persons and social ministry programs that attempt to include them in the community. Biblical teachings on the value and role of children provide impetus for child welfare services and child advocacy. Understanding these distinctive characteristics of the church context is just as important for effective social work practice as is understanding the culture, history, and current life experiences of an ethnic family requesting family service.

Often, the social worker will find not only commonalities but also basic conflicts between the values and knowledge of the social work profession and a congregation's or denomination's beliefs and practices. For example, Midgley and Sanzenbach (1989) have spelled out some of the basic conflicts between social work practice and fundamentalist Christian doctrines. The church social worker must find ways to live with and sometimes to challenge the contradictions inherent in being a social worker and a church leader. Such conflicts are not unique to the church context for social work practice but can be found in every host setting.

What are the Qualification for Church Social Work?

Church social work is not for every social worker who is a Christian, just as not every Christian is called to be a church leader. Social workers are also needed in public and other private, nonsectarian settings where they can live their faith through their work. Church social work is a highly demanding vocation, and one that requires some specific personal as well as professional qualifications:

1. First and foremost, the church social worker needs to be a Christian who loves the church in all its humanness as well as the ideal to which it strives. Churches are like any other human institution; there are problems, politics and personal conflicts. Grady Nutt, a Christian humorist, once said that the church is like Noah's ark: if it weren't for the storm outside, you couldn't stand the stink inside. I would add that church social workers, like other church leaders, often work below deck where the bilge can get pretty deep. Church leaders, including church social workers, must have a love for the church that can transcend the frustrations of fallible organizations and persons.

2. Church social workers often are the only social worker, or one of a very few, in the organization. Their work is often self-defined and requires creativity and the ability to envision what is not and plan and work toward the not-yet. Because so much of the work is often independent practice, a master's degree in social work which develops these abilities is frequently needed.

3. Church social workers are church leaders, relating social service and social action to the culture of the church community, which is rooted in scriptures and the history and doctrine of the church. At least some formal graduate theological education which provides knowledge of the Bible, theology, church history, and spiritual life can be enormously helpful. In addition, understanding the organizational distinctives of a voluntary, mission-driven organization is essential. Some graduate social work programs are now providing courses and concentrations in church social work that include this specialized content.

4. Church social workers do a great deal of public speaking and have opportunity to be influential if they can write for professional and congregational audiences about their work and its relationship to the mission and teachings of the church. They need to be prepared with skills of preaching, teaching, training, and writing.

5. Church social workers need specialized expertise in the arena of ministry in which they are employed, whether that is family therapy in a church child welfare or counseling agency, community organizing in an inner-city community center, administration in a denominational office of Christian social ministries, or any of the other myriad arenas for church social work practice.

6. Church social workers need personal warmth and a love for persons that is felt by others and draws people to them. They often do a lot of informal work with church leaders, members, and volunteers, and they need to be able to inspire, encourage, and motivate others to do the hard work of Christian social ministries.

7. Church social workers need a deep personal faith and a sense of calling to this challenging arena of professional practice. Sometimes church social workers find themselves in the heat of church or denominational conflicts which can be disheartening. Sometimes churches are unconscionably slow in living their mission as a people of faith and service. Sometimes churches are more social communities than they are the body of Christ. Sometimes church social workers see into the

heart of social injustice on the outside and ugly politics on the inside of churches. Church social work is not for the faint of heart, nor is it for those seeking nine- to-five employment.

8. Finally, church social workers need to be able to claim the truth that God does not call Christians, even church social workers, to be all that is required for the work before us; God calls us to be faithful. We are not ultimately judged on how effective our efforts have been to meet the needs of others or to create a just society, but on how faithful we have been to allow God to work through us as we do the best we can with what we have in the place we are.

The biblical stories of God's actions through history are always stories of limited, inadequate persons through whom God worked. These persons courageously lived into God's calling in the place they found themselves—Shiphrah and Puah, a couple of slave midwives who saved the Hebrew baby boys, including Moses; David, a little boy with a slingshot who felled a giant; Esther, a young Jewish wife of a ruthless king who risked her life to save her people; a nameless boy, a volunteer offering his meager lunch to help feed a hungry crowd of thousands. The great promise for church social workers is that we are not alone in facing the great challenges of social injustice, churches in internal conflict, and our own limitations.

References

Bacon, E. (1996). Presentation : Louisville Institute Conference, Louisville, KY.

Campolo, T. (1990). *The kingdom of God is a party*. Dallas: Word.

Carroll, J. W., Dudley, C. S., & McKinney, W. (Eds.). (1986). *Handbook for congregational studies*. Nashville: Abingdon.

Conn, H. (1987). *A clarified vision for urban mission: Dispelling urban stereotypes*. Grand Rapids: Zondervan.

Dudley, C. S. (1996). *Next steps in community ministry*: Alban.

Ferguson, J. (1992). The congregation as context for social work practice. In D. R. Garland (Ed.), *Church social work* (pp. 36-57). St. Davids: The North American Association of Christians in Social Work.

Filteau, J. (1993). Churches play critical role in national social welfare. *Intercom* (June-July), 5.

Garland, D. R. (1994). *Church agencies: Caring for children and families in crisis*. Washington, D.C.: Child Welfare League of America.

Garland, D. R. (1995). Church social work, *Encyclopedia of Social Work* . Washington, D.C.: National Association of Social Workers.

Garland, D. R. (1996). *Precious in His Sight: A guide to child advocacy for the churches*. (rev. ed.). Birmingham: New Hope.

Garland, D. R. (forthcoming). *Family ministry*. Downers Grove: Intervarsity Press.

Hessel, D. T. (1982). *Social ministry*. Philadelphia: Westminster Press.

Hinson, E. G. (1988). The historical involvement of the church in social ministries and social action. *Review and Expositor, 85*(2), 233-241.

Midgley, J., & Sanzenbach, P. (1989). Social work, religion, and the global challenge of fundamentalism. *International Social Work, 32,* 273-287.

Moberg, D. O. (1984). *The church as a social institution*. Grand Rapids: Baker Book House.

Wigginton, S. (1997). Roping off the pews: Boundary issues in family ministry. *Journal of Family Ministry, 1997*(2).

Wikler, M. (1986). Pathways to treatment: How Orthodox Jews enter therapy. *Social Casework, 67* (2), 113-118.

Wikler, M. (1990). "Fishbowl therapy": Hazards of Orthodox therapists treating orthodox patients. *Journal of Psychology and Judaism, 14* (4), 201-212.

CHAPTER 3

SOCIAL WORK'S LEGACY
THE METHODIST SETTLEMENT MOVEMENT

Sarah S. Kreutziger

Walter Trattner in his social welfare textbook *From Poor Law to Welfare*, critically asserts that religious settlements were little more than "modified missions....bent on religious proselytizing, rigorous Americanization, and the imposition of social conformity on lower class clientele" (1976, p. 17). I believe he vastly underestimates the scope and positive impact of religious settlements on the more highly publicized Social Settlement Movement and on social work itself. Starting in the mid-nineteenth century, in response to the demands of the industrialization of American cities and towns, the religious settlement workers created, financed, and staffed outreach programs to the most marginalized inhabitants of the inner cities. They formed Bible classes, kindergartens, industrial schools, clubs, loan banks, job bureaus, dispensaries, reading rooms, and other programs that laid the groundwork for later social reforms. In the process, they created the foundation for the beginning of modern social work. Religious settlements strengthened the cause of women's rights and paved the way for women to enter careers in social welfare. And, in the South, religious settlers led the campaign for racial and ethnic equality.

Many denominations sponsored these specialized city missions, but perhaps none was as well organized and tenacious as the Methodist Episcopal Church (now the United Methodist Church) in spearheading this form of mission outreach. For that reason, an examination of the Methodist Religious Settlement Movement not only shows the work of religious settlers as part of the religious settlement movement, but highlights as well the tension between the ideologies of Christianity and the emerging tenets of enlightenment liberalism. This tension forms social work values today.

Origins of the Methodist Religious Settlement Movement

City Missions

The religious settlement movement in American Methodism began in New York City "on the 5th of July, 1819, [when] 'a number of females' met at the Wesleyan Seminary...for the purpose of forming an Auxiliary Society to the Missionary Society of the Methodist Episcopal Church, which had been formed the previous April" (Mason, 1870, p. 82). While their original purpose was to support missionaries to the North American Indians, their work gradually focused on problems closer to home. By 1850, "the ladies of the mission," united in evangelistic pragmatism, began their work in the notorious Five Points of New York City surrounded by:

> ...miserable-looking buildings, liquor stores innumerable, neglected children by scores, playing in rags and dirt, squalid-looking women, brutal men with black eyes and disfigured faces, proclaiming drunken brawls and fearful violence. (Mason, 1870, p. 33)

The Five Points Mission was the earliest city mission and the precursor of latter settlement homes and community centers in the United States (Leiby, 1978; Magalis, 1973; Riis, 1962).

Led by evangelist Phoebe Palmer, one of the most famous women of her day, the ladies raised money for a building, appointed a paid missionary, and volunteered to conduct Sunday schools, church services, and a nursery for working women. Later, they opened a reading room as an enticement for men who habitually sought solace in taverns, started a medical dispensary, installed public baths for the tenement dwellers, and provided emergency food and shelter for the poor.

Another project of the Missionary Society was "rescue work." In 1833, the women formed the Moral Reform Society to help women who "were victims of sin and shame" (Ingraham, 1844, p. 39) find ways to support themselves other than prostitution. The Society hired city missionaries who were some of the first female social workers. The first and most famous was Margaret Pryor whose descriptions of her "walks of usefulness" became a best-selling book and did much to publicize their work.

Pryor's and Palmer's pleas to move into social reform were spoken in language of the "woman's sphere of action." This language can be appreciated best when we consider the assigned roles and relationships of that era. As homemakers whose responsibility was to build a "sanctified" (holy) society, women were exhorted by religious leaders to protect theirs' and others' homes by instilling spiritual values and righteous living in their children and other members of the household. Their special providence was to take care of other women and children who did not have similar resources or religious beliefs. It followed then, that other rescue work was directed at children. Charles Loring Brace, founder of a massive foster care system for destitute children, began his career at

Five Points Mission. His work there convinced him that "effective social reform must be done in the source and origin of evil, — in prevention, not cure" (Brace, 1973, p. 78). He founded the Children's Aid Society in 1853; an organization that relocated more than fifty-thousand children to rural homes to remove them from the real and perceived dangers of city life.

The Five Points Mission and similar agencies were part of a broader effort known as the City Mission Movement which had its roots in the New York Religious Tract Society. The tract societies distributed religious literature to convert the inner-city poor. In the 1830's, members of the Tract Society began holding prayer meetings and establishing Sunday schools for the children marked for evangelism (Smith-Rosenberg, 1971). As the volunteers became familiar with the living conditions of the residents, they carried food and clothing with them on their rounds and set up emergency funds. In time, they organized their welfare work into wards for distribution and created a new organization, the Society for the Relief of the Worthy Poor. This became the New York Association for Improving the Condition of the Poor. By 1870, forty full-time salaried missionaries were pioneering model tenements, summer camps for children, industrial training schools, and systematic "outdoor" relief. The Association was a forerunner of the New York Charity Organization Society, a pioneer of early professional social work.

The Institutional Churches

The rapid replication of the programs of the Five Points Mission was inspired by the challenge of the industrial age and the difficulties experienced by the men and women who immigrated to the United States to work in its factories. "Between 1860 and 1900, some fourteen million immigrants came to America and about another nine million, mainly from southern and eastern Europe...arrived between 1900 and 1910" (Trattner, 1979, p.135). The massive crowding, illnesses, and social problems created by the influx of largely unskilled, illiterate, foreign-speaking individuals was unparalleled in our history. In New York City, two-thirds of the population lived in tenements in 1890, while Chicago, then the fastest growing city in the world, packed inner-city residents near the putrid-smelling, unsanitary stockyards where slaughtered animal carcasses fouled water and air. Gangs and petty criminals, fortified by alcohol and other drugs, preyed on the new arrivals. The "urban frontier, like the rural frontier, was a dangerous place" (Seller, 1981, p. 50).

To the native-born Americans, the newcomers were dangerous in other ways. Their political attitudes, born out of feudal societies in which government was an agent of social control provided a challenge to American democracy. In the slums, the immigrants turned to old-world political traditions such as the "padrone," or political boss, who would manipulate the system for personal gain in exchange for votes. American ideals of patriotic civic action on the basis of self-denial and responsibility clashed with these attitudes (Hofstadter, 1955).

Americans were also concerned about the breakdown of traditional Protestant religious customs and beliefs founded on Puritanism which portrayed the United States as a "holy experiment" destined to create a new society as a beacon to the rest of the world (Winthrop, 1960; Woodbridge, Noll, & Hatch, 1979). Living sin-free, disciplined, temperate, hard-working lives was crucial to this cause. The immigrants, mostly Roman Catholic, drank, brought "continental ideas of the Sabbath" with them, displayed nomadic living habits, and wore fancy dress (Strong, 1893, p. 210). These practices severely distressed city evangelists. Even worse for their cause was the reality that many in the mainline denominations were becoming indifferent to the plight of the poor and abandoning the inner city churches.

The solution to these changes was to set up a specialized form of city missions in these abandoned churches to Americanize, and hence Christianize, the new arrivals by offering them resources and support. These citadels against the onslaught of massive social problems were called Institutional Churches. Programs and activities developed in these "open" or "free" churches (because there was no charge for the pews) were adopted by the social settlers and others following in their footsteps (Bremner, 1956). These churches viewed themselves as "institutions" that ministered seven days a week to the physical and spiritual wants of all the people within their reach. [They] sponsored clinics, free Saturday night concerts, self-supporting restaurants and lodging houses, wood yards for the unemployed, "fresh air work" for women and children, and "gold-cure" establishments for drunkards. There was a marked emphasis on practical education. Institutional churches sponsored libraries and literary societies and carried on kindergartens, trade schools, and community colleges (McBride, 1983, p. xi).

Although these churches have been described as similar to the secularized social settlements because they adopted many methods and educational theories of the "new charity" (Abell, 1962, p. 164), there is much evidence that the primary mission of the institutional churches was evangelism. While their programs were similar to non-sectarian charities, their ideology was quite different. The Methodist women who supported institutional work were motivated by Scripture. They were to feed the hungry, care for the sick, and clothe the poor (Tatem, 1960).

Methodist women carried these ideals into their work with the religious settlements and supported all of these missions through the structure and activities of the Home Missionary Societies.

The Home Missionary Societies

Almost without exception, the Home Missionary Societies were made up of white, middle-class women, better educated than most of their female contemporaries and freed from time-consuming house chores by the same industrial revolution that was creating the massive social problems in the cities and towns. While many other denominations were ministering to poor and oppressed individuals, the Methodists were the most zealous and well-organized. By 1844, when the Methodist Episcopal Church separated into the southern and northern branches over slavery, there were already 360 missionaries in the United States and one mission in Liberia supported by these societies (Norwood, 1974).

After the Civil War, the local mission societies joined together to build national organizations within the two divisions. The northern church established its missionary societies first in 1869, followed by the southern church nine years later, to aid foreign missions. The Woman's Home Missionary Society was founded in 1880 in the northern Methodist Episcopal Church to support missions within the United States. Their support of missions in the South, especially for the recently freed slaves, led to the founding of the southern church's Home Mission Society in 1880 (*Home Missions*, 1930).

Much of the philosophy undergirding the mission societies' work came from a societal view of women as the moral guardians of the home. In the North, missionary society members organized under the banner of "evangelical domesticity," the notion that the natural spiritual superiority of women gave them the authority to protect their homes and children from the evil influences of society (Lee, 1981). Countless women echoed the belief that "in every well-regulated family their [sic] mother is the potent influence in molding the little ones committed to her sacred guidance" (*Women's Missionary Society*, 1884, p. 4). Much of the reform activity therefore, was directed toward helping other women and children create barriers against the evils that would destroy the sanctity of the home.

In the South, the drive to purify homes was made more difficult by antebellum ideology. The plantation mentality that enslaved black women kept white women in bondage as well. A rigid, tightly-knit, hierarchical social order demanded obedience and submissiveness. As a result, religious activities for women stressed personal piety rather than the "social holiness" of evangelical service that northern women had channeled into abolition, women's rights, and other reforms (Thompson, 1972; Scott, 1970). The Civil War, despite its devastation, liberated southern women for reform activities previously denied them. Consequently, they poured their energies into "their appointed sphere": the churches. In time, the wives, daughters, and sisters of former slave holders joined with the wives, daughters, and sisters of slaves to establish agencies and organizations that promoted racial harmony and reinforced the cause of women's rights (Hall, 1979; Scott, 1984). A significant product of their work was the Methodist Religious Settlement Movement.

The Religious Settlements

Activities and Staffing

Methodist settlements, like their predecessors, often began as child care facilities for working mothers and expanded into kindergartens, sewing clubs, domestic labor training, homemaker clubs, rescue work for prostitutes, boys' athletic clubs, classes in cooking, play grounds, and religious services. Although they also included reading rooms, public baths, English classes, night school, dispensaries, lectures, concerts, music lessons, bookkeeping and banking classes, military drills, gymnastics, milk stations, saving associations, libraries, and "improvement clubs for men," — they were primarily geared to the needs of mothers and children (Woods & Kennedy, 1911).

The settlement houses were originally sponsored as an expanded mission project of the Women's Home Missionary Society (WHMS), the Chicago Training School for City, Home and Foreign Missions (CTS), and several independent associations. While the goal of the leaders of these organizations was still the sanctification of society through the changed lives of individuals, their work among the poor enlarged their vision of the difficulties that these individuals faced. City missionaries realized that society as a whole must be changed if their goal to evangelize the world was to be reached. Fed by the theology of the social gospel, which saw sin as systemic as well as individual, the city missionaries and their supporters created a broader, more far-reaching attack upon the barriers that kept all people from realizing their God-given potential.

Volunteers from the missionary societies and churches, along with a few paid city missionaries, ran many of the early missions; but the need for better training and education for their expanding work prompted missionary society leaders such as Lucy Rider Meyer, Jane Bancroft Robinson, and Belle Harris Bennett to advocate for biblically-trained women who would live in the neighborhoods among the disadvantaged in the same manner that foreign missionaries lived with citizens in the lands they served. After much planning, hard work, and many setbacks, the efforts of these women and others were realized by the 1880's in a new version of the home missionary: the deaconess.

Deaconesses were distinguished from the city missionaries by the clothing they wore, their communal living arrangements, their formal connection to the church, and their unsalaried service (*Deaconess Advocate*, February 1901). Easily recognized because of their dark dresses, starched bonnets tied with a large white bow, and brisk manner, the deaconesses took their calling seriously. Their task was to "minister to the poor, visit the sick, pray for the dying, care for the orphan, seek the wandering, comfort the sorrowing, [and] save the sinning..." (Thoburn & Leonard in Lee, 1963, p. 37). With the biblical deaconess Phoebe as their model, deaconesses went into the inner cities of the North and the factory towns and rural communities of the South as part of the twentieth century vanguard for the religious settlement movement. In the first thirty years of the Methodist diaconate, the Chicago Training School, founded by Lucy Rider Meyer, sent nearly 4,000 deaconesses and city missionaries to work in hospitals, schools, settlements, rescue homes, and churches. Forty of these institutions were started by CTS graduates (Brown, 1985).

In the South, Methodist settlements constituted from 30% to 100% of all settlements when the first national listing was compiled in 1911 (Woods & Kennedy, 1911). Settlements that served white populations were called Wesley Houses, after Methodism's founder John Wesley, and settlements that served African-Americans were known as Bethlehem Houses (Tatem, 1960). Settlement leaders worked with white American cotton mill employees in Georgia, French-Arcadians families and Italian immigrants in Louisiana, African-American farms workers in Tennessee and Georgia, European seafood workers in Mississippi, and Hispanic migrant workers in Texas and Florida (Nelson, 1909). Many of the settlements were headed by deaconesses who lived in the neighborhoods they served. In 1910, there were six Methodist deaconess training schools and ninety social agencies staffed by 1,069 deaconesses (Glidden, in Dougherty, 1988).

The Deaconess Mother Heart

The religious basis of the beliefs and values of the deaconess sisterhood was the Puritan vision of America's spiritual manifest destiny: America as the beacon to the rest of the world. Deaconess values were also formed from Wesleyan ideals of "perfecting" society through service and mission, cultural definitions of women's position and place, enlightenment views of scientific reasoning, and the emerging social gospel. Their declared goal was the salvation of the "household of faith": American society. The evils of unchurched people, drunkenness, pauperism, and negative influences from foreigners could be wiped out, they believed, with a return to Christian ideals based on the earlier promise of God's covenant with the "New Jerusalem," the United States. This heavenly pattern, imprinted upon America, would ensure the salvation of the world. As deaconess educator Belle Horton declared, "we must 'save America for the world's sake'" (Horton, 1904, p. 41).

Justification for women's entry into this noble endeavor came from church tradition and the Bible as expressed through the metaphor of the Mother Heart. The Mother Heart, as described by Meyer, was the nurturing, caring, feminine side of God understood and possessed by women. Deaconess sisterhood, reinforced by communal living arrangements and church connection, readily integrated the holistic social gospel tenets into their ideological center. Since building the Kingdom of God on earth required the sanctification of each home, it was important for churches to include the work of those whose specific mission was the care of God's "unmothered children": Women. This allowed the deaconesses, and by extension - all females - greater authority to be ministers to the whole of society. This expanded vision of women's role in the church and community helped set the stage for the ordination of women, suffrage, and other forms of women's rights. It also helped pave the way for women to enter paid careers as the profession of social work emerged from its two pioneer branches: the Charity Organization Societies and the Settlement Movements.

Religious Settlements and Social Settlements

The women who staffed the settlement homes and institutions were on the front lines of the home mission field. Because the early city mission and institutional churches had provided the model for service and intervention in the lives of the dispossessed for non-sectarian settlements and associated charities just as they had for the religious settlements, there was a great deal of exchange of information, ideas, education, and services. Meyer was a friend of social settlement leader Jane Addams and each knew and respected the other's work. Addams helped Meyer select the site for the CTS and was involved in the early plans. Meyer had wanted to put Addams on the School's Board of Trustees in 1892, but was voted down because: Hull-House was just then drawing the fire of the churches because it had been thought necessary to eliminate any direct religious teaching from its program and one or two members of the Training School Board protested against the presence of this "unChristian enterprise" (Horton, 1928, p. 182).

Addams discussed this experience in *Twenty Years at Hull-House* (1981) and the embarrassment it caused, in her words, to "the openminded head of the school" (p. 72). Addams compared the Training School favorably to the activities of the social settlements. Meyer and Addams continued to be friends throughout their careers and Meyer frequently spoke of Addam's work in the *Deaconess Advocate*, the journal of the CTS.

Despite opposition from church members who opposed the non-religious atmosphere of the social settlements, social settlement leaders continued to lecture regularly at the CTS and the students' field work included living as residents at Hull-House and other social settlements (Brown, 1985). By 1913, Meyers had supplemented the biblically-oriented lectures with textbooks by charity organization pioneers Edward J. Devine and Amos Warner (*Bulletin CTS*, January, 1914). By 1918, her students were working in the United Charities and Juvenile Protection Associations as "visitors" (*Bulletin CTS*, December, 1918), and were learning to think in the codified, scientific methods of the "new charity." Although religious motivation and language continued to be part of the curriculum, the new field of sociology and its promise of "perfecting" society through social engineering gradually supplanted the earlier emphasis on evangelism and proselytization in all the training schools. In time, it would become increasingly difficult to distinguish between the ideology and practices of those who graduated from the deaconess training schools and those who graduated from the university-based schools of social work. As deaconess education and values became less and less distinguishable from the values and methods of early professional social work, deaconess organizations began to lose the sponsorship of the church and other financial backers. Consequently, deaconess training schools were merged into schools of theology or schools of social work (Tatem, 1960; Nola Smee, telephone interview, July, 1995; address by Walter Athern, April 26, 1926, Boston University School of Theology Archives).

The Decline of the Methodist Religious Settlement Movement

While the movement toward non-sectarian liberalism characterized by scientifically-trained workers was initially moderated by the religious training of the settlers and other mission workers, the increasing centralization of reform activities and governmental intervention in social reform tipped the balance in favor of secularism. Additionally, "the spontaneous will to serve," so evident in earlier church volunteers, was subverted by the drive for professionalization. Previous values that had stressed compassion, emotional involvement, and vigorous love of humanity, according to social work historian Roy Lubove (1965), were "educated out" in preference for a "scientific trained intelligence and skillful application of technique" (p. 122). This new climate of professionalism at the beginning of the twentieth century changed the relationship between helper and those helped. Agencies became bureaucratic rather than evangelical, more contractual than spontaneous, and more removed from their clients.

One of the defining and continuing differences between the social settlements and the religious settlements was the pressure by churches on sectarian settlements to use their work for proselytizing (Doris Alexander, telephone interview, July, 1995; Davis, 1967). This pressure caused many of the settlements begun under religious auspices to sever their ties with their parent organizations. This was done to solicit community-wide support and to appeal to wealthy industrialists interested in ecumenical charities (Dubroca, 1955; Trolander, 1987). After World War I, with the rise of the Community Chest and other centralized social service funding, social settlement leaders were forced to answer to an organizational hierarchy that could dictate policy and programs. The net result was less emphasis on controversial community action (Trolander, 1987) and religious instruction. Funding from these centralized agencies also reinforced the drive to replace sectarian-trained workers with professional social workers.

Compounding these trends was social work's move into individual treatment and away from community development. Veterans of World War I suffering from battle-fatigue and shell shock required more than friendly neighborly relationships to help them cope with their personal and health-related problems. Red Cross workers treating military families discovered that Freudian psychoanalytic approaches and casework techniques developed by Mary Richmond, pioneer leader of the Charity Organizational Societies, were better suited to their needs. "Friendly visiting" gave way to therapeutic intervention as settlements were changed from community centers into mental health clinics.

This trend continued until by the early 1960's, professional social workers had replaced volunteers and religious settlement workers in many of the centers. The consequences of the move, according to one historian, led to greater emotional detachment between residents and the workers and less mutual concern and care. As she explained:

In place of spontaneity and being available around the clock, [social workers] made appointments and 'treatment plans.' Instead of seeking to do *with* the neighborhood, they sought to do *for* the neighborhood. Their 'professional' detachment from the neighborhood was not only physical, it was psychological. (Trolander, 1987, p. 39)

While Methodists followed similar practices related to staffing, there were some differences. Methodist deaconesses continued to reside in the settlements until the mid 1980's (Nola Smee, telephone interview, July, 1995) which helped to maintain the physical as well as the symbolic presence and sense of involvement in the neighborhoods that is part of the settlement legacy. Even when the settlers moved out, it was not so much because of their lack of dedication as it was from church policy and changing attitudes. The decline of religious settlers paralleled the decline of the deaconess movement as deaconesses began to retire and fewer and fewer women were willing to expend the level of commitment required for the diaconate as other opportunities for ministry and employment opened to women. The success of the deaconess crusade, the right of women to participate fully in the church and community, in other words, contributed to its decline (Betty Purkey, telephone interview, July, 1995).

Implications for the Future

While the history of religious settlements has remained in the shadows of the highly publicized work of social settlements such as Jane Addam's Hull-House (Addams, 1981; Davis, 1967; Leiby, 1979), the fact remains that these sectarian-sponsored organizations contributed much to the origins and success of early social work. Overlooked by most social work chroniclers were the hundreds of religiously-committed women, backed by an army of loyal supporters, who also moved into inner-city and rural neighborhoods to share their talents and service with the less fortunate. Methodist settlement leaders were typical examples of these women and their dreams.

The Methodist religious settlers' vision of society began with evangelical hopes for a holy nation undergirded by mutual concern for each other and love of God. This vision inspired the work that built hundreds of social welfare institutions and provided the support and financial resources to run them. When these front-line city missionaries were forced by the overwhelming task and changing times to create new ways of thinking and practice, they lost part of the religious underpinning that defined their vision. Despite these challenges and the decline of the deaconess movement, many of the original settlement houses survive as community centers and urban outreach stations for the churches. As such, they serve as reminders of what the church is capable of doing when the call for commitment, dedication, and sacrifice is answered. When, in the words of Bellah et al., (1985), we seek "the recovery of our social ecology [that] would allow us to link interests with the common good" (p. 287).

The religious and social settlers faced a society reeling from the effects of "wrecked foundations of domesticity" (Addams, 1972, p. 47) and other problems of societal dislocation and despair. Many contemporary people would agree that this century's end brings similar challenges. Family disorganization, international disruptions, population shifts, some with tragic consequences, and continuing disagreements over race, class, and gender create disunity and loss of purpose. Our country, like religious institutions and other social service professions, seems to be searching for a renewed vision and mission. Social work leaders Harry Specht and Mark Courtney (1994) join others calling for the profession of social work to return to its defining mission in the tradition of the settlement movements and the strong belief in the improvement of society. The history of the Methodist Religious Settlement Movement offers one avenue to reclaim that charge.

Notes

This chapter was rewritten from information from the author's unpublished dissertation research for Tulane University and research from a paper submitted to the School of Divinity at Duke University.

References

Abell, Aaron Ignatius. (1962). *The urban impact on American Protestantism 1861-1900.* Hamden: Archon.

Addams, Jane. (1981). *Twenty years at Hull House.* Phillips Publishing Co., 1910; reprint, New York: Signet Classic.

Addams, Jane. (1972). *The spirit of youth and the city streets.* New York: MacMillan Co., 1909; reprint, Urbana: University of Chicago Press.

Bellah, Robert N., Richard Madsen, William M. Sullivan, Ann Swidler & Steven M. Tipton. (1985). *Habits of the Heart: Individualism and commitment in American life.* Berkeley: University of California Press.

Brace, Charles Loring. (1973). *The dangerous class of New York.* New York: Wynkoop & Hollenbeck, Publisher, 1872; NASW Classic reprint, Washington, DC: NASW.

Bremner, Robert H. (1956). *From the depths: The discovery of poverty in the United States.* New York: New York University Press.

Brown, Irva Calley. (1985). *"In their times": A history of the Chicago Training School on the occasion of its centennial celebration, 1885-1985*. Evanston: Garrett Evangelical Theological Seminary.

Bulletin of the Chicago Training School for City, Home and Foreign Missions. (1914). 15(4).

Bulletin of the Chicago Training School for City, Home and Foreign Missions. (1918). 18(4).

Davis, Allen F. (1967). *Spearheads for reform: The social settlements and the progressive movement 1890-1914*. New York: Oxford University Press.

Deaconess Advocate. Vols. 14-29, 1898-1914.

Dougherty, Mary Agnes. (1979). The Methodist Deaconess, 1885-1918: A study in religious feminism. Ph. D. diss., University of California, Davis.

Dubroca, Isabelle. (1955). *Good neighbor Eleanor McMain of Kingsley House*. New Orleans: Pelican Publishing Co.

Hall, Jacquelyn Dowd. (1979). *Revolt against chivalry: Jessie Daniel Ames and the women's campaign against lynching*. New York: Columbia University Press.

Hofstadter, Richard. (1955). *The age of reform*. New York: Alfred A. Knopf.

Home Missions. (1930). Nashville: Woman's Missionary Council, Methodist Episcopal Church, South.

Horton, Isabelle. (1904). *The burden of the city*. New York: Fleming H. Revell Company.

Horton, Isaabelle. (1928). *High adventure—life of Lucy Rider Meyer*. New York: Methodist Book Concern.

Ingraham, Sarah R. (1844). *Walks of usefulness or reminiscences of Mrs. Margaret Prior*. New York: American Female Moral Reform Society.

Ladies of the Mission. (1854). *The old brewery and the new mission house at the Five Points*. New York: Stringer & Townsend.

Lee, Elizabeth Meredith. (1963). *As among the Methodists: Deaconesses yesterday today and tomorrow*. New York: Woman's Division of Christian Service, Board of Missions, Methodist Church.

Lee, Susan Dye. (1981). Evangelical domesticity: The Woman's Temperance Crusade of 1873-1874. In Hilah Thomas & Rosemary Skinner Keller, (Eds.), *Women in new worlds*, (pp. 293-309). Nashville: Abingdon Press.

Leiby, James. (1978). *A history of social welfare and social work in the United States*. New York: Columbia University Press.

Lubove, Roy. (1965). *The professional altruist: The emergence of social work as a career 1880- 1930*. Cambridge: Harvard University Press.

Magalis, Elaine. (1973). *Conduct becoming to a woman*. New York: Women's Division, Board of Global Ministries, The United Methodist Church.

Mason, Mary. (1870). *Consecrated talents: Or the life of Mrs. Mary W. Mason*. New York: Carlton & Lanahan.

McBride, Esther Barnhart. (1983). *Open church: History of an idea*. U.S.A.: By the author.

Nelson, John. (1909). *Home mission fields of the Methodist Episcopal Church, South*. Home Department, Board of Missions, Methodist Episcopal Church, South.

Norwood, Frederick A. (1974). *The story of American Methodism*. Nashville: Abingdon Press.

Riis, Jacob A. (1962). *How the other half lives: Studies among the tenements of New York*. 1890. Reprint, American Century Series. New York: Hill & Wang.

Scott, Anne Firor. (1970). *The southern lady: From pedestal to politics 1830-1930*. Chicago: University of Chicago Press.

Scott, Anne Firor. (1984). *Making the invisible woman visible*. Urbana: University of Illinois Press.

Seller, Maxine Schwartz. (1981). *Immigrant women*. Philadelphia: Temple University Press.

Smith-Rosenberg, Carroll. (1971). *Religion and the rise of the American city: The New York City Mission Movement, 1812-1870*. Ithaca: Cornell University Press.

Sprecht, Harry & Mark E. Courtney. (1994). *Unfaithful angels: How social work has abandoned its mission*. New York: The Free Press.

Strong, Josiah. (1893). *The new era or the coming kingdom*. New York: Baker & Taylor Co.

Tatum, Noreen Dunn. (1960). *A crown of service: A story of women's work in the Methodist Episcopal Church, South, from 1878-1940*. Nashville: Parthenon Press.

Thompson, Edgar. (1972). God and the southern plantation system. In Samuel Hill, (Ed.), *Religion and the solid South*, (pp. 57-91). Nashville: Abingdon Press.

Trattner, Walter I. (1979). *From poor law to welfare state*. (2nd. ed.), New York: Free Press.

Trolander, Judith Ann. (1987). *Professionalism and social change*. New York: Columbia University Press.

Winthrop, John. (1960). A model of Christian charity. In H. Shelton Smith, Robert T. Handy, & Lefferts A. Loetscher (Eds.), *American Christianity*, (pp. 98-102). New York: Charles Scribner's Sons.

Woman's Missionary Society of the Methodist Episcopal Church, South. (June): 1884.

Woodbridge, John D., Mark A. Noll, & Nathan O. Hatch. (1979). *The gospel in America*. Grand Rapids: Zondervan Publishing House.

Woods, Robert A. & Albert J. Kennedy, (Eds). (1911). *Handbook of settlements*. New York: Charities Publication Committee.

Archives

Boston University School of Theology.
Special Collections, University Libraries,
Boston, Massachusetts

CHAPTER 4

COMMUNITY PRACTICE: LESSONS FOR SOCIAL WORK FROM A RACIALLY-MIXED CENTRAL CITY CHURCH

Janice M. Staral

Social workers in the 21st century face the challenge of creating effective partnerships in order to respond to social problems. Developing these community coalitions requires an understanding of the history of problems and the nature of potential partners. The story of Reformation Lutheran Church, a racially-mixed church located in the central city of Milwaukee, Wisconsin, suggests strategies for developing community. These strategies are rooted in the settlement house tradition and reflect the religious beliefs of the church. This information was gleaned from participant-observer research conducted at the invitation of the church minister from 1991 to the present time.

Reformation Church was chosen as the focus of this study because the leaders of Reformation Church decided to remain at their original church location when faced with the problems of urban change and declining membership. During the past 20 to 30 years, leaders of other similar mainline churches chose to either close or sell their church buildings. Frequently, after the church closings, new churches were built in the outlying Milwaukee suburbs, following the out-migration of many of their church members. An example of this migration is illustrated by another Milwaukee Lutheran Church's decision to leave the central city. A note located in the Memorial Lutheran's 1992 Church Directory explains this movement to the suburbs:

> Rapid changes and population shifts took place in the inner-city during the 1950's and 1960's. In the summer of 1964, an offer to purchase the church by Mt. Moriah Baptist Church was accepted and the property was vacated by June 14, 1964. Groundbreaking for the new building in the suburb of Glendale began in October of 1965.

The leaders at Reformation Church, many of whom had also relocated to the nearby suburbs, wanted to continue to worship at their original site, but were concerned about their declining membership. These leaders were committed to social justice issues and believed that maintaining a church presence in the community was important. In 1985, they "called" a new pastor, a white male in his late thirties. He was encouraged to pursue strategies that would stabilize church membership, as well as be involved in the needs of the people in the Reformation Church neighborhood. The leaders asked for this specific pastor because he had a measure of success in his previous work in outreach ministries in the Uptown Chicago area. They hoped he could apply his experience to Reformation Church. The decision to hire this new pastor eventually resulted in church leadership which would pursue methods leading to neighborhood betterment and would change a largely white congregation to a racially-mixed one.

In this context, the goal of this chapter is to 1) *discuss* one church's response to urban change and decline, 2) *assess* and *examine* this response in terms of relevance and application to social work practice, and 3) *illuminate* the power religious institutions can have on a neighborhood. The role of the church is especially important in an era where federal and state budgets continue to be slashed and more expectations are being placed on the voluntary sector.

Understanding Urban Change

Urban America has changed dramatically in the last 30 years. Research conducted by Kasarda (1993), Abramson and Tobin (1994) and Massey and Denton (1993) suggest that many American cities have become increasingly segregated in terms of race and income. Such trends have been especially poignant in Milwaukee, a city distinguished by Abramson and Tobin as one of the most racially and economically segregated in the United States. This segregation has resulted in what the journalist, Joel Garreau (1991) has characterized as "edge cities," whereby the more affluent move their families and tax base beyond the city limits to areas that are "self-contained in terms of their social, economic, political, and cultural systems" (p. 14).

Urban communities have also been affected by deindustrialization, whereby family-supporting manufacturing jobs have been eliminated, relocated to outlying areas or moved to other countries (Bluestone & Harrison, 1982). Global restructuring, unemployment, and conservative economic policies (commonly known as supply-side economics, designed to boost profits) have affected all Americans, but especially the urban poor (Rose, 1997).

Various authors such as Murray (1984) and Mead (1986), have gained much public acceptance in their assertion that any aid to the poor only promotes dependence. The media portrayal of urban life as violent, infested with drugs and filled with gang-bangers contributes to the negative attitudes toward the urban poor. As the affluent become more self-contained, having minimal contact with the urban poor, it becomes much easier to objectify the poor and to "blame" them for the city's current social ills.

The History of Urban Change at Reformation Church

The reality of urban change can be seen directly through understanding the history and specific changes in the Reformation Church neighborhood. The Evangelical Lutheran Church of the Reformation, the official name of the church, was established in 1908. Two former pastors of Reformation characterized the church as a traditional, white, Lutheran Church, with middle to upper-class membership. Most of the members lived near the church, owning their homes or renting out the upper half of their duplexes to friends or family members. Most members were employed in various manufacturing or office jobs within the city.

Through the 1950's, Reformation Church maintained a roster of 2000 members and expanded its educational space for 600 Sunday School children in the congregation. The church appeared poised on a long-term successful expansion, but the forces of urban change were already beginning in the Reformation neighborhood. In the mid-1960's, numerous neighborhood homes were demolished as part a proposed freeway system which never materialized, leaving vacant, open lots. Local businesses and factories began to close or relocate, giving families further impetus to move to the suburbs and outlying areas.

The Reformation Church Neighborhood

By 1985, the neighborhood had changed dramatically in terms of racial composition, income level, crime, and home ownership. The congregation dwindled to 150 members, with no children for Sunday School. The remaining church-goers maintained their membership with Reformation Church, but no longer lived in the immediate neighborhood. Reformation Church had become a commuter church, having no significant membership from the church neighborhood.

The U.S. Census reports for the census tracts 90, 96, 97, and 98 that surround the Reformation neighborhood reveal marked changes in the period from 1960 to 1990 (see map). The following reveals these changes dramatically.

In the 1960's and 1970's, the Reformation Church neighborhood was virtually all white. By 1990, the neighborhood had become predominantly African American, with only about 12 percent white resi-

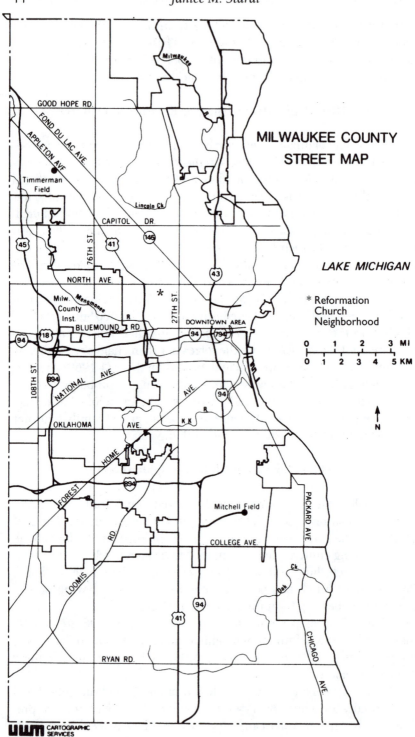

MILWAUKEE COUNTY
STREET MAP

LAKE MICHIGAN

* Reformation
Church
Neighborhood

0   1   2   3 MI
0   1   2   3   4   5 KM

N

GOOD HOPE RD.

FOND DU LAC AVE.

APPLETON AVE.

Timmerman
Field

Lincoln Ck.

CAPITOL DR.

76TH ST.

45   41   145

43

NORTH AVE.

Milw.
County
Inst.

Menomonee

27TH ST.

BLUEMOUND RD.

DOWNTOWN AREA

94   18   94   794

108TH ST.

894

NATIONAL AVE.

AVE.

94

OKLAHOMA AVE.

K K

HOME

894

FOREST

RD.

Mitchell Field

PACKARD AVE.

COLLEGE AVE.

LOOMIS

Oak Ck.

94

41

CHICAGO AVE.

RYAN RD.

UWM CARTOGRAPHIC
SERVICES

dents. The percentage of home ownership in the neighborhood changed from an average of 36.9 percent in 1960 to an average of 17.4 percent in 1990. Unoccupied, vacant housing increased from a vacancy rate of 2.7 percent in 1960, to 15.9 percent by 1990. Unemployment for males rose from an average of 3.9 percent in 1960 to 20.3 percent in 1990. The poverty rate rose from 13.8 percent in 1970 to 57.9 percent in 1990.

Data regarding crime in the Reformation neighborhood were difficult to interpret because the Police and Fire Commissions changed reporting procedures in 1980. However, data from 1984 to 1990 document a significant increase in crime in just six years. In 1984, there were 3,302 crimes in the four closest census tracts. By 1990, there were 4,088, a 23.8 percent increase. In 1984, three homicides occurred within the four census tracts. In 1990, 14 homicides occurred (*Milwaukee Fire and Police Commission Report*, 1984, 1990). The area clearly became more violent.

Despite the drastic decline in the neighborhood, it is still one of contrasts and contradictions. Some parts appear to be safe. These areas have rows of wooden frame duplexes and bungalows, typical of Milwaukee working class neighborhoods, with houses facing the city street and alleys behind. Some newly remodeled Habitat for Humanity houses are evident. Other homes are clearly in need of repair, with dilapidated porches, broken windows or screen doors. Within a few blocks of Reformation Church, there are abandoned homes and vacant lots, where homes have either burned down or been demolished.

A pastoral intern who lived next door to the church during her internship gave this researcher the following description:

> You hear shouting outside all the time. You see police throwing people on the ground. You hear shots many nights. When you hear shots, like when you hear a semi-automatic gun, you stay away from the windows. Sometimes the shots are just the teenagers shooting the rats in the alley. You hear screaming every night. Sometimes the screaming is just the teenagers playing around outside.

One of the peer ministers at Reformation described the neighborhood this way:

> I was on 46th Street first, then I moved. Then I got shot up in my house. It wasn't for me. My house was mistaken for the wrong house. There was a bullet laying at my baby's head. I was so scared, so I moved from there. That was 1985. Then I moved to 34th Street. I wanted to get out of the neighborhood, but it's getting bad all over.

A Holistic and Integrated Approach

Visitors coming to the church see a well built, large, white, stone structure. Carved depictions of Martin Luther and words from his "Here I Stand" speech during the time of the Reformation are prominent on the outside of the building. The outside brick of the church is free from graffiti typical of many other neighborhood buildings. There are glass windows on the lower side of the church walls. The glass windows are remarkable for they are some of the few glass windows in the neighborhood that are neither broken nor covered with iron bars. The sanctuary of the church, which occupies a smaller part of the building and seats about 300 to 400 people, reflects an earlier elegance. The church is built in the style of the old German Lutheran Church, with wood ceiling tiles, and dark, thick wood beams on the ceilings and sides. One side of the church is framed with intricately stained glass windows.

This picture of elegance contrasts with other areas of the church which need refurbishing. Furniture is comfortable, but worn. The inside of the church is a labyrinth of rooms, offices and classrooms, with a winding back stairs that connects its three levels. The quietness of the sanctuary contrasts with the activity and chaos which marks visiting areas and hallways.

Church members, community people, and strangers frequent the church during the week. On Sundays and during the week, there are contrasts in the people coming to the church, in terms of race, class, and physical and cognitive abilities. Some of the visitors come to assist and participate in church activities or to socialize. Others request, and sometimes demand, immediate help in the form of food, bus tickets, or other crises assistance. There is both an aura of safety, because most visitors are greeted warmly by staff and community people, and of caution because at times tempers flare and verbal confrontations occur. The violence of the streets is never far away.

Reformation Church's distinctiveness results from these contrasts, as well as its philosophy of what it means to do neighborhood outreach, or as the pastor would say, "to be church." According to the pastor "being church" means developing an integrated, holistic ministry, not one of providing various independent programs. Separating the various methods of Reformation Church outreach ministry is difficult because just like the chaos and the friendly greetings, the methods are interwoven and are affected by each other.

It is difficult to separate the various methods used by Reformation Church for neighborhood betterment, but defining the undergirding philosophy of this work is not. This philosophy is of special interest to social work because it parallels that of Jane Addams' time and her work in the settlement house movement a century ago. For example, the pastor and his family reside in the immediate neighborhood. The outreach methods directed by the pastor attempt to connect individual and community problems to collective action, and are directed at changing public policy. Like the social workers at Hull House, direct aid is provided, but used in the context of supporting individual empowerment or change.

Some social workers may also relate to the overarching values shared by the pastor and the members of Reformation Church, which are a deep faith in God and in the value and dignity of every individual. Biblical scripture is interpreted from the perspective of the poor and the marginalized, referred to in the Roman Catholic tradition as the "preferential option for the poor." Whereas some religious traditions draw a dichotomy between the spiritual and secular, the holistic ministry at Reformation rejects any dichotomy between these two spheres.

The overall philosophy of the pastor of Reformation Church is summarized well in a statement written in the church's monthly newsletter (*The Gleanings*, July-August 1991):

> Hopefully, Reformation does not minister *in* nor *to* the neighborhood, *but with the people!* In this approach, the community and congregation are partners. At times, through town hall meetings, the people of the neighborhood instruct the church. The people of the community, no matter how poor, are seen as people of worth and dignity who have potential and much to offer. Reformation needs to continually join with the people of the neighborhood as they discern and define and live out the kind of community they want.

Community Building

The methods used in Reformation's outreach ministries are well integrated, but the most distinctive feature and the one that supports the overall life of the church is that of "building community." The pastor explains that this community building means developing interdependent relationships among various church members and then extending these relationships to other people who live in the neighborhood. When questioning people at Reformation regarding their church, one of the most frequent comment is "we build community here; everyone is welcome and accepted."

During visits to the church it becomes easy to observe what the pastor means by developing community. During Sunday church services no separation is made between members and nonmembers. Both groups participate equally throughout the service, which includes receiving Holy Communion, which has some restrictions in many Lutheran Churches. Non-alcoholic wine is used for this sacrament, demonstrating concern for those in the community who may be struggling with alcoholism.

Children are encouraged to attend church services, regardless of whether they are accompanied by an adult. Volunteers serve a breakfast to the neighborhood children prior to the beginning of services. The young children sit with each other in the front pews or choose to sit with a favorite adult attending services. Sometimes babies or young children end up in the arms of various adults throughout the service. Early in the service, all children are invited to the altar for a special message. The teenagers, who sit in the back of the church, also participate in this weekly ritual.

In the summer, about 40 to 50 children who attend church services participate in the summer work program — raking, painting, and cleaning up trash at various neighborhood locations. The children spend about four mornings a week, for six weeks of work, earning $210 for the summer. They are supervised by adult members from Reformation, who live in the neighborhood and are usually African American. The summer program also includes field trips, and efforts directed at developing individual skills and building self-esteem.

The children demonstrate their connectedness to Reformation Church by convincing their mothers, and sometimes fathers or extended family members, to attend church with them. In contrast to the tradition of adults bringing their children to church, many adults in the neighborhood are brought to the church through their children.

Church members serve as greeters and stand outside of the church on the sidewalk to invite passersby to church, during both warm and cold weather. Midway through the service, the whole congregation is involved in the "passing of the peace," a ritual of greeting where the 150-200 people attending the service stand and move around to shake hands or hug anyone who is in attendance that Sunday. The "passing of the peace" usually lasts about 10 minutes. Likewise, after services, refreshments of cookies and juice are served to further encourage fellowship. With both the outward show of hospitality and the neighborhood grapevine, people begin to learn that Reformation Church is a place they will be welcomed.

This effort at building community is replicated throughout the week. The pastor calls the activities that occur regularly as "givens," activities scheduled on a regular, predictable basis to which community people can come without having to follow a church schedule. This is especially important to community people experiencing crises. When in crisis they may have to temporarily drop out of the various activities, but can then easily re-enter activities when their lives re-stabilize. Some of these events occur weekly, others occur on a monthly or twice a month basis. For example, community Bible studies occur on Tuesday and Thursday mornings at ten o'clock. Education night and gospel choir are scheduled every Wednesday night. Friday nights are reserved for an evening community meal. Other activities include house churches (small groups meeting in private homes for personal faith sharing and support), self-esteem classes, and game nights.

In addition to the givens, members and neighborhood people frequently come to the church during the week for casual visiting. The church has a small gathering room where people visit or wait to talk to the pastor. Through such informal and formal gatherings at the church, community people develop strong relationships with their neighbors and begin to form a positive connection to the church. During most days of the week and on Sundays, the church is a place of activity and one of the few safe places for visiting.

In this context of community, a source of support is available. For example, when one mother's house was firebombed and burned down, another member of Reformation "took in" the mother and her three children for three months, until she was able to find new accommodations.

Reciprocal Giving and the Peer Ministers

People in the community use the church frequently as a source of assistance, asking the pastor for free food, bus tickets, short-term loans, and sometimes counseling in solving personal or family problems. People are usually supplied with help if the church has adequate resources at the time. However, the pastor suggests that the person asking for help also be asked how he or she can contribute their talents or skills to the church.

This process of reciprocal giving serves a threefold purpose. First, it prevents the church from being seen as only a place for a "hand-out." Secondly, it begins to build a connection between the help seeker and the church. Thirdly, it underscores the reality that the help-seeker has something of value and worth to contribute. If the person requesting help expresses an interest in reciprocating, the minister will inquire about the person's talents or areas of interest, or if the person has no specific interest, the minister will invite the person to experiment with various activities. These activities could include: answering the church office phone, preparing rooms for meetings, monitoring and greeting visitors to the church, attending community social action meetings, or visiting the elderly in nursing homes.

The role of the "peer minister" has been developed through the process of reciprocal giving. A peer minister is someone from the community who has agreed to "volunteer" to do work at the church on a consistent basis with some of the various tasks detailed above. The presence of the peer ministers, usually African Americans who reside in the neighborhood, helps to build a stronger linkage and deeper trust between the church and the people in the community. Peer ministers frequently accompany the pastor or the parish nurse on initial home visits. The family visited is more receptive to the pastor or nurse because of the presence and familiarity of the peer minister.

In exchange for the services of the peer ministers, the pastor provides support to them in pursuing personal goals, such as developing leadership skills, becoming effective in dealing with family problems, obtaining additional education, or acquiring employment. In addition to the supportive counseling to achieve goals, the peer ministers also receive a cash allotment of forty dollars a week.

This linkage with the community has become quite important as many of the children who come to Reformation know who the peer ministers are. One peer minister explains that many of the children come to them for help with problems in their homes. She said, "they see us at church or they know our phone numbers and they call us if they need us."

In some cases, the needs of the person asking for help at Reformation are so complicated and entrenched, or the person is so overwhelmed that direct aid, referral to other agencies, or crisis help is not sufficient. In these instances, the pastor, church staff member, or peer minister engage in what they call, "walking with the poor," working intensely with that person. Instead of referring that person to a community resource, they accompany the person to the agency, helping them to fill out forms, preparing for meetings, and attending meetings with them. In "walking with the poor," the support person continues his or her involvement until the person seeking help has either resolved the problem or finally obtained the confidence, skills, or advocacy needed to overcome the previous barriers to accessing help.

Entering Into Coalitions

The pastor maintains the primary leadership role within the church, but involvement of the peer ministers and other church members is essential. Likewise, coalition-building with both people and organizations within and outside the Reformation Church neighborhood is an essential tool for the pastor's accomplishment of neighborhood outreach.

Participating in coalitions is important for Reformation in order to share information, collaborate on strategic planning, plan collective action, and share in a spirit of solidarity. Some of the coalitions the pastors and Reformation members have been involved in include: Northside Strategy, a group of ten central city Lutheran Churches; a pastor's group from the neighborhood Black Churches; and Milwaukee Inner City Congregation Allied for Hope (MICAH), a church-based social justice group.

Additionally, the pastor has developed relationships with the neighborhood librarian, the teachers and principal of the nearby high school, and some of the remaining local business people. These relationships have afforded mutual support, an exchange of resources, and facilitated people coming to Reformation Church for spiritual or material help.

Collective Action and Community Empowerment

Ernesto Cortez (1993), a faith-based community organizer and writer, provides insight regarding the legitimacy of the church's role in developing community, necessary in order to move toward collective action. He does this by referring to the Latin root word of religion, "re-legare," which means "to bind together that which is disconnected," (p. 303).

Hanna and Robinson (1994) elaborate further by providing a definition of community that explains how Reformation's nurturing of community can lead to collective action. They explain:

> When speaking of community we refer to a specific population defined in terms of geographic location, demographic characteristics, or group commonality, who share a degree of relationship with each other, as well as some experiences of self-interest which can be addressed on a collective basis (p. xii).

Reformation Church has used community building to initiate collective action in confronting the problem of drug houses in their neighborhood. In 1994, the congregation and its neighbors identified twenty-three suspected drug houses and made a map of the location of these houses. In conjunction with these efforts, the pastor worked with members from MICAH, eight area churches, the city housing authority, the media, and local politicians to raise public awareness of the drug houses. On Good Friday, the church coalition sponsored a neighborhood march including 200 marchers. As a result of this collaborative work and collective action, ten of the twenty-three identified drug houses were closed by the police within three months. Five continued under investigation. Twelve others were investigated, but drug activity was not substantiated. Although not all the alleged drug houses were closed, one neighborhood person said, "that at least her block was no longer controlled by the dealers and gangs." She said, "Before that time, we couldn't even go out." Members and neighbors shared a problem, addressed it together and garnered the satisfaction of tangible improvements.

Bridging Race and Class Barriers

Reformation Church is one of the few urban places where people of various classes, races, or abilities can be seen coming together. On Sunday morning, it is not unusual to see a black teenager help an elderly white woman down the church steps, or to observe a well-dressed, middle-income person sitting next to someone whose mental illness is apparent from the person's constant rocking motion, or to see the random hugging during the "passing of the peace."

The peer ministers sometimes talk about the neighborhood pressure they feel from other African Americans who criticize them for "having a white pastor." During a community Bible study, one African American male in his mid thirties, who had suffered from both severe depression and drug use, talked specifically about this criticism. "I don't care what they say," he said. "I don't care what color my pastor is, just that he is honest and is there for me." This testimonial was even more significant to those in the group who knew that he and the pastor had had numerous counseling sessions, some of which were very confrontative, but which eventually led to this man achieving two years of sobriety and control over his depression.

The bridge between race and class has also been built by the pastor's frequent guest preaching at various suburban churches at Sunday morning services. Reformation's pastor preaches an animated, revivalist style sermon, inviting suburban members to become partners in Reformation's urban ministry either through financial gifts or through personal visits to the church. The suburban members who respond to the invitation for a personal visit, usually express surprise at how openly they are welcomed. They also gain a new impression of the neighborhood from that of being a dangerous, alienating place to one where people in the community are poor, but working hard to make a difference in their community.

Other suburban members still too frightened to venture into Milwaukee's central city, respond to the pastor's request for financial help to support Reformation's direct aid to community people. In 1994, "suburban partners" contributed $70,000 to Reformation's overall church budget of $264,950. The invitation to become partners with Reformation helps to bridge the gap between class and race, as well as having the pragmatic effect of comprising over one quarter of the annual Reformation budget. Without this assistance, much of the direct aid, summer work programs, and money for the peer ministers would be impossible.

Implications for Social Work

The strategies utilized by Reformation Church have broad and varied implications for social work. The outreach work carried out at Reformation clearly parallels the generalist model of social work practice. The generalist social worker must intervene in individual difficulties, but also work collaboratively and collectively in confronting community problems. The social worker needs to know when referrals are not enough and when someone must "walk with the poor" until the problem is resolved or the client has gained the competence to resolve the concern.

Social workers need to develop stronger coalitions and discover new allies in dealing with urban problems. Just as "politics creates strange bedfellows," social workers need to forge new alliances with agencies, businesses and other professionals who share concern about the urban poor. Churches should also be included in these alliances, both in terms of providing meeting places and support, and in joining with social workers in advocating for social justice.

Like the work being done at Reformation Church, social workers need to find ways to develop community for their clients. This is especially important in an era of alienation, where people have become isolated and are in great need of mutual support. Social workers need to discern their clients' strengths and find ways in which help-seeking can be both empowering and rejuvenating for both social workers and clients alike.

Finally, social workers need to reclaim their own professional heritage, which includes solidarity with the poor, collective action as a force for social change, and religious roots. This heritage can sustain social workers in the face of today's tremendous challenges and support the social work value of actively working toward social justice.

References

Abramson, Alan J., and Tobin, Mitchell S. (1990). *The Changing Geography of Metropolitan Opportunity: The Segregation of the Poor in U.S. Metropolitan Areas, 1970 to 1990*. Washington D.C. Fannie Mae Annual Housing Conference.

Bluestone, Barry & Harrison, Bennett. (1982). *The Deindustrialization of America*. New York: Basic Books.

Cortez, Ernesto. (1993). Reweaving the Fabric: The Iron Rule and the IAF Strategy for Power and Politics. In Henry Cisneros (Ed.), *Interwoven Destinies*. New York: W.W. Norton Co.

Garreau, Joel. (1991). *Edge Cities: Life on the New Frontier*. New York: Doubleday.

Hanna, Mark G., & Robinson, Buddy. (1994). *Strategies of Community Empowerment*. New York: Edwin Mellen Press.

Kasarda, John D. (1993). Cities as Places Where People Live and Work: Urban Change and Neighborhood Distress. In Henry Cisneros (Ed.), *Interwoven Destinies*. New York: W.W. Norton Co.

Massey, Douglas S., & Denton, Nance A. (1993). *American Apartheid: Segregation and the Making of the Underclass*. Cambridge, Massachusetts: Harvard University Press.

Mead, Lawrence. (1986). *Beyond Entitlement*. New York: The Free Press.

Milwaukee Fire and Police Commission Research Services. *City of Milwaukee 1990 Crime Report*. City of Milwaukee, 1990.

Milwaukee Fire and Police Commission. *Crime in the City of Milwaukee 1984*. City of Milwaukee, 1984.

Murray, Charles. (1984). *Losing Ground: American Social Policy 1950-1980*. New York: Simon and Schuster.

Rose, Nancy. (1997). The Future Economic Landscape: Implications for Social Work Practice and Education. In *Social Work in the 21st Century*. CA: Pine Forge Press.

U.S. Department of Commerce. *Census Population and Housing, Census Tracts: Milwaukee*. Washington D.C.: U.S. Government Printing Office, 1973, 1983, 1993.

CHAPTER 5

SOCIAL WORK IN ACTION: INTEGRATING PEOPLE WITH MENTAL RETARDATION INTO LOCAL CHURCHES AND COMMUNITIES OF FAITH

Rick Chamiec - Case

Many individuals from various walks of life attach significant value and meaning to membership and participation in a local church or community of faith. There are a number of reasons for this. A community of faith, as the term suggests, often provides a **community**:

- which through its corporate life of worship and service assists persons to learn about, love, serve, honor, and enjoy God, whom they believe to be worthy of their ultimate commitment and devotion.
- to which a person feels that he/she "belongs" as a valued member.
- with which a person can identify and which helps him/her form a sense of identity.
- through which a person can reach out to others, enabling him/her to live out his/her shared beliefs and values by "giving back" to those in need.

Unfortunately, people with disabilities like mental retardation are notably under-represented in most faith communities (ANCOR, 1995). As a result, many people with mental retardation miss out on a rich opportunity to participate in a community group which could add significant value and meaning to their lives.

The under-representation of people with mental retardation in many local churches and communities of faith is caused by a number of factors. First of all, up until the past couple of decades, the majority of people with disabilities were placed in self-contained institutional settings outside the mainstream of local society. Many people in institutions lived their entire lives within the walls of that institution.

Yet even progress in assisting individuals with mental retardation to return to community settings in recent years has not done a great deal to reverse this unfortunate under-representation Due to the many decades of institutionalization, there is a very limited history of successful interactions, experiences, and relationships shared between people with disabilities and members of local communities of faith from which to learn and upon which to build. Often people with disabilities and members of communities of faith are just not sure how to relate in a healthy, meaningful way.

In addition, many of the activities and events which occur in communities of faith assume that all participants have a number of skills or abilities which people with mental retardation might not have. As a result, people with disabilities often feel excluded from many of these activities or events. For example, most adult education classes and Bible studies presuppose a participant's ability to read, talk fluently, and reason abstractly:

> . . . in most churches, religious education still means reading, writing, and rote memorization of Bible stories along with group discussion where participation requires a certain level of verbal fluency. (Webb-Mitchell, p. 32)

Also, most sermons or homilies are presented to reach individuals presumed to have at least a high school education. As such, forums and activities which occur in communities of faith are largely inaccessible or overwhelming to a person with mental retardation.

Lastly, there are often logistical barriers which block the participation of individuals with disabilities like mental retardation in communities of faith. For example, since many people with disabilities don't drive (and alternate forms of public transportation often don't run regularly on weekends), transportation to and from communities of faith can prove to be a significant obstacle. In addition, many worship services and group meetings are conducted in rooms which cannot be reached without climbing up or down a set of stairs. For individuals who might have limited mobility (the prevalance of physical disabilities in persons with mental retardation is significantly higher than in the general population), this can create an almost insurmountable barrier. Compared to many businesses and community organizations, churches have been slow to overcome a wide range of barriers which often prevent full participation of people with disabilities:

If supermarkets and bars are more accessible then altars, then we must all bear the shame. . . . Justice and love will triumph only when segregating walls are knocked down and the barriers of architecture, communication and attitudes are removed. Only then will people with disabilities become full participants in the celebrations and obligations of their faith. (Anderson, p. 44)

For a social worker providing services for people with mental retardation, this situation is one which almost literally cries out for the development of a potent social work intervention. In most cases, this reaction will be felt even more strongly by the Christian social worker, who can strongly empathize with any person who is prevented from full access and participation in a local church or community of faith.

This chapter will outline one Christian social worker's proposed approach addressing this significant issue, and in doing so, illustrate a number of key social worker roles, techniques, and perspectives which play a critical role in this intervention. Specifically, this chapter will describe an approach I have developed called the "Faith Connections Model." This model has been developed from a strengths/competence social work perspective, and calls upon a social worker to fulfill a variety of social work roles in its implementation. A sampling of these social work roles will include: consultant/facilitator, case manager/service broker, advocate, and teacher/trainer. In addition, this chapter will outline several ways in which key Christian beliefs and values play a critical role in the development and implementation of the "Faith Connections Model."

The Faith Connections Model

Simply put, the "Faith Connections Model" is a social work intervention which attempts to match the strengths, preferences, and stated desires of a person with mental retardation with a local church or community of faith. It takes seriously the many barriers which prevent fuller church inclusion described above, and develops strategies to overcome identified barriers to provide the target person with the opportunity to participate and/or become a member in a community of faith of his/her choice.

The 3 key stages of the "Faith Connections Model" are:
1. Exploring the Spiritual Dimension within an Overall Assessment Process
2. Community of Faith Development
3. Community of Faith Coaching

Stage 1: Exploring the Spiritual Dimension within an Overall Assessment Process:

Following the "Faith Connections Model," a target person's interdisciplinary team, facilitated by the social worker, seeks to define the individual's most significant strengths, gifts, interests, preferences, dreams, and capacities in all areas of his/her life (Mount, 1995). Unfortunately, while often looking at the physical, cognitive, emotional, and social dimensions of the person's life, many times assessments of persons with mental retardation do not include an exploration of the person's spiritual or religious dimension. It is a priority focus of the "Faith Connections Model" to include a rich spiritual component in the overall assessment process.

Important to this approach, the spiritual/religious component of the assessment process should, among other things, gather the type of information which allows the team to draw a picture of the type of community of faith (and specific faith community activities) in which the target person would like to become a participating member. It is critical that the social worker assist the team to focus primarily on what the target person can do well - **not** just on what he/she can't - and thus what he/she can bring to the community of faith.

Because of the target person's disability (not to mention the somewhat elusive task of identifying aspects of a person's "spirituality" in general), the spiritual component of this assessment requires more than simply asking the team to fill out a checklist during a hastily thrown-together team meeting. The social worker has to take the time to talk directly with the target person, as well as his/her family, friends, residential support staff (if applicable), and others who know the person well. In addition, the social worker may have to explore a number of creative approaches (role playing exercises, random observations of the person in selected activities, etc.) to help the team better understand the target person's deepest spiritual strengths, gifts, interests, preferences, dreams and capacities! Key areas to explore in the spiritual component of the overall assessment may include (but are not limited to): a. beliefs about God; b. spiritual/religious practices and traditions; c. beliefs about right and wrong; d life satisfaction assessment; e. values inventory; f. assessment of relationship with God and overall religious experience; and g. evaluation of spiritual mentors/"heroes."

It is also important to gather information regarding the target person's (or family's) current connections or prior experiences with local communities of faith. Often a great deal can be learned by reviewing what worked (as well as what didn't work) in any prior experiences for the target person.

Stage 2. Community of Faith Development:

While a good overall assessment helps to identify a person's strengths, needs, and preferences, simply gathering information is never a goal in and of itself. In stage 2 of the "Faith Connections Model," the social worker analyzes the results of (especially the spiritual component of) the assessment process and uses this information to seek a match between the strengths/preferences of the target person and the needs, culture, and resources of a selected local church or community of faith

However, before a social worker can begin to find such a match for a target person, he/she must first develop a pool of communities of faith which are potentially interested in and willing to support these types of connections. The social worker will often start by contacting local communities of faith and asking to meet with the appropriate clergy, staff, or lay leaders to present the "Faith Connections Model." In addition, it is often helpful for the social worker to participate in some of the activities or programs which are an important part of that community's life. Of course, it is equally important for the social worker to have contact with local communities of faith even when not specifically doing community of faith development. Some examples of regular contact might include: supporting church fund-raisers, co-sponsoring seminars and trainings with local communities of faith, etc.

Having identified a rich pool of communities of faith that seem genuinely interested in and committed to welcoming people with disabilities, the social worker begins community of faith development with the target person to select a few faith communities from that pool that he/she thinks might have potential as a match for that particular person. It is important to note that in seeking a match, the social worker may in some cases need to look beyond the boundaries of that person's familiar denomination or faith tradition.

Next the social worker facilitates some times for the target person (and other people important in the target person's life) to visit the selected communities of faith and optimally to join in on some of the activities which the target person has identified as important/desirable to him/her. It is often worthwhile for the team to plan out and structure even these brief initial visits. The more positive the initial impressions (for both the target person and the community of faith), the more likely that a positive connection will be made. From here, in most cases, the target person and important people in his/her life are able to decide which of the selected communities of faith (if any) seems to "fit" best. In general, the most reliable predictor of success is when all involved agree that the community of faith has the capacity and commitment to provide the support needed for the person to participate in that community.

Planning Supports

Once the target person (with the assistance of his/her family and/or other important people in his/her life) has indicated which community of faith he/she would like to focus on, the next step is for the social worker to convene the team to begin developing a plan of supports to help the target person integrate into the life of that community of faith.

The types of supports a person will benefit from generally vary from person to person, and can range from relatively minimal, informal supports to much more intensive, formal ones. However, one of the critical areas to include is an emphasis on the supports needed to assist the target person to make meaningful social connections within the community of faith. Without question, making meaning social connections is usually far and away the most significant factor contributing to a long term connection.

For clarity's sake, a support plan should include a listing of the specific supports which will be offered to the target person, the individual(s) who will provide each of the listed supports, and the approximate time frame(s) for implementing and then fading each of these supports. It is equally important to develop a support plan that neither over nor under-estimates the supports the target person might benefit from, and one that can be quickly and easily adjusted if necessary.

It is also critical that the person(s) who will provide each of the supports is familiar with the specific activities the person will participate in, and is enthusiastic about his/her role as a support provider. Most of the time the best candidates to provide supports are well-established and well-known members of that community of faith. However, there might be times when the support needed will have to be provided by a person(s) who is not a member of the community of faith. This is more likely to occur when a special level of expertise is needed that cannot be found within the community of faith (including examples such as interpreters, special educators, clinical specialists, etc.). In these cases the social worker is instrumental in helping the team locate and work with these individuals with special expertise.

Stage 3. Community of Faith Coaching:

Once the team has developed a support plan, the most critical stage of the process still remains - implementing the plan! The key element in implementing the support plan is the social worker's selection and training of a member of the community of faith to become the "community of faith coach." The "community of faith coach" (as the name implies) is the person who coordinates, assists, encourages, and provides direction for the various persons providing the supports identified in the support plan.

It is important that the "community of faith coach" is well respected by the other members of the community of faith, and has a thorough knowledge of both the strengths, needs, and preferences of the target person as well as culture, activities, and resources of the community of faith. He/she becomes the "inside" person who both provides on-going support to the other members of the community of faith, as well as maintaining communication with the social worker and team members to let them know how the target person is doing and when any additional assistance might be needed.

Often a member of the clergy or a committed lay leader is able to provide the name(s) of an individual(s) who has the potential to become a quality "community of faith coach." However, simply finding a willing and able candidate is only a small part of the job. It is up to the social worker to provide the hands-on training needed to equip him/her to fulfill this critical role.

The social worker needs to instill in the "community of faith coach" the following characteristics (among others):

- consistent use of a positive approach and frequent reinforcement.
- quickness to recognize and celebrate (even small signs of) progress.
- bias toward problem solving rather than blame-fixing.

In the end, a wisely selected and well-trained "community of faith coach" is the key to supporting the target person's connection with the community of faith on a long-term basis.

The Model at Work: Some Illustrations of the Faith Connections Model

Dave is a 52-year old man with mental retardation who has been living in a group home in a midwestern state for the past 17 years. He shares this house with four other individuals of varying ages with similar disabilities. Dave and his four housemates work together on a production unit in a day services program in the town in which they live. Dave gets along fairly well with most of his housemates, but doesn't seem particularly close to any of them. He appears to enjoy interacting the most with the staff members who work in the group home. Unfortunately, the turnover rate of staff is almost 50% each year, with few staff members staying more than a couple of years.

Dave has no family members who are currently active in his life. In fact, his social worker has not even been able to trace where Dave was born or where (or with whom) he grew up. At the same time, Dave

from time to time talks about the members of his family that he remembers including his grandmother, his aunt and uncle, as well as several
foster families. Often when he talks about his childhood years, he refers to some of the churches he attended when he was younger, and still
remembers many gospel hymns from his youth. He doesn't have many
possessions, but he does have a cassette player, and spends much of his
leisure time listening to (and singing along with) a collection of gospel
hymns and spirituals he has collected through the years.

During the last 15 years in his group home, Dave has only occasionally attended church, generally when the staff members who were working
on Sundays wanted to get out of the house for a few hours. However, even
when he and his housemates were taken to church, they would usually end
up going to the denomination or community of faith with which the staff
member on duty on any particular week felt most comfortable. When a
new social worker, Joan, began working for the organization, she requested
to be allowed to implement the "Faith Connections Model" approach for
people who seemed interested in participating in a local church or community of faith. When Joan was given the okay, she met with agency staff
members, who suggested that Dave would be a good person to work with
in this capacity. When Joan approached Dave, he responded enthusiasti-
cally to her offer, so she set up a team meeting to begin.

Stage 1

Joan worked with Dave and his team to define Dave's greatest
strengths, gifts, interests, preferences, dreams, and capacities in all areas of his life, including a strong focus on the spiritual dimension of his
life. Joan called a number of team meetings and set up several one-on-
one discussions with Dave and the staff who knew Dave best to find out
more about what was important to Dave. Joan and the team discovered
that Dave had many things he wanted to do, and much to contribute to
others that in his current life situation he was not able to contribute. A
number of important themes emerged from the assessment process. Some
of these the major included the following:

- Dave was an exceptionally friendly and patient person.
- Dave greatly enjoyed spending time with children.
- Dave loved singing, and had a strong voice that others liked to
  listen to.
- Dave wanted to spend more time with people who didn't live at
  his group home, or work in his production group.
- Dave didn't enjoy attending the churches his staff often took

him to as much as the churches he remembered attending when he was younger where the "people weren't afraid to dance and move around" when they worshipped.

- Dave had a strong faith in God (in spite of some very difficult times during his life), which he enjoyed sharing with others around him.

Stage 2

Joan focused on these themes as she began exploring for possible "matches" with the needs, cultures, and resources of several local communities of faith with whom she had spoken previously. After calling contacts from several promising congregations, presented Dave with a list of 3-4 communities of faith which she felt would be worth his exploring in person. She arranged for Dave and some of his favorite group home staff to visit these selected communities of faith during times when there were activities going on that she felt Dave might especially enjoy. Some of these identified activities included:

- Joining a congregation for an informal Sunday evening hymn sing.
- Helping out with games and serving refreshments at a church's children's Halloween party.
- Attending a church's annual fall picnic.
- Participating in a church's Sunday morning service in which the congregation's style of worship included lively singing, dancing, and plenty of "moving around."

Contacts from a couple of the churches called Dave at his group home before he visited, and most of the church contacts spoke to several of the members of the congregations, asking them to go out of their way to help Dave feel at home when he visited.

While most of the visits went fairly well, there was one church in particular that Dave seemed especially excited about. Fortunately, this church seemed equally eager to have Dave become more involved with them, and it was not long before more and more of Dave's visits were ending up scheduled for this church.

Planning Supports

Once it became clear that Dave was most drawn to this one church (the Memorial Baptist Church), Joan brought his team together with her contact from Memorial Baptist (Bob, who had agreed to be the "community of faith coach") to begin developing a plan of supports to assist Dave to integrate into the life of that community on a (hopefully) long-term basis. Because Dave had gotten off to such a good start at Memorial Baptist, he and his team did not feel that a large number of formal supports would be needed. However, they came up with a few important supports that they felt would be helpful for at least the first 6 months as Dave explored becoming a regular participant/member rather than just a visitor at Memorial Baptist. These supports included the following:

- Developing a pool of 3-4 families living near Dave's group home who could alternate giving him rides to and from worship services and other community of faith events. Dave in exchange agreed to wash each of their cars 1 time per month during the spring, summer, and fall seasons.
- Assigning a fellow tenor in the church choir (Dave wanted to sing in the church choir, and was also a tenor) to be Dave's mentor and to help him learn the weekly choir selections (especially the words to the songs), introduce him to the other members of the choir, "hang out" with him at choir rehearsals, etc.
- Arranging for Dave to assist Baptist Memorial's Youth Group Leader. This would include attending and helping out with youth group activities, making periodic phone calls to families notifying them of upcoming events, etc.

Within several weeks, with the pastor's assistance, Bob had recruited volunteers to provide each of these 3 supports. All of these volunteers had been members of the church for at least a year (except for one of the families which would be helping out with the transportation, and which had just joined Memorial Baptist 4 months ago).

Stage 3

It is worth mentioning that the speed with which volunteers were recruited to implement this support plan owed much of its success to the time Joan invested in training Bob as the "community of faith coach." During the first few months after implementing the support plan, Bob was encouraged to spend time each week observing the interactions between Dave and the other members of the community of faith. In addition, Bob called each of the support persons every other week to find out how things were going, and routinely talked with Joan to provide her with regular updates. Any time there were potentially significant issues, Joan would call the team together (which now included Bob) to either revise the support plan and/or make any other adjustments that might be needed.

After a little less than a year, the team was able to discontinue two of the formal supports, as they were replaced over time by more naturally-occurring sources. The exception was the transportation support, which the community of faith coach needed to continue to monitor and coordinate on an on-going basis. After attending Baptist Memorial for over a year, Dave became a member of the congregation, participating in a wide array of church activities several times a week. Most importantly, Dave consistently expressed strong satisfaction with his new friends in the congregation, and with the important role he felt he played at Baptist Memorial. Dave is an example of a person who, with the proper supports, was able to make a meaningful connection with a local community of faith on a long-term basis.

Key Social Work Perspectives and Roles Inherent in the Faith Connections Model

As is hopefully evident from this case study, the "Faith Connections Model" has been strongly influenced by a social work orientation and calls upon the social worker to fulfill a variety of social work roles in its implementation. This section of the chapter will highlight the reliance of the "Faith Connections Model" on the strengths/competency social work perspective, and outline four traditional social work roles which this model requires the social worker to assume.

Strengths/Competency Perspective

The strengths/competency perspective, which has become increasingly prominent in the field of social work in recent years (Miley, 1995), maintains that the best way to serve clients (taken as either an individual or a larger system) is to help them discover and build on their strengths, as opposed to identifying and trying to "fix" their weaknesses:

> Adopting a strengths perspective influences the way that social workers view client systems and involve them in the change process. Focusing on clients' strengths leads to an empowering approach that promotes clients' competence rather than working to erase their deficits. . . Strengths-oriented social workers believe that the strengths of all client systems - individual, interpersonal, familial, organizational, and societal - are resources to initiate, energize, and sustain change processes. (Miley, pp. 62-63).

This strengths/competency perspective is clearly a central emphasis of the "Faith Connections Model." First of all, in stage 1, the focus of the assessment process led by the social worker is on identifying the target person's most significant strengths and competencies in all areas of his/her life (including the spiritual dimension).

In addition, in stage 2, the social worker is called upon to analyze the results of (especially the spiritual component of) the assessment process and use this information to seek a match or fit between the **strengths/preferences** of the target person and the needs, culture, and resources of a selected local community of faith. In fact, one of the priorities in seeking this match is to identify a niche within the community of faith which the target person is able to fill due to the strengths he/she brings with him/her to apply to the applicable area.

In summary, the primary focus of the "Faith Connections Model" is to recognize, reinforce, and build on the target person's strengths and competencies to enable him/her to make a positive, valued, on-going contribution within that community of faith.

Key Social Work Roles

Effective social work practice requires that a social worker assume a variety of different roles and functions when implementing any number of social work interventions. Traditional social work roles include, among others, services broker/case manager, consultant/facilitator, teacher/trainer, and client advocate (Haynes & Holmes, 1994; Miley, 1995). The "Faith Connections Model" actively calls upon the social worker to assume a number of these traditional social work roles.

A. The Role of Case Manager/Service Broker

One of the important roles of the social worker is that of a broker of services or case manager. In many instances, a social worker's client does not know where or how to make (and maintain) connections with services or supports that he/she might need or from which he/she could benefit. A case manager is responsible to see that

> ...the client is (1) connected to the appropriate service provider(s) and that (2) appropriate services are actually being received... (T)heir primary roles and functions are to (1) identify the appropriate service providers, (2) link clients with those providers, (3) continue to coordinate services as needs change, and (4) continually monitor progress. (Haynes & Holmes, p. 287)

The "Faith Connections Model" relies upon the social worker to assume the role of case manager/service broker in at least two ways. First of all, in stage 2, the social worker serves as a broker to help connect his/her client with a community of faith from a pool of faith communities that he/she has recruited to support these types of connection. Secondly, once a match has been established, the social worker plays a key role in following along/monitoring the success of the match to help the client maintain this connection on a long-term basis.

B. The Role of Consultant/Facilitator

Another of the traditional roles of the social worker is that of a consultant/facilitator. Consultants/facilitators are responsible to work together with clients (as well as significant people within a client's system) to gather critical information and develop plans to help clients (at various levels) meet their identified service goals:

> As a function of social work, consultancy refers to social workers and clients conferring and deliberating together to develop plans for change…. Consultancy acknowledges that both social workers and clients systems bring information and resources, actual and potential, which are vital for resolving the issue at hand. Through consultancy, social workers seek to find solutions for challenges in social functioning with clients systems at all levels including individuals, families, groups, organizations, and communities. (Miley, pp. 16-17)

The "Faith Connections Model" relies upon the social worker to assume the role of consultant/facilitator in a number of ways. In stage 1, the social worker assists the client's team to work together to develop a rich initial client assessment (with an appropriate emphasis on the spiritual dimension). Then in stage 2, the social worker facilitates the team development of the support plan which defines the supports needed to overcome any barriers that might prevent the client from being fully integrated into the identified community of faith. Lastly, the social worker facilitates the team process of using feedback from the client and/or community of faith coach to make any needed adjustments to the support plan as the client begins to participate in community of faith on a regular basis.

C. The Role of Teacher/Trainer

One more of the traditional roles of the social worker is that of a teacher or trainer. A teacher/trainer develops an array of strategies to communicate key information and promote the acquisition of critical skills to their clients as well as those individuals/groups who support their clients:

> As teachers, social workers use learning strategies to promote skill development and enhance the information base of client systems.... Trainers provide instruction to... formal groups and organizations. (Miley, pp. 23-24)

The "Faith Connections Model" relies upon the social worker to assume the role of teacher/trainer in a number of ways. First of all, in stages 1 and 2, the social worker trains team members to define a target person's most significant strengths, interests, preferences, and dreams, and then to develop support plans to assist target persons to meet their aspirations. Secondly, under the "Faith Connections Model", the social worker is called upon to provide hands-on training for the community of faith coach, who in turn is instrumental in offering on-going direction and assistance to the supporting members of the community of faith.

D. The Role of Advocate

Yet one more of the traditional roles of the social worker is that of being an advocate for his/her clients. An advocate is one who speaks or acts to bring about change on behalf of or for the benefit of another:

> ...(t)he advocate is committed to ensuring that service delivery systems are responsive to clients' needs, and that clients receive all the benefits and services to which they are rightfully entitled.... (C)ase managers can and do engage in advocacy on behalf of specific clients who are not being served appropriately. (Haynes & Holmes, pp. 289-90)

The community of faith model relies upon the social worker to assume the role of advocate in one very important way. When developing a pool of communities of faith to participate in a "Faith Connections" project, the social worker advocates on behalf of persons with mental retardation as he/she reminds churches of their responsibility to welcome and support persons with disabilities in the life of their congregation - especially if persons with mental retardation are under-represented within that community of faith. This advocacy, of course, continues as the social worker assists with efforts to help target persons integrate into the on-going life of the community of faith on a regular basis.

The Contribution of Key Christian Beliefs/Values to the Faith Connections Model

In this last section I will outline several ways in which Christian beliefs and values have played a key role in the development of the "Faith Connections Model."

First of all, stage 1 of the "Faith Connections Model" stresses the importance of including a rich spiritual component within the overall assessment of the target person with mental retardation. This emphasis is driven by the Judeo-Christian belief that all persons are made in the image of God (Genesis 1), and as a result are spiritual/religious, as well as physical, cognitive, emotional and social beings. It is important to note that the "Faith Connections Model" does not attempt to introduce this spiritual/religious component as separate or distinct from the overall assessment process. Rather, it advocates that the spiritual/religious dimension not be excluded (as is often the case), but instead allowed to play its rightful role within the context of the development of an overall assessment of a person with mental retardation.

Secondly, the "Faith Connections Model" focuses on assisting persons with disabilities like mental retardation to become integrated into local churches and communities of faith. This emphasis reflects the Christian belief that significant value, meaning, and life satisfaction are associated with the spiritual growth and development which occur with and in a local church community. This is not intended to imply that facilitating participation and membership in a community of faith should be the sole or even primary focus of social work interventions for people with mental retardation. Rather, the "Faith Connections Model" argues that this critical focus (frequently neglected for people with disabilities) should be among those considered when addressing a target person's overall needs and service preferences.

Lastly, the case for churches and communities of faith to support the "Faith Connections Model" is strengthened by an appeal to the metaphor (found in Christian scripture) of the "Body of Christ" to support its case that communities of faith are strengthened as the diversity of its members is expanded:

> The body is a unit, though it is made up of many parts; and though all its parts are many, they form one body. So it is with Christ.... But in fact God has arranged the parts in the body, every one of them, just as he wanted them to be. If they were all one part, where would the body be? As it is, there are many parts, but one body. The eye cannot say to the hand, "I don't

need you!" And the head cannot say to the feet, " I don't need you!" On the contrary, those parts of the body that seem to be weaker are indispensable, and the parts that we think are less honorable we treat with special honor. (Selected verses from I Corinthians 12, New International Version)

This appeal is clearly consistent with the social work emphasis on the importance of diversity within all structures in a society.

In conclusion, it is worth noting that the "Faith Connections Model" represents an approach to a significant social work issue that highlights the cohesiveness of certain key social work and Christian values. While it has not been my experience that one will always find such a tight "fit" between current professional social work perspectives and Christian beliefs/values, the "Faith Connections Model" illustrates at least one case where such integration is alive and well!

References

ANCHOR - American Network of Community Options and Resources. *LINKS*, (1995). Volume XX, No. 1, p. 29 cites a 1994 survey of people with disabilities conducted by the Louis Harris polling firm.

Anderson, Robert C. (1994). A Comprehensive Look at Disability Laws and the Religious Community. *Exceptional Parent*, December, 43-44.

Faith Group Resources. (1994). *Exceptional Parent*, December, 38-39.

Gaventa, Bill. (1994). Religious Participation for All. *Exceptional Parent*, December, 22-25.

Haynes, Karen & Holmes, Karen. (1994). *Invitation to Social Work*. New York: Longman.

Hornstein, Becca. (1994). A Jewish Education for Every Child. *Exceptional Parent*, December, 29-30.

Miley, Karla Krogsrud, O'Melia, Michael, & Dubois, Brenda L. (1995). *Generalist Social Work Practice: An Empowering Approach*. Boston: Allyn and Bacon.

Mount, Beth. (1995). *Capacity Works: Finding Windows for Change Using Personal Futures Planning*. New York: Graphic Futures.

Webb-Mitchell, Brett. (1994). Toward a More Inclusive Protestant Sunday School: Making Religious Education Accessible to All. *Exceptional Parent*, December, 31-33.

CHAPTER 6

DIVERSITY: AN EXAMINATION OF THE CHURCH AND SOCIAL WORK

Lon Johnston

The weekend of October 11-13, 1996, I visited Washington, D.C., to participate in activities related to the display of the AIDS memorial quilt. In many different ways this weekend impacted my life far beyond anything I could have predicted or expected. Walking among the 40,000 quilt squares and watching the thousands of others who had come to see the quilt, I was reminded of how truly diverse God's creation really is. However, it was the interfaith service held at the National Cathedral on Sunday evening that forced me to re-examine how narrowly I had defined God and how limited I had become in understanding God. This service was entitled "The Journey Home: An Interfaith Service of Prayer and Healing." I entered the cathedral feeling very much alone. I had spent much of the weekend visiting my brother's quilt panel and grieving his death from AIDS in 1987, and I hoped to experience some kind of healing as I joined all of these other strangers for worship. From the call to worship by drum and chant by the Little River Drum to the call to prayer by the blowing of the shofar and the ringing of the Tibetan bowls, from the reading of the Baghavad Gita and of the Torah to the anthem sung by the Washington Gay Men's Chorus, from the New Testament and Buddhist readings to the anthem offered by the Voices of Inspiration of the Metropolitan African Methodist Episcopal Church, I was struck by the diversity of people gathered to participate in worshiping God.

One of the worship leaders asked us to look around us—he asked us to take a very good look at all the people seated in this great cathedral. As we looked into the eyes of strangers, the worship leader described what he was seeing: Christian, Jew, Muslim, Buddhist, male, female, gay, straight, African-American, white, Hispanic, Native American, Asian American. After he had finished his description, he reminded us that this was what heaven would look like. God's diverse creation would be gathered there. As I began to notice the multifaceted people gathered that Sunday evening, I felt a connection to the people around me. The loneliness I had brought to the service began to fade. The gender, race or ethnicity, religion or creed, or sexual orientation of the person did not matter; the important thing was that we were all symbolic of God's heterogeneous creation. As the service ended, hands joined throughout the cathedral, voices raised together in singing "We Shall Overcome," and individuals connected as the whole of God's diverse creation. All differences were set aside, and we experienced the joy and peace of belonging to the family of God.

This is a message that might be uncomfortable to some people who want to define God very narrowly and who refuse to believe that God is an inclusive God. The temptation to limit God's interaction with his creatures is one I believe Christians must avoid, not only within the religious world, but also within the secular social work profession. Many people, from both the secular and religious worlds, believe that theology and social work are incompatible, and emphasis is often placed on choosing one or the other. People in both worlds want to build walls that separate and divide rather than bridges that connect and support. However, there are many areas where theology and social work are very much in agreement, and there are other areas where tensions exist.

Some people may wonder why Christianity and social work need to have this dialogue in the first place. Why does it matter if tensions and suspicions exist between the two? Loewenberg (1988) gave one of the best answers to this question when he said:

> The religious belief (or lack of belief) of a chemist does not mean anything to the molecules, atoms, or electrons that he explores. An architect's religious beliefs (or lack of beliefs) does not affect the design of a building that he drafts. Or will the accountant who regularly attends church prepare one sort of profit/loss statement and his agnostic colleague another? But the religious beliefs of social workers may have meaning and relevance for those with whom they interact. And these religious beliefs (or lack of them) may influence what they do as practitioners. (p. 81)

Loewenberg is exactly right. If a social worker has no appreciation or understanding of the diversity of God's creation, then his or her practice will be influenced by that lack of inclusivity. On the other hand, to have such an understanding and appreciation will mean that a social worker views the gospel message as a message of inclusion, and his or her practice will be one based upon an acceptance and appreciation of all people as they are. The practice will be inclusive, just as the Bible is an inclusive book. To state this another way, the practice will be built on common grace. To view the Bible as being exclusive is to seriously misunderstand the message of God. Peter J. Gomes (1996) said:

...people beyond the little world of primitive Jewish Christianity see themselves and their story included in God's activity. When in John's gospel (John 10:16) Jesus says, 'And I have other sheep, that are not of this fold; I must bring them also, and they will heed my voice. So there shall be one flock, one shepherd,' this is a great mandate for inclusivity which these 'other sheep' recognize. As Jesus himself included among his own companions winebibbers, prostitutes, men and women of low degree, people who by who they were, by what they did, or from where they were excluded, so too does the Bible claim these very people as its own.

It is one of the unbecoming but unavoidable ironies of Christianity that Gentile Christians, who were excluded from the Jewish churches and who in time of the Roman persecution were themselves excluded from all hope in life, should themselves become the arch practitioners of exclusion. Even centuries of Christian exclusion, however, extending into our very own day, cannot diminish the inclusive mandate of the Bible, and the particular words of Jesus when he says, 'Come until me, all ye that labor and are heavy ladden and I will give you rest.' What Roman Catholic social theory teaches as the church's 'preferential option for the poor,' to the annoyance of Christians rich in the things of this world, is the same principle that extends the hospitality of the Bible, indeed preferential hospitality, to those who have in face been previously and deliberately excluded. So the Bible's inclusivity is claimed by the poor, the discriminated against, persons of color, homosexuals, women, and all persons beyond the conventional definitions of Western civilization. (pp. 22-23)

The Bible, comprised of the Hebrew and Christian scriptures, serves as the foundation for Christianity, and as Gomes has emphasized, those scriptures are inclusive. Social work is built upon professional values, and those values are also inclusive. It is sad that the secular social work profession only sees the exclusivity of organized religion, and it is equally distressing that organized religion views the inclusivity of professional social work as a threat to all that is sacred. There are differences between Christianity and professional social work that cannot be overlooked; however, these differences should not overshadow the large areas of common ground shared by them.

This chapter will focus on three areas of diversity: gender, sexual orientation, and multi- culturalism. The tensions and similarities that exist between the Christian church and social work will be examined in each of these areas.

Gender

Some of the earliest words recorded in the Hebrew Bible are found in the creation story (Genesis 1:27) where God is described as creating man "in his own image, in the image of God he created him; male and female he created them" (Revised Standard Version). Male interpretations of the Genesis story, often place the blame on Eve more than on Adam for bringing sin into this world, and such an interpretation reinforces the most divisive issue between men and women: power. Wallis (1995) said:

> As punishment women have been assigned a subordinate role to men...the control of women becomes a central male priority and has been the dominant characteristic of patriarchy (the subordination of women to men) from the earliest times....It is a structure of domination....In male dominated societies, the imbalance of power between women and men is deliberate—it is a system of both control and exploitation. As long as the differential of power between the genders is so great, various forms of violence and abuse will continue. When women earn only two-thirds the pay of men for the same job, when they are subject to sexual harassment on those jobs, when key social and religious institutions still refuse to grant half the population full dignity and equality, or when women must also bear the disproportionate weight of responsibility for child rearing, the power imbalance persists. (pp. 123-4)

The imbalance of power and the resulting inequality between women and men is an area where Christianity and social work should be able to stand united. Where would most churches be today if it were not for the women who are the majority of members, direct and staff most programs, give leadership and service in Christian education and social ministry, and influence and shape the moral and religious values of the homes (Gomes, 1996)?

When reading the Christian scriptures, especially the Gospels, it is important to remember these books "were all composed by men, or groups of men, and the new faith to which they testified was one which had risen from the male-oriented religion of Judaism. The readers and hearers of the Gospel...still were not part of a world in which females had equal rights and responsibilities with men" (Clark & Richardson, 1977, p. 32). However, a careful reading of the Christian scriptures reveals "quite a different picture from that which most people have of the sheltered, dependent Palestinian women of the first century" (Tucker & Liefeld, 1987, p. 20). We are told that women often traveled with Jesus, and the early church attracted many types of women, including those of high status. It is also clear that women held positions of importance within the first century church. Phoebe fulfilled the role of deaconess, Prisca was a prominent woman in the Roman congregation, and Mary took a great risk for Paul (Stark, 1996, p. 27). These women are examples of early Christians who somehow broke through the imbalance of power in the patriarchal society of that day.

Women have had the same influence upon and involvement in the social work profession. Where would the profession be without the persistent efforts of Mary Richmond in establishing some standards for professional education? The profession's commitment to the poor was demonstrated on a daily basis by Jane Addams and her female colleagues at Hull House (Morales & Sheafor, 1995). What about the everyday efforts of female social workers who visit abusive homes, comfort dying persons and their families, explain to children why their parents are divorcing, find safe places for elderly persons to live after being discharged from nursing homes, and listen to teenagers who feel threatened in their school environment?

Females comprise the majority of members of both the church and the social work profession. However, women have experienced oppression and exclusion in both these institutions as men have traditionally served in the roles of pastor, priest, deacon, and elder in the church, and men have been employed in the roles of supervisor and administrator in the social work profession. As stated earlier, the issue of unequal power between women and men in the church and in the profession cannot be denied.

It is more than ironic that women are found in such large numbers in the Christian church and social work while experiencing unequal access to power and position. A careful reading of scripture reveals Jesus' belief in the equality of all persons. While bound by the social mores of his time, Jesus did not discriminate in his treatment of women; in fact, his actions elevated women from second-class citizenship to positions of equality and honor. Just as Jesus modeled the way the church should relate to women, the Code of Ethics of the social work profession clearly states that all people are to be treated with dignity and respect (*NASW News*, 1996). There is to be no discrimination within the profession. All persons are to be viewed as equals, but unfortunately this is not always the case.

Several studies (Williams, Ho, & Fielder, 1974; Knapman, 1977; Sutton, 1982; York, Henley, & Gamble, 1987) found that male social workers tend to receive higher salaries than female social workers, and, in spite of the profession's statements to the contrary, this discrepancy continued throughout the 70's and 80's. Huber and Orlando (1995) describe similar inequities today. The question must be asked why a profession that prides itself upon its commitment to equality allows such an injustice to continue. A similar question can be asked of the church. If the Christian scripture is the basis for all that the church is supposed to do and be, then why do women continue to experience oppression, injustice, and inequality within the church? Again, the answer comes back to the issue of power. For equality and justice to occur within the social work profession and the Christian church, men have to be willing to share leadership roles at the risk of losing positions of influence and power.

These issues of power and influence have caused women to be hurt by the church, an institution that should be a healing, redeeming place for all people. Several years ago my wife and I joined a church that was very male dominated. Every time the pastor introduced us he covered my educational background and my present teaching position. Although my wife had a master's degree and was a highly accomplished professional in her own right, this pastor never acknowledged more than her name. Time after time this event repeated itself until one night, after my wife was left feeling discounted and invisible, she turned to me and said, "I never want to come back to this church again." I supported her decision, and we looked for another place to worship where women were seen as equals in God's creation. Sadly, this is not an isolated situation. Women experience these actions again and again in churches throughout this nation. Rather than being a safe, affirming place, some churches continue to oppress the majority of their members by such actions.

In light of this example, it is important to note that large numbers of men are supportive of the efforts of women to achieve equality. As noted by Tolman, Mowry, Jones, and Brekke (1986):

> The women's movement has raised men's consciousness about gender in two different...ways. Challenges to traditional sex roles by feminists have freed men to become more aware of the restrictions imposed by traditional male sex roles. In addition, consciousness of how men oppress women has grown from their relationships with women who confront their sexist behavior. (p. 63)

Men employed in the social work profession can utilize the principles developed by Tolman, et al. (1986) as they attempt to support and encourage the efforts of women seeking gender equality. The principles are:

1. **Develop a Contextual, Historical Understanding of Women's Experience.**
   Without the contextual and historical understanding, men are unable to comprehend the oppression that women have experienced. The ultimate goal is the attainment of empathy.

2. **Men Must Be Responsible for Themselves and for Other Men.**
   For men to continue to rely upon women for consciousness raising, "amounts to continued oppression of women by men....What is required is for men to assume responsibility for their own part in sexist injustice, both individually and collectively."

3. **Redefine Masculinity.**
   As men evaluate what they gain and what they lose with the ending of male dominance, they will necessarily be required to begin the process of redefining what it means to be male.

4. **Accept Women's Scrutiny Without Making Women Responsible.**
   Obviously many men support and encourage gender equality, but men must realize that their efforts will be closely watched by women because of the long history of oppression and dominance of women by men.

5. **Support the Efforts of Women Without Interfering.**
   Men need to understand that women must "define themselves and develop their own power base." Men must be careful that their supportive actions do not "confound or co-opt women's efforts."

6. **Struggle Against Racism and Sexism.**
   According to Tolman, et al. (1986), "Men must be sensitive to the ways in which issues of race and class influence commitment to gender equality. It is a mistake to assume that men, regardless of race and class, have the same resources or responsibilities for promoting an end to male dominance."

7. **Overcome Homophobia and Heterosexism.**
   As men fight to end prejudice and discrimination of gay men, they will discover new ways of relating to all men as equals. Some suggest this is a necessary first step for men in overcoming the dominance of women. Unless men can relate to other men as equals, they stand little chance of relating to women as equals.

8. **Work Against Male Violence in All Its Forms.**
Tolman, et al. (1986) indicate it is important that "...men actively confront how their own attitudes and behavior support violence, and not place all the blame for violence on the perpetrators of violent crimes."

9. **Do Not Set Up a False Dichotomy: Take Responsibility for Sexism.**
Men need to understand that their responsibility to address sexism does not end because they believe in and give support to gender equality. Men also have a responsibility to address the sexism that exists in the male-dominated society in which they live.

10. **Act at the Individual, Interpersonal, and Organizational Levels.**
Not only must men address gender equality at the individual level, but they must also confront sexism that is pervasive in all systems of society.

11. **Attend to Process and Product.**
If men are to truly make progress in supporting the goal of gender equality, they must be conscious of the ways they gather and organize themselves to address gender inequality. It is easy to fall back into old patterns that lead to continued female oppression even while developing ways to end that oppression.

It is important to note that while Tolman's suggestions are aimed at men, many women within the church and the social work profession have been socialized to believe in the sexist ideologies that permeate male-dominated American culture. The above suggestions can also be utilized by women who want to challenge their own thoughts and behaviors.

Sexual Orientation

While gender diversity continues to divide the Christian church and the social work profession today, it is probably safe to say the issue of sexual orientation creates the most heated debates between these two institutions. Heterosexual Christians can be found who support and work for the inclusion of people whose sexual orientation is different from theirs, and heterosexual Christians can also be found who describe homosexuality as an abomination and believe that homosexuals are not Christians. It is sad to say that similar views exist within the social work profession, a profession grounded in values and ethics of inclusiveness.

Today's religious climate has raised questions in the minds of many people regarding the ability of Christian social workers to openly and honestly address issues of inclusivity and diversity. There are some good reasons for these questions. At the 1997 annual meeting of the Southern Baptist Convention, messengers adopted a resolution to refrain from patronizing any movies produced by or theme parks operated by the Walt Disney Company due to the company's policy of providing health insurance to same sex partners of employees. Southern Baptists join the Assemblies of God, Presbyterian Church in America and American Family Association, among other groups, in boycotting Disney (Caldwell, 1997). In a recent survey of people who identified themselves as belonging to the Religious Right, Allen (1996) found that 78 percent of the respondents would prefer not to have homosexuals as neighbors. Is it any wonder that questions are raised as to whether Christian social workers will be able to uphold the values and ethics of the profession?

One way to answer this question is to note that there are diverse views within mainline Christian denominations regarding sexual orientation. Many religious groups, such as those mentioned above maintain that homosexuality is an abomination, while others, such as some Presbyterians and United Methodists, are conducting ongoing dialogues on the issue. The United Church of Christ even allows the ordination of gays and lesbians as ministers (Swindler, 1993).

It will not be an easy task, but the Christian church and the social work profession must work together to overcome the effects of **heterosexism**. The word "heterosexism" has been purposefully used rather than the more common word "homophobia." According to Mollenkott (1994, p. 145), "It is too easy for people to interpret a phobia as a morbid personal matter. A phobia can be someone else's private abnormality. To speak about heterosexism, however, bears witness that the basic phenomenon is public, institutionalized prejudice about gay, bisexual, and lesbian people throughout this society."

Where does this heterosexism come from? One source is the misuse of the Bible. Hays (1994) states:

> In terms of emphasis, it (homosexuality) is a minor concern, in contrast, for example, to economic injustice. What the Bible does say should be heeded carefully, but any ethic that intends to be biblical will seek to get the accents in the right places. Would that the passion presently being expended in the church over the question of homosexuality were devoted instead to urging the wealthy to share with the poor! Some of the most urgent champions of 'biblical morality' on sexual matters become strangely equivocal when the discussion turns to the New Testament's teachings about possessions. (p. 5)

According to Gomes (1996, p. 149), people tend to turn to the following six "select texts from the Old and New Testament...in seeking the Bible's teaching on homosexuality:"

1. Genesis 1–2	The Creation Story
2. Genesis 19:1–9	Sodom and Gomorrah, with the parallel passages of Judges 19 and Ezekiel 16:46–56
3. Leviticus 18:22 and 20:13	The Holiness Code
4. Romans 1:26–27	Regarded as the most significant of Saint Paul's views
5. I Corinthians 6:9	Pauline lists of vices
6. I Timothy 1–10	Pauline lists of vices

Noticeably absent from this list of scriptures are any references from the Synoptic Gospels (Matthew, Mark, Luke and John.) Most people look to these Biblical books when they desire to know what Jesus Christ had to say about specific issues of his day. According to Furnish (1994):

> Although these traditions include teachings on a number of specific topics, the matter of 'homosexual' relationships or practice is not among them....This silence of the Jesus traditions about same-sex practices does not mean that Jesus had nothing to say on the subject. It does suggest, however, that Jesus had nothing distinctive to say about it, and that 'homosexuality' was not a matter of special concern within the church that preserved and applied his sayings. (p. 23)

If the Synoptic Gospels contain no record of Jesus Christ addressing homosexuality and the entire Hebrew and Christian scriptures contain only six references to sexual orientation, an important question must be asked. Why does the church use the issue of homosexuality to divide and separate people instead of focusing on the biblical reality that all people are created in the image of God, and, thus all are joined together as part of that wonderful creation? Alexander & Preston (1996) describe what too often occurs within the church:

> Every Sunday morning, mainline Christian congregations across this country welcome into their fold new baptized Christians, children of God. Within the liturgy, these congregations pledge their undying support to accept, love, forgive, and nurture this person in the faith. Yet the church honors this covenant selectively. For what was supposed to be a means of unconditional love, grace, and justice becomes a conditional covenant for les-

bian and gay Christians—a compromise ending in silence, oppression, and judgment. It is this church that obstructs God's
grace and leads gay and lesbians to doubt that they are children of God. (p. xiii)

The sad fact is that the church is not alone in accepting people
selectively. The social work profession must also shoulder some of this
blame. Newman, White, and Stock-Linski (1995), in a panel presentation, indicated there is conflicting data related to student attitudes on
sexual orientation. They cite several studies that describe the existence
of homophobic attitudes among social work students. These attitudes
exist they feel because data indicate that large numbers of social work
programs have in the past made little effort to include curriculum content on sexual orientation. However, Black, Oles and Moore (1996)
administered the Index of Homophobia to 233 social work majors and
found that these students scored in the low-grade non-homophobic to
the low-grade homophobic range, with students becoming less homophobic as they progressed through their social work studies.

What is the result of the church and the social work profession
selectively accepting people based upon sexual orientation? The result
is heterosexism, and the outcomes can be devastating to homosexual
persons. One way heterosexism is exhibited is that people fail to see
homosexuals as people. Schmidt (1995, p. 37) said, "These are people
with faces, people with names, often Christian people, and...we must
never lose sight of their individual struggles, their individual pain, their
faces. If we neglect faces, we neglect the gospel." When we neglect
faces, we also neglect people, and that neglect leads to situations such
as the following.

A homosexual Christian, responding to an article in *The Other Side*,
a Christian magazine, wrote:

> Less than two months ago I was told by a sincere Christian (!)
> counselor that it would be 'better' to 'repent and die,' even if I
> had to kill myself, than to go on living and relating to others as
> a homosexual. (A friend of mine, told something similar by a
> well-intentioned priest, did just that)

> All I can do is pray that somewhere, someday, someone with
> compassion will begin the long, slow process of uncovering,
> discovery, and reconciliation of all who know Jesus Christ as
> Lord and Savior—both gay and straight.

Probably the most extreme example of Christians refusing to see
homosexuals as people with faces and names can be found by visiting

the web site of the Westboro Baptist Church of Topeka, Kansas. The address is www.godhatesfags.com. One of the questions posed at this web site is, "Why do we preach hate (of homosexuals)?" The response is, "Because the Bible preaches hate....What you need to hear is that God hates homosexual people, and that your chance of going to heaven is nonexistent unless you repent." Also located at this web site are pictures of members of the Westboro Baptist Church picketing funerals of persons who have died from AIDS. Members of the congregation can be seen standing in front of graves holding signs that say such things as "GOD HATES FAGS," "AIDS CURES FAGS," "THANK GOD FOR AIDS," "NO TEARS FOR QUEERS," "FAGS BURN IN HELL," and "GOD GAVE FAGS UP."

The face of Nicloas Ray West of Tyler, Texas, can not be forgotten. Nicloas was "brutally murdered for being gay. His torturers filled with the hate and poison of bigotry and their own estrangement shot him more times than could be counted by the coroner" (Alexander & Preston, 1994). Another face belongs to Bob (not his real name) who posted an email on the Internet describing his rejection by his family when they discovered he was gay. As a teenager he was kicked out of his home. Over twenty years later Bob does not even know where his parents are. A common friend talked with Bob's sister who said that his parents destroyed any evidence that Bob had ever existed—all pictures, personal belongs, etc.—and his parents tell people they only have two children: Bob's brother and sister.

How can people who call themselves Christians suggest to homosexuals that they are better off dead? How can people who call themselves Christians demonstrate at the funeral of persons who have died from AIDS? How can people murder someone for being gay? How can families turn their backs on their children? For many people, these are difficult questions to answer. Social workers try to answer these questions by looking to the profession's Code of Ethics and responding to all persons with dignity and respect, advocating for protection from hate crimes for homosexuals, and modeling the acceptance of all people as persons of worth. (*NASW News*, 1996, p. 1-4) This is not an easy task, but social workers belong to a profession that prizes the inclusion of all people. Christians who have committed themselves to following Jesus Christ also ought to believe in the inclusion of all.

As uncomfortable as it may be for some people, gay and lesbian issues are not going away. In fact, I believe that equal rights for gay and lesbian persons is the next civil rights battle to be fought in this country—in fact, we are already in the midst of this struggle. Gay and lesbian people deserve protection from losing their jobs simply because of their sexual orientation. Gay and lesbian people deserve the right to have access to a partner who is hospitalized, just as any family member would. Gay and lesbian people deserve the right to worship in ANY church without fear of rejection and condemnation. Gay and lesbian people deserve the right to live lives of integrity rather than becoming dehumanized as the victims of hate crimes. These are not any special rights. These are simply rights that are extended to ALL other persons—gay and lesbian persons should be included, not excluded. The Christian faith is very clear about who our neighbor is and how we are to treat that neighbor, and the social work profession is just as clear about relating to all person with respect and dignity. There is considerable common ground between the church and the social work profession, and this common ground can provide a foundation upon which the church and the profession can work together for the inclusion of gay and lesbian people in all spheres of society.

The organization known as P-FLAG (Parents and Friends of Lesbians and Gays) has identified ten specific acts people can do if they really want to make the world a better place for homosexuals. In discussing this list, Alexander and Preston (1996, p. 95) say, "You and I may not be able to do all of them yet, but we can pick at least one that we **can** do and start there." Some acts may very well cause value conflicts for some Christian social workers. However, all Christian social workers should be able to commit themselves to performing at least one item from the following list. Making that commitment would mean another step has been taken toward ending oppression and discrimination for gay and lesbian people. The ten acts are (P-FLAG, 1993):

1. Become a member of P-FLAG (or any other support group) and join with thousands of people from all walks of life, working to end discrimination against gays and lesbians.
2. Teach your children that being gay or lesbian is another means of expressing love.
3. If one of your family is gay or lesbian, be sure to let them know you love them just the way they are.
4. Don't tell anti-gay jokes. You just perpetuate the stereotypes about gays and lesbians.
5. Read our P-FLAG literature and find out more about what it is really like to be lesbian or gay in our society.
6. Be open with others about having lesbian or gay friends or family. Secrecy breeds shame.
7. If you overhear someone making an anti-gay comment, let them know you don't agree or approve.

8. Write Congress to protest any anti-gay legislation as you become aware of it.
9. Encourage open and honest discussion of gay and lesbian issues in your home, workplace, and church.
10. Stand with those who believe that discrimination against anyone is a crime against humanity—take a stand with P-FLAG.

Multiculturalism

While the dialogue between the Christian church and the social work profession regarding gender and sexual orientation is fairly recent, both of these groups have been addressing issues of race and ethnicity for many years. Certainly most mainline denominations have moved away from the days of segregated congregations and into a more inclusive environment. From its very founding as a profession, social work has also advocated for the equality of all persons, an end to oppressive acts, and social justice for all. However, it is important to note that areas of agreement and tension exist between the church and social work in relationship to race and ethnicity, or, as more currently referred to as issues of multiculturalism. Freeman (1996, p. 10) describes multiculturalism as two sides of one coin when she says, "Recognizing the universality of the human condition is one side of the coin of multiculturalism, and acknowledging and appreciating the unique culture and contributions of each ethnic group in this pluralistic society is the other side."

The results from a survey conducted by the National Opinion Research Center at the University of Chicago raise some questions regarding the openness to multiculturalism by Christians, specifically the group that has become known as the Religious Right. This survey found that "the Religious Right is 'deeply divided' from other Americans on a number of social issues..." (Allen, 1996). For example, fifty percent of the respondents said they would not vote for a Moslem for president and fourteen percent would not vote for a Jew. Fifty-four percent of the respondents said they would not want to have an atheist as a neighbor, and seventy-five percent said they would not vote for an atheist for president, even if "the candidate were otherwise well qualified."

How do these views impact Christians in the social work profession? Inference can be made that atheists, Moslems, Jews, and people from other minority groups might legitimately question a Christian social worker's ability to effectively provide assistance in a diverse and pluralistic society. Many people, unfortunately, assume that all Christians are equally intolerant. The Religious Right would argue they are not intolerant, but "from their faith comes....reluctance to accept as equal the beliefs and customs of others....it is not that they are intolerant, but they deem tolerance as a lesser value than Christian morality" (Allen, 1996). With Christian morality being more important than tolerance, the Religious Right is facing days ahead when their intolerance will be sorely tested. According to Gould (1996, p. 29), "The 1990 census shows that the racial and ethnic composition of the American population has changed more dramatically in the past decade than at any time in the 20th century, with nearly one in every four Americans identifying themselves as black, Hispanic, Asian...or American Indian." While the Religious Right is focusing on "Christian morality" as opposed to tolerance, the social work profession takes a different position regarding this trend. Gould (1996, p. 29) said, "...these trends certainly underscore the need for the social work profession to speak out publicly, to urge a societal commitment to the values of racial, ethnic, and cultural diversity—values that have been recognized as being part of the profession's 'system of ethics.'"

It is important to note that many Christian denominations support multiculturalism, but it is difficult to overcome the church's long history of intolerance toward people of other races and cultures. As with gender and sexual orientation, the Bible has been used by the white American majority (often Christians) to justify oppressive relationships with people who belong to a different racial or ethnic minority group, particularly African-Americans. According to Gomes (1996), in the summer of 1995 the Southern Baptist Convention publicly repented "for the role it had played in the justification of slavery and in the maintenance of a culture of racism in the United States." This repentance raises an important question:

> It is abundanently clear that the Southern Baptists rejected neither the faith nor the Bible of their mothers and fathers, but they have certainly changed their minds as to what scripture says and to what scriptures means....How is the moral consensus changed without changing the contents of the Bible? (p. 86)

The question needs to asked again: How is the moral consensus changed without changing the contents of the Bible? Will the views of the Religious Right someday change while still affirming the truth of scripture? There are no easy answers to these questions, but they must be given thoughtful attention in light of the fact that the United States is becoming a more heterogenous society. Not only must the church respond to the challenges this heterogeneous society presents, but the social work profession must also make adjustment (Kropf & Issac, 1992).

Breckenridge and Breckenridge (1995, p. 72) have identified several ways for the church to become more culturally aware without compromising its religious beliefs. They state: "It is not so much that we have to change our culture as that we must simply accept the culture of others. To accomplish such openness means that we do not insist on cultural sameness, but that we expand our ability to hear, see, and learn from other groups." This means that the church and the social work profession must change from thinking of society as a melting pot, "a metaphor that suggested that the United States was a country composed of many different ethnic groups, who had all somehow become blended or assimilated into 'Americans'" (Clark, 1994, p.3).

The idea of the melting pot has been replaced by another metaphor, that of the "tossed salad," a concept that according to Clark (1994) implies:

> that although many different groups live in the United States and may, indeed, consider themselves Americans, each also retains its own ethnic and cultural character and that this retention is both possible and desirable. Proponents of the tossed salad view believe that assimilation can be balanced with the preservation of identity; for them, the ideal is not for the elimination of differences but for an increased awareness of and respect for cultural and ethnic diversity. (p. 3)

There are adjustments that social workers and the Christian church can make in order to respond to this heterogeneous—tossed salad—society. One of the most important tasks is for individual social workers to work on becoming anti-racist. According to Wicker (1986, p. 37), "Racism can be unintentional and naively perpetuated by frontline workers because it is so institutionalized that we often do not notice it....we must be prepared to...have the courage to push ourselves, our co-workers, and our administrators to struggle effectively against racism. Passive acceptance of racist attitudes—even ones created by others—ensures the perpetuation of a racist system."

Wicker (1986) has identified a variety of ways social workers can work on their personal racism and has made suggestions that will enable social workers "to scrutinize their racism concerning citizens of a different color." These include:

Personal Work:
   1. Form non-hierarchical peer supervision groups at work to discuss basic definitions of racism and prejudice, then use a variety of...techniques...to help one another look at prejudice and racism in clinical work with people of color.

2. Read literature and nonfiction written by people of color to educate ourselves about people who are different and who live in different cultures.
3. Attend multicultural events....Support multicultural events in your community. Feel what it is like to be in the minority.
4. Attend "unlearning racism" workshops.

Working With Clients:
1. Ask the client how he or she feels about working with you.
2. Are you aware of and do you have information about the client's cultural heritage?
3. Ask yourself about your assumptions, hidden or blatant, about this client.
4. Be clear on how racism affects clients' lives on a daily basis. If you are a member of another minority group—gay, female, Jewish—try to identify the oppression of racism with the kind of oppression you have dealt with on a daily basis.
5. Interrupt racism in the therapeutic setting.....Interrupting internalized oppression— defined here as the oppressed taking on stereotyped views that the oppressor holds about them— with clients of color is essential.
6. Encourage clients to get involved in anti-racist organizations as a constructive way to deal with feelings of hopelessness and powerlessness.

The Christian church can also employ many of these same tasks. Breckenridge and Breckenridge (1995) support many of the tasks just described when they say:

> Christians must be willing to relinquish desire for societal control and let those who wish otherwise follow their own life path. This is very difficult, but we are reaching a point in our society where the church must decide whether its role is to be servant or conqueror.... For this reason, we argue that the critical place to begin is...with our feelings. We must develop a sensitivity which will recognize not only the rights of others, but also the presence of inferior feelings within ourselves. A large part of the answer is simply imitating Christ. (p. 253)

Imitating Christ! What a simple answer, and yet what a complex task for most Christians and social workers to do. It is hard to imagine Jesus Christ stating that he would not want to live next door to an atheist, Moslem, or homosexual. Since Jesus was a Jew it is even harder to imagine that he would exclude them as neighbors. So, why do Christian social workers struggle in their ability to imitate Christ when confronting multiculturalism? This is a very important question to ponder, and as answers are found, new and exciting ways of relating to God's diverse creation will begin to appear.

Summary

Issues raised in this chapter may have made some readers uncomfortable. Thinking about diversity issues related to gender, sexual orientation, and multiculturalism often stir value conflicts in the best of social workers. What are we to do with these conflicts? As indicated through this chapter, the Code of Ethics of the social work profession must be adhered to with all clients. However, adhering to the Code is sometimes easier said than done.

It is hoped that as social workers grow and mature, the church, as well as the profession, will be impacted in such a way that both of these great institutions become models of inclusion for the rest of society. Striving to reach this goal of inclusivity will benefit all of God's diverse and beautiful creation. There is only one way to start the process, and that is through imitating Jesus Christ. What does imitating Christ mean? I believe it means that we stand in the doors of our offices, arms opened wide, saying "Welcome; anyone who walks through these doors is accepted as a person of worth and dignity. Your race, ethnicity, gender, or sexual orientation takes nothing away from your personhood." Imitating Christ means that we also stand in the doors of our churches, arms opened wide, and offer the very same inclusive welcome to any who enters. Sometimes we may stand alone. That is allright. Jesus Christ often stood alone when he challenged the mores and oppression of his day. Other times we may be joined by people who share our commitment. No matter the number who join us, we must take the stand.

I believe those of us who gathered at the National Cathedral that October day were there not only to worship but to also take a stand. I'm convinced that Jesus stood with us, and had he been physically present there in the Cathedral he would have assured us all "Yes, this is what heaven looks like!" As Christians and social workers, let us live to spread that message of good news, inclusion, and grace.

References

Alexander, M.B. & Preston, J. (1996). *We Were Baptized Too: Claiming God's Grace for Lesbians and Gays.* Louisville, KY: Westminster John Knox Press.

Allen, B. (1996, October 2). Religious Right, America Deeply Divided. *The Baptist Standard*, p. 12.

Black, B., Oles, T., & Moore, L. (1996). Homophobia among students in social work programs. *Journal of Baccalaureate Social Work, 2,* 13-41.

Breckenridge, J. & Breckenridge, L. (1995). *What Color Is Your God?: Multicultural Education in the Church.* Wheaton, IL: Victor Books.

Caldwell, D.K. (1997, June 19). Baptists vote to boycott Disney Co. *The Dallas Morning News.*, p. 1A.

Clark, E. & Richardson, H. (1977). *Women and Religion: A Feminist Sourcebook of Christian Thought.* New York: Harper & Row.

Clark, I.L. (1994). *Writing About Diversity: An Argument Reader and Guide.* Fort Worth, TX: Harcourt, Brace & Company.

The National Association of Social Workers Code of Ethics. (1995, November). *NASW News, 41(10),* 17-20.

Edwards, A. (1996). Practitioner and client value conflict: Suggested guidelines for social work practice. *Social Work and Christianity, 23,* 28-38.

Freeman, E.M. (1996). I Am A Human Being. In Ewalt, P.L., Freeman, E.M., Kirk, S.A., & Poole, D.L. (Eds.), *Multicultural Issues in Social Work.* Washington, D.C.: NASW Press.

Furnish, V.P. (1994). The Bible and Homosexuality: Reading the Texts in Context. In J.S. Siker (Ed.), *Homosexuality in the Church: Both Sides of the Debate* (pp.18-35). Louisville, KY: Westminster John Knox Press.

Gomes, P.J. (1996). *The Good Book: Reading The Bible With Mind and Heart.* New York: William Morrow and Company.

Goodstein, L. (1996, June 13). Baptist Group Plans Boycott of Disney Company: Firm is Denounced for Policies on Gays. *Washington Post.*

Gould, K.H. (1996). The Misconstruing of Multiculturalism: The Stanford Debate and Social Work. In Ewalt, P.L., Freeman, E.M., Kirk, S.A., & Poole, D.L. (Eds), *Multicultural Issues in Social Work.* Washington, D.C.: NASW Press.

Hays, R. (1994). Awaiting the Redemption of Our Bodies: The Witness of Scripture Concerning Homosexuality. In J.S. Siker (Ed.), *Homosexuality in the Church: Both Sides of the Debate.* Louisville, KY: Westminster John Knox Press.

Huber, R. & Orlando, B.P. (1995). Persisting gender differences in social workers' incomes: Does the profession really care? *Social Work,* 40, 585-591.

Knapman, S.K. (1977). Sex discrimination in family agencies. *Social Work,* 22, 461-465.

Kropf, N.P. & Issac, A.R. (1992). Cultural Diversity and Social Work Practice: An Overview.In Harrison, D.F., Wodarski, J.S., & Thyer, B.A. (Eds.), *Cultural Diversity and Social Work Practice.* Springfield, IL: Charles C. Thomas.

Loewenberg, F.M. (1988). *Religion And Social Work Practice In Contemporary American Society.* New York: Columbia University Press.

Mollenkott, V.R. (1994). Overcoming Heterosexism—To Benefit Everyone. In J.S. Siker (Ed.), *Homosexuality in the Church: Both Sides of the Debate.* Louisville, KY: Westminster John Knox Press

Morales, A.T. & Sheafor, B.W. (1995). *Social Work: A Profession of Many Faces*. Boston: Allyn and Bacon.

Newman, B.S., White, J., & Strock-Linski, D. (October, 1995). *Populations at Risk: An Integrated Approach to Curriculum Building*. Panel presentation at the meeting of Baccalaureate Program Directors, Nashville, TN.

Parents and Friends of Lesbians and Gays. (1993). *Ten Simple Things You Can Do To Make A Difference*. [Brochure].

Scanzoni, L.D. & Mollenkott, V.R. (1994). *Is The Homosexual My Neighbor: A Positive Christian Response*. San Francisco: Harper.

Schmidt. T.E. (1995). *Straight & Narrow?: Compassion & Clarity in the Homosexuality Debate*. Downers Grove, IL: InterVarsity Press.

Stark, R. (1996). *The Rise of Christianity: A Sociologist Reconsiders History*. Princeton, NJ: Princeton University Press.

Sutton, J.A. (1982). Sex discrimination among social workers. *Social Work, 27*, 211-217.

Swindler, A. (1993). *Homosexuality and World Religions*. Valley Forge, Pennsylvania: Trinity Press International.

Tolman, R.M., Mowry, D.D., Jones, L.E., & Brekke, J. (1986). Developing a Profeminist Commitment Among Men in Social Work. In Van Den Bergh, N. & Cooper, L. (Eds.), *Feminist Visions for Social Work*. Silver Spring, MD: NASW Press.

Tucker, R.A. & Liefeld, W. (1987). *Daughters of the Church*. Grand Rapids, MI: Academie.

Wallis, J. (1995). *The Soul of Politics: Beyond "Religious Right" And "Secular Left"*. San Diego: Harcourt Brace and Company.

Wicker, D.G. (1986). Combating Racism in Practice and in the Classroom.. In Van Den Bergh, N. & Cooper, L. (Eds.), *Feminist Visions for Social Work*.. Silver Spring, MD: NASW Press.

Williams, M., Ho, L., & Fiedler, L. (1974). Career patterns: More grist for women's liberation. *Social Work, 19*, 466-466.

York, R.O., Henley, H.C., & Gamble, D.N. (1987). Sexual discrimination in social work: Is it salary or advancement? *Social Work, 32*, 50-55.

CHAPTER 7

CALLING: A SPIRITUALITY MODEL FOR SOCIAL WORK PRACTICE

Beryl Hugen

In making a career choice, many Christian students find the social work profession a good fit with their religious faith. Or at least at first glance it appears so. For example, as part of the application process for the social work program I teach in, students are asked to explain why they have chosen social work as a major. What motivates them to enter this field of study? Some answer the question by relating past experiences with social work services or role models who were social workers, but almost all describe a moderate or fairly strong religious impulse to serve people and society.

Many specifically relate their faith to their choice of social work—stating something like this: In being loved by God, they in turn wish to share some of this love with those who are poor or hurting or are in need of help of some kind. Some of these students believe that to be a Christian in social work they must work in an agency under religious auspices, whereas others plan to work in programs that do not have a specific religious base or affiliation, but are part of the larger community of governmental social welfare responses to those in need. Despite these differences, almost all are interested in finding ways to integrate their faith and their newly chosen field of study.

But it doesn't take long in their social work studies for these students to begin to recognize the complex tensions between their religious faith, agency auspices, and the secular values of the social work profession. This discovery is not surprising; social work is, after all, a secular profession. At times, students find the profession very critical of religion, even suspicious of anyone who claims to have religious motives for helping others.

This feeling is understandable, for in the last thirty to forty years, the social work profession has simply ignored religious insights and accepted the principle of separating the sacred and secular. Religion came to be seen as having no particular insight to offer or relevance for everyday professional practice. Because of this attitude, the recent professional literature does not offer much help to students in thinking through the relationship of religious faith and professional practice. It is ironic that social work, which claims as its unique focus the "whole person" in the whole environment, has for so long neglected the religious dimension of life.

Not only do students continue to come to the profession with religious motivations, but the roots of social work are largely grounded in religious faith (Devine, 1939). Social work originated and came of age under the inspiration of the Judeo-Christian traditions and the philanthropic and service motivation of religious people. As Leiby (1985) indicates, the Christian biblical command to love God and to love one's neighbor as oneself was directly translated into a sense of moral responsibility for social service. As the social work profession secularized in the 20th century, these earlier religious rationales and models for service were replaced by doctrines of natural rights, utilitarianism, and humanistic ideology.

Dealing with human need apart from religious motives and methods is actually a very recent development in the history of charity and philanthropy. The notion of a secular profession focused on responding to human suffering would have struck many of our professional ancestors as quite inconsistent and confusing. Many of them were religiously motivated and expressed their faith by means of social work as a vocation, a calling from God to serve their brothers and sisters who were in need. With their perception of social work as a calling, a vocation, they formalized a link between their religious faith and social work practice.

What is meant by viewing social work as a calling? Several recent articles have addressed this "old fashioned" concept of calling or vocation, sensing its power and value for current social work practice (Gustafson,1982; Reamer, 1992). However, these writers essentially have attempted to take the religious concept of calling and use it in a secular fashion. They have done so in order to provide a moral purpose for the profession—to counteract what they perceive to be the focus on self-interest inherent in the social work profession which has become increasingly professionalized, specialized and bureaucratic.

My intent in this chapter is to explain, or more accurately to reintroduce, the religious model of calling as used by Christian social workers, past and present, in linking Christian faith and professional social work practice. Both its attractiveness and shortcomings as a model will be addressed. My purpose is not only to help social workers and the profession understand or correct misunderstandings related to this model, but also help social workers better understand the broader issues related to the spirituality of social work practice, in that other religious models and spiritual traditions address many of the same integration of faith and practice questions. Also, reintroducing the model of calling will lead us to see the significance of how the perspectives and writings of our religiously motivated social work ancestors—of which there are many— -can contribute to the profession's current discussions regarding spirituality and social work practice.

Religion, Faith, and Spirituality

Before discussing the model of calling, it is helpful to define what is meant by the terms spirituality, religion, belief and faith. The profession has long struggled with this definitional dilemma. The dilemma has focused on how to reintroduce religious or spiritual concerns into a profession which has expanded beyond specific sectarian settings and ideologies to now include diverse sources of knowledge, values and skills, and how to respond to the needs of a much more spiritually diverse clientele. Addressing this dilemma, Siporin (1985) and Brower (1984) advocated for an understanding of spirituality that includes a wide diversity of religious and non-religious expressions, with such an inclusive understanding of spirituality encouraging social workers to reflect upon their clients both within and outside of particular institutional religious settings and ideologies.

From this beginning, Canda (1988a, 1988b) further developed a concept of spirituality for social work that incorporates insights from diverse religious and philosophical perspectives. He identifies three content components to spirituality—values, beliefs and practice issues— "all serving the central dynamic of a person's search for a sense of meaning and purpose, developed in the context of interdependent relationships between self, other people, the nonhuman world, and the ground of being itself" (Canda, 1988a, p. 43).

In the same vein, the work of James Fowler, known more for his model of faith development, is particularly instructive. Fowler (1981) states that to understand the "human quest for relation to transcendence," the key phenomenon to examine is not religion or belief but faith (p. 14). According to Fowler, who draws upon the ideas of religionist Wilfred Smith, *religions* are "cumulative traditions," which represent the expressions of faith of people in the past (p. 9). Included in a cumulative tradition are such elements as "texts of scripture, oral traditions, music, creeds, theologies," and so forth. *Belief* refers to "the holding of certain ideas" or "assent to a set of propositions" (p. 13). *Faith* differs from both religion and belief. Fowler describes faith as a commitment, "an alignment of the will...in accordance with a vision of transcendent value and power, one's ultimate concern" (p. 14). One commits oneself to that which is known or acknowledged and lives loyally, with life and character being shaped by that commitment. Defined in this way, faith is believed to be a universal feature of human living, recognizably similar everywhere, and in all major religious traditions.

What does faith consist of then? Fowler describes three components of what he calls the contents of faith. The first he terms *centers of value*, the "causes, concerns, or persons that consciously or unconsciously have the greatest worth to us." These are what we worship, things that "give our lives meaning" (p. 277). The second component of faith is described as our *images of power*, "the power with which we align ourselves to sustain us in the midst of life's contingencies" (p. 277): these powers need not necessarily be supernatural or transcendent. Finally, faith is comprised of "the *master stories* that we tell ourselves and by which we interpret and respond to the events that impinge upon our lives." Essentially, our master stories reveal what we believe to be the fundamental truths, "the central premises of [our] sense of life's meaning" (p. 277).

In discussing spirituality and faith, Fowler and Canda both emphasize its pervasive, all encompassing nature in an individual's life. Faith or spirituality is not a separate dimension of life or compartmentalized specialty, but rather an orientation of the total person. Accordingly, the three components of faith—centers of value, images of power, and master stories (Fowler, 1981) - and spirituality—values, beliefs, and practices (Canda, 1988) - exert "structuring power" in our lives, shaping our characters and actions in the world, including our work. Faith and spirituality are defined here as the essence of religion. Faith and spirituality take on a Christian religious meaning when the centers of value, images of power, and master stories of one's faith, the central dynamic of one's search for a sense of meaning and purpose, are grounded in the creeds, texts of scripture, and theology etc. of the Christian tradition. I will attempt to present the Christian religious concept of calling within these more inclusive frameworks of spirituality and faith.

Calling in Action

Perhaps the best way to develop an understanding of the religious concept of calling is to start with an illustration. Robert Coles, in his book *The Call to Service* (1993), tells of a six year old black girl who initiated school desegregation in the South in the early 1960's. Tessie, a first grader, each day facing an angry and threatening mob, was escorted by federal marshals to school. The mob almost always greeted her with a litany of obscenities. Tessie's maternal grandmother, Martha, was the family member who usually got Tessie up and off to school each morning.

Coles reports that one day Tessie was reluctant to go to school—claiming to feeling tired, having slipped and fallen while playing in a nearby back yard, and having a difficult time with a current substitute teacher. Tessie suggested to her grandmother that she might stay home that day. Her grandmother replied that that would be fine if Tessie truly wasn't well, but if she was more discouraged than sick, that was quite another matter. She goes on to say:

> "It's no picnic, child—I know that, Tessie—going to that school. Lord Almighty, if I could just go with you, and stop there in front of that building, and call all those people to my side, and read to them from the Bible, and tell them, remind them that He's up there, Jesus, watching over all of us—it don't matter who you are and what your skin color is. But I stay here, and you go—and your momma and your daddy, they have to leave the house so early in the morning that it's only Saturdays and Sundays that they see you before the sun hits the middle of its traveling for the day. So I'm not the one to tell you that you should go, because here I am, and I'll be watching television and eating or cleaning things up while you're walking by those folks. But I'll tell you, you're doing them a great favor; you're doing them a service, a big service."

> "You see, my child, you have to help the good Lord with His world! He puts us here—and He calls us to help Him out. You belong in that McDonogh School, and there will be a day when everyone knows that, even those poor folks—Lord, I pray for them!—those poor, poor folks who are out there shouting their heads off at you. You're one of the Lord's people; He's put His Hand on you. He's given a call to you, a call to service—in His name! There's all those people out there on the street." (p. 3-4)

Later Coles questions Tessie whether she understood what her grandmother meant by "how you should be of service to those people out there on the street." She replied:

> "If you just keep your eyes on what you're supposed to be doing, then you'll get there—to where you want to go. The marshals say, 'Don't look at them; just walk with your head up high, and you're looking straight ahead.' My granny says that there's God, He's looking too, and I should remember that it's a help to Him to do this, what I'm doing; and if you serve Him, then that's important. So I keep trying." (p. 4-5)

The heart of what Tessie had learned was that for her, service meant serving, and not only on behalf of those she knew and liked or wanted to like. Service meant an alliance with the Lord Himself for the benefit of people who were obviously unfriendly. Service was not an avocation or something done to fulfill a psychological need, not even an action that would earn her any great reward. She had connected a moment in her life with a larger ideal, and in so doing had learned to regard herself as a servant, as a person called to serve. It was a rationale for a life, a pronouncement with enormous moral and emotional significance for Tessie and her grandmother. This call was nurtured by the larger black community, her pastor, family, and the biblical values of love and justice—the stories of exile and return, of suffering and redemption—the view of the powerful as suspect and the lowly as destined to sit close to God, in His Kingdom.

Coles himself recounts how ill-prepared professionally he was to understand this family and their sense of calling:

> "I don't believe I could have understood Tessie and her family's capacity to live as they did, do as they did for so long, against such great odds, had I not begun to hear what *they* were saying and meaning, what *they* intended others to know about their reasons and values—as opposed to the motivations and reactions and "mechanisms of defense" I attributed to them. Not that there wasn't much to be learned by a psychoanalytic approach. Tessie and her companions, like human beings everywhere (including those who study or treat other human beings), most certainly did demonstrate fearfulness and anxiety; she also tried to subdue those developments by not acknowledging them, for instance, or by belittling their significance. Mostly, though, she clung hard to a way of thinking in which she was *not* a victim, *not* in need of "help" but someone picked by fate to live out the Christian tradition in her life. "I'm trying to think of the way Jesus would want me to think," she told me one evening. When I asked how she thought Jesus wanted her to think, she replied, "I guess of others, and not myself, I'm here to help the others." (p. 26)

Calling: The Meaning of Work

For some Christians, like Tessie and her grandmother, connecting one's work to the divine intentions for human life gives another dimension to the meaning and purpose of one's work and life. Certainly adequate pay, financial stability, social status and a sense of personal fulfillment remain significant criteria in choosing a career, but they are not the central motivation. The central motivation is the means by which one's Christian religious tradition has tied one's work and faith together, this concept of vocation, or calling.

Martin Luther originally formulated the notion of vocation or calling largely in reaction to the prevailing attitude toward work in medieval society. Medieval thinkers devalued work. They believed that in and of itself, work had little or no spiritual significance. They held, like the Greeks earlier, to the idea that the highest form of life, the form in which humans can realize their noblest potential, is the contemplative life of the mind. By thinking, we liken ourselves to God. Work was thus a hindrance to an individual's relation to God, which could be cultivated only in the leisure of contemplation. Because peasant serfs did most of the work in medieval society, and because the earthly character of their occupations prevented them from participating directly in the religious life, they received grace through the church by means of the sacraments.

Not only the life of productive work, but also the practical or active life, consisting of doing good to one's neighbor, was viewed by many medievals as an impediment to the true goals of the religious life. The activity given precedence was always the contemplative life. An early church father, St. Augustine (1950) wrote: "the obligations of charity make us undertake virtuous activity, but if no one lays this burden upon us, we should give ourselves over in leisure to study and contemplation" (p. 19). The need for the active or charitable life was temporary, whereas contemplation of God was eternal.

Luther's concept of vocation or calling fits neatly within the compass of this thought since he draws a basic theological distinction between the kingdom of heaven and the kingdom of earth. To the kingdom of heaven belongs our relationship to God, which is to be based on faith; to the kingdom of earth belongs our relationship to our neighbor, which is to be based on love. A vocation, properly speaking, is the call to love my neighbor that comes to me through the duties attached to my social place or *station* within the earthly kingdom. A station in this life may be a matter of paid employment, but it need not be. Luther's idea of station is wide enough to include being a wife or a husband, a mother or a father, a judge or politician, as well as a baker, truck driver, farmer or social worker. Thus, the call to love one's neighbor goes out to all in general. All of these callings represent specific and concrete ways of serving my neighbor, as I am commanded to do by God Himself.

What do we accomplish when we discharge the duties of our stations in life, when we heed the call of God to serve our neighbor in our daily tasks? Luther believed the order of stations in the kingdom of earth has been instituted by God Himself as His way of seeing to it that the needs of humanity are met on a day-by-day basis. Through the human pursuit of vocations across the array of earthly stations, the hungry are fed, the naked are clothed, the sick are healed, the ignorant are enlightened, and the weak are protected. That is, by working we actually participate in God's providence for the human race. Through our work, people are brought under His providential care. Far from being of little or no account, work is charged with religious significance. As we pray each morning for our daily bread, people are already busy at work in the bakeries.

Luther conceived of work as a way of serving others. He never recommended it as either the road to self-fulfillment or a tool for self-aggrandizement. We, of course, find it natural to assess the attractiveness of a particular job on the basis of what it can do for us. But Luther saw quite clearly that work will always involve a degree of self-sacrifice for the sake of others, just as Christ sacrificed himself for the sake of others.

During the time of Luther, and for many centuries preceding him, people thought of human society to be stable, static, and as incapable of change, as the order of nature itself. Shortly after Luther's time, however, European civilization underwent a dramatic transformation under the combined influence of a rapidly expanding market economy, accelerated urbanization, technological innovation, and vast political reorganization. In the face of these astounding changes on all fronts of social life, people soon saw that the structure of human society is itself in part a product of human activity, changeable and affected by sin. Once people recognized this fact, it became clear, in turn, that to the degree human activity is motivated by sinful desires and worldly ambitions, the society thus produced is also likely to be structurally unsound and in need of reform. For example, an economy based upon greed and a government based on the arbitrary use of power stand in just as much need of repentance as the individuals who are a part of them. For this reason, other reformers insisted that not only the human heart, but also human society must be reformed in accordance with the Word of God. The emergent vision of the Christian life at the dawn of modern social work practice, then, required not only that people obey God in their callings, but that the callings themselves be aligned with the will of God.

Calling Within Social Work

Although historically there have been many models of spirituality in social work, the calling model perhaps has been the most prominent, or at least the most extensively referred to in the social work literature. In fact, in the very early years, it was the dominant model. This dominance is certainly related to the fact that Protestantism was the dominant religious form at the time. Many early social workers in their writings refer to the relationship of their spirituality and social work within this calling model. Their response is not surprising, since many of them grew up in devoted religious families, many had theological training, and still others were very active as lay people in their churches. All found in their spiritual experiences something which gave impetus, meaning, and value to their work of service.

The following examples illustrate the prominence of the calling model and how it has been articulated and practiced by a variety of different leaders within the profession.

Edward Devine, a leader in the Charity Organization Society and the first director of one of the first schools of social work, records in his book *When Social Work Was Young* (1939) the early experiences in social work education and summarizes these experiences as follows:

> "The real start towards the professional education of social workers as such was made in 1898, when the Society launched its summer school of philanthropy with thirty students enrolled....
>
> For several years this summer school gathered from all parts of the country a substantial number of promising candidates, and a brilliant corps of instructors, who for one day, or sometimes for an entire week, expounded and discussed the fundamentals of the slowly emerging profession. Jane Addams, Mary Richmond, Zilpha Smith, Mrs. Glendower Evans, Graham Taylor, Jeffrey Brackett, John M. Glenn, Mary Willcox Brown, before and also after she became Mrs. John M. Glenn, James B. Reynolds, Mary Simkhovitch-a full roster of the lecturers in the school would be like a list of the notables in the National Conference of Social Work. Certainly no religious gathering could have a deeper consecration to that ideal of learning how to do justly, and to love mercy, and to walk humbly, which Micah described as being all that is required of us." (p. 125-6)

He ends the book by stating that in his opinion the spirit of social work finds its power, value, and purpose from the biblical Sermon on the Mount.

Richard Cabot (1927) addressed the model of calling more specifically in an article entitled "The Inter-Relation of Social Work and the Spiritual Life." He writes:

"religion is the consciousness of a world purpose to which we are allied...when I speak of the purpose being a personality, I speak of the person of God of whom we are children... I think it makes absolutely all the difference in social work to know this fact of our alliance with forces greater than ourselves. If a person wants to find himself and be somebody he has got to find his particular place in the universal plan. In social work, we are trying to help people find themselves, find their places and enjoy them. The chief end of man is to glorify God and to enjoy Him forever." (p. 212)

Cabot also articulated several spiritual powers applicable to social work practice that come to those who hold this faith: courage, humility and the ability to stand by people. He goes on to explain that the goal of social work is to:

"maintain and to improve the channels of understanding both within each person and between persons, and through these channels to favor the entrance of God's powers for the benefit of the individuals....

Unblocking channels is what social workers do. The sort of unblocking that I have in mind is that between capital and labor, between races, or between the members of a family who think they hate each other....

Spiritual diagnosis, I suppose, means nothing more than the glimpse of the central purpose of the person, unique and re-lated to the total parts of the world. Spiritual treatment, I sup-pose, is the attempt to open channels, the channels I have been speaking of, so as to favor the working of the world purpose. In this way social workers participate in the providence of God." (p. 215-16)

Perhaps the most prominent example of the power and dominance of the calling model is illustrated in Owen R. Lovejoy's presidential address to the National Conference of Social Work in 1920, entitled "The Faith of a Social Worker." In the speech he attempts to draw upon the foundations of faith of the members in order to aid in their approach to discussions during the Conference and to help create a real basis for unity. He begins by first disclaiming any intention of committing the Conference to any specific creed of social service. His desire, rather, is to discover "some of the those underlying principles which bind people together."

He states that all social workers have a philosophy of life, a faith, a "basic enthusiasm," and those who act on this faith can choose to:

"regard this as a sacred ministry and claim their commission as the ancient prophet claimed his when he said: "The Lord hath anointed me to preach good tidings to the meek, to bind up the broken hearted, to proclaim liberty to the captives, the opening of prison to them that are bound, to give a garland for ashes, the oil of joy for mourning, the garment of praise for the spirit of heaviness." Certainly this is not a slight task to which we are called, but the expression of a joyful faith carried with cheerfulness to those in the world most in need of it...a field of service based on the conviction that men are warranted in working for something corresponding to a divine order "on earth as it is in heaven." (p. 209)

He warns those "who look upon the visible institutions connected with their religion as the essential embodiment of faith," recognizing such a sectarian position frequently leads to imposing one's own values on others and proselytizing—similar issues we face today. He ends the address stating that the secret of their usefulness as social workers is found in the following litany.

God is a Father,
Man is a brother,
Life is a mission and not a career;
Dominion is service,
Its scepter is gladness,
The least is the greatest,
Saving is dying,
Giving is living,
Life is eternal and love is its crown. (p. 211)

It is difficult to imagine an address on such a topic being given today. Such was the significance of spirituality and the calling model in the social work profession at that time.

The calling model's chief apologist, however, was Ernest Johnson, a prolific writer and interpreter of Protestant religion and the social work profession. His writings detail the principles which he hoped would govern efforts to bring Protestantism to bear through the social work profession in meeting human needs. Recognizing that Protestantism had a majority position and influence in the culture, he strongly advocated, with some exceptions, for a pattern of social work based on the calling model. The result was to minimize the operation and control of agencies and social welfare enterprises by churches or religious groups and maximize Protestant participation in non-sectarian agencies.

Later in life he recognized that Protestantism, particularly when its pre-eminent position was beginning to wane, would never obtain complete cultural dominance or create an approximation to the ideal of a Christian society—the Corpus Christianum. The result, he lamented, would be only a partial transformation of the culture—and regrettably, a partial accommodation on the part of Protestantism to the culture. But despite this limitation, he still believed the Protestant pattern or model of influencing social work enterprises and social movements "indirectly" (through the means of one's calling or vocation) was essentially sound. Johnson (1946) states:

> "It [the calling model] affords the most effective channel through which our churches, in the midst of a religiously heterogeneous population, can bring to bear their testimony through community endeavor and make their impact on a secular culture. This means, however, a recovery of the sense of lay Christian vocation, which has been so largely lost. The major Protestant contribution to social work can be made, I believe, through the consciously Christian activities of persons engaged in non-sectarian enterprises and movements. In the existing situation in America a revival of a sectarian, possessive attitude toward social work would be definitely reactionary....
>
> In a word, then, we need to devise our social strategy in the light of our Protestant history, with its emphasis on freedom, and in the light of our cultural situation, which puts a premium on vocational work as Christian testimony. We can make our best contribution without seeking to enhance Protestant prestige, seeking rather to influence contemporary life and to meet human need through the activities of those whose lives have been kindled at our altars and nourished in our fellowship." (p. 2-4)

As Johnson relates, the calling model has not always functioned as intended. Already in 1893, one leader of the new social work profession, responding to the widening gap between religion and the emerging influence of scientific models in social work, characterized social work as "a revolutionary turning of thought in our society from a religious service to God to a secular service to humanity" (Huntington, 1893). Along this line of thought, Protestant theologian Reinhold Niebuhr (1932) grappled with the practical consequences of the calling

model for social work. With three-fourths of social workers then functioning under secular auspices, many had become "inclined to disregard religion." This development he regarded as a significant loss for
social work—"destroying or remaining oblivious to powerful resources
and losing the insights religion provided in keeping wholesome attitudes toward individuals" and "preserving the sanity and health in the
social worker's own outlook upon life" (p. 9). He believed social workers needed, therefore, a renewed sense of vocation or calling. In addition, this loss of calling partially contributes to what church historian
Martin Marty (1980) later referred to as "godless social service," or the
migration (privatization) of faith or spirituality from social work.

Conclusion

Because of our distance from the thoughts and assumptions of our
predecessors in social work and perhaps from the language of spirituality itself, efforts regarding such historical reflections as these may seem
awkward and archaic. The goal is not, however, to recreate the past, but
rather to identify the models of spirituality that guided our social work
ancestors and then to find ways to translate and apply the spirit of these
models to our present situation.

This model of calling offers significant insight into current discussions relating spirituality and professional social work practice. Within
this calling model, religious faith is not the private possession of an
individual, but is grounded in tradition and divine revelation, permeat-
ing the whole of life, connecting public and private spheres, and linking
the individual with the community. The model also places professional
techniques and methods in the context of larger goals and values that
give life meaning and purpose for both clients and practitioners.

Historically, religiously motivated persons and groups found their
faith propelling them into actions of concern for others, especially the
poor and the vulnerable in society. These social workers have affirmed
in a variety of ways their shared belief that the faith dimension of life
leads to a transcendence of individualism, and to a commitment to others—to social work practice motivated by a calling to a life of service.

The model presented is helpful to social workers from the Christian faith tradition, but also to others who seek to acquire a better understanding of the meaning and effects of spirituality in their own and
their clients' lives. A social worker's own cultivation of spirituality is a
crucial preparation for the competent application of knowledge and skills
in practice. The model is particularly helpful in taking into account the
distinctive values, sources of power and master stories of one particular

religious and cultural tradition, Christianity—represented by many persons like Tessie and her grandmother whom social workers daily encounter in practice, as well as by many social workers themselves.

Although the model does not resolve the tensions and conflicts which exist between the Christian spiritual tradition and the current largely secular profession, it does provide a beginning framework for integrating Christian spirituality and social work at both the personal and professional levels. The profession's roots are significantly tied to this particular model of spiritual/professional integration, and many social workers as well as clients continue to define their lives, personally and professionally, in the context of this Christian-based spiritual call to service. The Christian values of love, justice, and kindness; its stories related to the poor, the vulnerable, and those of liberation from oppression; and its emphasis on self-sacrifice, are the "passion of the old time social workers" that many find attractive and wish to bring back—albeit in a form more adaptable to a more diverse clientele and changed environment (Constable, 1983; Gustafson, 1982; Reamer, 1992; Siporin, 1982, 1985; Specht & Courtney, 1994).

References

Augustine, Saint. (1950). *City of God.* XIX, 19, New York: Modern Library.

Brower, Irene. (1984). *The 4th Ear of the Spiritual-Sensitive Social Worker.* Ph.D. diss., Union for Experimenting Colleges and Universities.

Cabot, Richard C. (1927). The Inter-Relation of Social Work and the Spiritual Life. *The Family,* 8(7), 211-217.

Canda, Edward R. (1988a). Conceptualizing Spirituality for Social Work: Insights from Diverse Perspectives. *Social Thought,* Winter, 30-46.

Canda, Edward R. (1988b). Spirituality, Religious Diversity and Social Work Practice. *Social Casework,* April, 238-247.

Coles, Robert. (1993). *The Call of Service.* New York: Houghton Mifflin Company.

Constable, Robert. (1983). Religion, Values and Social Work Practice. *Social Thought,* 9, 29-41.

Devine, Edward T. (1939). *When Social Work Was Young.* New York: Macmillan Company.

Fowler, James W. (1981). *Stages of Faith.* San Francisco: Harper and Row.

Gustafson, James M. (1982). Professions as "Callings." *Social Service Review,* December, 105-515.

Huntington, James. (1893). Philanthropy and Morality. In Addams, Jane, (Ed.), *Philanthropy and Social Congress,* New York: Crowell.

Johnson, Ernest F. (1946). The Pattern and Philosophy of Protestant Social Work. *Church Conference of Social Work,* Buffalo, New York.

Leiby, James. (1985). Moral Foundations of Social Welfare and Social Work: A Historical View. *Social Work,* 30(4), 323-330.

Lovejoy, Owen R. (1920). The Faith of a Social Worker. *The Survey*, May, 208-211.

Marty, Martin E. (1980). Social Service: Godly and Godless. *Social Service Review*, 54, 463-481.

Niebuhr, Reinhold. (1932). *The Contribution of Religion to Social Work*. New York: Columbia University Press.

Reamer, Frederic G. (1992). Social Work and the Public Good: Calling or Career? In Reid, Nelson P. & Philip R. Popple (Eds.), *The Moral Purposes of Social Work*, (11-33), Chicago: Nelson-Hall.

Specht, Harry & Courtney, Mark. (1994). *Unfaithful Angels*. New York: The Free Press.

Siporin, Max. (1982). Moral Philosophy in Social Work Today. *Social Service Review*, December, 516-538.

Siporin, Max. (1983). Morality and Immorality in Working with Clients. *Social Thought*, Fall, 10-41.

Siporin, Max. (1985). Current Social Work Perspectives on Clinical Practice. *Clinical Social Work Journal*, 13, 198-217.

CHAPTER 8

THE RELATIONSHIP BETWEEN BELIEFS AND VALUES IN SOCIAL WORK PRACTICE: WORLDVIEWS MAKE A DIFFERENCE

David A. Sherwood

In some circles (including some Christian ones) it is fashionable to say that what we believe is not all that important. What we do is what really counts. I strongly disagree. The relationship between what we think and what we do is complex and it is certainly not a simple straight line, but it is profound. Social work values, practice theories, assessments, intervention decisions, and action strategies are all shaped by our worldview assumptions and our beliefs.

I believe that a Christian worldview will provide an interpretive framework which will solidly support and inform commonly held social work values such as the inherent value of every person regardless of personal characteristics, self-determination and personally responsible freedom of choice, and responsibility for the common good, including help for the poor and oppressed. And it will challenge other values and theories such as might makes right, exploitation of the weak by the strong, and extreme moral relativism. In contrast, many other worldviews, including materialism, empiricism, and postmodern subjectivism lead to other interpretations of the "facts."

Worldviews Help Us Interpret Reality

What is a "Worldview?"

Worldviews give faith-based answers to a set of ultimate and grounding questions. Everyone operates on the basis of some worldview or faith-based understanding of the universe and persons— examined, or unexamined, implicit or explicit, simplistic or sophisticated. One way or another, we develop functional assumptions which help us to sort through and make some sort of sense out of our experience. And every person's worldview will always have a faith-based component (even belief in an exclusively material universe takes faith). This does not mean worldviews are necessarily irrational, unconcerned with "facts," or impervious to critique and change (though they unfortunately might be). It matters greatly how conscious, reflective, considered, or informed our worldviews are. The most objectivity we can achieve is to be critically aware of our worldview and how it affects our interpretations of "the facts." It is far better to be aware, intentional, and informed regarding our worldview than to naively think we are (or anyone else is) objective or neutral or to be self-righteously led by our biases which we may think are simply self-evident truth.

These worldviews affect our approach to social work practice, how we understand and help people. What is the nature of persons—biochemical machines, evolutionary products, immortal souls, all of the above? What constitutes valid knowledge—scientific empiricism only, "intuitive" discernment, spiritual guidance (if so, what kind)? What kinds of social work theories and practice methods are legitimate? What are appropriate values and goals—what is healthy, functional, optimal, the good?

To put it another way, we all form stories that answer life's biggest questions. As I become a Christian, I connect my personal story to a much bigger story that frames my answers to these big questions. Middleton and Walsh (1995, p. 11) summarize the questions this way:

1. Where are we? What is the nature of the reality in which we find ourselves?
2. Who are we? What is the nature and task of human beings?
3. What's wrong? How do we understand and account for evil and brokenness?
4. What's the remedy? How do we find a path through our brokenness to wholeness?

Interpreting the Facts

"Facts" have no meaning apart from an interpretive framework. "Facts" are harder to come by than we often think, but even when we have some "facts" in our possession, they have no power to tell us what they mean or what we should do.

That human beings die is a fact. That I am going to die would seem to be a reliable prediction based on what I can see. In fact, the capacity to put those observations and projections together is one of the ways we have come to describe or define human consciousness. But what do these "facts" mean and what effect should they have on my life? One worldview might tell me that life emerged randomly in a meaningless universe and is of no particular value beyond the subjective feelings I may experience from moment to moment. Another worldview might tell me that somehow biological survival of life forms is of value and that I only have value to the extent that I contribute to that biological parade (with the corollary that survival proves fitness). Another worldview might tell me that life is a gift from a loving and just Creator and that it transcends biological existence, that death is not the end of the story. Different worldviews lend different meanings to the same "facts."

The major initial contribution of a Christian worldview to an understanding of social work values and ethical practice is not unique, contrasting, or one of conflicting values, but rather a solid foundation for the basic values that social workers claim and often take for granted (Holmes, 1984; Sherwood, 1993). Subsequently, a Christian worldview will shape how those basic values are understood and how they interact with one another. For example, justice will be understood in the light of God's manifest concern for the poor and oppressed, so it can never be only a procedurally "fair" protection of individual liberty and the right to acquire, hold, and transfer property (Lebacqz, 1986; Mott, 1982; Wolterstorff, 1983).

The Interaction of Feeling, Thinking, and Behavior

Persons are complex living ecological systems—to use a helpful conceptual model common in social work—systems of systems, if you will. Systems within our bodies and outside us as well interact in dynamic relationships with each other. For example, it is impossible to meaningfully separate our thinking, feeling, and behavior from each other and from the systems we experience outside ourselves, yet we quite properly think of ourselves as separate individuals. The lines of influence run in all directions. What we believe affects what we experience, including how we define our feelings. For example, does an experience I might have of being alone, in and of itself, *make* me feel lonely, or rejected, or exhilarated by freedom, for that matter? Someone trips me, but was it accidental or intentional? I have had sex with only one woman (my wife Carol) in over fifty years of life. How does this "make" me feel? Are my feelings not also a result of what I tell myself about the meaning of my experience? But it works the other way too.

All this makes us persons harder to predict. And it certainly makes it harder to assign neat, direct, and one-way lines of causality. The biblical worldview picture is that God has granted us (at great cost) the dignity and terror of contributing to causality ourselves through our own purposes, choices, and actions. We have used this freedom to our hurt, but this also means that we are not mechanistically determined and that significant change is always possible. And change can come from many directions—thinking, emotions, behavior, experience. We are especially (compared to other creatures) both gifted and cursed by our ability to think about ourselves and the world. We can form purposes and act in the direction of those purposes. Our beliefs about the nature of the world, other persons, and ourselves interact in a fundamental way with how we perceive reality, how we define our own identity, and how we act.

If this is true in our personal lives, it is equally true as we try to understand and help our clients in social work practice. And it is no less true for clients themselves. What we believe about the nature of the world, the nature of persons, and the nature of the human situation is at least as important as the sheer facts of the circumstances we experience.

Worldviews Help Construct Our Understanding of Values

Cut Flowers: Can Values Be Sustained Without Faith?

One significant manifestation of the notion that beliefs aren't all that important is the fallacy of our age which assumes that fundamental moral values can be justified and sustained apart from their ideological (ultimately theological) foundation. Take, for example, the fundamental Christian and social work belief that all human beings have intrinsic dignity and value.

Elton Trueblood, the Quaker philosopher, once described ours as a "cut-flower" generation. He was suggesting that, as it is possible to cut a rose from the bush, put it in a vase, and admire its fresh loveliness and fragrance for a short while, it is possible to maintain the dignity and value of every human life while denying the existence or significance of God as the source of that value. But the cut rose is already dead, regardless of the deceptive beauty which lingers for awhile. Even uncut, "The grass withers, and the flower falls, but the Word of the Lord endures forever" (I Peter 1:24-25).

Many in our generation, including many social workers, are trying to hold onto values—such as the irreducible dignity and worth of the individual—while denying the only basis on which such a value can ultimately stand. We should be glad they try to hold onto the value, but we should understand how shaky such a foundation is. A secular generation can live off its moral capital only so long before the impertinent questions (Why should we?) can no longer be ignored.

Doesn't Everybody "Just Know" That
Persons Have Dignity and Value?

But doesn't everybody "just know" that human beings have intrinsic value? You don't have to believe in God, do you? In fact, according to some, so-called believers in God have been among the worst offenders against the value and dignity of all persons (sadly true, in some cases). After all, a lot of folks, from secular humanists to rocket scientists to New Age witches to rock stars, have declared themselves as defenders of the value of the individual. Isn't the worth of the person just natural, or at least rational and logically required? The plain answer is, "No, it's *not* just natural or rational or something everyone just knows."

I received a striking wake-up call in regard to this particular truth a number of years ago when I was a freshman at Indiana University. I think the story is worth telling here. I can't help dating myself—it was in the spring of 1960, the time the Civil Rights movement was clearly emerging. We were hearing of lunch room sit-ins and Freedom Riders on buses. Through an older friend of mine from my home town I wound up spending the evening at the Student Commons talking with my friend and someone he had met, a graduate student from Iran named Ali. I was quite impressed. My friend Maurice told me his father was some sort of advisor to the Shah (the ruling despot at that point in Iran's history).

The conversation turned to the events happening in the South, to the ideas of racial integration, brotherhood, and social justice. Ali was frankly puzzled and amused that Maurice and I, and at least some other Americans, seemed to think civil rights were worth pursuing. But given that, he found it particularly hard to understand what he thought was the wishy-washy way the thing was being handled. "I don't know why you want to do it," he said," but if it's so important, why don't you just do it? If I were President of the United States and I wanted integration, I would do it in a week!" "How?" we asked. "Simple. I would just put a soldier with a machine gun on every street corner and say 'Integrate.' If they didn't, I would shoot them." (Believable enough, as the history of Iran has shown)

Naive freshman that I was, I just couldn't believe he was really saying that. Surely he was putting us on. You couldn't just do that to people. At least not if you were moral! The conversation-debate- argument went on to explore what he really did believe about the innate dignity and value of the individual human life and social responsibility. You don't just kill inconvenient people, do you? I would say things like, "Surely you believe that society has a moral responsibility to care for the widows and orphans, the elderly, the disabled, the emotionally disturbed." Incredibly (to me at the time), Ali's basic response was not to give an inch but to question *my* beliefs and values instead. "Society has no such moral responsibility," he said. "On the contrary. You keep talking about reason and morality. I'll tell you what is immoral. The rational person would say that the truly *immoral* thing is to take resources away from the strong and productive to give to the weak and useless. Useless members of society such as the disabled and mentally retarded should be eliminated, not maintained." He would prefer that the methods be "humane," but he really did mean eliminated.

It finally sunk into my freshman mind that what we were disagreeing about was not facts or logic, but the belief systems we were using to interpret or assign meaning to the facts. If I were to accept his assumptions about the nature of the universe (e.g. that there is no God—Ali was a thoroughly secular man; he had left Islam behind—that the material universe is the extent of reality, that self-preservation is the only given motive and goal), then his logic was flawless and honest. As far as he was concerned, the only thing of importance left to discuss would be the most effective means to gain and keep power and the most expedient way to use it.

In this encounter I was shaken loose from my naive assumption that "everybody knows" the individual person has innate dignity and value. I understood more clearly that unless you believed in the Creator, the notion that all persons are equal is, indeed, *not* self-evident. The Nazi policies of eugenics and the "final solution" to the "Jewish problem" make a kind of grimly honest (almost inevitable) sense if you believe in the materialist worldview.

The "Is-Ought" Dilemma

Not long afterward I was to encounter this truth much more cogently expressed in the writings of C. S. Lewis. In *The Abolition of Man* (1947) he points out that both the religious and the secular walk by faith if they try to move from descriptive observations of fact to any sort of value statement or ethical imperative. He says "From propositions about fact alone no *practical* conclusion can ever be drawn. 'This will preserve society' [let's assume this is a factually true statement] cannot lead to 'Do this' [a moral and practical injunction] except by the mediation of 'Society ought to be preserved' [a value statement]" (p. 43). "Society ought to be preserved" is a moral imperative which no amount of facts alone can prove or disprove. Even the idea of "knowing facts" involves basic assumptions (or faith) about the nature of the universe and human beings. The secular person (social worker?) tries to cloak faith by substituting words like natural, necessary, progressive, scientific, rational, or functional for "good," but the question always remains— For what end? and Why? And the answer to this question always smuggles in values from somewhere else besides the facts.

Even the resort to instincts such as self-preservation can tell us nothing about what we (or others) *ought* to do. Lewis (1947, p. 49) says:

We grasp at useless words: we call it the "basic," or "fundamental," or "primal," or "deepest" instinct. It is of no avail.
Either these words conceal a value judgment passed *upon* the
instinct and therefore not derivable *from* it, or else they merely
record its felt intensity, the frequency of its operation, and its
wide distribution. If the former, the whole attempt to base value
upon instinct has been abandoned: if the latter, these observations about the quantitative aspects of a psychological event
lead to no practical conclusion. It is the old dilemma. Either
the premise is already concealed an imperative or the conclusion remains merely in the indicative.

This is called the "Is-Ought" dilemma. Facts, even when attainable,
never have any practical or moral implications until they are interpreted
through the grid of some sort of value assumptions. "Is" does not lead to
"Ought" in any way that has moral bindingness, obligation, or authority
until its relationship to relevant values is understood. And you can't get the
values directly from the "Is." It always comes down to the question—what
is the source and authority of the "Ought" that is claimed or implied?

The social work Code of Ethics refers to values such as the inherent value of every person, the importance of social justice, and the obligation to fight against oppression. It is a fair question to ask where those
values come from and what gives them moral authority and obligation.

A Shaky Consensus: "Sexual Abuse" or "Intergenerational Sexual Experience?"

For an example of the "Is-Ought Dilemma," is child sexual abuse a
fact or a myth? Or what is the nature of the abuse? Child sexual abuse is
an example of an area where there may seem to be more of a consensus
in values than there actually is. In any event, it illustrates how it is
impossible to get values from facts alone. Some intervening concept of
"the good" always has to come into play.

Fact: Some adults have sexual relations with children. But so what?
What is the practical or moral significance of this fact? Is this something we should be happy or angry about? Is this good or bad? Sometimes good and sometimes bad? Should we be encouraging or discouraging the practice? Even if we could uncover facts about the consequences of the experience on children, we would still need a value framework to help us discern the meaning or practical implications of those
facts. And to have moral obligation beyond our own subjective preferences or biases, this value framework must have some grounding out-

side ourselves. What constitutes negative consequences? And even if we could agree certain consequences were indeed negative, the question would remain as to what exactly was the cause.

In the last few years there has been a tremendous outpouring of attention to issues of child sexual abuse and its effects on adult survivors. I must say that this is long overdue and much needed. And even among completely secular social workers, psychologists, and other therapists there currently appears to be a high degree of consensus about the moral wrong of adult sexual activity with children and the enormity of its negative consequences on the child at the time and in later life. As a Christian I am encouraged, especially when I recall the self-described "radical Freudian" professor I had in my master's in social work program who described in glowingly approving terms high levels of sexual intimacy between children and each other and children and adults as "freeing and liberating" (that was the early 1970's).

However, if I look more closely at the worldview faith underlying much of the discussion of sexual abuse and its effects, the result is not quite so comforting to me as a Christian. The moral problem tends not to be defined in terms of a well-rounded biblical view of sexuality and God's creative design and purpose or an understanding of the problem of sin. Rather, it tends to be based on a more rationalistic and individualistic model of power and a model of justice which pins its faith on reason. Sexual abuse grows out of an inequity in power which a person rationally "ought not" exploit. Why not, one might ask.

But what if we take away the coercive element and get rid of the repressive "body-negative" ideas about sexual feelings? What if much or all of the negative effects of non-coercive sexual activity between adults and children is the result of the misguided and distorted social attitudes which are passed on to children and adults? Defenders of non-exploitive sexual activity between adults and children can (and do) argue that any negative consequences are purely a result of sex-negative social learning and attitudes. Representatives of a hypothetical group such as P.A.L. (Pedophiles Are Lovers!) would argue that what needs to be changed is not the intergenerational sexual behavior, but the sexually repressive social values and behavior which teach children the negative responses. These values are seen as the oppressive culprits. Then, the argument might go, should we not bend our efforts to eradicating these repressive sexual values and attitudes rather than condemning potentially innocent acts of sexual pleasure? Indeed, why not, if the only problem is exploitation of power?

You should also note that this argument in favor of intergenerational sexual behavior is not exclusively scientific, objective, or based only on "facts." It has to make faith assumptions about the nature of persons, the nature of sexuality, the nature of health, and the nature of values. By the same token, my condemnation of adult sexual activity with children is based on faith assumptions about the nature of persons, sexuality, health, and values informed by my Christian worldview. It is never just "facts" alone which determine our perceptions, conclusions, and behavior.

Right now, it happens to be a "fact" that a fairly large consensus exists, even among secular social scientists and mental health professionals, that adult sexual activity with children is "bad" and that it leads quite regularly to negative consequences. Right now you could almost say this is something "everyone knows." But it would be a serious mistake to become complacent about this or to conclude that worldview beliefs and faith are not so important after all.

First, not everyone agrees. Although I invented the hypothetical group P.A.L. (Pedophiles Are Lovers), it represents real people and groups that do exist. The tip of this iceberg may be appearing in the professional literature where it is becoming more acceptable and common to see the "facts" reinterpreted. In preparing bibliography for a course on sexual issues in helping, I ran across a very interesting little shift in terminology in some of the professional literature. One article was entitled "Counterpoints: Intergenerational sexual experience or child sexual abuse" (Malz, 1989). A companion article was titled "Intergenerational sexual contact: A continuum model of participants and experiences" (Nelson, 1989). Words do make a difference.

Second, we shouldn't take too much comfort from the apparent agreement. It is sometimes built on a fragile foundation that could easily come apart. The fact that Christians find themselves in wholehearted agreement with many secular helping professionals, for example, that sexual activity between adults (usually male) and children (usually female) is exploitive and wrong may represent a temporary congruence on issues and strategy, much more so than fundamental agreement on the nature of persons and sexuality.

But back to the "Is-Ought" dilemma. The fact that some adults have sexual contact with children, by itself, tells us *nothing* about what, if anything, should be done about it. The facts can never answer those questions. The only way those questions can ever be answered is if we interpret the facts in terms of our faith, whatever that faith is. What is the nature of the world? What is the nature of persons? What is the meaning of sex? What constitutes health? What is the nature of justice? And most important—why should I care anyway?

Worldviews Help Define the Nature and Value of Persons

So—Worldviews Have Consequences

Your basic faith about the nature of the universe has consequences (and everyone, as we have seen, has some sort of faith). Faith is consequential to you personally and the content of the faith is consequential. If it isn't *true* that Christ has been raised, my faith is worthless (I Cor. 15:14). And if it's *true* that Christ has been raised, but I put my faith in Baal or the free market or the earth goddess (big in New England these days) or Karl Marx (not so big these days) or human reason, then *that* has consequences, to me and to others. What are we going to *trust*, bottom-line?

In I Corinthians 15, the apostle Paul said something about the importance of what we believe about the nature of the world, the *content* of our faith. He said, "Now if Christ is proclaimed as raised from the dead, how can some of you say there is no resurrection of the dead? If there is no resurrection of the dead, then Christ has not been raised; and if Christ has not been raised, then our proclamation has been in vain and your faith is also in vain . . . If Christ has not been raised, your faith is futile and you are still in your sins . . . If for this life only we have hoped in Christ, we are of all people most to be pitied" (12-14, 17, 19).

I've been a student, a professional social worker, and a teacher of social work long enough to see some major changes in "what everyone knows," in what is assumed or taken for granted. "What everyone knows" is in fact part of the underlying operational *faith* of a culture or subculture—whether it's Americans or teenagers or those who go to college or social workers — or Southern Baptists, for that matter.

When I went to college, logical positivism was king, a version of what C. S. Lewis called "naturalism," a kind of philosophical materialism. It said that the physical world is all there is. Everything is fully explainable by materialistic determinism. Only what can be physically measured or "operationalized" is real (or at least relevantly meaningful). In psychology it was epitomized in B. F. Skinner's behaviorism.

I remember as a somewhat bewildered freshman at Indiana University attending a lecture by a famous visiting philosophy professor (a logical positivist) from Cambridge University (whose name I have forgotten) entitled "The *Impossibility* of any Future Metaphysic" (his take-off on Kant's title "Prologomena to any Future Metaphysic"). I can't say I understood it all at the time, but his main point was that modern people must permanently put away such meaningless and potentially dangerous ideas as spirituality, the supernatural, and any notion of values beyond subjective preferences. We now know, he said, that such language is meaningless (since not empirical) except, perhaps, to express our own subjective feelings.

In a graduate school course in counseling, I had an earnest young behaviorist professor who had, as a good behaviorist, trained (conditioned) himself to avoid all value statements that implied good or bad or anything beyond personal preference. When faced with a situation where someone else might be tempted to make a value statement, whether regarding spaghetti, rock and roll, or adultery, he had an ideologically correct response. He would, with a straight face, say "I find that positively reinforcing" or, "I find that negatively reinforcing." (I don't know what his wife thought about this kind of response) Notice, he was saying "I" (who knows about you or anyone else) "find" (observe a response in myself at this moment; who knows about five minutes from now) "that" (a particular measurable stimulus) "positively reinforcing" (it elicits this particular behavior now and might be predicted to do it again).

Above all, the idea was to be totally scientific, objective, and *value-free*. After all, values were perceived to be purely relative, personal preferences, or (worse) prejudices induced by social learning. And "everyone knew" that the only thing real was physical, measurable, and scientific. If we could only get the "facts" we would know what to do.

But this was, and is, a fundamental fallacy, the "Is-Ought" fallacy we discussed earlier. Even if facts are obtainable, they have no moral power or direction in themselves. If we say they mean something it is because we are interpreting them in the context of some values which are a part of our basic faith about the nature of the world.

Shifting Worldviews: The Emperor Has No Clothes

In the meantime we have seen some rather amazing shifts in "what everyone knows." I am old enough to have vivid memories of the 1960's and the "greening of America" when "everybody knew" that people under 30 were better than people over 30 and that human beings are so innately good all we had to do was to scrape off the social conventions and rules and then peace, love, and total sharing would rule the world. An astounding number of people truly believed that—for a short time.

In the '70s and early '80s "everybody knew" that personal autonomy and affluence are what it is all about. Power and looking out for Number One became the articles of faith, even for helping professionals like social workers. Maximum autonomy was the obvious highest good. Maturity and health were defined in terms of not needing anyone else (and not having any obligation to anyone else either). Fritz Perls "Gestalt Prayer" even got placed on romantic greeting cards:

I do my thing, and you do your thing.
I am not in this world to live up to your expectations.
And you are not in this world to live up to mine.
You are you and I am I,
And if by chance we find each other, it's beautiful.
If not, it can't be helped.

If you care too much, you are enmeshed, undifferentiated, or at the very least co-dependent.

And here we are at the turning of the millennium and, at least for awhile, it looks as though values are in. Time magazine has had cover stories on ethics. Even more amazing, philosophy professors and social workers are not embarrassed to talk about values and even character again. 'Family Values' are avowed by the Republicans and Democrats. The books and articles are rolling off the presses.

But we should not be lulled into a false sense of security with this recovery of values and ethics, even if much of it sounds quite Christian to us. The philosophical paradigm has shifted to the opposite extreme, from the modern faith in the rational and empirical to the postmodern faith in the radically subjective and relative, the impossibility of getting beyond our ideological and cultural horizons. Our culture now despairs of any knowledge beyond the personal narratives we make up for ourselves out of the flotsam of our experience and fragments of disintegrating culture (Middleton & Walsh, 1995). Postmodernism says each person pieces together a personal story through which we make sense out of our lives, but there is no larger story (meta-narrative) which is really true in any meaningful sense and which can bind our personal stories together.

It is remarkable, as we have seen, how rapidly some of these assumptions can shift. The seeming consensus may be only skin-deep. More importantly, unless these values are grounded on something deeper than the currently fashionable paradigm (such as a Christian worldview), we can count on the fact that they will shift, or at least give way when they are seriously challenged. It's amazing how easy it is to see that the emperor has no clothes when a different way of looking is introduced to the scene. Remember both enlightenment empiricism and postmodern subjectivity agree that values have no transcendent source.

What Is a "Person?"

Controversies regarding abortion and euthanasia illustrate the profound consequences of our worldview faith, especially for worldviews which deny that values have any ultimate source. Even more fundamental than the question of when life begins and ends is the question what is a person? What constitutes being a person? What value, if any, is there in being a person? Are persons owed any particular rights, respect, or care? If so, why?

If your worldview says that persons are simply the result of matter plus time plus chance, it would seem that persons have no intrinsic value at all, no matter how they are defined. From a purely materialist point of view, it may be interesting (to us) that the phenomena of human consciousness and agency have emerged which allow us in some measure to transcend simple biological, physical, and social determinism. These qualities might include the ability to be self-aware, to remember and to anticipate, to experience pleasure and pain, to develop caring relationships with others, to have purposes, to develop plans and take deliberate actions with consequences, and to have (at least the illusion of) choice. We may choose to define personhood as incorporating some of these characteristics. And we may even find it positively reinforcing (or not) to be persons. But then what? In this materialist worldview there are no inherent guidelines or limits regarding what we do to persons.

Do such persons have a right to life? Only to the extent it pleases us (whoever has the power) to say so. And what in the world could "right" mean in this context? But what if we do choose to say that persons have a right to life. What degree or quality of our defining characteristics do they have to have before they qualify? How self-conscious and reflective? How capable of choice and action?

It is common for people to argue today that babies aren't persons before they are born (or at least most of the time before they are born) and thus that there is no moral reason for not eliminating defective ones, or even just unwanted or inconvenient ones. And there are already those who argue that babies should not even be declared potential persons until they have lived long enough after birth to be tested and observed to determine their potential for normal growth and development, thus diminishing moral qualms about eliminating wrongful births. After all, what is magic about the birth process? Why not wait for a few hours, days, or weeks after birth to see if this "fetal material" is going to measure up to our standards of personhood? And at any point in life if our personhood fails to develop adequately or gets lost or seriously diminished through accident, illness, mental illness, or age, what then? Was my college acquaintance Ali right? Is it immoral to take resources from the productive and use them to support the unproductive? Do these "fetal products" or no-longer-persons need to be terminated?

A Solid Foundation

If I balk at these suggestions, it is because I have a worldview that gives a different perspective to the idea of what constitutes a person. I may agree, for example, that agency—the capacity to be self-aware, reflective, remember and anticipate, plan, choose, and responsibly act—is a central part of what it means to be a person. But I also believe that this is a gift from our creator God which in some way images God. I believe that our reflection, choice, and action have a divinely given purpose. This purpose is summarized in the ideas of finding and choosing God through grace and faith, of growing up into the image of Jesus Christ, of knowing and enjoying God forever. All of this says that persons have a special value beyond their utility to me (or anyone else) and that they are to be treated with the care and respect befitting their status as gifts from God. Even when something goes wrong.

Having a Christian worldview and knowing what the Bible says about God, the world, and the nature of persons doesn't always give us easy answers to all of our questions, however. And having faith in the resurrection of Jesus Christ doesn't guarantee that we will always be loving or just. But it does give us a foundation of stone to build our house on, a context to try to understand what we encounter that will not shift with every ideological or cultural season. I can assert the dignity and worth of every person based on a solid foundation, not just an irrational preference of my own or a culturally-induced bias that I might happen to have. What "everybody knows" is shifting sand. Even if it happens to be currently stated in the NASW Code of Ethics for social workers.

Some Basic Components of a Christian Worldview

Space does not permit me to develop a detailed discussion of the components of a Christian worldview here, but I would at least like to try to summarize in the most basic and simple terms what I perceive to be quite middle-of-the-road, historically orthodox, and biblical answers to the fundamental worldview questions I posed at the beginning (cf. Middleton & Walsh, 1995). This suggests the Christian worldview that has informed me and has been (I would hope) quite evident in what has been said. This little summary is not the end of reflection and application, but only the beginning.

1. *Where are we?* We are in a universe which was created by an eternal, omnipotent, just, loving, and gracious God. Consequently the universe has built-in meaning, purpose, direction, and values. The fun-

damental values of love and justice have an ultimate source in the nature of God which gives them meaning, authority, and content. The universe is both natural and supernatural.

2. *Who are we?* We are persons created "in the image God" and there-fore with intrinsic meaning and value regardless of our personal char-acteristics or achievements. Persons are both physical and spiritual. Persons have been given the gift of "agency"– in a meaningful sense we have been given both freedom and responsibility. Persons created in the image of God are not just autonomous individuals but are rela-tional–created to be in loving and just community with one another. Persons are objects of God's grace.

3. *What's wrong?* Oppression and injustice are evil, wrong, an affront to the nature and desire of God. Persons are finite and fallen–we are both limited in our capacities and distorted from our ideal purpose because of our selfishness and choice of evil. Our choice of selfish-ness and evil alienates us from God and from one another and sets up distortion in our perceptions, beliefs, and behavior, but we are not completely blind morally. Our self-centeredness makes us prone to seek solutions to our problems based on ourselves and our own abili-ties and accomplishments. We can't solve our problems by ourselves, either by denial or our own accomplishments.

4. *What's the remedy?* Stop trying to do it our way and accept the loving grace and provisions for healing that God has provided for us. God calls us to a high moral standard but knows that it is not in our reach to accomplish. God's creative purpose is to bring good even out of evil, to redeem, heal, and grow us up–not by law but by grace. "For by grace you have been saved through faith, and this is not your own doing; it is the gift of God–not the result of works, so that no one may boast. For we are what he has made us, created in Christ Jesus for good works, which God prepared beforehand to be our way of life." (Ephesians 2:8-10)

Why Should I Care? Choosing a Christian Worldview

Moral Obligation and Faith: Materialism Undermines Moral Obligation

To abandon a theological basis of values, built into the universe by God, is ultimately to abandon the basis for any "oughts" in the sense of being morally bound other than for purely subjective or cultural rea-sons. Normative morality that is just descriptive and cultural (This is what most people in our society tend to do), subjective (This is what I happen to prefer and do or It would be convenient for me if you would do this), or utilitarian (This is what works to achieve certain consequences) has no power of moral *obligation*. Why should I care? On materialist or subjective grounds I "should" do this or that if I happen to feel like it or if I think it will help me get what I want. But this is using the word "should" in a far different and far more amoral sense than we ordinarily mean. It is a far different thing than saying I am *morally obligated or bound* to do it.

Many will argue that reason alone is enough to support moral obligation. This is the argument used by Frederic Reamer in his excellent book on social work ethics, *Ethical dilemmas in social services* (1990), based on Gewirth (*Reason and morality*, 1978). If, for example, I understand that freedom is logically required for human personal action, then this theory says I am logically obligated to support freedom for other persons as I desire it for myself. But I have never been able to buy the argument that reason alone creates any meaningful moral obligation for altruistic behavior. Why *should* I be logical, especially if being logical doesn't appear to work for my personal advantage? Any idea of moral obligation beyond the subjective and personally utilitarian seems to lead inevitably and necessarily to God in some form or to nowhere.

The "Method of Comparative Difficulties"

Although it is logically possible (and quite necessary if you believe in a materialist universe) to believe that values are only subjective preferences or cultural inventions, I have never been able to completely believe that is all our sense of values such as love and justice amounts to. There are, in all honesty, many obstacles in the way of belief in God as the transcendent source of values. But can we believe, when push comes to shove, that all values are either meaningless or totally subjective? Elton Trueblood calls this the "Method of Comparative Difficulties" (1963, p. 73; 1957, p. 13).

It may often be hard to believe in God, but I find it even harder to believe in the alternatives, especially when it comes to values. It's easy enough to say that this or that value is only subjective or culturally relative, but when we get pushed into a corner, most of us find ourselves saying (or at least *feeling*), "No, *that* (say, the Holocaust) is really wrong and it's not just my opinion." (Cf. C. S. Lewis, "Right and Wrong As a Clue to the Meaning of the Universe," *Mere Christianity*, 1948)

Dostoevski expressed the idea that if there is no God, all things are permissible. C. S. Lewis (1947, pp. 77-78) said that "When all that says 'it is good' has been debunked, what says 'I want' remains. It cannot be exploded or 'seen through' because it never had any pretensions." Lust remains after values have been explained away. Values that withstand the explaining away process are the only ones that will do us any good. Lewis concludes *The abolition of man* (1947, p. 91):

You cannot go on "explaining away" for ever: you will find that you have explained explanation itself away. You cannot go on "seeing through" things for ever. The whole point of seeing through something is to see something through it. It is good that the window should be transparent, because the street or garden beyond it is opaque. How if you saw through the garden too? It is no use trying to "see through" first principles. If you see through everything, then everything is transparent. But a wholly transparent world is an invisible world. To "see through" all things is the same as not to see.

Seeing Through a Mirror Dimly:
Real Values But Only a Limited, Distorted View

So, I believe in God as the ultimate source and authenticator of values. I believe that real values exist beyond myself. And I believe these values put us under real moral obligation. To believe otherwise, it seems to me, ultimately makes values and moral obligation empty shells, subjective and utilitarian, with no real life or content. It may be true that this is all values are, but I find it very hard to believe. Belief in a value-less world, or one with only "human" (that is to say, purely subjective) values, takes more faith for me than belief in God.

But (and this is very important) this understanding of values as having ultimate truth and deriving from God is a very far cry from believing that I fully comprehend these values and the specific moral obligations they put me under in the face of a particular moral dilemma when these values come into tension with one another and priorities have to be made. Much humility is required here, an appropriate balance. At any given moment, my (or your) understanding of these values and what our moral obligations are is very limited and distorted. In fact our understandings are in many ways subjective, culturally relative, and bounded by the interpretive "language" available to us. And any particular place where I can stand to view a complex reality at best only yields a partial view of the whole. Remember the story of the blind men and the elephant ("It's like a snake," "It's like a wall," "It's like a tree").

We can see, but only dimly. God has given us light but we will only be able to see completely when we meet God face to face (I Cor. 13:8-13). In the meantime we are on a journey. We are pilgrims, but we are not wandering alone and without guidance. We see through a mirror dimly, but there is something to see. There is a garden beyond the window.

Love never ends. But as for prophecies, they will come to an end; as for tongues, they will cease; as for knowledge, it will come to an end. For we know only in part, and we prophesy only in part; but when the complete comes, the partial will come to an end. When I was a child, I spoke like a child, I thought like a child, I reasoned like a child; when I became an adult, I put an end to childish ways. For now we see in a mirror, dimly, but then we will see face to face. Now I know only in part; then I will know fully, even as I have been fully known. And now faith, hope, love abide, these three; and the greatest of these is love. (I Corinthians 13:8-13)

> Now we have received not the spirit of the world, but the Spirit that is from God, so that we may understand the gifts bestowed on us by God. And we speak of these things in words not taught by human wisdom but taught by the Spirit, interpreting spiritual things to those who are spiritual. Those who are unspiritual do not receive the gifts of God's Spirit, for they are foolishness to them, and they are not able to understand them because they are spiritually discerned. Those who are spiritual discern all things, but they are themselves subject to no one else's scrutiny. "For who has known the mind of the Lord so as to instruct him?" But we have the mind of Christ. (I Corinthians 2:12-16)

Now the Lord is the Spirit, and where the Spirit of the Lord is, there is freedom. And all of us, with unveiled faces, seeing the glory of the Lord as though reflected in a mirror, are being transformed into the same image from one degree of glory to another; for this comes from the Lord, the Spirit. (II Corinthians 3:17-18)

References

Gewirth, Alan. (1978). *Reason and morality*. Chicago: University of Chicago Press.

Homes, Arthur. (1984). *Ethics: Approaching moral decisions*. Downers Grove, IL: InterVarsity Press.

Lebacqz, Karen. (1986). *Six theories of justice: Perspectives from philosophical and theological ethics*. Minneapolis, MN: Augsburg Publishing House.

Lewis, C. S. (1947). *The abolition of man*. New York: Macmillan Publishing Company.

Lewis, C. S. (1948). *Mere Christianity*. New York: Macmillan Publishing Company.

Malz, Wendy. (1989). Counterpoints: Intergenerational sexual experience or child sexual abuse. *Journal of Sex Education and Therapy, 15*, 13-15.

Middleton, J. Richard & Walsh, Brian J. (1995). *Truth is stranger than it used to be: Biblical faith in a post-modern age*. Downers Grove, IL: InterVarsity Press.

Mott, Stephen. (1982). *Biblical ethics and social change*. New York: Oxford University Press.

Nelson, J. A. (1989). Intergenerational sexual contact: A continuum model of participants and experiences. *Journal of Sex Education and Therapy*, 15, 3-12.

Reamer, Frederic. (1990). *Ethical dilemmas in social service*. 2nd Ed. New York: Columbia University Press.

Sherwood, David A. (1993). Doing the right thing: Ethical practice in contemporary society. *Social Work and Christianity*, 20(2), 140-159.

Trueblood, David Elton. (1963). *General philosophy*. New York: Harper and Row.

Trueblood, David Elton. (1957). *Philosophy of religion*. New York: Harper and Row.

Wolterstorff, Nicholas. (1983). *When justice and peace embrace*. Grand Rapids, MI: Eerdmans Publishing Company.

CHAPTER 9

BATTLE BETWEEN SIN AND LOVE IN SOCIAL WORK HISTORY

Katherine Amato-von Hemert
Editorial Assistance, Anisa Cottrell

Is it heresy to discuss "sin" and "love" in the context of social work? Most social workers believe it is. This chapter, however, argues that it is impossible to understand the history of social work without understanding the pivotal roles that attitudes toward sin and love played in the founding institutions, actors and actions of American social work. Religiously-trained leaders dominated the pioneer decades of social work (Leiby, 1984). American social work is indebted to two social movements which straddled the launch of the twentieth century: the Charity Organization Society (COS) movement and the Social Settlement movement. Religious ideas influenced both primary threads of historical social work. The COS writings regarding human nature tend to emphasize the role of sin and the need to cultivate morally uplifting habits to combat it. Late nineteenth and early twentieth century Protestantism struggled with the influence of Calvinist Puritanism. Among the most liberal of these Puritans were the Unitarians, who counted among their members social leaders Josephine Shaw Lowell and Joseph Tuckerman. Social Settlement movement writings tend to emphasize the role of love in human relations and focus on the goal of creating an ideal community. Early twentieth century Protestant social gospel theology influenced many Settlement leaders, such as Graham Taylor and Robert Woods. The social work techniques that emerged from both movements are, in revised form, still apparent in contemporary social work. The COS legacy includes the individual-focused work of casework and clinical practice. The Settlement tradition spawned community organizing and group work. Social work technologies from both traditions grew from particular theologies.

The differences and conflicts between the Christian theologies of these two foundational social work movements will be discussed. The Puritan-based theology and the social gospel-based theologies are examined. These beliefs are explicitly and implicitly revealed in the documents written by social activists of the late nineteenth century and early twentieth century. In the 1930's, Protestant social critic and theologian Reinhold Niebuhr critiqued social work. His insights synthesize the schism between the love-based and sin-based competing visions of social work. Listen to the voices of those early social workers who sought to cure personal and social "ills." References to sin, love and justice are unmistakable in them.

Why are these issues relevant to social workers now? They are important because these same divergent understandings of human nature and of God's action in the world operate in the language that modern day social workers use to discuss social problems and to justify practice and policy decisions. By elucidating the theological concepts of "sin" and "love" as held by some of the diverse mothers and fathers of our profession, we can understand better how these same concepts affect our work as social workers today.

Sin

The idea of sin is relevant to the dispute between the Charity Organization Society movement and the Social Settlement movement because one of the hallmark differences between these groups' perspectives arose from their divergent beliefs about sin.

Charity Organization Society Perspective on Sin

The concept of "sin" has been defined in many ways. Sin can be conceptualized as individual, willful acts that are contrary to the will of God. It can also be viewed as a general state of alienation from God. This later perspective focuses less on human action and more on the human state of being. Many of the more liberal COS movement leaders were influenced by a form of Puritan theology which rejected the Calvinist doctrine of predestination.[1] This doctrine of predestination maintained that all people are sinful and thereby bring Divine wrath upon themselves. Some people are saved, not through their own merit but through God's love and mercy. In this way of thinking, everyone "deserves" damnation and salvation occurs through God's mercy. Adamantly against the idea that one can attain salvation through works, "works righteous", adherents of this doctrine believed that a person's eternal fate was sealed with Adam's fall. Viewing sinfulness as an ingrained and intractable personality trait logically results from these beliefs. Many charity leaders, however, felt that people could improve their situation, both on earth and in life after death. Their belief, called "Arminianism," originated during the Protestant Reformation as a reaction to the Calvinist doctrines of original sin and predestination. By embracing Arminianism, C.O.S. leaders affirmed the belief that people, regardless of their environment, could improve their situation, build their character, and work toward salvation through reforming their life.

The sin-related issue for these COS leaders included three significant features — attitudes toward character, attitudes toward salvation and particular images of poverty. Charity Organization leadership believed that people were born morally neutral; they were intrinsically neither good nor bad. They were born with the capacity to shape their own character and thus had a moral obligation to self-improvement. These Puritans trained their attention on habits and disposition. They believed bad habits enslaved the sinner to his/her vices, while good habits protected him/her against temptations. "Once a sinner had started down the path of bad habits, it was nearly impossible for him to return to the path of rectitude." This moral philosophy maintained an implicit tendency "to classify people as 'good' or 'bad'" (Howe, 1988, p. 111). At the same time, consistent with earlier forms of Puritanism, these leaders "judged men on the basis of their disposition rather than their deeds, their character rather than their individual acts. Character was hard to develop and not easy to change" (Howe, 1988, p. 111). Thus, the issue of salvation was of paramount importance. Unlike predestinarian theology, Arminianism contended that individuals had the freedom to work out their own salvation (Howe, 1988, p. 68). The conscience was autonomous and therefore needed to be trained to regulate the passions. Self-mastery was the aim of these training efforts.

> Sin consisted in a breakdown of internal harmony, an abdication by the higher faculties of their dominion over the lower. No longer was sinfulness considered inherent in the human condition; instead, it was an abnormal state of disorder, 'the abuse of a noble nature.' Sin represented a failure to regulate impulses that were not in themselves evil. (Howe, 1988, p. 60-61)

Individuals were charged with the responsibility to foster good habits to protect against sinfulness and to exonerate themselves for sinful actions.

The prevalent attitudes toward poverty of this time were derived from widespread beliefs about the human person and about salvation. Most nineteenth century Americans believed that poverty was the result of sinfulness or laziness. Poverty was viewed as either an act of God's punishment, or as a result of the individual's disposition or habits. The goal of charity was to teach the poor morally uplifting habits which would cause them to love and seek virtue. Tuckerman maintained, "the best resources for improving the condition of the poor are *within themselves,* they often need enlightenment respecting these resources more than alms." Regardless of whether poverty was punishment for sinfulness or the result of the individual's propensities, "the conditions of poverty could lead to sin" so Christians were obligated to help the poor improve their economic condition (Howe, 1988, p. 240).[2] "Charity was intended to reform and uplift the poor, not merely to mitigate their sufferings" (Howe, 1988, p. 239). Indiscriminate almsgiving was considered dangerous because alms were believed to "encourage indolence and wastefulness." Rationally disciplined educational approaches were "intended to be judicious and discriminating, designed to get to the root of problems" (Howe, 1988, p. 240). These perspectives on the individual, sin and poverty resulted in a moralistic charity.

The COS theology of sin provides additional insight into the expectations and hopes of the charity programs designed to serve the poor. Giving to the poor person "a friend not alms" makes sense when it is understood in the context of the belief that individuals needed to foster good habits to stave off sinfulness and to learn the love of virtue. Good habits could be taught within the relationship nurtured between a "friendly visitor" and an impoverished person. The assumption that poverty in some way resulted from sin leads reasonably to the conclusion that the development of virtue would eradicate poverty. This reading of the COS is not especially novel. What is of greater importance is consideration of its long term implications — the COS legacy.

Mary Richmond articulated the theory of social casework within the context of this COS theology.[3] Social casework placed particular importance on service to the individual, on social investigation and on the caseworker-client relationship.[4] All of these techniques assumed that sin plays a pivotal role in human nature. The priority attention given to the individual derived from the COS leaders' Arminian beliefs. Cultivating self-improvement was necessary because salvation resulted from individual effort. Social investigation was the practice of interviewing neighbors, family members and employers of potential service recipients in order to generate a detailed profile of need. This derived both from the rationalism of the theology as well as from the expectation that individuals in need may not necessarily be truthful about the specifics of their situation. One of the staunchest arguments on behalf of organizing the charity societies into COS's was the belief that fraud was rampant and duplication of requests for assistance could be reduced by greater communication among charity organizations.

Finally, the healing relationship between caseworker and client derived from the expectation that moral uplift is best achieved at close quarters. Accountability played an important role in this relationship and was therefore as much an opportunity for the caseworker to monitor and point out client's "bad habits" as well as for the client to learn good ones. These techniques, influenced by an understanding of the individual as a sinful being, have been passed down to contemporary social work (with modifications of course). Social casework's emphasis on service to the individual now holds a dominant position in current clinical social work practice. Its assumptions regarding human nature warrant closer attention; they may illuminate the current debates in the profession between those who seek to assist individuals psychotherapeutically versus those who engage in social reform. This line of inquiry may lead to additional insights when applied to the Social Settlement theology as well. Social Settlement leaders rejected many of these assumptions and created alternative institutions aimed to address social conditions of poverty. As in the case of the COS leaders, Settlement leaders had theological reasons for doing so. Contrary to the COS leaders, these Settlement advocates were more compelled by a theology focused on love rather than on one based on sin. This does not mean, however, that the Settlement leaders held no opinion on sin. The Social Settlement perspective on sin is just more difficult to tease out from within the overall love-focused sensibility.

Social Settlement Movement Perspective on Sin

The social gospel movement was an American religious phenomenon prominent during the early decades of the twentieth century. It aimed to move society toward a vision of justice; toward the incarnation of the "kingdom of God" on Earth. Its adherents focused more on societal reform and less on individual salvation. Social work practice which was influenced by social gospel theology acknowledged the existence of sin but viewed it as embedded within social relations which were subject to political, social and/or economic reform. A person who might have been seen by the COS leaders as "sinful" or in need of character reform was seen through the lens of the social gospel as a person at the mercy of an unjust, sinful society. The social environment caused people to receive fewer choices or to make unwise decisions. It is difficult to find explicit references to sin among Social Settlement writings and social gospel writings regarding social work. This theology's concern centered on issues of love; God's love for humanity, and our consequent love for one another. The individual was understood to be primarily defined by the social group (family, neighborhood, church or synagogue, industrial organization, etc.).

The most explicit shift in theological focus can be seen in the writings of the Anglican couple, Henrietta and Samuel Barnett. Prior to founding England's Toynbee Hall, the Barnetts were active in organized charity efforts. They became disenchanted and critical of the literal, evangelical appeals associated with the Charity Organization Societies. In 1882 Henrietta criticized the C.O.S.'s "materialist" reification of sin and hell and charged that, "religion has been degraded by these teachers until it is difficult to gain the people's ears to hear it" (Barnett, 1895a, p. 91). Within two years, her critique of the COS orientation included stronger appeals to the role love must play in charity and from then on, discussion of love received greater emphasis than attention to sin in all her writings. Her concern shifted to those charity workers who "fear the devil more than they love God; or, in other words, they fear to do harm more than they love to do good" and she claimed "personally, I doubt if anything but love for God will mean social reform" (Barnett, 1895b, p. 213, 219).

Graham Taylor, the founder of the Chicago Commons, a 100 year old social settlement house, is representative of the Social Settlement pioneers. In his first book, *Religion in Social Action* (1913), Taylor referred to sin fewer than one dozen times. If sin was an important dimension of Taylor's understanding of human character, his chapter, "Personality: a Social Product and Force," would refer to it. It does not. This omission is suggestive. In commenting upon the changes in Christian thought of the time, he noted that "the individual and the race are coming to be more inseparable in our consciousness of both sin and salvation" (Taylor, 1913, p. 97). Sin was viewed not as a feature of an individual's character or destiny but as a consequence of environmental influences. Salvation's goal "is more closely brought to bear upon turning the self from sin" (Taylor, 1913, p. 91) in order to train focus upon the promise of the Kingdom on earth. Sin was seen primarily as evil events spawned by evil circumstance.[5] This emphasis on the social leads to the assertion that "more and more men need to be convicted of and turned away from their social, industrial, and political sins, in order to be made conscious of and penitent for their personal sins" (Taylor, 1913, p. 100).

Walter Rauschenbusch, "the acknowledged professorial leader" of the social gospel movement (Marty, 1986, p. 288), spoke of those whom social workers serve as peoples who "have gone astray like lost sheep" (Rauschenbusch, 1912, p. 30). These are not people with sinful natures, they are people who have merely stepped off the path of righteousness. He spoke of the sacrifice and suffering intrinsic to social work's service to humanity with reference to the crucifixion of Jesus, claiming, "without the shedding of blood in some form there has never been cessation of sin"

(Rauschenbusch, 1912, p. 27). Above all, Rauschenbusch focused on the redemptive task and nature of social work (Rauschenbusch, 1912, p. 12-13, 26-27). A measure of the close linkage between social work and social religion at the beginning of this century comes from this text which to late twentieth century ears is quite shocking: "Social workers are in the direct line of apostolic succession. Like the Son of Man they seek and save the lost" (Rauschenbusch, 1912, p. 12). This pattern is consistent throughout the social gospel social work literature. The primary focus is on the social nature of individual life and whatever minimal references to sin that exist are located within this type of context. The concept of "social sin," as reflected in Taylor's statement above, fleetingly appears occasionally, though it is not fully developed. Conceptualizing sin was less important to the development of the Social Settlement movement. Social Settlement leaders emphasized love; something that the COS leaders did to a much lesser degree.

Love

It is also helpful to explore the contrasting perspectives on love found in writings from Charity Organization Society leaders with those found among Social Settlement movement leaders. COS leaders tended to view love as a remedy for evil while Social Settlement leaders discussed love in terms of both its personal expression and social necessity.

Charity Organization Society Perspective on Love

In 1890, Charles Stewart Loch reflected on the first twenty years of England's Charity Organization Society movement. He claimed, the "new movement," was vigorously dedicated to serve the best interests of the State, the stability of which was threatened by the existence of pauperism. "The new charity does not seek material ends, but to create a better social and individual life" (Loch, 1892, p. 6). Of the three forces at work in the new movement—a stronger sense of citizenship, a renewed commitment to remind the rich of their community obligations and a deepening religious consciousness—discussion of the need for a change in religious consciousness took precedence. Loch argued,

> Yet [religious communities'] efforts to improve the general conditions of the life of the poor were often but *feeble and transient*. Their charity was *not allied to any wider conception of citizenship*. It was too often, perhaps, the hopeless push and protest of the saint against the evils of a hopeless world, where he

had no abiding place; and then, *if zeal grew cold, it found a sufficient expression in a charity from which love had evaporated, and which was no better than the payment of a toll on the high road of life* (Loch, 1892, p. 7-8, emphasis added).

Loch criticized the instability of emotionally motivated charity. Charity motivated by mere sentiment, he claimed, is isolated from the larger concerns of "citizenship," undependable because "transient," and when its religious passion "grows cold," it is merely the scattering of coins among bystanders. The COS intent, therefore, was to improve upon such efforts by creating scientifically based systems of moral support which express commitment to a higher order of love. This love is a disciplined one. It demands development of virtuous habits. "The social life implies discipline. This may spring from habits grown almost instinctively and handed down from the past like heirlooms. . . .Or the discipline may be newly imposed in order to brace the individual, or the family, or the nation, to a new endeavor" (Loch, 1904, p. 190).

The love that motivated the COS enterprise assumed moral defect among the poor had to be uplifted. Reverend D.O. Kellogg, an advocate of "scientific charity" and organizing charity societies, addressed this issue in the *Journal of the American Social Science Association* in 1880.

Defective classes are not a social evil; but pauperism is, and it is a sign of moral weakness. The weak and depressed, and *all the victims of unsocial habits, need to be awakened to a proper love of approbation from their fellow men, to have their hearts kindled* to a sympathetic glow by neighborliness and respect; to be quickened to hope by examples among their associates of courage, versatility and self-reliance; to see a world of pleasure and honor opened to them in the companionship of the refined and the pure-souled. *To these add suitable industrial training; but without the other this will be of small avail.* (Kellogg, 1880, p.89, emphasis added)

"Industrial training" without moral regeneration was considered ineffective. Love's primary implications are personal rather than social. The "victims of unsocial habits" needed to learn or re-learn *love of virtue*. Kellogg was not interested in the charity worker's expression of love, or in charity as such, as an expression of love. Love may have motivated charitable action but it was primarily a redemptive ideal. As such, it entailed certain demands. These lead Kellogg to envision a relationship between love and science.

In Kellogg's view, the practice of charity must be scientific, not only to achieve greater effectiveness but because it is required by "the law of love" which is its originating impulse.

> Charity has its laws which can only be detected by a study of past experience. It is, therefore, a science,—the science of social therapeutics. Again, as art is the application of science, *it follows that there can be no true art of charity until its laws are formulated.* Until this is done, benevolence is not much else but quackery, however amiable its motive. Indeed *the true impulse of love cannot rest until it has found its science;* for it cannot stop short of effective methods and sound principles. (Kellogg, 1880, p. 86, emphasis added)

Love in this perspective, motivated not the particular practice of a single or collective group of charity workers—love was an ideal which required articulation and organization It was concerned with issues that can be discovered and formulated as law.

Social Settlement Movement Perspective on Love

A review of settlement leaders' writings reveals liberal use of a theologically influenced language of love.[6] Graham Taylor and Jane Addams are illustrative.[7] Taylor's first book, *Religion in Social Action* (1913), (for which Addams wrote the Introduction), reflects the influence of the social gospel thinkers of the time. Taylor spoke publicly and in print of his "social work" in explicitly theological terms throughout his career. In a 1908 review of the Social Settlement movement Cole stated, "Professor Graham Taylor defines a settlement as a 'Group of Christian people who choose to live where they seem most needed, for the purpose of being all they can to the people with whom they identify themselves, and for all whose interests they will do what they can'" (Cole, 1908, p. 3). After citing a second definition[8] which did not use religious language, Cole concluded that:

> In both of these definitions, brief as they are, the underlying spirit and purpose [of the Social Settlement movement] are emphasized. The spirit is one which may be shared by many who do not call themselves Christians. *It is a spirit of adventurous friendship which the Gospel of Christ has made familiar to the world. From this has arisen the purpose which may be described in a word as service through sharing.* Whatever the social worker may have in character, attainment, or experience, he draws upon in meeting the needs of the less fortunate" with whom he has contact (Cole, 1908, p. 3, emphasis added).

In the late 1930's Taylor spoke of a settlement house colleague as a "shepherdess of sheep without a fold, serving the one flock of the one Shepherd" who when she took "up the arms of *love* and *persuasion,* of *service* and *sacrifice,* she was moved by her *reverence for the sanctity and worth* of every human life, which *her religion told her was created in the image of God and capable of being restored to that image by grace* divine" (Taylor, 1937, p. x, emphasis added). The language of love, grace and sanctity of human life is the context in which the term "service" must be understood. This language is the most consistent thread found among Taylor's major works (Taylor, 1931; Taylor, 1936; Wade, 1964).

Jane Addams, the reformer most often associated with the Social Settlement movement, told the stories of Hull House's visitors to ever larger audiences as her platform became an international one. Even though religious language is less prominent in her work, Addams made clear her motivation and aim with reference to the words of "the Hebrew prophet [who] made three requirements from those who would join the great forward moving procession led by Jehovah. 'To love mercy and at the same time 'to do justly'. . ." (Addams, 1967, p. 69-70). The difficulty of this is great. Addams' solution was to advocate the prophet's third requirement,

> 'to walk humbly with God,' which may mean to walk for many dreary miles beside the lowliest of His creatures, not even in that peace of mind which the company of the humble is popularly supposed to afford, but rather with the pangs and throes to which the poor human understanding is subjected whenever it attempts to comprehend the meaning of life. (Addams, 1967, p. 70)

Creating a place that enabled the poor to mingle with the affluent so that individuals may share their common burdens was one of Addams' primary aims. Interestingly, her writings reveal virtual total silence on the question of individualistic sin or evil. (This is not uncommon among Settlement leaders as demonstrated previously). For Social Settlement leaders, love entailed a socially structured way of being. It was not an antidote to evil.

Sin, Love and Justice

Eminent social critic and theologian Reinhold Niebuhr's work on sin, love and justice as they relate to social work offers a way to bridge the schism between historic social work's emphasis on individual (sin-based) approaches and social (love-based) approaches. In 1928-29 Niebuhr gave a series of six lectures to social workers at the Columbia University School of Social Work. The book that anthologizes these pieces, *The Contribution of Religion to Social Work* (1932), bridges the sin-based theology which motivated the Puritan-oriented social reformers and the love-based social gospel oriented activists. In his lectures, Niebuhr challenged social work to rise above sentimentality, claiming, "social work, in its acceptance of philanthropy as a substitute for real social justice, and for all its scientific pretensions, does not rise very much higher than most sentimental religious generosity" (Niebuhr, 1932, p. 82).

For Niebuhr, the tension between love and sin is complicated and illuminated by his overarching emphasis on social justice. Instead of focusing on either sin or love in an exclusive and individualistic way, Niebuhr urged social work to adopt a more balanced view of human nature and to use its unique position in the community to further the aims of social reform.

> The fact that *social workers so frequently fail to think beyond the present social and economic system, and confine their activities to the task of making human relations more sufferable within terms of an unjust social order, places them in the same category as the religious philanthropists* whose lack of imagination in this respect we have previously deplored. *A great deal of social effort, which prides itself upon its scientific achievements and regards religious philanthropy with ill-concealed contempt, is really very unscientific in its acceptance of given social conditions.* (p. 80, emphasis added)

Niebuhr chastised social work for its piecemeal approach to socially embedded injustice. He believed this approach inevitably resulted from a misguided sentiment of love. Niebuhr charged that social work, "...builds a few houses for the poor, but does not recognize that an adequate housing scheme for the poor can never be initiated within the limits of private enterprise. Every modern society must come, even if slowly, to the recognition that only a state, armed with the right of eminent domain and able to borrow money at low interest rates, can secure ground and build such houses for the poor as they can afford to buy or rent" (*Contribution*, p. 80-81). Therefore he urged upon social work a realist approach to human nature which would issue in advocacy for social justice.

The question of justice is what launched Niebuhr's theology of love. Niebuhr considered love both in personal and social terms, though discussion of love's social implications predominate. Niebuhr's perspective on love is not Romantic. Indeed, his concern for the dangers or potential problems that arise from love dominates his treatment of the concept. This is perhaps the single most important contribution Niebuhr offered social work thought. For Niebuhr, several particular dangers inhere with the conventional philosophies of love. Of primary relevance to social work is the danger of sentimentality. Niebuhr's cautionary remarks to social work in *Contribution* derive from his years of experience ministering in a Detroit parish and working in numerous left-wing political struggles. He worked with social workers both in Detroit as well as after he wrote *Contribution*, when he was professor of social ethics in New York City (Brown, 1992; Phillips, 1957).

Niebuhr underscores four major dangers regarding love. First, romanticized love can quickly degenerate into sentimentality as referred to previously. This theme figures prominently in Niebuhr's critique of liberalism. An additional feature of this critique is that liberalism discredits the transcendent nature of love. Diminishing the province of love as known through relationship with God, eclipses the realistic sin/love paradox. Love expressed in human relational terms alone disguises the realities of sin because of its "blindness," and because it unduly inflates human capacity. A third danger of a sentimentalized conception of love is that it seduces people into self-righteousness and pride. Niebuhr illustrates this feature of love through extended commentary on the hypocrisies of philanthropy, wherein the selfish can convince themselves of their unselfishness by "giving of their superfluity." Finally, the Christian love ideal is always in danger of betraying its ethical imperative by sinking into social conservatism. In this case, the inherent perfectionism of idealized love restricts critical analysis of political and economic conditions because it potentially tarnishes the ability to express positive emotional responses.[9] It therefore maintains existing unjust economic and power distributions. All of these snares are embedded in the conflictual relation between love and justice, and he believed, commanded additional attention by the social work profession. These ideas were pivotal in the belief systems of the pioneers of social work.

Niebuhr made several recommendations for social workers related to the dangers of sentimentality. First, the unstable, transient nature of the sympathy which motivates a benevolent vocation should be connected with a vision of an ultimate value. Second, the "shrewder insights" of a religion, which understands the human personality to be paradoxically God-like yet finite, can defend against the sentimentality that an idealistic or personalized view of love fosters. Finally, he recommended that the Christian ideal of perfect love is "probably too high for the attainment of any nation" or any group, because groups will not sacrifice themselves to serve the interests of another group. Niebuhr concluded therefore, that groups should aspire to justice rather than to love. Implicitly, this suggests to social workers that they, even though motivated by sympathy, ought to seek justice rather than the impossible specter of an ideal self-sacrificing love.

Niebuhr speaks at length in *Contribution* and elsewhere of the dangers of sentimentality. But is sentimentality dangerous in social work? Three observations of social work trends confirms Niebuhr's hypothesis that sentimentality deteriorates and is therefore problematic for social work. The first observation is that the dual social work tradition from the COS and the Social Settlement movement are not equally represented in current social work practice. The individual-focused practices from the COS movement dominate the profession as evidenced by the debates regarding the "legitimacy" of private practice and the fact that the majority of current National Association of Social Work members do direct practice. Policy advocacy and groupwork, inherited from the Social Settlement pioneers, play minor roles in contemporary social work practice. Secondly, this narrowed focus has also privatized social work practice and its community roles. Social work roles in public welfare agencies are diminishing in all but management positions as incidence of private clinical social work is rising. The profession, rather than taking prominent roles in community advocacy, tends to look inward.

Niebuhr also recommended that social work subordinate its vocational aim to an ultimate ideal. Is this necessary? The risk of *not* having an ultimate guiding principle, implied by Niebuhr, is that an emotional and privatized motivation is not sturdy enough for the profession to weather expectable storms in its contact with the depths of human misery and social injustice. The decades of debate the profession has carried on regarding its identity, mission and values evidence analogous concern. Although the profession has grown (in size and sophistication) through these years of debate, no "ultimate value" has been settled upon. Social work's emotion-based motivation has survived. The problem is also that the debates over identity, mission and values all assume the same fundamentally sentimental presuppositions. Human beings are good. Period. They are finite and capable of great good; due to nature, nurture or some combination. When evil is encountered, the desire to, in language of the Social Settlement tradition, "turn the stray sheep back to the path," becomes the priority, and debate regarding the profession's aim resolves into debate about relative effectiveness of competing technique.[10] In addition, the field's tenacious defense of a principle of self-determination is seemingly due to the inability of the profession to articulate a secularized equivalent "doctrine of sin" to hold in tension with its generous estimation of human possibilities. This necessarily cursory review suggests that the act of debating professional identity may in fact lead the profession away from its intent to articulate its ultimate value, because it is predisposed to an image of human nature that is imbalanced.

Niebuhr's Critique of Social Work:
A Useful Prescription for the Profession?

Niebuhr's theological conception of love is useful to illuminate and critique social work's tradition. *Contribution* was written during the historic period when the social work profession was seeking to synthesize its dual traditions. Niebuhr critiqued both theologies which were at the basis of each strand in the tradition—the COS and the Settlement's. The outcome in the profession was the adoption of the practice from the COS tradition and the philosophy of the Social Settlement movement. This hybrid, while in theory would hold in tension the two conflicting theologies of which each is a product, in practice has given rise to interminable and seemingly irresolvable debate regarding the profession's mission, membership and values.[11] Given the overly positive estimation of human nature and the lack of agreement on an "ultimate" value to serve, the profession remains a conglomeration of factions. Unlike the Social Settlement workers who valued their role as "interpreters" of social conditions, current social workers tend to be embroiled in internal, professional disputes.

How might Niebuhr's insights assist? One resolution comes from paying closer attention to the historical moment in which *Contribution* appeared. As presented above, the theological differences between the COS and Settlement movements up into the post-W.W.I. period can be broadly construed as a conflict between an emphasis on sin and an emphasis on love. According to Niebuhr, sin is inevitable and love is "impossible." Given the tendency in social work to privilege one or the other, and the incumbent problems with this, something is needed to hold these two in fruitful tension. Drawing upon Niebuhr's recommendation, can *justice* serve this mediating function?

Niebuhr's realist approach to the individual in society holds in tension the "paradoxes of religion" (Niebuhr, 1932, p. 67). The primary paradox is the Christian insight that the human is both made in the image of God and is a sinner.

> This emphasis upon the sinfulness of man has been just as strong, in classical religion, as the emphasis upon his Godlikeness. It has *saved religion, at its best, from the sentimentality into*

which modern culture has fallen since the romantic period, with its reaction to dogma of man's total depravity by its absurd insistence upon the natural goodness of man. The *real religious spirit has no illusions about human nature. It knows the heart of man to be sinful. It is therefore not subject to the cynical disillusion into which sentimentality degenerates when it comes into contact with the disappointing facts of human history.* (ibid., p. 66, emphasis added)

From this perspective Niebuhr criticized both the classical or orthodox excessive attentiveness to human's sinful nature and the modern or liberal denial of sin. He chastised the likes of the charity organizers by indicting their moralism as counterproductive. Their excessive focus on the individual created blindness to the injustices of social conditions. He chastised the likes of the Settlement workers as hopelessly sentimental and therefore easily disillusioned and embittered. Consequently, Niebuhr urged upon the orthodox a greater measure of the loving forgiveness which the liberals prize as well as attention to social conditions; and he urged the liberals to greater mindfulness of the realities of sin. Proponents of both theologies easily succumb to self-righteousness. The orthodox charity worker who busily goes about the business of saving others' souls can easily forget the limitations of their own. The liberal who blithely confesses the sins of their group, from which they feel emancipated, is easily seduced by "the temptation to be humble and proud at the same time" (Niebuhr, 1957b, p. 120). Niebuhr commended to social work a moderate position which both acknowledges the realities of sin and posits human goodness while maintaining in tension the interaction between the individual and the group. Absent this, social conditions are not subject to critique, so reform of the structural causes of impoverishment and injustice is not possible. In sum, he cautioned social work to guard against the sentimentalism found among modern liberal religionists.

How might this critique and recommendation inform the understanding of historical social work? The pioneers of both the COS and the Settlement House movement represent poles along the continuum between "Sin" and "Love". In their attempts to eradicate human sinfulness and express divine love, respectively, they succumbed to the temptation to ignore the larger questions of social justice. By bridging the gap between love and sin with a strong critique of those who ignore social injustice, Niebuhr avoided the pitfalls of both extremes and oriented the discussion away from individual sin or love and toward the action of the whole. Contemporary social work would do well to follow his lead.

Notes

[1] Examples include Josephine Shaw Lowell and Joseph Tuckerman. See (Howe, 1988). These Unitarians were among the theological liberals of their day. They rejected the more conservative evangelical "revivalists." Tuckerman believed, for example, that "a Calvinist preacher who went into the slums teaching predestination and depravity did more harm than good" (Howe, 1988, p. 242). Both Calvinist Puritans and Unitarian Puritans were active in public life. Most relevant to social work's tradition is the Unitarian theology, however, it co-existed in a society still very much influenced by Calvinism and undoubtedly in practice reflected these influences (Cole, 1954).

[2] The city itself was also seen as fostering the conditions of sinfulness that led to pauperism. See Paine's 1893 text, "Pauperism in Great Cities: Its Four Chief Causes" for additional detail (Paine, 1964).

[3] She followed Josephine Shaw Lowell's work quite closely.

[4] Richmond uses the term "client" as early as 1917 in her classic text, *Social Diagnosis* (Richmond, 1917).

[5] Taylor offers the text of a letter from a pastor who works on the streets as an example of the impossibility of saving an individual if sinful environments are left untouched. "'Dear Pastor, In the first place, when we try to help a fallen brother, the odds against us are too great. Last night I believe that man was in earnest. When he said, 'I am tired of sin,' he meant it. . . .He went out from God's house, away from those commissioned to do his work. Where could he go but out into the cold, friendless streets of a great city? Then what? . . . .he was to shun the dram shop. He did this. He passed by seven, with the struggle which God only knows. The door of the eighth stood open. It did look warm and comfortable within. So he finally went in. . . Where could I have taken him? Cannot something be done to lessen these odds, to even things up, to give the Lord a fair show with a man who wants to be saved?'" (Taylor, (1913), p. 26).

[6] For an excellent review of the general role the social gospel played in the social settlement movement see: (Carson, 1990).

[7] Taylor is known to current social work students as the founder of the Chicago Commons settlement and the initiator of the social work courses that became institutionalized as the University of Chicago's School of Social Services Administration predecessor institution, the Chicago School of Civics and Philanthropy. Less known is the fact that Taylor was an ordained Protestant minister who accepted his teaching position at the Chicago Theological Seminary on the condition that he be allowed to set up a settlement house.

[8] The second definition is offered by Ada Woolfolk.

[9] One of Niebuhr's illustrations of this is of a good liberal minister in a Kentucky coal mining town who sided against the miners in a labor dispute on the grounds that strikes, because they were assertive, were contrary to Biblical love (Niebuhr, 1957a).

[10] Ehrenreich makes this case regarding social work between 1920 and 1945; see: (Ehrenreich, 1985).

[11] The inclusion of "membership" points to the mid-century debates regarding bachelor degree trained social workers and the earlier debates regarding volunteers and graduate-school trained social workers. See: (Popple, 1983). Specifics regarding the values debate fall beyond the scope of this study. For good summaries, see (Abbott, 1988; Berlin, 1990; Biestek, 1967; Faver, 1986; Gordon, 1965; Heineman, 1981; NASW, 1967; Reid & Popple, 1992; Timms, 1983; Weick, 1991).

References

Abbott, A. A. (1988). *Professional choices: Values at work.* National Association of Social Workers, Inc.

Addams, J. (1967). *Democracy and social ethics* (1902). New York: Macmillan Co.

Barnett, H. R. (1895a). Passionless reformers (1882). In S. A. Barnett & H. R. Barnett (Eds.), *Practicable socialism: Essays on social reform.* London: Longmans, Green & Co.

Barnett, H. R. (1895b). What has the Charity Organization Society to do with social reform? (1884). In S. A. Barnett & H. R. Barnett (Eds.), *Practicable socialism.* London: Longmans, Green & Co.

Berlin, S. B. (1990). Dichotomous and complex thinking. *Social Service Review,* 64(1), 64- 59.

Biestek, F. P. (1967). Problems in identifying social work values. In NASW (Eds.), *Values in social work: A re-examination.* Silver Spring, MD: National Association of Social Workers.

Brown, C. C. (1992). *Niebuhr and his age: Reinhold Niebuhr's prophetic role in the twentieth century.* Philadelphia: Trinity Press International.

Carson, M. J. (1990). *Settlement folk: Social thought and the American settlement movement 1885-1930.* Chicago: University of Chicago Press.

Cole, C. C. (1954). *The social ideals of the northern evangelists 1826-1860.* New York: Columbia University.

Cole, W. I. (1908). *Motives and results of the social settlement movement: Notes on an exhibit installed in the Social Museum of Harvard University.* Cambridge: Harvard University.

Ehrenreich, J. H. (1985). *The altruistic imagination: A history of social work and social policy in the United States.* Ithaca, NY: Cornell University Press.

Faver, C. A. (1986). Religion, research, and social work. *Social Thought,* 12(3), 20-29.

Gladden, W. (1894). *The church and the kingdom.* New York: Revell.

Gordon, W. E. (1965). Knowledge and value: Their distinction and relationship in clarifying social work practice. *Social Work,* 10(3), 32-39.

Heineman, M. B. (1981). The obsolete scientific imperative in social work research. *Social Service Review,* 55(3), 371-396.

Howe, D. W. (1988). *The Unitarian conscience: Harvard moral philosophy 1805-1861.* Middletown, CT: Wesleyan University Press.

Kellogg, D. O., Rev. (1880). The principle and advantage of association in charities. *Journal of Social Science, XII,* 84-90.

Leiby, J. (1984). Charity Organization Reconsidered. *Social Service Review,* (December), 523-538.

Loch, C. S. (1904). If citizens be friends. In C. S. Loch (Ed.), *Methods of social advance: Short studies in social practice by various authors.* London: Macmillan and Company Limited.

Loch, S. C. S. (1892). *Charity organization* (2nd ed.). London: S. Sonnenschein & Co.

Marty, M. E. (1986). *Modern American religion: The irony of it all 1893-1919.* Chicago: The University of Chicago Press.

Mathews, S. (1907). *The church and the changing order.* New York: Macmillan.

NASW (Ed.). (1967). *Values in social work: A re-examination.* Silver Spring, MD: National Association of Social Workers.

Niebuhr, R. (1932). *The contribution of religion to social work.* New York: Columbia University.

Niebuhr, R. (1933). Letter. *Christian Century, 50*(11), 363-364.

Niebuhr, R. (1957a). Religion and class war in Kentucky (1932). In D. B. Robertson (Ed.), *Love and Justice: Selections from the Shorter Writings of Reinhold Niebuhr.* Louisville, KY: Westminster/John Knox Press.

Niebuhr, R. (1957b). The confession of a tired radical (1928). In D. B. Robertson (Ed.), *Love and Justice: Selections from the Shorter Writings of Reinhold Niebuhr.* Louisville, KY: Westminster/John Knox Press.

Phillips, H. B. (1957). *The reminiscences of Reinhold Niebuhr [Microfilmed interview transcripts].* New York: Oral History Research Office Columbia University.

Popple, P. R. (1983). Contexts of practice. In A. Rosenblatt & D. Waldfogel (Eds.), *Handbook of clinical social work.* San Francisco: Jossey-Bass.

Rauschenbusch, W. (1912). *Unto me.* Boston: The Pilgrim Press.

Reid, P. N., & Popple, P. R. (Eds.). (1992). *The moral purposes of social work: The character and intentions of a profession.* Chicago: Nelson-Hall.

Richmond, M. E. (1917). *Social diagnosis.* New York: Russell Sage Foundation.

Taylor, G. (1913). *Religion in social action.* New York: Dodd, Mead and Co.

Taylor, G. (1931). *Pioneering on social frontiers.* Chicago: University of Chicago Press.

Taylor, G. (1936). *Chicago Commons through forty years.* Chicago: Chicago Commons Association.

Taylor, G. (1937). Introduction: Mary McDowell—Citizen. In C. M. Hill (Ed.), *Mary McDowell and municipal housekeeping.* Chicago: Chicago Council of Social Agencies.

Timms, N. (1983). *Social work values: An enquiry.* London: Routledge & Kegan Paul.

Tucker, W. J. (1911). *The function of the church in modern society.* Boston: Houghton, Mifflin.

Wade, L. C. (1964). *Graham Taylor: Pioneer for social justice, 1851-1938.* Chicago: University of Chicago Press.

Weick, A. (1991). The place of science in social work. *Journal of Sociology and Social Welfare, 18*(4), 13-34.

CHAPTER 10

THE POOR WILL NEVER CEASE OUT OF THE LAND?
OR
THERE WILL BE NO POOR AMONG YOU?
A CHRISTIAN PERSPECTIVE ON POVERTY

Beryl Hugen

To advocate for the poor in the context of today's debates on welfare reform is not easy. In fact, it can be quite an intimidating task. But it apparently has always been a difficult and somewhat unpopular task to defend the poor. Daniel Boorstin, in his book *The Creators: A History of Heroes of the Imagination*, on the artistic history of Western civilization, states that with the birth of rhetoric or speech, it became customary in learning the art, to take as a topic the defense of the poor. This was done, he says, because it was considered an excellent, if not the best, test of an orator's skill.

More striking than the difficulty in defending the poor, however, is the implied assumption that there will always be the poor to defend. This too is not a new idea. The writer of Deuteronomy said, "The poor will never cease out of the land." Every Western society since has had within it people who cannot or do not support themselves and are dependent on others for help. While no accurate count of the poor can be made since definitions of poverty vary, probably in most societies the number of all adults who are poor has never fallen below five percent. The estimates of poverty during the Depression of the 1930's—even those that showed fifty percent of the population below the poverty line—do not appear particularly large from a historical or international perspective. In the 1930's America was a phenomenally rich country by world standards. When the Russians viewed the film *The Grapes of Wrath*, they marveled that the Okies had cars. Humorist Will Rogers quipped that the United States was the only nation in history that went to the poorhouse in automobiles.

At certain times the percent of the population living in poverty has been very high, as for instance in the latter days of the Roman Empire, and at present it is probably not much higher or lower than the average over the years. Societies have from time to time launched campaigns to eliminate poverty, the most recent being Lyndon Johnson's "War on

Poverty" in the 1960's. Although small gains were made, the problem persists. Nor, as far as I am aware, has the problem ever been reduced to what might be thought of as its irreducible minimum: those who are handicapped, sick, or victims of disaster.

This chapter attempts to trace historically the motives, principles and values of Christians who have over the centuries, tried to help, support, and sometimes to control or reform this unassimilated group in society. I will not attempt to explain why the poor are poor. The causes of poverty are relevant only when what is perceived as the cause of poverty affects how the poor are treated.

For example, there have been many theological explanations. St. Ambrose thought that inequalities in possessions were a result of the Fall. St. John Chrysostom of the early church believed God permitted poverty so that the well-to-do would have someone to give to, and therefore earn their reward in Heaven. Some Puritans held that the poor were the non-elect, who were deemed an insult to God.

Most common, historically, have been moral explanations. The poor have consistently been accused of laziness and intemperance. John Locke, the philosopher of liberty, wrote in 1696 that the increase of the poor could only be caused by "the relaxation of discipline and the corruption of manners." The Reverend Jerry Falwell alleges that material wealth is God's way of rewarding those who do his will—and presumably, poverty is His way of punishing those who don't. Lack of thrift has often been charged to the poor. Occasionally, the moral onus has rested on the well-to-do, who were seen as exploiting the poor. This can be seen in several early twentieth century "social hymns," such as Walter Russell Bowie's *Holy City Seen of John* and Frank North's *Where Cross the Crowded Ways of Life*, both of which speak of greed. But these are exceptions to the general rule.

There have also been sociological and economic explanations, ranging from the effects of the Enclosure Acts in England, to technological unemployment and economic maladjustments, such as the Depression of the 1930's, and disasters such as the Black Death in the 14th century and the potato famine in Ireland in the 1840's. In the twentieth century there has been some recognition that an economic system that favors the majority of the people may at the same time leave part of the population poor; so, for example, the battle against inflation may increase unemployment or a free market depress wages. But these theories and explanations are only significant for our purposes as people come to believe in them.

I will also not attempt to describe in detail the various mechanisms and institutions humankind has devised to cope with the poor. These programs, mechanisms, and institutions, as well as the laws under which they were developed, generally reflect the Christian motives, values, and principles of helpers. Suffice it to say that in the history of Western civilization from Biblical times to the present day—society has used at least the following mechanisms: the hospice, the allocation of the tithe, settlement laws, overseers of the poor, the workhouse, subsidization of wages, work-relief, less-eligibility, social insurance, public assistance, public provision of certain benefits such as education or health care, graduated taxation, the distribution of surplus commodities, soup kitchens, and mutual aid societies. A complete list would be significantly longer.

Drift and Revival

Crucial to understanding the historical development of Christian responses to poverty is the fact that programs to combat poverty may start with one set of ideals or motives, but gradually become diverted from their original intention without changing too much in form. For example, this is what has happened to Aid to Families with Dependent Children (AFDC) in the United States, for many years the program most people referred to when they thought about welfare. It was originally conceived as a long-term income replacement program, strictly financial, enabling single parents to stay at home with their children. It soon began to take on rehabilitative overtones, requiring that the single parents work if at all possible, and urging recipients to exert every effort to become self-supporting as soon as they could.

This theme of a gradual change in direction or meaning in human institutions, indeed in any principle or motive, though maintaining similar form or language, is one that is central. We possess an almost infinite ability to distort our values and stated principles. Progress in dealing with poverty, therefore, has not always been a continually upward process, with perhaps a plateau or two on the way, or even a series of hills and valleys, but rather a series of new starts and a wandering away from the direction of that start. Progress occurs most often when a new idea is born, or when either a major happening (such as the Reformation, a World War, a great Depression) or some person or theory (the impact of Freudian psychology) forces people to reconsider their assumptions. There is then a return to the original direction and a new direction built upon that one. This is similiar to the role played by the prophets in the Old Testament - to bring the people back to essentials: "What does the Lord require of you, but to do justice, to love kindness, and to walk humbly with your God." Indeed, the Old Testament can be read as a paradigm of this drift and revival process. It is with this process in mind that I will explore the Christian impulse to help the poor.

Why Help?

Societies have given a variety of reasons why human beings are willing to help those who cannot help themselves. There have been societies where the poor and the sick were simply left to starve or die of disease, and at times this has even been suggested, in theory at least, to be desirable, as in the works of the Social Darwinists who thought that in feeding the victims of famine we only contribute to the "population explosion," thus ensuring still greater famine. Socio-biologists ascribe the motive to help to an instinct for the preservation of the species, but always have problems explaining why certain species seem to care for the sick and the wounded, while other species clearly do not. Humanists believe helping the poor is somehow characteristic of humankind as we have evolved as social creatures.

Christians believe that God commands it. There have been in the course of Western history, at least four principles, or conscious motives, upon which Christians have based their efforts for helping the poor and less fortunate.

From the Hebrew world came the ideal of justice, basically a religious concept. It held that every human being, as a child of God, had certain rights to a small part of God's blessings. No person or class of persons had the right to take everything. The entire concept was wider than this—including the use of just weights and measures and prohibiting using one's superior status or power to take advantage of the poor. The writer of Exodus commanded that the fields not be gleaned "so that the poor may eat." Proverbs praises the man "who knows the rights of the poor." The word "rights" is significant—it establishes something that personal judgment cannot deny. Micah puts justice before kindness, as does the Old Testament as a whole. Numerous references to justice are made in the Old Testament, and although all of these do not refer to the poor, the poor were certainly included, often specifically. It is not surprising that many of the strongest advocates for a strictly "rights" program of public assistance have been Jewish.

To the Hebrew ideal of justice, early Christianity added love, or charity—which in its original meaning included the concept of valuing or thinking well of its recipient. Love in its purest form is best described in I Corinthians 13, which emphasizes that love does not insist on its own way and has a capacity to endure. Love's mainspring is responding to God's love. Having been greatly loved by God, Christians could do little else than love in return. They also believed that one must love one's enemies as well as one's friends, and accepted the apostle Paul's statement that "there is now no distinction since all have fallen short of the glory of God."

But early Christianity encountered both the Greek and the Roman world. The Greek's believed persons were self-fulfilled only if they were involved with others. Although this had largely to do with involvement in community affairs, it also referred to helping those in distress. From the Roman world came the idea that those more fortunate had a responsibility, even a duty, to help the poor. This sense of "noblesse oblige" was practiced so assiduously in Rome one writer calculated that in the later days of the Roman Empire 580,000 people were receiving some sort of public subsidy, and only 90,000 were self-sufficient, a ratio of more than six to one (Uhlhorn, 1883).

These four principles—justice, love, self-fulfillment, and responsibility—all arose initially from noble sentiments. All at times and to some extent have been distorted. They also have had to compete with two other principles, both basically good. The first is that one's actions should produce some moral good, the other being the need for order in society. These two principles, in turn, like the original four, have often times been distorted.

The need for order in society was strong in the Middle Ages, but rarely was argued for directly, perhaps because it was simply assumed. During this time the need for order was based on the belief that God had ordained the status quo. As the nineteenth century hymn *All Things Bright and Beautiful* puts it, in a verse rarely sung today, "The rich man in his castle, the poor man at his gate / God made them, high or lowly, and ordered their estate." Christians during this period accepted society as it was, believing it had been ordained as such.

The Directions of Diversion

What has happened, at various times, to these original four principles?

Responsibility to help the poor can very easily become paternalism and colonialism—the "White Man's Burden" or the company town. It can be used to justify intruding into the lives of those for whom one assumes responsibility, usually with the intent of "doing them good." Frequently it has involved an elite who see themselves as morally superior and wiser than the people they wish to help. Often it has been used to exercise social control.

Self-fulfillment through helping others has been perverted in two directions. On the one hand, it often takes the form of the desire for gratitude from the person being helped, or to be loved and thanked by them. On the other hand, it may involve pity for the poor, an emotion that always involves a belief in one's own superior fortune or kindness. It is essentially patronizing and demeaning, less concerned with the real needs of the people it serves than with feeling good about serving. A peculiar turn that self-fulfillment took, quite early in its history, was when self-fulfillment began to mean not feeling good in this world, but earning salvation in the next.

But the principle perverted most was Christian love, or charity, as the debasement of the latter word testifies. The original impulse was apparently comparatively short-lived. It flourished for a while, as we know from the book of Acts, overcoming distinctions of wealth, citizenship, and of slave or free status. It greatly enhanced the status of women. But what was possible in the small closed community of the early church could not be carried out in the world at large and by the time of Constantine "the idea of equalizing social conditions for love's sake had pretty much disappeared" (Troeltsch, 1931, p. 37). Charity or love began to mean doing good by exhorting the poor to greater frugality or morality.

Of the four principles, the one perverted least is that of justice. What perversion has occurred is found in rigid categorizing rules: the failure, that is, to temper justice with mercy. There is considerable debate today on how far commutative justice, that which is owed to persons simply by the fact of their existence or being children of God, should go. Does it include, for instance, the right to a minimum income or to health care? Certainly commutative justice needs to be balanced to some degree by distributive justice, or that which is owed to persons in relation to their contribution to society. The problem has been that for the most part, commutative justice has had to take very much of a back seat to distributive justice.

These four principles, in pure or perverted form, have had periods of either great popularity or little influence. Yet they constitute the basic Christian motives for caring for and helping the poor.

A Historical Look

How have these principles or motives been acted upon in history? In what specific ways have these principles or motives been distorted? What is the Christian record regarding treatment of the poor?

As we have seen, the idea of equalizing social conditions for love's sake did not last long. The early church soon recognized the poor would not "cease from the land" and would need individual assistance. This was accomplished by the giving of alms and by distributing the tithe.

But immediately the question arose: Were these "poor" people really in need? Were not some of them, at least, merely pretending to be poor? And would they spend what was given to them for their support in immoral living? This was then, and is still today, an important question that preoccupies us. Johnny Cash sings of the "Welfare Cadillac." Because there are always a few who abuse any system, we tend to suspect all.

The writers in the early church usually stressed helping the poor even at the risk of assisting some who were undeserving. Clement of Alexandria, at the beginning of the third century, said, "For by being fastidious and setting thyself to try who are fit for thy benevolence, and who are not, it is possible that thou mayest neglect some who are the friends of God." At the end of the fourth century, St. John Chrysostom, wrote, "And yet be we as large hearted as we may, we shall never be able to contribute such love towards man as we stand in need of at the hand of a God that loveth man." On the basis of this theology, Chrysostom asserted that "the poor have only one recommendation: their need. If he be the most perverse of all men, should he lack necessary food, we ought to appease his hunger." He even had empathy for those who asked for alms unnecessarily, recognizing that the poor might be tempted more than the rich. Regarding the moral effect of giving on the recipient, Chrysostom said one could not and should not judge (Uhlhorn, 1883).

Notwithstanding Chrysostom's empathy with the supposed impostor, he was much more concerned with the hardness of heart of the giver than with the effects of his charity. And despite his understanding of the unmerited grace of God, Chrysostom was not free of the belief that man, through his own efforts, could win treasure in heaven. He believed that the poor were "useful" to the rich so that the rich might get rid of their material excess and so win that treasure.

Gradually, love for one's neighbor drifted toward and was superseded by self-love—charity became useful as a means to earn salvation. So strongly was this believed that Augustine warned against the assumption that one might obtain a license to sin through giving alms. This assumption was a major heresy of the medieval church. Yet, in one respect at least, the medieval church protected the poor. Only the church was large enough and universal enough to speak for those who were outside the system. The feudal system, through its reciprocal responsibilities, could be counted on to take care of most people. But it was not structured to care for the sick, the migrant, or the fugitive. It is significant that the three services most typical of the church at that time were the hospital, the hospice, and sanctuary. With the fragmentation of the church following the Reformation, this safeguard was lost and did not appear, in America, at least, until the federal government assumed something of this role in the 1930's.

Toward Judgmentalism

Nothing in the theology of the Reformation in itself should have led to a contempt for the poor, a desire to reform them or make life so miserable for them so that they would reform themselves. But this attitude began to dominate the relationship between rich and poor for the next two centuries or more.

The Reformation theology in which 'works' were totally ineffectual might have dried up the generosity of the rich, but it should not have led to the utter contempt for the poor. All men were sinners—there was now "no distinction,"— nothing a man could do to earn favor with God. This would seem to be a breeding ground for humility and not for sweeping judgments on one's fellows. Yet it proved to be exactly the opposite. Not only were the poor despised, but they were treated as if each one of them had the characteristics of the least worthy.

There have been a number of explanations, both theological and economic, for what happened. Some point to Luther's emphasis on work as a necessity. Yet, Luther did not have in mind the necessity to engage in a gainful occupation at whatever wages are offered. He argued that a worker was fulfilling God's intention as well, or better, than the man given to the contemplative life.

It took the development of the new capitalist economy, however, to translate this involvement in worldly affairs into a demand that the first duty of human beings was to earn their own living. Those among the poor who either could not find work or were too sick to work were the natural victims of this demand. Consequently, those who could not or did not work were naturally seen as inferior or unfit.

But this new evaluation of work was not the sole factor operating. Max Weber (1930) believed that the crux of the matter was found in the doctrine of election and the "absolute duty" of the elect to "consider himself chosen, and to combat all doubts as temptations of the devil, since lack of self-confidence is the result of insufficient faith." This meant one could be sure one was of the elect only if one was actively engaged in doing work. As a corollary, those who did not or could not work showed they were not of the elect. This led to a hatred of those who did not or could not work as being an insult to God. But to look for evidences of election in human behavior was to deny and distort the whole rationale of Calvin's election doctrine. It meant that God chose those who pleased Him through their activities, and led to the identification of worldly success with election. It opened the door to the possibility that it was human beings and not God who determined their election.

The Poor and the Social Order

During the transition period between the end of the feudal system and the full establishment of market economies, most nations developed laws or systems of public relief. In England these were called poor laws. It was a period of great hardship for the poor, many of whom were uprooted from the land and became destitute. The measures set up as public relief were always accompanied by stricter and stricter laws against begging and leaving one's settlement or residence. One could be branded, enslaved, or even executed (on a third offense) for begging. Public relief sprang not so much from compassion for the poor, but primarily to avert public disorder.

In 1601 the Poor Law declared all able-bodied poor must do some kind of work to earn their sustenance; the sustenance itself was provided by the parish—the local unit of administration in England. For some time both church-sponsored charity and public relief co-existed. In many communities, a public overseer of the poor was appointed. By 1750, however, rural poverty began to rise dramatically, driven by an unprecedented occurrence—a permanent surplus in labor in the countryside accompanied by a boom in trade. To meet this great distress and encourage employers to hire more workers, the poor laws were modified to subsidize wages, creating a guaranteed minimum income of sorts. Under this new system a man received relief, even if he was working, if his wages fell below the family subsistence income. With his meager income now guaranteed whatever his wages - and with the added certainty that he could never make more than a guaranteed subsistence income - the laborer had little motivation to satisfy his employer. Conversely, an employer could now obtain labor at minuscule wages; whatever he paid, the subsidy from the poor rates brought the laborer's income up to the guaranteed minimum scale. There was no easy way out of this vicious cycle. Poverty had become very expensive.

The best Christian minds in England at the time grappled with this problem of poverty. The general consensus was to abolish the Poor Laws (wage subsidies and outdoor relief) and replace them with workhouses (indoor relief), guided by the principle of less-eligibility. According to this principle, if the living conditions and assistance rates of persons maintained at public expense were equal to or better than the lowest paid persons maintained at their own expense, calamity would be inevitable. Living conditions and assistance for the poor, therefore, should be made *less* than what the lowest paid *eligible* worker received. Also recommended was to make the conditions of relief so odious, humiliating, and forbidding that one would do anything short of starving to avoid it. When the new Poor Law of 1834 came into being, this was the rule that was followed. The only thing worse than dependency would be death itself. The law of 1834 was the most important piece of social legislation passed in the nineteenth century. The English poor were compelled to be "independent" and were forced into the competitive labor market. They were now free and independent in a new and unheard of way. They were solely responsible for themselves.

When the new law went into effect it was greeted with great anger. No piece of legislation in English history has probably ever been so hated or despised. One of England's greatest writers was on hand to comment on this monumental development. In his novel *Oliver Twist*, Charles Dickens gives a blistering satire on the new Poor Law and the principles that animated it, including the awareness that independence in the scheme of political economy was easily convertible into isolation and abandonment. What was learned, perhaps, was that it is possible to degrade people by caring for them and to degrade people by not caring for them.

Control of Pauperism

The major thrust of welfare policy by the early nineteenth century became, therefore, to control pauperism or dependency. In the public mind, being poor and being a pauper were different. Paupers were characterized by their moral degeneracy, drunkenness, vice, and corruption. They were outcasts, no different than criminals. The dividing line between the poor and the paupers was the ability and willingness to work. Those who could support themselves, but didn't, crossed the line from being poor to being paupers.

The goal of welfare policy was to prevent the poor from crossing that line. The poor were seen as precariously balanced on the brink of moral disaster, and one sure way to tip the balance and send a family downward into pauperism was the indiscriminate giving of aid. Therefore, the public policy was to reform those poor who applied for relief. Incentives for reforming would-be applicants were either a government's denying assistance or making the conditions of accepting relief extremely onerous. The methods used to try to reform the poor and spur them to independence were nearly all negative. Kindness towards them was suspect. It would tempt the poor to be content with their state. To receive relief, a family was required to go to the poorhouse where the humiliating conditions were designed to deter applications for relief. Deterrence was thought to be rehabilitative. This was the nineteenth century's attempt to reform the poor. To help take people out of poverty would not have made sense to this generation, for they truly believed in taking the poverty out of people.

The belief that one can stop people from being or becoming poor by making them miserable is one that persists today. George Gilder (1981), believed by some to have provided the theological justification for the Reagan administration's economics, is quoted as saying that for the poor to succeed and cease to be poor, they "need most of all the spur of their poverty," — hence the "crucial goal should be to restrict the [welfare] system as much as possible, by making it unattractive and even a bit demeaning."

Evangelical Revival

The religious revivals of the middle eighteenth and early nineteenth centuries could have counteracted the rigidities of these capitalist-puritan beliefs, but did not. Because evangelical revivalism emphasized love rather than justice and was essentially individualistic, it did not further an understanding of the plight of the poor. Evangelicalism was not, according to Niebuhr (1932), a true "religion of the disinherited." Although it appealed to all classes, it remained largely middle class. It was selective in its view of sin, emphasizing personal sins such as irreverence and intemperance rather than collective ones such as oppression and injustice. It was also more impressed by the vices to which the poor had succumbed than by the evils to which they had been subjected. The sins of which evangelicals convicted the rich and the poor were very different.

The main impact of the evangelical movement on the rich may have been to restore for a time the prominence of self-fulfillment as a motive for helping others. While not so blatant, perhaps, as in medieval times, the motive is obvious. The philanthropy of the wealthy during the first part of the nineteenth century was the bridge in many cases between their business dealings and their Christian conscience. Throughout the nineteenth century the charitable response of the American people was almost as generous as their pursuit of gain was selfish. Charles Wesley's solution was to get all one can, save all one can, and give all one can.

The two streams of giving and getting converged at the end of the nineteenth century in the gospel of wealth. This doctrine harmonized with the major tenets of individualism, and through the idea of stewardship, endowed individualism with moral sanctity. It was Andrew Carnegie who in word and deed gave the gospel of wealth its classic expression. Believing that enormous differences in the economic conditions of men were normal and beneficial, Carnegie asserted that wealth was a sacred trust to be administered by the person possessing it for the welfare of the community. The aim of the millionaire, he declared, should be to die poor. For all its undoubted romantic appeal the gospel of wealth did not solve or help understand poverty, for Carnegie was not seeking to correct poverty, but to justify wealth. The weakness of the approach lay in its failing to recognize that the suffering the wealthy generously relieved with one hand, was in many instances, but the product of the ills they sowed with the other.

Science and Advice

By the late nineteenth century there was a great deal more interest in the conditions of the poor. This took various forms. One, which was primarily humanitarian but had a strong religious base, consisted largely in the founding of missions in poor neighborhoods. Part of the motive of these missions was a genuine concern to improve the conditions under which the poor were compelled to live and part was a desire to reform the character of the poor. Many social welfare organizations of this period had their origin in religious missions of this form.

Alongside these was another form, the scientific Association for Improving the Condition of the Poor, with its concept of "friendly visiting." They operated with a conviction that what the poor needed was the "influence" (primarily moral advice) of the visitor and not material relief. Part of this feeling was religious, that spiritual things were much more important than material. Principles of the society were put forward as, "FIRST, the moral elevation of the poor; and SECOND, ...the relief of their necessities" (Brown, 1855).

Jesus' use of Deuteronomy 8:3, or rather the partial statement, "Man does not live by bread alone," was often quoted in support of the primacy of intangible services, as if Jesus was condemning bread, despite his asking for it in the Lord's Prayer. To elevate intangible services over the practical is poor theology, but it became the primary attitude of helpers during this period.

As social conditions for the poor worsened under the impact of the Industrial Revolution and America also had to contend with a vast influx of immigrants, social reformers turned to Charity Organization Societies (COS). In many ways these organizations continued what the Association for Improving the Condition of the Poor had done, favoring friendly visits over material relief. In fact, the detection of fraud is listed as the Society's first function, ahead of the adequate relief of the honest poor (Gurteen, 1882).

Applicants for assistance who could pass the rigid examinations of the COS agents were certified as worthy and referred to a cooperating agency for the relief of their needs. Thus, when prospective contributors to the New York COS asked how much of their donation would go to the poor, the director was able to answer proudly, "Not one cent." It saw as the principal cause of pauperism the "misdirected charity of benevolent people" (Gurteen, 1882, p. 170).

Birth of Social Work

It did not take long before America, with its tradition of individual responsibility and its belief in technology, carried the scientific claims of the Charity Organization Society to their logical conclusion and developed a new science, that of social casework.

The person most responsible for developing this new "science" of social casework was Mary E. Richmond. She had been a Charity Organization Society worker; in fact, her first book was entitled *Friendly Visiting Among the Poor* (1899). Richmond greatly enlarged and enhanced the art of investigation. Her method was to ask literally dozens of questions about an individual and his or her relationships. In a later book Richmond described the three most successful casework policies as the following: "encouragement and stimulation, the fullest possible participation of the client in all plans, and the skillful use of repetition" (Richmond, 1922, p. 256).

It is the second of these that is significant. For the first time, the poor or deviant person being studied was given some part in his or her own treatment. Richmond elaborated on this principle and gave it the name by which it is still known: "self-determination." The next step was obvious, the training of professionals. In 1897 Richmond had already made the first plea for a School of Applied Philanthropy. Social casework and social work became almost synonymous.

The new profession of social work was now ready for Freud. Here was an acceptable scientific theory that explained much of what had puzzled caseworkers when clients did not respond to reason, and here also was an answer to the moralism of earlier social work practice which was then beginning to fall out of favor.

A New Definition of Justice

Mary Richmond, as we have seen, had enunciated a pragmatic principle that she called self-determination. Freud gave scientific sanction to the principle. Finally, it became recognized as a philosophical and eventually a religious belief.

Self-determination as a principle certainly produced a much more humane treatment of the poor. At times it may have led to indulgence, to protecting people from the law or the natural consequences of their actions. At times, in Freudian terms, it liberated the id at the expense of the superego. But it did much to counter the disregard for human dignity that had been taken for granted as part of the fate of anyone who asked for help - submission to the will of the helper and restrictions on his freedom to manage his own life. It was a great corrective to pride arising out of exercising social control.

Self-determination did more. Politically it helped to develop a welfare system that established, for the first time, a legal right to assistance. While social workers were developing their theories of self-determination, the government in the United States was reacting to the Depression with a relief system that seemed to promise some dignity to the poor.

What was really new in the Social Security Act of 1935 were the categories of public assistance - at that time Old Age Assistance, Aid to the Needy Blind, and Aid to Dependent Children. These spelled out for the first time a legal and enforceable right to assistance if certain eligibility conditions were met. The act set aside the goal of earlier welfare reformers who had tried to change human nature, and accepted the fact that government will always be engaged in spending for welfare. What was conceded was that the poor will always be with us.

It is true that the law did not guarantee the adequacy of assistance. The principle of less eligibility could still be practiced. There was also resistance from those who could not accept the idea that the poor had the right to live their lives free from efforts to reform or rehabilitate them. Nevertheless, the moral right had now been given statutory form protected by a system of appeals or fair hearings in which due process was to be observed. Money payments were interpreted to mean unrestricted payments which the recipient could spend as he or she wished, free from social control. With the passage of the Social Security Act, the federal government became, in fact, the protector of the rights of the poor and of the least popular among them—a role not unlike that of the medieval church.

The public, however, found commutative justice hard to accept. Most of them still thought of assistance as a "dole" and were convinced that many of the recipients of public assistance were cheats. Less eligibility was still rife in the system. The grants rarely, if ever, were sufficient for more than minimum health and decency, and many states paid only a fraction of their own estimate of minimum needs. Despite the federal government's insistence that clients should be the principal source of information about their situation, as they are, for instance, in paying income tax, they were subjected to a degrading and often rigorous investigation, which almost assumed that they intended to lie or to cheat.

The Services Solution (rehabilitation)

As a result, by 1956, "services" again became an integral part of these programs. Probably there is no clearer indication of the way basic programs were changed than the revisions made in the Aid to Dependent Children (ADC) program. This was the year in which parents and other caretakers of dependent children were officially recognized as recipients, and the name of the program changed from Aid to Dependent Children to Aid to Families with Dependent Children. The goals of the program were no longer simply to provide a parent with the money to care for her children. They became rehabilitative goals, incumbent on the parent. The "right to assistance" and the unrestricted money grant were still the law, but they had been modified in practice as well as in the announced purpose of the program.

At the beginning of the 1960's, social workers and others persuaded Congress that the answer to the rising costs of welfare was more social services to those in need. The outcome was President Johnson's "War on Poverty." The "War on Poverty" did not abolish poverty. An assessment in 1976 estimated there had been substantial progress in overcoming poverty, measured in absolute terms—that is, reaching a minimum level of well-being. However, there was no progress either in the ability of people to do without government help or in the incidence of relative poverty. In other words, living standards had improved and the welfare system was more generous, but economic inequality remained (Plotnick, 1976). Nevertheless, by 1980, something of a floor had been placed beneath most of the poor—a somewhat shaky floor perhaps, but some assurance that most would not be without adequate food or medical services.

Back to the Poor Law

The actions of the Reagan/Bush administration that came into power in 1980 were not simply an attempt to cut back on welfare programs in order to reduce federal spending. They were an attempt to return America to the principles of controlling pauperism, principles that were current a hundred or two hundred years ago. Clinton campaigned with the promise to "end welfare as we know it." Identifying solutions to dependency had become high politics, with governors, legislators, and policy experts attempting to win public approval for their welfare reform proposals.

The proposals were all very similar. All emphasized that poor women, specifically AFDC recipients, must be coerced to break the habit of dependency on the state. Most solutions relied on market coercion, and a few on a combination of both market and state coercion. Charles Murray (1984) recommended simply abolishing income supports, forcing poor mothers to expose themselves to the curative discipline of the labor market. Lawrence Mead (1985) was less optimistic about the ability of the poor to respond to market sanctions, and called instead for an "authoritative work policy" that would include systematic monitoring by government, along with rewards and sanctions to force the poor to behave in socially-approved ways. Yet, ironically, even the government's own research studies indicated while the range of tested pilot welfare-to-work programs modestly improved people's income, they proved unlikely to move most people out of poverty (Gueron & Pauly, 1991). In fact, for many, they were worse off and without any lasting protection.

In 1997, Congress passed the Personal Responsibility Act, ending over fifty years of federal legal protection for many poor persons. Although early outcomes show a decrease in welfare roles, the effects on poverty rates and on the poor themselves are not as clear or optimistic.

This brief historical review highlighting the motives and attitudes of helpers has shown how easily our best motives, even our cherished Christian values, can very easily be diverted or distorted. As can be seen, we frequently have lost our direction or have been diverted from the goal of properly caring for the poor.

Biblical Principles and Attitudes

What are the biblical principles and attitudes related to poverty? What is our responsibility in caring for the poor? Will we always have the poor with us? What does the Bible really have to say about poverty?

First of all, one of the central, if not *the* central social concern of the Bible is the plight and suffering of the poor. Yet, interestingly enough, the Bible almost never addresses the poor themselves, but rather the nonpoor. The Bible asks the prosperous to set right the condition of the poor.

Amos saw firsthand the terrible oppression of the poor. He saw the rich "trample the head of the poor into the dust of the earth" (2:7), and perceived that the lifestyle of the rich was built on the oppression of the poor (6:1-7).

Many other biblical texts assert how God lifts up the poor and disadvantaged. God aids the poor, but the rich He sends away empty. He actively opposes the rich, not because they are rich, but because they oppress the poor and neglect the needy. Jesus clearly warns against the possession of wealth, and almost every time Jesus offers an opinion about riches, it is negative. Jesus' advice to the rich young ruler (Luke 18:18-30) calls for him to abandon his possessions, and give them to the poor. Either God or wealth is one's master or "employer" (Matthew 6:24). In the parable of the rich man and Lazarus, the rich man was found guilty for neglecting the poor man at his gate (Luke 16:19-31).

Psalm 146 is one among many passages relating God's concern for the hungry and the oppressed. Indeed, care for the poor is central to the nature of God. God not only acts in history to liberate the poor, but He identifies with the weak and destitute.

Luke pictures the Good News as a message of salvation for the poor, sick, sorrowful, weak, lowly and outcast (4:18-19). The parable of the Good Samaritan (Luke 10:25-37) and of the Last Judgment (Matthew 25:31-46) are two of the better known lessons by Jesus on this subject. A living faith is one that demonstrates compassion for those in need: "If a brother or sister is ill-clad and in lack of daily food, and one of you says to them, 'Go in peace, be warmed and filled,' without giving them the things needed for the body, what does it profit?" (James 2:15-16)

The biblical message is clear, poverty exists because we try to serve both God and money, and the love of self is more important than love of neighbor. In short, the cause of economic poverty is found in moral poverty, but not the morality of the poor. In the Bible, moral poverty, described as misplaced hope, distorted love, and perverted faith in money and in oneself, is found with those who are not poor. A true Christian explanation of poverty in affluent America, therefore, is to be found not in the concept of the culture of poverty, but in the concept of the culture of wealth.

Concluding Reflections

The God of the Bible is not a neutral God. The above biblical passages show how pervasive concern for the poor is in the Bible. The Bible depicts God as on the side of the poor, God biased in favor of the poor. This conclusion is hard to contest. Nevertheless, some comments and clarifications are in order.

First of all — although the Bible says many times that God is on the side of the poor and that Jesus identifies himself with the poor, what difference does this make? As long we read these texts merely as if they were saying something beautiful about God, an additional attribute of God, they will make very little if any difference. But all true *theo*-logy, that is speaking about God, is also *anthropo*-logy. These texts are not to be read as if they were speaking only about God. The biblical authors always speak of God as He reveals Himself to us, as He manifests Himself to us, and challenges us. Therefore, every text that says that God is on the side of the poor should also be read as a challenge addressed to us: you who say you believe in the God of the Covenant, who say you are on His side, should be where the Bible says that God is, namely on the side of the poor. To identify, to know, to meet the poor — is to identify, to know, to meet God.

Second, it is clear from the biblical message that poverty has to be opposed and its main causes, injustice and oppression, have to be counteracted. This calls for unrelenting work for justice. The concrete ways and means to attain justice will certainly differ in every given situation. But the biblical texts clearly suggest that this action for justice will include a concrete willingness to share what one has (Luke 3:11; 19:8), and the true measure of this sharing is not the "surplus" of the haves, but the need of the have-nots.

Lastly, in the course of this study of the poor, the central place of the Covenant needs to be made clear. Texts challenging God's people to do justice in the Old Testament are given as conditions of the Covenant. The Old Testament prophets fiercely attacked social injustice in order to recover the lost ideal of the Covenant. The reference point for all biblical texts on social justice is the Covenant community, a people equal among themselves and equal before God, among whom there shall be no poor.

The title of this chapter comes from a verse in Deuteronomy. Deuteronomy comprises the so-called Deuteronomic Code of Law (Deut. 12-26) edited within the framework of two discourses attributed to Moses, represented as both prophet and lawgiver. The central theme of Deuteronomy is the election of Israel as the people of God by means of the Covenant. Deuteronomy's prescriptions concerning the sabbatical year (Deut. 15:1-11) are as follows:

> (1) At the end of every seven years you shall grant a release. (2) And this is the manner of the release: every creditor shall release what he has lent to his neighbor; he shall not exact it of his neighbor, his brother, because the Lord's release has been proclaimed. (3) Of the foreigner you may exact it; but whatever of yours is with your brother your hand shall release. (4) *But there will be no poor among you* . . . (7) If there is among you a poor man, one of your brethren, in any of the towns within your land which the Lord your God gives you, you shall not harden your heart or shut your hand against your poor brother, (8) but you shall open your hand to him, and lend him sufficient for his need, whatever it may be .... (10) You shall give to him freely, and your heart shall not be grudging when you give to him; because for this the Lord your God will bless you in all your work and in all that you undertake. (11) *For the poor will never cease out of the land* (you will have the poor always with you); therefore I command you, You shall open wide your hand to your brother, to the needy and the poor, in the land.

At the beginning of this biblical passage stands an old precept (verse 1), which is legally interpreted (verse 2), and then developed like a sermon (verses 3-11). This sermon invites us to meet the poor at all times with an open hand and an open heart. The interest of the *law-giver* is satisfied when he has made an ordinance obligatory. But the *prophet* is concerned with the conscience of the people at whom the law is aimed. In this context, the covenant ideal of a people equal before God and equal among themselves is expressed: "there will be no poor among you" (verse 4). But, considering the way people are running things, the *prophet* sadly concedes that in reality "the poor will never cease out of the land" (verse 11). The presence of the poor, therefore, is not to be considered a fact of life which we should accept as unavoidable. On the contrary, it is to be considered a scandal, contradicting God's vision of the human community, and therefore, must be counteracted by all means.

As Christians in social work we have a similar responsibility to respond to the problems of poverty and wealth in our communities and the world. With poverty rates rising and the gap between the haves and have-nots continuing to widen, will we as Christian social workers respond obediently to God's Word? Will we advocate for the poor and work for God's ideal "that there will be no poor among you." Or will we also distort God's ideal, or simply minimize the goal, finding the task too difficult or unpopular? Being a Christian in social work provides the unique opportunity to respond to this significant Christian challenge.

Notes

I am indebted and wish to acknowledge Alan Keith-Lucas's book *The Poor You Have With You Always*(1989) for much of the outline, themes and many of the illustrations offered in this chapter. Portions of the chapter are descriptions from this book. I refer the reader to his book for a more complete and detailed analysis of this topic.

References

Alexander, Cecil. (1845). All Things Bright and Beautiful. In *Hymns Ancient and Modern*, 1924 edition.

Brown, James. (1855). Confidential Instructions to Visitors of the AICP. In Ralph Pumphrey & Murial Pumphrey (Eds.), *The Heritage of American Social Work*. New York: Columbia University Press.

Gilder, George. (1981). *Wealth and Poverty*. New York: Basic Books.

Gueron, Judith M. & Edward Pauly with Cameron M. Lougy. (1991). *From Welfare to Work*. New York: Manpower Demonstration Research Corporation.

Gurteen, Humphreys S. (1882). A Handbook of Charity Organization. In Ralph Pumphrey & Muriel Pumphrey (Eds.), *The Heritage of American Social Work*. New York: Columbia University Press.

Mead, Lawrence. (1985). *Beyond Entitlement: The Social Obligations of Citizenship*. New York: Free Press.

164   *Beryl Hugen*

Murray, Charles. (1984). *Losing Ground.* New York: Basic Books.

Niebuhr, Reinold. (1932). *The Contribution of Religion to Social Work.* New York: Columbia University Press.

Plotnich, Robert D. (1976). Progress Against Poverty? *Social Welfare Forum*, 104-115.

Richmond, Mary E. (1899). *Friendly Visiting Among the Poor.* New York: Russell Sage Foundation.

Richmond, Mary E. (1922). *What is Social Case Work?* New York: Russell Sage Foundation.

Troeltsch, Ernest. (1931). *The Social Teaching of the Christian Churches.* Translated by Olive Wyon, New York.

Uhlhorn, Gerhard. (1883). *Christian Charity in the Ancient Church.* Edinburgh.

Weber, Max. (1930). *The Protestant Ethic and the Spirit of Capitalism.* London.

CHAPTER 11

WHEN SOCIAL WORK AND CHRISTIANITY CONFLICT

Lawrence E. Ressler

His name is Emory and he is a Christian. To be more specific, he is a Mennonite. He may not look like what you expect a Mennonite to look like, but he is. When Emory was young, his family followed more traditional customs. They drove only black cars, for example. His dad wore a plain coat and his mom wore a white bonnet and dark stockings. They had no radios or televisions. His relatives, who have remained committed to traditional Mennonite customs, would not approve of the mustache he now wears, the television, stereo, computers, and gold colored car he has. What is more important to know about Emory, however, is that while he has abandoned many of the traditional customs, he still has the soul of a Mennonite. It is the framework that provides structure and purpose to his living. A story might help illustrate the influence that being Mennonite has on his life.

When Emory was about 13, he earned money by mowing lawns. One day, when he went to mow a lawn for a customer, he found another boy at the same house with a lawnmower. Emory informed the boy he had been hired to do the mowing, to which the boy replied he had been hired to do it. Emory insisted the job was his and before he knew what happened, the other boy drew back and hit Emory squarely on the jaw, knocking him to the ground. Emory got up and did what he thought was proper. He turned his face to one side and said, "Here, do you want to hit this side too." After all, Jesus had said, "Turn the other cheek." To Emory's surprise, the boy hit him a second time. Rather than fight about the lawn, Emory got up and went home. Even as an adolescent, Emory was guided by the Mennonite commitment to nonviolence.

Emory's personal sense of history begins in January 1525 when Conrad Grebel and Felix Mantz chose to be rebaptized as adults in Zurich, Switzerland. They did so based on their reading of the Bible. The choice to be a Christian, they believed, should be a voluntary adult decision rather than a procedure imposed on infants as was the custom of the day. Such an idea ran counter to official church policy and the law that required infant baptism. This issue may not seem significant today, but at that time adult baptism was considered both heresy and treason.

Adult baptism was considered so egregious during the sixteenth and seventh centuries that it could result in capital punishment.

The adult baptisms of Grebel and Mantz marked the beginning of the Anabaptist (rebaptizer) movement which was an extension of the Protestant Reformation begun by Martin Luther in 1517. The word Mennonite was given to followers of Menno Simons, an Anabaptist leader in Holland in the latter part of the sixteenth century. Menno Simons and his followers were deeply committed Christians who desired to use the Bible as a guide to living, particularly the New Testament and the teaching of Jesus. Over the years, a distinctive Mennonite theology and life style developed. This included such things as nonconformist living, service to others, community accountability, and simple living. The visible application of this theology included dressing distinctively, rejecting some technology, a worldwide voluntary service system to help people in need, and living a modest lifestyle. Central to their belief system was a commitment to nonresistant love which was to be put into consistent and practical action. Love, following the teaching of Jesus, was to be extended even to one's enemies.

Anabaptists, including Mennonites, were so empowered by and committed to their faith, that while they would not kill to preserve their beliefs, they were willing to die for them. The commitment to their faith was put to the greatest of tests. Anabaptists were persecuted for several hundred years in Europe because of their beliefs and lifestyle with over 3000 men, women, and children being burned to death, drowned, and beheaded (Bracht, 1837). Take Michael Sattler and his family who were rebaptized in 1525, for example. The Sattlers were arrested, tried, found guilty of heresy and treason, and instructed to recant. Because Michael would not, his tongue was cut out and red hot tongs were applied three times to his body. When he continued to refuse to abandon his beliefs, he was driven to the countryside and had red hot tongs applied five more times to his body. When he still would not renounce his Anabaptist beliefs, he was burned at the stake. His wife and sisters were later drowned because they also would not recant (Baergen, 1981).

In Emory's own direct family, his grandfather seven times removed was sentenced to prison in 1710 for his religious beliefs. The family, along with many other Mennonites, came to America in 1715 primarily in search of religious freedom. James Madison specifically mentions the "Menonists" in the influential apology for religious liberty written in 1785 entitled "Memorial and Remonstrance" (Gaustad, 1993, p. 145). For Emory's ancestors, the First Amendment to the Constitution was a welcome end to several hundred years of religious oppression.

Like his ancestors, Emory has no interest in killing to protect his rights. While Emory cannot state for certain that he would take persecution to the point of death for his beliefs, in his soul he would want to. Religious beliefs are as dear to Emory as they were to his ancestors. Emory may not look like what you would expect a Mennonite to look like, but the teachings of Christ, respect for the Bible, the Mennonite theology, and a lifestyle which emerges from them are as important to him as those who dress and live in a distinctive manner.

Emory is also a social worker. He has a bachelor's degree, a master's degree, and a doctorate in social work. He has worked as a social worker in both religious and secular settings and has attended or worked in social work educational institutions for two decades. Emory has also had leadership roles in both the National Association of Social Workers (NASW) and the North American Association of Christians in Social Work (NACSW).

Emory is equally committed to his faith and the social work profession. He has found the social work profession to a be a particularly meaningful vocation. His motivation for social work is related to his understanding of what it means to be a faithful follower of Christ. I John provides a particularly clear connection between his theology and his interest in social work:

> We know love by this, that he laid down his life for us—and we ought to lay down our lives for one another. How does God's love abide in anyone who has the world's goods and sees a brother or sister in need and yet refuses help? Little children, let us love, not in word or speech, but in truth and action. (I John 3:16-18)

Emory is an example of what can be called a Christian social worker. While Emory is comfortable with the label, others are not. The phrase Christian social worker, for some, is an oxymoron. Rather than see social work and Christianity as allies, Christianity, for them, is viewed as a major barrier to accomplishing social work ideals. The linking of Christianity and social work, for some social workers, is a troublesome connection.

There are, in other words, points of tension between social work and Christianity. The purpose of this chapter is to explore the reasons for the conflict between Christianity and social work. In addition, several suggestions for reducing the tension between the two are offered.

Spirituality and Religion

To fully understand the tension between Christianity and social work, it is important, first of all, to distinguish between spirituality and religion.

Definitions

Spirituality, in the popular social work use of the term, refers to "the basic human drive for meaning, purpose, and moral relatedness among people, with the universe, and with the ground of our being" (Canda, 1989, p. 573). Human beings from this perspective are viewed as more than physical beings determined by their basic drives as Freud suggested, by the economic system as Marx believed, or by the environment as Skinner argued. A spiritual perspective holds that at the core of the human being is a search for meaning, the desire to know, and the yearning to be connected.

Spirituality is distinguished from religion which is defined as "an institutionally patterned system of beliefs, values, and rituals" (Canda, 1989, p. 573). Religion involves the organization of ideas about the relationship of the supernatural world and the natural world. It also includes the organization of activities and people that stem from an understanding of the supernatural and natural worlds. Whereas spirituality is largely philosophical in tone and speaks to human nature issues, religion is more sociological and theological. Spirituality is a personal phenomenon while religion is a social phenomenon.

A Typology

Using contemporary definitions, an analysis of spirituality and religion results in a fourfold typology. The first category could be called **Spiritual and Non- Religious**. This would include people who are actively engaged in a search for or have found meaning and connection in life. They do so, however, outside of a religious framework. They do not attend a church and are not involved in what is considered religious activities. Meaning in life and connectedness come from non-religious sources such as nature, a job, special relationships, or even the mundane aspects of daily living that are approached with a spiritual attitude. The second type could be designated **Religious and Disspirited**[1]. This would be typical of people who go to church, follow religious rituals, and even support the religious organization. Their life, however, has no meaning and they do not feel connected to others. They may be involved in religious activity but it does not provide meaningful structure or purpose for life. The third classification could be referred to as **Disspirited and Non- Religious**. This would involve persons who are not consciously purposeful about life nor connected. They may well feel aimless and isolated from others. They also are not involved in religious activities, do not embrace a religious belief system, and are not part of a religious community. The fourth category could be called **Spiritual And Religious**. This would consist of persons whose meaning in life is related to their religious experience. Emory, described earlier, is in this category. The person of Jesus Christ and the Bible as well as an awareness of the Holy Spirit give form and substance to his life. The Mennonite theology helps organize how he understands the world, history, and the future, and it influences how he lives. Going to church, reading the Bible, praying, singing, worshiping with others, and attending church conferences provide inspiration and motivation. His religion is a source of hope and strength.

Spirituality, Religion, and the Social Work Profession

After decades of neglect, the topic of spirituality has become increasingly popular in social work in recent years. Spirituality, for example, is being addressed more frequently in social work journals. A keyword search in the Social Work Abstracts, for example, found 70 entries related to spirituality in the past 20 years with 86% published in the last 10 years. After being dropped from the Council on Social Work Education's (CSWE) curriculum policy statement in 1970, the term spirituality has been reinserted in the 1996 revision (Marshall, 1991). An organization called the Society for Spirituality and Social Work has been developed complete with a newsletter, chapters across the country, and an annual convention. Although the change is not yet evident, there is also some indication that social work textbooks, which have seriously neglected spirituality (Cnaan, 1997), are beginning to address the topic (e.g. Bullis, 1996). In sum, the concept of spirituality appears to be gaining support in the profession.

The topic of religion, like spirituality, has been largely ignored in social work for the greater part of the twentieth century (Cnaan, 1997; Loewenberg, 1988). There appears to be an interesting paradox with respect to recent attitudes in the social work profession related to religion, however. On the one hand, there is increasing recognition of the importance of religion to clients and colleagues. This is evident most notably in the revised 1996 NASW Code of Ethics where religious diversity has been given increased status. Religion is now included as one of the groups which social workers are implored to be sensitive to along with race, ethnicity, national origin, color, sex, sexual orientation, age, marital status, political belief, and mental or physical disability. Social workers are instructed in the NASW Code of Ethics to "obtain education about and seek to understand the nature of social diversity and oppression" related to religion as well as diverse groups (1.05). Social workers are further instructed to "avoid unwarranted negative criticism of colleagues" related to religion (2.01), to "not practice, condone, facilitate, or collaborate with any form of discrimination" on the basis of religion (4.02), and are required to "act to prevent and eliminate domination of, exploitation of, and discrimination against any person, group, or class" on the basis of religion (6.04). In other words, respect for religious diversity seems to be of equal importance to other types of diversity.

At the same time, there has been significant tension in the profession with respect to religion, especially those who are in the **Spiritual** and **Religious** category. Alan Keith- Lucas highlighted the crux of the matter with this question in 1958, "What happens, then, to the social worker who is not content with religious generalizations and who really believes and acts by what he says in his creed?" (Keith-Lucas A., 1958, p. 236). Keith-Lucas, who wrote prolifically about the integration of Christianity and social work for 40 years, believed that with careful theology and a good understanding of social work the two were compatible. He states, "The task of beginning to make such a synthesis will not, however, be an easy one. It will require an exploration for those willing to undertake it, of what theology really teaches and not what most people take for granted that it teaches, or remember from Sunday School...It must be intellectually rigorous, conducted by people who are amateurs neither in religion nor social work. It will have to do with the 'hard paradoxes' rather than the 'easy correspondences'" (p. 236).

Not everyone has taken Keith-Lucas's position. In spite of clear evidence that social workers do not feel adequately prepared to deal with religious issues which arise in social work practice (Joseph, 1988; Sheridan, 1992), some social workers resist giving increased attention to the topic. Clark (1994), for example, argues, "If we want the social work profession to maintain its political and technological gains, we must not move religion to a position of central importance" (p. 15). Increased attention to religion in social work, Clark argues, will place the profession on a "slippery slope."

One of the most visible and volatile clashes in social work took place recently between the Council on Social Work Education (CSWE) and religiously-affiliated institutions. At the center of the conflict was an accreditation standard developed in 1982 which extended mandatory nondiscrimination to political and sexual orientation. The requirement that sexual orientation be included in the social work program nondiscrimination statement conflicted with a policy in some religiously-affiliated institutions that prohibits sexual intimacy outside of marriage[2]. Interestingly, the CSWE acknowledged in a publicly distributed memorandum that the sexual orientation requirement was added knowing that it violated the religious beliefs of some institutions (CSWE Commission on Accreditation, 1996).

From 1982 to 1995, the conflict was dormant because the policy was not enforced. That changed beginning in 1995 when a number of schools were told by CSWE that they would not be accredited if they did not comply with the standard. A number of religiously-affiliated schools responded by threatening a lawsuit on several accounts. First, the 1982 standard was viewed as a violation of the profession's commitment to religious diversity and being denied accreditation was seen as a violation of the principle of social justice. Second, denying accreditation to religiously-affiliated institutions for policies related to their religious beliefs was interpreted as a violation of the First Amendment guarantee of religious freedom. Third, since eliminating religiously-affiliated institutions from accreditation would result in their students being ineligible for state licenses, anti-trust concerns were raised.

The CSWE Commission on Accreditation (COA) made an attempt to resolve the conflict by proposing an exemption to the nondiscrimination standard similar to the American Bar Association and the American Psychological Association. In part, the proposed revision read, "Religious institutions that qualify for religious exemption under federal laws and regulations may apply for an exemption if they cannot comply with these standards" (CSWE Commission on Accreditation, 1996). Concern was raised by both religiously-affiliated institutions that would benefit from the revised standard and gay and lesbian advocates who favored having sexual orientation in the standard. The common concern, however, came from very different sources. Religious affiliated institutions feared a social stigma if granted an exemption. Gay and lesbian advocates saw the proposal as abandoning historic commitments to the oppressed. As a result of the negative and widespread feedback, the COA withdrew the proposal.

A second effort to resolve the dilemma was attempted in 1996 by removing the 1982 nondiscrimination standard entirely and replacing it with a new standard. The proposed standard called for "specific, continuous efforts to provide a learning context in which understanding and respect for diversity (including age, color, disability, ethnicity, gender, national origin, race, religion, and sexual orientation) are practiced" (CSWE Commission on Accreditation, 1997). The proposal was received favorably by the religiously-affiliated institutions who had expressed dissatisfaction with the 1982 standard. The proposal was resisted by gay and lesbian advocates who wanted a policy that required nondiscrimination based on sexual orientation. The second statement was approved by the CSWE Board of Directors by a narrow margin in June of 1997. While a new policy has been put into place, the debate uncovered a significant level of animosity among some social work educators and practitioners toward religious persons and institutions, especially those whose spirituality stems from a more conservative theology.

Why the Conflict Between Social Work and Christianity?

At one level, there seems to be a natural compatibility between Christianity and social work. Take the six core values and related ethical principles espoused in the newly revised NASW Code of Ethics, for example. Related to the value of **Service** is the following ethical principle, "Social workers primary goal is to help people in need and to address social problems." For Christians, this brings to mind the statement of Jesus, "Whoever wishes to be great among you must be your servant, and whoever wishes to be first among you must be your slave just as the Son of Man came not to be served but to serve, and to give his life a ransom for many" (Matt 20:26-28). The value of service appears to be highly esteemed in both social work and Christianity.

The second of the social work values is **Social Justice** with the ethical principle stated as follows, "Social workers challenge social injustice." Some theologians, such as Donahue (1977) argue that justice is the central theme in the Bible. The admonition of Micah 6:8 seems to fit quite nicely with the NASW principle. "He has told you, O mortal, what is good; and what does the LORD require of you but to do justice, and to love kindness, and to walk humbly with your God."

The third NASW value is **Dignity and Worth of the Person** and the fourth value is **Importance of Human Relationships**. The related ethical principles are that "Social workers respect the inherent dignity and worth of the person" and that "Social workers recognize the central importance of human relationships." Both of these principles appear to have striking Christian parallels. The most dominant symbol in Christianity, the cross, is a powerful reminder to Christians of God's unconditional love. The NASW commitment to social relationships seems compatible with Jesus' admonition to love your neighbor as yourself (Luke 10:27). Indeed, Christians are called to love one's enemies and to do good to those who hate them (Luke 6:27).

The fifth and sixth values are **Integrity** and **Competence** with the related ethical principles being "Social workers behave in a trustworthy manner" and "Social workers practice within their areas of competence and enhance their professional expertise." While the Bible does not speak to these issues directly, they would easily fit the Christian imperative to be holy (Ephesians 1:4) and to be above reproach (I Timothy 5:4).

In other words, at the principle level of the NASW Code of Ethics, there exists what appears to be an easy fit between social work and

Christianity. At this level, social work appears to be a natural profession for Christians who want to help.

Incompatible Christian Issues

While similarities can be demonstrated between Christianity and social work at the value and ethical level, there are many areas of difference, some of which result in significant tension. Some of these differences derive from Christian tradition and thought.

Spiritual Reductionism

One source of tension between social work and Christianity stems from a strain of thought I will call spiritual reductionism. Reductionism, according to Babbie (1995), is an overly strict limitation on the kinds of concepts and variables to be considered as causes in explaining a broad range of human behavior" (p. 93). Spiritual reductionism is rooted in the ancient Greek philosophy of gnosticism that embraced a dualistic view of the world. To oversimplify, the material world was seen as evil while the spiritual world was viewed as good. Gnostics believed they had secret knowledge which would lead people to return to the goodness found in the spiritual world.

In a similar way, contemporary Christian spiritual reductionism has a bifurcated view of existence. The material world, including the human body, is viewed as fallen, doomed, and temporary. The spiritual world, including the human soul, is eternal. Heaven and Hell are places where good and bad reign for eternity. The ultimate destiny of the soul depends on spiritual decisions made prior to death. Since the soul is viewed as eternal and the material world as temporary, saving a person's soul is the only action that really matters.

Spiritual reductionism can have a significant impact on how Christians conduct themselves. For example, shortly after I moved to a new house once, two representatives from a local church knocked on my door. Bluntly they asked, "Are you a born again Christian?" I was shocked by their directness and was speechless. I mumbled something and they went away. The only issue that concerned them was my spiritual welfare. I suspect I said yes and that seemed to be all they were concerned about.

This type of theology can also have a direct impact on social attitudes about social work. Dwight Moody and Billy Sunday, famous turn of the century evangelists for example, spoke out actively against social work arguing that it detracted from the more important work of saving souls (Loewenberg, 1988). Moberg (1977), in *The Great Reversal: Evan-*

gelism and Social Concern, examines the split between "fundamentalists" and "social gospelers" that took place between 1910 and 1930. He
describes in considerable detail the rejection of social welfare concerns
by fundamentalists who embraced a gnostic-like theology.

Christian spiritual reductionism can impact the practice of social
work as well. Food, clothing, or shelter, for example, may be used as a
means to an end. Material needs may be addressed only as a way to get
to the spiritual aspect of clients which is viewed as the more important
aspect. Christian spiritual reductionism can also result in a myopic assessment of problems. Placing a higher value on the spiritual dimension
than other aspects may result in the belief that if spiritual problems are
resolved, other problems will dissipate. It can also reduce intervention
strategies to those which address spiritual issues. Furthermore, Christian spiritual reductionism can result in a dependence on religious language when working with clients. Not only may the social worker rely
heavily on religious language when assessing problems, they may establish client use of religious language as a measure of success. Finally,
working in contexts which prohibit the use of religious language for
legal or other reasons, may lead to employment frustration for spiritual
reductionistic social workers because of their inability to deal with what
they consider to be the most important area of life.

Unbalanced Social Work Practice

A second tension between social work and Christianity stems from
an understanding of evangelism that has the potential to clash with the
profession's commitment to client self-determination. I received a letter
once from a Christian social worker who shared this dilemma:

> It is the dying person who seems content without "religion"
> that truly frustrates me. I fear for his/her death based on my
> own spiritual beliefs that death without Jesus Christ equals
> Hell. Yet, I continue to practice my commitment to not force
> discussion about his/her spiritual apathy in honor of my pro-
> fessional value: self-determination. So I ask the following ques-
> tion: How can I profess to be a Christian and practice ethical
> social work? (personal correspondence, 1996)

The more a person's theology emphasizes evangelism and Hell,
the more difficult it may be to remain committed to the social work
value of self-determination. If one believes "death without Jesus Christ
equals Hell," the most caring act one could engage in would be to lead
the person into a saving knowledge of Christ and into eternal life. The

more intense the conviction, the more extreme the measures may be to "save" people. Indeed, in its most extreme form, forcing someone to confess their sins is interpreted as a loving act even if causing pain is necessary. Sadly, some Christians have used beating, torture, drowning, and burning people to death in an effort to save their souls.

Religious Tyranny

A third source of tension between social work and Christianity results from a phenomenon I will call religious tyranny. Religious tyranny, like other types of tyranny, imposes one way of doing things on others. It ignores diverse perspectives and may even be threatened by them. Whether the social policies are unintentionally insensitive to diverse groups or intentionally controlling, the result is the same; a second class of citizenship results.

One form of religious tyranny stems from a belief that the United States is or should be a Christian nation. Elsen (1954) illustrates this conviction:

> Let us be honest. Our kind of democracy depends on religion. It depends on the Christian religion. Its ideas are Christian ideas. Its ideals are Christian ideals. Its goals are Christian goals. Allow Christian faith and practice to languish, and democracy as we know it begins to disintegrate. (p. 175)

Numerous American colonies in the eighteenth century in fact had laws that were deferential to Christianity including Connecticut, Delaware, Georgia, Maryland, Massachusetts, New Hampshire, New Jersey, North Carolina, Pennsylvania, South Carolina, and Vermont. The South Carolina constitution, for example, stated, "The Christian Protestant religion shall be deemed, and is hereby constituted and declared to be, the established religion of this State" (Gaustad, 1993, p. 171). Numerous colonies limited public offices to persons who would affirm Christianity. Pennsylvania, for example, required the following: "Each member [of the legislature], before he takes his seat, shall make and subscribe to the following declaration, viz: 'I do believe in one God, the creator and governor of the universe, the rewarder to the good and punisher of the wicked. And I do acknowledge the Scriptures of the Old and New Testament to be given by Divine inspiration'" (Gaustad, 1993, p. 170).

State sponsored religion was declared illegal for all of the entire nation in 1868 when the Fourteenth Amendment to the Constitution was adopted[3]. The Fourteenth Amendment required that states honor the Constitutional bill of rights including freedom of religion in the

First Amendment which states, "Congress shall make no law respecting an establishment of religion, or prohibiting the free exercise thereof" (Gaustad, 1993, p. 44).

Neither the First Amendment nor the Fourteenth Amendment, however, have eliminated the belief for some that Christianity should be the preferred religion and that laws and legislators need to be consistent with it. The most visible advocate in recent years is Pat Robertson, the president of the Christian Broadcast Network, who ran for president in 1992. He states in a recent book, "There is absolutely no way that government can operate successfully unless led by godly men and women operating under the laws of the God of Jacob" (Robertson, 1991, p. 227).

This issue is for some Christian social workers one of the most troubling dilemmas. The NASW Code of Ethics calls on social workers to be dually committed to clients and to the general welfare of society (e.g. NASW Code of Ethics, 1.01, 6.01). Consequently, if one believes that Christianity is the one true religion and that biblically supported lifestyles are necessary to achieve a healthy society, there is a sense of obligation to advocate for Christian ways of doing things. At the same time, the Code of Ethics calls for respect for diversity. These two standards result in a perplexing ethical dilemma for some.

It needs to be pointed out that this is not just a Christian dilemma. All social workers have a vision of what constitutes the general welfare of society. Each social worker must wrestle with the tension between the patterns which are consistent with this vision and ideas or practices that are at odds with it. This tension was illustrated most clearly to me at a seminar focused on religious fundamentalist families that I attended. A social worker convinced of the rightness of egalitarian family structure indicated she would never be able to work with a family that had a hierarchical structure. Her vision of what constitutes a healthy family system was at odds with a model that others embrace. Her dilemma was fundamentally the same as that faced by many Christians.

Oppressive Aspects of Social Work

There is, however, another side to the social work and Christianity tension that is less frequently acknowledged in the profession. The tension between social work and Christianity can also stem from an aspect or body of social work thought that is religiously oppressive and lacks commitment to religious diversity. Ironically, some social workers, in their attempt to pursue social justice for certain groups, condone prejudice and discrimination against certain religious groups with whom they disagree.

Social Work Secularism

Secularism is a way of thinking that denies or ignores the spiritual dimension of life and discredits the value and contribution of religion. While there is widespread agreement that social work has a religious foundation (Niebuhr, 1932; Marty, 1980; Goldstein, 1987; Loewenberg, 1988; Midgley, 1989; Keith-Lucas, 1989), it is also clear that social work was significantly influenced by the progressive mindset of the late nineteenth century which promoted a positivist worldview and devalued spirituality and religion. Empirical evidence and logic, the twin pillars of science, were embraced in the social sciences as superior ways of knowing.

Karl Marx, Emile Durkheim, and Sigmund Freud, key social scientists upon which social work theory relied during much of the twentieth century, all viewed religion with suspicion and doubt. Religion for Marx was oppressive, for Durkheim was a social construction, and for Freud a neurotic impulse. With respect to social work, friendly visiting was replaced with scientific charity, while religiously motivated compassion and caring gave way to social diagnosis.

Evidence for the secular influence in social work is provided by Cnaan and Wineburg (1997). In reviewing papers given at the CSWE Annual Program Meeting, they found that only 30 out of 1500 (2%) papers given at the CSWE Annual Program Meeting from 1990 - 1994 dealt with religion and service delivery, with only 2 papers addressing "contemporary concerns of religiously based social services" (p. 7). Their study found that, with few exceptions, the 20 most popular texts "made no mention of any congregational or sectarian aspect of social work with the exception of the obligatory Charity Organization Societies" (p. 8). Furthermore, their study found that only 10 of 50 social welfare syllabi reviewed mentioned religiously-affiliated social service provision.

Positive sentiments from social work pioneers about spirituality and religion have been largely expunged from historical accounts of social work. Seldom acknowledged, for example, is Jane Addam's view of the critical role of Christianity in the settlement house movement. Referring to Christian humanitarianism, she states, "Certain it is that spiritual force is found in the Settlement Movement, and it is also true that this force must be evolked and must be called into play before the success of any Settlement is assured" (Addams 1910: p.124, as quoted in Garland, 1994, p.81).

Likewise, little has been said about the positive attitude the renowned Mary Richmond had about the role of the church. She states:

After all has been said in objection to past and present methods of church charity, we must realize that, if the poor are to be effectively helped by charity, the inspiration must come from the church. The church has always been and will continue to be the chief source of charitable energy; and I believe that, to an increasing degree, the church will be the leader in charitable experiment and in the extension of the scope of charitable endeavor...The church has always been the pioneer in such work. (Richmond, 1899, p. 174-175)

Cnaan and Wineburg (1997) conclude that a "bias of omission" related to religiously-based social service provision exists in social work.

A second aspect of social work secularism is related to the broader church/state legal issue. While there has been no Supreme Court decision that has directly addressed the relationship of religion and social work, the profession has been influenced by the secular philosophy advanced by the Supreme Court in other arenas, the most significant of which have taken place in education. The dominant church/state philosophy endorsed by the Supreme Court in the twentieth century was first articulated by Justice Black in 1947 when he wrote, "The First Amendment has erected a wall between church and state. That wall must be high and impregnable" (Eastland, 1993, p. 67). This philosophy has resulted in Supreme Court decisions that have consistently ruled against religion in the public arena. Carter (1993), in a recent bestseller about politics and religion, concludes that the law has trivialized religion and needs to move towards a more accommodating stance.

Since the growth of the social work profession has been closely correlated with the growth of the welfare state, the "high and impregnable wall" philosophy suggested by Justice Black has had a significant impact on how religion was dealt with by social workers. Namely, religion in publically funded agencies has been treated as a phenomenon outside the purview of social work. In order to observe the "high wall" separation of church and state, religious issues, if acknowledged at all, were seen as best dealt with by religious representatives. While no study has been completed to document the impact of the "high wall" philosophy on social work, there is a wealth of anecdotal evidence from social workers in public agencies who report being strictly forbidden to address religious or spiritual issues, to use religious language, or to pray with clients even if it was in the client's best interest and desired by clients. While dealing with religious issues is surely a complicated professional matter, the principle strategy followed by the profession was to refuse to deal with them.

The secularization of social work practice has gone beyond social workers working in publicly funded agencies, however. Religious-free social work practice has been presented as the only responsible professional position. There have been individuals and organizations over the years who have explored and supported an accommodating philosophy of religion but with little public acknowledgment and presented only in obscure literature. Most notable among those addressing the relationship of Christianity and social work is the North American Association of Christians in Social Work (NACSW) which has been in existence since 1950 and has published the journal *Social Work and Christianity* since 1974. As for individual contributions, Alan Keith-Lucas was by far the most productive writer on the integration of faith and social work (Ressler, 1992). In general, however, little attention has been given to the relationship of religion and social work even in private agencies not constrained by the First Amendment.

Religi-phobia and Religious Discrimination

Religious prejudice and discrimination are reported with surprising frequency by religiously active social workers. While no study has been completed to evaluate the full extent of the problem, one small study (Ressler, 1997) found that 12 of 18 persons (67%) who placed themselves in the **Spiritual** and **Religious** category had experienced prejudice or discrimination within the profession. For example, the respondents reported the following:

> They act like you are a fanatic if your religion permeates your life...In a board meeting, I heard someone talking about "those born-again' folks in a derogatory manner. There have been times that born-again [persons] are accused of extreme behaviors and portrayed as lunatics, when in fact, the person may have had difficulty without born-again affiliation...My religious values, especially my personal interpretation of scripture concerning homosexuality, resulted in my being told by a supervisor that I shouldn't be a therapist because I couldn't be objective enough to work with gay and lesbian clients...A vivid memory occurred as an undergraduate when a professor jumped on me in the classroom for including Scripture in a paper. A peer was ridiculed in the classroom for her faith by another instructor...Mostly subtle beliefs that Christian values are somehow different than those of others and should never be expressed.

Religious discrimination has made inroads into some social work institutions which has resulted in screening out of students with certain religious belief systems. The social work faculty at St. Cloud State University, for instance, in 1992 developed a position paper entitled, "The S.C.S.U Social Work Department's Position on Attitudes Towards Gay and Lesbian People" (St. Cloud State University Department of Social Work, 1992). Referring to themselves as gatekeepers for the profession, the position statement attempted to outline what was expected of students related to gay and lesbian people. The initial paper stated, "The only legitimate position of the social work profession is to abhor the oppression that is perpetuated in gay and lesbian people and to act personally and professionally to end the degradation in its many forms...Many of our students come from religious backgrounds that do not accept homosexuality...It is not okay in this case to "love the sinner and hate the sin"...Students who have predetermined negative attitudes towards gay and lesbian people, and who are not open to exploring these values will not find this program very comfortable and should probably look elsewhere for a major" (p. 2).

The social work program also required that student applicants participate in an admission interview that "made a point of examining students' attitudes towards homosexuality" (Hibbard, 1994, p. 1). With the support of the Christian Legal Society, the American Jewish Congress, American Jewish Committee, the Center for Individual Rights, the Intercollegiate Studies Institute, and the Minnesota Civil Liberties Union, the statement and interview was challenged by some students. As a result, the statement was revised and reference to a student's religion was dropped. The interview has been replaced with an "admissions meeting in which students 'formally introduce' themselves to the department" (p. 1).

Social Work Tyranny

Hidden in the question about religious values being in conflict with social work values is an issue which the social work profession needs to address. Some social workers advocate a form of professional tyranny with the notion that there is one correct social work worldview and one set of values in social work that all must agree with. Social workers, they believe, who do not accept this worldview and agree with the popular application of social work values should be censured or even banished from the profession.

This argument was made by the University of Buffalo with respect to the CSWE non-discrimination statement on sexual orientation described earlier. The faculty at the University of Buffalo signed a petition that stated, "We, the faculty at the University of Buffalo, are disappointed and outraged at CSWE's proposal to exempt social work programs at religious institutions from nondiscrimination on the basis of sexual and political orientation...If these programs want to receive CSWE accreditation, they must be held to nondiscrimination policies" (State University of New York at Buffalo, School of Social Work, 1996).

Jones (Parr, 1996) in her argument against allowing religious institutions to be exempt from the sexual orientation non-discrimination standard suggested that programs that did not comply should, among other things, be "explicitly identified by CSWE in its listing of accredited programs" and "should be monitored with particular diligence and asked to demonstrate their efforts in these areas at an additional time midpoint between accreditation site visits" (p. 310). Her recommendation that there be public identification of those who are different and that there be close monitoring of their behavior are reminiscent of tactics advocated by oppressive dictators.

The tone in the NASW lesbian and gay issues policy has a similar exclusivist and intolerant tone. The policy statement reads, "NASW affirms its commitment to work toward full social and legal acceptance and recognition of lesbian and gay people. To this end, NASW shall support legislation, regulations, policies, judicial review, political action changes in social work policy statements, the NASW Code of Ethics, and any other means necessary to establish and protect the equal rights of all people without regard to sexual orientation" (p. 163). There is no recognition of diversity among groups and no room for variation. The position is dictatorial.

Where to From Here

The current tension between social work and Christianity, in other words, has both a Christian aspect and a social work aspect. Reducing the tension involves adjustments from both the Christian community and the social work community.

Christian Adjustments

First, Christians need to embrace a wholistic Christian understanding of creation that acknowledges the spiritual dimension of life but with a balanced view of the world, including the psychological, social, biological, economic, political, and environmental aspects. Christians who have a wholistic theology will likely find much in common with the person in environment framework which undergirds social work.

Second, it is important for Christian social workers to develop a theology of evangelism that does not abandon self-determination. Most Christian theologies view self-determination as a basic human right and one that God has afforded to each of us. If, as most Christians believe, God provided humans with the ability and responsibility to choose, including the freedom to make bad decisions, surely Christian social workers need to allow clients to make their own choices. Self-determination is a sound Christian principle even for evangelicals, as well as a central social work value.

The self-determination dilemma may also involve a mistaken assumption about what self-determination in social work means. Self-determination does not mean that a social worker does not confront and cause discomfort when working with clients. Self-determination means, that first, you do what you do with the awareness and consent of the client, and second, that you respect the right of clients to make their own decisions.

Third, Christian social workers will need to develop a confident understanding of their own role and the contribution of Christianity in society while remaining committed to diversity, even if laws and individual behavior do not fully support a Christian sense of morality. This begins with a Christian humility that holds we "see through a glass darkly" and that "all have sinned and fallen short of the glory of God." It further acknowledges that God permits humans to live in ways that violate His intended plans. Finally, the temptation to impose Christian values can be reduced by interpreting the Christian role as one of salt and light rather than conquerors.

Having said this, Christians need to be afforded the right of others to participate in public conversation about what constitutes the general welfare and to be involved in the political process.

Social Work Adjustments

There are adjustments the social work profession can make as well to reduce the tension. This involves, first of all, adopting positions on social issues which are inclusive rather than exclusive. Interestingly, on the abortion and euthanasia issues, the social work profession has made a conscious effort to respect and accommodate diverse values. For example, on the abortion issue the 1996 NASW position statement relates that, "In acknowledging and affirming social work's commitment to respecting diverse value systems in a pluralistic society, it is recognized that the issue of abortion is controversial because it reflects the different value systems of different groups. If the social worker chooses not to participate in abortion counseling, it is his or her responsibility to provide appropriate referral services to ensure that this option is available to clients" (NASW, 1994, p. 3). For the individual, diversity is acknowledged and honored. With respect to social policy, the position is moderate. "In states where abortion services are not available as one option, those members of NASW who so desire may work toward legalization, planning, funding, and implementation of such services" (p. 3).

With respect to the euthanasia position, the NASW policy states, "In acknowledging and affirming social work's commitment to respecting diverse value systems in a pluralistic society, end of life issues are recognized as controversial because they reflect the varied value systems of different groups. Social workers should be free to participate or not participate in assisted-suicide or other discussion concerning end of life decisions depending on their own beliefs, attitudes, and value systems" (p. 59). Social worker diversity is respected individually. With respect to social policy, the position is conservative. "It is inappropriate for social workers to deliver, supply, or personally participate in commission of an act of assisted suicide when acting in a professional role" (p. 60).

Furthermore, if the profession is going to respect religious beliefs, then it will have to allow for diversity among institutions. This is the position that the Commission on Higher Education has taken. In a recent publication they state, "The Commission respects and honors the diversity of institutions it accredits and recognizes institutional limits created by law, government, or religious tenets. It does not find the diversity of its member institutions incompatible with the principles of equity and diversity within those institutions" (Commission on Higher Education, April 1996, p. 1).

Toward a Common Agenda

The fact that there are differences between Christianity and social work should not be a surprise to either Christians or social workers. For Christians, the very nature of the created world assumes differences between people and groups by extension. The belief in sin and redemption, the Kingdom of God and the Kingdom of this world presumes differences between the Christian and non-Christian. Likewise, the social work profession supports the notion of differences through its concept of diversity. Differences are to be expected.

Furthermore, neither Christians nor social workers should be surprised that some differences result in tension. Jesus warned His disciplines many times of the likelihood of conflict (e.g. John 15:18-19).

Likewise, the NASW Code of Ethics acknowledges the reality of tension between social workers with different points of view. The Purpose of the NASW Code of Ethics includes this statement, "Reasonable differences of opinion can and do exist among social workers with respect to the ways in which values, ethical principles, and ethical standards should be rank ordered when they conflict."

The reality of tension does not need to lead to destructive interaction, however. Christians are called to live at peace with everyone as much as is possible (Romans 12:18) and to pray for leaders so that "we may live peaceful and quiet lives in all godliness and holiness" (I Timothy 2:1-2). The social work profession, for its part, has a section in the NASW Code of Ethics that requires responsible handling of conflict between colleagues (2.03, 2.04).

Tensions exist in part because the differences reflect differing values. Tensions also reflect the fact that not all things are of equal worth and policies and actions make a difference in the lives of people in society. Tensions exist over differences because things matter. The goal, therefore, is not to eliminate all differences since this is impossible. The goal is not even to eliminate all tension since this, too, is not possible. The goal is to reduce the tension as much as possible and to avoid oppressive behavior while making room for as much freedom as possible.

Reducing tension requires differing parties respect each other and engage in dialogue about the differences we see and the tensions we feel. It is particularly critical to listen to those who see injustice and feel oppressed. Listening, it needs to be pointed out, does not mean one agrees nor does it necessarily resolve the tensions. It does, however, provide information which may lead to wiser, healthier, and more empathic decisions.

Christians must insist on their right to live according to their faith but they must extend the same right to others. The goal is to find solutions which make room for as many as possible. This can only happen when people with differences learn to work together to find solutions. Resolving conflict in a way that brings people together is a great challenge of life. How can we be one and yet many? How can we find unity in our diversity? These are not simple questions and there are no simple answers. It seems that social workers and Christians ought to be among those best able to model constructive conflict management. Trying will surely get us closer to living in peace than not trying.

Notes

[1] Since philosophically, all people are viewed as spiritual much like they are sociological and psychological, the term disspirited is used rather than non-spiritual. The fact that a person has no meaning in life or feels unconnected does not mean they are non-spiritual. It rather indicates a negative spirituality.

[2] It should be noted that the concern of faith-based programs tends not to be sexual orientation but sexual behavior. The policies include heterosexual behavior outside of marriage as well as homosexual and bi-sexuality.

[3] There is a debate among Constitutional scholars as to whether the First Amendment prohibits favoring religion in general or one particular state favored religion. The majority on the Supreme Courts since 1947 have favored the religion in general point of view. There has been a minority point of view that argues the intent of the First Amendment was to prohibit one state authorized religion.

References

Babbie, E. (1995). *The practice of social research*. Belmont, CA: Wadsworth.

Baergen, R. (1981). *The Mennonite story*. Newton, KS: Faith and Life Press.

Bracht, T. (1837). *Martyrs' Mirror*. Lancaster, PA: D. Miller.

Bullis, R. K. (1996). *Spirituality in social work practice*. Washington, D. C.; London: Taylor & Frances.

Canda, E. (1989). Response: Religion and social work: It's not that simple. *Social Casework, 70*, 572-574.

Carter, S. (1993). *The culture of disbelief: How American law and politics trivialize religious devotion*. NY: Basic Books.

Clark, J. (1994). Should social work address religious issues? No! *Journal of Social Work Education, 30*(1), 13-15.

Cnaan, R. &., Wineburg. (1997, March 7). Social work and the role of the religious community. Council on Social Work Education. Chicago.

Commission on Higher Education. (April 1996). *Statement concerning the application of equity and diversity principles in the accreditation process*. 3624 Market Street, Philadelphia, PA 19104: Middle States Association of Colleges and Schools.

CSWE Commission on Accreditation, J. N., Chair. (1996, January 22). [Proposed Changes in Accreditation Standards] (Memorandum to Deans and Directors). 1600 Duke Street, Alexandria, VA 22314.

CSWE Commission on Accreditation, J. N., Chair. (1997, February 20). [Proposed Revision to Standard 3.0] (Memorandum to Deans and Directors of Schools of Social Work). 1600 Duke Street, Alexandria, VA 22314.

Donahue, J. (1977). Biblical perspectives on justice. In John Haughty (Ed.), *The faith that does justice*, 68-112.

Eastland, T. (1993). *Religious liberty in the supreme court: The cases that define the debate over church and state*. Washington, DC: Ethics and Public Policy Center.

Elsen, E. (1954). *America's spiritual recovery*. Westwood, NJ: Fleming H. Revell.

Garland, D. (1994). *Church agencies: Caring for children and families in crisis*. Washington, D.C.: Child Welfare League of America.

Gaustad, E. (1993). *Neither king nor prelate: Religion and the new world 1776-1826*. Grand Rapids, MI: Eerdmans.

Goldstein, H. (1987). The neglected moral link in social work practice. *Social Work, 32*(3), 181-186.

Hibbard, J. A., Jungman. (1994). St. Cloud Drops "Attitude" Screening. *The Minnesota Scholar.*

Joseph, M. (1988). Religion and social work practice. *Social Casework, 69*(7), 443-452.

Keith-Lucas, A. (1989). Southern comfort. *Social Services Insight, 4*(8), 1-5.

Keith-Lucas, A. (1958). Readers comments. *Social Casework,* 236-238.

Loewenberg, F. M. (1988). *Religion and social work practice in contemporary American society*. New York: Columbia University Press.

Marshall, J. (1991). The spiritual dimension in social work education. *Spirituality and social work communicator, 2*(1), 12-15.

Marty, M. E. (1980). Social service: Godly and godless. *Social Service Review, 54*(4).

Midgley, J., Sanzenbach. (1989). Social work, religion and the global challenge of fundamentalism. *International Social Work, 32*(4), 273-287.

Moberg, D. (1977). *The great reversal: Evangelism and social concern*. NY: Holman.

NASW. (1994). *NASW Speaks: NASW Policy Statements*. Silver Spring, MD: Author.

Niebuhr, R. 1. (1932). *The contribution of religion to social work*. New York: Pub. for the New York School of Social Work by Columbia University Press.

Parr, R. &., Jones. (1996). Should CSWE allow social work programs in religious institutions an exemption from the accreditation nondiscrimination standard related to sexual orientation. *Journal on Social Work Education, 32*(3), 297-313.

Ressler, L. (1992). Theologically enriched social work: Alan Keith-Lucas's approach to social work and religion. *Spirituality and Social Work Journal, 3*(2), 14-20.

Ressler, L. (1997). Spirituality and religion [A survey of 90 MSW students]. Roberts Wesleyan College.

Richmond, M. (1899). *Friendly visiting among the poor.* Montclair, NJ: Patterson Smith.

Robertson, P. (1991). *The new world order.* Dallas: Word.

Sheridan, M., Bullis. (1992). Practitioners' personal and professional attitudes and behaviors toward religion and spirituality: Issues for education and practice. *Journal of Social Work Education, 28*(2), 190-203.

St. Cloud State University Department of Social Work. (1992, April 29). [The S.C.S.U. Social Work Department's Position on Attitudes Towards Gay and Lesbian People]. St. Cloud, MN.

State University of New York at Buffalo School of Social Work. (1996, February 17, 1996). Petition to the CSWE Board of Directors distributed publically at the Council on Social Work Education Annual Program Meeting. Washington D.C.

CHAPTER 12

INCORPORATING RELIGIOUS ISSUES IN THE ASSESSMENT PROCESS WITH INDIVIDUALS AND FAMILIES

Mary P. Van Hook

Understanding how people interpret events in their lives and the world around them is essential in social work practice with individuals, families, and community groups. The implicit and explicit beliefs of the family and the wider group help shape these interpretations. Religious beliefs and practices influence these interpretations for many individuals, families, and community groups. As a result, understanding how religion shapes people's experiences can be important in social work practice. Including religious issues in the assessment process can also guide the social worker in developing appropriate interventions. The role of religion can be especially salient when people are wrestling with crises and critical junctures in their lives (for example, Loewenberg, 1988; Joseph, 1988; Carlson & Cervera, 1991; Austin & Lennings, 1993; Mailick, Holder & Waltaher, 1994). These events are frequently occasions that prompt people to seek social work help. Such occasions can also be times in which important value choices and issues of meaning are involved. Ignoring religious issues can risk overlooking potential resources and strains in the lives of some client systems. This chapter uses a variety of theoretical approaches to demonstrate how incorporating religious issues in the assessment process can help social workers better understand client systems and develop more effective interventions.

Religion in this chapter refers to "the institutionally patterned system of beliefs, values, and rituals" (Canda, p. 573, 1988). It has both a belief and an organizational participation dimension. A religious person is one who "belongs to a faith group, accepts the beliefs, values, and doctrines of that group, and participates in the required activities and rituals of the chosen group" (Loewenberg, p. 33, 1988). Since people are influenced by family and cultural traditions, the impact of religion can emerge through acceptance of or struggling with aspects of the religious element in these traditions. Religion is a multi-faceted phenomena including beliefs, interpersonal relationships at the family and community level, rituals, and social organizations. As a result, it is helpful to draw upon a variety of theoretical perspectives in analyzing the impact of religion on the lives of people. While this chapter discusses a variety of theoretical approaches to understand religious issues, some aspects will emerge as more important than others in working with a specific client system. It would not be realistic or even necessary for social workers to incorporate all these dimensions in their ongoing assessment of a specific client system or situation. The chapter suggests possible ways to elicit this information as part of the ongoing assessment process, and the nature of information that might be relevant to specific theoretical frameworks or situations. In view of space limitations, this chapter will emphasize individuals and families and will discuss communities and organizations only as they shape them. The case illustrations used demonstrate how incorporating religion from at least one of a variety of theoretical perspectives can be useful in the assessment process and can guide in the development of effective interventions.

Although the emphasis in this chapter is on the assessment of the client system, there is growing recognition that the nature of the relationship between the social worker and the client system is influenced by the characteristics of both the client system and the worker. This interaction process suggests that a religious self-assessment by the social worker can also be important in the assessment and intervention process. Social workers bring to the helping relationship beliefs and practices that influence how they perceive problem situations and possible solutions.

Religious Beliefs

Since it is impossible to do justice to the vast diversity of the world's religions, the following discussion will be limited to the major monotheistic religions of Christianity, Islam, and Judaism. These groups share a core belief in a divine being with an existence separate from human beings with the possibility of a personal relationship between human beings and the divine. As a result, they must answer questions involving how the divine relates to human beings and the world as a whole, and how human beings in turn should relate to the divine and each other. Clients might not be immediately aware of the nature of these underlying beliefs, but this awareness may emerge in the course of exploration regarding the meaning attached to behaviors and more readily recognized beliefs (Miller, 1988). While social workers do not necessarily need complete information about the religious beliefs of their clients, asking clients if they have any religious beliefs that might relate to the presenting problems can both provide useful information and let the client know that these beliefs have a legitimate place in social work efforts with them. The following represent some major themes that might be present in these religious traditions.

"His eye is on the sparrow": This phrase from the Gospel song reflects the belief that God is intimately involved in everything that happens in life. Beliefs about the involvement of God range from this intimate involvement to only remote involvement in major events. Questions of good and evil, free will versus determinism or fatalism, and the intentions of God are raised by these beliefs. These beliefs become especially salient, perhaps comforting or troubling, as people must deal with tragedy in their lives (Kushner, 1981; Smedes 1982). Why did God allow my child to die or my husband to leave me? Why did God allow me to get AIDS? How can I trust a God who would allow this terrible thing to happen to me? Can I gain comfort from believing that nothing happens by chance, that there is a purpose in everything? Is God punishing me for something I did? Is God here for me as I walk through this valley of despair?

Exploring with clients their beliefs in this area can reveal sources of comfort as well as alienation from God and from organized religion. People might be reluctant to voice their anger, doubts, and sense of alienation to other people out of fear that family members and their support system within the church and the community will condemn them for these thoughts and emotions. The experience of raising these issues with someone who can listen without judgment and understands the pain can be an important first step in the healing process. It can also provide an occasion to explore with clients the possibility that there might be other people in their lives who could also understand and accept their views.

God as love/as judgment: Religious traditions vary in terms of whether they view God as relating to people primarily on the basis of judgment against sinful people and a sinful world, or on the basis of love and grace. For members of traditions focused on judgment, feelings of self-worth can be viewed as suspect at best. On the other hand, feeling loved as a "child of God" can be a great source of comfort and self-worth to people. God's love can also be viewed as a gift of grace or something to be earned through specific works and sacrifices. When God's love is linked to works and sacrifice, people may worry that they have not done enough. Yet accepting love as a gift of grace can be difficult for many people even when official religious beliefs affirm this position (Smedes, 1982; Tournier, 1962; Phillips, 1963). Exploring what is the basis of legitimate self-worth within the client's religious tradition can be particularly helpful in working with clients experiencing low self-worth. This exploration can be useful not only with people who are currently religious, but also with those who as adults rejected the religion of their childhood and their family, because they may still be struggling with deeply entrenched views in this area.

Human nature as good/evil: Human nature can be considered to be primarily sinful, neutral, or good. Although viewing human beings as evil has been considered antithetical to the social work belief that people are capable of good and positive changes (Sanzenbach, 1989; Loewenberg, 1988), this can sometimes be a false dichotomy. Even religious traditions that view human nature as essentially sinful can allow for positive change through divine redemption and grace (Smedes, 1982). Understanding and respecting the client's sense of dependence on God for this change can be important.

God of dialogue/God of answers: The divine can be viewed as welcoming dialogue with human beings or requiring their unquestioning acceptance. Tevye in "The Fiddler on the Roof" asks God why he could not have made him a rich man instead of a poor man. Tevye is comfortable with being in an ongoing and sometimes complaining dialogue with God. For some people, questioning God for letting a child die or a factory close would be very difficult. Feelings of anger toward God for these events would create guilt or perhaps fear of retribution. While it may be useful to indicate to such people that sometimes even devoutly religious people feel angry with God, the social worker must also understand their reluctance to acknowledge these feelings personally because of their fear that doing so might come at a very high price.

Basis/Context for Religious Beliefs

In addition to specific beliefs, religious groups also vary in terms of the legitimate basis for their religious beliefs. For some groups, the legitimate basis for religious beliefs can be limited to a literal interpretation of the sacred text, while for others it can include tradition. These later groups adopt a less literal view of interpretation and/or are willing to include the insights of science, history, and culture. Understanding this perspective enables the social worker to identify the types of information that clients and their reference groups would consider valid. A strongly fundamentalist Christian, for example, would not be swayed by social science or cultural information in terms of the scriptural passages regarding sex roles that contradicted their interpretation of the Bible.

Organizational context of beliefs: Although membership in a specific religious denomination plays a less important role in defining beliefs of individuals than it did previously, understanding the belief system of specific groups can give some insight into potential sources of pain or support on particular issues. This is particularly true if the group holds highly specific views on an issue (Loewenberg, 1988). As an example, Mark returned home to his parents in the terminal stages of AIDS. His parents belonged to a conservative church that viewed homosexuality as a grievous sin and AIDS as God's punishment for those who have sinned. Understanding the strain experienced by his parents who were caught between their love for their son and the tenets of their church and religious support system can be important in responding to the pain experienced by Mark and his family.

Families living in rural areas can experience a compounding of stigma (McGinn, 1996). Mrs. James, a Roman Catholic woman, sought counseling for depression following the birth of a baby born blind. For years she had been dreading God's punishment for her earlier divorce and marriage outside the church. When her baby was born, she was convinced that this was God's punishment on her. Fortunately a referral to understanding Roman Catholic sisters and a priest helped her recognize that the church did not teach that God would punish her baby in this way.

In working with grieving families facing a death in the family, understanding how their religious group views life after death can identify potential sources of support or additional grief. Families who are Baptist or Jehovah's Witness, for example, are likely to derive very different types of comfort from their religious beliefs in dealing with the death of a child from Sudden Infant Death Syndrome.

Social Support: The social support systems of individuals and family members can be an important resource as they seek to cope with a variety of stressful life events. As a result, understanding potential sources of support and possible barriers to using these sources can be extremely important in the process of helping people cope. Social support in this context includes both emotional and material support. Religion can play an important role in the social support system of clients. Religion can influence this support basis through the nature of the resources available—a caring church congregation or specific programs offered by religious groups. The nature of these supportive networks can also be influenced by the ethnic traditions of the individuals involved. As indicated in a subsequent discussion in this chapter regarding racial/ethnic groups, African Americans have a strong tradition of interdependence in which the church plays a central role (Hines & Boyd-Franklin, 1982).

In addition to understanding basic group traditions regarding the role of the church community, it can also be important to identify how the nature of the problem might effect potential sources of help within the church. Religious groups vary in terms of their attitudes toward specific life difficulties and the type of help that is viewed as appropriate. Typically problems relating to a death or illness in the family are likely to evoke sympathy and support. Yet if the illness is due to AIDS acquired through a homosexual relationship, attitudes of judgment regarding the illness may diminish either actual support or people's willingness to seek help due to fear of judgment (McGinn, 1996). Attitudes toward divorce, alcoholism, and mental health problems can influence either actual available support or the client's perceptions about seeking such help. A recent study of economically distressed farm families revealed a mixed picture regarding available support from the church. The attitudes of church members and the economically hurting family members toward this extremely complex problem made it difficult for some people to seek or receive the help they needed (Van Hook, 1990). Use of an eco-map that identifies potential sources of support and strains can be useful in eliciting information from clients about the role of the church in this regard.

Personality Theories

Several important personality theories can help social workers understand the interplay between religion and the experiences of clients. An understanding of this interplay can help the social worker develop effective helping approaches. This section discusses how aspects of cognitive-behavioral and psychodynamic/ego psychology can be used in this regard.

Cognitive behavioral: According to contemporary cognitive-behavioral theory, our beliefs influence our behavior, our emotions, and our thoughts. Religious beliefs can influence the core beliefs that are especially influential in this process. Helping based on this theory uses a collaborative partnership between the client and the social worker to identify the nature of these beliefs and to test out their accuracy. The process begins with a series of questions asked of and with the client. These questions are designed to identify how the client views the world. These might include questions such as, "What do you think would happen if you told your parents that you want to switch to social work as a major?" The client and worker also engage in a process of testing these beliefs by a series of further questions or activities. The client, for example, might tell her or his parents about the switch to a social work major and the reasons for doing so to test out what really will be the parents' reaction.

Miller (1988) describes the use of this approach with a male seminary student with a strong sense of duty who was suffering from depression. His initial attempt was to help the man through progressive relaxation of the muscles of this body and scheduling of pleasant activities. This approach was unsuccessful because it did not fit with the client's sense of purpose in life. Miller then used a common approach in cognitive treatment. A person is asked to keep a record of when a certain problem arises, the situations in which the problem occurs, and the person's reaction to these events. The student was asked to record the situations in which he felt depressed, his self-statements in these situations, and his resulting emotions. Several crucial themes emerged. Three potentially healing religious themes surfaced in this process: "Even servants have to be restored" (in response to his relentless driving of himself), "Grace" (a message he wished to communicate to others but did not fit with his own driving perfectionism), and "Focus on others" (which was impeded by his worry about himself). The social worker used this understanding to develop a more effective helping strategy with John. John began to experiment with replacing his driven perfectionism with alternative self-statements that were consistent with important elements of his core religious belief system. "1. — Even Jesus took time to rest and recharge, 2. — If I want to serve, I also need to take care of myself, 3. — God, through Jesus Christ, accepts me as I am, 4. — Don't worry about how people are evaluating me. Focus on their needs instead. And 5. — I have good news to share." Within this context John was able to use the techniques of relaxation and scheduling of pleasant events because these efforts were compatible with efforts to change the way he was thinking — a process called "cognitive-restructuring" (Miller, 1988).

Cognitive-behavioral strategies like these can also help clients identify other issues that might be camouflaged by religious thoughts and interpretations of events. Sue's parents, for example, contacted their pastor because their daughter Sue felt that she was demon possessed. The pastor assured the family that God would not let this happen to one of His children and suggested they contact a mental health program. Sue, age 13, was able to identify the thoughts, emotions, and bodily sensations that she associated with being demon possessed. The social worker asked her to keep a log identifying the situations in which she had the sensations that made her feel that she was demon possessed. The following week she returned for counseling pleased that she had discovered the nature of the problem. She experienced it when she was lonely and afraid the other children in her new community would not want to be her friends. She and her family had recently moved to the community and she was experiencing the anxiety of trying to make friends in her new school and community. Her insight clearly established the direction for counseling and gave her a very different view of herself and her problem.

Psychodynamic/ego psychology: One important aspect of psycho-dynamic/ego psychology is the theory of object relations. According to object relations theory, people gradually identify a sense of self separate from the world around them. A child, for example, quite early on becomes clear that there is a "me" that is separate from others. In the course of this process, children internalize a series of mental images (objects) of the people who are important to them. These internalizations are subjective and reflect how the child has experienced these other people. These subjective interpretations in turn influence how children view themselves as well as experience the world around them and subsequent relationships with other people. A child who has experienced parents and other caretakers as loving and meeting his needs is likely to view himself as lovable and to trust that other people will also be loving and trustworthy. On the other hand, a child who has experienced abuse is likely to distrust that other people will love her or meet her needs appropriately.

From an object relations perspective, the concept of God is not an illusion. Instead it represents an important reality. Part of being human is our capacity to create nonvisible realities (Rizzuto, 1979). The concept of God develops very early in a child's psychological development in the context of the child's developing a sense of separation from nurturing parents (Fuller, 1988). Although God is often called the "Heavenly Father," a child's concept of God represents more than just an internalization of the father. It involves a combination or gestalt of many powerful factors: the characteristics of the mother and the father, the dynamics of the twofold need to merge with a higher power and yet at the same time to experience oneself as autonomous, and the general social, historical, and religious background of the family (Fuller, 1988). As a result, children develop an image of God that reflects their own experiences with significant individuals and their own developmental needs. Belief in a powerful God can serve as an important transition object as children develop a growing sense of separation from their parents (Fuller, 1988). The internalization of an all powerful and all knowing God with the power to judge based on parental relationships can be a source of considerable distress if it is based on rejecting parental experiences and a source of comfort when based on trusting or caring relationships with these individuals.

Because these internalized views (objects) of other people color a person's relationships with others and their view of themselves, understanding the client's early and basic view regarding God and the impact of this perspective on their lives can be important. Questions about one's experiences with parents as well as about how one views God can provide important clues in this area. Joyce illustrates how early family relationships combined with the belief system of the group profoundly shaped her view of God, herself, and others. She was a member of a strongly religious group that stressed God's judgment and the sinfulness of human beings. Yet most members of this group manage to live relatively satisfying lives. In contrast, she lived a life preoccupied with fear of the rejection of others and of God. She was convinced that she was completely unlovable and totally undeserving of any happiness. Exploration of her life revealed that her image of God was shaped in part by a realistically very frightening relationship with her father. Her father, who has been in a nursing home for several years, had suffered severely during World War II and later immigrated to the United States. After his move to the United States and while the children were growing up, he frequently had paranoid delusions in which Joyce and another sibling were Nazi soldiers. He would then try to attack them and her mother would have to hide them from their father. As a result of these events and their rural setting, the family was generally isolated from other families so there were few other adults to serve as benign and protective role models that might create a balance in her life. By the time she entered school she was so traumatized that she withdrew from others and experienced herself as the object of ridicule. For Joyce, her early experience of terror and rejection by her father and her mother's inability to protect her from the emotional trauma created a strong introject of a powerful and rejecting God. At an intellectual and beliefs systems level her perspective was further reinforced by the doctrines of her religious group, but her early life experiences set the stage for her sense of fear. She needed a helping relationship that demonstrated that she was a person deserving of concern, and to help her with her difficulty in trusting others.

Family Issues

The family plays a primary role in the formation of religious beliefs. These beliefs are further shaped by relationships within the family and family events. Family rituals in turn reinforce these religious beliefs and practices. As a result of the key role of the family, understanding the interaction between family and religious issues can be especially fruitful (Dudley & Dudley, 1986; Friedman, 1985; Cornwall, 1987; Joseph, 1988; Loewenberg, 1988; Raider, 1992). This section examines families in terms of life-cycle issues, rituals, and family patterns and rules.

Families can be understood in terms of the development of the family over time — the life-cycle of the family. This process in turn is influenced by the developmental process of individual family members. As children enter adolescence, it becomes important for them to establish their own sense of identity. While the family is important in this sense of identity, adolescents frequently need to distance themselves from their parents in various ways. Some adolescents do so by distancing themselves from their parent's religious beliefs, practices, and rituals. This process can be the source of considerable tension within the family.

Families also face important transitions in the life-cycle of the family. Transitions that involve the breaking of old bonds and identities and the establishment of new ones are frequently marked by rituals, including religious ones (Friedman, 1985). Baptism in the Christian tradition and circumcision (*bris*) in the Jewish tradition represent the entry of a child into the religious community, and the assumption by parents of the responsibilities of raising the child in the religious traditions. Confirmations, Bar Mitzvahs, and other religious rites symbolize growth and approaching adulthood and the personal adoption of an identity within religious groups. Weddings mark the establishment of new commitments and boundaries with the accompanying need to create a new family structure. Religious rituals surrounding death help family members relinquish the lost family members and bind remaining family members together. The inability to carry out these rituals, on the other hand, can be the source of great distress (Harari & Wolowelsky, 1995; Friedman, 1985). Asking family members about the nature of pertinent rituals and how family members experienced these rituals can open the door to important information in this area.

Examining how individuals maintain and experience religious and other family rituals can provide clues to the nature of relationships within the family system, but also the extent to which family members are tied to their religious traditions. Harari and Wolowelsky (1995) describe how exploring changes in family observance of religious rituals following a death in the family can be an entrée into possible changes in family roles generally. This can be the opportunity to identify, for example, who are the individuals that others turn to in difficult times, and shifts in power within the family due to illness or the response to a death.

It is always important to explore what these family religious rituals mean to family members. Clients can be asked what these rituals mean to them, how they experienced them, and how they felt participating (or not participating) in them. These rituals convey messages of belonging or alienation. They can be sources of healing or further occasions to evoke the memory of an aching void or the pain of disrupted relationships. Exploring which family members are included or excluded from important family rituals also provides valuable information about family coalitions, cohesion or disengagement in the family, reasons for cutoffs in families, and family communication patterns.

Because family religious rituals frequently are invested with great meaning, failure to carry out previously treasured rituals or the institution of new rituals can be a source of considerable tension within an extended family. For immigrants, especially the elderly, difficulties in carrying out the religious rituals that were important in their home country can be a source of distress. Tensions can also be present if younger family members become acculturated and subsequently devalue these rituals. The Li family who came to the United States as refugees following the Vietnam war illustrate these tensions. They were later joined by her parents and extended family. When Mrs. Li became pregnant the extended family wanted her to carry out a religious ceremonial ritual that members of their traditional group viewed as an essential protection for a baby during pregnancy. While this ritual continued to be vitally important to Mrs. Li's parents and other relatives, Mr. and Mrs. Li had changed their religious beliefs and refused to carry it out because they felt it was not necessary, and doing so would violate their new religious beliefs. The extended family became frantic, fearing that the baby would be born deformed and were very angry with the Li's for their actions. Although the baby was born without any birth defects, this event contributed to lasting tensions within the family system.

Social workers also need to be alert to ways that religious rituals can be used to control other family members. Religious rituals are one of the ways family members use to enforce family patterns and rules on other members. One way this can be done is by excluding family members from important family rituals, for example, a Bar Mitzvah or Christening, if family members are viewed as straying from family beliefs or practices.

The K family illustrates how the religious ritual of prayer can be used in a coercive manner. Mrs. K and her husband had agreed to an amicable divorce but her parents were furious with her because of this action. Mrs. K was eager to explain to her parents the reasons for her action and to find some way to maintain a relationship with her parents. As a result, a meeting was arranged between Mrs. K, her parents, the minister (who was supportive of Mrs. K's decision) and the social worker. Mrs. K's parents continued to be adamant in terms of their disapproval of her actions with her mother indicating she would rather have Mrs. K dead than divorced. With no resolution of the issue, her mother indicated at the end of the meeting that she wanted to have a closing prayer and launched upon one designed to make Mrs. K feel guilty of letting both her parents and God down. Fortunately the pastor was sensitive to this issue and offered a second prayer that spoke of forgiveness and reconciliation.

Families not only generate a sense of identity but also loyalty to the family group and members. Contextual family therapy points out the power of these family legacies or loyalty and obligations from one generation to the next (Broszormenyi-Nagy, 1986). As a result, individuals feel obligated to believe or act in a certain way in response to these family legacies. Family loyalty issues can emerge in powerful and sometimes painful ways in family groups. These issues frequently come to the fore as people begin to establish their own way of understanding the world ("worldviews" — including religious beliefs) appropriate to their own family and personal existence. In his book *Blood of the Lamb,* novelist Peter DeVries (1960) tells a poignant story of a man whose beloved daughter dies of cancer. As an adult he had rejected the religious beliefs of his childhood and family and raised his daughter as an atheist. After her death he again becomes attracted to a religious faith. Now he cannot accept this faith out of a sense of loyalty and obligation to his dead child. He cannot accept a faith that he denied her. Clients who have rejected the religious beliefs of their family members may struggle with a sense of betrayal to their family tradition.

Individuals change and establish their own identities in the history of families. This process can also create the risk of alienation from the family. Religious issues have been the source of intense emotional cutoffs in families whereby family members either totally or partially eliminate contact with another family member. If the client is aware of previous cutoffs in the family history due to religious intermarriage or departures from the family's religious beliefs and practices, they too may fear abandonment by family members.

Genograms are an effective way to identify religious themes within families (Raider, 1992). A genogram is a visual map of the family as it exists through several generations. It can reveal intergenerational expectations within families. A genogram, for example, that reveals a long line of family members who served the church in various ways can suggest unfulfilled expectations and issues of betrayal on the part of a person who has left the family church and religion. In contrast, as one minister's wife said after doing a genogram, "I realize I had to either become a minister or marry one." For her, the genogram confirmed a pattern that was consonant with her current life choices. The impact, however, would be quite different for an individual who had left the church or was struggling with the religious tradition of the family. Genograms also reveal cutoffs within families due to religious reasons. Use of a genogram can not only help identify and objectify family patterns but also be an occasion to examine how similar or different a client's current situation is from past events in the family.

Ethnicity

Studies of ethnicity reveal the important role of religious beliefs, practices, and organizations in the lives of many groups. These beliefs shape expectations regarding relationships among family members, ways that events are experienced, and the nature of acceptable resources. The growing body of literature regarding ethnicity reveals how important religion is in shaping the lives of members of these groups. The following represent several religious themes which are present in the ethnic traditions of client systems. In this context, it is important to remember that such themes run the risk of becoming stereotypes, and social workers always need to explore the perspectives and experiences of specific individuals and families (Caple, Salcio, & Cecco, 1996; Yellow Bird, Fong, Galindo, Nowicki & Freeman, 1995; McGolderick & Giordano, 1996).

Confucian ideas and beliefs about filial piety and sense of respect for elderly persons have strongly influenced Chinese, Japanese, and Koreans (Browne & Broderick, 1996). As a result, it is especially important to demonstrate respect for family members of authority and not to expect family members to provide information that would be demeaning to other family members in the assessment process. To do so would be to ask family members to bring shame to the family (Shon, 1982).

Ethnicity can influence views regarding the nature of illness and health and appropriate healers. Beliefs in the connection with the spiritual world, the nature of both "natural" and "supernatural" illnesses suggest the important role that folk healers (*curandero*) can play, especially for elderly Mexican-Americans (Applewhite, 1996). Folk healing traditions combining Spanish Catholic practices with African and other belief systems can be present in some Cuban families (Bernal, 1982). Traditional healers can also be important for Native Americans (Attneave, 1982). In addition, Al-Krenawi and Graham (1996) describe the importance of traditional healing rituals and healers for the Bedouin people.

Religious beliefs and organizations have long played essential roles for African Americans. The church has served as a source of dignity and self-esteem, as a mutual aid society, and as a focal point for activism for social change. Church leaders have played central roles within African American communities. As a result, eliciting information about religion and the church may identify important emotional, spiritual, and material resources for African American individuals and families. In terms of community practice, assessing the presence and roles of the church within the African American community can help discover essential resources for mobilizing people and other community resources (Hines & Boyd-Franklin, 1982).

The Roman Catholic church and beliefs have traditionally played an important role in the life of Irish individuals and families. Irish Catholicism has historically emphasized the need for personal morality while viewing human nature as intrinsically evil. Sin and guilt have been strong elements. Prior to Vatican II the church held a strongly authoritarian stance with people in terms of morality, and the role of the priest is still very influential (McGolderick, 1982).

Jewish families vary widely in terms of their adherence to Jewish rituals and beliefs. "Familism" which makes the family and the procreation and raising of children central, remains important to the Jewish traditions of all groups. It is useful to elicit from Jewish clients how they view their family obligations and how their current actions fit with the expectations of their family and cultural group. Discovering how Jewish clients observe religious rituals can also be an important clue to how closely they identify themselves with the Orthodox, Conservative, and Reform groups, and the salience of these traditions for the life of the family (Herz & Rosen, 1982; Friedman, 1985).

Defensive Use of Religion

Religion can protect people from anxiety in ways that help people cope more effectively or can contribute to problems in functioning. According to ego psychology, people protect themselves from being overwhelmed by anxiety or guilt by defense mechanisms. These defense mechanisms can be thoughts, feelings, and actions. As Brenner points out (1981), virtually any aspect of life can be used as a defensive mechanism to ward off anxiety. An individual with terminal cancer might not be able to believe the words of the doctor about the seriousness of the illness. This sometimes also takes the form of people avoiding dealing with painful personal issues by putting them in religious terms or context (York, 1989). For example, a parent who cannot deal with his own rage and is physically abusive to a child, might rationalize this behavior by saying that a parent must exercise proper discipline because "sparing the rod would spoil the child."

Religious involvement in symptoms and problems can sometimes be readily identified in clients as problematic, for example, the individual who is obviously psychotic and out of touch with reality and who talks about being a special messenger of God. Typically the situation is less obvious. There are times in which religion is used defensively to avoid acknowledging other personal problems. In evaluating the role of religion in this regard, it is important to view the religious beliefs and practices of the client in the context of the total life and functioning of the client. The individual who finds it hard to believe that she has a terminal illness might initially be less anxious because her religious beliefs help to cushion the shock. The denial of the seriousness of the illness becomes problematic, however, if she continues to refuse treatment for the illness, spends large amounts of money or goes through a series of doctors in order to find someone who says that the problem is not life-threatening, or refuses to seek treatment because "God will protect me."

In assessing the role of religion, social workers and others in the helping professions must also be aware of how their own views about religion are affecting their evaluation of deviance and pathology. They need to be aware of the danger that they will use their own beliefs as the basis for viewing the religious beliefs and practices of a client as pathological (Bindler, 1985). There is always the danger of the process called "countertransference," whereby the social worker reacts to clients based on the social worker's own life experiences and personal issues, rather than the reality of the client's situation. Because religious issues can evoke strong feelings, social workers need to be alert to the danger of this process when dealing with religious clients or religious issues generally. A social worker, for example, who is reacting negatively to the religious practices of his own parents risks being overly judgmental of a client whose religious beliefs and practice mirror those of the parents. Defensive uses of religion can sometimes be identified because these religious concerns are more intense or effect more of life than is typical of others who belong to a similiar religious group. Peter's situation demonstrates how religious views can protect against other life concerns. He was preoccupied by his religious obligation to forgive an abusive father. He felt that his religion obligated him to forgive him but he had difficulty doing so. The issue became especially acute when his father became ill and needed his help. While his religious belief system included the theme of forgiveness, he seemed to be placing unduly harsh expectations on himself. Further exploration revealed that his religion protected him against having to acknowledge his ambivalence toward his father. He yearned for a sense of closeness while he feared being hurt again. This understanding permitted the social worker and Peter to work together to learn ways that he could cope with his father during the illness, and in the process to come to terms with the reality of his relationship with his father.

Or consider the situation of Joan, who could virtually talk of little else than her fear that she had committed the "unpardonable sin" and was, therefore, dammed by God. While this belief was a part of her religious group's belief system, most members rarely think about it or

can easily dismiss it because they have been taught that people who
have committed it do not worry about doing so. As a result, her religious preoccupation met the criteria of being an undue preoccupation
accompanied by rigidity, ongoing unhappiness, and lack of productivity. As the helping process unfolded, it became apparent that her obsession represented a desperate way of eliciting interest from others, including the social worker. Even when Joan had realistic issues in her
life that would naturally elicit interest from others, she would fall back
on her obsession of the unpardonable sin. Her story included a sister
who had been severely mentally ill for years and a brother who had
recently been arrested for attempted murder. As a child, she had felt
ignored by her parents because her father was preoccupied with religion and her mother with her sister's illness. The social worker's understanding of the role of this religious obsession in the total economy of
her life and demonstration of interest in other aspects of Joan's life helped
her to diminish substantially her obsession. The social worker helped
Joan experience that it was possible to relate to others on the basis of
healthy aspects of her person.

Spero (1985) suggests several characteristics of religious beliefs
and practices that might suggest the presence of a disordered psychological need or conflict.

1. The individual's total religious affiliation, or the current intensity and sense of religious meaning and conviction, is of relatively recent and rapid onset. It has also involved the person in
   severing of one or more significant family, social, or professional
   ties and roles.

2. The individual's past history includes numerous religious "crises"
   or episodes of changing religious affiliation or levels of belief.

3. The individual's religious behaviors and beliefs indicate that the
   person remains or has returned to a way of relating to God and
   others that is more immature than is appropriate for one's age.
   This can be evidenced by several themes.

   a. There is a predominance of immature themes of relationships
      that do not fit with developmentally appropriate relationships
      with other people. This might be evidenced by an adult who
      does not believe that she must prepare herself for a profes-
      sional service role because she believes "God will provide
      the way."

   b. There is lack of integration between the individual's mode of religious expression and adaptive ego functioning—the individual may be careful in the use of money in most of the areas of their life, but gives without questioning the value of a program, if it is described in religious terms.

c. The individual is unable to successfully accomplish appropriate psychosocial tasks— a young man who neglects his own young children because he spends so much of   his time helping the youth program in the church.

4. The religious individual is preoccupied either with a directly acknowledged or intellectually masked fear of back-sliding. The individual then becomes very rigid, and extremely concerned with a rigid interpretation of belief and behavioral codes to deal with such fears. Sometimes this takes the form of strict interpretations of religious laws even when others in the group typically follow more lenient interpretations of the laws.

5. Continued unhappiness and unproductivity following religious conversion or awakening. The individual has turned to religion to conquer a drinking problem that persists despite growing religious zeal designed to conquer the drinking.

6. Excessive idealization of a religious movement or leader, and the use of such idealization to resolve problems of autonomy, identity, impulse control, and so forth. The Jonestown, Waco (Texas) and recent Heaven's Gate tragedies represents extreme cases of this pathological use of religion. People gave up their individuality, their possessions, and their own and their children's lives because they had idealized their religious leaders.

Because religious groups vary widely in terms of beliefs and practices, an assessment of the defensive use of religion might require further study about the groups involved or perhaps conversations with relevant religious leaders. As with cultural groups, lack of this understanding can lead to either one of two errors: attributing personal pathology to the religious group or evaluating members of a group that is different from one's own experience as disturbed.

Conclusion

As suggested by previous discussions, assessment includes an analysis of the fit between the client and possible types of interventions. Religion can influence the nature of interventions that are viewed as ac-

Mary P. Van Hook

ceptable by clients. As with other cultural issues, it may be necessary to interpret interventions from the perspective of the religious views of clients. The example of the seminary student who could not use relaxation and pleasure scheduling until after cognitive interventions made these acceptable, illustrates the need to place interventions in an appropriate context. Understanding religious beliefs and practices can also identify potential sources of healing within the religious tradition. Prayer, for example, might be an important source of comfort for many Christians. It may also be important as a source of support, to reconnect people with important religious rituals within their religious traditions.

Religion is a multi-faceted phenomena that can influence the lives of people in many complex ways. Incorporating religious issues in the social work assessment process helps identify ways in which religion can be either a resource or a strain for clients, provides meaning for present and past life events, and points to the types of interventions that might be helpful in managing their problems. Many theories from social work and psychology further this understanding. The specific nature of the appropriate theoretical perspective will depend on the nature of the problem situation. The importance of social work practitioners being aware of their own religious beliefs and those of other ethnic and cultural groups in order to make appropriate assessment and intervention decisions is becoming a prerequisite for competent professional practice.

References

Al-Krenawi, A. & Graham, J. (1996). Social work and traditional healing rituals among the Bedouin of the Negev, Israel. *International Social Work,* 38, 365-377.

Applewhite, S. (1996). *Curanderissmo*: Demystifying the health beliefs and practices of elderly Mexicans Americans. In P. Ewalt, E. Freeman, S. Kirk, & D. Poole (Eds.), *Multicultural issues and social work.* Washington, DC: NASW Press.

Attneave, C. (1982). American Indians and Alaska Native families: Emigrants in their own homeland. In M. McGolderick, J. Pearce, & J. Giordana (Eds.), *Ethnicity and Family Therapy.* New York: Guilford Press.

Austin, D. & Lennings, C. (1993). Grief and religious belief: Does belief moderate depression. *Death Studies,*17(6), 487-496.

Bernal, G. (1982). Cuban families. In McGolderick, J. Pearce, & J. Giordana (Eds.), *Ethnicity and family therapy.* New York: Guilford Press.

Bindler, (1985). Clinical manifestations of religious conflict in psychotherapy. In M. Spero (Ed.), *Psychotherapy of the Religious Client.* Springfield: C.Thomas.

Boszormenyi-Nagy, (1986). Transgenerational solidarity: The expanding context of therapy and prevention. *American Journal of Family Therapy*, 14(3), 195-212.

Brenner, C. (1981). Defense mechanism. *Psychoanalytic Quarterly*, Oct. 557-569.

Browne, C. & Broderick, A. (1996). Asian and Pacific Island Elders: Issues for social work practice and education. In P. Ewalt, E. Freeman, S. Kirk & D. Pool (Eds.), *Multicultural issues and social work*. Washington, DC: NASW Press.

Canda, E. (1988). Spirituality, religious diversity, and social work practice. *Social Casework*, 69, April, 238-247.

Caple, S. Salcio, R. & Cecco, J. (1996). Engaging effectively with culturally diverse families and children. In P. Ewalt, E. Freeman, S. Kirk, & D. Poole (Eds.), *Multicultural issues and social work*. Washington, DC: NASW Press.

Carlson, B. & Cervera, D. (1991). Incarceration, coping, and support. *Social Work*, 36(4), 279-85.

Cornwall, M. (1987). The social basis of religion: A study of factors influencing religious belief and commitment. *Review of Religious Research*, 9(1), 4-56.

DeVries, P. (1960). *The Blood of the Lamb*. Boston: Little, Brown.

Dudley, R & Dudley, M. (1986). Transmission of religious values from parents to adolescents. *Review of Religious Research*, 28(1), 3-15.

Friedman, E. (1982). The myth of Shiska. In M. McGolderick, J. Pearce, & J. Giordano (Eds), *Ethnicity and family therapy*. New York: Guilford Press.

Friedman, E. (1985). *From generation to generation: Family process in church and synagogue*. New York: Guilford Press.

Fuller, R. (1988). *Religion and the life cycle*. New York: Haworth Press.

Harari, V. & Wolowelsky, J. (1995). Family therapy after a death in the traditional Jewish family. *Journal of Family Therapy*, 17, 243-251.

Herz, F. & Rosen, E. (1982). Jewish Families. In McGolderick, J. Pearce, & J. Giordana (Eds.), *Ethnicity and family therapy*. New York: Guilford Press.

Hines, P. & Boyd-Franklin, N. (1982). Black families. In McGolderick, J. Pearce, & J. Giordana (Eds.), *Ethnicity and family therapy*. New York: Guilford Press.

Joseph, M.V. (1987). The religious and spiritual aspects of clinical practice: A neglected dimension of social work. *Social Thought*, 13(1), 12-23.

Joseph, M.V. (1988). Religion and social work practice. *Social Casework*, 70(Sept), 447-457.

Kunshner, H. (1981). *When bad things happen to good people*. New York: Avon.

Loewenberg, F. (1988). *Religion and social work practice in contemporary American society*. New York: Columbia University Press.

Mailick, M. Holden, G. & Walther, V. (1994). Coping with childhood asthma: A caretaker view. *Health and Social Work*, 19(2), 103-111.

McGinn, F. (1996). The plight of rural parents caring for adult children with HIV. *Families and Society*, (May), 269-278.

McGolderick, M. (1982). Irish families. In M. McGolderick, J. Pearce, & J. Giordana (Eds.), *Ethnicity and family therapy*. New York: Guilford Press.

McGolderick, M & Giordano, J. (1996). *Ethnicity and family therapy*. New York: Guilford Press.

Miller, W. (1988). Including clients' spiritual perspectives in cognitive behavior therapy. In Wm. Miller & J. Martin (Eds.), *Behavior therapy and religion: Integrating spiritual and behavioral approaches to change*. Thousand Oaks: Sage.

Phillips, J. (1963). *Your God is too small*. New York: MacMillan.

Raider, M. (1992). Assessing the role of religion in family functioning. In L. Burton (Ed.), *Religion and the family: When God helps*. New York: The Haworth Pastoral Press.

Rizutto, A. (1979). *The birth of the living god*. Chicago: University of Chicago Press.

Smedes, L. (1982). *How can everything be all right when everything is all wrong.* New York: Harper and Row.

Spero, M. (1985). Diagnostic guideline for psychotherapy with the religious client. In M. Spero (Ed), *Psychotherapy of the religious client.* Springfield: Charles C. Thomas.

Tournier, P. (1962). *Guilt and Grace.* New York: Harper and Row.

Van Hook, M. (1990). Family response to the farm crisis: A study in coping. *Social Work,* 35(5), 425-431.

Yellow Bird, M., Fong, R., Galindo, R., Nowicki, J. & Freeman, E. (1996). The multicultural mosaic. In P. Ewalt, E. Freeman, S. Kirk, & D. Poole (Eds.), *Multicultural issues in social work.* Washington, DC: NASW Press.

York, G. (1989). Strategies for managing the religious-based denial of rural clients. *Human Services in the Rural Environment,* 13(2), 16-22.

CHAPTER 13

DOING THE RIGHT THING: A CHRISTIAN PERSPECTIVE ON ETHICAL DECISION-MAKING FOR CHRISTIANS IN SOCIAL WORK PRACTICE

David A. Sherwood

You are on the staff of a Christian Counseling Center and in the course of a week you encounter the following clients:

1. A minister who became sexually involved with a teen-age girl at a previous church several years ago. His current church is not aware of this. He says he has "dealt with his problem."
2. A Christian woman whose husband is physically abusive and who has threatened worse to her and their young child if she tells anyone or leaves him. She comes to your office with cuts and bruises, afraid to go home and afraid not to go home. She doesn't know what she should do or can do.
3. A single mother who is severely depressed and who is not taking adequate care of her two young children, both under the age of four. She denies that her personal problems are affecting her ability to take care of her children.

The list could easily go on. Helping professionals, Christian or otherwise, are daily confronted with issues that are immensely complex and which call forth judgments and actions that confound any attempts to neatly separate "clinical knowledge and skill," our preferred professional roles and boundaries, and, fundamentally, our world-view, faith, moral judgment, and character. Much as we would like to keep it simple, real life is messy and all of a piece. All kinds of things interconnect and interact. How would you respond to clients like the ones I just mentioned?

Christian social workers need to know who they are and what resources they have to do the right thing as children of God—personally, socially, and professionally. What are our resources and limits in choosing and acting ethically as Christians who are placed in helping relationships with others? I will try to review briefly a Christian perspective on:

- When we have a moral problem.
- Conditions under which we choose and act.

- Faith and the hermeneutical spiral (understanding God's will).
- How the Bible teaches us regarding values and ethics.
- A decision-making model which integrates the deontological (ought) dimensions with the teleological (purpose and consequences) dimensions of a problem.
- The fundamental role of character formed through discipleship and the guidance of the Holy Spirit.

We cannot devise or forcibly wrench out of the scriptures a set of rules which will simply tell us what to do if we will only be willing to obey. It appears that God has something else in mind for us as He grows us up into the image of Christ. Ultimately, "doing the right thing" results from our making judgments which grow out of our character as we are "changed into his likeness from one degree of glory to another; for this comes from the Lord who is the Spirit" (II Cor. 3:18).

When Do We Have a Moral Problem?

When do we have a moral "problem?" I would argue that value issues are so pervasive in life that there is virtually no question we face that does not have moral dimensions at some level. Even the choice regarding what brand of coffee to use (or whether to use coffee at all) is not a completely value-neutral question. However, for practical purposes I think it is helpful to realize that moral "problems" tend to be characterized by the following conditions:

1. **More than one value is at stake and they are in some degree of conflict.**

    This is more common than we would like to think. It need not be a conflict between good and bad. It is more usually differing goods or differing bads. A maxim that I drill into my students is "You can't maximize all values simultaneously." Which is to say life continually confronts us with choices and to choose one thing *always* means to give up or have less of something else. And that something else may be a very good thing, so serious choices are usually very costly ones. A familiar, lighthearted version of this is the adage "You can't have your cake and eat it too." This is one of life's truisms which is very easy to forget or tempting to ignore, but which is at the heart of all value and moral problems. No conflict, no problem.

2. **There is uncertainty about what values are, in fact, involved or what they mean.**

    For example, what are all the relevant values involved in a decision regarding abortion? And what, exactly, is meant by choice, right to life, a person? Where do these values come from? What is their basis? How do they put us under obligation?

3. **There is uncertainty about what the actual facts are.**

What is the true situation? What are the relevant facts? Are they known? Can they be known? How well can they be known under the circumstances?

4. **There is uncertainty about the actual consequences of alternative possible choices and courses of action.**

Often we say that choices and actions should be guided by results. While it is true that their morality is at least in part influenced by their intended and actual consequences, Christians believe that God has built certain "oughts" like justice and love into the creation and that results always have to be measured by some standard or "good" which is beyond the naked results themselves. It is also crucial to remember that consequences can never be fully known at the time of decision and action. The best we can ever do at the time is to *predict*. We are obligated to make the best predictions we can, but we must be humbled by the limitations of our ability to anticipate actual results. However, unintended consequences turn out to be every bit as real and often more important than intended ones, especially if we haven't done our homework.

Under What Conditions Do We Have to Choose and Act?

Given this understanding of a moral "problem," it seems to me that real-life value choices and moral decisions are always made under these conditions:

1. **We have a problem.**

An actual value conflict is present or at least perceived. For example, we want to tell the truth and respect our dying parent's personal rights and dignity by telling him the prognosis but we don't want to upset him, perhaps hasten his death, or create possible complications for ourselves and the hospital staff.

2. **We always have significant limitations in our facts, knowledge, understanding, and ability to predict the consequences of our actions.**

What causes teen-age, unmarried pregnancy? What policies would lead to a decrease in teen-age pregnancy? What other unintended consequences might the policies have? Correct information and knowledge are very hard (often impossible) to come by. As Christians we know that human beings are both finite (limited) and fallen (liable to distortion from selfishness and other forms of sin). The more we can do to overcome or reduce these limitations the better off we'll be. But the beginning of wisdom is to recognize our weakness and dependence.

3. **Ready or not, we have to decide and do *something*, at least for the time being, even if the decision is to ignore the problem.**

   Life won't permit us to stay on the fence until we thoroughly understand all the value issues, have all the relevant data, conduct a perfectly complete analysis, and develop a completely Christ-like character. So, we have to learn how to make the best choices we can under the circumstances.

4. **Whatever decision we make and action we take will be fundamentally influenced by our assumptions, world-view, faith'*whatever* that is.**

   "Facts," even when attainable, don't sustain moral judgments by themselves. They must be interpreted in the light of at least one faith-based value judgment. Where do my notions of good and bad, healthy and sick, functional and dysfunctional come from? Never from the "facts" alone.

5. **We would like to have definitive, non-ambiguous, prescriptive direction so that we can be completely certain of the rightness of our choice, but we never can.**

   Not from Scripture, not from the law, not from our mother. We want to *know* without a doubt that we are right. This has always been part of the allure of legalism, unquestioning submission to authorities of various stripes, and simplistic reduction of complex situations. The only way (to seem) to be saved by the law is to chop it down to our own puny size.

6. **We may not have legalistic, prescriptive formulas, but we *do* have guidance and help.**

   Doing the right thing is not just a subjective, relativistic venture. God knows the kind of help we really need to grow up in Christ and God has provided it. We need to be open to the kind of guidance God actually gives instead of demanding the kind of guidance we think would be best. What God has actually given is Himself in Jesus Christ, the story of love, justice, grace, and redemption given witness in Scripture, the Holy Spirit, and the community of the church, historically, universally, and locally.

7. **Ultimately, doing the right thing is a matter of identity and character.**

   In the last analysis, our morality (or lack of it) depends much more on *who* we are (or are becoming) than what we know or the procedures we use. We must become persons who have taken on the mind and character of Christ as new creations. And it turns out that this is precisely what the Bible says God is up to'growing us up into the image of Christ, from one degree of glory to another. The "problem" of making and living out these moral decisions turns out to be part of the plot, part of God's strategy, suited to our nature as we were created. Instead of fight ing and resenting the hardness of moral choice and action, maybe we should *embrace* it as part of God's dynamic for our growth.

Faith and the Hermeneutical Spiral

Walking By Faith Is Not Optional

Christian or not, consciously or not, intentionally or not, we all inevitably approach understanding the world and ourselves on the basis of assumptions or presuppositions about the nature of things. Walking by faith is not optional. All human beings do it. We do have some choice (and responsibility) for what we continue to put our faith in, however. That's where choice comes in.

Is love real or a rationalization? Does might make right? Do persons possess inherent dignity and value? Are persons capable of meaningful choice and responsibility? Are human beings so innately good that guilt and sin are meaningless or destructive terms? Is human life ultimately meaningless and absurd? Is the physical universe (and ourselves) a product of mindless chance? Is there a God (or are *we* God)? These are a few of the really important questions in life and there is no place to stand to try to answer them that does not include some sort of faith.

Interpreting the Facts

Like it or not, the world, life, and scripture are not simply experienced or known directly. Things are *always* interpreted on the basis of assumptions and beliefs we have about the nature of the world which are part of our faith position. Knowingly or not, we are continually engaged in hermeneutics, interpretation on the basis of principles.

My interpretation of the meaning of scripture, for example, is strongly affected by whether or not I believe the Bible is a strictly human product or divinely inspired. It is further affected by whether or not I assume the Bible was intended to and can, in fact, function as a legal codebook providing specific prescriptive answers to all questions. My beliefs about these things are never simply derived from the data of the scripture only, but they should never be independent of that data either. In fact, a good hermeneutical principle for understanding scripture is that our interpretations *must* do justice to the actual data of scripture.

The same is true regarding our understanding or interpretation of the "facts" of our experience. The same event will be seen and interpreted differently by persons who bring different assumptions and expectations to it. On the day of Pentecost, the Bible records that the disciples "were filled with the Holy Spirit and began to speak in other tongues as the Spirit enabled them" (Acts 2:4). Some in the crowd didn't know anything about the Holy Spirit, but were amazed by the fact that they heard their own native languages. "Are not all of these men who are speaking Galileans? Then how is it that each of us hears them in his native tongue" (Acts 2:7-8). Some, however, heard the speech as drunken nonsense and said, "They have had too much wine" (Acts 2:13). Different interpretive, hermeneutical frameworks were in place, guiding the understanding of the "facts."

As a child, I occasionally experienced corporal punishment in the form of spankings from my mother (on one memorable occasion administered with a willow switch). The fact that I was spanked is data. But what did those spankings "mean" to me? Did I experience abuse? Was I experiencing loving limits in a way that I could understand? The experience had to be interpreted within the framework of the rest of my experiences and beliefs (however formed) about myself, my mother, and the rest of the world. And those "facts" continue to be interpreted or re-interpreted today in my memory. In this case, I never doubted her love for me or (at least often) her justice.

The Hermeneutical Spiral

We come by our personal faith position in a variety of ways'adopted without question from our families, friends, and culture; deliberately and critically chosen; refined through experience; fallen into by chance or default'or, more likely, it comes through some combination of all of these and more. However it happens, it is not a static, finished thing. Our interpretation and understanding of life proceeds in a kind of reciprocal hermeneutical spiral. Our faith position helps order and integrate (or filter and distort) the complex overload of reality which we confront. But at the same time reality has the capacity to challenge and at least partially modify or correct our assumptions and perceptions.

Once the great 18th century English dictionary-maker, writer, conversationalist, and sometime philosopher Samuel Johnson was asked by his biographer Boswell how he refuted Bishop Berkeley's philosophical theory of idealism (which asserted that the physical world has no real existence). Johnson replied, "I refute it *thus*." He thereupon vigorously kicked a large rock, causing himself considerable pain but gaining more than enough evidence (for himself, at least) to cast doubt on the sufficiency of idealist theory as a total explanation of reality.

This is a hermeneutical spiral. You come to interpret the world around you through the framework of your faith, wherever you got it, however good or bad it is, and however embryonic it may be. It strongly affects what you perceive (or even look for). But the world is not a totally passive or subjective thing. So you run the risk of coming away from the encounter with your faith somewhat altered, perhaps even corrected a bit, perhaps more distorted. Then you use that altered faith in your next encounter. Unfortunately, there is no guarantee that the alterations are corrections. But, *if* the Bible is true, and *if* we have eyes that want to see and ears that want to hear, we can have confidence that we are bumping along in the right general direction, guided by the Holy Spirit.

How Does the Bible Teach Us?

The Heresy of Legalism

For Christians, the desire for unambiguous direction has most often led to the theological error of legalism, and then, on the rebound, to relativism. Legalism takes many forms but essentially uses the legitimate zeal for faithfulness to justify an attempt to extract from the Bible or the traditions of the elders a system of rules to cover all contingencies and then to make our relationship to God depend on our understanding and living up to those rules.

It is theological error because it forces the Bible to be something that it is not—an exhaustive theological and moral codebook yielding prescriptive answers to all questions. It distorts the real nature and meaning of God's self-revelation in the incarnation of Jesus Christ, the Holy Spirit, the Scriptures, and even nature. Taken to its extreme, it effectively denies the gospel of justification by faith in Jesus Christ and substitutes a form of works righteousness. It can take the good news of redeeming, reconciling love and distort it into a source of separation, rejection, and condemnation.

The paradigm case in the New Testament involved some of the Pharisees. Jesus had some very strong words for them. When the Pharisees condemned the disciples for breaking the Sabbath by gathering grain to eat, Jesus cited the example of David feeding his men with the temple bread, also a violation of the law, and told them, in effect, that they were missing the point of the law' "The sabbath was made for man, not man for the sabbath" (Mk. 2:23-28). In the parable of the Pharisee and the tax collector Jesus warned about those who "trusted in themselves that they were righteous and despised others" (Lk. 18:9-14). He talked of those who strain out gnats and swallow camels, careful to tithe down to every herb in their gardens but neglecting the "weightier matters of the law, justice and mercy and faith" (Mt. 23:23-24). When a group of Pharisees condemned the disciples because they didn't wash their hands according to the Pharisees' understanding of the requirements of purifica tion, saying "Why do your disciples transgress the tradition of the elders?" Jesus answered "And why do you transgress the commandment of God for the sake of your tradition? . . . For the sake of your tradition you have made void the word of God. Hear and understand: not what goes into the mouth defiles a man, but what comes out of the mouth" (Mt. 15:1-11).

The Heresy of Subjective Relativism

If the Bible isn't a comprehensive lawbook out of which we can infallibly derive concrete, pre scriptive directions for every dilemma, what good is it? Aren't we then left to be blown about by ev ery wind of doctrine, led about by the spirit (or spirits) of the age we live in, guided only by our subjective, selfish desires? This is a good example of a false dichotomy, as though these were the only two alternatives. Either the Bible is a codebook or we land in total relativism. Yet this is the conclusion often drawn, which quite erroneously restricts the terms of the discussion. Once we cut loose from the deceptively certain rules of legalism it is very easy to become the disillusioned cynic—"I was tricked once, but I'm not going to be made a fool again." If the Bible can't give me all the an swers directly then its all just a matter of human opinion. So the false dilemma is stated.

The Orthodoxy of Incarnation—What if God Had a Different Idea?

Such conclusions assume that, to be of any practical use, God's revelation of His will can only be of a certain kind, an assumption we are more likely to take *to* the Bible than to learn *from* it. It as sumes that divine guidance must be exhaustively propositional, that what we need to be good Christians and to guide our moral lives is either specific rules for every occasion or at least principles from which specific rules can rationally be derived. What if such an assumption is wrong? What if it is not in keeping with the nature of God, the nature of human beings, the nature of the Bible, the nature of the Christian life?

What if the nature of Christian values and ethics cannot be adequately embodied or communicated in a book of rules, however complex and detailed? What if it can only be embodied in a life which is fully conformed to the will of God and communicated through the story of that life and its results?

What if God had to become a man, live a life of love and justice, be put to death innocently on the behalf of others, and raise triumphant over death to establish the kingdom of God? What if the Bible were book about that? A true story of how to become a real person?

The point I am trying to make is that if we go to the Bible for guidance on its *own* terms, not de ciding in advance the nature that guidance has to take, what we find is neither legalism nor relativism but precisely the kind of guidance that suits the kind of reality God actually made, the kind of crea tures we actually are, the kind of God with whom we have to do.

We learn that ethical practice has more to do with our identity, our growth in character and virtue than it does with airtight rules and that the Bible is just the kind of book to help us do this. It may not be as tidy as we would like. It may not be as easy as we would like to always tell the good guys from the bad guys. We may not always be able to act with the certain knowledge that we are doing just the right (or wrong) thing. But we will have the opportunity to get closer and closer to the truth of God, to grow up into the image of Christ. Growth is not always comfortable. But the Bible tells us *who* we are, *whose* we are, and *where* we're going.

God is Bigger Than Our Categories but the Bible is a Faithful Witness

The reality of God and biblical truth shatters our categories. At least, none of them, taken alone, can do the God of the Bible justice. Taken together, our categories have the potential to balance and correct each other. Human language can only carry so much divine freight in any particular car.

We are *all* susceptible to distorted use of Scripture. We need the recognition that we (*all* of us) always take preconditions to our Bible study which may seriously distort its message to us. In fact, we often have several *conflicting* desires and preconditions at work simultaneously. For example, we have the hunger for the security of clear-cut prescriptive answers ("Just tell me if divorce is always wrong or if I have a scriptural right to remarry") *and* a desire to be autonomous, to suit ourselves rather than submit to anyone or anything ("I don't want to hurt anyone, but my needs have to be met").

So, how do I think the Bible teaches us about morality? How does it guide us in making moral judgments in our professional lives? Struggling to rise above my own preconditions and to take the Bible on its own terms, to see how the Bible teaches and what the Bible teaches, I think I am beginning to learn a few things.

God's Project: Growing Us up into the Image of Christ

It seems to me that God is trying to reveal His nature and help us to develop His character. And it seems that the only way He could do that is in *personal* terms, creating persons with the dignity of choice, developing a relationship with a nation of them, becoming one of us Himself, revealing His love, grace, and forgiveness through a self-sacrificial act of redemption, and embarking on a process of growing persons up into His own image. The process requires us to be more than robots, even obedient ones. It requires us to make principled judgments based on virtuous character, to exercise wisdom based on the character of Christ. Neither legalism nor relativism produce this.

According to the Bible, growing us up to have the mind and character of Christ is an intrinsic part of God's redemptive project. We are not simply forgiven our sins that grace may abound but we are being rehabilitated, sanctified—being made saints, if you will. The theme is clear, as the following passages illustrate.

In Romans 6:1-2, 4 Paul says that, far from continuing in sin that grace may abound, we die to sin in Christ, are buried with him in baptism, and are raised that we too may live a new life. Romans 12:2 says that we do not conform to the pattern of this world but are to be transformed by the renewing of our minds which makes us able to test and approve what God's will is. II Corinthians 3:17-18 says that where the Spirit of the Lord is, there is freedom and that we are being transformed into His likeness with ever-increasing glory. Ephesians 4:7, 12-13 says that each one of us has been given grace from Christ to prepare us for service so that the body of Christ might be built up until we all reach unity in the faith and knowledge of the Son of God and become mature, attaining to the whole measure of the fullness of Christ. I John 3:1-3 marvels at the greatness of the love of the Father that we should be called children of God and goes on to affirm that, although what we shall be has not yet been made known, we do know that when Christ appears we shall be like him. In Philippians 2, Paul says that, being united with Christ, Christians should have the same servant attitude as Christ, looking out for the interests of others as well as ourselves. Then he makes this remarkable conjunction—"Continue to work out your own salvation with fear and trembling, for it is God who works in you to will and to act according to his good purpose."

And in I Corinthians 2 Paul says that we speak a message of wisdom among the mature, God's wisdom from the beginning, not the wisdom of this age, revealed to us by His Spirit. He explains that we have received the Spirit who is from God that we might understand what God has freely given us. He concludes, "Those who are unspiritual do not receive the gifts of God's Spirit for they are foolish ness to them, and they are unable to understand them because they are spiritually discerned . . . But we have the mind of Christ."

A Key: Judgments Based on Wisdom Growing Out of the Character of Christ

It would seem that the key to integrating Christian values into professional practice (as in all of life) is making complex judgments based on wisdom growing out of the mind and character of God, incarnated in Jesus Christ.

In our personal and professional lives we face many complex situations and decisions, large and small. Real-life moral dilemmas confront us with having to make choices between (prioritize) values that are equally real (though not necessarily equally important—remember Jesus' comments on keep ing the Sabbath versus helping a human being). Whatever we do, we cannot fully or equally maximize each value in the situation. (If the father embraces the prodigal son and gives him a party, there will be some who will see him as rewarding irresponsibility.) Whatever we do, we have to make our choices on the basis of limited understanding of both the issues involved and the consequences of our actions. Moreover, our decision is complicated by our fallen nature and selfish desires.

In situations like this, the answer is not legalism (religious or scientific) or relativism. The *mind* of Christ helps us to figure out *what* to do and the *character* of Christ helps us to have the capacity (i.e. character or virtue) to actually *do* it. It seems to me that in the very process of struggling through these difficult situations we are dealing with a principle of growth that God has deliberately built into the nature of things. The people of God are continually required to make decisions based on principles embodied in our very identity'the character of who we are, whose we are, and where we are going.

These virtues are not just abstract ones but rather they are incarnated in the history and *character* of Jesus Christ. Love and justice are the fundamental principles but we learn what they mean because Jesus embodies them. (Yes, keep the Sabbath but don't let that keep you from helping someone.)

How should a Christian social worker respond when a client says she wants an abortion? How should parents respond when an unmarried daughter tells them she is pregnant? How should a church respond to a stranger's request for financial aid? Should I be for or against our Middle Eastern pol icy? Should my wife Carol and I invite her mother to come and live with us? How much money can I spend on myself? It appears I have some complex judgments to make in order to live a life of love and justice.

So, one of God's primary dynamics of growth seems to be to place us in complex situations in which decisions based on judgment are required. These decisions require our knowledge of the character of Christ to make and they require that we be disciplined disciples at least beginning to take on the character of Christ ourselves to carry them out. It seems to me there is a deliberate plot here, daring and risky, but the only one that works, which fits the world as God made it.

Can the Preacher Have a Boat?

Permit me a personal example to illustrate the point. I remember a lively debate in the cafeteria as an undergraduate in a Christian College over whether or not a preacher (i.e. completely dedicated Christian) could have a boat. The issue, of course, was stewardship, our relationship and responsibility toward material wealth, our neighbors, and ourselves.

Being mostly lower middle class, we all easily agreed that a yacht was definitely an immoral use of money and that a row boat or canoe was probably o.k. But could it have a motor? How big? Could it possibly be an inboard motor? How many people could it carry? It was enough to cross a rabbi's eyes. Since we believed the Bible to contain a prescriptive answer to every question, we tried hard to formulate a scriptural answer. But we found no direct commands, approved apostolic examples, or necessary inferences that would nail it down.

What we found was much more challenging—things like:

> The earth is the Lord's and the fullness thereof (Psa. 24:1)
> Give as you have been prospered (I Cor. 16:2)
> What do you have that you did not receive (II Cor. 4:7)
> Remember the fatherless and widows (Jas. 1:27)
> Don't lay up treasures on earth (Mt. 6:19-20)
> Follow Jesus in looking out for the interests of others, not just your own (Phil. 2:1-5).

Plenty of guidelines for exercising love and justice, lots of examples of Christ and the disciples in action—in other words, no selfish relativism. But no iron-clad formulas for what to spend or where—in other words, no legalism.

Instead, every time I turn around I am faced again with new financial choices, fresh opportunities to decide all over again what stewardship means—plenty of chances to grossly rationalize, distort, and abuse the gospel, to be sure. But also plenty of opportunities to get it right this time, or at least better. To grow up into the image of Christ.

Gaining the Mind and Character of Christ

So, only persons of character or virtue can make the kind of judgments and take the actions required of us. To do the right thing we need to be the right kinds of persons, embodying the mind and character of Christ.

The most direct route to moral practice is through realizing our identity as Christ-Ones. In Galatians 2:20 Paul said "I have been crucified with Christ and I no longer live, but Christ lives in me. The life I live in the body, I live by faith in the Son of God, who loved me and gave himself for me" and in Galatians 5:13-14 he said "You were called to freedom, brothers and sisters; only do not use your freedom as an opportunity for self-indulgence, but through love become slaves to one another. For the whole law is summed up in a single commandment, 'You shall love your neighbor as yourself.'"

The mind and character of Christ is formed in us by the Holy Spirit as we submit to God's gen eral revelation in creation (Romans 1-2), written revelation in Scripture (II Tim. 3:15-17), and, ultimately, incarnated revelation in Jesus Christ (John 1:1-18; Col. 1:15-20). We can only give appropriate meaning to the principles of love and justice by knowing the God of the Bible, the Jesus of incarnation, and the Holy Spirit of understanding and power. This happens best (perhaps only) in the give and take of two living communities—Christian families and the church, the body of Christ.

What we have when this happens is not an encyclopedic list of rules that gives us unambiguous answers to every practical or moral issue we may ever encounter. Neither are we left in an uncharted swamp of selfish relativity. And, it should be noted well, we are not given a substitute for the clear thinking and investigation necessary to provide the data. The Bible and Christ Himself are no substitute for reading, writing, and arithmetic (or practice wisdom, theory, and empirical research)'getting the best information we can and thinking honestly and clearly about it.

Instead, what we have then is the enhanced capacity to make and carry out complex judgment that is more in harmony with God's love and justice than we could make otherwise. We are still limited. We still know in part and "see but a poor reflection as in a mirror" (I Cor. 13:12).

We may be disappointed that the Bible or Christ Himself don't give us the kind of advice, shortcuts, or easy black-and-white answers we would like, but what they give us is much better—the truth. Do you want to live a good life? Do you want to integrate your Christian values and your professional helping practice? Do you want to do what is right? The only way, ultimately, is to know God through being a disciple of Christ. This doesn't mean that only Christians can have good moral character—God's common grace is accessible to all. But it really is *true* that Jesus is the way, the truth, and the life (John 14:6). God is the one who gives *content* to the idea of "good." The mind of Christ is really quite remarkable, filling up and stretching to the limit our humanity with God.

Lord, help us to know
> **who** we are,
> **whose** we are, and
> **where** we are going.

An Ethical Decision-Making Model

Given this understanding of the human situation, how God is working with us to grow us up into the image of Christ and the proper role that the Bible plays in giving us guidance, I would like to briefly introduce an ethical decision-making model for Christian helping professionals. It is a simple "problem-solving" model which assumes and is no substitute for developing the mind and character of Christ. It is simple only in concept, not in application. And it is what we need to do in all of our lives, not just in our work with clients.

Deontological and Consequentialist/Utilitarian Parameters

Ethical judgments and actions can generally be thought of as being based on two kinds of criteria or parameters—deontological and consequentialist/utilitarian. These are philosophical terms for describing two types of measuring sticks of whether or not something is good or bad in a moral sense and either ought or ought not to be done.

Deontological Parameters—The "Oughts"

Deontological parameters or criteria refer to moral obligation or duty. What are the moral imperatives or rules that relate to the situation? What are the "oughts?" For the Christian, it can be summed up by asking "What is the will of God in this situation?" Understanding the deontological parameters of an ethical dilemma we face is extremely important. But it is not as simple as it may first appear. Some think that ethics can be determined by deontological parameters only or that deontological parameters operate without consideration to consequences in any way. For example, the commandment "Thou shalt not lie" is taken to be an absolute, exceptionless rule which is to be obeyed in all circumstances and at all times, regardless of the consequences. By this principle, when Corrie Ten Boom was asked by the Nazis if she knew of any Jews, she should have led them to her family's hiding place.

Trying to answer all moral questions by attempting to invoke a particular deontological principle in isolation, even if it is biblical, may wind up leading us into actions which are contrary to God's will. That is the legalistic fallacy which we discussed before. Normally we have an ethical dilemma because we are in a situation in which more than one deontological principle applies and they are in conflict to some degree. Do we keep the sabbath or do we heal? The Ten Commandments or the Sermon on the Mount, for example, contain deontological principles that are vitally important to helping us understand the mind of Christ and doing the will of God. But they cannot be handled mechanistically or legalistically or we will become Pharisees indeed. Does "turning the other cheek" require us to never resist evil in any way?

Most Christians properly understand that God's will is fully embodied only in God's character of love and justice, which was incarnated in the person of Jesus Christ. Love and justice are the only "exceptionless absolutes" in a deontological sense. The moral rules and principles of scripture provide important guidelines to help us to understand what love and justice act like in various circumstances, but they cannot stand alone as absolutes nor can they be forced into a legal system which eliminates the need for us to make judgments.

Consequentialist/Utilitarian Parameters—The "Results"

For God and for us, moral reality is always embodied. Part of what this means, then, is that the deontological "oughts" can never be completely separated from the consequentialist/utilitarian parameters. The consequentialist/utilitarian parameters refer to the results. Christian ethical decisions and actions always have to try to take into account their consequences. What happens as a result of this action or that, and what end is served?

Many people (quite erroneously) believe that moral judgments or actions can be judged exclusively on the basis of their results. Did it have a "good" or desired result? Then it was a good act. If we value the end we implicitly accept the means to that end, no matter what they might be (say, terrorism to oppose unjust tyranny). This is just as much a fallacy as the single-minded deontological judgment. Pure utilitarianism is impossible since there must be some deontological basis for deciding what is a "good" result, and this can never be derived from the raw facts of a situation. And "goods" and "evils" must be prioritized and balanced against one another in means as well as the ends.

It is a fact that some adults engage in sexual activity with children. But so what? What is the moral and practical meaning of that fact? Is it something we should encourage or prevent? Without some standard of "good" or "health" it is impossible to give a coherent answer.

Another major limitation of consequentialist/utilitarian criteria in making moral judgments is that at best they can never be more than guesses or *predictions* based on what we *think* the results might be, never on the actual consequences themselves. If I encourage my client to separate from her abusive husband, I may think that he will not hurt her or the children, but I cannot be sure.

So, ethical and practical *judgments* are always required. They aren't simple. And they always involve identifying, prioritizing, and acting on *both* deontological and consequentialist/utilitarian parameters of a situation.

The Model: Judgment Formed By Character and Guided By Principle

1. **Identify and explore the problem:**
   What issues/values (usually plural) are at stake?
   What are the desired ends?
   What are the alternative possible means?
   What are the other possible unintended consequences?
2. **Identify the deontological parameters:**
   What moral imperatives are there?
   What is the will of God, the mind of Christ?
   What are the principles at stake, especially in regard to love and justice?
   Are there any rules or rule-governed exceptions, biblical injunctions, commands, or codes of ethics which apply?
3. **Identify the consequentialist/utilitarian parameters:**
   What (as nearly as can be determined or predicted) are the likely intended and unintended consequences?
   What are the costs and benefits? How are they distributed (who benefits, who pays)?
   What must be given up in each particular possible course of action? What values will be slighted or maximized?
4. **Integrate and rank the deontological and consequentialist/utilitarian parameters:**
   What best approximates (maximizes) the exceptionless absolutes of love and justice?
5. **Make a judgment guided by character and act:**
   After gathering and analyzing the biblical, professional and other data, pray for wisdom and the guidance of the Holy Spirit.

Make a judgment and act growing out of your character as informed by the character of Christ.

Refusing choice and action *is* choice and action, so you must do the best you can at the time, even if, in retrospect it turns out you were "sinning bravely."

6. **Evaluate:**

Grow through your experience. Rejoice or repent, go on or change.

Character Formed through Discipleship and the Guidance of the Holy Spirit

Ultimately, ethical Christian practice depends on one thing—developing the mind and character of Christ. It depends on our growing up into the image of Christ. This begins in the new birth as we become new creations in Christ. We are filled with the Holy Spirit and called to a life of discipleship in which we bring every thought and action in captivity to Christ (II Cor. 10:5). We present our bodies "as a living sacrifice," not conformed to this world, but "transformed by the renewal of your mind" (Rom. 12:1-2). We hunger and thirst after righteousness. We seek to know God's will through scripture, the guidance of the Holy Spirit, and the community of the church. We identify with Jesus and the saints of God down through the ages. We daily choose to follow Christ as best we know and can. We repent and confess to our Lord when we fall. We thankfully receive his grace. We choose and act again.

Certainly piety is not a substitute for the discipline of professional training, careful research, and thoughtful analysis. Rather, the use of all of these is simply a complimentary part of our stewardship and discipleship. The most solid possible assurance that we will do the right thing in our personal lives and in our professional practice is our discipleship, growing to have more and more of the character of Jesus Christ, as we make judgments more in harmony with God's character and Spirit.

We become a "letter from Christ . . . Written not with ink but with the Spirit of the living God, not on tablets of stone but on tablets of human hearts, . . . ministers of a new covenant, not in a written code but in the Spirit; for the written code kills, but the Spirit gives life . . .Now the Lord is the Spirit, and where the Spirit of the Lord is, there is freedom. And we all, with unveiled face, beholding the glory of the Lord, are being changed into his likeness from one degree of glory to another; for this comes from the Lord who is the Spirit" (II Cor. 3:3, 6, 17-18).

Notes

This chapter was previously published in *Social Work and Christianity*, 20(2), 1993.

References

Adams, Robert M. (1987). *The virtue of faith*. New York: Oxford University Press.

Hauerwas, Stanley. (1981). *A community of character: Toward a constructive Christian social ethic*. Notre Dame: University of Notre Dame Press.

Hauerwas, Stanley and Willimon, William H. (1989). *Resident aliens: Life in the Christian colony*. Nashville: Abingdon Press.

Holmes, Arthur. (1984). *Ethics: Approaching moral decisions*. Downers Grove, IL: InterVarsity Press.

Keith-Lucas, Alan. (1994). *Giving and taking help*. Botsford, CT: North American Association of Christians in Social Work.

Keith-Lucas, Alan. (1985). *So you want to be a social worker: A primer for the Christian student*. Botsford, CT: North American Association of Christians in Social Work.

Lewis, C. S. (1947). *The abolition of man*. New York: Macmillan.

Lewis, C. S. (1943). *Mere Christianity*. New York: Macmillan.

MacIntyre, Alasdair. (1984). *After virtue: A study in moral theory*. 2nd Ed. University of Notre Dame Press.

Mott, Stephen C. (1982). *Biblical ethics and social change*. New York: Oxford University Press.

O'Donovan, Oliver. (1986). *Resurrection and the moral order: An outline for evangelical ethics*. Grand Rapids: Eerdmans.

Osborne, Grant R. (1991). *The hermeneutical spiral: A comprehensive introduction to biblical inter pretation*. Downers Grove, IL: InterVarsity Press.

Pinnock, Clark. (1984). *The scripture principle*. New York: Harper and Row.

Sire, James W. (1980). *Scripture twisting*. Downers Grove, IL: InterVarsity Press.

Sherwood, David A. (Spring-Fall 1981). Add to your faith virtue: The integration of Christian values and social work practice. *Social Work and Christianity*, 8, 41-54.

Sherwood, David A. (Spring 1989). How should we use the bible in ethical decision-making? Guidance without legalism or relativism. *Social Work and Christianity*, 16, 29-42

Sherwood, David A. (Fall 1986). Notes toward applying Christian ethics to practice: Growing up into the image of Christ. *Social Work and Christianity*, 13, 82-93.

Smedes, Lewis. (1983). *Mere morality*. Grand Rapids: Eerdmans.

Swartley, Willard M. (1983). *Slavery, sabbath, war, and women: Case issues in biblical interpre tation*. Scottsdale, PA: Herald Press.

Verhay, Allen. (1984). *The great reversal: Ethics and the new testament*. Grand Rapids: Eerdmans.

CHAPTER 14

HOSPICE: AN OPPORTUNITY FOR TRULY WHOLISTIC SOCIAL WORK

John E. Babler

The field of social work provides many diverse opportunities for practice and most students wonder what type of practice setting will fit them best. For Christians, the contemplation of practice settings may include consideration of variables such as their own spiritual gifts, their theology of helping, the openness of various social work settings to Christians sharing their faith, and God's call on their life. This chapter will present information about hospice, a social work practice setting that should be of particular interest to Christians in social work.

The Seminary where I teach exists to provide theological training to men and women called to vocational ministry. The department in which I teach focuses on preparing students for ministries of helping. The importance of both demonstrating *and* declaring faith in Jesus while helping is modeled and taught. God calls me personally to overtly express my Christianity when helping others and to teach them that His Word is sufficient to solve problems in living. God continually reminds me what a great resource He has provided in the Bible. Of all the books we have available to us it alone is living and active (Hebrews 4:12) and inspired by God and useful for teaching, reproof, correction and training in righteousness (2 Timothy 3:16-17).

Several years experience in hospice social work and completion of a dissertation on spiritual care in hospice causes me to be excited about hospice as a practice setting for Christians in social work. It is a practice setting that can be a good fit for Christians in social work.

Hospice: History and Overview

Throughout history, writings of philosophers, theologians, and poets have detailed and explored a universal human fascination with and fear of death (Munley, 1983). Missinne (1990) contends that Ameri-

Scripture taken from the New American Standard Bible, c. 1977, by The Lockman Foundation.

can attitudes concerning death are negative. In facing death, people are exposed to their weaknesses and encounter feelings such as hostility, denial, and embarrassment. Possessions and physical beauty no longer are important. Death is democratic, the one thing we all have in common is that we all will die. Many of us "fear death far less than...a long and painful dying that leaves us incapacitated, helpless, totally dependent on the good will of strangers—bereft of dignity, comfort, and human warmth" (Bulkin & Lukashok, 1988).

According to Munley (1983), the rapidly advancing medical technology in our society coupled with urbanization and the lack of contact with dying people makes dealing with death even more complex. Dying in America is often a clinical experience filled with machines, tubes, unknown people, strange surroundings, and limited family contact. In contrast, the end of life for a hospice patient is filled with familiar surroundings, close (sometimes constant) support of family and friends, and wholistic care by committed professionals.

Hospice care can be a positive alternative to a "technological" death. Hospices were common in the Middle Ages where they served a variety of purposes. The typical medieval hospice was a combination guest house and infirmary where all who entered were given food, shelter, and care until they died or set out again on their journeys, refreshed and renewed (Munley, 1983). Ley and Corless (1988) emphasize the fact that these medieval hospices had strong Christian roots. They were dedicated to the Scriptural injunctions of Matthew 25 to feed the hungry, give drink to the thirsty, welcome the stranger, clothe the naked, and visit the prisoner as well as to the early church practice of burying the dead. The medieval view that death is a transformation and the belief that what happens to the mind and the spirit are as important as what happens to the body provided the foundation for the modern hospice movement (Stoddard, 1991).

Dame Cicely Saunders was the driving force behind the beginning of the modern hospice movement. Saunders was first trained as a nurse and then her interest in terminally ill patients led her to be trained as a medical social worker, and finally as a physician. As a physician at a hospice operated by the Irish Sisters of Charity, she began to integrate the wholistic care concepts of hospices of the past with modern pain control techniques. She opened St. Christopher's Hospice in London in 1968. St. Christopher's has become a model of modern hospice care and is an international education and research center that attracts hospice professionals and those interested in hospice from around the world (Munley, 1983).

St. Christopher's was "founded on the ancient Christian concept of hospice dating back to the fourth century A.D.—a place to care for pilgrims and travelers, the poor, the sick, and the dying" (Ley & Corless,

1988). Strong religious affiliation was one of the major characteristics of the development of the hospice movement in England, but in the United States a more pluralistic and secular tradition exists and the religious aspect may not appear to be so significant (O'Connor, 1986).

The hospice movement in the United States has Elizabeth Kubler-Ross as its "lightning rod." Her commitment to meeting the needs of the dying and their loved ones as demonstrated by her life and teaching and her book *On Death and Dying,* helped many in the medical community to see the need hospice could fill. Hospice Incorporated in New Haven, Connecticut and Hospice of Marin in Marin County, California were among the first hospice programs in the United States. Hospice of Marin was begun by committed professionals who volunteered their time to care for terminally ill cancer patients in their homes (Stoddard, 1991; Munley 1983).

Less than twenty years since its humble beginnings in this country, hospice has grown and changed significantly. No longer dependent upon volunteers, hospices employ many to meet the needs of the terminally ill and their families. Hospice services are covered by Medicare, Medicaid, and many private health insurance plans. The National Hospice Organization currently represents over 1600 hospice organizations. In the midst of change and growth, many of the emphases of the past continue on today. Among these are the inter-disciplinary team approach to providing care and a continuing emphasis on the necessity of treating the whole person. The National Hospice Organization sums up this emphasis as a standard for hospices, stating that a specially trained team of hospice professionals and volunteers work together to meet physiological, psychological, social, spiritual, and economic needs of patients and families facing terminal illnesses (National Hospice Organization, 1994).

Hospice does nothing to hasten or slow the process of death. A common sentiment is that hospice does not deal with death, but rather with making the end of one's life as positive as possible. An appropriate understanding of hospice stresses a "good death" or "the good in dying" (Jennings, 1997). Due to a belief that people should not suffer needlessly, palliation or pain control is a major priority of hospice. Sometimes, very large doses of pain relievers such as morphine are required to keep the patient comfortable.

Since hospice has a very high success rate at keeping patients comfortable, it serves as a positive alternative to the argument that assisted suicide is necessary to keep people from dying painful deaths. Hospice takes very seriously the other needs of patients and their families, as well. These needs are widely varied and may relate to emotional support, financial struggles, out of home placement, spiritual issues, personal hygiene of the patient, counseling, crisis intervention, and grief.

The interdisciplinary team of hospice professionals and volunteers work together to meet the wholistic needs of the hospice patient and the patient's family, friends, and co-workers. Requirements for hospice admission include a diagnosis of a terminal illness with less than six months to live and a desire to *not* seek further curative treatment. After admission to a hospice program, assessments are made of the patient and family by the various team members and the team designs and implements a care plan for the family.

The inclusion of social work services as a part of hospice care is required and social workers are a vital part of the hospice team (National Hospice Organization, 1994). The comprehensive skills that a social worker has obtained through education and experience find many applications in hospice care. The team approach allows social workers a voice in a wide variety of issues, and ongoing relationships with other professionals, hospice patients, and their families and friends provide abundant opportunities for intervention.

Hospice: Meeting Psychosocial Needs Through Social Work

The National Hospice Organization (1994) provides the following guidelines for the availability and scope of social work services:

1. Social work services should be offered to every patient/family/significant other.
2. A thorough social work/psychosocial assessment should be done by a social worker at the time of admission or as soon as possible thereafter. The social worker should be involved in the initial and ongoing care planning.
3. Social work services should be reflective of traditional social work roles and include, but not be limited to: psychosocial assessment, counseling, consultation, education, resource and referral services, advocacy, and discharge planning.
4. The scope of services should be clearly defined in the policies and procedures of the organization or social work department.
5. Ongoing social work services should be provided based on the social work assessment and plan of care. Additionally, services may be initiated upon referral at any time by any member of the interdisciplinary team, the patient or family. (p.1)

While the above guidelines provide a foundation for hospice social work, published articles that address social work in hospice are rare (MacDonald, 1991). Those that have been written focus primarily on the roles and functions of hospice social workers (Quig, 1989; Rusnack,

Schaefer, & Moxley, 1988). There continues to be a need for research that clarifies the importance and efficacy of social work in hospice (Richardson, 1997).

Social workers are a necessary component of hospice care. Strengths brought to the hospice team include a focus on the patient as not only a part of a family, but as part of a community and society. Social workers have many varied opportunities to practice social work roles in hospice, but there is a need to formalize the interventions and skills as well as outcomes sought and achieved. The advocacy role of the social worker in hospice is vital in the current environment of health care reform. The demands of reform give social workers in hospice the opportunity to clarify their importance to the health care industry as well as the profession (Richardson, 1997). The practice of social work in hospice is emotionally intense and very demanding. It requires well developed skills and an ability to be flexible based on the needs and demands of others.

Social work in hospice is accomplished at several different levels. First and foremost is the work that is accomplished with the patients, families and loved ones. This work requires excellent assessment skills as well as wisdom to know which problems require intervention and which issues are normal for people facing their own mortality. Sometimes the social worker is called on to assist the family in group problem-solving. Knowledge of group dynamics as well as an ability to work with groups is necessary. Social workers also practice advocacy for patients and families with other hospice team members during team meetings and in other settings. Since hospice social work requires the social worker to make their own schedule and do home visits, self-discipline is a must.

Hospice social workers are frequently called on to present grief workshops and work with bereaved family members. This requires public speaking skills and compassion as well as an understanding of grief. Networking and crisis intervention round out the responsibilities of hospice social workers.

Gambrill (1997) emphasizes the importance of nonverbal behaviors such as facial expression, gaze, posture and position, proximity, gestures, touch, and physical appearance. These nonverbal communications are even more important and less defined in hospice work. People who are receiving hospice services all have different needs, but all are in "chronic crisis" and many are ultra-sensitive to nonverbal as well as verbal communication.

Hospice provides a setting where a social worker will have the opportunity to use almost all the skills learned in the classroom and field education. It also provides the opportunity to use skills in spiritual care that, unfortunately, are not typically a part of social work.

Hospice: An Opportunity for Truly Wholistic Social Work

As has been mentioned, the hospice movement in the United States does not have the same strong emphasis on religious affiliation as hospices in England. Despite the differences, the religious and spiritual components of hospice in the United States are vital to caring for the dying. By accepting patients with no hope of recovery and offering them hope of spiritual restoration, hospice has called forth the spiritual force in society by challenging the mortality of humans (O'Connor, 1986). Even for patients who have not been active in a church or synagogue, religious concerns often become important as death nears and they may welcome the opportunity to discuss religious matters with a chaplain, pastoral counselor, friends, family, or staff members (Rhymes, 1993).

While there is agreement that spiritual needs of hospice patients and families are important and need to be addressed and that hospice programs need to provide spiritual care, the spiritual care component of hospice care is the most undefined area of service (Meogrossi, 1991). Missinne asserts that providing spiritual care is as important as meeting biophysical and psychosocial needs (Missinne, 1990).

Ed Holland of Methodist Hospital in Minneapolis describes one way hospices attempt to meet the spiritual needs of patients and families. Chaplains in his program are the designated spiritual care providers. In this approach, the chaplains are the team members who provide spiritual care (Holland, Hay, & Rice, 1991). This approach is similar to the medical model utilized at most hospitals of referring all spiritual needs to the chaplain and is the preferred approach of many medical personnel.

In this medical model of spiritual care, if a patient or family member expresses any sort of spiritual concern it is referred to the chaplain. If a team member observes anything he or she believes needs spiritual intervention it is referred to the chaplain. The chaplain acts as a liaison between the patient/family and the mental health professionals on the team. The chaplain is responsible for spiritual/emotional support, pastoral counseling, acting as liaison to community clergy, acting as support group facilitator, providing grief instruction and counseling, coordinating bereavement services, and facilitating religious rituals and worship.

In addition to the familiarity that medical professionals have with it, the acceptance of the referral approach to spiritual care by some hospices may be motivated by a focused definition of spiritual caregiving. A narrow definition of spiritual care "includes specifically priestly acts, administration of sacraments, prayers, Scripture reading, and talking about explicitly religious or theological concerns: theodicy, sin, forgiveness, salvation, and eternal life" (Irion, 1988). Acceptance may also be motivated by the lack of definition of the chaplain role as pointed out by True Ryndes, "You experience role-blurring a great deal with some of the team members, especially social work..." (Schwarz, Schmoll, Ryndes, & Hay, 1991).

Christian social workers who find themselves working in a hospice that utilizes this referral approach to spiritual care will struggle with role-blurring with the chaplain. The overlap of the responsibilities mentioned above with social work are obvious. The social worker who is committed to helping the whole person will also be responsible for providing spiritual/emotional support. Social workers are trained and equipped in advocacy and often serve as liaisons to various individuals and institutions in the community. Social workers have advanced skills in group work and many have had course work that covers issues of grief. While this role-blurring may be frustrating, Christian social workers are equipped to deal with it on two different levels.

Social workers receive education and experience in dealing with role difficulties in practice. Conflict can occur around issues of age, race, ethnicity, culture, and authority. The skills utilized by a young, single social worker to deal with concerns expressed by a mother of four seeking help parenting can be transferred to a situation where a chaplain doubts the ability of a social worker to intervene in a particular situation. Other skills and emphases inherent in social work such as the importance of honest communication are also beneficial in dealing with role confusion. Although social work skills and training can be helpful in dealing with role-blurring, the Christian social worker is equipped to deal with the issue even more effectively. Christians have Jesus' example of servant-leadership (as when He washed the disciples feet in John 13:1-15) as a foundation upon which to build relationships. This servant-leadership avoids the power struggles or "turf wars" that are so common in role-blurring between professionals and additionally is a witness to the world that we are Christ's disciples (John 13:34-35).

Milton Hay of San Diego Hospice describes another way hospices attempt to provide spiritual care to patients and families. This approach emphasizes using all team members to provide spiritual care and sees pastoral care as a religious specialization. He explains that at San Diego Hospice, spiritual care is the *broader* application of the work of the chaplains in the Department of Pastoral Care. Assessments are completed by a team consisting of a nurse and a social worker. The intake social worker completes the initial spiritual assessment. This is a part of the overall psycho-social assessment and includes questions about religious beliefs and involvement as well as questions about feelings and emotions related to the impending death of the patient. When a spiritual "problem" is identified, the ongoing social worker is responsible for resolving it. One of the options the social worker has available is referral to a chaplain. The patient's and family's spiritual needs are continually re-assessed and addressed, but not all see a chaplain. Spiritual assessment and intervention by non-chaplain team members is always appropriate and referrals to chaplains can be made by any team member. These referrals are coordinated by the social worker who works closely with the chaplains regarding spiritual issues (Holland, Hay, & Rice, 1991).

This inter-disciplinary team approach fits well with general hospice philosophy. Hospice is not anti-specialization, but it encourages specialists to adopt a team approach that values role flexibility, "...in a hospice, a social worker may carry a tray, a maintenance worker may comfort a patient, and a physician may promise a prayer" (Munley, 1983).

It almost goes without saying that hospice workers and volunteers should respect spiritual and religious views different than their own. "Hospice provides spiritual care services that are consistent with patient/family beliefs and desire for service..." (National Hospice Organization, 1993). The provision of spiritual care in hospice needs to take into account the patient's and family's right to self-determination. No matter what conclusion the hospice program comes to regarding who will provide spiritual care utilizing which approach, if the patient and family conclude their spiritual needs are not being met, the spiritual care component is not successful.

Truly wholistic social work includes meeting the spiritual needs of clients. Hospice as a field provides opportunities for Christians in social work to be exposed to and meet spiritual needs. The greatest need every individual has is for a personal relationship with Jesus Christ. For those who already have a relationship with Jesus, the greatest need is to grow to become more like Him through discipleship. Social workers pride themselves on helping the whole person. However, most social workers focus only on meeting the physical and emotional needs of their clients. To help the whole person, the Christian social worker must be committed to the practice of evangelism and discipleship. Truly wholistic social work both demonstrates and declares the Good News of Jesus. Hospice can at times provide opportunities for the Christian social worker to overtly engage in evangelism and discipleship.

I have frequently heard that if you give a man a fish you feed him for a day, but if you teach him to fish you feed him for a life time. It wasn't until a recent mission trip to the Philippines that I heard the complete version of this illustration. If you give a man a fish you feed him for a day, if you teach him to fish you feed him for a lifetime, but if you introduce him to the Creator of the fish he will be fed for eternity. Hospice is one practice setting that can at times provide opportunities for Christians in social work to meet needs at all three levels.

The Bible calls us to witnessing and ministry. In Mark 1:17 Jesus commands us to follow Him and promises to make us fishers of men. Jesus tells us to go and make disciples and promises to be with us (Matthew 28:19-20). Acts 1:8 shows that witnessing is not just voluntary or mandatory, but is inevitable. If Christ is in our hearts, He will be in our talk (Atkinson & Roesel, 1995). Ministry unto the least is presented to people of every nation as ministry unto Jesus (Mt. 25:31-46).

People that the social worker will encounter in hospice are in crisis. Either a loved one or they themselves are dying. When people are in crisis and facing the issue of death, they frequently have questions and are open to spiritual issues. I remember caring for a young single woman (I'll call her Ellen) whose 3 month old baby (I'll call her Jennifer) was dying. Over the months we got to know each other I not only demonstrated Christ's love for her, but I verbally presented the Good News of Jesus.

Ellen was a nineteen year old single mother who did not finish high school, she lived with her parents in a rural setting away from her friends, her parents did not approve of the baby's father, and she was making life and death decisions for Jennifer. She had many physical, spiritual, and emotional needs. In my role as hospice social worker I had the opportunity to walk with Ellen through this crisis and meet some of her many needs. I accomplished many traditional social work tasks. I advocated for her and for Jennifer with doctors, children's hospital staff, The Ronald McDonald House, and governmental agencies. I counseled her regarding difficult decisions she had to make. I counseled with the entire family and attempted to facilitate and improve communication. I sat with her and her family during the last few hours of Jennifer's life. I attended the funeral and encouraged Ellen as she continued her life after the death of her dear daughter.

But my "intervention" with Ellen was so much more than just traditional social work—focusing on meeting physical and emotional needs while ignoring the spiritual. Through an emphasis on true evangelism, which includes both demonstration and declaration of the Gospel, Ellen's ultimate need was met. Throughout our relationship we talked about God and heaven and faith until one visit I shared with her the plan of salvation. God convicted her of her sin, she responded in humble repentance and asked Jesus to be her Lord and Savior. She was truly changed by God and began to exhibit the spiritual fruit that only God can develop (Gal. 5:22-23).

At Southwestern Seminary we call the combination of demonstration and declaration of the Gospel with the meeting of physical and emotional needs Ministry-Based Evangelism. The focus of Ministry-Based Evangelism is to develop a relationship through which needs are met in the name of Jesus and true evangelism takes place. As my experience with Ellen demonstrates, hospice can provide a unique opportunity for the Christian social worker to do truly wholistic social work.

Many of the people I encountered in hospice were committed Christians. As I attempted to meet their needs I was able to disciple and challenge them from God's Word. People in crisis have many questions and God has provided everything we need for life and Godliness (2 Peter 1:3). The idea of discipling someone who is more mature is a challenge that can best be met by making sure our counsel is from God's Word (Heb 4:12, 2 Ti. 3:16-17).

Many Christian professionals who have studied the behavioral sciences have become accustomed to looking first to science for answers and often ignore the greatest resource available—The Bible. Providing not only the foundation for our service, The Bible is the living truth (Heb 4:12) that God uses to change lives. I have found it very important to share actual Scripture verses rather than just Biblical insight. Some of the verses I have found helpful to share with hospice clients are listed below.

For Evangelism:

John 14.6 Jesus said to him, I am the way, and the truth, and the life; no one comes to the Father, but through Me.

Rom. 3:23 For all have sinned and fall short of the glory of God.

Rom. 6:23 For the wages of sin is death, but the free gift of God is eternal life in Christ Jesus our Lord.

Rom. 10:9-10 That if you confess with your mouth Jesus as Lord, and believe in your heart that God raised Him from the dead, you shall be saved; for with the heart man believes, resulting in righteousness, and with the mouth he confesses, resulting in salvation.

To Show That God Understands Grief and is Compassionate:

Is.53:3-4 He was despised and forsaken of men, a man of sorrows, and acquainted with grief; and like one from whom men hide their face, He was despised, and we did not esteem Him. Surely our griefs He Himself bore, and our sorrows He carried; yet we ourselves esteemed Him stricken, smitten of God, and afflicted.

2 Chr.30:9 For if you return to the Lord, your brothers and your sons will find compassion before those who led them captive, and will return to this land. For the Lord your God is gracious and compassionate, and will not turn His face away from you if you return to Him.

Ps.22:24 For He has not despised nor abhorred the affliction of the afflicted; neither has He hidden His face from him; but when he cried to Him for help, He heard.

Ps.25:6 Remember, O Lord, Thy compassion and Thy loving kindnesses, for they have been from of old.

Ps.31:7 I will rejoice and be glad in Thy loving kindness, because Thou hast seen my affliction; Thou hast known the troubles of my soul.

Ps.40:11 Thou, O Lord, wilt not withhold Thy compassion from me; Thy loving kindness and Thy truth will continually preserve me.

Ps.51:1 Be gracious to me, O God, according to Thy loving kindness; according to the greatness of Thy compassion blot out my transgressions.

Ps.103:8 The Lord is compassionate and gracious, slow to anger and abounding in loving kindness.

Ps.103:13 Just as a father has compassion on his children, so the Lord has compassion on those who fear Him.

Ps.111:4 He has made His wonders to be remembered; the Lord is gracious and compassionate.

Ps.116:5 Gracious is the Lord, and righteous; yes, our God is compassionate.

Pr.28:13 He who conceals his transgressions will not prosper, but he who confesses and forsakes them will find compassion.

Lu.15:20 And he got up and came to his father. But while he was still a long way off, his father saw him, and felt compassion for him, and ran and embraced him, and kissed him.

Jn.11:35 Jesus wept.

Heb.4:15 For we do not have a high priest who cannot sympathize with our weaknesses, but One who has been tempted in all things as we are, yet without sin.

The above verses are just a small sample of all that the Bible says to those in hospice. I encourage you to look them up and read them in context to better understand their application for hospice social work. It is my prayer that whatever social work setting you find yourself in, you will search the Scriptures and allow them to provide the foundation and the vehicle for helping people.

Conclusion

The world would have us believe that death is something to fear and that those facing the death of themselves or a loved one will receive little comfort or hope. For many years hospice has provided comfort for dying patients and their families. Christian social workers in hospice have an opportunity to provide both comfort and hope. The Bible provides many verses that tell us about our hope and encourage us to share it (Rom. 15:4; 1 Pet. 3:15; Col. 1:5; Tit. 2:13; He. 6:18-19; 1 Pet. 1:3). We can share the message that "God is able to do exceeding abundantly beyond all that we ask or think, according to the power that works within us (Eph. 3:20)." Finally, in the midst of our own grief in helping people facing death, as members of God's family we can rest on and share the family secret: "And WE KNOW that God causes all things to work together for good to those who love God, to those who are called according to His purpose (Rom. 8:28)."

References

Atkinson, Donald A. & Charles L. Roesel. (1995). *Meeting Needs Sharing Christ*. Lifeway Press: Nashville, TN.

Bulkin, Wilma & Herbert Lukashok. (1988). Rx for Dying: The Case for Hospice. *New England Journal of Medicine*, February 11, 378-80.

Gambrill, Eileen. (1997). *Social Work Practice*. Oxford University Press: NY.

Holland, Milton Hay & S. Rice. (1991). Don't Put a Round Plug in a Square Hole! Developing an Effective Spiritual Care Model for Your Hospice. Tape recording of presentation made at National Hospice Organization's First National Conference on Spiritual Care in Hospice, Kansas City, MO.

Irion, Paul E. (1988). *Hospice and Ministry*. Nashville: Abingdon Press.

Jennings, Bruce. (1997). Individual Rights and the Human Good in Hospice. *The Hospice Journal*, 12(2), 1-8.

Ley, Dorothy & Inge Corless. (1988). Spirituality and Hospice Care. *Death Studies*, 12,101-05.

MacDonald, Douglas. (1991). Hospice Social Work: A Search for Identity. *Health and Social Work*, 16 November, 274-80.

Meogrossi, Romuald J. (1991). A Comparison of Patient Satisfaction of Persons Treated in Church-related and Nonchurch-related Hospices. D.P.C. dissertation, Loyola College in Maryland.

Missinne, Leo. (1990). Death & Spiritual Concerns of Older Adults. *Generations, 14* Fall, 45- 49.

Munley, Anne. (1983). *The Hospice Alternative*. New York: Basic Books.

National Hospice Organization. (1994). *Standards of a Hospice Program of Care*. Arlington, VA: National Hospice Organization.

O'Connor, Patrice. (1986). Spiritual Elements of Hospice Care. *Hospice Journal*, 2 Summer, 108-19.

Quig, Lois. (1989). The Role of the Hospice Social Worker. *The American Journal of Hospice Care*, 6 (July/August),22-23.

Rhymes, Jill. (1993). Hospice Care in the Nursing Home. *Nursing Home Medicine*, 1 (November), 16.

Richardson, Joan. (1997). Embracing The New, Guarding The Past. *The Hospice Professional*, Spring, 13-14.

Rusnack, Betty, Sarajane McNulty Schaefer, & David Moxley. (1988). "Safe Passage": Social Work Roles and Functions in Hospice Care. *Social Work in Healthcare*, 13, 3-19.

Schwarz, Jack, Betty Schmoll, True Ryndes, & Milton Hay. (1991). The State of the Art of Spiritual Caring in the 1990's Science of Hospice. Tape recording of presentation at National Hospice Organization's First National Conference on Spiritual Care in Hospice, Kansas City, MO.

Stoddard, Sandoll. (1991). *The Hospice Movement*. New York: Vantage Books.

CHAPTER 15

SPIRITUALLY SENSITIVE ASSESSMENT TOOLS FOR SOCIAL WORK PRACTICE

Timothy A. Boyd

In the social work endeavor, assessment has been a mainstay of the social workers' effective helping of clients. Without proper and thorough assessment, it is difficult to know how to structure and implement intervention strategies that fit the individual client. Effective assessment individualizes the intervention plan, and allows it to be tailored to the specific needs of the client—effective interventions flow out of effective assessments.

The hallmark of social work assessment, and the thing that differentiates it from assessments done by other disciplines, is its emphasis on a holistic picture of the client. Social work assessment focuses on the person-in-situation, and insists on the exploration of the interactions between the person and the various systems that affect that person. The assessment, therefore, is transactional in nature. It is a fluid, dynamic, and ongoing process, rather than a static product. The results of this kind of assessment leads the worker to a complex, multi-faceted understanding of the client, rather than to a diagnostic category based upon symptoms and their configuration. While social workers can and do use diagnostic systems such as the DSM-IV (Diagnostic and Statistical Manual of the American Psychiatric Association), they often feel torn between the need to work within the prevailing classification systems of modern therapy, and the need to describe the client in more holistic terms. Many social workers find difficulty with an emphasis on the medical model-based systems that tend to classify people according to symptoms rather than describing them in a way that includes strengths, resources, coping skills and the environmental forces that impinge upon their lives. As Goldenberg (1983) states, assessment needs to "obtain a picture of a person's strengths, assets, and adaptive functions as well as weaknesses, deficits, and dysfunctions; to look beyond the individual alone in order to see and understand his or her behavior and experience within a broader context" (p. 82-83).

In order to have a truly multi-dimensional assessment and a complete picture of the clients' functioning, it is necessary to gather data and understandings of the total person, both internal and external. This requires multiple sources of information. Rauch (1993) says, "assessment can be defined as the process of gathering, analyzing, and synthesizing salient data into a multi-dimensional formulation that provides the basis for action decisions" (p. XIV). It includes both the factors that maintain a problem as well as the resources that can be mobilized for change. Jordan and Franklin (1995) list five factors that encompass a multi-dimensional assessment:

- The nature of the clients' problems
- The functioning of clients and significant others (strengths, limitations, personality assets and deficiencies)
- The motivation of clients to work on their problems
- The relevant environmental factors that contribute to the problem
- The resources that are available or are needed to ameliorate the client's difficulties (p. 3)

Since professional social work values and works with many dimensions of a client's life, it would seem logical that social work assessments would be inclusive of all the following; the biological, psychological, social-cultural, *and* religious/spiritual dimensions. In fact, Jordan and Franklin (1995) make the assumption that well-qualified practitioners are knowledgeable about numerous assessment methods. It is curious, however, that most social work assessment texts and writings seem to ignore or give cursory examination to the religious/spiritual dimension, while affording a thorough examination of the other dimensions. An exploration of the various assessment tools, tests, and surveys used in the field reveals a paucity of resources that social work practitioners can utilize in their attempts to do holistic assessments. On the positive side, there does seem to be a growing awareness in the field of the importance of the religious/spiritual dimension, and an attempt to integrate this perspective into social work education and practice. Perhaps this will result in the development of a variety of assessment tools that can be used to explore this dimension.

Evidence of the growing awareness of the importance of the religious/spiritual dimension in assessment can be seen in the change that was enacted in the fourth edition of the Diagnostic and Statistical Manual (DSM-IV) (1994). The fourth edition, in a change from the third, included a V-Code (which describes additional conditions, other than clinical disorders, that may be the focus of clinical attention) for Religious and Spiritual Problems (p. 685). The Manual states that this category can be used when the focus of clinical attention is a religious or spiritual problem, and gives examples such as loss or questioning of faith, problems associated with conversion to a new faith, or the questioning of spiritual values (p. 685). The P-I-E System (Person In Environment System, 1994), which is one of the newest classification systems, has been developed by social workers and has the endorsement of the NASW (National Association of Social Workers). P-I-E has a category under "Voluntary System Problems" for problems related to religious groups. These problems could involve lack of a religious group or choice, lack of community acceptance of religious values, or other religious group problems (1994, p. 32). The P-I-E Manual also lists religious discrimination and religious member role problems as possible sources of client distress. Both the DSM-IV and the P-I-E System, however, only focus on the problematic aspects of a person's religious/spiritual life, and do not address the beneficial effects.

Religion is of prime importance in the lives of a majority of Americans. Gallup surveys indicate that 2/3 of the population of the U.S. consider religion to be important or very important in their lives (Religion in America, 1985). A Gallup poll (Gallup & Castelle, 1989) revealed that 94% of the U.S. population believes in God and report their relationship with God has influenced their beliefs. 40% of Americans attend religious services one time per week and 60% have a religious membership of some sort (Bellah et al, 1985, p. 219). Bullis (1994) cites a 1988 study done by Greif and Porembski that illustrates one example of how religion plays a key role in the coping response of a population in crisis. Bullis said that the researchers "looked at the coping mechanisms of individuals, families, and friends faced with the crisis of AIDS" and found that "a renewed or continued faith in God, both for themselves and the person with AIDS, was a factor, if not the most important factor for 9 out of 11 respondents" (p. 12). Derezotes (1995) succinctly summed up the importance of this issue when he said that "the social worker has a responsibility to assess each client's unique spiritual development and religiosity, and to provide interventions that reflect both developmental levels and religious doctrines and rituals" (p. 11).

Is there a difference between the religiosity of social workers and the population in general? A study by Bergin and Jensen (1990) found that 44% of their sample of clinical social workers were regular religious service attendees, 83% said that they tried hard to live by their religious beliefs, and 46% said their whole approach to life was based upon their religion (contrasted to 72% of the general public). Bergin's conclusion, in another article (1991), was that therapists are generally more religious than would be expected, although less so than the general public. In light of this finding, Bergin (1991) puzzled over his findings that only 29% of therapists rated religious content in the process of psychotherapy as important in guiding and evaluating treatment with many or all clients. Bergin conjectured about a "religiosity gap" be-tween clients and therapists, and suggested that this gap may explain why people in distress often prefer counsel from clergy rather than coun-sel by mental health professionals (citing a 1981 study by Veroff, Kulka, & Donovan).

A survey done by Elhiany, McLaughlin, Brown, and Bertucci (Un-published paper) used a sample of 30 social work educators, 30 practitio-ners, and 90 social work students. They found that 96% of the educators, 93% of the practitioners, and 92% of the students felt that client religious and spiritual beliefs are important in treatment, but only 8% of the educa-tors, 13% of the practitioners, and 15% of the students said that they dis-cuss a client's in-depth religious and spiritual beliefs during an initial as-sessment. Also reported was that 37% of the educators, 43% of the practi-tioners, and 30% of the students felt that these beliefs should be discussed only when the client presents the issue to the worker. Another survey which presents an apparently different conclusion, was carried out by Bullis (1992) with a sample of 116 clinical social workers in Virginia. On a 5-point scale (1=Not at all to 5=Always) respondents had a mean of 3.57 on the factor of "Frequency of Use of Religion or Spiritual Factors in Assessment." Respon-dents also had a mean of 3.77 on a 5-point scale (1=Not at All Important to 5=Extremely Important) on the factor of "Importance of Religious and Spiri-tual Factors in Assessment."

It appears that, although a majority of social workers are religiously or spiritually involved themselves, many may be reluctant for a variety of reasons to pursue an in-depth exploration of spiritual and religious issues in their client's lives. Bergin (1992) wondered if this reflects "that such matters have not been incorporated into clinical training as have other modern issues such as gender, ethnicity, and race" (p. 396). An-other factor might be located in a concern on the part of social workers that a more focused exploration of religious/spiritual issues might lead to an imposition of personal values on the client, which would be a violation of the ethical principle of self-determination. Perhaps there is some avoidance of these issues related to the ongoing debate over the functional versus dysfunctional aspects of religion. A number of theo-rists, most notably Sigmund Freud and Albert Ellis, have written about the immaturity inherent in an individuals' need for involvement in reli-gion. As many practitioners have been influenced by these ideas in their professional training and development, an ambivalence may have been created in many professionals who now fear being too positive toward religious involvement. In addition, personal observations of the nega-tive effects of dysfunctional belief systems on clients may also reinforce this reluctance.

Importance and Relevancy of Religious/Spiritual Assessment

For the purposes of this chapter, a distinction will be made between religion/religiosity and spirituality. In religion, people usually have some kind of identification or affiliation with an institutional structure. Such an affiliation involves religious roles, practices, doctrines, and identities. Spirituality is a broader, less well-defined term that refers to a person's attempt to find meaning in their life, to move toward higher states of consciousness, or to transcend themselves. It may or may not find expression in some form of institutional membership, beliefs or practices. Spirituality is a universal — every person has a spiritual self. Dombeck and Karl (1987) state that "every person can be understood to have a spiritual life, although some persons do not subscribe to any established religion" (p. 184). All persons have worldviews, belief systems, and value systems that orient their life decisions.

In addition to assessing information regarding a person's religious affiliations and the actual content of their spirituality, it is important to assess the process whereby their spiritual identity was developed, and how that identity is translated into principles for living. These more complex dimensions may require somewhat more sophistication in the assessment process, but are key to a holistic understanding of the person's capacities for change and growth. Victor Frankl (1968) went as far as to say that "the proper diagnosis can be made only by someone who could see the spiritual side of man" (p. ix).

The social worker who is sensitive and informed about a persons' religious/spiritual life is better equipped to engage and develop rapport with a client, as well as to develop intervention strategies that will be successful. Netting (1982) states that ethical decision-making in both micro and macro practice often includes an understanding of religious values. If a social worker is reluctant to explore religious/spiritual issues that are important to a client, it leaves the unspoken message that these issues are to be avoided, and subsequently, clients may be hesitant to offer information about such concerns. To ask about a person's religious beliefs, values, and affiliations is to affirm their importance. It is important to note that clients are affected by what we ask or do not ask, and by the manner in which we ask and by our responses to their verbalizations.

In a review of the empirical literature from 1974 to 1987 on religious counseling, Worthington (1986) suggests that highly religious clients have two fears about participating in psychotherapy with non-religious therapists; first, that their values will be challenged, and second, that they will be misunderstood and misdiagnosed. This fear may have some basis in reality. A study done by Gartner, Harmatz, Larson, and Gartner (1990) found evidence that religiously and politically extreme patients were assigned psychiatric diagnoses more frequently than patients whose religious and political views were unknown. In an article by Canda (1988), in which he describes the results of interviews with 18 social workers who had demonstrated knowledge concerning spirituality and social work, he reports comments relating to the importance of religious/spiritual self-awareness on the part of practitioners. A comment given by one of the interviewees was that a "social worker has to be in touch with [her] own feelings...about spiritual [and] religious beliefs [and] be aware of [her] own unresolved issues about institutional religion," and that a "social worker must be comfortable with his/her beliefs in order to learn appropriate skills for exploring these issues without the distortions of countertransference" (p. 244). Canda, in the article, reminds social workers that clients sometimes have spiritually significant experiences that sound unfamiliar and bizarre, but that it is important to not confuse insights achieved during peak experiences or altered states of consciousness with psychopathology (p. 246).

Another advantage of a thorough religious/spiritual assessment of clients at intake is in the awareness gained which can facilitate an optimal matching of client to worker. Research has demonstrated that clients prefer a counseling approach consistent with their worldview (Lyddon & Adamson, 1982). Denton (1990), in an article on the religiously fundamentalist family, said that religion for these families tends to permeate every aspect of family life (including interpersonal relationships, roles, family boundaries, relationship to community, and help-seeking behaviors). Denton expressed the belief that unique assessment skills are needed in working with these families, because they are so different from other families. He further described the ethical dilemma that is encountered when the therapist believes that the families' beliefs are pathological, or perceives the families' problems to be caused by their religion (p. 10).

A possible benefit for clients in being asked to participate in a religious/spiritual assessment can be found in the effect of the procedure itself. The worker's initiative to explore spiritual issues may act as a catalyst for clients to recognize and grapple with the questions of worth and meaning that underlie their life experiences. Sensitive and well-timed inquiries can serve to help clients enter a process of self-reflection, look beyond their circumstances to the broader context, and evaluate the principles and values they use to give direction to their lives. The worker's interest in these issues may help deepen the client's interest in their own spiritual journey. Being asked a timely question can promote a substantive dialogue between worker and client about religious issues that are at the heart of the client's dilemma.

Lastly, the exploration of a client's religious affiliations can help both worker and client discover linkages to religious social support systems that may be advantageous in the identification of resources to aid the helping process. Religious leaders, clergy, and spiritual healers can be utilized as consultants to the worker, and can serve as reinforcement and support for the changes that a client is attempting to make. Abbot, Berry, and Meredith (1990) list five ways that religion can be an asset to family functioning:

- By enhancing the family's social support network
- By sponsoring supportive family activities and recreation
- By promoting supportive family teachings and values
- By providing family social and welfare services
- By encouraging families to seek divine assistance with personal and family problems (p. 443)

Dimensions of Religious/Spiritual Assessment

Just as there are several dimensions to a holistic assessment of clients, there are also several dimensions within a holistic assessment of religious/spiritual life. Attempts to explore these dimensions allows the worker to develop a more robust or texture-filled assessment. The assessment of the religious/spiritual life of clients ranges from the more basic collection of factual information to a more sophisticated assessment of factors such as level of religious development and spiritual maturity. It may be useful to assess a client's categorical religious affiliations (what kind of religious institutions or denominations the client is involved with), but it is also vital to know the degree to which he/she is involved in that group, the degree of commitment she/he has to the group, and the amount of support received from the group. Doing a holistic assessment does not mean that the worker has the goal of exploring every conceivable religious/spiritual question, but rather, crafts the assessment in light of its' overall purpose or usefulness. The worker always maintains an integrative focus with the client's presenting and ongoing problems. The assessment must be well integrated with the intervention goals, and should be prescriptive of treatment. This is part of the art of assessment — knowing what to explore and when to explore it.

Because assessment is an ongoing process, the worker does not need to pressure the client or themselves into finding out all there is to know. An effective assessment unfolds over time, depending on a number of factors. Because religious/spiritual issues are usually very personal and clients experience a sense of vulnerability about them, workers must approach their exploration with utmost sensitivity and discretion. This is especially true for those clients who have had negative or harmful experiences in their past religious/spiritual life. An astute worker possesses the skills to effectively assess persons from a wide range of religious systems and personal backgrounds, which often requires study into the cultural context of those systems.

The social work setting (where the assessment is being carried out) is also important to the manner in which an assessment is conducted. First, and most obvious, are the particular parameters for practice that have been established by the agency or organization. It is important that the worker be in concert with the practice guidelines of their agency.

There are some social work settings where religious/spiritual factors are especially cogent, by virtue of the variety of religious issues that regularly surface. Two examples can be found in work with elderly clients and hospice clients. Issues related to the afterlife, doing life reviews (an examination of life events and relationships carried out as a means of coming to terms with their life), and emotional responses to the process of aging and/or dying are regularly encountered with these populations, especially as they confront their own impending death. Religious/spiritual issues come to the forefront for many people at these times. Watson, Howard, Hood, and Morris (1985) demonstrated that intrinsic religiosity (religion as a master motive in one's life) is significantly associated with age.

Another setting which has traditionally involved the spiritual dimension in the process of help is the field of chemical dependency. The 12-Step program, with it's focus on the relationship between the chemically dependent person and their "higher power," naturally requires the assessment of religious/spiritual issues. In addition to this setting, there are certain other population groups in which religious affiliations seem to be of particular centrality to the socio-cultural matrix of the client. For example, many immigrant clients find a strong source of personal stabilization in their identifications with their religious groups as they negotiate the process of transitioning and acculturation.

Social workers assess client religious/spiritual issues also with regard to both the functional and dysfunctional effects on the individual. This involves some judgment on the part of the worker related to what may have a positive effect on client functioning, as well as what may have a negative impact. This aspect of assessment gauges a clients's "health" from a spiritual perspective. The judgments are slippery, and the worker must attend to their own countertransferences and biases in order to remain objective. The classification process can become subjective, for example, when a client's group affiliation is called a "cult," a term which is often experienced by clients as a pejorative or inaccurate description. The label "fundamentalist," as another example, carries the same kind of subjective coloring. While some clients may welcome such a descriptor, others might feel misunderstood. It is important in the assessment process, therefore, to explore the client's own meanings and evaluations. What kind of designations, labels, and descriptions do they give (ascertaining their own descriptive words and metaphors)? Workers serve their clients well by being sensitive to their use of language. Some clients may be comfortable with assessment questions that are contextualized in "religious language" while other clients are more comfortable with less religiously oriented language. Canda's (1988) interviews with social workers led him to the conclusion that spiritually sensitive practitioners attuned themselves to the specific beliefs and needs of the clients without imposing their own beliefs, and were able to maintain an appreciation for the diverse spiritual beliefs of their clients, yet maintained a strong commitment to their own beliefs (p. 245).

A number of studies have established a clear correlation between religiosity and a person's general sense of well-being. Koenig, Kvale, and Ferrel (1988) found a significant positive correlation between intrinsic religiosity, organizational religious activity, ability to cope, and morale. Koenig, George, and Siegler (1988) discovered a positive relationship between religious behaviors and well-being, and Willits and Crider (1988) also identified a relationship between religiosity and overall well-being and satisfying relationships. In exploring the beneficial aspects of a religious/spiritual orientation, the worker may want to know such things as how the client's religious/spiritual connections:

- Foster pro-social attitudes and behaviors (help the client maintain fulfilling relationships with others)
- Help to maintain positive support networks with their environment
- Foster growth, health, and life-style improvements
- Give comfort and solace in time of crisis
- Give help in problem solving and ethical decision-making
- Provide stability at times of stress and loss
- Provide goods and resources, social services, and social opportunities

The worker will also need to explore how people use their beliefs in the process of coping. Religious/spiritual defense mechanisms can serve a purpose in the clients' attempts to negotiate their life events, even if they may not be the most functional ways to do so. Although past negative religious/spiritual experiences may cause a client to be indifferent, or even hostile toward their background, the client is still effected by what has been experienced and internalized. An assessment of negative religious/spiritual experiences can be vital in the selection and utilization of interventions. Client willingness and readiness to incorporate and act upon certain interventions depends upon what meaning those experiences have to them.

A thorough assessment of religious/spiritual issues will not only identify the beliefs and practices of an individual, but will also explore how those beliefs and practices are operationalized in the client's life. A consideration in this regard is the degree that a client has a committed or consensual faith; ie. what degree of commitment does she/he have to the beliefs and doctrines of their religious affiliation or group. This understanding may help explain how a person can identify with a particular religious group, but not necessarily be invested in meeting the behavioral expectations of the group. It is important to remember that there is within religious groups a significant amount of diversity among adherents, such that one cannot assume that people from a particular faith group are homogeneous in their commitments to their beliefs and practices.

A prime issue for consideration in the assessment of families is the way that religion permeates family life. Denton (1990) outlines five major questions for consideration in family assessment:

- Is religion used for extrinsic (social) or intrinsic (spiritual) purposes?
- Do family members vary in their investment in the religious community and belief structure?
- Is the family enmeshed in the church community?
- To what degree is the problem given a religious interpretation, which will dictate the   extent to which the worker will have to make use of religious beliefs in order to change the family system?
- To what degree is religion used as a control mechanism? (p. 10-11)

The family assessment will need to examine, therefore, the way family structure, roles, and boundaries are effected by the family's religious system, with these considerations having major implications for intervention planning.

Religious/spiritual assessment usually incorporates three time dimensions — past, present, and future. The historical perspective (past) explores such things as the events, experiences, and individuals that have shaped a person's life. The present dimension explores how a person is currently manifesting their spiritual self — their current beliefs and affiliations. The future dimension focuses on the person's hopes and desires for spiritual growth, their spiritual "vision," their anticipation about the afterlife, and issues such as "How will I raise my children in regard to their spiritual life?"

Lastly, the social worker may need to take a developmental perspective when doing the assessment, focusing on understanding the level or stage of the client's moral and spiritual development. The developmental dynamics of spiritual well-being can be difficult to measure, however. Canda (1988) called for criteria that would establish a client's level of moral and spiritual development, but also cautioned that the development of these criteria requires much work. He states that "perhaps a client's spiritual development can be evaluated according to their life satisfaction, degree of caring and love in relationship with others, capacity for sophisticated moral reflection, and willingness to come to terms with morality and other challenges to their sense of meaning and purpose," but cautions that "these criteria should not be used to reduce the client's spirituality to externally observable behavior" (p. 246). It is generally safe to conjecture that a client's level of spiritual development will be a key factor in their responses to the challenges of life. How clients respond to problems, life choices, value conflicts, and suffering, for example, is intimately related to the internalized principles of worth and meaning that they have developed.

Techniques

The techniques used in the assessment of religious/spiritual issues vary little from those used in assessment in general. In fact, some of the most widely used social work tools can be usefully translated into more specific applications in religious/spiritual assessment. Perhaps the simplest is the time line, which allows the client and worker to see the process of development in the client's spiritual life. A time line can be drawn upon which the key religious/spiritual experiences can be depicted (membership in groups, key mentors/spiritual guides/leaders, baptism/conversion/communion/Bar-Mitzvah/rites of passage, etc.). Bullis (1996) suggests that the time line can be "supplemented with photographs or a collage of pictures and drawings" (p. 35).

The genogram can also be adapted for use in a religious/spiritual assessment utilizing the same procedures used for a family system or genetic genogram. Bullis (1996) says that spiritual genograms are a kind of family tree which charts — those persons, places, ideas and experiences that have formed one's spiritual identity or lack thereof (p. 34).

Another tool, the eco-map, can be adapted for use. The eco-map is generally used to identify how a person relates to the variety of systems that impact his/her life, and the "rate, direction, and mutuality of resource exchanges" (Mattaini, 1993, p. 22). One could include the religious/spiritual systems as part of this larger systemic review, or could devote one specific eco-map to a more detailed depiction of the religious/spiritual subsystems and relationships.

Additional assessment techniques could be implemented using drawings, collages, and sculptures. One could ask an adult to draw a picture depicting their current spiritual identity, or a child to draw a picture of what God is like. The family sculpture technique could be modified to depict a family's spiritual life at present, or to show the type of spiritual life a family identifies as a desired goal (with each family member having a chance to do their own sculpture). In addition to these tools, there are other surveys, questionnaires, and tests that can be utilized, although a survey done by this author found the selection to be quite limited. Some of these available tools cover a wider range of religious/spiritual dimensions, but have limited depth, while others focus intensely only on a specific religious/spiritual dimension, but have limited range.

A Comprehensive Religious/Spiritual Assessment Tool

Following is a multi-dimensional religious/spiritual assessment tool that can be utilized with clients. It is designed to cover a range of issues, and includes a variety of questions of an exploratory nature that could be utilized. Appropriate use of this tool, however, is dependent on it's modification to the individual situation. The assessor needs to have a well-conceived rationale for what issues will be addressed, and when in the helping process those issues may be most appropriately explored. Questions can be modified and adapted to fit the specific client and situation (utilizing appropriate use of language, terms, and metaphors). Appropriate use for most clients would require careful limited selection of relevant issues (it is not intended to be given in its entirety).

I. RELIGIOUS AND SPIRITUAL HISTORY

1. Religious Upbringing

a. How would you describe your religious upbringing? Growing up, what were the religious and spiritual beliefs of your parents? Your siblings? Your extended family? How invested were they in them? What would you consider to be the most important beliefs they held? What were their religious and spiritual practices? What kinds of words would you use to describe your religious upbringing (strict, liberal, conservative, permissive, punishing, positive, negative, nurturing, deprivational, stunting, stimulating, non-existent)?

b. What kind of religious and spiritual training did you receive? What have you retained from this training? If you are not still practicing your earlier faith, why not?

c. Who would you consider to be your spiritual ancestors?

2. Life-Shaping Experiences

a. What kinds of experiences, events, persons, events, and crises shaped your religious and spiritual identity...positively...negatively?

3. Conversion/Peak/Mystical Experiences

a. Have you had anything you would describe as a "conversion experience?"

b. Have you ever experienced something you would call a "mystical" experience?

4. Spiritual Crises and Emergencies

a. Have you had any crises of faith...belief in your life? How did you handle them? How are you different now?

5. Current Social Environment

a. What are the beliefs and practices of the significant others in your life (spouse, partner, children, friends)? How do religious/spiritual issues affect your relationships?

b. What approach or religious/ and spiritual orientation are you using in your child- rearing? Are others (spouse) in agreement on the approach? What are the most important spiritual beliefs that you would like to instill in your children?

c. What relationships do you currently have that positively...negatively affect your spiritual self? How do other key people in your life view your faith? How does that affect you?

d. Do you have any clergy/church leaders/counselors that you respect...trust...confide in?

II. CURRENT BELIEFS AND PRACTICES

1. Religious Identity

a. Do you identify with any particular religion or faith? Would you consider yourself a religious person?

2. Commitment Level

    a. How central is your religion in your life? Your faith?

    b. How committed are you to your particular religion/faith?

3. Religious Identifications/Affiliations/Involvements

    a. Do you attend a particular church/synagogue/mosque/etc.? Do your friends attend the same place of worship that you do? Do you keep in touch with people from your religious group? How invested are you in your religious community? What is the attitude of your religious group toward outsiders?

    b. What kinds of social support do you receive from your religious community? What kinds of resources and opportunities are made available to you (financial, recreational, goods and services, other)?

4. Codification of Beliefs

    a. What are your most important beliefs? Do you adhere to any particular code... commandments... doctrinal requirements? Do you find that you are able to follow them? Do you have any sacred writings... books... scriptures from which you receive instruction? Do you read these writings? Are there any particular characters from these writings that you identify with?

    b. How, and to what extent, does your religious belief system have rules and/or norms about marriage... child-rearing practices... divorce... abortion... premarital sex... cohabitation... contraception... sex roles...? How do these beliefs affect your family life?

    c. What is sin? What would be the worst sin one could commit?

    d. What are your beliefs about human nature... human responsibility?

    e. What are your beliefs about an afterlife? How is it determined what happens to a person after their death? What do you believe will happen to you?

5. Rituals, Images, Symbols, Behavioral Enactments, Observances, Practices

    a. What have been some of the most significant religious rituals that you have participated in (baptism, communion, Bar-Mitzvah, rites of passage, membership, etc.)?

    b. Do you pray? How? How often? What do you pray about? What are your expectations about what will happen when you pray? Do you find it helpful to pray?

    c. How do you prefer to worship?

d. Do you participate in any kinds of "healing" rituals? What are your beliefs about healing?

e. What other kinds of religious rituals do you participate in?

6. *God Image, Theodocies*

a. Do you have a belief in a higher power? What name do you use for the Supreme Being? Do you have faith (trust) in this being? How do you experience God? What is your understanding about God?

b. What is God/Allah/Other like? What kinds of thoughts... feelings... memories... words come to your mind when you think of God?

c. How does God communicate to humans... to you?

d. Does God intervene in the events of this world? How? How does God regard human suffering? How concerned is God about your problems?

7. *Concepts of Evil and the Demonic*

a. Do you believe in evil beings? What names, if any, do you use for them? How do these beings/forces affect the world....your life? Have you ever had any experiences with the demonic that have affected your life?

III. SPIRITUAL MATURITY AND DEVELOPMENT

1. *Development Through Stages of Life*

a. As you have gotten older, how has your faith changed? Can you think of times that you have received help from your faith, as you have struggled with life events?

b. What kinds of spiritual conflicts are you now dealing with?

2. *Effect of Religious/Spiritual Identity on Life Style*

a. How do your beliefs affect your behavior? How do you decide what is right or wrong? How do you go about decision-making? How does your faith affect the way you handle guilt...fear?

c. Do your spiritual beliefs affect your ideas and practices regarding "forgiveness?"

d. How does your faith help you to cope with your current life circumstances?

e. How do your beliefs affect your physical health or self-maintenance?

3. Meaning of Life Issues

a. What gives your life meaning (makes life worthwhile)? Are you hopeful about the future... Why? When you get discouraged, what renews your sense of hope... vitality... purpose? Have you had any particular experiences that have shaken... affirmed your optimism? How satisfied are you with your life? Why do you think you are alive (what is the purpose)?

b. What are your goals for spiritual growth? What is your "growing edge?"

c. What does death mean to you? Are you afraid to die? What do you think happens after one dies? What do you believe will happen to you when you die? Have you thought about your own death? Have you experienced the death of someone you were close to?

d. How does your faith motivate you?

e. What is your ideal of mature faith?

4. Moral Frame of Reference

a. What are your key values? How did you develop them?

References

Abbot, A., Berry, M., & Meredith, W. (1990). Religious belief and practices. *Family Relations, 39,* 443-48.

American Psychiatric Association. (1994). *Diagnostic and Statistical Manual of Mental Disorders.* Washington, D.C.: American Psychiatric Association.

Bellah, R., Madsen, R., Sullivan, W., Swidler, A., & Tipton, S. (1985). *Habits of the Heart.* N.Y.: Harper Row.

Bergin, A. (1991). Values and religious issues in psychotherapy and mental health. *American Psychologist, 46*(4), 394-403.

Bergin, A., & Jensen, J. (1990). Religiosity of psychotherapists: A national survey. *Psychotherapy, 27,* 3-7.

Bullis, R. (1996). *Spirituality in Social Work Practice.* Washington, D.C.: Taylor and Francis.

Canda, E. (1988). Spirituality, religious diversity, and social work practice. *Social Casework, 69*(4), 238-47.

Canda, E. (1989). Religious content in social work education: A comparative approach. *Journal of Social Work Education,* Winter, 36-45.

Denton, R. (1990). The religiously fundamentalist family: Training for assessment and treatment. *Journal of Social Work Education,* Winter, 6-14.

Derezotes, D. (1995). Spirituality and religiosity: Neglected factors in social work practice. *Arete, 20,* 1-15.

Dombeck, M., & Karl, J. (1987). Spiritual issues in mental health care. *Journal of Religion and Health, 26,* 183-97.

Elhiany, A., McLaughlin, S., Brown, P., & Bertucci, G. (1997). *The role of religion and spirituality in social work education and practice.* Unpublished Paper.

Frankl, V. (1968). *The Doctor and the Soul.* N.Y.: Knopf.

Gallup, G. (1985). *Religion in America* [Report # 236]. Princeton, N.J.: Gallup Organization.

Gallup, G., & Castelle, J. (1989). *The People's Religion: American Faith in the 90's.* N.Y.: McMillan.

Gartner, J., Harmatz, M., Larson, D., & Gartner, A. (1990). The effect of patient and clinician ideology in clinical judgment: A study of ideological transference. *Psychotherapy, 23,* 98-106.

Goldenberg, H. (1983). *Contemporary Clinical Psychology (Second Edition).* Monterey, CA.: Brooks Cole.

Jordan, C., & Franklin, C. (1995). *Clinical Assessment for Social Workers.* Chicago: Lyceum.

Karls, J., & Wandrei, K. (1994). *Person-In-Environment System.* Washington, D.C.: NASW Press.

Koenig, H., George, L., & Siegler, I. (1988). The use of religion and other emotion-regulating strategies among older adults. *The Gerontologist, 28,* 301-10.

Koenig, H., Kvale, J., & Ferrel, C. (1988). Religion and well-being in later life. *The Gerontologist, 28,* 18-28.

Lyddon, W., & Adamson, L. (1982). World view and counseling preference: An analogue study. *Journal of Counseling and Development, 71,* 41-47.

Mattaini, M. (1993). *More Than a Thousand Words: Graphics for Clinical Practice.* Washington, D.C.: NASW Press.

Netting, E. (1982). Social work and religious values in church-related social agencies. *Social Work and Christianity, 9*(1-2), 4-20.

Rauch, J. (1993). *Assessment: A Source Book for Social Work Practice.* Milwaukee, WI: Families International.

Veroff, J., Kulka, R., & Douvan, E. (1981). *Mental Health in America.* N.Y.: Basic Books.

Watson, P., Howard, R., Hood, R., & Morris, R. (1985). Age and religious orientation. *Review of Religious Research, 29,* 271-80.

Willits, F., & Crider, D. (1988). Religion and well-being: Men and women in the middle years. *Review of Religious Research, 29,* 281-94.

Worthington, E. (1986). Religious counseling: A review of published empirical research. *Journal of Counseling and Development, 64,* 421-31.

CHAPTER 16

THE FIELD OF CHILD WELFARE: SUFFER THE LITTLE CHILDREN

Gary Anderson

Social work practice takes place in a variety of settings and fields of practice. One of the most complex and challenging fields for social work is the field of child welfare. With the specter of abused and neglected children and the complications of working with multiple systems, this field of practice poses value questions and emotional dilemmas in addition to clinical and policy challenges for the social worker. Child welfare settings are some of the few places in which social workers are the predominant profession. It is also a field of practice that employs high numbers of social workers. Whether employed in child welfare or not, all social workers need to have some knowledge about child maltreatment and the system designed to respond to child abuse and neglect as all social workers have a professional and legal responsibility to recognize and report suspected child maltreatment.

There is a strong and positive relationship between child welfare and religion. Compassion for children and a commitment to family life are common ground for the Christian community and professionals concerned about the well-being of children. But there is also a degree of tension. Some in child welfare might question the church's vigilance in protecting children from abuse or neglect as demonstrated by the sexual abuse of children by clergy or other religious authority figures. Some might view various religious viewpoints as encouraging parents to be abusive and practice severe physical punishment in disciplining children. Hence child welfare authorities may view religion and churches as failing to see and appreciate child maltreatment and even at times allowing or encouraging such treatment. Conversely, religious people might be suspicious of the state's role and potential intrusiveness in parenting and interfering with the autonomy and integrity of the family. The Christian social worker in child welfare might find herself or himself in a position in which there is a shared concern for children and families, but also misunderstanding and, at times conflict, between the child welfare system and religion.

This chapter will begin with a brief description of the history, continuum and goals of the child welfare system. The congruence and tensions in child welfare and religion will then be explored. Finally, their common values and mission will be highlighted.

History

The American system of child protection and child welfare began in the earliest days of the United States as society responded to children who were orphaned or abandoned by their parents. Children were often placed in congregate care facilities—or orphanages—for at least part of their life to grow up under adult protection and supervision. There were a number of other responses to caring for mistreated or abandoned children. For example, in the mid-1800's Charles Loring Brace developed Orphan Trains to transport and place young children and sibling groups from Eastern cities with potential parents and homes in the Midwest and West (Cook, 1995).

In 1873, a child protection system was launched by the case of Mary Ellen in New York City. This young girl was being beaten by her stepmother and a "friendly visitor" tried to intervene to protect the child. There was no agency charged with protecting children from intrafamily abuse so the case was investigated by the Society for the Prevention of Cruelty to Animals. Soon after presenting this case in court, the private agency Society for the Prevention of Cruelty to Children was created. By the mid-1900's the child protection function was accepted by public child welfare agencies (Costin, 1991).

By the early 1900's the use of orphanages began to be replaced by using volunteer homes and families recruited to take in mistreated children. These homes—called foster homes—became the placement of choice from the 1950's to the present day. Although foster homes provided a family-like setting for vulnerable children, concern was expressed about the length of time children remained in temporary foster care, and the impact of separations and loss upon children. Research and practice experience pointed to the harmful effects of what was referred to as "drifting" in foster care, with no timely outcome or stable family life for the child. This drift was compounded by multiple placements for the same child, and inattentiveness to the needs of the child once in the foster home. After three decades of documenting the problems with placement of children in foster care and the length of the time that children spent in out-of-home care, the federal permanency planning law was passed in 1980. This law (Public Law 96-272) established permanency planning as the prevailing philosophy, value and strategy for child welfare. In the early 1990's there was a growing commitment to family preservation and family support legislation and funding to prevent the unnecessary placement of children in out-of-home care. Throughout the development of these child welfare systems in the United States the church has had a prominent role as sponsor and auspices for private child welfare services (Garland, 1994). For example, the child welfare agencies in New York City, apart from the city and state agencies, have been organized in three federations: Protestant, Catholic, and Jewish agencies.

Continuum of Care

The child welfare system in the United States has evolved to include a number of services in a continuum of care. This continuum suggests that there is a progression of seriousness, treatment need, and service commitment and cost from one service level to the next. This continuum includes:

- *Family Support Services*— the counseling and concrete services that provide supportive assistance to a family in response to a crisis, or absence of resources that if present would reduce stress or increase the ability of the family to meet the needs of its children.
- *Child Maltreatment Prevention Programs*— counseling and other services designed purposely to address and reduce the risk of child abuse or neglect.
- *Family Preservation Services*— oftentimes intense and short-term services targeted to families that are experiencing a crisis that has the potential to result in serious harm to the child, and that would result in out-of-home placement.
- *Crisis Nurseries/Respite Care*— special projects to provide relief for stressed parents who need to have some immediate and short-term assistance to provide some time away from their children/infant.
- *Emergency Shelters*— homes or residences with the capacity to house children for a number of days or weeks who need to quickly be removed from a dangerous setting. These settings could have a diagnostic capacity to determine the special needs of children awaiting placement in another setting. The shelter could also be a transitional setting providing an interim placement for a child while a proper setting is developed or identified. Children might be reunited with their families after a brief separation, assessment of the family, and the introduction of needed services.
- *Foster Care*— these are homes and family settings that provide temporary care for children who are unable to be with their parent(s). Foster homes can be provided by volunteer families

who are generally licensed and supervised by the agency and provided a modest board payment to meet the needs and expenses associated with the child in care. These homes can also be kinship or relative homes—the child is placed with a relative who provides a safe home for the child. Therapeutic foster homes are designed for children and youth with specific emotional and mental health challenges that require the special supervision and treatment resources that specially trained parents and professional staff can provide. Children generally enter foster care through a court order issued by the family or youth court in response to a petition alleging child abuse or neglect that was submitted to the court by a child protective service worker. Some children are voluntarily placed through an agreement between the child's parents and the child welfare agency.

- *Group Homes*— sometimes young people are placed in these congregate care facilities that provide a home-like atmosphere for a small number of youth supervised by live-in house parents or rotating staff members.
- *Residential Treatment Facilities*— provides housing, education, and counseling for young people in a congregate care setting that may be organized around dormitories or cottages. Residential treatment facilities are often responsible for helping young people with a number of challenges in addition to child maltreatment. These challenges could include working with young people with emotional, mental health, educational or developmental disabilities.
- *Adoption Services*— when it is determined that children cannot be reunited with their family, the legal system may terminate parental rights or parents may voluntarily relinquish their rights and the child welfare agency seeks to find an adoptive family for the child.

Intertwined in each service are relationships with other fields of practice, disciplines, and helping systems. For example, many out-of-home placements and services require court involvement, such as petitioning the court for custody, submitting case plans and the periodic review of these plans, and potentially, hearings, or trials to examine evidence and make recommendations. Health, mental health, and juvenile probation and law enforcement are some of those systems that interact extensively with child welfare service delivery.

The child welfare system encompasses a number of varied services and settings that are designed to separately meet the child and family's needs or provide a continuum of care if the child's needs change or intensify over time. Regardless of the setting, the American child welfare setting has a number of primary goals in service provision.

Goals

The American child welfare system has three primary goals: (1) making certain that children are *safe*; (2) working to secure *permanency* for children; and (3) when children are involved with the child welfare agency, it is the agency's goal to strengthen the child's *well being* while the agency is responsible for the child (Williams, 1996).

The first goal of child welfare is the *physical safety* of the child. The Child Protective Service division of the public child welfare agency is charged with responding to reports from the public and professionals alleging or suspecting that a child is in some form of danger. The perpetrator may be the child's parent or guardian, or another relative, adult or child/adolescent. Threats to safety include the physical abuse of children, a number of types of child neglect (including physical, medical, educational, or supervisory neglect), and the sexual abuse of children or threats to seriously harm or kill children. By law, professionals are required to report suspected child abuse and child protective service workers are empowered to investigate abuse and take steps to remove children from situations in which they are at serious risk or have been abused or neglected. For example, for show-and-tell, a kindergarten boy lifted the back of his shirt and showed his class the bruises and lash marks on his back as a result of a punishment from his father that morning. The school teacher immediately contacted the principal; who then called the child abuse hotline number to report the incident. A child protective service worker was assigned the case, proceeded to the school, witnessed the bruises, contacted the family court to obtain a temporary order of placement, and took the boy to a foster home that day. With the child physically safe, the work with the parents was begun by the worker.

The second goal of *permanency* is defined as providing children with family connections or the potential for a safe, stable and lifetime family. The commitment to permanency was informed by the research in child development that documented the effect of separation and loss on children, the impact of a child's sense of time and its correlation with length of stay in out-of-home care, and concern about children drifting in foster care. This drift was the tendency of children to remain in out-of-home care for long periods of time, typically years, without a viable plan to reunite the children with their families or provide another permanent option for the child. With foster care drift came the increased possibility of a child experiencing a number of foster care homes and placements. The outcome of long and ill-defined stays in foster care and multiple placements could include detrimental effects on the child's mental health and social adjustment resulting in the need for more intense placements. Without a commitment to permanency planning the child's psychological safety was at risk. For example, when the kindergarten boy was placed in foster care, the child welfare worker understood that this was a temporary arrangement to keep the child physically safe. Having accomplished some degree of safety, the goal of permanency became the worker's priority. So, the worker immediately began an assessment of the parents and family to form a judgement about the appropriateness, necessary steps and timing of reunification of the family. Family reunification is one means of achieving the goal of permanency. If the parents were unable or unwilling to provide a safe home for the child, another option for permanency, such as adoption, would be explored. For some older adolescents, a goal of establishing one's independence after age 18 or a guardianship arrangement might be considered in addition to reunification or adoption (Maluccio, et al, 1986).

The third goal of child welfare is to address the **well being** of children served by agencies or in out-of-home care. For example, when children are placed in foster care, the agency should provide for the medical care of the child and provide counseling or other support services to address the mental health needs of the child. Also needed is the assurance that children are receiving an appropriate education, recreation, and socialization.

These are worthy goals but their implementation has often been incomplete, at best. With regard to safety, the child welfare system has been buffeted by criticisms from two sides. Critics have charged that it has either responded too slowly, resulting in children being left in family situations that are dangerous because these situations were not reported to the authorities, or, if reported, the child protection sytem did not respond quickly, thoroughly, or decisively. Others have identified another troubling outcome. The child protection system has often moved too quickly, without adequate evidence, and unnecessarily intruded into family life and at least temporarily traumatically separated parents and children. The overrepresentation of minority children in foster care has added the concern that discriminatory practices have unfairly heightened this intrusiveness into families of color in the United States (Anderson, 1997).

With regard to permanency goals, the failure to implement permanency planning strategies and to internalize the necessity of permanency has allowed children to drift without their biological families and without the connection to another family that could become their psychological home. Some children in out-of-home care have not been well taken care of and their educational, health or mental health needs have not been adequately addressed.

The goals of the child welfare system are admirable. Their implementation is essential as they address the basic safety and mental health of the child. They provide a common focus for program planning, clinical practice and professional commitment.

Congruence with Christianity

A commitment to the safety of children, to their connection with loving adults and family members, and to the well being of children seems to be completely congruent with a Christian world and life view. For good reasons Christian churches provided early leadership in providing child welfare services. For a Christian social worker, working with vulnerable children and families would appear to be a natural expression of one's Christian beliefs and values.

The faith of the Jewish nation, its relationship with Jehovah, and its value on human life contrasted with the idolatry in Canaan where some worshipped Molech and required the human sacrifice of children. In Jesus' ministry (Matthew 19:13-15), he welcomed young children who were being kept away by the disciples. He spoke of the need to become like little children with an innocence of faith and response to the gospel (Matthew 18:2-6).

The connection between children and parents in families was respected and valued. When Jesus saw the grieving widow at Nain following the casket of her son, he understood her need for family and the importance of the parent and child relationship (Luke 7:11-17). This was also evidenced in other miraculous actions, including raising the daughter of Jairus (Luke 8:40-56). Among his final words on the cross, Jesus was concerned about his mother and proclaimed that John and Mary were to be as parent and child—preserving family ties and relationships (John 19:25-27). Throughout scripture there is the admonition to be sensitive to and assist the fatherless and the orphan (for example, James 1:27). One of the most serious threats by Jesus in his teaching was the warning against causing the stumbling of a child (Matthew 18:4-6).

It is consistent with scripture and the example of Jesus to be concerned with the safety and well-being of children and to strengthen their connections to family. The continuing leadership role of Christian organizations in the care of children is understandable and laudable. But this relationship between child welfare and Christianity is not without conflict and tension.

Tensions

That Christian people would have genuine compassion for the well-being of children seems natural based on the compassionate example of Jesus, the Christian ethic of love, and specific scriptural admonitions to care for children without parents or basic necessities. However, historically there have been a number of areas in which there is tension between the professional child welfare community and religion. Several topics of tension include: (1) the definition of child abuse and neglect; (2) the causes of child maltreatment; and (3) the view of the world.

1. *Definition.* In the United States there is no national child abuse and neglect law or definition. The definition of abuse and neglect varies from state to state. These definitions are oftentimes general and vague thus allowing multiple interpretations of conditions described as "harm" and "injury". This lack of clarity or allowance for a range of definitions reflects a conflict of values, or at least differing viewpoints, with regard to parenting, child raising, and discipline. The sanctity of the home and parents' rights to raise their children in the manner they choose may be in conflict with the value of protecting children from harm, and society's obligation to protect children and monitor parenting on behalf of children.

Consequently, within a community it is possible to find some persons who define abuse as significant injury that is life threatening or results in wounds and broken bones, whereas other community members might define any physical punishment as abusive. It is on this point that some criticize religion as allowing, if not promoting child abuse. The frequently cited "spare the rod and spoil the child" is viewed with horror by some child welfare professionals and viewed as the literal truth and interpreted as a directive to physically punish their children by a number of Christians (Meier, 1985; Radbil, 1974). In the public sector, corporal punishment is sometimes viewed as child abuse. Although few, if any, Christians would argue that the Bible promotes excessive or injurious physical punishment, the child welfare professional might be concerned about the support of physical punishment and failure to sufficiently warn against excessive punishment (Dobson, 1970; Lovinger, 1990; Wiehe, 1990). Defining only extreme, life endangering physical harm as abuse (particularly combined with a belief that child abuse could not occur in a Christian family) could lead to the failure to recognize and respond to potentially harmful situations (Pagelow & Johnson, 1988).

Specific areas of concern involving religion and child maltreatment have also been identified. In the mid-1980's the American Humane Association began to collect information on child abuse and neglect in cults and religious sects (AHA, 1984). Issues of medical neglect by parents who failed to secure critical medical treatment due to the family's religious beliefs have also been identified (Anderson, 1983; Bullis, 1991).

2. *Causation.* Broader than the issue of physical punishment, religion has at times been portrayed as providing the context or belief system that contributes to child abuse and neglect (Garbarino & Ebata, 1983; Garbarino & Gilliam, 1980; Kadushin, 1980; Salter, et al, 1985). The Bible is full of examples of killing infants and children, from the proclamation of the Egyptian Pharaoh in the days of Moses to the declaration of Herod the Great during Jesus' infancy. Yet it is not just jealous rulers who order the killing of children. The great flood drowned children, Abraham was asked to sacrifice Isaac, the death angel killed the firstborn children, the invading Israelites killed whole populations of children, and Jepthah's sacrifice was his adolescent daughter. Children suffer because of the actions of their parents.

A number of theories of child abuse point to the role of an authoritarian or patriarchal family structure in creating an atmosphere in which children (and sometimes women) are viewed as subservient to fathers and husbands (Horton & Williamson, 1988; Peek, Lowe & Williams, 1991). Equating patriarchy with authoritarian parenting styles, concern is expressed about physical abuse of children, emotional abuse or neglect, and a climate in which child maltreatment is justified or allowed. The child is expected to be obedient to the parent (Alwin, 1986). He or she is not allowed to display a "willful spirit" (Fugate, 1980; Hutson, 1983). The shaping of the child's will (sinful nature) and spirit, and discipline required for achieving maturity need to be firmly enforced by the parent (Hyles, 1974; Rice, 1982; Williams & Money, 1980). The implied relationship between patriarchal excess and child maltreatment is particularly noted in cases of child sexual abuse as the father or stepfather's actions are described as related to one's sense of power or powerlessness in the family and community (Pellauer, Chester & Boyajian, 1987). Parental actions are justified as preserving a family hierarchy, breaking the child's willful spirit, or responding to the child who is born in sin and needs to learn submission to authority (Walters, 1975; Miller, 1985).

3. *Viewpoint.* The first two dynamics—supporting physical punishment and providing a rationale or fertile ground for child maltreatment—portray religion as part of the child abuse problem. This "world-life view" describes religion as irrelevant to the problem of child abuse and neglect, and the church's attention to the spiritual world, the inner world, and the afterworld as diluting or replacing attentiveness to the

physical, material and present-day needs of children. Or there may be denial that a religious or Christian family would maltreat a child. Consequently, the church's knowledge of and support for public child protective and child welfare systems might not be present or strong.

Response

The child welfare system is intended to provide comprehensive assistance to children who are abused and neglected. This mission is informed by the permanency planning law—the commitment that children need to be raised in families with the potential of lifelong relationships. The Christian commitment to love one's neighbor and care for the helpless is congruent with this mission. There is a reasonable response to the critics of religion that affirms the critical role of Christians in social work and the Christian church in the child welfare service community.

There is a range of perspectives on Biblical passages that provide instruction in the raising of children. However, the abuse of children (or women) is not condoned (Alsdurf & Alsdurf, 1989; Campbell, 1985; Tomczak, 1982). The church has a crucial role in educating parents and supporting families. While acknowledging the authority of parents and the necessity to discipline children, there is also the admonition to love children and not provoke children to wrath due to one's parenting behavior.

While attentive to the physical and psychological needs of children and families, attention to the spiritual needs of parents and children does not have to be neglected or separated from its real life consequences. For example:

A child abuse investigation discovered that a father had sexually molested his son and daughter. Picked up at their Christian school, the children were placed in emergency foster care and the child protective service worker immediately scheduled an appointment to meet with the parents.

During this first interview, the father told the child protective service worker that the abuse had ended in recent months as he had a conversion experience and was now a genuine Christian. The worker expressed appreciation for this decision by the father but stated that the father's statement of belief needed to be demonstrated consistently by his actions. The father responded "Yes! faith without works is dead!"

With his wife's support and the worker's support, the father confessed his guilt in court, entered counseling, apologized to his children, and visited his children, who remained in foster care while he followed the court's order and case plan. Within six months, the family was successfully reunited as the father completed all required actions.

The church can support the spiritual, physical, and psychological needs of the family and recognize their connections.

Finally, the church and Christian individuals and organizations have historically and currently make a crucial contribution to services for children and families. Through its educational ministries, support services, and assistance to families, the church provides a significant network and number of family support services whose critical role in family preservation and the prevention of stress that may contribute to risk of child maltreatment, has not been fully recognized. The provision of formal child welfare services, such as foster care, group home care and residential treatment, and adoption services is frequently provided by private, church-related organizations under contract to the state's public child welfare agencies. These service providers are essential to meeting the need for placements and homes for children and young people who are removed from their homes or need to be placed in specialized settings to meet their safety and mental health needs. In addition to services provided by Christian or church-related organizations, there are significant numbers of foster parents and adoptive parents, licensed and approved by public agencies, whose motives, coping ability, and compassion are inspired by their religious faith and convictions and supported by their membership and involvement within faith communities.

One of the model programs that promotes a partnership between one's church and religious faith and the needs of children is the One Child One Church adoption initiative that encourages each church to encourage at least one of its member families to adopt at least one child waiting for a permanent home. This initiative, that began in an African-American congregation in Chicago, has been supported nationally by the federal government.

Why should a family care for its children? Why should a community care about the treatment of the children in its member families? The Christian response is simple and clear: affirming that children are God's creation and precious in His sight. Parent's are responsible for the nurturing of their children, and have reason to grieve or take pride in their children's accomplishments. In addition, the community's obligation to provide for children, particularly those without parents, is strongly affirmed in the Bible.

Conclusion

The child welfare system in the United States is a continuum of services designed to support families and protect children. When protection requires the removal of children from their parent's custody, the child welfare system's guiding philosophy of permanency planning informs plans and strategies to reunite children with their families. If this is not possible, the child welfare worker should develop another option that provides the possibility of a home and lifetime family for the child. Child welfare includes a professional concern for the child's well-being, including the child's physical health, mental health, educational and social needs.

The role of religion and the church has at times been presented with some concern regarding its impact on child abuse and neglect and responsiveness to at-risk children. The Church can serve as a primary source of family support and family preservation services for vulnerable families. Its members have a motive for becoming foster and adoptive parents, and a means of coping with the challenges of new parenting through prayer and the social support of the church. Church child welfare agencies have a long history of caring for children and families in crisis. This field of practice provides a setting in which a Christian social worker can express her or his care for children and commitment to families.

References

Alsdurf, J. & Alsdurf, P. (1989). *Battered Into Submission*. Downers Grove, Il: InterVarsity Press.

Alwin, D. (1986). Religion and Parental Child-Rearing Orientations. *American Journal of Sociology, 92*, 412-440.

American Humane Association. (1984). Child Abuse and Neglect in Cults and Religious Sects. *Protecting Children, 1*, 17.

Anderson, G. (1997). Achieving Permanency for All Children in the Child Welfare System. In G. Anderson, A. Ryan & B. Leashore (Eds.), *The Challenge of Permanency Planning in a Multicultural Society*. New York: Haworth Press.

Anderson, G. (1983). Medicine vs. Religion: The Case of Jehovah's Witnesses. *Health and Social Work, 8*, 31-39.

Bullis, R. (1991). The Spiritual Healing Defense in Criminal Prosecutions for Crimes Against Children. *Child Welfare, 70*, 541-558.

Campbell, R. (1985). *How to Really Love Your Child*. Wheaton, Il: Victor.

Cook, J. F. (1995). A History of Placing Out: The Orphan Trains. *Child Welfare, 74*, 181-199.

Costin, L. (1991). Unraveling the Mary Ellen Legend: Origins of the "Cruelty" Movement. *Social Service Review, 65*, 203-223.

Dobson, J. (1970). *Dare to Discipline*. New York: Bantam Books.

Fugate, R. (1980). *What the Bible Says About Child Training.* Tempe, AZ: Aletheia.

Garland, D. (1994). *Church Agencies: Caring for Children and Families in Crisis.* Washington D.C.: Child Welfare League of America.

Horton, A. & Williamson, J. (1988). *Abuse and Religion: When Praying Isn't Enough.* Lexington, MA: Lexington.

Hutson, C. (1983). *The Why and How of Child Discipline.* Murfreesboro, TN: Sword of the Lord.

Hyles, J. (1974). *How to Rear Children.* Hammond, IN: Hyles-Anderson.

Lovinger, R. (1990). *Religion and Counseling: The Psychological Impact of Religious Belief.* New York: Continuum.

Maluccio, A., Fein, E. & Olmstead, K. (1986). *Permanency Planning for Children— Concepts and Methods.* London and New York: Tavistock and Methuen.

Pagelow, M. & Johnson, P. (1988). Abuse in the American Family: The Role of Religion. In A. Horton & J. Williamson (Eds.), *Abuse and Religion: When Praying Is Not Enough.* Lexington, MA: Lexington.

Peek, C., Lowe, G. & Williams, L.S. (1991). Gender and God's Word: Another Look at Religious Fundamentalism and Sexism. *Social Forces, 69,* 1205-1221.

Pellauer, M., Chester, B. & Boyajian, J. (1987). *Sexual Assault and Sexual Abuse: A Handbook for Clergy and Religious Professionals.* San Francisco: Harper and Row.

Rice, J. (1982). *God in Your Family.* Murfreesboro, TN: Sword of the Lord.

Smith, E. (1995). Bring Back the Orphanages? What Policymakers of Today Can Learn From the Past. *Child Welfare, 74,* 115-142.

Tomczak, L. (1982). *God, the Rod, and Your Child's Bod.* Old Tappan, NJ: Revell.

Wiehe, V. (1990). Religious Influence on Parental Attitudes Toward the Use of Corporal Punishment. *Journal of Family Violence, 5,* 173-186.

Williams, C. (1996). *Keynote Speech: Mississippi Permanency Partnership, A Vision.* Jackson, Mississippi, June, 1996.

CHAPTER 17

ADOPTION AND ME:
A NARRATIVE APPROACH

Mary Vanden Bosch Zwaanstra

Change, move, dead clock, that this fresh day
May break with dazzling light to these sick eyes.
Burn, glare, old sun, so long unseen,
That time may find its sound again, and cleanse
What ever it is that a wound remembers
After the healing ends.
       "Small Prayer" - Weldon Kees (1975)

"Outta my way, lady." Our fifteen year old son made his way to the back door. Dressed in jeans and a cowboy hat, Karl clutched a sleeping bag under one arm and a duffel bag and radio in the other hand. His jacket pockets were stuffed with his treasures. The runaway season was upon us again.

Beginning when he was around ten, fall evoked disaffection and restlessness in him with what was familiar and familial. Issues and events varied but the result was always the same. By the time of his November 11 birthday the stage was set. There would be a fight and he would leave.

This narrative explores a family's experience with adoption. I am the narrator and the mother. I relate the story from my perspective. It could, and perhaps someday it will, be told from the perspective of my husband or from that of any of our children: Karl, born in 1964; Kerrie, born in 1967; and Matthew, born in 1969. Karl is our son by adoption; Kerrie and Matthew are birth-children. Only Karl was "planned"; the others came along quite unexpectedly. In the third year of our marriage we joined the ranks of the infertile, having been informed that "it was statistically unlikely" that we would ever have children born to us. Adoption was the "cure" for our fertility problem. As is the case with policy arrangements generally, the practice of adoption produces both intended and unintended consequences. This narrative is about policy and its affects. Living it propelled me into the social work profession.

At one month of age Karl entered our family with a one page document detailing his birth weight and development since birth. He had gained two pounds, slept through the night and should be strapped on the changing table since he was a very active baby. That was the extent of it. Adoption practice in 1964 was grounded in two beliefs: nurture counted infinitely more than nature and anonymity was best for all members of the adoption triad. If their adult offspring were to be allowed access to identifying information, Michigan birth-parents were legally required to file the requisite written permission with the state. Few signed since they were not encouraged to do so. The professional community believed the birth-mother could and should release her child and go on with her life. Neither the adopted person nor the family established by adoption required more than a legal release from her. Everyone involved would live happily ever after.

We bought unquestioningly into this belief system. Without objecting to the quality or quantity of information supplied us, we took Karl into our hearts and acted like the parents we longed to be. Objecting to or even questioning adoption practice arrangements was not thinkable because it would challenge the authority of scientifically informed professional practice. More weighty was the power differential between the professional and the applicant-parent. The worker held the power to give or withhold the child. What prospective, hopeful parent-to-be with no other options would presume to challenge so potent a force?

We heard bits and pieces of information about Karl's birth-parents verbally related by the social worker in the Christian agency with which we chose to work. His mother was a college student, a biology major; his father was preparing to be a draftsman. They were from different religious backgrounds. The father disappeared when told of the pregnancy. The mother went to a "maternity home" to await the birth of her baby, hoping to keep her secret and spare her family embarrassment. It was standard fare in 1964. No written documentation of Karl's close or extended family history was offered, nor requested. We knew that Karl was born by Cesarean Section after an extended labor. Little was said about the quality of the pregnancy or labor and nothing about the specific events necessitating the Section. We were warned that he might have some "questions about his origins" as a teen. As our life together unfolded, we discovered that we needed all the information we could get. When Karl developed asthma there was "no recorded family history of asthma." When he became addicted to drugs and alcohol, we were reluctantly informed that his father and both grandfathers "perhaps" had alcohol problems.

Two explanations are germane. The agency and its workers were loath to dispense pertinent information; their primary loyalties were to secrecy commitments made to the birth-mother. In addition, information gathered was scanty and superficial; it was not considered important in the era which viewed the newborn as a blank slate upon which nurture would write the defining tale. Karl's early life in our family was manageable. It was pleasurable. He smiled easily and slept little during the day. He seemed unusually strong and loved to stand on his feet. He took to applesauce and pulled faces at meat. He was allergic to milk but we found a soybean formula that worked well. We responded to this busy, beautiful child by developing new schedules and priorities to match his need for action and attention. Beyond the necessities, Karl's life was filled with touching, talk and play. We walked him during his daily fussy time. We read books and explored the world. We sang and played peek-a-boo. He loved animals and we entertained a series of furry and crawly creatures over the years. He was loved. As time went on his intensity and impulsiveness gave us some pause. But we had both been raised in stable homes with positive parenting models. I was a pediatric nurse and my husband a seminary professor. We reassured ourselves that while we made mistakes, we were very adequate parents. Faith, hope and love would see us through. It would turn out all right.

In the months after we became a nuclear family, our church published its yearly directory. Karl's name was not included. We asked why. The answer was that he was not really "ours" until the adoption was legally finalized after a year. Until then he was not officially part of the fellowship and he could not be baptized as most newborns are in our church. In spite of its ostensible support of adoption and rich covenant theology, it was apparent that there were some rules about inclusion and exclusion of which we had been unaware. In the recesses of our minds we became aware that certain things were different for the adopted as compared with the non-adopted.

In preschool and kindergarten Karl was aggressive with other children. He hit, kicked, spat and fought. We were appalled and worried. We had him tested by a professional who found Karl to be of normal intelligence but socially immature. Time, it was suggested, was the antidote. We then spent a sabbatical year in the Netherlands and he attended kindergarten again. Karl's social skills needed more time to develop, we thought. He learned the Dutch language quickly. We lived in close quarters in a crowded society which valued privacy and decorum. Karl threw rocks at a car and we dealt with irate neighbors. He pried up a man-hole cover and dropped it on his three year old sister's toe causing much pain and loss of a toenail.

Upon our return, Karl entered first grade in the neighborhood Christian school with a new group of children. In second grade there were more children than could be accommodated in our neighborhood school and some children were selected to be bussed. Karl was one of them. Many parents strongly objected to this arrangement since they would have children in two schools. Karl was, however, an uncomplicated choice for the school since he was the only child attending from our family. At the new school he had to adapt to a new environment and reference group. At first it was difficult for him. He stayed for two years. He had the same teacher both years. She liked him and set firm but friendly boundaries. Then he was selected to return to the school close to home for fourth grade. That fall he looked forlorn. While driving home from a piano lesson he told me he felt like standing in the middle of the street and letting a car run him over. He could not elaborate on the misery he was feeling. At bedtime we talked again. He said solemnly, "I peed on the bathroom floor at school today and the teacher made me clean it up." I asked why. He cried and said, "Mom, if I don't do dumb things nobody pays any attention to me. No one wants to play with me or be my friend." The next morning, with a heavy heart, I called the teacher. She dismissed his feelings and my concerns: "Children work these things out best by themselves." Later, the principal judged that I was guilty of over-protecting my son. In his opinion it was a common fault among adoptive parents. There would be no help in the school system.

Karl's investment in the family had decreased markedly by the time he was eleven. He was using marijuana, though we were unaware of it at the time. The fall runaways began. At first he simply disappeared when it was time to cut the birthday cake and serve it to friends and neighbors, returning later in the evening. By the time he was fifteen he was gone for two weeks at a time. Then he began to run whenever there was a major conflict. We called the police, who never found him. I gave him the phone number and address of the local shelter for runaways and picked him up when he was ready to return. We talked, cajoled and set limits. But Karl preferred to be outside the limits, wherever they were set. Gradually fall became a fearful and chaotic time for all of us. Karl's behavior was disruptive. He was destructive. He slashed the orange chairs in the family room and sold his dad's gold class ring for the cash. We virtually stopped entertaining. Karl's unpredictability made our other children reluctant to have friends in to play or spend the night. In our isolation we felt like failures and freaks. Only other families had the luxury of normalcy. No other Christian family could possibly be like ours, we thought.

I began to read everything I could get my hands on about adoption. I became a sleuth. I became a pest at the adoption agency which maintained a stonewalling posture. I discovered much that surprised me. I learned that adoptive children were over-represented in the mental health system and first came across the term "restless wanderer" in reference to adopted persons (Sorosky, Baran & Pannor, 1975). I read about studies being done in

Scandinavia that followed adopted-away offspring of persons with mental illness. A genetic link to personality and behavior, particularly alcohol abuse and mental illness, was postulated. From John Bowlby (1969) I learned about loss, grief and attachment in the very young. From Rene Spitz (1965) I learned about infant-maternal bonding and the helpful effects of maternal regression in the service of forming a secure bond. From Thomas Verny (1981)I learned about the perils and importance of the intrauterine environment and prenatal period in human development. Verny states that an "emotional set-point," established at this time, is difficult to alter later. A sympathetic physician searched Karl's maternity home and hospital records and confirmed my suspicion that fetal distress had been a factor in the Cesarean decision. From Erik Erikson (1968), himself an adopted person, I learned how identity is shaped and how crucial it is to healthy development. I concluded that adoption policy and practice were based on politics and tradition and not on scientifically grounded principles. Slowly I began to trade isolation for openness. I discovered that ours was not the only adoptive family, Christian or otherwise, in distress. We organized a support group for adoptive families, many of which remain friends to this day. We tried to educate ourselves about what was happening to us and our children since we found little knowledgeable help in the professional community. I applied to graduate school in social work.

That fall I entered my graduate program; Karl turned fifteen. He continued to be moody and morose after running away in November. We called the adoption agency, but they had no help or insight to offer. On New Year's Eve Karl overdosed. We brought in the new year at the local emergency room. Karl was embarrassed and remorseful. He wanted to come home. We removed his bedroom door from its hinges and kept a suicide watch while, during the next two days, Karl descended into the depths again. We had to commit him. At the Christian psychiatric hospital family therapy was mandated. Our daughter cried, "How can I face my friends? They'll think I have a crazy brother and that I'm crazy too." Assumptions about the state of our marriage and family structure guided treatment. Our pathologies were labeled. We heard that Karl was the "identified patient," the "symptom bearer" in our family. When I suggested that Karl's adoption played a role, that he might have a biochemical disorder, my thinking was dismissed as inconsequential to the treatment plan. After a month, he was discharged home, no longer suicidal but singularly disinterested in continued treatment, which soon stopped. At home he kept to himself and to friends we did not know. We coped but with difficulty. Several years later we learned that long-term hospitalization of Karl was considered but rejected by the professional staff of the psychiatric hospital. They supported this decision by citing the possible iatrogenic effects of hospitalization on Karl and our own coping strength. Their thoughts and opinions were not shared with us. Neither were our ideas, opinions and preferences solicited.

When I applied for my first M.S.W. field practicum, the coordinator recommended that I not divulge the ongoing family crisis. It would, he believed, be looked upon with disfavor by social service agencies. I would be considered "sick." It was still the era of the "schizophrenegenic mother." Unable to compartmentalize my life so neatly or with integrity I gave voice to the stressors and found a warm welcome first in a gerontology program and later in a program for the persistently mentally ill and their families. Here I discovered, and came to fully appreciate, that cornerstone of social work thinking, the "person-in-environment." My clients, their families and the mental health system were powerful teachers. I was touched by the courage and strength of many clients and families.

Karl began high school the next fall. He played soccer with vigor. We went to his games and cheered along with the other spectators. As soccer season ended and November approached, the familiar pattern began again. Karl's drug use increased, and he carried a knife. He avoided questions. He came and went from home at will. He was involved in incidents of petty vandalism and harassment of younger neighborhood children. He refused to participate in activities with the family. He took the car for a drive though he had no license. Karl discovered he was physically stronger than his dad and became verbally threatening. He fantasized about our deaths. We were afraid that he would harm us. We slept behind locked doors. We visited a counselor at the juvenile court where we learned that to get help we would need to obtain release from our legal, parental responsibility for his behavior, supervision, and care. Essentially this legal process would declare us unfit parents and Karl, a Ward of the Court. Somehow we couldn't take that step. We were not bad parents and we would not abandon our son. Beyond a legal contract we had entered into a covenant, committing ourselves to be parents to him. We would seek help where we could find it and depend on available supports to ride out the storm.

On a 1979 November afternoon, after school and before either of us were home from work, Karl ripped the telephone from the wall, put his knife through a door, and verbally threatened his siblings. When he ran away it was a relief. All of us were completely exhausted. We rejected committing Karl because of the stigma and ineffectiveness of treatment. From some fellow adoptive parents we heard of a boarding school, run by a group of American Christians, for behaviorally disordered youngsters in the mountains of the Dominican Republic. We spoke to its representatives; we agonized. We found some aspects of the program not to our liking, but after considering the available options, made arrangements to enroll him. There were theological differences. The quality of the educational program was inferior to that of the local high school. It was costly and we couldn't really afford it. But the cost in suffering for the family as a whole from having him at home we judged to be greater. Karl wanted out of our family and was intrigued by the adventure of the "D.R.". He left in January, 1980 for what would be a year and a half stay and completion of a high school course of study. In spite of the criticism of some social workers and Karl's school, who thought we had "overreacted" and decided "prematurely," we were at peace. We knew our son was safe, and we felt safe too. We shed our tears and got on with our lives.

The program in the Dominican Republic was strictly behavioral. Karl earned privileges when he met the behavioral standards and lost them when he didn't. He ran once. But he knew neither the language nor the geography and quickly learned that conformity was his only ticket out. The rest of the family visited Karl there during his first summer. It was exciting to see him doing so well. He expressed some ambivalence about being in the program but pleasure with the progress he was making in school. By this time he had earned the right to be in a leadership role in his house and was rightly proud of this accomplishment. In the fall he wrote, describing the sadness he felt: "When my birthday comes I think about my birth parents. I wonder who they were and who I am. I feel like a variable that has no end. I could be anything or I could be nothing." One year later he returned for good.

We looked forward to Karl's return. But within twenty-four hours of his arrival large motorcycles and strange friends appeared in the driveway. Once again he was testing boundaries. He did not ask for advice or permission. He expressed no hostility. He simply pursued his own agenda in his own way. We were terribly disappointed but felt helpless to counter his personal choices. That fall he became eighteen. He commented, "I'm free at last." I replied, "Your dad and I are free too." That he was on his own, legally an adult, was understood by all of us. He entered college that fall and stayed for two years, finishing only a fraction of his courses and poorly at that. Typically he began a semester with enthusiasm that waned halfway through and finally evaporated altogether. His friends were not serious students. He was finally not allowed to return.

Karl lived at home infrequently after that, preferring the company of those with very different values from our own. He rapidly became a poly-drug abuser. His primary drug of choice was alcohol. He moved frequently often leaving things behind that had once been precious to him. I had given the children christmas tree ornaments each year, commemorating a trip or a special memory. Dated, these marked the history of their early years. Karl's collection was lost or stolen or perhaps disposed of during this period.

During his twenties Karl existed marginally. He worked sporadically at several low paying jobs where his attendance was often spotty. He married and divorced three times. He fathered a male child who was placed in an adoptive home. He dismissed his antisocial, self-destructive behavior, stating he would be dead before he was thirty anyway, so what difference did it make. Karl's nihilistic spirit was painful for us. We had tried to instill a love of life and of faith in him. But now we considered the possibility that he might destroy himself and perhaps others as well. Death seemed a distinct possibility and we thought about where we might bury him. We prayed that God would heal him or take his life and committed him to God's care. I wished that he could die while wanting for him the best that life can give. At times I wished that I could die too.

In the fall of 1994 as his third marriage disintegrated, Karl was jailed after his first DUI (Driving Under the Influence) arrest. This resulted in a stiff fine and loss of his driver's license. Shortly thereafter he elected to see a psychiatrist who listened carefully and told him he had likely been anxious and depressed throughout his life; his substance use/abuse was his attempt to self-medicate his fluctuating moods. The drug Paxil was prescribed. We could see how different Karl was within a week. He was initially ambivalent about this change. He did not know himself apart from the depressed state and had to learn to accept unfamiliar feelings and a more positive relational style. Gradually the clouds lifted and a different future seemed possible. After twenty years of substance abuse he was sober and could begin the process of rebuilding his life. He became both a successful full-time employee and college student, earning excellent grades while working full time. He moved in with a woman and her eight-year-old daughter. They enjoyed fixing up their house and planting flowers in the yard. We enjoyed an occasional picnic with them in their back yard around the umbrella table he gave her for Mother's Day last year. We gave thanks for these miracles in Karl's life and prayed for stability and future well-being.

But concerns about adoption policy and practice remain for me. I am repelled by the persistent romantic version of the adoption story. A bumper sticker, "Adoption not Abortion," in my opinion, typifies a simplistic approach to the complex realities of adoption. Open adoption is a move in the right direction since it recognizes the importance of both birth and adoptive parents to the adoptee. However, I remain concerned about the earlier generation of adoption triad members who must live under the onus of the closed system. Many remain in need and in pain, confined by earlier policy which, supported by the likes of Ann Landers, limits their well-being by denying them crucial information. In Michigan it is now legal for members of the adoption triad to engage an intermediary to search for another triad member with whom they desire contact while maintaining confidentiality. When Karl's birth-mother was contacted by the agency intermediary, she was indignant. Under no circumstances, distant or close, did she want anything to do with him. He would have been satisfied with so little from the woman whose abdomen bears the C-Section scar.

I am also concerned about current adoption practice. Somewhere there is a young child in an adoptive family. He is Karl's son. How much do they know about his genetic heritage and vulnerabilities? Do they know he is at-risk for depression and alcohol abuse? Are they teaching moderation or abstinence? Recent research suggests that co-occurring mental disorders and addictive disorders typically show up in genetically predisposed persons around the age of eleven (Kessler, Nelson, McGonagle, Edlund & Frank, 1996) Grafting a child to a family tree of strangers is a worthy endeavor. But it cannot be done without sufficient, reliable information. Whose responsibility is it to know and convey such information?

It is, furthermore, not ethically correct social work practice to place a child and leave the family to fend for itself. In this era of shrinking infant adoption and burgeoning international and "special needs" adoption, the practice of "place and run" is unconscionable. "Special needs" is often a euphemism for damaged, neglected, multiply-abandoned children who have often seen, heard and otherwise experienced what no child ever should. Of course these children need and deserve homes. However, the agency and the adoptive family must commit to collaboration with each other for the sake of the child for as long as it takes. And it may take a lifetime! In my opinion, the needs of the adoptee take ethical precedence over the claims of the birth-mother, the adoptive family or the agency. Adopted persons are precisely those with the most to lose and the least power. The state must also share the responsibility. The availability of post-adoption services in agencies, mandated in social policy is absolutely essential. In my experience, these are often considered an expendable luxury by administrators and politicians. In Michigan it is becoming very difficult to get Adoption Subsidy for special needs kids. It has always been nearly impossible in infant adoptions. This is short-sighted and cruel to all those whose lives are irrevocably affected. Social work advocacy is required here. Who will advocate for this marginalized group if not social workers? Who will demand that policy serve adopted persons in such a way that they can reach their full human potential? Professional helping that ignores environmental issues, including the policy and practice link, cannot rightly be called social work practice.

Diversity sensitive social work practice demands that the particular concerns of adoption triad members be heard and attended to by professionals tirelessly pledged to sort out situational complexities and act in the best interests of the members in creative ways. Much can be done when workers are willing to take risks rather than opt for "what we have always done." This also means rejecting traditional practices not supported by current knowledge. Perhaps we did not understand the interplay between nature and nurture correctly in 1964. But we now know that it is not an either/or question. We know that genetics plays a far greater role than we thought possible (Cadoret, Yates, Troughton, Woodworth & Stewart, 1995). We also know that a rupture of the first maternal-infant relationship often leaves a scar, remnant of a wound without conscious memory or words. Practice has not fully taken into account the effects of this rupture which every adopted person has experienced. Although rebellious youngsters appear similar, I would argue, with Cline (1979), that the underlying issue for adoptees is more often their failure to attach rather than their having been inadequately parented.

Professionals should be willing, and would do well, to accept knowledge from those closest to the issue: members of the adoption triad itself. We know and arrive at truth in different ways. One of these ways is through experience. Yet social work has been reluctant to take seriously the experientially acquired knowledge of persons closest to adoption. I passionately wish I could say that all the professionals we worked with over time listened carefully and demonstrated a spirit of consistent, supportive helpfulness. Some have done so and we are grateful for them. But in fact, the most helpful people have been the fellow strugglers, the adoptive families, who have lived out their innocently made commitments to parent children who are a mystery to them. These are the people who, more than anyone else, heard our grief and graced us with their presence and care. They gave us what we needed most — a shoulder to cry on and the hope that we would survive.

And we have survived. This story is one of hope even as it is one of pain. Our marriage is still intact and we are reasonably healthy. Karl's life is more stable. His siblings are also grown. Each is married and has children. It is, they say, unlikely that they could or would adopt. They have memories and some of them are painful. Because they experienced hurt in their relationship with Karl, they believe they could not bring needed objectivity to an adopted child. Each of us has coped in various ways. Some have opted for therapy while others have not. Our younger children maintain some distance from their brother. We have accepted the reality that they may never be warm friends.

Perhaps you are wondering why I would want to tell this story publicly. Simply said, it has long been a goal. Throughout this experience I often said, "Someday I'm going to write a book!" Perhaps this effort is the beginning of that project. But there are more compelling reasons. I am convinced that this is a story that must be told. Alcoholics Anonymous has a saying: secrets make you sick. In our family this document has provided opportunity for unpacking the past, a past not easily raised. This has been healing for each of us. I was fearful about giving it to Karl. He was doing so well. Would it set him back? Would he respond angrily or defensively? On the contrary, he was appreciative. He had no memory of some of the incidents described. We talked about hurts and gave and received apologies. We discussed parenting since he is now in a position to occupy the parenting role with his partner. He showed it to a co-worker, an adoptive parent struggling with a teen, as a means of encouragement and support. It cemented a friendship between them. It is my hope that parents with difficult children will understand that they are not alone, that things change, that they and their children can have relatively healthy relationships after the storms have passed.

Living this story has, furthermore, profoundly shaped the way I view the practice of social work. I am skeptical about claims of professional expertise. Although the social worker has acquired certain skills and understandings about people and the social environment, the worker doesn't know everything. The client is the expert in matters pertaining to their lived experience. When I wanted attention paid to adoption issues, genetics and biochemistry, I was not, I believe, trying to usurp the prerogatives of the worker or call into question the worker's competence. Nor was I attempting to deny any family problems. As a primary stakeholder and a thoughtful human being I considered my perspective important to the goals we were working on together. I expected to be a participant on the team; the deficits driven, worker-as-expert model didn't promote that. More than any hired helper, I longed for my son to be well and for the pain to end. Being a professional helper requires humility in balance with knowledge. It is my hope that clients and professionals alike will be encouraged to value and respect each other in the important relationships they forge together and do all they can to make these relationships humane.

Just as social work does not have all the answers to adoption's challenges, neither does the faith community. Many churches and Christians find emotional problems disturbing and difficult to respond to while physical problems are more readily accepted. As a result they find it hard to faithfully walk beside families in which there is an acting out youngster. Doesn't scripture, after all, instruct parents to train up children in the right way and infer the promise that children will then do the right thing? And isn't an acting out child evidence that the parents have failed in some fundamental way? Christians speak generally about "family values," but what does this buzz phrase have to say to families with difficult children? I support efforts to make and keep families strong and safe for all members. But I also feel for families that don't measure up to the model Christian family. We often carry shame, experience loneliness and grieve in isolation, while continuing to rub elbows with fellow church members either unable or unwilling to care sensitively or inured to our pain. Our grief is not only for ourselves but for our children who suffer, whose suffering we are powerless to end. We grieve because we long for wholeness, for God's shalom, for them, for us, for our families. We grieve because our prayers go unanswered and because we feel alienated from other Christians and from God.

It would probably be fair to say that most Christians oppose abortion and support adoption. I agree with them in general. Yet I often find this stance naive and superficial. While Christians rally to causes which support the right of the fetus to continued life, as a group they are far less concerned about how the child fares after it is born. How often have Christians rallied to demand that justice be done with regard to Adoption Subsidy funds or the right of adoptees to all of the available information about themselves held by various agencies? It seems to me that a consistent pro-life stance demands that the Christian community be at least as vigorous in advocating for measures to assure that adoptees have opportunities to become all that God desires and intends them to be.

There is little awareness, in my experience in the faith community, of the particular issues confronting adopted persons and their families. For example, those who are not adopted have difficulty putting themselves in the adoptee's experience of having very limited knowledge of their own history, or knowing a painful history. Most of us know what kind of people we came from, we have pregnancy and birth stories that are ours alone, we know how the pieces of our family tree fit together. Most of us know that our parents, siblings, grandparents and other extended family are part of who we are. We know ourselves by particular, sometimes peculiar ancestors, historical events and geographical locations. But none of this is true for the adopted person. The longings of the adoptee to know him/herself fully are both appropriate and normal, and do not imply rejection of the family by which the adoptee was "chosen." That Christians have all been chosen or adopted by God in Christ (Romans 8, 9; Ephesians 1) is sometimes used to normalize adoption, and to some extent the comparison works. However God's adoption is not the same as human adoption conducted according to the rules established by society. God adopts us, the human creatures he knows with the creator's perfect knowledge, out of pure grace. We continually turn away from him. He remains faithful to us. And He supplies us with a multitude of stories, recorded in the Old and New Testaments, designed to teach us who we are in relation to him. In human adoption neither are our motives so pure nor are our available resources so well designed. Still each of us—families, professionals, the Christian community—commits to diligently do the best we can with the limited information and finite resources we have at the time, trusting that God, who knows the whole, will bless our faithfulness.

References

Bowlby, J. (1969). *Attachment and loss*. New York: Basic Books.

Cadoret, R. J., Yates, W. R., Troughton, E. Woodworth, G. & Stewart, M. A. (1995). Adoption study demonstrating two genetic pathways to drug abuse. *Archives of General Psychiatry, 55*, 42-52.

Cline, F. W. (1979). *Understanding and treating the severely disturbed child*. Evergreen Consultants in Human Behavior.

Erikson, E. H. (1968). *Identity, youth, and crisis*. New York: W.W. Norton.

Kessler, R. C., Nelson, C. B., Mc Gonagle, K. A., Edlund, M. J., Frank, R. G., & Leaf, P. J. (1996). The epidemiology of co-occurring addictive and mental disorders: Implications for prevention and service utilization. *American Journal of Orthopsychiatry, 66*, 17-31.

Kees, W. (1975). Small Prayer. In D. Justice (Ed.), *The Collected Poems of Weldon Kees*. Lincoln: University of Nebraska Press.

Sorosky, A.D., Baran., A., & Pannor, R. (1975). Identity conflicts in adoptees. *American Journal of Orthopsychiatry, 45*, 18-27.

Spitz, R. A. (1965). *The first year of life: A psychoanalytic study of normal and deviant development of object relations*. New York: International Universities Press.

Verny, T. (with Kelly, J.) (1981). *The secret life of the unborn child*. New York: Summit Books.

ABOUT THE CONTRIBUTORS

Katherine Amato-von Hemert received a BA in History/Women Studies/Drama from Lake Forest College, a MA in General Studies in the Humanities, and a MA and PhD from the School of Social Services Administration, University of Chicago. Currently she is on the faculty of the College of Social Work, University of Kentucky, and an adjunct Professor at Lexington Theological Seminary. Her professional interests are researching the intersection of Christian congregation life and social service policy and program, the Medieval and Reformation history of poverty and social responses to it, along with the variety of religious influences in the history of the social work profession. Presently she is directing a research project examining Caucasian and African-American Protestant churches in four states (KY, CA, CO, GA) regarding congregational attitudes toward poverty and social welfare policy.

Gary R. Anderson received a BRE from Cornerstone College (Grand Rapids, Michigan), a MSW from the University of Michigan, and PhD from the School of Social Services Administration at the University of Chicago. Presently he is a Professor at Hunter College School of Social Work, of the City University of New York, in New York City. He has social work practice experience as a child protective service worker. He has published extensively in the areas of child welfare, ethics, and health care. He is currently the Principal Investigator for the National Resource Center for Permanency Planning at Hunter College and has recently been appointed Editor of the journal *Child Welfare*.

John E. Babler earned a BGS from the University of Texas at Dallas, a MSSW from the University of Texas at Arlington, and a MA and PhD from Southwestern Baptist Theological Seminary, Fort Worth, Texas. He is Assistant Professor of Social Work and Ministry-Based Evangelism at Southwestern Baptist Theological Seminary in Fort Worth, Texas. He has had direct practice experience in hospice social work, administration, and consulting for several years. Previous to his hospice experience, Dr. Babler worked as an administrator in a residential children's home, as an inner-city missionary, and on several church staffs. He has researched and written extensively in the area of spiritual care in hospice.

Timothy A. Boyd holds a BA from Wheaton College, a MA from the School of Social Services Administration at the University of Chicago, and a MA and PsyD from Rosemead Graduate School at Biola University. Currently he is an Associate Professor of Social Work and Psychology at Roberts Wesleyan College, Rochester, New York. His professional interest areas are cross-cultural psychology and international social work, counseling and education sevices for clergy and missions, and mental health services.

Rick Chamiec-Case earned a BA in Philosophy from Wheaton College, a MAR in Religion from Yale Graduate School, and a MSW from the School of Social Work at the University of Connecticut. He is presently Senior Vice President at ARI of Connecticut, whose mission it is to provide homes, jobs, and opportunities for people with disabilities and their families. He has several previous practice experiences in administrating clinical, case management, quality assurance, family support, staff training, and management information services for people with disabilities like mental retardation. He has written and presented at conferences on various topics addressing the integration of faith with different management and disability issues. He currently is the Executive Director of the North American Association of Christians in Social Work.

Diana Garland received her BA, MSSW, and PhD degrees all from the University of Louisville. She currently is Professor of Social Work at Baylor University in Waco, Texas. Her interests include church social work, family ministry, and child welfare. She is currently directing a national research project funded by the Lilly Endowment which is studying the characteristics of families in congregations and faith as a dimension of family life experience. She also serves as Editor of the *Journal of Family Ministry*. She has authored, or co-authored, or edited fourteen books, including *Church Social Work*, *Precious in His Sight: A Guide to Child Advocacy* and *Church Agencies*. In 1996, Dr. Garland received the Jack Otis Whistleblower Award from the National Association of Social Workers to honor her public stance against unethical practices of the administration of The Southern Baptist Theological Seminary.

Beryl Hugen received a BA from Calvin College, a MSW from Western Michigan University, and a PhD from the University of Kansas. He is currently a Professor of Social Work and Practicum Coordinator in the Department of Social Work and Sociology at Calvin College. He has practice experience in a variety of mental health and child welfare settings. Professional areas of interest include mental health (family and chronic mental illness), program evaluation, the integration of Christian faith and social work practice, child welfare, and social work history. Presently he serves on the Board and as Special Publications Editor for the North American Association of Christians in Social Work.

Lon Johnston holds a BA from Baylor University, a MSSW from Kent School of Social Work, University of Louisville, and a PhD from The Southern Baptist Theological Seminary. Presently he is Professor and Chair of the Department of Social Work and Sociology at the University of Mary Hardin-Baylor, Belton, Texas. His direct social work practice experience is in child welfare, medical social work, and inner-city churches. Professional interests include HIV issues, multiculturalism and human diversity, the homeless, and oppressed and vulnerable populations. He has been recognized by both professional and academic organizations for excellence in teaching and campus leadership.

Sarah S. Kreutziger earned a BA from Columbia College (South Carolina), a MSSW from the University of Tennessee, and a DSW from Tulane University. Presently she is Assistant Professor and Director of the Center for Life-Long Learning at Tulane School of Social Work. Previous social work practice experience has been as Director of Communications for the Louisiana Conference of the United Methodist Church and as a psychiatric social worker. Her research and practice interests are women's spirituality and religious beliefs and its impact on Amercian values, ethics, and social institutions, along with clinical services to individuals and families in health care and substance abuse. She has been recognized as social worker of the year in Florida and received several volunteer service awards.

Lawrence E. Ressler received a BSW from Eastern Mennonite College, a MSW from Temple University, and a PhD from Case Western Reserve University. He is currently a Professor of Social Work, Associate MSW Program Director, and Associate Division Chair of the Social Work and Social Sciences Division at Roberts Wesleyan College, Rochester, New York. His social work practice experience has been in individual, family, and organizational counseling, and mediation. Professional areas of interest include conflict management, research, church/state relationship, and family counseling. He has held leadership roles in NASW and in social work education at the state level, and served as President of the North American Association of Christians in Social Work.

David A. Sherwood received his BA from David Lipscomb College (Nashville, Tennessee), a MSW from Bryn Mawr Graduate School of Social Work, and a PhD in Social Work from the University of Texas at Austin. He is currently Professor of Social Work, MSW Program, at Roberts Wesleyan College, Rochester, New York. His professional interests include the integration of Christian faith and social work practice, ethics, practice with individuals and families, and social work in health care and with the elderly. He has written several articles on ethics and topics related to the integration of Christian faith and social work practice. Dr. Sherwood has served on the Board and as President of the North American Association of Christians in Social Work. He currently is the Editor of the journal *Social Work and Christianity*.

Janice M. Staral holds a BSW from the University of Wisconsin-Milwaukee, a MSW from the University of Michigan, and a PhD from the University of Wisconsin-Milwaukee. She presently is an Assistant Professor at Marquette University in the Social Work Program, within the Department of Social and Cultural Sciences. She has a particular professional interest in how social work can collaborate with churches in order to be a force for social change and social justice.

Mary P. Van Hook earned a BA from Calvin College, a MSW from Columbia University School of Social Work, and a PhD from Rutgers University. She currently is an Associate Professor of Social Work at Grand Valley State University (Grand Rapids, Michigan). Her social work practice experience includes clinical and supervisory roles in mental health and family and children's services. Her professional interests include family coping, integration of mental and general health care, incorporating religious issues into social work practice, and international issues regarding women and children. Dr. Van Hook presently is Editor of the journals *Rural Community Mental Health* and *Practice Forum of Health and Social Work*. In addition, her article "Christian Social Work" will appear in the next edition of the *Encyclopedia of Social Work*.

Mary Vanden Bosch Zwaanstra holds a Diploma in Nursing(RN) from Blodgett Memorial Medical Center School of Nursing (Grand Rapids, Michigan), a BA from Aquinas College (Grand Rapids, Michigan), and a MSW from Western Michigan University. She presently is an Associate Professor in the Social Work Program at Calvin College. Her practice experience has involved hospital nursing and social work, along with work in gerontology and mental health. She has been involved in education in both nursing and social work, including being the Dean of

Students at Reformed Bible College (Grand Rapids, Michigan). She has served on several Boards and community organizations. Her most extensive practice experience has been as an adoptive parent and consumer of social services.

Christianity
and Social Work

*Readings on the Integration of
Christian Faith and
Social Work Practice*

Beryl Hugen, Editor

NORTH AMERICAN ASSOCIATION
OF CHRISTIANS IN SOCIAL WORK

NACSW provides opportunities for Christian fellowship and professional learning, encourages professional
standards among Christian workers and agencies,
recruits Christian students to enter the social work
profession, and promotes a Christian philosophy of
social work and the development of professional
literature reflecting a Christian perspective. The
Association's services include:

* An Annual Convention and Training Conference;
* *Catalyst*, a bimonthly newsletter;
* *Social Work and Christianity*, a semi-annual refereed
  journal;

A growing array of publications including books,
  monographs, videos, etc.;

* Chapters in twelve states and in Canada.

For more information:
NACSW, Box 121, Botsford, CT 06404-0121
Phone/Fax: (203) 270-8780. Email: NACSW@aol.com

ISBN 0-9623634-6-4